I0820509

TOJO

TOJO

THE RISE AND FALL OF JAPAN'S MOST CONTROVERSIAL WORLD WAR II GENERAL

PETER MAUCH

THE BELKNAP PRESS OF
HARVARD UNIVERSITY PRESS
CAMBRIDGE · MASSACHUSETTS
LONDON · ENGLAND
2026

Printed in the United States of America
First printing

EU GPSR Authorised Representative
LOGOS EUROPE, 9 rue Nicolas Poussin, 17000, LA ROCHELLE, France
E-mail: Contact@logoseurope.eu

LIBRARY OF CONGRESS CATALOGING-IN-PUBLICATION DATA
Names: Mauch, Peter (Peter Cameron), author.
Title: Tojo : the rise and fall of Japan's most controversial World War II general / Peter Mauch.
Description: Cambridge, Massachusetts ; London, England : The Belknap Press of Harvard University Press, 2026. | Includes bibliographical references and index.
Identifiers: LCCN 2025029718 (print) | LCCN 2025029719 (ebook) | ISBN 9780674495197 (cloth) | ISBN 9780674303843 (epub) | ISBN 9780674303850 (pdf)
Subjects: LCSH: Tōjō, Hideki, 1884–1948. | Prime ministers—Japan—Biography. | Generals—Japan—Biography. | Japan—Politics and government—1912–1945.
Classification: LCC DS890.T57 M38 2026 (print) | LCC DS890.T57 (ebook)
LC record available at https://lccn.loc.gov/2025029718
LC ebook record available at https://lccn.loc.gov/2025029719

To the memory of my grandparents

CONTENTS

Note to Readers

Asian names are rendered with the family name first—for example, Tojo Hideki. The only exception is in notes citing Asian authors who have published in English and have put their given name first—for example, Sadao Asada.

Transliteration of Japanese names and terms follows the Hepburn system. In Japanese titles cited in the notes, macrons indicate long vowels (e.g., Tōjō).

All quotations in English that come from Japanese sources are my own translations.

Transliteration of Chinese names follows the pinyin system. In a few select cases, older and better-known alternative romanizations are used (for example, Chiang Kai-shek rather than Jiang Jieshi).

CHRONOLOGY

July 30, 1884	Tojo Hideki born in Tokyo to Lieutenant General Tojo Hidenori and Chitose (née Tokunaga).
1899–1902	Cadet at the Tokyo Regional Military Preparatory School.
1902–1904	Cadet at the Central Military Preparatory School.
1904–1905	Member of the seventeenth class of the Military Academy
April 1905	Attached to the Third Imperial Guard Infantry Regiment in Tokyo; then (July 1905) to the Fifty-Ninth Infantry Regiment in Port Arthur; then (April 1906) back to the Third Imperial Guard Infantry Regiment. Promoted to second lieutenant (April 1905) and then first lieutenant (December 1907).
April 1909	Married Ito Katsuko.
October 1909	Instructor at the Military Academy.
1912–1916	Member of the twenty-seventh class of the War College. Promoted to captain (June 1915).
August 1917	Appointed Army Ministry adjutant, then (July 1919) to the Forty-Eighth Infantry Regiment.
August 1919	Study in Switzerland.
August 1920	Promoted to major.
July 1921	Study in Germany.
November 1922	Lecturer at the War College (also attached to the General Staff, beginning in October 1923).
August 1924	Promoted to lieutenant colonel.
March 1926	Attached to the Military Affairs Bureau's Army Affairs Section.
March 1928	Assigned to the Economic Mobilization Bureau's Mobilization Section.
August 1928	Promoted to colonel.
August 1929	Commander, First Infantry Regiment, Tokyo.
August 1931	Chief, Organization and Mobilization Section, Army General Staff.
March 1933	Attached to the Army General Staff. Promoted to major general.
August 1933	Transferred to Military Research Division, Army Ministry.
March 1934	Deputy commandant, Military Academy, Tokyo.
August 1934	Commander, Twenty-Fourth Mixed Brigade, Kurume.

September 1935	Provost marshal, Kwantung Army; concurrently chief, Police Affairs Department, Kwantung Bureau.
December 1936	Promoted to lieutenant general.
March 1937	Chief, Kwantung Army staff.
May 1938	Vice army minister; as of June 1938, concurrently chief, Army Aeronautical Department.
December 1938	Inspector general of Army Aviation; as of February 1940, concurrently extraordinary military councillor.
July 1940	Army minister; concurrently general secretary, Manchukuoan Affairs Bureau.
October 1941	Prime minister, promoted to general. Concurrent appointments: army minister (October 1941–July 1944); home minister (October 1941–February 1942); foreign minister (September 1942); commerce and industry minister (October 1943); munitions minister (November 1943–July 1944); army chief of staff (February 1944–July 1944).
July 1944	Imperial Army reserve list.
September 1945	Arrested as war criminal suspect.
November 12, 1948	Sentenced to death.
December 23, 1948	Executed by hanging.

TOJO

INTRODUCTION

TOJO HIDEKI. His bristling, mustached countenance was, from the moment he led Japan into hostilities in the Pacific, the face of his nation's participation in World War II. An army general who had devoted his career to understanding warfare, Tojo orchestrated the national war effort until mid-1944. By that time repeated battlefield losses and the dawn of a sustained aerial bombardment campaign against the home islands so crippled him politically that Emperor Hirohito consented to Tojo's deposition from power. Some twelve months later, in the wake of the aerial bombardment campaign that culminated in the US atomic bomb attacks on Hiroshima and Nagasaki, the emperor rejected the army's arguments for a decisive home island battle against invading enemy forces. Tojo, too, pushed for a decisive home island battle; the emperor, however, insisted on surrender. This paved the way for the first foreign military occupation in Japan's long history, and Tojo determined to take responsibility in what he called "the Japanese way."[1] He bungled his suicide attempt and fell captive to the wartime enemy. The irony was bitter: He had, several years earlier, issued a death-before-dishonor military code that counseled explicitly against the "disgrace of becoming a prisoner."[2] He now earned the bitterest derision and contempt among his countryfolk. "He is a pathetic human being," spat a junior high school teacher in tones that resonated throughout Japan.[3]

In April 1946 the enemy hauled Tojo and twenty-seven of his contemporaries before the International Military Tribunal for the Far East—the so-called Tokyo trial—to defend themselves against a raft of criminal charges. These included not just conventional war crimes like maltreatment of prisoners of war but also the novel crime of having conspired to wage aggressive war in Asia and the Pacific. Tojo "regretted" and accepted responsibility for any atrocities that occurred while he sat atop the army's chain of command. But he angrily denounced the Tokyo trial as a "political trial" and a "victors' tribunal" that, he insisted, existed for the base purpose of shifting all blame for the war onto the vanquished.[4] He ferociously defended Japan's wartime actions, and willingly took responsibility for every decision made during his time as prime minister. He so dominated the proceedings that the Tokyo trial became known colloquially as the Tojo trial.[5] Tojo laughed scornfully when the International Military Tribunal president, William Flood Webb, sentenced him to death, and he marched to the gallows confident that Japan's future generations would reject the Tokyo trial's findings.[6] He believed that the "truth" about Japan's participation in World War II would eventually surface and, when that day arrived, he anticipated his own phoenix-like rise from the ashes of the Tokyo trial.[7]

That last thought was doubtless consoling for a man whose lifework lay in tatters, but it failed utterly to account for the domestic origins of Tojo's ugly image in Japanese war memory. Long before the war had ended, people had whispered about the propriety of Tojo atoning for the unfolding catastrophe by committing ritual suicide.[8] In the early aftermath of the war, Tojo's family members were forced to travel significant distances just to buy basic commodities, for nearer to home, where their faces were familiar, they were turned out of stores empty-handed. "I have nothing to sell to Tojo's family!" was the storekeepers' common refrain.[9]

After the guns fell silent, memoirists joined the wider public in blaming and scapegoating Tojo. Former Prime Minister Konoe Fumimaro's posthumously published papers pinpointed Tojo as the leading militarist standing athwart Konoe's own "struggle for peace."[10] Former Imperial Navy officers sought to salvage their service from the wreckage of war memory. They framed their appraisals of Tojo—whose decades of army service culminated in his appointment as army minister during the war—in what has subsequently been called a "villainous army and virtuous navy narrative."[11] To cite but one example, Suzuki Kantaro, a retired admiral who was prime minister at the end of World War II, portrayed Tojo and his ilk as "shogunate-like warlords" sitting atop a "despotic government" that disregarded the emperor's desire for peace, "misled" the people, isolated Japan from "world opinion," and pushed the nation along an "aggressive" and "belligerent course."[12] Army memoirists were few, but Tanaka Ryukichi portrayed his former boss as the ultimate victor of the murderous factionalism that had roiled the Imperial Army in the 1930s, and as a single-minded "dictator" with no tolerance for dissent. In Tanaka's retelling, once Tojo decided on war against the Anglo-American powers, his cabinet ministers behaved like "well trained cats" and marched "full speed" into war.[13]

Early postwar scholarship in Japan also pinpointed Tojo as the individual primarily responsible for the nation's plight. Miyatake Gaikotsu, a journalist turned popular historian, wrote of Tojo's prime ministership as the culmination of the military's takeover of the government and insisted that "nothing could have been more disadvantageous for the nation, nor more ill fated for the people."[14] Best-selling political scientist Maruyama Masao wrote in 1949 of "the Tojo dictatorship," which "suppressed" and "forcibly dissolved" opposition voices while aggregating to itself "unprecedented authority" and leading the nation into an irrational war.[15]

In this way Japanese public memory of Tojo coalesced around an image of him as the personification of the wartime militaristic state that had oppressed ordinary Japanese people and led them into a devastating war that ended in crippling defeat. Little changed over the ensuing decades. Tojo's widow, Katsuko, continued to receive hate mail from embittered countryfolk into at least the 1960s.[16] When Yasukuni Shrine decided in the late 1970s to enshrine Tojo and other war criminals alongside Imperial Japan's war dead, reactions ranged from bewilderment to "absolute opposition" to the enshrinement of those who had "led the people into war" and "drove Japan to ruination."[17] Emperor Hirohito reflected the national mood when he noted in a private conversation that the latest additions to the shrine were people who had victimized practically all other Japanese; he obeyed the dictate of his "heart" and never again visited Yasukuni Shrine.[18] Yet, by that point, most of the other war criminals had dropped out of the public consciousness; nationwide criticism of the shrine's actions focused with laser-like intensity on the enshrinement of the ever-identifiable Tojo. Military historian Hata Ikuhiko commented on time's apparent inability to heal the deep wounds Tojo had evidently inflicted and pondered the Japanese public's refusal to "restore" Tojo's "honor."[19]

A small minority has since sought to vindicate Tojo. Leading the charge around the turn of the century was his granddaughter, who took direct issue with the prevailing "diabolical" (*gokuaku hido*) image of Tojo. She traced this back to the Tokyo trial and criticized the government for having done nothing in the intervening decades to "reenlighten" the Japanese people.[20] Others joined the fray. They regarded Tojo as a talismanic figure who could inspire contemporary Japanese society to throw off the shackles of the so-called "Tokyo trial view of history" and its perceived corollaries, including a lack of "love of their own country," diminished "pride in the national flag," and a nationwide "complex" that stemmed from its condemnation as an "aggressor nation."[21] Tojo is, in this reckoning, a figure in whom Japanese society ought to take pride.[22] Such arguments made little impression on the wider Japanese public, however, and thus Tojo's name remains for most Japanese—in the words of historian Furukawa Takahisa—a "byword for evil."[23]

THE PRESENT VOLUME IS a military biography of General Tojo. Some readers will regard it as a biography of the man against the backdrop of Japanese military history; others will, perhaps, see it as a study of the Imperial Japanese Army through the conceptual lens afforded by Tojo. Either way, it moves beyond the narrow confines of the Tokyo trial and might best be considered an examination of the rise and fall of Japanese militarism and its enduring "symbol" in Tojo.[24] The aim is to reconstruct as fully as possible the ideas, beliefs, and assumptions that animated Tojo, as well as the contexts in which he acted.

The time seems right for this undertaking. The last book-length study of Tojo in English was written by US historian Robert Butow in 1961; it made judicious use of Tokyo trial sources and argued that Tojo was neither a conspirator in chief nor a dictator but instead "one among many and not even the first among equals."[25] A wealth of sources has become available in the intervening years. These include the memorandums and letters that Tojo himself penned in the final days of World War II and during his subsequent incarceration; there are also the diary accounts of his wartime secretaries.[26] There are military sources, including the collected telegrams, memorandums, and other materials pertaining to the campaign in Inner Mongolia that Tojo led in the early stages of Japan's undeclared war against China.[27] There is also the 102-volume *Senshi sosho* (War history) series, which quotes liberally from the army and navy archives and which remains almost criminally underused by all but the merest handful of naval and military historians.[28] Then there are sources relating to the emperor whom Tojo served with an admixture of reverence, awe, and diligence. These sources include the official sixty-volume record of Hirohito's reign, his own postsurrender "monologue," and his courtiers' diaries.[29] Drawing on these sources, Japanese scholarship has recently broken a long-standing virtual silence on Tojo, and there is at present a minor Tojo boom taking place among Japanese historians. The prevailing view can be characterized as follows: Tojo's wartime authority was considerably less than autocratic—one recent study holds that he could only present publicly or "act" as a dictator—because he operated within a byzantine decision-making process in which authority and responsibility were fragmented across multiple layers of bureaucracy. This broad scholarly consensus also holds that Tojo was not a visionary leader but was instead a bureaucratic politician and administrator.[30]

This book draws inspiration from these and other scholarly works, but it seeks to reframe the prevailing view of Tojo's leadership. First and foremost, it portrays Tojo as the army's single most effective political operator since such luminaries as Yamagata Aritomo (1838–1922), Katsura Taro (1848–1913), and Tanaka Giichi (1864–1929). Tojo possessed more than political instinct. Partly by accident and partly by design, he spent his entire military career cultivating, honing, and refining his capacity for bruising political battle. He thrived on conflict, yet he was not just a backroom brawler. Nor was he just a political wrecking ball. Tojo was incisive, assertive, and confrontational, and none of his contemporaries—inside the Imperial Army or out—could match him. He had an eye for the minutest detail, and he was peerless in his ability to navigate and manipulate the complex administrative structures of army and state. Tojo's performance as army minister in the cabinets of Prime Minister Konoe Fumimaro during 1940 and 1941 was masterful. He contributed ultimately to Konoe's political downfall and then took the dual appointments of army minister and prime minister; he added a raft of other ministerial appointments and eventually also took on the role of army chief of staff. No soldier before him had stood astride Japan's bifurcated decision-making structure and simultaneously taken on leadership of both policy and operations. Even within the army, many muttered about the immensity of the powers he was accruing, but Tojo stared his opponents down. The term *political animal* does not do Tojo justice; he was the *apex political predator* in wartime Japanese politics. Only a precipitously failing war effort eventually brought him down. Stated simply, Tojo was the single most accomplished political operator in Tokyo's halls of power during the first two decades of Hirohito's reign (1926–1945).

Tojo's political skill set was an asset for an officer championing national mobilization. He recognized early in his career that warfare was evolving and that World War I seemed to herald a new era. Until then, warfare had been limited in geographical scope, fought with clear and finite objectives, and of relatively short duration and limited impact on the home front. But in World War I it instead became what German general Erich Ludendorff would in the mid-1930s label "total warfare" (or what military philosopher Carl von Clausewitz had, almost one hundred years earlier, called "absolute warfare)."[31] War aims in this new era were imprecise and veered toward the infinite; writer H. G. Wells found a receptive audience in at least the English-speaking world when he declared World War I to be "the war that will end war."[32] Combatants had, accordingly, dispensed with limits on what they were willing to commit to the fight. Technological advancements, and especially the advent of the machine gun, had rendered the battlefield offensive ineffective and thereby ensured a grinding war of almost unending attrition whose reverberations were felt far beyond the battlefield. To cite an example that Tojo himself studied firsthand in the immediate aftermath of World War I, German defeat was, in part, due to material shortages that had crippled the home front. The changing nature of warfare required new approaches to preparation for war. Generals in an earlier era had understood mobilization to mean enlisting men into active service and training and equipping them for battle. Tojo and like-minded Japanese generals never overlooked the importance of men and morale, but they also understood that mobilization for total war was an all-encompassing national project. Victory in total war depended on a government's capacity to harness a nation's strength in its totality, and Tojo's military career involved long stints in bureaus dedicated to such tasks as economic mobilization. A watershed moment came during his posting to occupied Manchuria with the Kwantung Army in the mid-1930s. From his position in the capital city of Xinjing, Tojo was centrally involved in not just military matters but also political, economic, industrial, scientific, technological, financial, commercial, and diplomatic issues as they impacted the Japanese puppet state of Manchukuo. Ultimately, after he rose to a ministerial position in Tokyo, Tojo believed it was only right and proper that he exercise the army's voice in all such matters. Nothing less, he believed, would prepare Japan for total war.

Tojo was far from alone in his pursuit of national mobilization. He was not even the leading intellect among what historian Michael Barnhart has called Japan's "total war officer[s]."[33] Even so, the present study rejects the broad scholarly consensus that regards Tojo as lacking in vision. Such criticisms trace back to his enemies within the Imperial Japanese Army; foremost among them was the mercurial Ishiwara Kanji, who frequently denounced what he regarded as Tojo's myopia. Ishiwara underestimated Tojo; historians continue today to do so. It might plausibly be suggested that Tojo's vision has remained hidden in plain sight, for he envisioned nothing more and nothing less than Japan in a state of perpetual preparedness for total war. This vision stretched far beyond the battlefield and required the integration of policies and operational planning in times of both war and peace. It was what a later generation would recognize as "grand strategy."[34]

To assert that Tojo had a vision—or a grand strategy—is to laud neither the man nor his vision. Total war required total security. Domestically, Tojo envisioned something akin to a "garrison state" or a "military state" in which soldiers concerned themselves with not just their traditional accoutrements but also with the management and regulation of "large-scale civilian enterprise" in order to maximize the entire nation's "fighting effectiveness."[35] This meant a greatly expanded role for a military that already wielded considerable political clout. Indeed, Tojo envisioned the army enlisting the entire nation and preparing it for total war. In this way he neatly upended Georges Clemenceau's oft-quoted line about war being "too important for the generals."[36] As Tojo saw it, war—and indeed, preparing for war—was too important for civilians.

Tojo never rose above his military training and outlook, and even as prime minister he imposed distinctly military solutions on practically all issues he confronted. Once the war began, he favored the imposition of martial law not because of unrest on the home front but because it would ensure that Japan became something akin to a nation at arms. Although the emperor restrained this particular predilection, Tojo nonetheless became a practitioner par excellence of what historian Koketsu Atsushi has labeled "kenpei politics."[37] Tojo's prime ministership was, in other words, defined by his use of Japan's feared gendarmerie or military police as instruments of compulsion and coercion. The level of control may not have matched that in Nazi Germany or the Soviet Union, but the effect on wartime Japanese society and culture was stultifying. In the assessment of liberal journalist Kiyosawa Kiyoshi, "everything" was "regulated" and, by at least early 1944, a "stillness like death" permeated all aspects of Japanese society.[38]

Abroad, Tojo's vision involved military opportunism and aggression, beginning in the 1930s with Manchuria and Mongolia, then the rest of China, and, ultimately, the resource-rich colonial regions of Southeast Asia. Military action against such relatively weak opponents should not, Tojo reasoned, involve Japan in total warfare. Prompt, decisive action was the order of the day, and it was designed both to facilitate access to natural resources and to construct for Japan a strategically impregnable position in what Tojo came to call Greater East Asia. His blind spots were numerous: In China, Tojo failed to see—until it was far too late—that the Japanese Army could win all the battles and occupy vast tracts of Chinese territory without ever being able to deliver the knockout blow. He also failed, at least initially, to accept that aggression in Southeast Asia would likely plunge

Japan into total war against the incomparably powerful United States. Over time he came to accept the Imperial Navy's insistence on Anglo-American inseparability and allowed that a Japanese attack on the British Empire in Southeast Asia would bring the United States into World War II. Tojo then used this to his political advantage. During the Japanese-US negotiations of 1941, he held his naval counterparts to account: If they believed it was impossible to emerge victorious from war in the Pacific, he insisted they say so. Then and only then would he adjust army policy to ensure against the calamitous possibility of Japan going to war without prospect of victory. The admirals could not, however, bring themselves to confess US naval superiority. Nor, despite their best efforts, could they change the terms of the debate as set by Tojo. Tojo's aptitude for political battle so overwhelmed the admirals that they withered before him. This set Japan on a disastrous course: it plunged headlong into a war which it could not win and which took it to the brink of national annihilation.

AT THE INNERMOST CORE of Tojo's vision for Japan was the *kokutai;* a notoriously ambiguous term, it connotes Imperial Japan's governing structures as well as a distinctly Japanese spirit. It is variously translated as "national polity," "national essence," or "national principles."[39] Fundamental to the *kokutai* was a "sacred" and "inviolable" emperor, who under the Meiji Constitution combined in himself the "rights of sovereignty" while also maintaining "supreme command" of the armed services.[40] The relationship between emperor and armed services was amplified by the Imperial Rescript to Soldiers and Sailors, which likened uniformed officers to the emperor's "limbs" and encouraged them to "look up" to the emperor as their "head."[41] The *kokutai* also "united" the entire nation as "one great family nation in heart," which out of "deep faith" observed "spontaneous obedience" to the Imperial will.[42]

Tojo understood the *kokutai* to require direct Imperial rule: a system of governance in which the emperor's voice was determining. His military colleagues also spoke of direct Imperial rule, and although the term meant different things to different soldiers; at the very least they could all point to that defining moment in modern Japanese history known as the Meiji Restoration of 1868, which had stripped the feudal-era shogun of all his powers and prerogatives, and putatively returned—or restored—them to the Meiji Emperor. They could also agree that certain understandings of the *kokutai,* including the official theory that the emperor was merely an organ of the state and therefore akin to a constitutional monarch, were anathema.[43] It mattered little that Emperor Hirohito himself supported the organ theory.[44] Military officers attributed such thinking to wrong-headed and even "evil advisers" around the emperor; soon after the Showa era began with Hirohito's ascension to the throne in 1926, these officers launched a series of coups d'état with a view to eliminating those advisers and implementing direct Imperial rule.[45] That the army would play the key role in advising the emperor was a foundational assumption; the coup plotters were, in this sense, aiming at a military dictatorship in which a supposedly autocratic emperor was beholden almost solely to the generals. For these officers, direct Imperial rule came with such caveats as to render the term practically meaningless.

The coup attempts all failed. The dream of direct Imperial rule nonetheless remained, and Tojo—a sworn enemy of the army's coup plotters—took it on himself to implement it. Here again, historians are guilty of misreading Tojo: They regard him and indeed his entire generation as creatures of and beholden to ossified institutions bequeathed by their Meiji-era forebears. According to this view, Tojo and his contemporaries lacked the standing to dispense with custom and convention and were unable to reinterpret and reshape the relationships between and among the various institutions of Imperial prerogative. Often cited in this regard is Tojo's inability to overcome the hallowed principle of the "independence of the supreme command." In concrete terms, there was no provision for a prime minister to join the army and navy chiefs of staff in meetings of the supreme command apparatus known in wartime as Imperial General Headquarters. Thus it was, for example, that Tojo only learned of the navy's Pearl Harbor attack plan days before it was launched. Even then, he learned this privileged information not as prime minister but instead in his capacity as a general-rank officer serving as army minister. According to accepted wisdom, Japan's complex decision-making process made it all but impossible for Tojo's generation to integrate civil, military, and maritime affairs into a single, coherent wartime strategy under the person of the emperor.[46]

Had such a case been put to Tojo, he himself would doubtless have acknowledged the challenges he faced. As I have already noted, he ultimately broke with precedent and assumed the role of army chief of staff while still serving as prime minister and army minister. At one level, this was a power grab, born of a sense that he was better equipped than his contemporaries to get things done. Yet it owed also to Tojo's frustration with the difficulties inherent in crafting wartime strategy even as the supreme command clung zealously to its independence from the cabinet. After the war had been fought and lost he went so far as to advocate constitutional revision that would place the supreme command under ministerial control. As if to further complicate matters, Tojo was also highly conscious of the problems posed by the fractious relationship between Japan's armed services. During the war, he pleaded with the emperor to order a thoroughgoing reform of Imperial General Headquarters so that its component parts—the Army and Navy General Staffs—ceased operating independently of each other. In other words, Tojo regarded Japan's divided military and maritime command structure as injurious to the creation of a coherent wartime strategy, and he recognized that only the emperor's direct intervention could possibly resolve the issue.[47]

That last anecdote is wonderfully illustrative of Tojo's emperor-centric approach to administration and decision-making. His efforts lacked the romance and drama of a military coup, because he concerned himself for the most part with small steps, incremental adjustments, and successive approximations. He practiced the art of what the Meiji Constitution made possible, and over time, he worked to shape and systematize administrative structures and processes in an effort at constructing a composite of wills between and among the emperor, his cabinet ministers, and his chiefs of staff.

At the individual level Tojo was extraordinarily deferential and consistently offered complete and unyielding fidelity to the emperor's express will. Examples abound; suffice it here to cite his preparedness, on the eve of his prime ministerial appointment, to order the immediate withdrawal of all Japanese troops from China in the event Hirohito ordered him to do so. Yet Tojo was no mere automaton. He reported to the throne with unparalleled frequency, and the emperor later recalled how Tojo spoke "plainly" and tried to draw out and understand his own position on matters.[48] In this way Tojo engaged his emperor in a genuine two-way dialogue and tried to fulfill his constitutional duty of "encouraging" what was "proper" and "discountenancing" what was "improper."[49]

Tojo's positioning ensured that he played a central role in shaping the emperor's will. To return to the language of the Imperial Rescript to Soldiers and Sailors, Tojo very much regarded himself as one of the emperor's "limbs" and, as such, believed it was only right and proper that he do much of the legwork before the emperor reached any decision. This, in turn, magnified and maximized Tojo's influence. He could certainly lay claim to the emperor's trust.[50] On the eve of the Pearl Harbor attack, Tojo was satisfied that, because he had reported "without omission" to Hirohito, the opening of hostilities was "based on His Majesty the Emperor's decision."[51] Others around the throne agreed: the emperor ultimately accepted—even if only regretfully—that diplomacy had run its course and war was the only way forward.[52] Yet even as he sought to bend the emperor to his will, Tojo remained fiercely loyal to him. It was a loyalty he preserved until the very end: in large part, he accepted full responsibility at the Tokyo trial because he believed this would shield the emperor from being tried as a war criminal. This was his final service to emperor and nation, and he approached it with a fierce and uncompromising dignity.

The emperor, for his part, saw much in Tojo that was praiseworthy. He told his courtiers in early 1946 that Tojo had been a "diligent" worker who paid "meticulous" attention to detail. Perhaps most impressive of all, Tojo possessed a rare—almost unique—ability to impose order on an obstinately reckless army in which a spirit of *gekokujo* (insubordination) otherwise reigned supreme. The emperor also found much to criticize in Tojo. For one thing, he saw at least some truth in the Japanese people's perception of Tojo as a "tyrant" or "despot." This the emperor attributed to two factors: First was Tojo's penchant for holding "too many positions": besides serving as prime minister and army minister and later as army chief of staff, Tojo also served at varying times during the war as foreign minister, home minister, munitions minister, commerce and industry minister, and Greater East Asia minister. The second factor was Tojo's "overuse" of the *kenpei* to silence domestic dissent.[53]

Various other factors combined to lower Tojo in the emperor's estimation. Tojo's role in the opening and again in the endgame of the war in the Pacific theater also left a lasting impression. After the guns had fallen silent, Hirohito held Tojo directly accountable for having ignored international law and thereby ensuring that the nation marched to war in the Pacific without issuing a declaration of war. Then, in the final days of war, Tojo himself lurched out of control and opposed the emperor's decision to surrender. Tojo quickly forsook this position, returned to his characteristic fealty, and supported the decision to surrender. The emperor nonetheless found Tojo's trenchant opposition difficult to forgive or forget.[54] As a whole, the emperor viewed Tojo with what can only be called ambivalence. He told Grand Steward Tajima Michiji on July 14, 1950, of the two "faces" or "sides" he had always seen in Tojo: one had been "quite good"; the other was "very bad."[55]

THE PRESENT VOLUME TAKES its cue from the emperor and presents Tojo as neither wholly good nor wholly bad—neither hero nor villain. Instead it seeks to understand how Tojo became the man he was when he ascended to the prime ministership in October 1941. At fifty-seven years old, he had spent over four decades in service to the Imperial Japanese Army. During that time, he worked to transform military administration, outmaneuvered dozens of military rivals, redefined the army's relationship to the emperor, and honed his unparalleled ability to channel the army's immense institutional strength so that he possessed the single most powerful voice in the Japanese decision-making process. Yet by 1945 he had become the face of national defeat—the man who had dragged Japan into an irrational war that ended in national ruination.

This book looks beyond the stereotypes—Tojo as war criminal, Tojo as tragic hero, Tojo as middling bureaucrat—and considers instead the story of his formation, his motivations, and his lead role in Japan's crushing defeat. It also treats Tojo as a fascinating point of entry into a breathtakingly wide array of events and issues in Japanese military history. No other figure so starkly highlights the transition from Meiji- through Taisho- to Showa-era military leadership, the intensity of factional politics within the Imperial Army, or the military doctrines and strategies that guided Japanese military thinkers in the decades before the Second World War.

The origins of this story, however, lie with the generation of military men who preceded and influenced Tojo, including his father Tojo Hidenori, one of the Imperial Army's finest early generation staff officers. Indeed, Tojo's youth as part of a vaunted military family would come to shape his trajectory in profound ways. It is, then, to this chapter of his life we must now turn, paying particular attention to Tojo's doctrinal and educational inheritances, as well as the genesis of his lifelong hatred for the army's founding father, Field Marshal Yamagata Aritomo, and those who followed in his footsteps.

1
TOJO'S YOUTH
1884–1912

ON JULY 30, 1884, Tojo Chitose bore her husband, Hidenori, a son. It was the seventeenth year of the Meiji Emperor's reign, and the birth took place in Tokyo's Kojimachi ward, a mere stone's throw from the Imperial Palace in central Tokyo. Only a few decades earlier, the palace had been the shogun's castle, the ward home to shogunal retainers, feudal lords, and wealthy merchants. Since the collapse of the Tokugawa Shogunate's system of controls and the restoration of political power to the Imperial throne in 1868, some of the ward's large, landscaped gardens had given way to an army parade ground, while others had been converted to such novelties as dairy and beef farms. The bovine presence reflected a newfound fascination with all things Western and presented an interesting case study of the national attempt at modernizing in accord with new practices and knowledge sought—to borrow the words of the Imperial Charter Oath of April 1868—from "throughout the world."[1] More prosaically, the farms provided gainful employment for small numbers of samurai who might otherwise have found no role for themselves in Japan's postfeudal order.

The plight of Japan's samurai class was a vital part of the newborn baby's recent family history. His paternal grandfather, Hidetoshi, had been a retainer of the Morioka feudal domain (which cut across modern-day Akita, Aomori, and Iwate Prefectures in Northern Honshu). A practitioner of the Hosho school of Noh theater, he had received an annual stipend of 160 koku of rice (one koku is approximately five bushels), which placed him at the higher end of the domain's middle-ranking samurai. A change in domain hierarchy in the early 1850s signaled a dramatic career change, and Hidetoshi received orders to immerse himself in the teachings of the neo-Confucian scholar Tojo Ichido. He did so with gusto, and in August 1856 adopted Tojo as his surname.[2]

Tojo Hidetoshi's life and career prospects plummeted after the Morioka domain chose to remain loyal to the moribund Tokugawa Shogunate and fought a losing campaign against Imperial forces during the Boshin Civil War of 1868–1869. The new Imperial government seized the domain and imposed harsh penalties on the feudal lord, and the impact on the Tojo family was immense. Tojo Hidetoshi lost his retainer's status and his stipend; to make ends meet, he opened a school that taught paying students an eclectic mix of Noh theater and neo-Confucianism.[3]

His firstborn son and heir, Tojo Hidenori, saw little future in such endeavors. Born in December 1855, at about the same time his father was reinventing himself as a neo-Confucian scholar, Tojo Hidenori left the family home in the early 1870s for the capital, Tokyo. He opted for a career in the new Imperial Japanese Army, and in April 1873 entered the Noncommissioned Officers Training Unit. He graduated eighteen months later, and received his first posting to the Kumamoto garrison on the island of Kyushu. Tojo Hidenori was then transferred to the Fourteenth Infantry Regiment in 1877, distinguishing himself in the Seinan War against Saigo Takamori's rebellious samurai army. This civil war signaled a bloody end to the samurai class, and within the Imperial Army it embedded the concept of the service as the ultimate arbiter of the emperor's will and state affairs. For Tojo Hidenori it offered opportunity: In the early aftermath of the war he was recalled to Tokyo, where he received his commission and was promoted to the position of second lieutenant.

After a brief posting as an instructor at the Army Toyama School in Tokyo, Tojo Hidenori engaged in operational planning on the Army General Staff in the early 1880s. He had found his vocation; indeed, he so impressed his superiors that he was given the opportunity to join the inaugural class of the new War College in Tokyo. Here his humble noncommissioned career origins placed him well outside the norm. His classmates, including Akiyama Yoshifuru, Iguchi Shogo, and Ishibashi Kenzo, had all followed the military's elite educational pathway, which began at the Military Academy and now included the War College.[4]

During their third and final year at the college, Tojo Hidenori and his classmates had the good fortune to study under the "father of modern military education in Japan," Major Klemens Wilhelm Jakob Meckel, a Prussian officer.[5] The Imperial Japanese Army had, after a brief flirtation with the French military model, self-consciously modeled itself after its Prussian counterpart, and Meckel's arrival at the War College reflected the strong German influence. Meckel brought an unwavering belief in the superiority of men and morale over technology and firepower. This fed his insistence on the need for tight infantry formations, iron discipline, and relentless attack from the very outset of war. Meckel advocated for mobilization before any declaration of war, and he emphasized the efficacy of peacetime drills, maneuvers, war gaming, and training. And he insisted that military history was not made up of tales of valor and heroism but instead involved a careful examination of lessons to be learned from the past.

Meckel sought to adapt his own convictions to Japan's situation and to lay the foundations of Japanese military doctrine and strategic thought. In one lecture, which he published under the title "Yasenho haisu beki no setsu" (The theory that field artillery should be abolished), Meckel insisted that Japan's topography had deeply influenced the Japanese way of war. The fact that steep, rugged mountains cover approximately three-fourths of Japan's principal islands meant, in Meckel's reading of history, that the Japanese had themselves long since recognized the impracticality of "waging war with field artillery." Feudal Japan's emphasis on courage in hand-to-hand combat was, in his estimation, a laudable tradition that placed the nation in good stead in a world in which the infantry continued, in Meckel's estimation, to reign militarily supreme. Meckel nonetheless insisted that the Japanese Army must recognize its weakness and must therefore adopt an essentially "defensive" posture. "Offensive" warfare was, he felt, permissible only against China. The Chinese were, like the Japanese, ardently pursuing military modernization, but Meckel emphasized that the Qing dynasty had focused not on strengthening its infantry but instead on costly field artillery. This he dismissed as a "waste of money and labor" and "unwise" in a world in which the "powerful ate the flesh of the weak." His conclusion virtually presented itself: the Japanese Army ought to focus on building its infantry arm and preparing to wage offensive war against the doctrinally unsound Chinese military.[6]

Meckel's influence was hardly electrifying. His lectures, delivered in German, had a reputation for turgidity and impenetrability. And he was a most exacting taskmaster. Of the twenty-one who entered the War College's first class, only ten graduated; Meckel cast away those he deemed dull, unconscientious, or inattentive to their studies. He held Tojo Hidenori, however, in the highest esteem, regarding him as the Japanese Army's "preeminent" young officer.[7] True to Meckel's assessment, Tojo Hidenori graduated first in his class in December 1885. He then taught at the college, where he remained under Meckel's influence and established himself as one of the Imperial Army's leading young staff officers. Then, in a sure sign that his star was rising, Tojo Hidenori was ordered in March 1888 to Germany, and spent the subsequent eighteen months attached to the German General Staff.[8]

After returning to Tokyo, Tojo Hidenori was posted to the General Staff. There he engaged in operational planning through the early 1890s. During the Sino-Japanese War of 1894–1895, he worked closely under the Imperial Army's chief of staff, General Kawakami Soroku, and in the final weeks of the war, he served under the chief of the combined staff, Prince Komatsu Akihito. After the war he undertook a lightning tour of Russia, presumably to observe and discern Russian intentions in Northeast Asia. Tojo Hidenori returned to Tokyo and replaced Lieutenant Colonel Uehara Yusaku as head of the General Staff bureau charged with compiling the official military history of the recent war. In a manner befitting one of Meckel's foremost disciples, he insisted that this history must not merely flatter the army's upper echelons; it must instead be written with a view to instructing future generations in the art of troop movement and war strategy.[9] Even as he presided over preparation of this official history, Tojo Hidenori also taught at the War College. The lessons of the Sino-Japanese War were a prominent feature of his classes.

Tojo Hidenori's career stalled at the dawn of the new century. In what was an almost unimaginably incongruous appointment, he was transferred in May 1901 to command the inconsequential Eighth Infantry Brigade in Hyogo Prefecture. He then served, without distinction, in the Russo-Japanese War of 1904–1905 and was retired from active service at the rank of lieutenant general in November 1907. Some regard his early retirement as the result of poor battlefield performances during the Russo-Japanese War and of his subsequent ill health.[10] There may, perhaps, be some element of truth in this, but it fails to account for the fact that this brilliant staff officer was frozen out of operational planning positions years *before* the Russo-Japanese War.

The most plausible explanation for the inglorious end to Tojo Hidenori's career rests with the army's so-called *hanbatsu* personnel practices of nepotism and cronyism that entrenched in positions of power officers from the former Choshu feudal domain (present-day Yamaguchi Prefecture). Attributable to the leading role Choshu had played in the downfall of the Tokugawa Shogunate and in the Meiji Restoration of 1868, these *hanbatsu* personnel practices were championed by Field Marshal Yamagata Aritomo, a leading soldier and statesman and himself a former Choshu samurai. Tojo Hidenori had, while still a relatively junior officer, confronted Yamagata and demanded an end to nepotism and cronyism. His arguments for a meritocratic military succeeded only in making him a target of Yamagata and his cronies, including generals Katsura Taro, Kodama Gentaro, and Terauchi Masatake (the latter hailed from the Satsuma domain, but he assiduously cultivated Yamagata's patronage). As early as the mid-1890s, even as Tojo Hidenori prepared the Japanese Army's official history of the Sino-Japanese War, he had clashed repeatedly—and, by all accounts, heatedly—with Terauchi, who was serving as army vice chief of staff and who saw no good coming from critical appraisals of senior officers' wartime decisions. Tojo Hidenori now found himself a marked man. The imperturbable Kawakami, a non-Choshu general with a well-earned reputation as a fine military strategist, valued Tojo Hidenori's abilities and shielded him from the vindictive Choshu generals.[11] Yet Kawakami's death in 1899 removed the only real obstacle between the Choshu generals and their quarry. In 1901, Kodama signed off on Tojo Hidenori's transfer to Hyogo Prefecture; Terauchi banished him from active service in 1907. Following his enforced retirement, Tojo Hidenori published numerous books as a military commentator. He died an embittered man in 1913.

His wife, Chitose, was born into the Tokunaga family in 1861. The daughter of a True Pure Land Buddhist priest, she had grown up in the contemplative surroundings of Mantokuji Temple in the historic city of Kokura on Kyushu. She was a pious woman, and engaged at least occasionally in standard True Pure Land practice, chanting "Namu Amida Butsu" (I take refuge in Amida Buddha). It seems almost axiomatic that she kept, in adulthood, a household altar encasing Buddhist images and memorial tablets for deceased ancestors. Whatever Chitose's level of religiosity, it did not preclude her marrying someone from an altogether different religious tradition. (Many decades later, after the war had been lost and after Tojo Hideki had rediscovered Buddhism, he recalled not only his mother's Buddhism but also his father's identification with Shinto, the native Japanese belief system.)[12]

Chitose first met Tojo Hidenori in the mid-1870s, when he was posted to the Fourteenth Infantry Regiment (based on Kyushu). The two married in 1878, when she was still a teen. She ultimately gave birth to seven sons and two daughters. Hideki was her third son; her two elder sons had both died in infancy. The family doctor attributed the deaths to Chitose's lead-based cosmetics: her lead-laden breastmilk had, he surmised, poisoned the children. Rather than risk subjecting their third child to the same fate, Hideki's parents put him out to nurse. He returned to his birth parents' household some five months later, after he had been weaned. For this reason, the family register records his birthdate as December 30, 1884.[13]

Little is recorded about Tojo Hideki's earliest years. It is known that his mother rejected common practice among military families and refused to allow a housemaid to raise her child. (Some believe this was probably due to a nervous disposition, exacerbated by the loss of her first two children.)[14] It is also known that the young family moved first to Samoncho and a few years later to nearby Sugacho, in Tokyo's Yotsuya ward, which was home to many military families. It was also, if one of Japan's best-known ghost stories is to be believed, home to a female phantom named Oiwa. Her vengeful malevolence must surely have helped young mothers, like Chitose, in their efforts at frightening any undesirable behaviors out of their children.[15]

Tojo Hidenori's posting to Germany occurred when Hideki was only three years old. It was unthinkable for a soldier to take his family abroad; Chitose remained behind with Hideki and newborn baby daughter Hatsue. Joining them was her aging father-in-law Tojo Hidetoshi, who had torn himself from the family home in the former Morioka domain and would now live out his final years with his son's family in Tokyo.

Hideki began his formal education at Yotsuya Elementary School in September 1890. Two years later, his family again moved, this time to Okubomachi (present-day Nishi Okubo). Various military installations, including the Army Research and Development Command and an army firing range, were in the area, and military families were common. In the meantime, Hideki had moved at his father's insistence to the aristocratic Gakushuin Elementary School. Here many of his well-heeled classmates traveled to school by rickshaw. Some ate lunch in the school canteen, while others had freshly cooked meals brought to them by household maids during lunch hours. Hideki must have felt positively spartan as he walked to and from school—it was at least a forty-five-minute walk each way—and carried his own lunch.[16]

Hideki lasted little more than a year at Gakushuin. A recent study plausibly suggests this was likely due to a hard-learned lesson in snobbery: A military officer's lofty status in Meiji society meant nothing to the scions of Japan's noblest families, who refused to accept a military officer's son as one of their own.[17] He moved to Aoyama Higher Elementary School, which had quite a large number of military officer's sons, for the school shared a neighborhood with the Imperial Army's First and Third Infantry Regiments and an Imperial Guard firing range was also nearby. It was in this more familiar setting that Hideki completed his elementary school education.

Hideki's time at Aoyama Higher Elementary School coincided with Japan's war against China. A youth like Hideki could not help but be swept up in the wave of patriotic fervor to which the war gave rise; everyone, after all, was talking about the war.[18] His father, a staff officer responsible for the war's operational planning, must have explained to his young son that Japan was fighting China for the right of influence on the Korean Peninsula. Questions abounded: Would traditional Chinese concepts of regional order prevail? Would Korea remain, as it had for centuries, a Chinese vassal state? Or would Japan displace China and impose on Korea instead a relationship modeled after Western nations' relationships with the non-Western world? Would the war vindicate Japan's determined pursuit—since the Meiji Restoration of 1868—of modernity? Would Japan's Imperial forces emerge victorious over their vastly more numerous Chinese opponents? His mind awash with such questions, Hideki decided at this time to strike out on a career as a military officer.

Yet he did not want to replicate his father's unorthodox path to military commission. Hideki would instead tread the service's elite educational pathway, which now included not just the Military Academy and the War College but also, as a first step, the Military Preparatory School. Successful completion of the first year of junior high school was the minimum standard of education for entry; in September 1898 Tojo Hideki entered Johoku Junior High School, which had earned a reputation as a nursery for aspiring cadets.[19] In his first twelve months there, he sat and passed the military preparatory school entrance exam.

The Military Preparatory School had first opened its gates in 1887, and it offered a soldier's preparatory training, as well as a junior high school education. The school had initially been under the direct authority of the army minister, but by Tojo's time it had come under the authority of the inspector general of military training. Outside the military, some worried that the school's provenance undermined what was otherwise a centrally controlled education system. Many pointed to the martial training that was part of the standard civilian junior high school curriculum and questioned whether and why this was inadequate for the army's purposes. The Imperial Army was unmoved, at least partly because it sought to cordon off aspiring officers from the supposedly antithetical democratic trends unleashed by the new Imperial Diet and the dreaded political parties. To this end, cadets memorized the Imperial Rescript to

Soldiers and Sailors, which the Meiji Emperor issued in 1882; it forbade "meddl[ing] in politics" and emphasized the "essential duty of loyalty" to the emperor.[20] The Military Preparatory School instilled in its cadets two basic concepts: (1) the army as the ultimate executor of the emperor's will, and (2) the cadets themselves as the army's future elite. Despite the school's external critics, the army deemed it a success, and in 1897 it opened regional schools in Hiroshima, Kumamoto, Nagoya, Osaka, Sendai, and Tokyo. It also established the Central Military Preparatory School, where graduates of the six local schools received a further two years of military training and education.[21]

Decades later, the Showa Emperor complained bitterly about his officers and the education they had received in the Meiji-era military preparatory schools. He criticized his generals for conflating the army's outlook with the nation's best interests, and accused them of seeing things "superficially," attributing this to what he called the "unsatisfactory" and indeed "blinkered" education they had received in the schools. The emperor was critical of what he believed was the schools' focus on independence of action, for however necessary such independence might be on the battlefield, it was having a baneful effect on the nation's policymaking processes. The generals, in the emperor's estimation, seemed all too prepared to act first and later present the government with faits accomplis (as we shall see, Tojo himself was not altogether immune from such behavior). As far as the emperor was concerned, the schools had instilled in officers an unpredictable "arbitrariness" and a wrongheaded conviction that the "ends justified the means."[22]

Such concerns were, however, far in the future when fifteen-year-old Tojo Hideki entered the Tokyo regional Military Preparatory School in September 1899. He and the other cadets were immediately placed into one of two companies. Each company was formed of six platoons comprising first-, second-, and third-year cadets. A third-year cadet commanded each platoon. The lifestyle was predictably regimented: a bugle woke cadets every morning at 0530 hours, and cadets moved from one activity to the next at the call of a bugle until lights-out at 2100 hours. In Tojo's time, the school's educational priorities were fourfold: physical fitness; respect for emperor and love of country; cultural knowledge; and a soldierly steadfastness founded on self-discipline.[23] Considerable focus was placed on preparatory military training, which included calisthenics, marching, reconnaissance, horse riding, swimming, and marksmanship. General education classes included history, geography, literature, cartography, arithmetic, science, foreign languages, and the Chinese classics.[24]

Tojo did not distinguish himself academically. He spoke to a later generation of cadets about what he regarded in hindsight as his "failings." He freely admitted to having been "inattentive" to his studies, and to having received particularly poor grades in German and composition. He related how he had held books in "contempt" and recalled how he had not been among the academically high-achieving cadets to whom the school granted weekend leaves of absence. He spoke of the scoldings to which Superintendent Lieutenant Horii Takasumi had subjected him for his academic underperformance. He nonetheless graduated, and in September 1902 he matriculated to the Central Military Preparatory School. Here each cadet's arm of service was decided, and Tojo entered the most prestigious arm, the infantry. He began to "take responsibility" for his grades and his future. Most important, he learned the value of rote learning and detailed note-taking, and on May 31, 1904, he graduated equal third in the school's infantry arm. The lesson was not lost on Tojo, who remained to the end of his days an avid note-taker.[25]

The military preparatory schools played host to some notable dignitaries during Tojo's time there. Far and away the most memorable guest was the Meiji Emperor, who graced the school's graduation ceremonies with his Imperial presence in May 1903, and again when Tojo graduated in May 1904.[26] The pomp and ceremony served to remind the cadets—if indeed they needed reminding—of the Imperial Army's frequent and fierce professions of loyal service to the emperor and of their own role as the emperor's "limbs."[27] It is not at all difficult to imagine Tojo, who remained to the end of his days unstinting in his loyalty to the emperor, exulting in these Imperial visits. He was, however, less than enthused by the visit of one of his father's tormentors. General Terauchi Masatake, an army minister (and Yamagata protégé) also came to the Central Military Preparatory School to address the cadets. Tojo did not listen to a word. Instead he glowered at Terauchi and muttered to himself about the "bullying" to which the Choshu generals and their lackeys were subjecting his father.[28] Tojo never forgave and never forgot his father's mistreatment. His hatred for Choshu was lifelong and deep.

Tojo and his fellow Central Military Preparatory School graduates subsequently formed the crux of the Military Academy's seventeenth class. Established in 1874, the academy followed on from the military preparatory schools as the military's next elite educational step, and its educational standards were the same as that of Meiji-era normal schools. The focus was, however, almost solely on professional military subjects and military training. Cadets took classes in military tactics, military organization, weapons training, fortifications, geography, horse riding, swordsmanship, calisthenics, and battlefield sanitation. Only foreign language classes, including Chinese, English, French, German, and Russian, were taught by civilian instructors.[29]

Tojo and his preparatory school classmates would ordinarily have waited until March 1905 before entering the academy; in the interim, they would have received postings to the garrisons. Yet the military hierarchy felt an acute need for an influx of junior officers, as Japan had gone to war with Russia in February 1904. As had been the case in Japan's previous war, against China, this war was again fought over the future of Korea, for the Russians had in the intervening years replaced the Chinese and were competing with Japan for dominance over the Korean Peninsula. The manpower needs and the costs of the war were almost unimaginably high:

A Tojo family portrait, undated but likely taken between June 1904 and May 1905. Tojo Hideki is standing third from left in the back row. His father is standing in the back row, center, and his mother is seated in the front row, third from left. His grandfather is also seated in the front row, third from right.

Tojo Hidenori and three of his sons. The photo is undated, but was likely taken between June 1904 and May 1905. Tojo Hideki is standing to his father's left.

Over the course of the conflict, the Japanese Army mobilized twenty-five (seventeen active and eight reserve) divisions. It sent approximately one million men to the front, and of those, some eighty-four thousand died on the battlefield and another 143,000 were seriously wounded.[30] Field Marshal Terauchi Masatake (who in 1904 was serving concurrently as army minister and inspector general of military training) thus pushed forward the seventeenth class's entry to the academy to June 1, 1904. The need to fast-track their education was pressing, so vacations and weekends were eliminated and the Military Academy's two-year curriculum was condensed into eleven busy months.[31]

Two events from Tojo's time at the academy deserve mention. The first was an official visit by Prince Karl Anton of Hohenzollern-Sigmaringen on September 19, 1904, which served as a powerful reminder of the ties that continued to bind the German and Japanese Armies and also aimed at guarding against the possibility of increased Russo-German cooperation.[32] The second event pitted Tojo against a cadet who had entered the Military Academy not via the military preparatory school system but instead via a civilian school.[33] Such youths were locatable across all Military Academy years and were derisively referred to as "d's," or "donkeys." On one occasion, a member of the seventeenth class tightly slammed shut the lunchbox of a company commander who had the misfortune of being a "donkey." The unwitting company commander struggled unsuccessfully to open his lunchbox against the humiliating backdrop of his subordinates' roaring laughter. Struggling to contain his anger, the "donkey" commander singled out Tojo and demanded to know the cause of his mirth. "It was funny," a disdainful Tojo responded, "so I laughed." The enraged commander then struck out with his fists. A classmate recalled that, throughout the prolonged beating, an unbowed Tojo stood at attention and glared at his assailant.[34]

Tojo's final days at the Military Academy in March 1905 included an excursion to the Imperial Palace. The graduation ceremony was held on March 30 in the emperor's august presence, and he personally awarded binoculars to the top eight graduates.[35] Tojo just missed this distinction, for he graduated tenth in his class. He did not have long to nurse any disappointment at this near miss, however; within weeks of graduation he was commissioned as a second lieutenant and assigned to the Imperial Guard's Third Division, based in Tokyo's Akasaka district. Then, in July, he was posted to the Fifty-Ninth Infantry Regiment, which formed part of the Fifteenth Division and had been ordered to the Asian continent. Tojo did not, however, see combat in the Russo-Japanese War. The Fifty-Ninth served as a garrison force at Port Arthur (present-day Lushun, China) and the Japanese Army had pushed Russian forces as far north as Changchun. Both Japan and Russia had, moreover, long since accepted US President Theodore Roosevelt's formal offer of mediation to end the war, and the Portsmouth Peace Conference began only weeks after Tojo's arrival in Manchuria.

The peace conference confirmed that Japan had won the war and, by so doing, had carved out for itself a position as the preeminent continental power in East Asia. By the terms of the Treaty of Portsmouth, Russia recognized Japan's "paramount political, military, and economic interests" in Korea. (Japan would formally annex Korea in 1910.) Russia transferred to Japan the balance of its twenty-five-year lease on the Liaodong Peninsula (which the Japanese subsequently renamed the Kwantung Leased Territory), and ceded the southern half of the island of Sakhalin to Japan. Russian forces that had remained in Manchuria since the Boxer Rebellion of 1900 withdrew, and Russia transferred to Japan the right to the railroad connecting Changchun and Port Arthur, as well as several connecting lines and spurs. (In 1906 the Japanese established the South Manchuria Railway to operate the railways taken over from the Russians.)

The Treaty of Portsmouth was not well received in Japan. Violence broke out on Tokyo's streets after it became apparent that the treaty made no provision for an indemnity from Russia. During the so-called Hibiya Riot of early September 1905, rioters torched three-fourths of Tokyo's police boxes and destroyed buildings and streetcars around the capital. To restore order, the government declared martial law.[36] The nation's soldiers—Tojo almost certainly included—were more realistic in their appraisal of the treaty than were the rioters. They well recognized that not only the Imperial Army but the nation itself was on the verge of exhaustion and unable to continue the war.[37] Besides, the army had achieved practically everything it had hoped to achieve. As General Hayashi Senjuro put it many years later, the military had pushed the Russians out of Korea and had then aimed to "drive Russian troops out of Manchuria." Attainment of this aim, even in the absence of indemnities, was "enough."[38]

Tojo returned to Tokyo in September, soon after the Hibiya Riot. The following April he returned to the Imperial Guard's Third Division (which had, in his absence, been pressed into martial law service during the riot). In December 1907 he was promoted to first lieutenant. By this time Tojo was developing a reputation as a "scholarly" and "frugal" young officer of "good character" who possessed a filial "pride" in his father's accomplishments.[39] These traits made him an eminently eligible late Meiji-era bachelor, and his parents sought a suitable bride.

Just such a woman arrived in the form of Ito Katsuko. The daughter of a Kyushu landlord, she was distantly related to Tojo's mother and had boarded, as a normal school student, at the temple in which Tojo's mother had been raised. She was an intelligent young woman, and earned entry to Japan Women's College in Tokyo, where she studied Japanese literature. Her father drew on the familial connection, wrote the recently retired Tojo Hidenori, and explained that Katsuko needed a guarantor as well as a place to board. Tojo's father granted both requests. In so doing he implicitly acknowledged an unstated—but presumably no less obvious—request that he attend to Katsuko's future marriage prospects.[40]

Tojo Hideki and Katsuko married on April 11, 1909. He was twenty-five and she nineteen. Tojo's parents added a room to their family home for the young couple. In a not unusual happenstance, Katsuko became almost immediately responsible for managing a household that included her grandfather-, parents-, brothers-, and sisters-in-law and nieces and nephews.[41] The demands on Katsuko's time were great and, despite her efforts, she seemed unable to meet her mother-in-law's expectations. At issue was Chitose's unwavering belief that a woman's place was not in the study hall but in the home; two months into married life, Katsuko withdrew from her final year of college. Even this seemed not to placate the domineering Chitose, and within months, Tojo spoke with his father about the need to move. The young couple did so with the patriarch's blessing.[42]

The difficult relationship between his mother and wife was an unwelcome distraction for Tojo Hideki, who was deep in preparation for the War College entrance exam. There was good reason to seek entry to the college. For one thing, Tojo almost necessarily must have keenly felt the weight of expectation that accrued to the son of the officer who graduated atop the college's inaugural class. He was also ambitious, and ambition demanded a college education; the War College was the final step in the military's elite educational pathway. A graduate, immediately identifiable by the prominent badge he wore on his right breast, was by no means guaranteed promotion to general rank, but nonentry to the college practically ensured early retirement at or around the rank of colonel.

Entry to the college was a formidable process. Aspiring entrants had to have served in the military for two years and attained a rank of either first or second lieutenant. They were required to have a robust academic record from their time at the Military Academy, and a subsequent record of exemplary conduct. They needed to demonstrate good health during an extensive physical examination, and their superiors needed to be convinced of their devotion to duty. The upper age limit was twenty-eight.[43] In Tojo's time, some two thousand officers sought entry annually. In April of each year they sat a written test that ran the gamut of questions on algebra, fortifications, troop movements, weapons, tactics, and operations.[44] The one hundred officers with the highest marks on the written exam then took an oral exam, conducted in December by college instructors, and the fifty best-performing officers gained entry to the college.

As was the case with all aspiring students to the college, Tojo needed significant preparation time. He sought and attained the active support of his commanding officer, Colonel Shiba Katsusaburo, who transferred Tojo to the Military Academy in October 1909. Tojo's duties there were light: three times each week, he drilled cadets of the academy's twenty-fourth class; by happy coincidence, his father had recently published a drill manual. The younger Tojo (who seemed by now to have forgotten his earlier contempt for the written word) pored over his father's book, and sought as best he could to follow its Meckelian emphases on infantry, attack, and training. Most fundamentally, he based his actions on his father's twin insistences that the "most urgent and indispensable requirement of war" was maintenance of "discipline and order," and such discipline and order must be "taught in peacetime" so that they would "not be eradicated on the battlefield."[45] Tojo Hideki was perhaps too exacting a drillmaster, for the cadets hated him and regarded him as "neurotic." He learned over time not to be overly zealous, and the cadets came eventually to hold him in high regard.[46]

When not drilling on the parade ground, Tojo spent his time studying, deep in preparation for the entrance exam. Even so, he did not expect to pass the exam on his first attempt. He understood, as he put it to his father, that failure on the first attempt was almost an unwritten rule and that officers were expected to take the entrance exam multiple times before they entered the college.[47] Sure enough, he failed the written exam on his first attempt in April 1910, and he failed again the following year. Facing the upper age limit, Tojo now had one final chance. He redoubled his efforts over the next twelve months, aided by First Lieutenants Nagata Tetsuzan, Obata Toshiro, and Okamura Yasuji. These men had all been a year ahead of Tojo in the Military Academy and were his closest friends. As we shall see, in the 1920s Tojo and these officers formed a number of clandestine associations, before their relationships broke down amid disagreements over military strategy.[48] But in April 1912, with their help, Tojo passed the written exam.[49] He took the oral exam that December and was the fifth-highest performer among college entrants.[50]

This all took place against the backdrop of the death in July 1912 of the Meiji Emperor. Tojo's reaction to the end of the Meiji era is undocumented, although he almost certainly shared in nationwide feelings of pride at the era's significant progress and achievements. Japan was no longer a feudal backwater on the fringes of world politics but could now count itself among the world's great powers. It boasted a constitutional government, a highly efficient and centralized bureaucracy, a rapidly growing and technologically advanced industrial sector, and a powerful army and navy. By virtue of its successful wars against China and Russia, Japan also possessed a burgeoning empire, with colonies in Korea and Taiwan and a sphere of interest in Manchuria.

It also seems fair to suggest that Tojo, at the end of the Meiji era, reflected on the Imperial Army's basic strategic outlook. The military's initial postwar annual operational plan, sanctioned by the Meiji Emperor in April 1906, designated Russia as the Imperial Japanese Army's most likely enemy and Manchuria as the likely battlefield. The plan, which remained basically unchanged over subsequent years, called for a fast-moving offensive against Russian troops in northern Manchuria, a deliberate attack against Harbin with the intention of engaging the enemy there in a decisive battle, and the severance from Russia of the far eastern end of the Trans-Siberian Railway between Vladivostok and Khabarovsk.[51] The Meiji Emperor had, one year later, sanctioned the Imperial National Defense Policy, which enshrined the concept of Russia as the Imperial Japanese Army's hypothetical enemy (and the United States as the Imperial Japanese Navy's hypothetical enemy). The policy called for armament expansion on a massive scale. According to the policy, it was imperative that the army expand from nineteen to twenty-five active divisions (while also maintaining another twenty-five reserve divisions); the navy was to expand its fleet to include eight new battleships and eight new cruisers (the so-called eight-eight fleet).[52]

Tojo left to posterity no contemporaneous record that might shed light on various issues that arose from these operational and strategic concepts, and we are thus compelled to make some educated guesses. There is every reason to believe that Tojo agreed wholeheartedly with Russia's designation as the army's most likely enemy, if only because no other nation could hope to dislodge Japan from its hard-earned position on the continent. He doubtless also joined most military officers in professing bewilderment at the navy's refusal to fall in line behind the army's insistence on Russia as *the* hypothetical enemy. He almost certainly celebrated the army's toppling of the cabinet of Prime Minister Saionji Kimmochi—set in motion by Army Minister Uehara Yusaku's ministerial resignation in December 1912—after the cabinet took a "navy first, army second" approach to funding and showed more enthusiasm for the navy's expensive but popular shipbuilding programs than for the army's professed need for two new divisions.[53]

Tojo's father died some eighteen months after the Meiji Emperor. He had been suffering from ill health for some time, and in his final years moved from Tokyo to the healing climes of the hot spring resort town of Odawara. His death on his fifty-eighth birthday, in December 1913, caused nary a ripple in the army that had discarded him. Tojo might have been forgiven had he contrasted the silence that surrounded his father's passing with the nationwide commentary that followed the passing of another Meiji-era general: Nogi Maresuke's act of *junshi* (following his lord into death) by means of ritual suicide on the day of the Meiji Emperor's funeral in September 1912—the general was joined by his wife, Shizuko—recalled for many Japan's "half-forgotten" feudal past.[54] For Tojo it almost certainly recalled Nogi's Choshu origins and the privileges this accident of birthplace seemed still to bestow in the Imperial Japanese Army.

Whatever the depth of Tojo's discontent at the Choshu officers' ongoing domination of the Imperial Japanese Army, it would be at least another ten years before he was able to act on it. In the intervening years he was to study military art and science at the War College. He then spent several years in central Europe, seeking lessons from World War I. Tojo emerged from these experiences with contradictory views about the next war Japan was likely to fight. For one thing, he recognized the likelihood of a protracted war of attrition, which would test not merely the fighting capabilities of the Japanese soldier but indeed Japan's overall national strength. He also wondered whether Japan could avert such an unsettling possibility by forcing on its opponent a cataclysmic decisive battle, fought as soon as possible after the opening of hostilities.

2
THE MAKING OF A POLITICAL OFFICER
1912–1929

TOJO HIDEKI ENTERED JAPAN'S Taisho period as a typical, elite-level, young army officer. His education in the military preparatory schools and later the Military Academy had kept him at arm's length from what many in the Imperial Japanese Army regarded as "subversive" ideologies associated with the ongoing processes of industrialization, urbanization, and modernization; Tojo, like practically all of his professional military colleagues, looked askance at the dislocations created by such imported ideas as individualism, liberalism, materialism, consumerism, utilitarianism, democracy, socialism, communism, and anarchism.[1] Political consensus, too, seemed distressingly distant to uniformed officers in the Japanese Army. Responsibility was divided between and among institutions so that contributions to decisions were made not just by the army but also its sister service, the Imperial Japanese Navy, and the various bureaucracies. There was also the Imperial Diet, which, to the army's chagrin, enjoyed the constitutional privilege of approving the budget. Diet politicians had not only evinced a willingness to challenge the army's plans for expansion; their predilection for debate and mutual opposition posed challenges for soldiers and their prioritization of domestic unity, order, and stability.

It would nonetheless be a mistake to assume that Tojo concerned himself much with the social ferment, cultural dynamism, and political upheaval that was such a feature of the early Taisho period. In December 1912 he entered the War College as a member of its twenty-seventh class. The college purported to foster the development of staff officers, field officers, and commanders; its educational emphases included not ideological debate and political discussion but instead the "science of advanced strategy and tactics" and "the various academic disciplines indispensable to military research."[2] The three most critical professional military subjects were, in order of descending importance, military science, military history, and operational staff planning. Also included were military geography, military transport, weapons training, fortifications, accounting, and battlefield sanitation. All of these subjects were, almost without exception, taught by middle-echelon officers who had themselves graduated from the War College five to ten years earlier. General education subjects also had a place in the curriculum: horsemanship was emphasized, as was foreign-language education (Chinese, English, French, German, and Russian). Other subjects included history, mathematics, statistics, and national and international law; these were taught by both officers and civilians.[3]

Military science occupied pride of place in the War College curriculum. Instructors set questions that were based on broad strategic principles and, by way of response, each student officer researched actual historical case studies. These case studies, which student officers discussed and debated at considerable length with instructors during one-on-one consultation periods, were designed to shed light on the strategic principles under investigation. Minute historical details were the order of the day. Once the instructor was satisfied with each student officer's case study, the student officer formulated a response to the original question. This response drew freely from the rich, granular detail of the student officers' case studies, but it was also designed to provide an overarching perspective and enable a clear view of particular strategic precepts. In this way the War College classroom purported to produce a stream of highly competent and meticulous planners of battlefield strategy and operations.[4]

During Tojo's time at the War College, the Russo-Japanese War provided the principal focus for both the war science and war history classrooms. The multivolume official General Staff history of the war, which was published publicly between 1912 and 1915, made up the principal text.[5] This official history steered clear of criticisms of the top brass by altogether omitting discussion of Imperial General Headquarters decision-making. It read instead as an operational combat history, and even at this level, it adhered closely to the editorial policy of avoiding criticism and instead burnishing the army's prestige.[6] Tojo and his War College classmates, on this basis, studied intensively the First Army's early success in pushing Russian forces back along the Yalu River near Dandong, the capture of Nanshan, and the Manchurian campaign that followed. Supplementary texts, including college instructor Major Tamon Jiro's *Yo ga sanka shitaru Nichi-Ro seneki* (The Russo-Japanese War in which I participated), provided further detail on these and other battles.[7] In this way Tojo and his fellow student officers studied such strategies as the battlefield offensive, surprise attacks, night attacks, encirclement, and turning maneuvers.[8]

The emphasis in the War College classroom was very much on the offensive. The spirit of the age was perhaps best captured by Tojo's friend and reputed "strategic demon," Obata Toshiro, who graduated in December 1911: "Attack is the only way . . . to achieve victory! Defense is nothing more than a temporary measure on the transition to the offense. Attack! Attack! Just go on the attack!"[9] During Tojo's time at the War College, few saw any need to question this emphasis. This might be, from the vantage point of historical hindsight, a curiously mistaken view. It certainly seems to fly in the face of the diabolically high attrition rates that Russian artillery and machine guns had inflicted on General Nogi Maresuke's Third Army during its assault against Port Arthur in early 1905. Yet this and other such examples from the Russo-Japanese War were either dismissed as anomalous or—even if only indirectly—attributed to Nogi's disastrous generalship.[10] In this latter regard, Tojo and his colleagues were unsurprisingly warned off the frontal attacks that Nogi (and other commanding officers) had pursued with reckless abandon during the war. Ideas for minimizing losses during the offensive were encapsulated by such slogans as "Bullets before bayonets," "Bombard before the signal to attack," and "Advance in stealth, not out in the open."[11]

Such reasoning may seem wrongheaded, particularly in light of the static trench warfare and mass slaughter that would very soon characterize the European battlefields of World War I. Yet the emphasis on the offensive drew on an educational tradition that traced back at least as far as the Prussian Army's Jakob Meckel, and which held the fighting abilities of the Japanese infantryman in higher regard than it did firepower. Now the experiences of the Russo-Japanese War seemed to have validated such concepts. One of Tojo's instructors, Major Muro Kenji, excoriated the "fallacy," which he said had taken hold in some quarters on the eve of the Russo-Japanese War, that held that technological advances in firepower had resulted in the defensive displacing the offensive as the "decisive" factor in modern warfare. Muro insisted that Japan's victory over Russia confirmed the ongoing primacy of the "decisive battle," replete with massed infantry charges and hand-to-hand combat.[12]

Another of Tojo's instructors, Shiba Kotaro, who aside from the foreign-language staff was one of the War College's very few civilian faculty members, reached similar conclusions. The Russo-Japanese War had, he explained, not undermined but instead reemphasized the infantry's integral role as the "mainstay" of the army. Shiba argued that firepower had not in any way changed this situation; to the contrary, he argued that the infantryman's "adoption of [powerful] firearms" had in fact increased his value and had reinforced the imperative of the infantry-led offensive.[13]

Tojo could hardly escape this overwhelming emphasis on the offensive. Nowhere did this emphasis receive fuller treatment than in the new infantry manual (*hohei soten*) that the army published in 1909.It emphasized the primacy of the Japanese infantryman over and above weaponry and firepower, the efficacy of close combat, a spirit of relentless attack, and the intangible quality of élan. Europe's major continental powers were developing their own offensive-oriented strategies; the Japanese Army's emphasis on attack was nonetheless extreme. So, too, was the insistence on forging its foot soldiers' courage under fire. In this regard, the new manual highlighted the role of "moral education" (*seishin kyoiku*). This involved imbuing the men with reverence for Japan's notoriously nebulous *kokutai,* which in this context referred to the unique essence of Japanese society, to the Imperial institution and the emperor's divinity, and to each individual soldier's absolute loyalty to the throne.[14]

An offensive spirit fired by Japanese tradition and patriotic fervor was everywhere. A training manual published in 1909 noted that battle ought ideally to end in bayonet charge, adding that peacetime training for this purpose improved "physical fitness," "spiritual vigor," and "self-confidence."[15] The war field duty manual of 1907 equated "military spirit" with *yamato damashii* (the spirit of Japan)—and also with the mythologized but self-sacrificing samurai tradition *bushido* (the way of the warrior).[16] Another publication equated the "soldier's spirit" with "loyalty, decorum, valor, loyalty, and frugality" and attributed these characteristics, in turn, to both *yamato damashii* and *bushido.*[17]

In the War College classroom, Tojo was exposed to the centrality of spiritual qualities in war. One textbook quoted journalist Shiga Shigetaka, who attributed victory in the Russo-Japanese War to the Japanese infantryman's fealty to *bushido* and courage under fire.[18] Another textbook put the case clearly: If two armies of equal size and strength clashed, then the army with greater "spirit" or élan would win. The spiritual factor was so important that a numerically inferior army could draw on its spiritual strength and defeat a much larger but spiritually inferior opponent. The Imperial Japanese Army during the Russo-Japanese War provided the "most glaring example" of this dynamic in recent times. The War College classroom considered various other examples in which élan proved decisive and, true to the army's newfound confidence in a distinctly Japanese way of war, case studies included the feudal-era Battle of Okehazama, in which Oda Nobunaga's vastly outnumbered samurai force defeated an immense army commanded by Imagawa Yoshimoto.[19]

A second feature of military science as Tojo learned it at the War College requires attention. It was, in a word, narrow in its approach. Tojo and his classmates became expert at, for example, moving troops and encircling an enemy force, but their instructors never encouraged them to lift their gaze far beyond the battlefield. Grand strategy and war leadership were not taught at the War College. Similarly, matters such as political imperatives or economic implications of a wartime decision received no attention in the college classroom. Nor, for that matter, did the imperative of military administration. The interplay between the civilian politician and the soldier on matters of crucial concern to both—including the all-important decisions for war or peace—was not part of the War College curriculum. Naval strategy and joint operations received only the most perfunctory attention; there was no opportunity for student officers to join their counterparts from the Naval War College in consideration of, for example, joint army-navy operations.[20] All this owed to army tradition, which rested on a deliberate attempt at keeping military matters distinct and apart from outside interference; and also the assumption that strategic principles learned at the War College provided the basis for larger-scale operational planning and military policy planning, and ultimately for war leadership and national strategy. Either way, this particular feature of the War College education left student officers like Tojo ill equipped to deal with the epochal changes in warfare that loomed on the near horizon.

THERE WAS ONE EXCEPTION to the rule concerning the narrowness of the War College education. This took the form of Tojo Hidenori's *Senjutsu fumoto no chiri* (Strategic dust that has accumulated at the foot of a mountain).[21] This was the elder Tojo's magnum opus, published in two volumes in 1910. At the behest of the college superintendent (and the elder Tojo's close friend), Lieutenant General Iguchi Shogo, it was required reading at the War College. The younger Tojo pored over his father's words and regarded them as something akin to a sacred text.[22]

The book opened, in the tradition of the great Prussian military philosopher Carl von Clausewitz, with an examination of the phenomenon of war. Like Clausewitz, the elder Tojo wrote of war as a natural and ineradicable feature of human society. The elder Tojo presumed (again like Clausewitz) that an understanding of war's "essence" (*jittai*) would contribute to success in future wars. In explaining that essence, the elder Tojo drew almost word for word on Clausewitz's famous insistence that war was the continuation of politics. As Tojo Hidenori wrote, "War is the continuation of foreign policy." He elaborated: "Speaking simply from the military point of view, the sole purpose of war is to 'exterminate the enemy.'" This most basic military objective was, however, a means to an end. The elder Tojo explained that exterminating or eliminating enemy forces was ultimately an effort at "compelling another nation to recognize what the nation claims as its own right." He discussed several possible such claims, including the "seizure of territory," the "gaining of complete independence," and the "struggle for political control."[23]

The younger Tojo and his War College classmates were accustomed to poring over battlefield histories in their search for technical information that would help them arrive at strategic precepts or even clearly written rules for action. They were not at all accustomed to books that compelled them to consider anything much other than the question of *how* to wage war. To be sure, the elder Tojo's book included such material and offered instruction on, for example, night attacks and moving troops over long distances. Yet much of the book represented a neat departure from the student officers' standard reading fare, insofar as battlefield instruction was of decidedly lesser concern than was theoretical speculation. The elder Tojo's discussion of "war potential" provides a case in point. He acknowledged that a nation's armed services were the main, and most obvious, gauge of war potential. He nonetheless insisted that a commander ignored at his own peril other indicators of war potential, including everything a nation might harness to fight a war. Chief among these, according to the elder Tojo, were the people's "physical strength, energy, and intellect." He nominated energy as the most important of these, and reckoned it included "powers of endurance," "patriotism," and a "work ethic." Tojo Hidenori was little less impressed by the need for nations to develop their people's intellectual capacities and, in particular, people's ability to remain abreast of scientific and technological advances (he specifically cited development of the airplane) in order to fulfill a nation's war potential.[24]

The elder Tojo's opus suggested a holistic approach to the study and understanding of war. Battlefield strategy and tactics remained a central, but not his sole, concern; military objectives were but part of a broader and indeed underlying set of national objectives. On these grounds, the elder Tojo reasoned that warfare required not a narrowly defined military approach but instead a national approach that comprehended and harnessed the full field of a nation's "human activity."[25] His analysis made up the genesis of what would be the younger Tojo's enduring professional interest in a nation's latent power potential and the means by which that potential might be channeled into a war effort.

WORLD WAR I BROKE out in Europe in August 1914, roughly halfway through Tojo's second year at the War College. Japan entered the war as Britain's ally, and a single Japanese Army division required only a few weeks to dispossess Germany of its Qingdao Fortress on China's Shandong Peninsula. The fighting was limited in scope, time, objectives, and intensity, and its doctrinal impact was hardly epochal. In the War College classroom, Tojo and his peers studied the fighting in Shandong only sparingly. They spent little time studying the Imperial Japanese Navy's successful maritime operation against Germany's defenseless central Pacific Ocean possessions, including the Caroline, Marianna, and Marshall Islands; they devoted even less time to wartime diplomacy, including the infamous Twenty-One Demands that the Japanese government issued in January 1915 in a bald attempt at semicolonizing China.[26]

Of greater interest to Tojo and his classmates was the war's epicenter in Europe, where the fighting was taking place on an unprecedented scale. A select few Japanese Army officers saw in the war in Europe a need for a new understanding of warfare, one that resonated with the themes broached by the elder Tojo in his magnum opus. To cite but one example, Major Mitake Kakutaro argued, as early as December 1914, that the war in Europe involved vastly more than a mere competition of arms. He insisted that the war had instead become a test of overall national strengths, so that each European power was drawing on its "moral potential," its "economic and financial" strength, its domestic politics, its diplomacy, and its commerce. Governments had also to contend with their people's livelihoods, as well as their national industrial output. Japan was geographically removed from all of this and had, Mitake argued, a golden opportunity to study war as it impacted not just the armed services but the nation as a whole, including its politics, business, industry, and education.[27]

The War College did not take up this challenge during Tojo's time there. It seemed too close in time to gauge the war's overall impact with any degree of accuracy or certainty. Did the trenches on the Western Front mark a fundamental break with the recent past? Had the defensive displaced the offensive as the defining feature of modern warfare? Or, might the stalemate in western Europe seem less impressive in historical retrospect? As we shall see, Tojo later, as a War College instructor, taught the German opening-of-war-gambit known as the Schlieffen Plan. He also taught about the need for sustained interaction between the government and the military. But as a student officer at the War College he remained within the intellectual confines set by his instructors. They looked for lessons in the war in Europe that reinforced the college's preexisting educational emphasis on pure operational planning and battlefield strategy. The advent of aerial warfare provided one of the few points of departure insofar as it shifted the emphasis to technological innovation, and the college in Tojo's third and final year instituted annual inspection tours of a nearby balloon squadron that was home to the army's fledgling airplane fleet. Tojo and his colleagues were invited at this juncture to ponder airplanes' battlefield roles, including reconnaissance, bombing, and fighting. In this way the focus remained, to borrow the words of the army chief of staff, General Hasegawa Yoshimichi, on the "immensity" of airplanes' contribution to the most immediate task of battlefield victory.[28] Even as they considered this potentially precedent-shattering technological innovation, Tojo and the other student officers were not in any way disabused of the notion that wars were won and lost by soldiers (the contribution of sailors was generally an afterthought). At least so far as the War College was concerned, warfare remained almost the sole prerogative of the army, and the input of other institutions and sections of society remained less studied and little understood. Decades later, after Japan's surrender in World War II, Tojo identified and acknowledged this as a "deficiency" in his education. The War College, he lamented, had not really caused him to lift his gaze beyond the battlefield and beyond narrowly conceived "strategy and tactics."[29]

TOJO WAS PROMOTED TO the rank of captain in June 1915, and graduated from the War College six months later. The top six graduates in his class, including Captains Imamura Hitoshi and Homma Masaharu, received sabers from the emperor.[30] Tojo ranked an entirely respectable eleventh out of fifty-six graduates. He returned briefly to the Imperial Guard's Third

Division, where he served as a company commander, before he was posted in August 1916 to the Army Ministry. There, as a junior adjutant in the secretariat, he served as aide to the army minister, Lieutenant General Oshima Ken'ichi.

Key to add at this juncture is a brief outline of the military's triangular organizational structure, which included the Army Ministry, the General Staff, and the Inspectorate General of Military Training. The Army Ministry was an administrative organ, responsible for budgets and personnel, and it made up the juncture at which the military encountered politics. The General Staff, the most prestigious of the three branches, was the military's command organ and was responsible for all operational planning. The Inspectorate General was responsible for all of the army's education apparatuses (except the War College, which remained under the auspices of the General Staff). Each branch maintained its independence from the others, and the equality of the three branches was a bedrock principle. Symbolizing and enshrining this independence and equality was the right of direct access to the throne maintained by each branch's leader: known collectively as the army's *san-chokan* (big three), they were the army chief of staff, the army minister, and the inspector general of military training.

Tojo's posting to the Army Ministry was something of an anomaly. A recent War College graduate like Tojo might reasonably have expected to spend at least a few years engaged in operational planning on the General Staff. There, however, the influence of the former Choshu feudal domain remained particularly strong, and some were concerned lest Tojo become a target on account of lingering Choshu enmity toward his father.[31] It was not immediately apparent to Tojo, but the posting fundamentally shaped his outlook and career. While the majority of his contemporaries who were

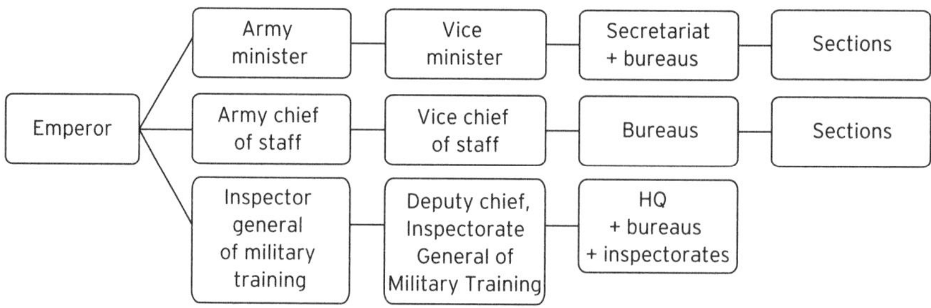

The Imperial Japanese Army's triangular organizational structure

posted to the General Staff engaged in the pure, untrammeled strategic thinking for which the War College had trained them, Tojo—by force of circumstance—concerned himself instead with all the extramilitary factors that necessarily affected army planning and policy. He quickly memorized by rote the army's regulations concerning everything from conscription to budgets to personnel.[32] Tojo otherwise proved himself possessed of an admirable administrative capacity as he organized papers, filed and generated reports, distributed correspondence, wrote letters, fielded phone calls, and answered questions and requests. He was involved in no decisions of any import but worked instead to ensure the Army Ministry's smooth day-to-day functioning.

Two episodes during Tojo's time in the Army Ministry seem particularly noteworthy. The first involved revisions to the Imperial National Defense Policy, which the Taisho Emperor sanctioned in June 1918. The revised policy required no input from a mere Army Ministry adjutant like Tojo, but it certainly crossed his desk. The most notable revision was that of China's inclusion as a hypothetical enemy (Russia remained the Imperial Army's foremost potential enemy, and the United States remained likewise for the Imperial Navy). China's inclusion owed to a perception of it not as a threat but instead as an opportunity. It had descended into what one observer has aptly called the "chaos of warlordism" and, as was the case when the Japanese government issued the Twenty-One Demands, China seemed unlikely to withstand any sustained outside pressure.[33] Within the Japanese Army this gave rise to a particularly powerful opportunistic streak: uniformed military officers saw an opportunity not only to consolidate the southern Manchurian foothold that Japan had earned in the Russo-Japanese War but also to strengthen its hold over Manchuria and Mongolia in their practical entirety. The purpose was twofold: On the one hand, Manchurian and Mongolian bases would facilitate operations against the Russians and would maximize the Japanese army's chances of securing victory in the Russian Far East decisively and expeditiously. On the other hand, Manchuria and Mongolia were veritable storehouses of natural resources that could potentially feed industries—including munitions industries—and thereby prepare Japan for the possibility of protracted warfare. Tojo's immediate reaction to the revised Imperial National Defense Policy is not recorded anywhere, but given that he agitated in subsequent years for the conquest of Manchuria and Mongolia, it can be safely assumed that he was in basic agreement with its identification of China as an opportunity.[34]

The Siberian intervention was the other particularly noteworthy episode during Tojo's time as adjutant. As had been the case with the revisions to the Imperial National Defense Policy, Tojo did not contribute to the decision to intervene in Siberia, but he was a firsthand witness to the politics in which the top brass had necessarily to engage in order to get the intervention off the ground. Launched in August 1918, it was animated by antagonism for Russia's recent Bolshevik Revolution, and it involved British, French, Japanese, and US forces in an ostensible effort at rescuing the Czech Army, which was stranded in Siberia. The Japanese Army saw in the Siberian intervention an opportunity to cement and expand Japan's continental position at the direct expense of its principal hypothetical enemy in Russia. To that end, it nursed the threefold aim of fostering support for a pro-Japanese and anti-Bolshevik government in southeastern Siberia, controlling the Chinese Eastern Railway and the Trans-Siberian Railway east of Irkutsk and incorporating the Amur River basin into Japan's economic network. Others in the Japanese government baulked at the army's ambitions. They worried that Japan might earn international opprobrium—the Americans were particularly mistrustful of Japan's motives—and they also worried that Japan might find itself hopelessly and inextricably entangled in Russia's bewildering political landscape.[35]

Such issues were beyond Tojo's purview when he was ordered in late 1918 to undertake an inspection tour of the Twelfth Division, which was at the vanguard of Japanese involvement in Siberia. So, too, were battlefield operations, if only because there was nothing in the way of operations on which Tojo might report. The Twelfth Division was, when he arrived, guarding against any underground Bolshevik activity and otherwise trying to pacify the local population. For this reason, Tojo directed his focus to managerial and logistical issues, including health, housing, diet, policing, and finances. He reported on the so-called Spanish flu epidemic that had taken hold among the troops, and on the capture of Russian-owned barracks along the Amur and Ussuri Railways. He reported on supply demands, which he expected would increase during the harsh Siberian winter, as well as on the inadequacy of interpreters who were supposed to facilitate negotiations between the Twelfth Division's officer complement and the local populace. He reported on the need for greater levels of "special" funding to buy intelligence and collaboration, and on the need for a greater *kenpei* (gendarmerie or military police) presence.[36] Here, again, Tojo's field of vision differed fundamentally from the pure strategic concepts that might normally occupy the thoughts of a recent War College graduate. It was not necessarily apparent to him, but he was transitioning into quite a different kind of army officer.

FOLLOWING HIS INSPECTION TOUR, Tojo returned to Tokyo. Little did he know that the Siberian expedition would come over time to divide the army, and also antagonize broad segments of Japanese society. And he did not foresee the army returning home from Siberia empty-handed. But that final outcome would be some three and a half years in the future. Tojo moved, in the meantime, to a very different assignment: He was ordered in August 1919 to Bern, Switzerland, where he spent nearly two years and, during his time there, was promoted to major.[37] He was transferred in July 1921 to Germany and remained there for a little over twelve months, returning to Tokyo, via the United States, in November 1922.

Throughout his three-and-a-half-year European sojourn, Tojo took German-language classes to supplement and extend the German he had learned at both the Military Academy and the War College. He immersed himself in evaluations of the German Army's wartime performance, and he mixed with other Japanese Army officers in central Europe. Most important, he and his professional military colleagues in the German-speaking world sought out lessons from the German wartime experience from which Japan might profitably learn.

At least some of those lessons made familiar reading for any soldier knowledgeable in Japanese military doctrine. For example, a December 1919 analysis of German infantry tactics during the early stages of the Battle of Verdun emphasized the centrality of the infantry, of an attacking spirit, and of the decisive battle. Basing their analysis on Captain Cordt von Brandis's *Die Stürmer von Douaumont: Kriegserlebnisse eines Kompagnieführers* (The stormers of Douaumont: War experiences of a company commander), Japanese officers in the German-speaking world insisted that infantry had to be well trained, "strict military discipline" was a necessity, and the infantryman's strength of "spirit" and "body" was an absolute requirement. They allowed that coordination with other military arms was necessary, and that the infantry should charge only after a concentrated burst of artillery fire had struck "terror" into the enemy. They also accepted that "every means" of reconnaissance had also to be "exhausted" before the infantry launched an assault. Yet, only the infantry could dislodge the enemy from their battlefield position. "Infantry should fire in a spirit of single-handedly destroying the enemy," ran this analysis, "and should charge with a feeling of being completely unaffected by gunfire." The nature of the charge was of the utmost importance. If the troops advanced with "determination," they could overpower an enemy force of "superior" strength, but if the charge was characterized by "hesitation and vacillation," the consequences would be "disastrous" for the attacking force.[38]

Such analysis affirmed preconceived notions in the Japanese Army about the primacy of men and morale on the battlefield. It would nonetheless be a mistake to assume that the army learned nothing tactically from the trench warfare that had been such a feature of the war in Europe. On the basis of reporting by Tojo and other officers in Europe, the Japanese Army took a new approach to equipping its infantry units so that regiments that had hitherto been armed only with rifles and fixed bayonets were by the end of the decade reinforced with mortars and flame throwers, and battalions were equipped with machine guns, sniper rifles, and grenade launchers. The Japanese Army also sought to minimize losses during an offensive by replacing its traditional close-order infantry formations with more scattered formations and by also experimenting with a vertical formation (as opposed to an easily-mowed-down horizontal formation). Efforts were also made to maximize the effectiveness of any attack by emulating the German efforts at locating and exploiting weak points in enemy defensive lines. With such innovations, the Japanese Army continued to place its faith in the offensive.[39]

The other great lesson for Japan, according to Tojo and his professional military colleagues in Europe, involved the irreducible necessity of national mobilization. They insisted that the European war had tested not just military strength but "national strengths," so that each combatant had drawn on "all available knowledge" and "all available strength." Concretely, "national mobilization" involved the control of a nation's resources and functions in their entirety so that they could be put to the "most effective use" in pursuit of victory. Each nation had necessarily to mobilize its people so that the "entire people's strength" was controlled and used in time of war. Similar endeavors were required vis-à-vis a nation's industries, communications, finances, and science and technology.[40]

Decades earlier, when the elder Tojo was earning his stripes as a staff officer, Meckel had emphasized the importance of mobilizing before war. Now the younger Tojo and his professional military colleagues in Europe were striking a remarkably similar tone. But whereas Meckel in an earlier era had envisioned military mobilization, Tojo and his colleagues in central Europe in the early aftermath of the world war envisioned national mobilization. Leading the charge was Nagata Tetsuzan (who was one of the men who had helped Tojo prepare for entry to the War College). Nagata had been in Germany when the war began and thereafter observed much of the war from neutral Denmark and later Sweden. He spent the immediate postwar years in Austria and in mid-1921 was posted to Switzerland. His influence over Tojo was electrifying.

Nagata had a most sophisticated understanding of the demands of modern, total war. In his analysis, Japan had to prioritize the procurement of materials and plan the development of such industrial capacity as would meet the army's demand for weapons, ammunition, and other war-related products. Sophisticated rail and highway networks were a must, and airplanes, with all their potential, seemed destined to play a role in future wars. Power-generating installations were of vital importance. So, too, was a highly skilled labor force with the scientific and technological capacity to develop the destructive capacity of ordnance and ammunition. Nagata was no less convinced of the need to imbue the civilian population with a nationalistic, martial spirit. Total war, in his estimation, required nothing less than a total national effort.[41]

Tojo proved the most faithful of all Nagata's followers. He felt bound by unbreakable bonds of friendship, and like many of his contemporaries, he felt something akin to awe for Nagata's remarkable powers of intellect. Certainly, Nagata's total war theories enabled Tojo to take a long-term view of—and formulate lessons from—the unprecedented situation he encountered in postwar Europe. There was one other factor that contributed to Tojo's fealty to Nagata's cause: Nagata professed a determination to break Choshu's domination of the army's upper echelons. One biographer attributes this less to conviction than to shrewd calculations about the following it might earn Nagata among disaffected officers like Tojo.[42] Principled or otherwise, Nagata's anti-Choshu stance alone might have been enough for Tojo. He unabashedly regarded himself as Nagata's right-hand man, and remained so until Nagata was cut down by a sword-wielding junior officer in November 1935.

It is appropriate here to pause and consider a conspiratorial meeting held in the Black Forest town of Baden-Baden in late October 1921. Three conspirators were involved: Majors Nagata Tetsuzan, Obata Toshiro, and Okamura Yasuji. These were the same three men who had helped Tojo prepare for the War College entrance exam some ten years earlier. Nagata was the ringleader and was the attaché to Switzerland; Obata was the attaché to Russia (but was living in Berlin because the Russians refused to admit him entry to the country), and Okamura was in Europe following a tour of China. The three men discussed the total war theories of Germany's wartime chief of staff, General Erich von Luderndorff, including his insistence on mobilizing all the nation's resources—including human resources—in an effort to win the war. They also, at Nagata's behest, agreed on the need to break Choshu's stranglehold on the Japanese Army's personnel decisions, the better to reorganize the military so that it was able to direct national mobilization in an era of total war. These two concepts were intricately interrelated: Continued Choshu dominance of the army's upper echelons meant, in the conspirators' view, that the army would remain locked in its outmoded ways. This would necessarily impact its ability to reorganize itself—and indeed the nation—in ways conducive to modern, total warfare. Days after concluding the so-called Baden-Baden agreement, Okamura contacted Tojo and invited him to join this clandestine effort at military modernization. Tojo did not give it a moment's thought and pledged his unstinting cooperation.[43]

TOJO RETURNED TO TOKYO in late 1922. The following year, he and the other Baden-Baden conspirators (all of whom returned to Japan at roughly the same time) invited Lieutenant Colonels Itagaki Seishiro and Komoto Daisaku to join them in pursuit of their Baden-Baden objectives. Their anti-Choshu grievance seemed well justified, for despite the death in February 1922 of Japan's leading soldier, statesman and Choshu godfather, Field Marshal Yamagata Aritomo, Choshu dominance of the army seemed alive and well. Preeminent next-generation Choshu general Tanaka Giichi served as army minister from 1918 until ill health intervened and he resigned in 1921. His health returned and he reemerged as minister in 1923. Holding the ministerial seat during the interval was Lieutenant General Yamanashi Katsuzo, who was not a Choshu officer but was regarded, fairly or otherwise, as a Tanaka puppet. Lieutenant Generals Ugaki Kazushige and Tsuno Kazusuke served successively in the early 1920s as vice minister; both were Tanaka protégés and the latter was a Choshu officer. The all-important post of Military Affairs Bureau chief in the early 1920s belonged to Major General Sugano Hisaichi, who was another Choshu officer. General Kawai Misao, who was appointed army chief of staff in 1922, was a Tanaka ally and was regarded as a Choshu proxy.

Tojo had in the meantime been sent to teach military history at the War College, and he took proactive steps to shape the military's future elite in ways that eroded Choshu power. He followed the lead of his friend and mentor Nagata, who was also serving as a college instructor. He and Nagata recruited other instructors to the cause, and used their oversight of the oral component of the college entrance exam to rig the system and summarily fail young Choshu officers. Lieutenant Horike Kazumaro later recalled the bullying to which he was subjected when he took the oral exam in December 1924 because Tojo and the other instructors mistakenly believed he was a Choshu native. They changed their tune dramatically when they realized their mistake, and the atmosphere became almost chummy as Horike passed the oral exam.[44] The War College, which had hitherto admitted between three and five Choshu officers annually, admitted no Choshu officers for the three years that Nagata and Tojo served there as instructors.[45]

Nagata's and Tojo's actions did not—could not—affect the fortunes of Choshu officers who were already at the top of the army's ranks. Yet, by denying young Choshu officers a place in the War College, Tojo denied the next Choshu generation a future place in the military's highest echelons. He did not take kindly to suggestions that he was acting improperly. Some years later, Captain Tsuchihashi Yuitsu told Tojo that "bullying" Choshu officers was an "anachronism" and that the "discrimination" to which he had subjected young Choshu officers at the War College was "ludicrous." Tojo lost his temper. His mentor Nagata physically held Tojo back from Tsuchihashi, as Tojo shouted about his hatred for Choshu officers and the "grudges" they bore.[46]

As a college instructor Tojo was not only breaking Choshu's grip on the army but was also educating and training the military's future elite. He taught military history and, unsurprisingly, lectured on Germany's participation in World War I. For this purpose, he drew on several hundred German-language books and magazines that he had collected during his time in Europe and which he now donated to the War College library.[47] Among his lecture topics were the German opening-of-war gambit known as the Schlieffen Plan, and the need for coordination between and among the government and the high command. Tojo's approach to each of these topics provides some insight into the evolution of his thinking about war.

The Schlieffen Plan was an obvious lecture topic for Tojo given his recent European experience. Named after Germany's long-serving army chief of staff, Count Alfred von Schlieffen, the plan had been designed to extricate Germany from the strategic nightmare of a simultaneous two-front war against France and Russia. It called for a massive offensive from the outset of hostilities that aimed at the rapid capture of Paris and simultaneous annihilation of the French Army. That objective achieved, Germany would turn the full force of its arms eastward, against the slow-to-mobilize Russians.

In the War College classroom, Tojo invited his student officers to consider not failings in the Schlieffen Plan itself but instead failings in its implementation. In particular, he held the German First Army commander, General Alexander von Kluck, to account for having plunged "headlong" and indeed "recklessly" in pursuit of retreating French forces even as he neared Paris. In this way, and in a manner utterly "contrary" to the Schlieffen Plan, the First Army swung north of Paris (rather than southwest, as intended) and passed into the River Marne Valley. Here the French halted their retreat, gathered their forces, and launched a counterattack. Now it was the Germans' turn to retreat, and they went as far as the lower Aisne River before digging trenches and halting the French counterattack. Tojo's conclusion was telling: "The German army did not lose strategically," he insisted. The Schlieffen Plan had been fundamentally sound, but poor decisions by field officers locked Germany into a four-year war of attrition; the Germans eventually lost the war because they ran out of resources.[48]

Tojo's attraction to the Schlieffen Plan can be readily explained. The appeal lay primarily in the fact that the plan represented the high-water mark of precisely the kind of operational planning taught at the Japanese Army's War College. It was meticulously detailed and deliciously precise. It was also glorious in its grandiosity. It was predicated on relentless attack and was (to borrow the words of military historian Basil Liddell Hart) a "conception of Napoleonic boldness." Yet, just like the military science classes at the War College, the Schlieffen Plan also showed scant regard for the "wider political, economic, and moral factors which are inseparable from the military factors on the higher plane of strategy that is aptly termed 'grand strategy.'"[49]

In a separate lecture, Tojo departed from the War College's emphasis on battlefield operations and strategy and addressed the issue of grand strategy. The army could not, he insisted, arrive at a wartime strategy unless and until it gave sustained attention to not only military factors but also all of the other aspects—political, economic, financial, commercial, diplomatic, and industrial—that played an integral role in the making of grand strategy in an era of total war. In this regard, Tojo accepted that the Army General Staff's jealously guarded independence of the government was right and proper in peacetime, but he insisted that war "interrupted" usual decision-making processes. He proposed that, in wartime, the cabinet and the supreme command (which in wartime drew together the Imperial Army and Navy General Staffs) had necessarily to liaise and cooperate. This would, Tojo argued, guard against the calamitous possibility of the armed services "recklessly forcing the state to do the impossible in the name of 'military / naval necessity.'" In other words, anything less than meaningful consultation and careful calibration between and among the army and navy chiefs of staff, the prime minister, army minister, navy minister, and foreign minister in wartime would be to the detriment of—or even "destroy"—the decision-making process.[50] In this way Tojo was pointing to the reality whereby "in an age of total war, the independence of the supreme command was outmoded and behind the times."[51]

The biographer is compelled here to pause. Did Tojo remain wedded to the offensive, and to the short, decisive war that the Schlieffen Plan promised? How did that square with the understanding of total war at which he had arrived and which, in his estimation, required a broad approach to questions of national defense and strategy? What, precisely, was Tojo? Was he a conservative? Or was he a reformer? The answer seems to lie somewhere in between. He was conservative insofar as he hoped for a decisive battle, fought soon after the outbreak of hostilities, which would enable the Japanese Army to play to its strengths—including the troops' presumed fighting abilities—while averting an unwanted and debilitating war of attrition. He was also a reformer, for he had himself witnessed Europe's scarred battlefields and was a firm believer in the totality of modern warfare. He was, as historian J. P. Clarke has written in a different context, among the "'reformers' [who] sometimes seemed reactionary," but he was also among the "'conservatives' [who] sometimes seemed progressive."[52]

Tojo was, in this way, a creature of his times. The glaring contradictions that informed his own outlook on war also informed the Japanese Army's evolving strategic outlook, as summarized in revisions to the Imperial National Defense Policy. This latest set of revisions received Imperial sanction in February 1923, and stressed the need to prepare for total war while also emphasizing efforts at averting a war of attrition by taking the offensive from the war's outset and seeking a decisive battle as soon as practicable after the outbreak of hostilities.[53]

TOJO WAS TRANSFERRED IN March 1926 to the Army Ministry's powerful Military Affairs Bureau. He served with the Army Affairs Section, which was responsible for the political questions arising from the army's organization, troop dispositions, troop dispatches, and requisitions. This was a sure sign he had been marked for a bright future, for, outside the General Staff, this was one of the choicest possible assignments for an officer of his rank. It also served, once again, to keep Tojo at arm's length from the purely strategic considerations of a staff officer.

Discerning Tojo's personal contributions to the Army Affairs Section's activities is nonetheless difficult, because its archived paperwork tends not to record individual authorship. It nonetheless stands to reason that Tojo participated in preparations for the Shandong expeditions of 1927 and 1928, which purported to protect Japanese lives, rights, and interests in Shandong Province against Chinese leader Chiang Kai-shek's National Revolutionary Army. It also seems entirely reasonable to assume that Tojo was in agreement with that large number of army officers who hoped that the expeditions would ensure that Chiang did not gain sway over Shandong and its neighboring provinces. There is, in other words, every reason to believe that Tojo joined many military officers in eyeing the Shandong Peninsula and north China more broadly.[54]

Within months of Tojo's arrival at the Army Affairs Section, the Taisho Emperor died. His reign had been short and, at least in comparison with that of his illustrious father, uninspiring. His physical and mental health had long since seemed unequal to an emperor's tasks, and his first-born son, Crown Prince Hirohito, had been serving as regent since November 1921. Tojo seems unlikely to have nursed any particular feelings of nostalgia at the passing of the Taisho era, although the emperor's death yielded an unusual and interesting assignment: Tojo was included in December 1926 on the army's ad hoc Imperial Funeral Management Committee. Under the leadership of Major General Abe Nobuyuki, the committee directed the armed services' involvement in the emperor's funeral.[55] Incidentally, it brought Tojo for the first time into sustained contact with naval officers. Interservice cooperation was, according to the gentlemanly Abe, exemplary and indeed "efficacious."[56]

Tojo remained with the Army Affairs Section for two years before he succeeded his friend and mentor Nagata in March 1928 as head of the Mobilization Section of the Army Ministry's Economic Mobilization Bureau. The bureau had been established by Army Minister Ugaki Kazushige as recently as 1926; it evinced the army's determination to take the lead on what it regarded as the pressing issue of national mobilization. Tojo was now responsible for preparing studies on all matters related to mobiliza-

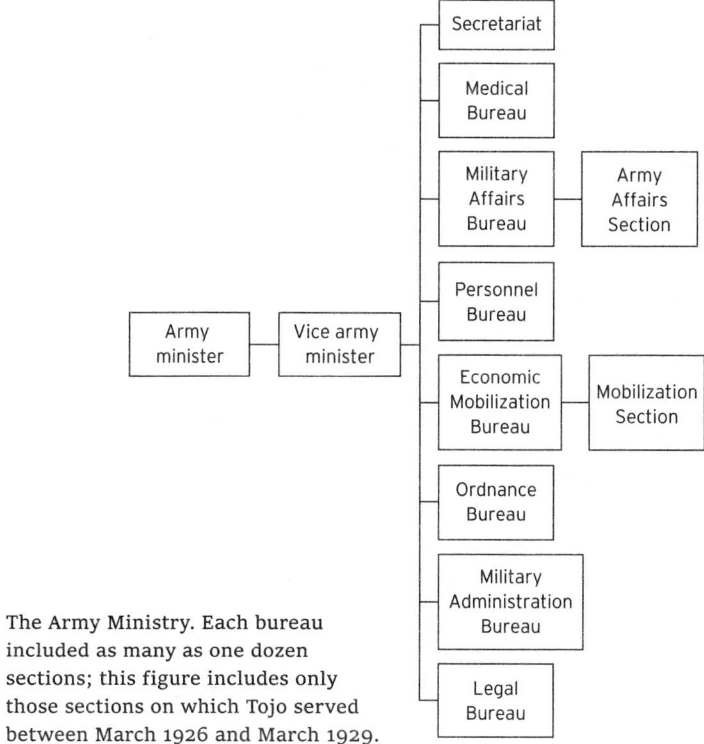

The Army Ministry. Each bureau included as many as one dozen sections; this figure includes only those sections on which Tojo served between March 1926 and March 1929.

tion, including the draft, the requisition of materials, and the oversight of munitions industries.[57] For Tojo, the post continued his transition to military modernizer and total war officer, and it also meant he could now contribute materially to his earlier Baden-Baden pledge concerning reorganization of the army and nation in preparation for the demands of total war.

In one of his first tasks in this new assignment, Tojo reported on a mobilization drill undertaken by the Second Division. Tojo, who had in the meantime been promoted to colonel, headed a team of Tokyo-based officers who proceeded to divisional headquarters in Sendai to observe and study the distribution of weapons, uniforms, provisions, medical provisions. and other resources during the drill. Collating the data and reaching conclusions was a time-consuming exercise; not until November did Tojo report to Army Minister Shirakawa Yoshinori on the lessons learned. Those lessons included the need to identify and provide in advance for the army's wartime needs. Doing so, Tojo averred, would greatly reduce the need for ad hoc procurement programs following the outbreak of war. Stockpiling programs were, in his view, vital, and they needed to account for the likelihood of damages to portions of stockpiled goods. He acknowledged that such measures would entail peacetime restrictions on civilian use of materials, and he seemed to assume that the army ought to have the controlling voice in any steps Japan might take toward managing its economy and guiding its industrial output.[58]

Another lesson that Tojo took from the mobilization drill was the need to educate all officers about the material demands of modern warfare. There was, he wrote, a gulf separating the commanding officers' understanding of the need to prepare economically for war, and the junior officers' prioritization of manpower and morale to the virtual exclusion of all else. He attributed the difference to the junior officers' education, which terminated at the Military Academy. Tojo was struck by the junior officers' morale and fighting spirit (he referenced the reputation they had earned for their almost fanatical devotion to the *kodo* [Imperial way]), but he also noted their inability to grasp the overriding importance of harnessing the economy to the military's distinct needs. His proffered solution was for the long term: the Military Academy must, he insisted, include in its curriculum the irreducible need to allocate resources so that the army was equipped appropriately and prepared for war.[59]

THROUGHOUT HIS TIME IN the nation's political nerve center in Tokyo, Tojo continued to meet with his fellow Baden-Baden conspirators. In mid-January 1927 Itagaki, Nagata, Obata, Okamura, and Tojo met at a French restaurant in Shibuya (in central Tokyo) called Futaba. Under Nagata's informal leadership, this restaurant became their regular haunt, and they began referring to themselves as the Futaba Club.[60] This was a clandestine study group, where discussion centered on the twin Baden-Baden causes of breaking Choshu power and modernizing the army so that it could lead a national effort at preparing for total war. They began recruiting like-minded officers from among the graduates of the Military Academy's fifteenth through eighteenth classes (all recruits had subsequently graduated from the War College).[61]

In late 1927 Nagata and Tojo joined a second clandestine officers' association, known variously as the Nameless Club, the National Policy Club, and the Thursday Club. Led by Suzuki Teiichi, it drew its membership primarily from the Military Academy's twentieth through twenty-fifth classes. Membership was restricted to War College graduates, and included Ishiwara Kanji, Murakami Keisaku, Nemoto Hiroshi, and Tsuchihashi Yuitsu. The club focused on questions of national policy, and over time, developed a distinctive focus on Japanese policy toward Manchuria and Mongolia.[62]

The Japanese presence in South Manchuria had evolved since the early aftermath of the Russo-Japanese War. The Office of the Kwantung Governor-General had been established in Port Arthur in the early aftermath of World War I, and had moved from military to civilian control in 1919. At that same time, the force that garrisoned the Kwantung Leased Territory and the railway zones established its own, independent command structure. Thus was born the Kwantung Army.[63] Alongside it stood the semigovernmental South Manchuria Railway Company, whose scale of activity went well beyond freight and passenger services. The railway company operated coal mines at Fushun and Yantai, as well as harbor and port facilities at Andong, Port Arthur, and Yingkou. It maintained warehouses for goods and hotels for travelers, ran schools and hospitals, and managed utilities along its rail lines. It even collected taxes.[64] Moreover, Japan had, by means of the Twenty-One Demands, extracted China's agreement to a seventy-five-year extension on all its Manchurian leases.

Uniformed army officers in the mid- to late 1920s found reason for concern about Japan's position in Manchuria. They fretted about the steps Japan had taken toward a two-party system of government, and the parties' refusal to take a bipartisan approach toward China and toward Japan's special rights and interests in Manchuria. The Minseito (Democratic Party) cabinets of 1924 to 1927 had evinced a willingness to see China united under Kuomintang leader Chiang Kai-shek. Championed by Foreign Minister Shidehara Kijuro, these policies sought Sino-Japanese amity as a basis for expanded Japanese commercial activity in China. Policies of the subsequent Seiyukai cabinet, led by retired Choshu general Tanaka Giichi, worked from the premise that Manchuria and Mongolia were areas of Japan's special interest and distinct from the rest of China. Tanaka, who served concurrently as foreign minister, accepted that Chiang Kai-shek might unify China but he was adamant that unification must not extend north of the Great Wall into Manchuria and Mongolia. There Tanaka believed that Japan's best interests were served by a policy of support for Manchurian warlord Zhang Zuolin.[65]

It was against this backdrop that Tojo addressed the Thursday Club in March 1928. He opened with the observation that Japan undertook all "war preparations" with a view to hostilities against the Soviet Union. He next insisted that the first and most important step in preparations for war against the Soviets was the "establishment of complete political control over Manchuria and Mongolia" and added that a "defensive posture" in the Pacific region was a necessary component of what must be the national policy of guarding against US entry into any Japanese-Soviet war; this insistence peremptorily subordinated the navy's strategic outlook to that of the army. Reinforcing this approach were Tojo's twin beliefs that the next war would be fought for national "survival" and that the United States could be convinced to remain out of any Japanese-Soviet war because it had enough for its own national survival in North and South America. (This was, as we shall see, a prototype of the foreign policy concepts that would inform Tojo and others in the summer of 1940). Finally Tojo noted that war against China did "not require serious consideration." China remained weak and would be unable, for the foreseeable future, to assert itself in any meaningful way. Japan should, Tojo stated, see China through the lens of "resource acquisition."[66]

One short exchange in the subsequent question-and-answer period was particularly interesting. An unnamed officer asked whether Japan should simply "take" Manchuria and Mongolia, and Tojo answered in the affirmative. At the end of the meeting, the Thursday Club delivered its "verdict," which quoted Tojo's analysis almost word for word. It added that Japan had no choice but to take Manchuria and Mongolia in order to complete its program for national survival. It acknowledged that this placed Japan on a crash course with the Soviet Union, which was pursuing a policy of expansion "to the [Pacific] Ocean." It was dismissive of Chinese sovereignty and noted, in any case, that neither the Manchu nor Mongols were ethnically Han Chinese. According to this self-serving logic, the conquest of Manchuria and Mongolia ought not to include any great affront to Chinese sovereignty. Finally, the Thursday Club agreed that such an approach should affect the vital interests of neither Britain nor the United States and that it should be sufficient to adopt a "defensive posture" toward the United States and to resolve any issues with Britain diplomatically.[67]

This position differed from that of the Tanaka cabinet in a number of ways. For one thing, Tojo and his Thursday Club colleagues were convinced of the inevitability of war against the Soviet Union, and regarded Manchuria and Mongolia as a strategic necessity for Japan in such an event; Tanaka seemed to hope that a Japanese-Soviet war might be avoided, and hoped that Manchuria might provide a buffer zone between the two nations. Tojo's conception of political dominance over Manchuria and Mongolia seemed not to leave any future for the warlord Zhang Zuolin, whereas Tanaka continued to regard him as a useful client. Zhang, to be sure, presented problems: his forces had captured Peking in 1926, and Zhang himself remained there, south of the Great Wall, and nursed ambitions of his extended rule across at least North China. In May 1928 Tanaka confronted Zhang with a choice: He could remain in Peking and prepare for the disarmament of his forces by Japan's Kwantung Army, or he could return to Manchuria and abandon his dreams of adding North China to his realm. In this latter instance, Tanaka assured Zhang that the Kwantung Army would not disarm his forces, and he would at least retain control over Manchuria.[68]

Zhang's warlord army could not possibly stand up to the Kwantung Army's finely honed fighting prowess, so he made the obvious choice and in early June took the train back to the Manchurian capital of Mukden. He was assassinated en route: a Kwantung Army staff officer and Futaba Club member, Colonel Komoto Daisaku, planted a bomb under a South Manchurian Railway bridge at a crossing point with the Chinese-owned Peking-to-Mukden line on which Zhang was traveling. Komoto had not informed his superiors of the plot, but he anticipated that Zhang's assassination would spark unrest and thereby provide the Kwantung Army with a pretext to occupy Manchuria in its entirety. Komoto had, on his own authority, deliberately and self-consciously acted in direct contravention to Tanaka's policy.[69]

How best to handle the bombing wracked Tokyo. Tanaka wanted the perpetrator punished. He informed the emperor of this in late December 1928, and the emperor made it clear that this accorded with his own wishes.[70] Tojo had no way of discerning his emperor's mindset, but he understood—and rejected—the thinking of the Choshu general and prime minister, Tanaka. Tojo met with other Tokyo-based Futaba Club members on January 12, 1929, and discussed "rescue plans" for Komoto. Incredulous at the notion that anyone in Tokyo was even thinking about punishing Komoto, Tojo followed up a few days later with a "confidential conversation" with Baden-Baden coconspirator and Futaba Club member Okamura concerning Komoto and Zhang's assassination.[71] In mid-February Tojo took up Komoto's case with the Kwantung Army staff officer, Lieutenant Colonel Ishiwara Kanji.[72] Other Futaba Club and Thursday Club members were similarly active in their efforts at sparing Komoto the ignominy of being hauled before a military tribunal.

The army minister, General Shirakawa Yoshinori (who was a Tanaka protégé) eventually bowed to the pressure bubbling up from within the military. Shirakawa reported to the emperor in late March and asserted that Komoto had acted on no authority but his own and had, in fact, taken "independent initiative." He nonetheless added that the army intended to take only light administrative action against Komoto. In the face of the army's intransigence, Tanaka, too, backed down. He advised the emperor in late June that Komoto would face nothing more than the military's internal "administrative disciplinary procedures." This so angered the emperor that he demanded Tanaka's prime ministerial resignation. Over the ensuing weeks, the emperor fretted about the constitutionality of his action. He also worried about instilling "discipline" back into the Imperial Japanese Army.[73] Tojo and his closest military associates were marching to a different beat: They celebrated the fact that Komoto escaped any real punishment, but they brooded over decision-makers' refusal to take the opportunity presented by Komoto's actions. Manchuria remained firmly in their sights.

TOJO WAS, BY THE late 1920s, an intensely political officer. He himself would have regarded the label as insulting and out of step with the Imperial Rescript to Soldiers and Sailors and the Japanese soldier's traditional disavowal of any interest in politics. His dislike of the label makes it no less accurate. He was, for one thing, unapologetically engaged in a systematic attempt at ending Choshu's domination of the Japanese Army's upper echelons. Joining him in his political activities were fellow members of several clandestine officer clubs. These were more than single-issue associations and, with Tojo near the forefront, they worked assiduously in defiance of not only the army hierarchy but also state policy. The emperor later lamented the lack of action taken to reinstill discipline in the army following Zhang Zuolin's assassination.[74] Tojo was far from alone, but he was from the outset a key figure within the army pushing in a very different direction from that of his emperor.

Tojo's view of politics extended beyond the army. This owed primarily to his views about the changed nature of twentieth-century warfare. He had become, to borrow a term coined by historian Michael Barnhart, a "total war officer."[75] The transition was imperfect, and he clung to some concepts—including the early decisive battle—that were the pet projects of the army's more traditional officers. Yet, unlike the traditionalists, Tojo accepted that the next war would in all likelihood repeat the experience of the last and would become a grinding war of attrition fought across a period of years. Such a war would test more than Japan's mere military prowess, and Tojo was convinced that total warfare would stretch to the breaking point all possible indices of Japan's national power, including its commercial, financial, economic, political, diplomatic, naval, and industrial strength. Preparations for this likely eventuality were, in Tojo's estimation, nonnegotiable. This awareness seemed *not* to spawn in Tojo a predilection for sustained contact with colleagues from outside the army; like so many graduates of the military preparatory schools, he seemed simply to presume that the army—or to be more precise, like-minded total war army officers—knew best. This mindset contributed to Tojo's politicization, for it burnished in him the belief that the army had not only the right but indeed the imperative to intervene and engage in decisions and discussions that might traditionally have been considered outside the army's province. The vision remained unformed and embryonic, but Tojo was envisioning a future in which the army deployed its immense institutional strength and imposed itself on the Japanese decision-making process in such a way as to maximize the chances of victory in a total war.

3
SHIFTING FORTUNES
1929–1935

PROMOTION TO THE GENERAL ranks of the Imperial Japanese Army required a command post. For Tojo Hideki this came in the form of a transfer, in April 1929, to the First Infantry Regiment. He remained at regimental headquarters, near Roppongi in central Tokyo, until August 1931. This was one of the more prestigious posts to which a colonel like Tojo might aspire. The regiment had been formed in January 1874 and was, per its title, the Japanese Army's inaugural infantry regiment. Its mission, as defined by the Meiji Emperor when he presented the regiment with its colors in December 1874, was to develop its "soldierly cooperative unity" and its "power and authority" in order to "safeguard the nation."[1] True to its founding ideals, the regiment boasted a proud battlefield history and had fought with distinction in the Seinan War, the Sino-Japanese War, and the Russo-Japanese War. In Tojo's time, it consisted of nine rifle companies, a command company, and several support companies.

This was Tojo's first extended assignment with troops since the late Meiji period. His basic mission was to prepare the men for war; to this end, he was no less beholden to discipline and drill than the next commanding officer. Tojo sought to improve the physicality of even the weakest soldiers and drilled the regiment to something closely approximating parade ground perfection. His regiment attained such exacting standards that his immediate superior, the First Division commander, Lieutenant General Masaki Jinzaburo spoke openly of Tojo as Japan's "best regimental commander."[2]

Combat preparation required more than parade ground marching. Tojo was now, to quote the military's handbook for squad administration, personally responsible for "all lines of regimental business," including personnel, mobilization, weaponry, finances, and the health of his men and horses.[3] He embraced these responsibilities and took sustained interest in the regiment's procurement, storage, and distribution of material resources. He participated with what can only be imagined as vigor, relish, and forthrightness in the drafting of divisional reports on such matters as equipment, mobilization, and management of medical supplies.[4]

Tojo found it difficult, at least initially, to connect with his subordinate officers. This was partly a product of the system in which he operated. His subordinates (accurately) regarded him as belonging to the army's operational and political nerve center, and they resented the fact that his regimental posting was impermanent and but a step on his career path. To borrow the words of historian Leonard Humphreys, unit officers regarded the regimental commanders as "distant, inaccessible, the source of change and perturbation, the higher-ups who coldly and impersonally controlled their lives."[5] The difficulties in connecting were also partly due to Tojo's personality, for his subordinates generally regarded him as overbearing, more attuned to the needs of conscripts than to his officers' goals and motivations. Certainly he was punctilious to a fault: one subordinate later recalled a parade ground scolding from Tojo because he had not yet committed to memory the names of conscripts who had arrived only a day or two earlier.[6]

Over time, Tojo revealed a softer side in his dealings with his subordinates. He spent considerable time, energy, and effort educating them in the demands of modern warfare. He also extended an extraordinary degree of patronage to Lieutenants Akamatsu Sadao, Kato Takashi, and Suzuki Yoshikazu, actively assisting them in their preparations for the War College entrance exam. On one occasion he went so far as to call on the Akamatsu household and, recalling how the discord between his wife and mother had impacted his own efforts at preparing for the War College exam, asked the young officer's mother and wife to ensure that he had much time to study. (Akamatsu became one of Tojo's favorites, and served him in various capacities over the ensuing years). Tojo also regularly invited not only Akamatsu, Kato, and Suzuki, but also lieutenants Koda Kiyosada, Ishiguro Teizo, Nishi Hisashi, and Usuda Kanzo to his household for convivial and morale-boosting dinners.[7]

Tojo's solicitude for the enlisted men was another outstanding feature of his regimental command. There was, perhaps, little wonder that his troops referred to him as the "kindly commander."[8] One time Tojo rebuked his regimental quartermaster for a series of unpalatable meals that, he insisted, could only "stick in the men's throats."[9] He thoroughly disliked hazing and sought to eradicate corporal punishment in the barracks.[10] He insisted that each of the conscript's fathers and older brothers be personally invited to the regiment's annual presentation of colors, and amid the salutes, processions, and festivities, he reassured the recruits' family members that the officers and men were as close as "fathers and sons and brothers." Tojo also established a regimental committee to help his troops find gainful employment when they had completed their two years' service and returned to civilian life.[11]

The patrician attitude Tojo assumed in his dealings with the conscripted men and their families reveals another side to him. It was not a case of his putting on airs. Tojo held to an idealized notion of the uniformed officer as a paragon of virtue who commanded—not demanded—respect from all with whom he came in contact. This Tojo regarded as important, because the individual officer and particularly the regimental commander represented the principal point of contact between civil society and the military as an institution, and common cause between the army and people was all the more integral in this era of total war.

THROUGHOUT HIS TIME WITH the First Infantry Regiment Tojo remained, alongside Nagata Tetsuzan, in the Futaba Club, and joined yet another clandestine officer association, the One Evening Society, which was the result of a merger between the Futaba and Thursday Clubs. Besides Tojo, its more notable members included the original Baden-Baden conspirators Nagata Tetsuzan, Obata Toshiro, and Okamura Yasuji; Komoto Daisaku, who had assassinated warlord Zhang Zuolin; and Itagaki Seishiro, Muto Akira, Tanaka Shin'ichi, and Tominaga Kyoji.

At its inaugural meeting in mid-May 1929, the One Evening Society agreed on a three-point plan of action. Its members would seek, first, to control the Japanese Army's personnel decisions in an effort to ensure that they and like-minded officers filled all key positions in Tokyo. The society would focus, second, on "resolution of the Manchuria-Mongolia issue," and, third, it would seek every opportunity to raise the fortunes of the military's three leading antiestablishment generals—namely, Lieutenant Generals Araki Sadao, Hayashi Senjuro, and Masaki Jinzaburo.[12] The three goals were intricately interwoven: With the trio of Araki, Hayashi, and Masaki atop the army and middle-ranking officers like Nagata and Tojo filling important section-level posts, the army would be in a perfect position to resolve the Manchuria-Mongolia issue and pursue other policies the One Evening Society deemed important.

Infusing the One Evening Society's agenda was a confidence that had not hitherto been discernible. Only a few years earlier Nagata and Tojo had rigged the War College's entrance examination process to deny young officers from the former Choshu feudal domain a future at the top of the military. Now in Nagata's and Tojo's sights were officers already at the top. Of particular interest were upper-echelon officers who belonged to the so-called Ugaki faction. Named after General Ugaki Kazushige, the faction included both the army minister, General Shirakawa Yoshinori, and the army chief of staff, General Suzuki Soroku, as well as the officers immediately beneath them, including Abe Nobuyuki, Hata Eitaro, Kanaya Hanzo, Koiso Kuniaki, Minami Jiro, Ninomiya Harushige, and Tatekawa Yoshitsugu.

For many in the One Evening Society and indeed across the Imperial Army as a whole, anti-Ugaki sentiment owed to the disarmament policies Ugaki had championed in the mid-1920s. He had, as army minister, deactivated four infantry divisions and spent the savings on mechanizing and otherwise modernizing the Japanese Army. This had inverted the military's traditional emphasis on men over materiel, and it earned Ugaki an unyielding hatred among many of his professional military colleagues. Tojo's enmity toward Ugaki owed to more primal instincts: Ugaki was General Tanaka Giichi's foremost protégé and therefore, in Tojo's view, a Choshu proxy. Old grievances burned brightly in Tojo's anti-Choshu bosom, and he regarded, by association, all members of the Ugaki faction as tainted.[13]

The One Evening Society first flexed its muscles in early 1930, when it learned that the all-important post of chief of staff would soon be vacated. Incumbent and key Ugaki ally General Suzuki Sosoku was retiring, and Ugaki wanted to replace him with another factional supporter. Nagata and Tojo worked in opposition to Ugaki. It was too soon to hope that Araki, Hayashi, or Masaki might succeed him; Nagata and Tojo hoped instead that the inspector general of military training, General Muto Nobuyoshi (an earlier-generation anti-Choshu officer), would, in a lateral move, become chief of staff and that Araki would be appointed his deputy.[14] Nagata and Tojo enlisted the active assistance of the army's oldest and most venerable anti-Choshu officer, Field Marshal Uehara Yusaku. Their method was disarmingly simple: Uehara, as a prestigious but largely powerless military councilor, was expected to rubber-stamp personnel decisions, but with Nagata and Tojo goading him, Uehara fought a desperate rearguard action against Ugaki's presumptive nominee, Lieutenant General Kanaya Hanzo. Uehara retracted his opposition only after the emperor expressed his dismay at the unprecedented intervention.[15] Days later, Kanaya was appointed chief of staff. Nagata and Tojo congratulated themselves over drinks for having at least fired a shot across the military establishment's bow.[16]

TOJO REMAINED WITH THE First Infantry Regiment in March 1931, when senior army officers actively engaged with right-wing extremist Okawa Shumei and planned a coup d'état. The plan began with a mob surrounding the Imperial Diet, and the Japanese Army would act as if to suppress the mob but would instead seize the Diet. Coup planners assumed that the cabinet would collapse, the emperor would name Ugaki the next prime minister, and a military dictatorship would ensue. Underpinning the coup plans was a belief that party politicians were contemptible, corruptible, and cravenly beholden to narrow, partisan interests, as well as a decades-old conviction that the army ought to be the ultimate arbiter of state affairs. Lieutenant Colonel Hashimoto Kingoro, the Russia Section chief on the General Staff, was the most centrally involved. He organized the Cherry Society, which brought together radicalized young officers. The army's upper echelons—and, in particular, officers who had coalesced around Ugaki—were at least informed of the coup plans. This included the vice chief of staff, Lieutenant General Ninomiya Harushige, and the vice army minister, Lieutenant General Sugiyama Hajime, as well as their immediate subordinates, including Major Generals Koiso Kuniaki and Tatekawa Yoshitsugu. Even Ugaki flirted with Okawa.[17]

Tojo refused to engage the coup plans. He ordered his regimental subordinates to dissociate themselves from right-wing coup agitators like Okawa Shumei. He refused to accept extralegal action, insisting that the army must necessarily remain within the limits of the constitution. "It is out of the question," Tojo declared on one occasion, "for the emperor's troops to deploy without [the emperor's] permission."[18]

Tojo's opposition to the coup was not in and of itself enough to sway army policy; his seniority was not such that his voice was determining. Still, his was among the voices of mid- and higher-ranking officers who worked to wean the army away from the planned coup. Principal among them was Tojo's friend and mentor, Major General Nagata Tetsuzan. Joining Nagata and Tojo were fellow members of the Futaba Club and the One Evening

Society, all of whom remained steadfastly opposed to Ugaki and the coup. Tojo met with his old friends Nagata and Okamura, as well as Doihara Kenji, on March 15, 1931, to discuss what they regarded as the poisonous influence exercised over young officers by right-wing ideologues like Okawa Shumei.[19] Their stance was principled insofar as they all professed fidelity to proper constitutional process. Also informing their efforts was a shared confidence in the future. "Wait just a while," Tojo told the One Evening Society in early 1931. "Our time, with Nagata at its core, will come." Then, he assured his colleagues, everything would "start to happen."[20]

One further motivation underpinned the actions of Tojo and his confidants in the Futaba Club and One Evening Society. Both associations, it will be recalled, had long since called for the use of force in Manchuria and Mongolia. The Manchurian-Mongolian issue remained in early 1931 their first priority, and they were concerned lest domestic upheaval divert attentions away from the continent. Their representations ultimately contributed to the army leadership's decision to dissociate itself from the planned coup. When the so-called March Incident ended not with a bang but with a whimper, Tojo and his contemporaries might have been forgiven for believing in the fundamental correctness of their position on Manchuria and Mongolia.[21]

TOJO WAS TRANSFERRED IN August 1931 to the Army General Staff, where he headed the Organization and Mobilization Section. Here, again, he had the opportunity to organize the army and nation for total war. Most immediately, he had to contend with a powder-keg situation in Manchuria. His predecessor, Colonel Yamawaki Masataka, had participated on a committee that had prepared a "general outline of a solution for the Manchurian problem." The outline's coauthors were section-level chiefs from the Army Ministry, the General Staff, and the Inspectorate General of Military Training; included among them was Tojo's mentor, Nagata Tetsuzan (who headed the Army Affairs Section of the Army Ministry's powerful Military Affairs Bureau). This outline anticipated the likely possibility of a continued rise in "anti-Japanese activities" in Manchuria and echoed concerns within the army for the future of Japanese rights and interests there. It stated that, unless the situation changed dramatically, military action would "probably be necessary." It predicted that such action was likely by spring 1932 and called for a concerted effort to prepare both Japanese public opinion and "foreign understanding" of Japan's aims.[22]

This twelve-month time frame required a degree of patience singularly lacking among Kwantung Army officers. Whereas Nagata (closely followed, as ever, by Tojo) was animated by the twin imperatives of building domestic support and guarding against international opprobrium for any military action in Manchuria, Kwantung Army officers were convinced of the need for prompt action. On September 18, 1931, Colonel Itagaki Seishiro and Lieutenant Colonel Ishiwara Kanji (both One Evening Society members) launched the so-called Manchurian Incident by bombing the South Manchurian Railway just outside Mukden. They blamed Chinese bandits and thereby created a casus belli. Within hours the Kwantung Army had seized Mukden. When the cabinet of Prime Minister Wakatsuki Reijiro—including Army Minister Minami Jiro—learned what was happening, it adopted a policy of nonexpansion of the incident, but the Kwantung Army ignored the cabinet. Ishiwara and Itagaki paid provocateurs to launch anti-Japanese demonstrations in the areas surrounding Mukden, which set the stage for the expansion of hostilities. Within days, all of Manchuria south of Mukden and east of the Peking-Mukden Railway was under the Kwantung Army's control.[23]

Some officers in Tokyo were in active connivance with the Kwantung Army; most belonged to the One Evening Society. Tojo remained a key member of the society, very much involved in efforts at ensuring that the Kwantung Army's efforts did not go to waste. He met on September 21 with Colonels Isogai Rensuke, Okamura Yasuji, Shigeto Chiaki, and Watari Hisao; all were section chiefs in either the Army Ministry or the General Staff, and all but Shigeto were members of the One Evening Society. Under discussion

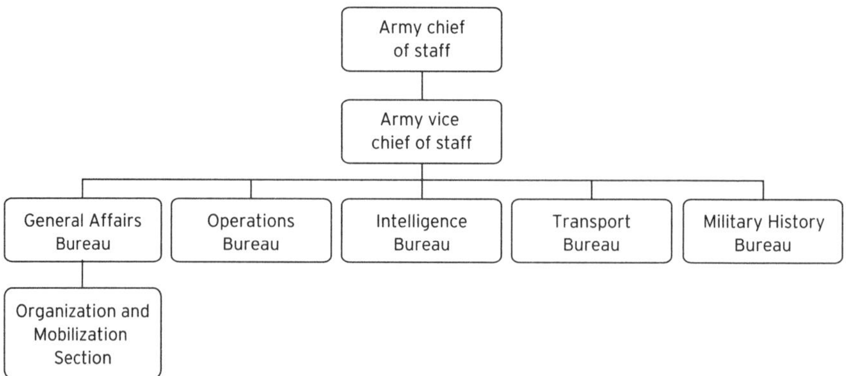

The Army General Staff. Each bureau included multiple sections; this figure includes only the section on which Tojo served between August 1931 and August 1933.

was the unfolding Manchurian situation, and agreement was forthcoming on the perceived need to ensure that state policy did not hinder but instead capitalized on the Kwantung Army's actions.[24] That same day, Korean Army commander (and darling of the One Evening Society), Lieutenant General Hayashi Senjuro, dispatched forces under his command across the border into Manchuria. He acted independently and on no authority but his own, directly defying state policy.[25]

On September 24, Tojo met again with Isogai, Okamura, Shigeto, and Watari. This time they were joined by Colonel Imamura Hitoshi and Major General Tatekawa Yoshitsugu. The latter had just returned from Kwantung Army Headquarters and explained the "truth" of the unfolding incident in Manchuria.[26] Truthfully or otherwise, Tatekawa disavowed complicity in Ishiwara's and Itagaki's actions. He insisted that the Japanese Army—and the government as a whole—must not play the role of "firefighter" in Manchuria but must instead take "full responsibility" and see the incident through to its conclusion.[27] Tojo and his fellow staff officers were in fundamental agreement with this assessment. They met again on September 25 and agreed it was necessary to proceed with the "establishment of a new, independent administration" in Manchuria, with a view to the "construction of an independent state." During a freewheeling discussion, Tojo emphasized that such steps were necessitated by ongoing preparations for war against the Soviets, which in turn was attributable to the need to defend Korea as well as Japan's rights and interests in Manchuria against the Soviet Union.[28]

All the while, the Kwantung Army worked to reorganize the region's governance. It dismantled the Northeastern Governmental Affairs Council, which had exercised at least nominal control over Manchuria under warlord Zhang Xueliang (the Young Marshal, as he was known, had replaced his assassinated father), and it sought to convince Manchurian Chinese elites to cooperate in administration and governance. The Kwantung Army was aided in this endeavor by the Chinese government's policy of nonresistance and by the Young Marshal's scrupulous adherence to that policy. According to historian Rana Mitter, "It was a fact that [Zhang] had ordered troops not to resist the Japanese; faced with that order ... why should anyone else [in Manchuria] feel an obligation to oppose the Japanese?"[29] Thus it was that, within days of the September 18, 1931, explosion that sparked the incident, public order maintenance committees staffed by Manchurian Chinese elites and guided and surveilled by Japanese advisers emerged in Mukden and elsewhere. Dozens of these committees mushroomed across Manchuria; over the ensuing months, they amalgamated and evolved and provided the basis for provincial governments. Tojo was a keen student of these machinations and later sought to apply them in Inner Mongolia.

EVEN AS THE SITUATION in Manchuria unfolded, Japanese Army officers in Tokyo involved themselves in another planned coup. Lieutenant Colonel Hashimoto Kingoro was again a central organizer, and the Cherry Society was again involved. Plans included a mid-October attack on the Diet and the assassination of all the Wakatsuki cabinet members. The aim of the so-called October Incident was a military dictatorship under the presumed leadership of the deputy inspector general for military training (and another One Evening Society darling), Lieutenant General Araki Sadao.

Tojo's response to the planned coup echoed his response to the abortive March Incident. At an October 16 meeting that included the Imperial Army leadership, Tojo agreed with majority opinion, which counseled deployment of the *kenpei* (gendarmerie or military police), the arrest of the coup plotters, and a suppression of the coup. Araki's was the only dissenting voice; he explained that he had prevailed on the coup plotters, and although they had not agreed to call off the coup, they had at least agreed to postpone it. Araki argued, on these grounds, that the army ought not to take any action against the plotters. Amid a bewildering mix of rumor, innuendo, and misinformation, Tojo and others received an anonymous tip that specifically charged Araki with having lied about any agreement to postpone the coup. According to the information they received, the coup would indeed go ahead as planned. Tojo convinced his colleagues of the need to inform Army Minister Minami, who deployed the *kenpei*. Twelve officers were detained.[30]

The October Incident ended, as had the March Incident before it, tamely. Tojo met on the evening of October 17, 1931, with like-minded middle-ranking officers, including his old friends Nagata and Okamura. They congratulated themselves for their role in having deflated the coup, but also wondered whether the army was rendering itself "uncontrollable." They spoke of the need to "purify" the army and "reorganize the nation."[31] These twin prescriptions differed little from the ten-year-old Baden-Baden pledge, although purification now seemed to target not only officers who engaged in *hanbatsu* [clan or factional] personnel practices but also radicalized younger officers.

The October Incident was but the latest event in which radical elements within the Imperial Army hoped to drag the military, and indeed the nation, in directions that seemed otherwise unlikely, unfeasible, and even unpalatable. It presents a useful point at which to pause and consider Tojo's response to the rise of radicalism within the Japanese Army. Had Tojo not supported Komoto following the unauthorized assassination of Manchu warlord Zhang Zuolin? Had he not also supported the conquest of Manchuria, which the Kwantung Army launched in brazen defiance of government policy? Why, then, did he refuse to accept the unauthorized deployment of troops during the March and October Incidents? How did Tojo reconcile his acceptance of the Kwantung Army's radicalism with his staunch opposition to any domestic move that might be deemed unconstitutional? The inconsistencies should not be explained away. It might nonetheless be noted that he seemed entirely willing to grant field commanders and garrison forces the prerogative of independent initiative, but he was utterly unwilling to grant that same prerogative to units stationed in Tokyo. Tojo seemed, in other words, willing to accept radical action outside Japan but refused to concede the need for any such action domestically.

There were limits to Tojo's tolerance of the Kwantung Army's defiance. Days after the October Incident was defused, he received intelligence from the *kenpei* linking the coup plotters and the Kwantung Army. The suggestion was that the Kwantung Army had welcomed the prospect of a new, army-centric cabinet led by Araki. The failure of the October Incident had, according to this intelligence, left the Kwantung Army impatient and pondering a declaration of independence from Tokyo. In this telling, the Kwantung Army intended to build an independent Manchurian-Mongolian state and serve as its military. Some were doubtful as to the reliability of this intelligence, but Tojo prevailed on the army leadership to dispatch a mission to Manchuria as a precautionary measure. It is difficult to measure the effectiveness of this action, but the Kwantung Army remained within the Japanese Army's chain of command.[32]

IN MID-DECEMBER 1931 the Wakatsuki cabinet reflected on several months of unabated aggression in Manchuria, admitted its inability to control the army, and resigned en masse. The army's "big three"—outgoing army minister, General Minami Jiro; the chief of staff, General Kanaya Hanzo; and the inspector general of military training, General Muto Nobuyoshi—proved unable to agree on Minami's ministerial successor. Minami and Kanaya wanted Lieutenant General Abe Nobuyuki, who identified (if only loosely) with Ugaki. The curmudgeonly Muto instead wanted Lieutenant General Araki Sadao, who remained a favorite of the One Evening Society. Tojo's friend and mentor, Nagata Tetsuzan, prevailed on the army leadership to forward both names to incoming Prime Minister Inukai Tsuyoshi; it was only proper, Nagata insisted, to let the prime minister decide. Nagata, Tojo, and their One Evening Society colleagues did not leave things to chance. They drew on their connections, contacted those who might be able to influence Inukai, and built support for Araki. In this way the society made good, at least in part, on its earlier pledge to support and promote the fortunes of the trio of Araki, Hayashi, and Masaki as they moved up into the military's highest echelons. Araki was appointed minister on December 13, 1931. Nagata, Tojo, and their One Evening Society colleagues could now consider themselves kingmakers—or, at least, minister makers.[33]

Within days of his ministerial appointment, Araki began a personnel sweep. He went straight to the top and removed Chief of Staff Kanaya. Recall that there had been intense politicking that resulted in Kanaya's appointment; Tojo and others who had fought that appointment now rejoiced in his ousting. Few other officers lamented the loss of Kanaya, for he was an alcoholic and widely regarded as unfit for the demands of his office. Over the ensuing weeks, Araki targeted all officers associated with Ugaki. This led to a clean sweep of the highest positions in the Army Ministry and the General Staff. Vice Chief of Staff Ninomiya Harushige and Operations Division Chief Tatekawa Yoshitsugu, as well as Vice Minister Sugiyama Hajime and Koiso Kuniaki, the director of the Military Affairs Bureau, were all reassigned to the field.

Araki installed the French-educated field marshal and Imperial family member Prince Kan'in Kotohito as chief of staff. Prince Kan'in was only ever supposed to be a figurehead; daily staff duties were expected to devolve to his deputy. To that post Araki appointed his friend and ally Masaki, who had been Tojo's direct superior during Tojo's time with the First Infantry Regiment. Two of the three officers the One Evening Society had hailed as the leaders of a new era in the military were now in positions of the highest leadership.

The One Evening Society was rewarded handsomely for having supported Araki during the minister-making process, and many key appointments went to the society's members. Nagata was appointed chief of the General Staff's Intelligence Division, and Major General Yamaoka Shigeatsu was appointed chief of the Military Affairs Bureau. Colonel Obata Toshiro became the chief of the Operations Section, and a few weeks later was reassigned to head the Transport and Communication Division. Replacing him in the Operations Section was One Evening Society member Lieutenant Colonel Suzuki Yorimichi, and One Evening Society colleague Colonel Yamashita Tomoyuki was appointed chief of the Army Affairs Section. Tojo remained chief of the General Staff's Organization and Mobilization Section.

TOJO AND HIS One Evening Society colleagues now considered themselves part of a much wider faction within the Imperial Army. Known as the *kodoha* (Imperial way faction), it drew inspiration from a rich army tradition—in which Tojo was steeped—of extolling the uniqueness of the Imperial line and trumpeting the superiority of the Japanese spirit. Araki and Masaki, who led the faction, were its chief spokesmen. They freely used the term *kodo* (Imperial way) and built a cult following among the army's junior officers, who were (as Tojo had once noted) particularly reverential in their treatment of the emperor, the Imperial line, and the Imperial way. A pronouncement, which Araki made a few weeks after his ministerial appointment, is indicative of the crude cultural nativism that was a defining feature of the faction's public discourse:

> What is Japan's true nature? It was gifted by [the Sun Goddess] Amaterasu at Japan's very foundation, and is none other than the great ideal to which the three sacred treasures [mirror, sword, and jewel] give expression.... The mirror symbolizes justice, the jewel means love, and the sword manifests courage. In other words, justice, love, and courage as revealed by the three sacred treasures are our nation's founding ideals. This is ... the way of the emperor. Since the time of the gods, the way of the emperor has been truly clear and unmistakable. It is the so-called true "kodo".... To protect this path, to brighten this path, and to proceed down this path! This is the ideal of the Japanese people as Imperial subjects. This has to be our duty. With the sovereign and people united, with the cooperation of the higher and lower classes, and with high ideals, we will make new efforts day by day. Herein resides the essence of our "kokutai" [national essence, spirit].[34]

The appeal of such pronouncements, particularly among the army's junior officers, was magnetic. Tojo hoped this might provide Araki and Masaki with leverage over the army's radicalized elements and facilitate the reimposition of military discipline. Such pronouncements also promised to unify the military and civilian society—integral in an era of total war. Tojo and his One Evening Society colleagues had good reason to identify with the Imperial way faction.[35]

Tojo also found cause for satisfaction in Araki's Manchurian-Mongolian policies. Whereas his ministerial predecessor had equivocated on the Manchurian-Mongolian issue, Araki was utterly unambiguous about Japan's objectives. According to a policy paper prepared days after Araki's ministerial appointment, Manchuria-Mongolia had to be made "separate and independent" from China's nationalist government in Nanjing and had to become a Japanese "protectorate."[36] Recall that Tojo had espoused a similar position in an address to the Thursday Club in March 1928; he now celebrated Araki's continental objectives.

Tojo also identified with Araki's most immediate Manchurian objective. On taking office, Araki was insistent that the "Jinzhou issue" had to be "quickly straightened out."[37] Manchu warlord Zhang Xueliang had, at the outset of the Manchurian Incident, removed his forces from Mukden (and elsewhere in Manchuria) to Jinzhou in southwestern Manchuria. Should Jinzhou fall to the Kwantung Army, Zhang's forces could reasonably be expected to retreat out of Manchuria and into North China. This would remove the last vestige of the Young Marshal's Manchurian presence, marking the end of any realistic claim to Manchuria that either Zhang or the Chinese nationalist government in Nanjing could reasonably make.

On December 22, 1931, the Kwantung Army announced its intention to advance on Jinzhou. It offered Zhang's forces the opportunity to withdraw unmolested. Zhang took the opportunity, and the majority of his forces had left Jinzhou for Hebei Province in North China by New Year's Day 1932. The Kwantung Army occupied Jinzhou on January 3, and advanced as far as the Great Wall at Shanhai Pass, where it established contact with an existing Japanese garrison. Manchuria was now, for all intents and purposes, severed from China proper.

Early signs of disunity in the Imperial way faction emerged in the immediate aftermath of Jinzhou's capture. Tojo's friend and mentor, Nagata Tetsuzan, fired the opening salvo. Nagata remained mindful of international opinion, and he was adamant that Japan must not by its actions in Manchuria isolate itself irrevocably from the Western powers. It seems possible that Nagata was particularly affected by a January 7, 1932, diplomatic note from US Secretary of State Henry Stimson. The note made clear the US refusal to recognize any Sino-Japanese agreement that impaired US treaty rights, "including those which related to the territorial and administrative integrity of China." Nagata now argued for an end to all military operations in Manchuria. He approached Araki and recommended issuance of an Imperial rescript applauding the troops and announcing an end to hostilities. Araki, however, would have none of it. He castigated Nagata and like-minded officers in the army's middle echelons for their "extremely short-sighted" approach and insisted that operations must not end any time soon.[38]

Nagata took his concerns to the chief of staff, Prince Kan'in. Whereas Araki had been dismissive, Prince Kan'in proved receptive. He was, perhaps by virtue of family ties, more finely attuned to the emperor's solicitude for Japan's international position than Araki (whose loyalty to the Imperial way had self-evident limits). Prince Kan'in secured from the emperor an Imperial rescript on January 8, but it did not reflect the sense of crisis that had animated the emperor since the beginning of the Manchurian Incident. A rescript was not the vehicle with which the emperor should voice his fear for the damage done to orderly and proper decision-making processes. Nor was it the vehicle with which to fret openly about the possibility of Japan's becoming an international pariah. Instead the rescript lauded the Kwantung Army for having "proclaimed, at home and abroad, the majesty of the Imperial forces" and for having laid the "foundations of peace in the Orient." It applauded the Kwantung Army for having suppressed the "bandits" and for having ensured "security" across Manchuria. The rescript made clear that it was now time to halt any further military operations.[39]

Tojo was dispatched to Mukden to deliver the Imperial rescript to the Kwantung Army. He met on January 8 with his brilliant if impetuous One Evening Society cadre, Lieutenant Colonel Ishiwara Kanji. Tojo insisted it was time to "extract troops" from Manchuria, and specified that the forces that the Japanese Korean Army commander, Hayashi Senjuro, had dispatched in support of Kwantung Army operations would have to return to Korea. He set a most stringent deadline of January 20, 1932, for the central military authorities sought to avoid the ire of fiscally minded members of the Imperial Diet and also to make a favorable impression in the League of Nations. Ishiwara accepted that the Korean Army troops would eventually have to leave Manchuria, but he contended that they must remain for the purpose of "bandit suppression" until at least late February or early March.[40]

Tojo also raised with Ishiwara the state of central military authorities' planning for Manchuria's future. Specifically, he spoke of plans for a peak Japanese control agency, which would be located within Kwantung Army headquarters. Named the Special Affairs Unit, it would cooperate with the semigovernmental South Manchurian Railway Company as it oversaw Manchuria's economic and industrial development. This plan bore the fingerprint of officers like Tojo insofar as it sought to develop Manchuria in ways that complemented and bolstered Japan's drive to economic self-sufficiency. It also expressed the frankly utilitarian motives driving officers like Tojo in Tokyo. The contrarian Ishiwara, who was developing an altogether more idealistic pan-Asian ideology, was unimpressed. He refused to accept that the Kwantung Army chief of staff ought to lead the Special Affairs Unit or take an alternative suggestion to the effect that the unit might best be led by a civilian.[41]

Tojo returned to Tokyo without having secured Ishiwara's agreement on any substantive issues. It is not difficult to imagine him fuming at Ishiwara's intransigence. Indeed, one commentator quotes him as follows: "Shit! That Ishiwara! He doesn't give a damn about the right of Supreme Command! He thinks the Kwantung Army has authority over the Army General Staff! At this rate, the army will collapse in disorder."[42]

IN THE AFTERMATH OF Tojo's Manchurian mission, the fighting spread to Harbin (in northern Manchuria) and also to Shanghai. The Kwantung Army's decision to capture Harbin reflected its confidence in the likelihood of ongoing Soviet military inaction; the spread of fighting to Shanghai was a product of the army's desire to shift the Western powers' attention away from Manchuria.[43]

Tojo continued to enjoy easy access to Araki and Masaki. He met with the latter on February 7 and with the former on February 14, 1932. In both instances he spoke of the so-called Shanghai Incident, and his involvement in preparation of the Ninth Division (stationed at Kanazawa) for deployment thereto. With Araki he spoke also of the propriety of dispatching Colonel Okamura Yasuji to Shanghai. Tojo found himself locked in a dispute with Obata Toshiro on precisely this issue. In Obata's estimation, Okamura's status as an expert on China made him an obvious choice for dispatch. Tojo took no exception with Okamura's reputation—he, in fact, admired Okamura's connections with China's warlords—but Tojo wanted Okamura to remain in Tokyo, in his position as chief of the Personnel Bureau's Appointments and Assignment Section. As Tojo put it to Araki, personnel decisions were critical to the ongoing issue of the army's "reform," which was ultimately more important than the Shanghai Incident. Tojo was unable to convince Araki of the soundness of his position, and Okamura received orders to leave for Shanghai.[44]

Days thereafter, Obata sent a subordinate to Tojo's office to request that he mobilize not only the Ninth Division but also the Eleventh and Fourteenth Divisions. Tojo was livid; he had been neither consulted nor apprised. He stormed into Obata's office and asked, "Are you ready to fight alone [in Shanghai]?"[45] There was, however, little Tojo could do. The Shanghai Expeditionary Army, which included not only the Ninth but also the Eleventh and Fourteenth Divisions, occupied Shanghai's Wusong Forts on March 3, 1932, and then declared a unilateral ceasefire. Okamura involved himself in the subsequent Sino-Japanese truce negotiations, before the talks shifted from Shanghai to Geneva. An armistice was agreed to in Geneva on May 5.

Violence returned very soon thereafter to Tokyo. On May 15, young naval officers joined with Military Academy cadets and the usual assortment of right-wing extremists in yet another round of political violence. Prime Minister Inukai Tsuyoshi was shot and killed, and with him went the era of political party cabinets. Araki, who remained as army minister in the cabinet of the new prime minister, retired admiral Saito Makoto, spoke eloquently in defense of the assassins. They were, in Araki's estimation, "pure and naïve young men" who had acted "in the sincere belief" that they were spilling blood "for the benefit of Imperial Japan."[46] Tojo shared no particular love for Inukai, but his response to the so-called May 15 Incident was consistent with his response to earlier such incidents: He deplored the departure from constitutional process and lamented the breach in military discipline. On the night of the incident, Nagata and Tojo summoned a radicalized junior officer, Lieutenant Colonel Suganami Saburo, whom Nagata accused of having played a behind-the-scenes role in the plot. Suganami insisted that he had instead sought to prevent the violence. For Tojo, Suganami's admission of foreknowledge was tacit acknowledgment of involvement, and he moved to restrain Suganami physically. Tojo was called off by the coolheaded Nagata, and although the meeting ended without any further ado, Suganami called subsequently on Obata's patronage. In this way the Baden-Baden conspirators were descending into disunity and strife, with Nagata at one end, Obata at the other end, and Okamura and Tojo caught in the middle.[47]

THE LEAGUE OF NATIONS had, in the meantime, sent a commission of inquiry to China and Manchuria to judge the situation. The final report sought to be evenhanded: It recommended the withdrawal of Japanese troops, but it also condemned warlord Zhang Xueliang's regime and saw good reason to offer Japan generous treaty rights and privileges in Manchuria. The league's deliberations mattered little. Establishment of the nominally independent state of Manchukuo was announced on March 1, 1932. China's last emperor, known in the West as Henry Pu Yi, had been spirited from his abode in the Japanese concession in Tianjin and was made chief executive of this new state. Japan extended diplomatic recognition some six months later and secured, in solemn treaty form, Manchukuo's recognition of its existing rights and privileges. It also undertook to provide for Manchukuo's security. For this latter purpose, both nations agreed to a continued Japanese military presence in Manchukuo.[48]

While the foreign ministry worked to shore up Manchukuo diplomatically, the army reconsidered the likelihood of a Japanese-Soviet war. It is easy to see why this might have been the case: the Japanese-Soviet buffer zone in northern Manchuria had now disappeared, and the Japanese and Soviet armies now confronted each other directly along the ill-defined Manchukuoan-Soviet border. The possibility of war arose during deliberations on the army's annual operational planning. One of the original Baden-Baden conspirators, Major General Obata Toshiro, was among the most vociferous, insisting that a preventive war against the Soviet Red Army was not only possible but indeed desirable. In Obata's estimation, this required a crash mobilization program that included the acquisition of manpower, procurement of equipment, training of the expanded army, creation of new divisions and other units, and ultimately the transport of these new units to the combat zone. The alternative, Obata argued, was an ever-increasing Japanese-Soviet military imbalance and, eventually, absolute Soviet military superiority.[49]

Nagata Tetsuzan responded caustically to Obata's call for a preventive war. He regarded Obata's thinking as simplistic in the extreme. He remained beholden to a concept of warfare that reached beyond the battlefield and calculations of relative troop strengths. In other words, he remained convinced that twentieth-century warfare was ultimately a test of overall national strength. For this reason, Nagata argued for a cautious stance toward the Soviet Union, at least until Japan had successfully implemented a long-term war preparation program that involved economic plans and annual industrial output goals in Manchukuo, all of which would boost Japan's war preparations.[50]

The relationship between Nagata and Obata deteriorated precipitously. Tojo was left to ponder the decades-long history he shared with the two men. Both had, along with Okamura, helped Tojo prepare for the War College entrance exam. Both were also, along with Okamura and subsequently Tojo, coconspirators at Baden-Baden. Both had, again alongside Okamura and Tojo, been founding members of the Futaba Club, and both were One Evening Society members. Now their relationship was in a state of collapse. Tojo joined Okamura and sought, for a time, to mediate the conflict, but it was to no avail. This was due, at least partly, to Obata's complete lack of respect for Tojo (he later commented that he had "from the outset" regarded Tojo as lacking in "ability," "character," and "insight").[51] Obata also knew that he enjoyed the patronage of Araki and Masaki, and he felt no particular need to step away from his hardline anti-Soviet stance. Nagata, for his part, remained convinced of the soundness of his position and would not budge.

Tojo stood by Nagata. His principal protagonist was the One Evening Society member, Obata protégé, and Operations Section chief, Lieutenant Colonel Suzuki Yorimichi, who was responsible for determining the granular details of Obata's call for preventive war against the Soviets. He figured that Japan must open war when the Red Army maintained no more than four or five divisions in the Soviet Far East. Japan's initial aim was the force's "annihilation," which in Suzuki's estimation would require all three Kwantung Army divisions and both Korean Army divisions, as well as another seaborne division (for a total of six divisions). The Imperial Japanese Army would then send a further two divisions to the Soviet Far East. These extra divisions' task was threefold: mopping up operations, destruction of all air fields, and control of all fortresses in and around Vladivostok. The Japanese Army would in the meantime send nine divisions to Harbin, three divisions to Heilongjiang Province in the north, four divisions to Heilongjiang Province in the west, and one division each to Jehol Province and the island of Sakhalin, for a total of twenty-six divisions. All except the division in Sakhalin would fight a decisive battle on the Manchukuoan-Soviet border, and if everything went according to Suzuki's plans, Japanese forces would occupy all key points east of Lake Baikal. Finally, two divisions would remain in the home islands as a defensive measure against possible US entry into the war. All told, Suzuki's plan required the mobilization of all of the Japanese Army's twenty-eight divisions.[52]

Tojo opposed Suzuki vociferously. The two engaged regularly in screaming matches, and Tojo professed astonishment at the shortsightedness of officers like Suzuki, who failed to see that war against the Soviets would require more than battlefield planning. "The victor in modern warfare," Tojo insisted, "will be the state that controls all instruments of operations, including military force, economics, ideology, and politics." He insisted that Manchukuo's development was of interest to the Imperial Army precisely because it would enable the army to fight the Soviets in what would almost necessarily be total war. Fighting the Soviets at the outset of that development process seemed extreme folly. Tojo cited the enormous costs involved in Manchukuo's industrial and infrastructural development and questioned whether war against the Soviets would divert funding from this program. He also recalled the army's earlier Siberian expedition, which had come at great cost but ultimately offered no rewards whatsoever.[53]

Suzuki behaved as though he were a protected species. He enjoyed not only Obata's patronage but ultimately that of Araki and Masaki. For better or for worse, Tojo began earning a reputation for his "anti-Araki spirit."[54] In March 1933 Araki moved against Tojo, shifting him out of the Organization and Mobilization Section and instead merely attaching him to the General Staff. This left Tojo with very little to do other than wait for his next assignment. (In this same personnel reshuffle, Araki transferred Nagata out of Tokyo altogether). Tojo was, to be sure, simultaneously promoted to major general, but this was small consolation. Five months later, Araki transferred Tojo to the Army Ministry's Military Research Division, were he was charged with little other than collecting and collating newspaper articles related to army affairs. Tojo began to see himself following his father into enforced early retirement, and rued the irony whereby his own fate was being determined by the army's foremost anti-Choshu officer.

NAGATA NOW SPLIT FROM the Imperial way faction and led the internal opposition thereto. Tojo stood firmly behind Nagata, and Major General Umezu Yoshijiro became a key ally. Younger officers, including Muto Akira and Tominaga Kyoji, joined them. They made common cause around the need for long-term war planning and preparation, as well as military discipline. They did not necessarily see themselves as a faction or group, but their opponents in the Imperial way faction referred to them pejoratively as the *toseiha* (control faction).[55]

Nagata and Tojo began looking at Araki's personnel policies with a jaundiced eye. Yamaoka Shigeatsu had proved an utterly uninspired choice as director of the powerful Military Affairs Bureau, a clear case of the wrong man in the wrong place. Araki had forced several good officers, including Major General Nakamura Kotaro and Colonel Imamura Hitoshi, out of Tokyo. He had unfairly dismissed former Vice Minister Ninomiya Harushige. More recently, he had (as Nagata put it) "demoted" Tojo.[56] Even more pernicious was the favoritism Araki bestowed on officers from the former feudal domains of Saga and Tosa (which had in the meantime become Saga and Kochi Prefectures, respectively). Practically all of Araki's appointees hailed from these domains, or were at least connected closely with an officer from one of them. Nagata and Tojo—and, indeed, many others—now questioned whether Araki's tribalism was any better than the Choshu tribalism he had just displaced.[57]

Meanwhile, military operations in Manchukuo had recommenced. In January 1933 the Kwantung Army took Shanhai Pass, the strategic pass in the Great Wall on the Tianjin-Jinzhou Railway where the wall meets the ocean. This seemed to indicate a possible Japanese interest in areas south of the Great Wall, most immediately in Hebei Province. In late February the Kwantung Army moved instead against the Inner Mongolian province of Jehol; the entire province fell in less than one week. Now a Japanese advance westward into two other Inner Mongolian provinces, Chahar and Suiyuan, also seemed a possibility. The Kwantung Army chose instead to take the fight to Chinese forces south of the Great Wall, in adjoining Hebei Province.

Tojo's fall from grace meant that his contemporaries neither sought nor recorded his opinion on the capture of Jehol and the Shanhai Pass and the subsequent advance into Hebei Province. Did Tojo agree with the large number of Japanese Army officers who saw Jehol as an integral part of the new Manchurian state? Did he view the Jehol campaign as a logical continuation of the Manchurian Incident? Did he see Manchukuo's subsequent annexation of Jehol as appropriate and necessary? Did he agree with operations south of the Great Wall? Did he, for that matter, agree with the efforts of the Japanese Army's so-called Tianjin Special Service Agency, which sought to cobble together an alliance of warlords in Hebei and surrounding provinces in an effort to establish a regime in North China independent of the Chinese nationalist government in Nanjing?

Questions also surround Tojo's reception of the Tanggu Truce, the conclusion of which on May 31, 1933, ended the Jehol campaign. He trusted the acumen of his old friend Okamura Yasuji, who headed the Kwantung Army delegation at the truce negotiations: What did he make of the truce provisions? Now that the truce gave the Kwantung Army the right to garrison specified locations within the Great Wall and the main passes along it, did Tojo regard Manchukuo's boundaries as complete and secure? The truce also established a demilitarized zone in northeastern Hebei Province, giving the Japanese Army what historian Shimada Toshihiko has called a "firm foothold" there. Did Tojo recognize this as a desirable or even necessary first step into North China?[58] Or did he worry that this might divert attention away from the Inner Mongolian provinces of Chahar and Suiyuan? It is difficult to reach firm conclusions regarding these questions.

One can comment, with a far greater degree of certainty, on Tojo's understanding of the international reaction to the Manchurian Incident and the subsequent Jehol campaign. One of the more meaningful tasks Tojo undertook during his time with the Military Research Division was preparation of an army volume that formed part of a larger series titled *Hijoji kokumin zenshu* (Nation in crisis: Collected works).[59] Tojo gathered together a group of contributors, including Colonel Iimura Jo, Major General Sakurai Tadayoshi, Colonel Sakai Takashi, and Colonel Yokoyama Isamu. All focused on the presumed Soviet threat, and all were at least sympathetic to the control faction's insistence on due preparation for total war. Tojo's own contribution, titled "Shohai no bunkiten wa shisosen" (The battle of ideas: At the juncture of victory or defeat), opened with some observations about the changed nature of warfare. Wars of yesteryear—Tojo specifically cited the Russo-Japanese War—had been pure clashes of arms, but he insisted that "modern war" extended beyond the battlefield to include not only clashes of arms but also clashes of ideologies, politics, and economics. The nation best able to unify and control the traditional and nontraditional weapons at its disposal, he wrote, would emerge the "victor."[60]

Tojo was adamant that this was not merely a wartime endeavor. Indeed, he insisted that there was no longer a "clear distinction" between war and peace, and that before and after a clash of arms, nations would engage each other politically, ideologically, and economically. To clarify this last point, he wrote, "Declarations of war will not necessarily appear in future wars." Tojo noted that the Western powers had been waging an undeclared political and ideological war against Japan since the end of World War I and the results were discernible everywhere. He wrote of what he regarded as Japan's defeats at the Washington Naval Conference (1921–1922) and the London Naval Conferences (1930 and 1935) and the naval armament limitation treaties concluded there. This had, in turn, given rise to pressure for a reduction in military armaments and costs, which took the form of Ugaki's disarmament policies. And Tojo charged the Western powers with having caused a precipitous rise in anti-Japanese sentiment in China. "It must be said," he wrote, "that the Manchurian Incident was Japan's unavoidable line of defense vis-à-vis the encircling offensive directed against Japan by the Great Powers."[61]

Having portrayed the Manchurian Incident as a defensive action against the Western powers' ideological and political offensives, Tojo celebrated diplomat Matsuoka Yosuke's actions in leading the Japanese delegation's withdrawal from the League of Nations General Assembly on March 27, 1933. "It is truly a matter of national pride," he wrote, "that we were able to bring this ideological and political war to a conclusion through the final efforts of the plenipotentiary Matsuoka." With this stirring declaration of victory over the League of Nations, Tojo turned his attention to Japanese-Soviet relations. The Soviets, fighting an ideological war, sought nothing less than Japan's "Bolshevization." Tojo overlooked the substantial ideological gulf dividing the Soviet Union and the United States and insisted that the Soviets were connecting with the United States, as well as China, in an anti-Japanese coalition.[62]

Tojo concluded with some thoughts about what Japan ought to do in the face of a hostile international environment. He disparaged the two-party political system that had flourished in the 1920s insofar as it divided Japanese society into "factions," "schools," or "groups." He looked instead to the establishment of a "supreme national organ" that could unite and provide internal coherence to Japan's military, diplomacy, and politics. He also professed his belief in the creation of a "new Japan" and, naturally enough for an army officer who focused on the ever-present Soviet threat and the need to develop Manchukuo, he insisted this "new Japan" must work from the basis of a "continental policy" informed by a self-conscious attempt at guarding against "evil influences" from abroad.[63]

DURING TOJO'S TIME IN military limbo, the Araki-Masaki era entered its early demise. The initial sign came, somewhat counterintuitively, in the form of Masaki's promotion in June 1933 to full general. Prince Kan'in (who remained unexpectedly proactive) responded to the promotion by insisting that Masaki be removed from the General Staff. Masaki fought the move, but Prince Kan'in insisted on strict adherence to the precedent whereby the vice chief of staff remained a lieutenant general. Masaki became, against his wishes, a prestigious but mostly powerless military councilor. Prince Kan'in next named—and got—his preference for Masaki's successor: Lieutenant General Ueda Kenkichi, who was aligned with neither the Imperial way faction nor the control faction but with General Ugaki Kazushige.

Ueda's appointment coincided with a rapprochement between the Nagata-led control faction and the Ugaki faction. Nagata, Tojo, and their control faction colleagues suddenly proved willing to concede that their earlier assumptions about the Ugaki faction's Choshu leanings were overblown. They also continued to insist that Araki's purge of Ugaki faction officers had resulted in some very poor choices as their replacements. Ultimately, the key issue bringing the two factions together was a shared loathing for the Imperial way faction.

All the while, Araki was losing the support of the Imperial Army's young officers. They continued to revel in his Imperial way discourse but despaired at his inability to steer the army's agenda (or what might more properly be called the Imperial way faction's agenda) through the cabinet. Araki proved unable to convince his ministerial colleagues to agree to the Imperial way faction's pet rearmament programs. Nor did the Saito cabinet accept (among other things) any particular need to prepare for the worst in Japan's relationship with the Soviet Union. Araki was floundering at the cabinet level. Perhaps fortuitously, he came down in late 1933 with a severe flu; by January 1934 it provided him with the pretext he needed to resign his ministerial post.[64]

Araki hoped and believed that Masaki would succeed him. The army's junior officers agreed: Masaki was no less effusive than Araki in his treatment of the Imperial way, and there was hope in his ability to press the army's agenda on the cabinet. Yet the chief of staff, Prince Kan'in, once again showed an independent streak, insisting instead on Lieutenant General Hayashi Senjuro. Araki must now have wondered (had he not done so already) as to the wisdom of having appointed a prince to the army's "big three," for it was difficult to argue against an Imperial family member. Prince Kan'in got his way, and Hayashi was appointed minister. Masaki, by way of consolation, was appointed inspector general of military training.

Tojo had reason for cautious optimism. Hayashi was the third officer, alongside Araki and Masaki, in whom Tojo and his One Evening Society colleagues had, several years earlier, placed their hopes. Hayashi had, in the meantime, remained conspicuously aloof from Araki and Masaki's Imperial way discourse. For Tojo, an improvement in his own personal situation seemed at least possible. Tojo called on Hayashi on January 31, 1934, and urged him to "expel" a number of Imperial way faction officers, including the hopelessly ineffectual vice minister, Yanagawa Heisuke. Word of this approach reached Masaki, who now spoke of the need to place Tojo under "surveillance."[65]

An undaunted Tojo continued to offer Hayashi advice on personnel matters. In mid-February he suggested the need to recall both Nagata and Obata to the army's political and operational nerve center in Tokyo. He was, in effect, requesting the recall of two leading officers from either side of the army's Imperial way faction / control faction divide. This was a fascinating suggestion that owed to Tojo's belief that he might somehow mediate peace between two of his oldest friends. It also seems to indicate that, at least as far as Tojo was concerned, there remained some scope for the fusion of the two men's strategic outlooks. He probably reasoned that Japan had, first, to complete its preparations for total war, per Nagata's arguments, and then to enact the military operations being championed by Obata. Certainly such an approach would have fit with the most recent revisions to the Imperial National Defense Policy, which made clear the need to prepare for total war, as well as the desirability of a decisive battle fought soon after the outbreak of hostilities. Whatever the case, Tojo told Hayashi that Nagata and Obata's "era" was looming, and he insisted that, without them, the army could achieve nothing of substance.[66]

Hayashi revealed himself to be at least partly receptive to Tojo's suggestions. In April he appointed Nagata director of the all-important Military Affairs Bureau. He did not, however, return Obata to the army's strategic and political nerve center; he moved him instead to the vice superintendent position at the War College. Later that year, he swept out of Tokyo several Imperial way faction members, including Vice Minister Yanagawa; the provost marshal, Lieutenant General Hata Shinji; and the Army Affairs Section director, Colonel Yamashita Tomoyuki. Rumor had it that Hayashi would also shift Tojo out of his pointless role in the Military Research Division and appoint him head of the Army Ministry's Economic Mobilization Bureau. All but the most hardened Imperial way faction officers regarded Tojo as the right man for this position. Yet, at the last moment, Masaki prevailed on Hayashi to transfer Tojo instead to the Military Academy, where he was under Masaki's purview.[67]

Masaki now drew a target on Tojo. By May 1934 Masaki was complaining about Tojo "rebelling" against him. In July he began wondering whether Tojo should be issued a "stern warning," or even be "expelled." He spoke openly of "the Tojo problem." It is not clear what the problem was, but Imperial way faction officers were fretting about Hayashi having made common cause with Nagata, Tojo, and the control faction. These same young officers told Masaki that Nagata and Tojo had played a behind-the-scenes role in the "establishment of the current cabinet."[68] The charge was baseless but serious insofar as the young officers were vitriolic in their hatred for the recently installed cabinet of the prime minister (and retired admiral), Okada Keisuke.

The relationship between Masaki and Tojo gave way to mutual recrimination, personal hostility, and hatred. On July 31 Masaki summoned Tojo to his office and charged him with actions Masaki found "distressing." Tojo returned fire. Masaki's ire was, he said, "beyond comprehension," and he accused Masaki of "taking revenge" on him for no good reason. Masaki was indeed intent on revenge: He wanted Tojo moved out of Tokyo, and he prevailed on Hayashi to do just that. Masaki broke the news to Tojo on August 2, 1934, that he was being transferred to Kurume, in distant Kyushu, where he would command the inconsequential Twenty-Fourth Mixed Brigade. Before leaving Tokyo, Tojo joined a gathering of like-minded officers and "disparaged" Masaki for having engaged in factional infighting, squandering the army's institutional "power."[69] These were the words of a man who seemed convinced he would share his father's fate. Tojo now fully expected to serve out a few meaningless years in Kurume before being banished to the Imperial Army's reserve list.

Factional brawling at the Imperial Army's nerve center continued unabated, but Tojo, now in Kyushu, was considerably removed from it. That changed on August 12, 1935, when the Imperial way faction's Lieutenant Colonel Aizawa Saburo brandished his sword and hacked to death Tojo's great friend and mentor, Nagata Tetsuzan (who was posthumously promoted to lieutenant general). On receiving the news, Tojo returned immediately to Tokyo. This involved no small degree of personal risk, for rumor had it that Tojo was next on the Imperial way faction hit list. On his arrival in the capital, Tojo paid his respects to Nagata's bereaved family, who gave him the uniform Nagata had been wearing when he was murdered. Tojo returned to his hotel room in central Tokyo, dressed himself in Nagata's bloodstained uniform, and vowed revenge.[70]

TOJO'S BLOOD-SOAKED OATH OF vengeance provides eloquent testimony to his churning emotions in the dark days of mid-August 1935. He had lost his greatest friend and mentor, the control faction had lost its leader, and the army had lost its foremost intellectual, an officer almost certainly destined to rise to the "big three" level. This was internal army politics at its fiercest, and Tojo could not have been more centrally involved.

It is at least reasonably common among scholars to engage, however tentatively, in counterfactual reasoning and wonder whether Nagata might have steered Japan away from its calamitous involvement in World War II. But that was not to be. It remained for Tojo and his factional allies to realize Nagata's vision of national mobilization, which involved organizing peacetime Japan so that it could shift seamlessly in time of need to a war footing. In Nagata's own words, published after his death, such an effort required peacetime "control" of all human, material, and financial resources at Japan's disposal. It also required a population imbued with patriotic fervor and a steadfast martial spirit so it could cope with the deprivations demanded by modern war.[71]

As much as Tojo owed his fallen friend, he was no mere Nagata clone. He was less concerned by the possibility of international opprobrium than was Nagata. Tojo had, in 1934, already discerned Japan's encirclement by a hostile Sino-Soviet-US coalition and already mulled the possibility of a recourse to arms without bothering to issue a declaration of war. He continued to believe in the efficacy of a decisive battle fought as soon as possible after the outbreak of hostilities. Yet the notion that Tojo might rise atop not only the Japanese Army but the nation's decision-making processes was well beyond what even the most far-sighted observer might have ventured in the period immediately after Nagata's assassination.

4
RESURRECTION IN MANCHUKUO
1935–1938

IN THE EARLY AFTERMATH of Nagata Tetsuzan's murder, Tojo Hideki was appointed the Kwantung Army's provost marshal, which required a move to the Manchukuoan capital of Xinjing. It was a most welcome change of scenery. The transfer did more than remove him from the charged atmosphere inside Japan; it also placed him in what Kishi Nobusuke called "a truly unique modern state" and "the hope of East Asia," and what Hoshino Naoki called a "new paradise" where Han Chinese, Japanese, Koreans, Manchu, and Mongols worked together in ethnic harmony.[1] Kishi and Hoshino were technocrats with whom Tojo forged close working relationships in Xinjing; their shared vision of Manchukuo doubtless owed at least as much to aspiration as to reality. Even so, Manchukuo presented for many Japanese an exhilarating experiment in modernization, and it was *the* destination for many of Japan's best and brightest and also for vast quantities of Japanese capital. Xinjing was a showcase and a truly metropolitan modern capital built on the hitherto nondescript provincial town of Changchun. Carefully planned and zoned, Xinjing included paved roads, waterworks, sewage systems, handsome park spaces, and thousands of new buildings ranging from government offices and business offices to private dwellings. The most impressive building in this modern and attractive capital city was Tojo's new workplace, the Kwantung Army Headquarters.

Tojo's order to Xinjing came not from General Hayashi Senjuro, who took responsibility for Nagata's murder and resigned his ministerial post, but instead from his successor, Lieutenant General Kawashima Yoshiyuki. Tojo's remit as provost was wide. He was responsible not only for military law enforcement but also maintaining Manchukuo's internal security and public order, criminal investigations and penal law enforcement, and all espionage activities. He oversaw the political activities of the mass political organization known as the Concordia Association, which was designed to promote pan-Asian ideals, a Confucian system of government, and Manchukuoan nationalism, and he surveilled individuals, organizations, and thoughts deemed antithetical to Manchukuoan national identity. Tojo was given oversight of all state mechanisms that were supposed to enhance cooperation between and among Han Chinese, Japanese, Koreans, Manchu, and Mongols. He played a key role in overseeing and devising public policies, including labor laws and subsidy programs designed to facilitate farming and cropping practices that met the Kwantung Army's needs. And he was charged with keeping Manchukuo free from the influence of either Chiang Kai-shek's Kuomintang or the Chinese Communist Party.[2]

Many Japanese Army officers looked askance at the *kenpei* (gendarmerie, military police) and at the post Tojo now assumed atop the Kwantung *kenpei*. The provost marshal was not in any way responsible for the operational planning the Imperial Japanese Army continued to prioritize and lionize, and although Tojo outranked the lieutenant colonels and colonels who served as Kwantung Army staff officers, his position was in many ways less prestigious. Yet, as we have seen, Tojo was a different kind of army officer. He was intensely political and a military administrator par excellence. It was almost as though his entire career had molded him for the provost marshal role. This, coupled with his imposing personality, made Tojo a formidable operator. It was hardly surprising that, in the period after Tojo's arrival, the provost marshal position "suddenly became most powerful."[3]

When he came to Xinjing, Tojo stepped into a roiling dispute concerning police organization and jurisdiction. The Kwantung Army had long since sought unification under the provost marshal's leadership of police units not only in Manchukuo but also in the Kwantung Leased Territory. Whatever the merits of this approach, it smacked of a power grab, and the Police Affairs Bureau of Manchukuo's Ministry of Civil Affairs, the Foreign Ministry's Consular Police, and the Kwantung Police Bureau (based in Port Arthur) each fought to maintain its separate existence. The bureaucratic turf war had escalated in 1934 to the ministerial level in Tokyo. The Japanese Army had at one stage threatened to take matters into its own hands and impose what it regarded as the Kwantung Army's commonsense approach. The Kwantung Police Bureau was particularly active in its opposition, and in October 1934 some fifteen hundred civilian police in Port Arthur threatened to resign in protest if their force was subsumed by the Kwantung

Army's *kenpei*.[4] None of this was Tojo's doing, but he resolved the issue soon after his arrival in Xinjing. His solution was simple: Tojo remained provost marshal and served concurrently as head of the Kwantung Police Bureau. This represented a clear step toward the Kwantung Army's push for unification of the various police forces while maintaining at least a modicum of independence for the Kwantung Police Bureau. Opposition to the move remained, but it subsided quickly and civilian police work in and around Port Arthur continued under Tojo's leadership.[5]

TOJO AWOKE ON THE morning of February 26, 1936, to news of yet another coup attempt in Tokyo. The telegram he received that morning has been lost to history; precisely what he learned, and from whom he learned it, is not apparent. It might be assumed that the information he received was scant, if only because the situation in Tokyo was exceedingly fluid. He probably learned that two Tokyo-based army units with which he had a close personal association—the Third Imperial Guard Infantry Regiment and the First Infantry Regiment—had attempted a coup d'état. It must not have escaped him that the coup attempt had been launched even as Nagata's murderer stood before a military tribunal and sensationally insisted he had acted on no motive other than love of country.

It is impossible to say with certainty whether Tojo learned immediately of the coup leaders' assassination targets, including the former lord keeper of the Privy Seal, Makino Nobuaki; Prime Minister Okada Keisuke; the current lord keeper of the Privy Seal (and former prime minister), Saito Makoto; Genro (senior statesman) Saoinji Kimmochi; Grand Chamberlain Suzuki Kantaro; the finance minister (and former prime minister), Takahashi Korekiyo; and the inspector general of military training, Watanabe Jotaro. Nor is it clear if Tojo learned of the rebel troops' seizure and occupation of a one-square-mile area that included the Army Ministry; the General Staff offices; the Imperial Diet building; the Tokyo Metropolitan Police Headquarters; other government offices; several foreign embassies; and the official residences of the prime minister, army minister, and several other ministers.[6]

It seems unlikely that Tojo was informed of the coup leaders' precise goals and wishes on the morning of February 26. But, on the basis of earlier failed coup attempts, he knew full well that the coup leaders must be calling for direct Imperial rule, which in their estimation required the suspension of the Meiji Constitution, the imposition of martial law, and a military dictatorship. He was well aware, on the basis of experience, that the coup attempt was attributable to young officers. And he understood the likelihood of the coup leaders receiving at least the sympathy—and quite possibly the active support—of high-ranking *kodoha* (Imperial way faction) officers, including generals Araki Sadao and Masaki Jinzaburo (both of whom were military councilors) and Army Minister Kawashima. Even so, Tojo would probably have been surprised to learn that, on the morning of the attempted coup, Kawashima submitted the coup leaders' manifesto to the emperor and advised the emperor of the need for a new "strong" cabinet that met the young officers' demands.[7]

Tojo presented a striking contrast to Kawashima and indeed many others in Tokyo. He refused either to flirt with the coup leaders or to sit on the proverbial fence. So, too, did the Kwantung Army's commander in chief, Minami Jiro. Even so, taking a strong stand in opposition to the coup, as Tojo did, required no small degree of personal courage, for there was no guarantee that the coup would be suppressed, and the coup leaders dealt summarily with their opponents. Major Katakura Tadashi, who had long since followed Nagata and Tojo in the control faction, tried on February 26 to speak with the coup leaders; he was shot in the head as he tried to enter the rebels' de facto headquarters in the army minister's residence.

In Xinjing, Tojo immediately put the Kwantung *kenpei* on high alert. He ordered every unit under his command—not just in Xinjing but also in Chengde, Harbin, Mukden, Qiqihaer, and Yanji—to monitor all incoming mail and packages. He ordered close surveillance of all active duty army officers, as well as civilians with known right-wing sympathies. As a result, the Kwantung *kenpei* uncovered a plot to launch a similar coup attempt in Manchukuo. Tojo ordered suppression of the coup and, within days, forty Kwantung Army officers and 1,082 civilians—including technocrat Haraguchi Sumichika and Great Unity Academy instructor Ito Makoto—were arrested.[8] By his actions, Tojo ensured that Manchuria remained a place of order and calm.

In Tokyo the attempted coup of February 26, 1936, was suppressed. The key figure was the Showa Emperor, who repeatedly and angrily denounced the coup as a criminal mutiny. At the Imperial Army's political and operational nerve center in Tokyo, the vice chief of staff, Lieutenant General Sugiyama Hajime, was among the coup's most important opponents. By February 29 the rebel leaders had either committed suicide or surrendered, and the troops returned to their barracks. Some months later, a military tribunal sentenced thirteen young officers and four civilians to death; they were executed in July. A handful of officers were sentenced to life imprisonment; one or two other minor participants received lesser sentences. In what was for Tojo an intensely satisfying outcome, a new military tribunal was established for Nagata's murderer, who was sentenced to death in May and executed on July 3, 1936.

The Okada cabinet had in the meantime taken responsibility for the rebellion and resigned. Career diplomat Hirota Koki led the next cabinet, and the Japanese Army named General Terauchi Hisaichi as its cabinet-level representative. Terauchi forced the Imperial way faction's highest-ranking officers—including Araki, Kawashima, Obata Toshiro, and Yanagawa Heisuke—into early retirement. He placed Masaki under effective house arrest, and targeted officers from the pro-Choshu faction of Ugaki Kazushige, including generals Koiso Kuniaki, Minami Jiro, and Tatekawa Yoshitsugu. Hayashi, who was more closely associated with the control faction than any of his contemporaries, was removed from active service. Various other full-ranking generals, including Abe Nobuyuki and Hishikari Takashi, who had only ever played peripheral roles in the military's factionalism, were also placed on the army's reserve list.[9]

Tojo presumably felt little remorse at the purge of most Imperial way faction officers. He almost certainly shed no tears when he learned of Masaki's fate. He probably accepted the other generals' enforced retirements as a distasteful but almost inevitable outcome of the February 26 Incident. He doubtless only wished that an officer other than Terauchi had been chosen for the task, for Terauchi's father was the very man who had ended Tojo's father's career. Did Tojo worry lest the army was turning back to its old reliance on Choshu officers and their proxies in the aftermath of the February 26 Incident? It is impossible to say with certainty, but old jealousies and hatreds died hard with Tojo.

The February 26 Incident exercised a twofold impact on Tojo's career. First, he earned recognition as one of the relatively few general-rank officers who stood, from the outset, steadfastly opposed to the coup. It would be a mistake to draw a direct line from the February 26 Incident to Tojo's ministerial appointment several years later. But it would equally be a mistake to ignore the February 26 Incident. It was no coincidence that two of the coup's opponents, Sugiyama and Tojo, would later serve in the Japanese Army's "big three." A second impact is also discernible: Tojo emerged from the February 26 Incident with a newfound appreciation—even admiration—for the *kenpei*. Officers under his command had provided a constant stream of information and intelligence that had proved integral to his efforts throughout the incident. His subsequent reliance on the *kenpei* became so great that, following the outbreak of war against Britain and the United States, he became a practitioner par excellence of so-called *kenpei* politics, relying on surveillance and intimidation to quash dissenting voices and opinions.[10]

In the immediate aftermath of the incident, Tojo demanded a massive supplementary budget, and argued "heatedly" with anyone who disagreed with him regarding the expansion of police powers in Manchukuo. When the Kwantung Bureau of General Affairs secretary, Ono Rokuichiro, indicated a disinclination to grant this wish, Tojo stormed out of Ono's office and threatened to resign. There was no need to make good on the threat, for as Tojo knew full well, the Kwantung Army was the real power broker in Xinjing. Ono soon relented, and Tojo got his increased budget and powers.[11]

TOJO'S REMIT WAS WIDE. He even moved beyond his formal responsibilities and took a sustained interest in the ongoing effort to industrialize Manchukuo's economy. He became a key member of the so-called *ni-ki san-suke* (two -ki and three -suke) group, which drew its membership from the institutions most centrally involved in Manchukuo's economic development. Tojo represented the Kwantung Army, while the Manchukuo Department of General Affairs director general, Hoshino Naoki, and his deputy, Kishi Nobusuke, represented the Manchukuoan bureaucratic apparatus. Nissan conglomerate founder Ayukawa Yoshisuke and South Manchuria Railway (SMR) president Matsuoka Yosuke represented the two most plentiful sources of capital investment, as well as the engine for Manchukuo's heavy industrialization.[12] Here Tojo revealed himself as willing to accept the advice of the economic and financial experts and overturned his initial opposition to Ayukawa's insistence on abandoning existing industrial development models and relaxing state controls in Manchukuo.[13]

That decision had far-reaching ramifications. It heralded a new approach in which the Kwantung Army ended its three-decades-long reliance on the SMR for capital ventures and industrial development and instead actively sought foreign capital, materials, and technology via Ayukawa's Nissan conglomerate. Matsuoka fought a desperate rearguard action in defense of the SMR, but to no avail; Tojo discarded him like a spent shot. In November 1937 the Kwantung Army compelled the SMR to turn over most of its nonrailroad administrative rights to the state of Manchukuo, and in subsequent months, the SMR's nonrailroad enterprises were transferred to Nissan.[14]

DURING TOJO'S TIME IN MANCHUKUO, the cabinet of Prime Minister Hirota Koki joined with Nazi Germany and concluded the Anti-Comintern Pact. Tojo can be assumed to have welcomed the pact, primarily because it presented the Soviets with a giant diplomatic pincer movement, with Germany confronting it from the west and Japan doing so from the east. One is given to wondering whether Tojo foresaw the pact widening its scope so that Germany and Japan squared off also against Britain; here it might be noted that the Imperial National Defense Policy was revised in 1937 so that Britain was included alongside China, the Soviet Union, and the United States as a hypothetical enemy. Such issues were not, however, part of Tojo's remit in Xinjing, where his civilian contemporaries were taking note of his abilities. Ono's successor as general affairs secretary, Takebe Rokuzo, felt that Tojo's "breadth of vision" was perhaps narrow but he admired his courage and was certain that Tojo would, in the future, "carry the army." Takebe emerged from one meeting with Tojo and Lieutenant General Itagaki Seishiro convinced that these two men would soon assume "supreme leadership of the army."[15]

Tojo was promoted to lieutenant general in December 1936. The promotion was, he told his wife, Katsuko, "completely unexpected." He recalled that his father had been promoted to lieutenant general only on the day of his enforced retirement, and he freely admitted he was "not nearly as smart" as his father.[16] Then, on February 25, 1937—the eve of the first anniversary of the February 26 Incident—Tojo learned that he would presently replace Itagaki as Kwantung Army chief of staff. The appointment, which became official on March 1, 1937, confirmed that Tojo's career trajectory had taken a most positive turn.[17]

Tojo had not long settled into his new post when a rising star in Japanese politics, the aristocratic Konoe Fumimaro, was appointed prime minister. Konoe's cabinet was inaugurated on June 4, 1937. The Kwantung Army took the opportunity to dispatch its new chief of staff to Tokyo to explain to Konoe its views on policy toward China. In typically forthright fashion, Tojo insisted that any "adjustment in diplomatic relations" with what he dismissively called the "Nanjing regime" was "impossible." "If we allow ourselves a resort to armed force," he said, "I must say that the most

Kwantung Army officer complement, undated, but almost certainly sometime between March 1937 and May 1938, at Kwantung Army headquarters in Xinjing, Manchukuo. Tojo is seated in the front row, fifth from right. Seated directly to Tojo's right is the Kwantung Army commander, Ueda Kenkichi; to Ueda's right is Itagaki Seishiro.

advantageous measure is to eliminate the threat to our rear by dealing them such a blow that they will be unable to stand again."[18] Three points seem especially noteworthy: Tojo's prioritization of the Soviet threat and the insistence that China menaced the Kwantung Army's rear guard from behind; his disavowal of diplomacy vis-à-vis the Kuomintang (Chinese nationalist) government in Nanjing; and his belief in the need to eliminate the Chinese threat before defeating the Soviet enemy.

Tojo was still in Tokyo when his ordering of continental priorities was challenged by an incident on a section of the Manchukuo-Soviet border marked by the Amur River. The border was vague, and clashes were far from uncommon; literally hundreds of incidents had occurred through the early to mid-1930s. The Amur River boundary was characterized by a peculiar ambiguity, for although Sino-Russian treaties had in the 1800s set the median line of the river's principal channel as the boundary, subsequent shifts in the river channel had ramifications for the median line. This, in turn, called into question the sovereignty of hundreds of islands dotting the river, and this was indeed the case for Chinamho and Kanchatzu

Islands. This ambiguity set the scene for the Kanchatzu Island Incident, which military historian Alvin Coox has called the "worst border crisis" of the year 1937.[19]

Tojo remained in Tokyo when a detachment of some twenty Soviet soldiers landed on June 19 on Kanchatzu Island. The Soviet soldiers ordered off the island its sole inhabitant—a Manchukuoan lighthouse keeper—as well as a motley crew of Manchukuoans panning for gold. That night, another forty Soviet soldiers chased a few dozen Manchukuoans off nearby Chinamho Island. The next day, a small group of Manchukuoan police and soldiers met with gunfire when they tried to come ashore at Kanchatzu Island to investigate.[20]

Tojo returned to the continent on June 21. He was briefed on the situation, and he concluded that the Soviets would back down if the Kwantung Army confronted them with superior force. He believed that the threat of hostilities alone should convince the Soviets to reconsider their recent actions. There was a possibility that the Soviets would respond militarily and hostilities would ensue. In that instance, Tojo believed, the Kwantung Army had to hurl a preponderance of power at the Soviets, score a quick and decisive victory, and then negotiate a return to the status quo. Securing the agreement of the Kwantung Army commander, General Ueda Kenkichi, posed no real difficulty: Ueda was nicknamed the Virgin General in reference not only to his unmarried status but also the distance he kept from the army's factionalism and politics. He reported to the central military authorities in Tokyo regarding the need to hurl a preponderance of force at the Soviets on Chinamho and Kanchatzu islands. The army vice chief of staff, Lieutenant General Imai Kiyoshi, responded on June 24, 1937, "The future impact of Soviet forces' illegal seizure of . . . Manchukuoan territory is likely to be serious. You are therefore instructed to maintain the old order by appropriate measures." Tojo needed no further prompting. He dispatched to the Amur River's south bank the Forty-Ninth Infantry Regiment (First Division), the Fourth Air Company (Eleventh Air Regiment), and the Third Light Bomber Company (Tenth Air Regiment).[21] Tojo concentrated overwhelming force against the few dozen Soviet troops on Chinamho and Kanchatzu Islands.

The Soviets responded by concentrating military strength on the Amur River's north bank. The Kwantung Army and the Red Army were on a collision course before cooler heads prevailed. The central military authorities in Tokyo began questioning the wisdom of so much as the prospect of a Japanese-Soviet war, particularly given that "military preparedness vis-à-vis the Soviets" remained "incomplete."[22] The vice minister, Lieutenant General Umezu Yoshijiro, cabled Tojo on June 26 and advised that confidence in the efficacy of a military solution had evaporated. Consensus in Tokyo had instead gelled around the need for the foreign ministry to take immediate diplomatic steps to bring an end to the "illegal" Soviet occupation of Chinamho and Kanchatzu Islands.[23]

Tojo was unimpressed with this sudden about-face. In his response to Umezu, which he addressed also to Vice Chief of Staff Imai, Tojo maintained that an "amicable settlement" via diplomacy was "impossible." The fundamental issue, he insisted, was the Soviet "attitude." The Soviets seemed unwilling to accept the illegality of their actions, and Tojo was convinced that only military action seemed likely to cause any "reflection" on their part. But that was not all. Japan could not, he wrote, enter diplomatic negotiations on Manchukuo's behalf and still maintain that Manchukuo remained an "independent" nation. Japan's "diplomatic participation" was therefore, in Tojo's estimation, disadvantageous and potentially disastrous. Military action would, in contrast, fall within existing Japanese-Manchukuoan agreements concerning "joint defense" and would not undermine Manchukuoan sovereignty.[24] His logic was unimpeachable.

Diplomacy in Moscow undermined Tojo's arguments. Deputy Foreign Minister Boris Stomonyakov told Japanese Ambassador Shigemitsu Mamoru on June 29 that his government was ready to withdraw troops if Japan would do likewise.[25] This was music to the ears of the central military authorities in Tokyo. Umezu cabled Tojo on June 29; he chose not to address any issues Tojo had raised and simply affirmed the Japanese government's decision to pursue "diplomatic negotiations" with the Soviets.[26]

The border incident might have ended there. But Tojo ignored his government's pivot to diplomacy, and events in the vicinity of Chinamho and Kanchatzu Islands outpaced the efforts of decision-makers in Tokyo and Moscow. On June 30, 1937, three Soviet gunboats steamed into the southern channel between the disputed islands and the Manchukuoan shore, opening fire on Japanese forces on the Amur River's south bank. The Forty-Ninth Infantry Regiment responded in kind, sinking one ship and heavily damaging another.[27]

Mutual recriminations ensued. Japanese diplomats protested the "incomprehensible" actions of the Soviets, and Soviet diplomats protested the damage to their gunboats.[28] Meanwhile, Tojo and his professional military colleagues in Xinjing refused to accept that they had done wrong. In an unrepentant cable to Tokyo, they argued that the incident was attributable in the first instance to the "illegal" Soviet occupation of the islands. They added that the Soviets compounded the issue by concentrating forces in the islands' vicinity. They insisted that diplomatic negotiations concerning the withdrawal of Japanese and Manchukuoan forces from the area impinged on the hallowed "right of supreme command." And they questioned the diplomatic wisdom of withdrawing forces from the south bank of the Amur River, for doing so would merely indicate "acceptance" of Soviet actions, effectively admitting that Chinamho and Kanchatzu Islands were Soviet territory.[29]

The Soviets opted to resolve the incident diplomatically. On July 2 Soviet Foreign Minister Maxim Litvinov reprised his deputy's earlier proposal, according to which Soviet forces would withdraw from the islands and their vicinity, on the understanding that Japanese forces would also withdraw from the south bank of the Amur River.[30] The Japanese government breathed a sigh of relief, but Tojo and his fellow officers in Xinjing seethed with discontent. They reminded Tokyo that the Soviets had illegally occupied Manchukuoan territory and had then concentrated forces on the Amur River's north bank. Soviet gunboats had entered identifiably Manchukuoan waters and opened fire on Japanese troops on the south bank. Against this backdrop, Tojo and his colleagues deplored the "unequal" Soviet proposal for a "mutual withdrawal" from the immediate vicinity of Chinamho and Kanchatzu Islands. Agreement to such a proposal, they argued, would mean that the Soviets were making decisions that were properly the prerogative of the Supreme Command in Tokyo. They worried about the dangerous precedent this would set and were concerned that Tokyo's insistence on de-escalating the situation would merely encourage the Soviets to attempt ever more serious border incidents. Tojo and his colleagues counseled that Japan must, "to the bitter end," avoid a "humiliating" or "defeatist" posture. Concretely, they insisted that Japan demand unilateral Soviet withdrawal from the islands and the vicinity. This was, in their estimation, nonnegotiable and should therefore take the form of an ultimatum. Japan should, in the event the Soviets balked, be prepared to "terminate negotiations."[31]

The Japanese Foreign Ministry chose not to follow this unsolicited advice, and in Moscow, Litvinov and Shigemitsu persisted with the Soviet proposal. Not to be ignored, Tojo and his colleagues in Xinjing released a statement on July 3 that sought to reaffirm the basic Kwantung Army position. It opened with what Tojo regarded as a statement of simple fact—namely, that the Soviet "invasion" of Chinamho and Kanchatzu Islands was illegal and the fundamental cause of the ensuing conflict. The Soviets had "recognized" their "misdeed" and, as a result, had "pledged to . . . withdraw troops from both islands and their vicinity." The Kwantung Army, the statement pronounced, hoped that the Soviets would carry out their commitments "faithfully," and stood ready to take "resolute action" in common cause with the fledgling Manchukuoan Army if ever again the Soviets "violated Manchukuoan territory."[32]

The Soviets declined to respond to this provocative statement. They had evidently decided they wanted a peaceful resolution to the border conflict, and the Litvinov-Shigemitsu channel doubtless seemed more likely to yield the desired results than did any public spat with the Kwantung Army. By the evening of July 4, Soviet troops had left Chinamho and Kanchatzu Islands, and by the following morning, all Soviet gunboats had withdrawn from the surrounding waters.[33] Tojo subsequently called back Kwantung Army forces. Thus ended a "large-scale" border incident that the Army General Staff in Tokyo recognized had the potential to "develop into an all-out Japanese-Soviet conflict."[34]

In the immediate aftermath of the Kanchatzu Island Incident Tojo remained defiant. "I've always been of the opinion that any incident should be resolved locally, if at all possible," he told his wife, Katsuko. He seemed neither to notice nor care that Shigemitsu's diplomacy in Moscow had contributed to the incident's resolution. Tojo conceded that he had ignored and "disobeyed" orders from Tokyo and intensified the incident rather than contained it, and he admitted he was therefore guilty of *gekokujo* (insubordination). He allowed, in yet another nod to the memory of his father's enforced early retirement, that he now seemed likely to be "stood down" from active duty. Yet he expressed no regrets. "I've always wanted to make a meaningful exit from the military," he told Katsuko, and recounted his belief that the Soviets, as a result of his act of *gekokujo,* were likely to think twice before sparking another incident along the Amur River border.[35]

Contrary to Tojo's expectations, the central military authorities in Tokyo took no disciplinary action against him. The incident nonetheless left a lasting impression on him. For one thing, it confirmed his belief in bringing superior force to bear from the outset. This seemed the best way to keep things quick and decisive. As he put it to Katsuko, committing troops "little by little" out of a misplaced sense of caution merely encouraged the enemy to do likewise. Under these circumstances, things could—and, in Tojo's estimation, generally did—"get out of hand." It was far better, he said, to "make a big move" and "show one's resolve" from the outset. This, he believed, served to "blunt" the enemy's "will to fight" and paved the way for what he called "good results." He regarded the Kanchatzu Island Incident as a "good example" of precisely this dynamic.[36]

MOST IMMEDIATELY, THE KANCHATZU Island Incident convinced Tojo of the Soviets' fundamental unwillingness to challenge the Japanese position on the continent. The ramifications were enormous, and they became apparent on July 7, 1937, when Japan's Tianjin Garrison Army clashed with Chinese forces near Marco Polo Bridge on the outskirts of Peking. Satisfied that the Japanese Army need not concern itself with the threat of a two-front war against China and the Soviet Union, and equally convinced that Chinese leader Chiang Kai-shek would come on his knees to the negotiating table if only Japan applied a preponderance of force, Tojo posited himself as a proponent of quick and decisive military action and expansion of the Japanese Empire into North China and Inner Mongolia.

It is perhaps necessary to consider the extent of Japanese influence beyond Manchukuo. First, recall Tojo's earlier involvement in the Shandong expeditions of the 1920s; Japanese interests in that province remained extensive. Manchukuo's annexation of Jehol Province meant that one Inner Mongolian province had already been detached from China's nationalist government in Nanjing; it meant also that Manchukuo shared borders with both Hebei Province in North China and the Inner Mongolian province of Chahar. The Tanggu Truce had provided for a demilitarized zone in Hebei, creating inroads for the Japanese. Sino-Japanese agreements had, in the meantime, brought both Chahar and Hebei Provinces nearer to Japanese control. The He-Umezu Agreement of June 10, 1935, had removed Hebei from the Kuomintang's political and military control; the Qin-Doihara Agreement of June 27, 1935, had resulted in the demilitarization of northern and central Chahar Province, so that only southern Chahar, inside the Great Wall, remained under the control of Chinese warlord Song Zheyuan.

Governing councils in both Chahar and Hebei declared autonomy from Nanjing. Then, in December 1935, a Kwantung Army–backed Mongolian force took six Chahar districts—including Zhangbei—immediately north of the Great Wall. The Mongols accepted advisers from Manchukuo and introduced the Manchukuoan yuan as their official unit of currency. By June 1936 an Inner Mongolian government was established and concluded a mutual assistance treaty with Manchukuo. In December 1936 the Inner

The photo is undated, but Tojo here is likely patrolling Manchukuo as the Kwantung Army's chief of staff, sometime between March 1937 and May 1938.

Mongolian Army launched an invasion of neighboring Suiyuan Province. This was actually a covert Kwantung Army operation, which was ill conceived and stunningly unsuccessful. It nonetheless indicated that Kwantung Army ambitions stretched beyond Chahar to Suiyuan Province.[37]

Against this backdrop the Kwantung Army leadership—Tojo included—met on July 8, 1937, and discussed the Marco Polo Bridge Incident. Agreement was readily forthcoming on four key issues. First, the incident provided a perfect opportunity to settle the North China issue. Second, the Soviet Union seemed highly unlikely to intervene. Third, Japan needed to strike militarily not just in Hebei Province but also farther west, in Chahar Province. And, fourth, the Kwantung Army must overcome any reluctance on the part of the central military authorities in Tokyo and ensure that full use was made of this opportunity. The Kwantung Army leadership cabled the General Staff in Tokyo for permission to send the First and Eleventh Mixed Brigades and an aviation unit to reinforce the Tianjin Garrison Army. Meanwhile, Tojo dispatched a staff officer, Captain Tsuji Masanobu, to incite what he regarded as the inexplicably passive and "indecisive" Tianjin Garrison Army. Tojo cabled the Tianjin Garrison Army chief of staff, Major General Hashimoto Gun, on July 10 and informed him that an infantry unit from the Eleventh Mixed Brigade had moved to the Great Wall's eastern terminus at Shanhai Pass and now awaited deployment in Hebei Province. The order to dispatch those forces across the Manchukuoan border into North China arrived on July 11.[38]

In Tokyo, the cabinet of Prime Minister Konoe Fumimaro adopted a policy of nonescalation in what it labeled the North China Incident (in reference to the continued escalation in the fighting, it adopted the term "China Incident" from early September).[39] Tojo and his Kwantung Army colleagues lambasted what they regarded as the cabinet's "weak attitude"; they wanted a "truly momentous decision."[40] General Ueda cabled Tokyo on July 13 and relayed the Kwantung Army's stance. He acknowledged that a localized, temporary solution to the fighting in Hebei Province might prove possible, but he saw no real benefit therein. Indeed, such a solution could only "hinder" Manchukuo's political and economic development, as well as Japan's preparations for war against the Soviet Union. Far better, he wrote, would be to recognize that the incident's fundamental cause was the Chinese government's "anti-Manchukuo, anti-Japanese" policies, and to respond with an "unflinching attitude" and a determination to "wipe out the root cause of this evil." He called for the removal, once and for all, of any Kuomintang presence—military or political—in North China.[41]

The Konoe cabinet was unmoved by such counsel and continued to regard a local truce as the best possible outcome. The central military authorities agreed with this approach. Indeed, the Military Affairs Bureau director, Major General Ushiroku Jun (who, like Tojo, was a member of the Military Academy's seventeenth class), met on July 23 with the Naval Affairs Bureau director, Vice Admiral Toyoda Soemu, and the director of the Foreign Ministry's Greater East Asia Bureau, Ishii Itaro, and affirmed the need to "persist" in "nonexpansion" of the incident. All were agreed also on the necessity of continuing the search for a "localized solution."[42]

Tojo and his Kwantung Army colleagues continued to argue otherwise. In a policy paper dated July 24, 1937, they insisted that Japan had been given a "heaven-sent opportunity" to pursue a "proactive strategy" and reach a "fundamental solution" to the "North China issue." The solution, so far as the Kwantung Army was concerned, practically wrote itself: Use the North China Incident to deliver a "decisive blow" against Chinese forces in

Kwantung Army officers greet the army chief of staff, Prince Kan'in Kotohito (*seated, center*). The photo is undated, but it is almost certainly taken sometime between March 1937 and May 1938. Tojo is in the front row, second to the right of the seated prince.

Hebei and Shandong Provinces, and create in those provinces a "climate" conducive to the "establishment of an independent regime." With targeted Japanese and Manchukuoan assistance, including the provision of advisers and funding, it seemed reasonable to the Kwantung Army to expect the emergence within six months of a government in Hebei and Shandong Provinces that would separate itself from the Kuomintang in Nanjing. In a sign that this would not satiate their collective appetite, the Kwantung Army officers wrote of their expectation that this new government would, over time, rule also over Shanxi Province. To the west, Tojo and his colleagues were equally insistent on the need to pursue, in "conjunction with this North China policy," what they called "political machinations" in the Inner Mongolian provinces of Chahar and Suiyuan.[43]

Tojo and his professional military colleagues in Xinjing failed to see why Japan should not take the opportunity that now presented itself in North China and Inner Mongolia. In their collective opinion, the Japanese Army possessed more than enough strength to overwhelm its Chinese opponents. European powers, Britain, and the United States were unable to intervene militarily. The Soviets had the capacity to intervene yet had proved in the recent Kanchatzu Island Incident their unwillingness to "take the offensive" against the Japanese Army.[44]

Even allowing for the likelihood of nonintervention by the Western powers, the Kwantung Army leaders recognized the considerable scale of military operations they were prescribing. Tojo and his colleagues acknowledged that it would be necessary to place Japan on a war footing, to undertake all preparations for national mobilization, and to prepare the people "spiritually" for the demands—and possibly the deprivations—of modern total war. These not inconsiderable requirements demanded some explication of the extent of Japan's interests in North China and Inner Mongolia. This Tojo and his uniformed colleagues were only too willing to provide. They insisted that resolute disposal of the North China Incident would provide the basis for the implementation of all Japanese foreign policy. They seemed not to consider that, outside the army, such a continent-centric foreign policy vision might seem anything but axiomatic. Most particularly, the North China Incident provided the opportunity to "strengthen Manchukuo's foundations," to move toward a Japan–Manchukuo–North China economic bloc and to "establish a basis for a fundamental resolution of the Soviet issue in the future."[45]

Tojo was not content merely to send this document to the central military authorities. He wanted to reinforce the message and, on July 27, dispatched his deputy, Major General Imamura Hitoshi, as well as a staff officer, Colonel Tominaga Kyoji, to Tokyo. He expressly instructed Tominaga to "whip up" the central military authorities and to arouse them from what he regarded as their stupor.[46]

The Kwantung Army had in the meantime received from the Tianjin Garrison Army a request for reinforcements. By way of an interim response, on July 27 Tojo dispatched the so-called Tsutsumi detachment (named after the company commander, Lieutenant Tsutsumi Yutaka) and a mixed brigade to the western Jehol rail point of Chengde. From there deployment to the Sino-Japanese fighting in Hebei Province was but a short rail trip; so, too, was the regional city of Tolun in the Inner Mongolian province of Chahar. There was little mistaking Tojo's priorities: he placed the forces in Chengde on standby for a "rapid advance" into Tolun. There is even a fascinating suggestion, in a Kwantung Army report, that some forces actually began assembling in Tolun. This was an act of *gekokujo,* for the dispatch of troops across national boundaries required the emperor's approval. The General Staff scrambled and received the emperor's approval for the Tsutsumi detachment's deployment to Tolun. It nonetheless relayed its displeasure and took the opportunity to remind the Kwantung Army leadership of the national policy of nonescalation. It insisted that troops in Tolun must engage in nothing other than defense of Manchukuo's westernmost border; it explicitly forbade any further advances into Chahar Province.[47] Tojo was oblivious to the General Staff's importuning. He and his professional military colleagues in Xinjing continued to believe in the efficacy of major-scale military operations in North China, as well as in Inner Mongolia. They conceded that such operations were "not without two or three faults," but they were satisfied that these faults would pale in insignificance once Japanese forces scored a series of "repeated victories" on the battlefield.[48]

Tojo cabled Tokyo on July 30 and argued for the expansion of operations as far west as Pingxingguan in Suiyuan Province and Datong in Shanxi Province (both located on the Peking-Suiyuan Railway). He was firmly rebuffed, as the General Staff reaffirmed its commitment to the search for a prompt end to the fighting in Hebei Province. The Kwantung Army leadership shrugged its institutional shoulders and ordered the Tsutsumi detachment to leave Chengde and join the fighting in and around Tianjin. This involved crossing the Manchukuoan border into North China's Hebei Province, but the Kwantung Army sought approval only after the troops had boarded the train. For the second time in three days, the General Staff scrambled to secure Imperial sanction. It thereby "legitimized" the Kwantung Army's action, even as the Tsutsumi detachment made its way by rail into Hebei Province, where it participated in the Sino-Japanese fighting until August 2, 1937.[49]

On August 2 the Tsutsumi detachment returned briefly to Manchukuo, received reinforcements, and on August 5 rerouted to Tolun. That same day, the ever persistent Tojo requested permission for the Tsutsumi detachment to advance, via the Zhangjiakou-Tolun Railway, from Tolun to Zhangbei. He learned via back channels that his request had divided the General Staff in Tokyo. The Operations Section chief, Colonel Muto Akira, "recognized the necessity" of the move and supported Tojo. The chief of staff, Prince

Tojo's battles: the Kanchatzu Island Incident and the Inner Mongolian Campaign, 1937

Kan'in Kotohito, took advice instead from Muto's direct superior, Major General Ishiwara Kanji, the Operations Bureau chief, who argued that the proposed Zhangbei advance was but the first move in a wider Kwantung Army plan to conquer Inner Mongolia. On Ishiwara's advice, Prince Kan'in "completely disagreed" with the move.[50] Prince Kan'in's opposition to the Zhangbei advance evaporated over the ensuing days because China's Central Army began moving into Chahar and Suiyuan Provinces, where it posed a clear threat to the Tianjin Garrison Army's right flank.[51]

The General Staff informed Tojo on August 7 of a change of heart, approving the Tsutsumi detachment's Zhangbei advance. That same day the Kwantung Army and the Tianjin Garrison Army received from the vice chief of staff, Lieutenant General Imai Kiyoshi, a forewarning of a major change in the General Staff's overall attitude. The General Staff, Imai wrote, now recognized the need to clear Chahar Province of Chinese forces. He added that it should prove "strategically advantageous" to "occupy" Kalgan, situated just inside the Great Wall in southern Chahar. This latter objective, according to Imai, could profitably be assigned to Lieutenant General Itagaki Seishiro's Fifth Division, recently sent from Hiroshima to reinforce the Tianjin Garrison Army.[52]

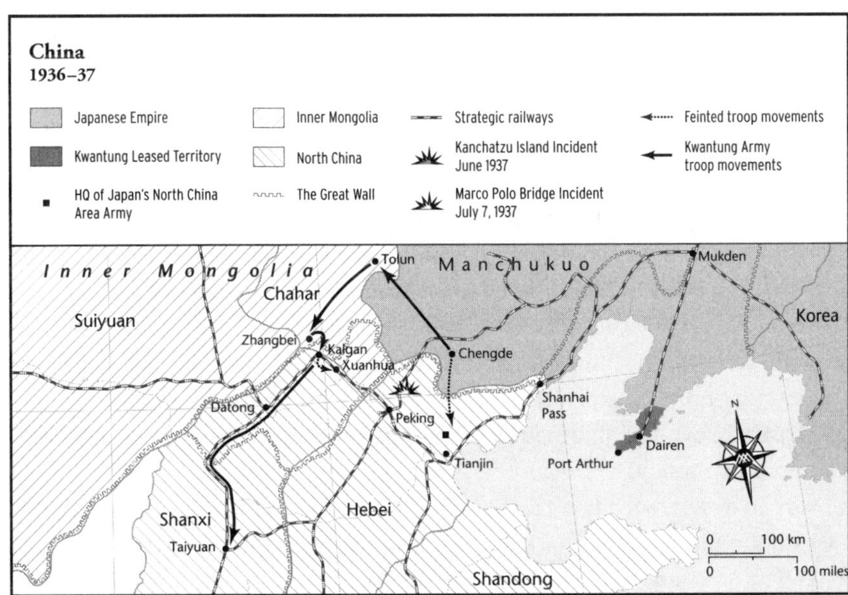

Tojo's battles: the Kanchatzu Island Incident and the Inner Mongolian Campaign, 1937 (*detail*).

Three points in particular made an impression on Tojo and his military colleagues in Xinjing. First, the General Staff may have accepted the need for military action in Chahar Province but had by no means shifted over to the Kwantung Army's hawkish opportunism. It instead remained overtly focused on securing the flank of the Tianjin Garrison Army, which was bearing the brunt of the fighting in the Peking-Tianjin area in Hebei Province. Second, the General Staff seemed to be dividing duties in Chahar Province so that the districts south of the Great Wall were the Tianjin Garrison Army's responsibility and the districts north of the wall were the Kwantung Army's responsibility. Third, this division of duties seemed designed specifically to contain the Kwantung Army and to impede any moves farther west, particularly into Shanxi Province, the northeastern districts of which were virtually indistinguishable from southern Chahar.

Tojo readied for battle on two fronts. There was the forthcoming battle against Chinese forces in Chahar Province, and there was a battle between and among the Kwantung Army, the Tianjin Garrison Army, and the central military authorities over primacy in and the direction of the Chahar campaign. This second battle would go a long way toward determining the objectives for which Japan fought. Would Japanese forces in Chahar seek merely to protect the Tianjin Garrison Army's flank? Would Chahar Province be artificially divided into north and south, for seemingly no good reason other than the Japanese Army's internal politics? Or would the Japanese Army seize the opportunity and seek to peel Inner Mongolia and North China away from Kuomintang control?

The Tianjin Garrison Army chief of staff, Major General Hashimoto Gun, cabled the General Staff on August 8 and indicated agreement with Imai's basic points. He added one minor proviso—namely, that the occupation of Kalgan would require not only Itagaki's Fifth Division but also the Eleventh Independent Mixed Brigade. The General Staff agreed, and as a necessary prelude on August 8 ordered the Eleventh to the vital Manchukuo–North China route known as the Nankou Pass. There its role was to clear northwestern Hebei Province of Chinese forces and thereby lay the groundwork for an advance into Chahar and eventually Kalgan (both Kalgan and Nankou were on the Peking-Suiyuan Railway). Tojo believed he was in a race with the Tianjin Garrison Army to Kalgan, and to ensure that he did not lose that race, he ordered the Second and Fifteenth Mixed Brigades to Zhangbei, and the so-called Oizumi detachment to Guyuan County in southern Chahar. The General Staff was compelled, once again, to legitimize Tojo's actions retroactively. As it did so, Tojo mounted a case for the return of the First Mixed Brigade and the aviation unit from the Tianjin Garrison Army to the Kwantung Army.[53]

On August 9, 1937, the General Staff issued Imperial Army Order Number 712 to both the Kwantung Army and the Tianjin Garrison Army. The order read, in part,

1. The Tianjin Garrison Army Commander-in-Chief should, at the appropriate time and with a powerful corps, sweep Chinese forces away from the areas east of Kalgan.
2. The Kwantung Army Commander-in-Chief should use the necessary force to facilitate the aforementioned operations in Hebei Province and Inner Mongolia.

Tojo and his military colleagues in Xinjing cabled the General Staff and expressed their bewilderment at this order, which assigned the Kwantung Army a supplementary role in the forthcoming Chahar campaign. The Operations Section chief, Colonel Muto Akira, who had earlier revealed himself sympathetic to the Kwantung Army's cause, wrote that same day and explained that the General Staff had, all along, envisioned the Tianjin Garrison Army playing a key role in the Chahar campaign.[54]

Tojo and his Kwantung Army colleagues were of a very different mindset. They aimed to establish in Kalgan an "autonomous" Mongolian government that would rule over Chahar in its entirety. Its fundamental policies would, in their conception, include "defense of the people," "rejection of warlordism," the "overthrow" of Chiang Kai-shek's Kuomintang, "Japanese–Han Chinese–Mongolian concord," and "defense against communism." They planned to establish a special affairs agency (*tokumukikan*), directly subordinate to the Kwantung Army commander in chief, and to dispatch Japanese and Manchukuoan advisers with "creative talent" and also the "ability to control" the new Mongolian government in its planning and functioning. Underpinning all planning was the base concept of the Kwantung Army as the primary defender or protector of a new Mongolian state.[55]

In the finest tradition of the Kwantung Army, Tojo determined to defy the central military authorities. On August 14 he activated the Chahar Expeditionary Force. It comprised the Second and Fifteenth Mixed Brigades (already in Zhangbei), the First Mixed Brigade (which Tojo wrested back from the Tianjin Garrison Army), and the Second Air Division. Tojo himself took personal command of the force. For a chief of staff to assume command authority, as Tojo now did, was unprecedented and shattered what military historian Hata Ikuhiko has called an "unwritten rule" in Japan's armed services. Gaining the approval of his immediate superior was not difficult: The mild-mannered "virgin general" Ueda Kenkichi was never going to restrain the increasingly self-assured, assertive, and even overbearing Tojo. And, so far as Tojo was concerned, a reputation as a swashbuckler who by his own acuity had fostered Inner Mongolian independence from China provided the most likely means of avoiding his father's fate and ensuring his promotion to full general.[56]

Tojo initially established his headquarters in Tolun. On the eve of the campaign his basic strategy entailed transporting the corps in its entirety from Tolun to Zhangbei via the Zhangjiakou-Tolun Railway; launching a "lightning" campaign and clearing Chinese forces from Zhangbei and surrounding districts, as well as all Great Wall passes in the vicinity of Zhangbei; "pursuing" Chinese forces that would presumably retreat in the direction of Kalgan and thereby provide a pretext to continue the Tojo corps' "lightning" tactics as it advanced on Kalgan; engaging and bolstering the Tehua-based Inner Mongolian independence movement so that it was truly independent of the Kuomintang in Nanjing; and taking the fight deep into Shanxi Province and thereby creating a distinguishable and defensible line against any Chinese attempt at retaking Inner Mongolia.[57]

OVER THE ENSUING DAYS, the Kwantung Army leadership prepared a document titled "Jikyoku shori yoko" (Outline of disposal of the current situation) that set forth, clearly and unambiguously, the Kwantung Army's view of the Chahar campaign, including its scope and objectives. General Ueda forwarded the outline to the central military authorities in Tokyo on August 14, promoting it as the best way out of a Sino-Japanese conflict that—Tokyo's ill-founded optimism notwithstanding—showed no signs of ending anytime soon. Ueda went so far as to insist that, in the absence of a major change in Japanese policy, the current Sino-Japanese conflict could not possibly be confined to the North China region. He added, somewhat ominously, that the conflict would continue to expand until it had become "all-encompassing."[58]

The Kwantung Army's outline located the Chahar campaign within a broader alternative strategy that stretched across Chahar, Hebei, Suiyuan, Shanxi, and Shandong Provinces. It called, in short, for a "fundamental solution" of what it called the "North China issue." Such a solution demanded, in the first instance, a commitment to large-scale military operations. The basic military objective, in the estimation of the Kwantung Army, was to be the "destruction" of China's Central Army and all other Chinese forces in North China. Tojo's fingerprint on the document is easily discernible: He sought to secure a quick victory—and to avoid a debilitating war of attrition—by securing central army authorities' immediate commitment to a decisive battle. The Kwantung Army's outline called for a concentration of "superior" strength, including air power, and for operations that would "repulse and mop up" Chinese forces in Chahar and Hebei Provinces. These operations would be characterized by "agility, speed, and fearlessness" and would cause the nationalist government in Nanjing to "lose the will to fight." As if to reinforce this last point, the Kwantung Army's outline insisted against "diplomatic negotiations" unless and until Chiang Kai-shek "surrendered."[59]

The political objective of such a military campaign presented itself readily enough. Japan's "ultimate aim," according to the Kwantung Army's outline, was an autonomous North China regime that encompassed Chahar, Hebei, Shandong, Shanxi, and, Suiyuan Provinces. As an interim measure, the outline indicated a need to "guide" and "assist" in the establishment of two smaller-scale regimes that would later merge and form a single North China regime. The outline located the first regime's seat in Peking and argued that it ought to rule over Hebei and Shandong Provinces, and subsequently also over Shanxi Province. This regime would relate to the Japanese Tianjin Garrison Army in a manner not dissimilar to the relationship between Manchukuo and the Kwantung Army. The outline located the second regime's seat in Kalgan and argued that it ought to unite and rule over a united Chahar Province, and subsequently also over Suiyuan Province. Just as the envisioned Peking regime would relate to the Tianjin Garrison Army, the envisioned Kalgan regime would relate to the Kwantung Army.[60]

The Kwantung Army's outline emphasized that the envisioned Peking and Kalgan regimes must deliver good governance. It insisted that both regimes had necessarily to "brighten" the prospects of those they would govern. This required a two-pronged approach that borrowed heavily from the Manchukuo precedent. First, the new regimes would repeat Manchukuo's co-optation of local elites at the political, bureaucratic, and military levels so that, for example, an existing Inner Mongolian military government would continue to function and preserve order and thereby serve as a nucleus for the Kalgan regime's formation. Second, the new regimes would require Japan's administrative and technical "guidance" and "support." Bureaucratic advisers from Japan and Manchukuo would build state structures, while engineers and others would develop transportation and communications networks and "electrical grids." Japanese military "occupation" was also deemed necessary.[61]

The Kwantung Army leadership also addressed itself, in the outline, to the overarching purpose of expansion into North China. The issue of operations against the Soviet Union remained (as always for the Kwantung Army) the "primary consideration," and the outline argued that an independent North China would contribute in two essential ways to Japan's preparations for such operations. First, a North China independent of the Chinese nationalist government in Nanjing would—in combination with a suitably "chastised" Chiang Kai-shek—secure the Kwantung Army's rear flank and reduce or remove the need to plan for the possibility of two-front operations against the Chinese and the Soviets. Second, in a longer-range impact, the outline foresaw North China's incorporation into what it called a "Japan-Manchukuo-North China economic bloc." Here again Tojo's input was discernible, for he (and other total war officers at the Kwantung Army Headquarters) identified an opportunity to repeat and expand on Manchukuo's technocratic experiment and to engage in state-planned economic development and state capitalism in North China. In this regard, Tojo and others nursed the basic expectation that the military's needs would receive first priority, and they looked with eager anticipation to North China's conformity to the pattern established in Manchukuo by creation of such heavy industries as the Dowa Automobile Manufacturing Company, the Manchuria Arsenal Corporation, the Manchuria Chemical Industry Company, the Manchuria Petroleum Company, and the Showa Steel Works.[62]

For all its comprehensiveness, the Kwantung Army's outline paid precious little attention to the possible impact a program of territorial conquest in North China might have on Japan's relationships with the great powers, and especially Britain, France, and the United States. It conceded the necessity of avoiding "so far as possible" any injury to the powers' business interests and capital ventures in North China. Otherwise, in an implicit acknowledgment of the likely negative reaction to a renewed round of Japanese aggression and conquest, the Kwantung Army's outline merely noted it would be necessary to guard against the powers' material support for Chiang. Finally, the outline insisted that no offer of "mediation" by any of the powers could possibly be accepted before Chiang had surrendered. In other words, Tojo and his professional military colleagues in Xinjing were convinced that Japan's military and political objectives in North China overrode any concerns for Japan's relationships with the Western powers.[63]

ANIMATED BY THE CONCEPTS contained in the outline, Tojo moved his command post to Zhangbei on August 18. He had, in the meantime, dispatched a Kwantung Army staff officer, Colonel Tanaka Ryukichi, to the seat of the Mongol Military Government in Tehua. Tanaka had been deeply involved in that government's formation in 1936; Tojo now instructed him to "guide" the Inner Mongolian Army as it fought alongside the Tojo corps in the forthcoming campaign to clear Zhangbei and surrounding districts of Chinese forces.[64]

Tojo cabled Vice Chief of Staff Imai and Vice Minister Umezu on August 19, 1937. He explained that, in the absence of "any instructions" from Tokyo, he was now preparing to "cope with the situation by taking measures based on [the Kwantung Army's outline]." Concretely, he noted that operations to capture Kalgan were now imminent. He added that the Kwantung Army was preparing to base in Kalgan a "special service agency" to oversee Mongolian efforts at uniting northern and southern Chahar Province. He signed off with a request that the central military authorities "acknowledge" the Kwantung Army's outline.[65]

Tojo received a response from Umezu within twenty-four hours. It explained that the Army Ministry and General Staff had reached agreement on how best to manage the Sino-Japanese conflict in North China. Efforts were now being made to ensure that the army's position became a matter for "Imperial decision," and Umezu noted that it was inappropriate to comment on policy before the emperor gave his official sanction. He nonetheless stated outright opposition to the idea of "uniting northern and southern Chahar" and of placing any new Mongolian government under the "leadership of a special service agency in Kalgan responsible to the Kwantung Army." He ordered Tojo to confine operations to the areas north of the Great Wall that were already "controlled by the [Inner Mongolian] Silingol and Chahar leagues."[66]

Had Tojo followed Umezu's orders, the Kwantung Army's contribution to the Chahar campaign would have ended very soon thereafter. The fast-moving Tojo corps' main axis of attack was south of Zhangbei along the Great Wall, and by August 22, the corps had cleared all of the wall's passes in Zhangbei's vicinity. It also cut Chinese forces' principal supply line to Suiyuan Province; fighting north of the wall ended on August 23, when the Tojo corps "encircled" Chinese forces in Zhangbei.[67] That same day, the Second Mixed Brigade pursued Chinese forces as they fled south of the Great Wall toward Kalgan. This aligned precisely with Tojo's aims, and he had no intention of calling a halt to the pursuit. He cited, as his reason for disobeying Umezu's orders, the unexpectedly stiff resistance put up by the Chinese Central Army's Eighty-Ninth Division in the vicinity of the Nankou Pass and the inability of Itagaki's Fifth Division and the Independent Eleventh Mixed Brigade to break through that resistance and advance into southern Chahar. Tojo noted that his corps' advance into southern Chahar would threaten the Chinese Eighty-Ninth Division's rear flank. In this way he argued he was acting within the spirit of Imperial Army Order Number 712 insofar as he was supporting the main theater of operations in Hebei Province.[68]

The Tojo corps occupied Kalgan on August 27, 1937. A minor drama had arisen some three days earlier, when the Independent First Mixed Brigade commander, Major General Sakai Takashi, did "not recognize the opportunity" awaiting the Tojo corps.[69] This was a euphemistic way of expressing Sakai's opposition to the forthcoming occupation of Kalgan unless and until reinforcements arrived. One Tojo biographer attributes this episode to a personality clash between Sakai and Tojo, and also to Sakai's conviction that Tojo was "sacrificing" his own troops in a campaign that ultimately aimed at little other than burnishing Tojo's image as an all-conquering war hero.[70] There is doubtless more than a hint of truth in Sakai's assessment, but it is important to note that he underestimated Tojo's commitment to the lightning campaign and to continuous forward movement designed to catch the enemy unaware and off balance. Sakai also seems to have lost sight of Tojo's concern that the central military authorities in Tokyo might divide Chahar Province and his belief that he could short-circuit such thinking if only the Tojo corps occupied Kalgan before the arrival of Itagaki's Fifth Division and the Independent Eleventh Mixed Brigade. In short, it seems fair to conclude that Tojo was motivated not only by personal ambition and visions of his individual war glory but also by a deep-seated professional conviction concerning the way in which war ought to be fought, as well as by a belief that the force that occupied Kalgan would almost invariably enact its own planning for postwar Chahar.

Following the occupation of Kalgan, the Tojo corps moved east via the Peking-Suiyuan Railway and on August 28 occupied Xuanhua. It now coordinated its actions with Itagaki's Fifth Division, which on August 27 opened an attack on Huailai County in southern Chahar. Tojo himself remained in his new command post in Kalgan, from which he cabled the central military authorities in Tokyo, informing them of the "public order work accompanying the attack on Kalgan." He reported that preparations had been made to send from Manchukuo at least ten highly experienced bureaucrats, fifty peacekeeping troops, a medical team numbering at least ten, a handful of financial experts, thirty officers from the Manchukuoan Army's gendarmerie, and approximately one hundred Manchurian police officers. He specifically referenced the Kwantung Army's outline, explaining that he was acting in accord with its emphasis on a fundamental solution of the North China issue. Concretely, he noted that he was concerned with the threefold task of the restoration of law and order across northern and southern Chahar Province, "effective" cooperation with Japanese forces in Hebei Province, and "political maneuvers" in North China.[71]

Umezu's response arrived in Kalgan one day later. It rejected the Kwantung Army's call for a fundamental solution of the North China issue and explicitly disavowed Tojo's "political maneuvers" in Chahar Province. It forbade Tojo from "enacting maneuvers to merge southern Chahar with Inner Mongolia [in northern Chahar]." It insisted that any "agency" purporting to "maintain peace and order" in southern Chahar must include no officials from Manchukuo but instead only locals. Finally, it allowed that Chinese forces should not be permitted to return to southern Chahar. In this regard, it ordered Tojo to lay the groundwork so that southern Chahar could be made a "demilitarized zone."[72]

Tojo completely ignored Umezu's cable. He contacted Umezu and Vice Chief of Staff Imai on August 30, referring them to the cable he had sent two days earlier and informing them of his "actions to restore peace and order in Chahar Province." Specifically, "real progress" was already being made on the dispatch of dozens of "Japanese and Manchukuoans" to his command post in Kalgan. He looked ahead to the eventual withdrawal of his command post and insisted that it would be "necessary" to leave in Kalgan an officer to oversee and "guide" the Japanese and Manchukuoan contingent in their efforts at restoring order. To facilitate this "urgent" process he named Sakai Takashi as his preferred candidate.[73] (This was, incidentally, Tojo's way of dealing with what he regarded as Sakai's recalcitrant and ongoing opposition to his war leadership.) Days later, Tojo advised the central military authorities of the imminent establishment of an autonomous government in southern Chahar. He had established a committee comprising local elites, and under his watchful eye, they were engaged in careful study of education policy, public works, and the costs involved.[74]

Tojo had completely outpaced the central military authorities. In Tokyo they had insisted all along that the Great Wall should demarcate responsibilities in Chahar Province so that the Kwantung Army was responsible for areas north of the wall and the Tianjin Garrison Army was responsible for areas south of it. (On August 31 the General Staff established the North China Area Army; it incorporated the Tianjin Garrison Army and recently arrived reinforcements into its order of battle and, in the central military authorities' thinking, assumed responsibility for southern Chahar). Tojo had acted as if perfectly ignorant of central army policy and had established a Kwantung Army–backed, Kalgan-based Mongolian regime that aimed to rule all of Chahar Province. The army authorities in early September tried to retake control of the situation. The General Staff drafted, and the Army Ministry on September 4 agreed to, an "outline of management of Chahar and Mongolia" by means of which they sought to rein in Tojo and reimpose control.[75]

The centrally drafted outline included several points with which practically any Japanese soldier would readily have agreed. Among these points was the insistence that the army sought in Inner Mongolia a regime that would of its own volition cooperate with Japan and Manchukuo in "defense against communism." In its foreign relations, the new regime should "align" with Japan and Manchukuo in its stance toward both the Soviet Union and the Soviet-sponsored Mongolian People's Republic (generally referred to as Outer Mongolia). Domestically, the new regime should provide for the Mongol people's "peace and prosperity." To these ends, the outline maintained that Japan and Manchukuo must necessarily "assist" the new regime by furnishing it with finances, weapons, and materials.[76]

Most important, the outline addressed the question of whether Inner Mongolia encompassed Chahar Province only in part or in its entirety. The central army authorities came down on the side of those in the military who believed that the Great Wall served as a dividing line between northern and southern Chahar. The outline explicitly and forthrightly forbade any attempts at "merging" the north and south; it tried to put Tojo back in his box by reinforcing the idea that the Great Wall served as the dividing line between the Kwantung Army's sphere of responsibilities in the north and the North China Area Army's sphere of responsibilities in the south.[77] Tojo gave this outline barely a moment's thought. The very day it landed on his desk, he attended a founding ceremony for the

Kalgan-based South Chahar Autonomous Government, which he had fostered and supported.[78]

It was as though Tojo never even saw the central authorities' outline. He contacted Umezu on September 7 and reiterated the need for a Japanese military commander in southern Chahar. It would, he wrote, be necessary to establish "control" and the South Chahar Autonomous Government could then properly devote its attentions to "governance" and "administration." Even then, Tojo asserted, the Imperial Japanese Army would continue to play a role. He anticipated establishment of a Japanese consulate in Kalgan, and he expected the South Chahar Autonomous Government to remain under the "direction" of a Japanese Army officer and a Special Service Agency posted to that consulate.[79] Umezu responded on September 8, insisting that any form of "military administration" must be "avoided," and he was adamant that the South Chahar Autonomous Government not be placed under a Japanese Army commander.[80]

JAPANESE MILITARY LEADERS REMAINED optimistic about the prospect of an early end to the conflict, and they prevailed on Kwantung Army Headquarters to try and prevent Tojo from widening the sphere of the conflict beyond Chahar Province. "Do not," the Kwantung Army cabled Tojo on September 1, "take Datong [in Shanxi Province]."[81] Tojo's gaze had, however, shifted westward along the Peking-Suiyuan Railway, into northeastern Shanxi Province. He was in essential agreement with his staff officers, who insisted on Japan's inability to "compel China to surrender unless [Japanese forces] advanced into Shanxi." From his command post in Kalgan, Tojo once again disobeyed orders and on September 2 "unofficially" directed the Second Mixed Brigade to move against Shanxi Province's northern districts, including Tianzhen and Yanggao. Here the Tojo corps connected with Itagaki's Fifth Division (which had itself ignored orders in taking the fight to Shanxi Province) and, by September 7, "cleared" the districts of Chinese forces. The resistance in Yanggao proved unexpectedly fierce, and there is at least a suggestion that the Tojo corps responded by rounding up and massacring as many as five hundred men.[82]

Tojo now established his command post in Shanxi Province, and his force, along with Itagaki's Fifth Division, invaded the regional city of Datong on September 13. They continued to advance southwest, through rugged mountain terrain toward the provincial capital of Taiyuan (which was also the terminus of the Peking-Suiyuan Railway). All told, the Tojo corps advanced nearly four hundred miles in three weeks. This was blitzkrieg or lightning warfare at its dizzying best, and Tojo returned to Kwantung Army Headquarters in Xinjing on September 20.[83]

Tojo was satisfied that his corps had attained most military objectives and confident that all remaining territorial objectives were within reach. Sure enough, the campaign ended soon thereafter, with the Kwantung Army controlling Chahar and Suiyuan Provinces and the northern half of Shanxi Province. Tojo seemed unconcerned by either Chinese forces' southward retreat or the continuation, intensification, and magnification of Sino-Japanese fighting in areas well beyond North China and Inner Mongolia. This is, perhaps, defensible given that battles in Shanghai and elsewhere lay well beyond the Kwantung Army chief of staff's jurisdiction. It must nonetheless be recalled that Tojo and his professional military colleagues in Xinjing had repeatedly insisted, in communications with the central military authorities in Tokyo, that their preferred military solution—namely, the injection of preponderant force across North China and Inner Mongolia—would bring the incident to an early conclusion. Call it an honest mistake, or perhaps a miscalculation of Chinese intent; either way, the consequences were grave, for the Japanese Army now found itself in a war in which it won most battles but from which it could not extricate itself. Tojo was hardly solely responsible, but his personal responsibility was hefty.

Tojo had little time for such reflection; he was too busy furthering the cause of Inner Mongolian autonomy. His sensitivity to the Inner Mongolian nationalist movement was on full display during an October 16, 1937, conversation with the Foreign Ministry's Sawada Renzo and Togo Shigenori, as well as the Manchukuoan General Affairs Agency director, Hoshino Naoki. On this occasion Tojo explained that the South Chahar and North Shanxi Autonomous Governments had been established in Kalgan and Datong, respectively. He spoke also of the intention to establish in Suiyuan Province a third autonomous government. He voiced outright opposition to inclusion of these Mongolian autonomous governments in North China. In Tojo's formulation, two separate regimes must become independent of the Chinese nationalist government in Nanjing. He foresaw a North China regime encompassing Hebei and Shandong Provinces, as well as the non-Mongolian southern Shanxi Province; he foresaw also an Inner Mongolian federation that incorporated the South Chahar Autonomous Government, North Shanxi Autonomous Government, and Mongolian Autonomous Government. There should be, he stated, a "united council" that included members from each of these three autonomous governments; the council would be responsible for regulating the governments' approaches to such "common issues" as railways and a currency system. He foresaw a need for Japanese troops to remain in and defend Inner Mongolia, and also for Japanese advisers to work with the autonomous governments.[84]

Weeks later Tojo traveled to Hohhot (the Mongolian name for what had hitherto been called Guisui, in Suiyuan Province) and looked on approvingly as Mongolian Princes Yun and Teh announced the foundation of the Mongolian Federated Autonomous Government. He spoke with a subordinate about replicating the Manchukuo precedent and entrusting a Kwantung Army Special Affairs Unit or Agency (he used the terms *tokumubu* and *tokumukikan* interchangeably) with "guidance" of this new government. He spoke of the need to prioritize "defense against communism," "ethnic harmony," and development of a "particularly close relationship" with Manchukuo, and he held up "political independence" as the ultimate aim. This seemed uncontroversial and indeed justifiable because, as Tojo put it, Inner Mongolia was "geographically and ethnically" separate and distinct from China. To justify the effort and expenditure, he simply noted that Inner Mongolia would become an essential component of operational planning vis-à-vis China and the Soviet Union.[85]

Tojo was outstripping Japanese decision-makers with more than just his prognoses for Inner Mongolia. His view of Chiang Kai-shek, the Sino-Japanese hostilities, and their impact on Japan's relationships with the Western powers was considerably more strident than most in Tokyo were willing to entertain. He wrote the central military authorities in late November and defined Japan's aim as "Sino-Manchukuo-Japanese co-prosperity"; he tied to this aim Japan's anticommunist policies, its fidelity to the concept of ethnic concord, and its pursuit of Sino-Japanese friendship. In contrast, he portrayed Chiang Kai-shek as pursuing a procommunist, anti-Japanese, and denial-of-Manchukuo stance. Japan must not, he insisted, negotiate with Chiang; it should instead collaborate with various regional regimes and facilitate their collaborating and thereby creating a new central government. He argued that North China and Inner Mongolia must necessarily remain distinct and separate from this new Chinese government, and he posited that Japan and Manchukuo must assist in their "economic construction." In a separate cable several days later, Tojo conceded that he was advocating a policy of "divide and conquer." He acknowledged the likelihood of Japanese policies attracting Anglo-American opprobrium, and he thought this could be countered by securing German and Italian recognition of any new central government in China.[86]

TOJO'S FINAL MONTHS IN Xinjing were dominated by a bitter personal feud with his newly appointed vice chief of staff, Major General Ishiwara Kanji. The two men had known each other since at least the late 1920s, when they were both members of the One Evening Society. As we have seen, they had clashed in early 1932 over the issue of troop withdrawals from Manchuria and also over the Kwantung Army's subsequent role in Manchukuo. Ishiwara had, following the Marco Polo Bridge Incident, been one of the key voices of caution on the General Staff and had argued incessantly for the incident's nonescalation. In this way he adopted a position that was the polar opposite of that taken by Tojo. In the interim, Ishiwara had considered representing Lieutenant Colonel Aizawa Saburo as he awaited trial for Nagata's murder. Ishiwara was, apparently, "impressed with the burning convictions that had led Aizawa to wield his sword."[87] This last piece of Ishiwara's biography was, so far as Tojo was concerned, decisive. It mattered little to Tojo that Ishiwara had eventually turned down Aizawa's request; Ishiwara had, by identifying on some level with Nagata's murderer, made himself Tojo's sworn personal enemy.

Ishiwara arrived in Xinjing in late September 1937, only days after Tojo returned from the war front. Tojo convened a meeting of Kwantung Army staff officers to greet his new deputy, using the occasion to put Ishiwara in his place. He announced that Ishiwara would henceforth assist in matters such as operational planning and logistics. He added a cautionary note: Ishiwara must not, Tojo insisted, involve himself in any "Manchukuo-related affairs." These Tojo demarcated as his own responsibility. Ishiwara responded with uncharacteristic calm. "As directed by the chief of staff, I will touch on Manchukuoan military matters [only] as they relate to operations," he said. "But I will not touch other matters relating to security, transportation, or political affairs."[88]

The irascible Ishiwara proved unable, over the ensuing weeks and months, to follow his own counsel. He bristled at the system of governance that had developed in Manchukuo. He insisted on the removal of the Kwantung Army's system of controls, and he called for self-governance for Manchukuo. He nursed high hopes for the Concordia Association and the role its pan-Asian ideology ought to play in building a sense of nationhood among the Han Chinese, Japanese, Koreans, Manchu, and Mongols. He fulminated in private and in public against the "guidance" the Kwantung Army provided the Concordia Association and against what he regarded as the "stifling controls" imposed on the Manchukuoan government, leveling his frustrations at his immediate superior, Tojo.[89]

Tojo shared none of Ishiwara's idealism. He prioritized effective administration and what he regarded as good governance. The system in which he participated, in his estimation, provided just that.[90] The locus of the decision-making process was the weekly "Wednesday meeting," at which Tojo met with an assortment of civilian Japanese bureaucrats. He aired the Kwantung Army's views at the outset of each meeting, which formed the basis of subsequent discussion. Conclusions were forwarded to the executive branch of the Manchukuoan government for adoption. Implementation then fell on the bureaucracies, which were headed by Japanese officials. That Manchukuo enjoyed no real autonomy from Japan—and, most particularly, from the Kwantung Army—seemed not to trouble Tojo in the slightest. Besides, his enmity for Ishiwara meant that he would not and indeed could not accept the latter's arguments and ideas.[91]

Ishiwara held Tojo personally responsible for what he regarded as Manchukuo's stunted political development. The insults he hurled at Tojo were legion: He referred to him variously as "that mental defective Tojo," the "uneducated Corporal Tojo," "private first-class Tojo," "the sissy who could do nothing but use the *kenpei*," and "Sergeant Tojo."[92] On one occasion, he told Tojo to his face that he had the "pettifogging mentality of a sergeant." On another occasion, after learning that Tojo was funneling official Kwantung Army funds to the Manchukuo Women's National Defense Association (which was run by Tojo's wife, Katsuko), Ishiwara publicly accused Tojo of corruption. Former Ishiwara protégé Colonel Katakura Tadashi pleaded with Ishiwara to take a more "conciliatory" approach in his dealings with Tojo.[93] It was to no avail. Tojo responded by calling on the contacts he maintained in the highest levels of the Kwantung *kenpei*, prevailing on them to surveil Ishiwara.[94]

THE UNDECLARED WAR IN China continued to expand. The Imperial Japanese Army had in early September 1937 launched a general offensive in Shanghai, which had long been a flashpoint in Sino-Japanese relations but was very far removed from North China. Soon thereafter, air battles were being fought over the Chinese nationalist capital at Nanjing. The pressure on Nanjing was such that the Chinese government in early October shifted its capital to Wuhan in Hubei Province and then subsequently to Chongqing in Sichuan Province.

Scoring repeated battlefield victories in North China and in the Yangtze River basin was one thing, but bringing an end to the hostilities was another matter altogether. The question of an exit strategy divided uniformed army officers. In Tokyo, Army Minister Sugiyama Hajime parroted the hard-line approach of his subordinates (who referred to him as the "toilet door" because he moved in whichever direction his hawkish subordinates pushed). He argued against peace negotiations with Chiang Kai-shek and for the establishment of local regimes, autonomous governments, and councils across occupied zones in China. In this way, he argued, Chiang could hope—at best—to emerge from the fighting as the leader of but one of these local regimes. The Army General Staff, which continued to adhere to the approach established by Ishiwara Kanji, was of a very different mindset. It had no confidence in the Japanese forces' ability to compel enemy forces to engage in a war-ending decisive battle, and argued for peace negotiations with Chiang Kai-shek. It reckoned that Japan's peace terms should not go beyond four basic demands: the Chinese nationalist government's formal recognition of Manchukuo; a Sino-Japanese agreement for joint defense against communism, for which purpose it foresaw a postwar Japanese military occupation of North China and Inner Mongolia; an end to anti-Japanese activities in China; and China's incorporation into a Sino-Japanese-Manchukuoan economic and trading bloc.[95]

The Kwantung Army—with Tojo at the forefront—refused to stay out of this debate. Tojo was, for one thing, bullish about the prospect of total victory in China. Japan ought, he wrote in late November 1937, to "sever" all contact with what he referred to derisively as the "Chiang regime." He saw no good coming from peace feelers, negotiations, and the like. He insisted instead that Japan ought to "nurture local regimes, cooperate with them, and develop a sentiment conducive to the establishment of a new central government."[96]

Organization of the provisional government of the Republic of China in Peking soon followed. Tojo now staked out a position at variance with majority opinion in the Japanese Army. He cabled the North China Area Army and demanded consideration of "conflicts of interest" in the forthcoming effort to "guide" North China's separation from Chiang's nationalist government. His purport was twofold: First, he was implying—none too obliquely—that Inner Mongolia remained within the Kwantung Army's bailiwick. Second, he was warning against any unwanted intrusion or interference therein. Tojo was insisting, in short, that Inner Mongolia remain separate and distinct from any North China regime.[97]

Japanese forces entered the nationalist capital of Nanjing in mid-December 1937. Even as they visited unspeakable miseries on that unfortunate city and its residents, Tojo and his professional military colleagues in Xinjing clarified their position in communications with both the North China Area Army and the central military authorities in Tokyo. The Kwantung Army believed, they wrote, in the need to "eradicate Chiang Kai-shek's regime." It did not, however, plan for the establishment of a new "central" government in China. Instead it sought throughout China's regions a series of "loosely connected" and "self-governing bodies" that would "govern by law and reason rather than by military force."[98]

A few weeks later the Japanese government issued a declaration in Prime Minister Konoe's name. It made apparent the Konoe cabinet's refusal to deal any further with China's nationalist government, and it clarified a determination to look instead to the establishment of a new Chinese government with which Japan would cooperate for the "adjustment of Sino-Japanese relations and the building of a rejuvenated China." Known as the *aite to sezu* (no deals with [the nationalist government]) declaration, it caused consternation in the Army General Staff. Tojo's initial reaction to the statement has been lost to history, but he doubtless applauded Konoe's declared intention not to deal with Chiang Kai-shek's nationalist government. Yet, given his enthusiasm for the emergence of only loosely connected regional regimes across China, he probably did not welcome Konoe's emphasis on the emergence of a new Chinese government.

TOJO WAS RECALLED TO Tokyo in May 1938. His Manchukuoan interlude had lasted, all told, a little over two and a half years. It was an exhilarating period, and it revitalized his military career. Tojo's accomplishments were essentially threefold: He had cordoned Manchukuo off from the February 26 Incident. He had, at least in his own estimation, forced the Soviet Union to back away from a border dispute with Manchukuo. And he had fostered Inner Mongolian autonomy from the Chinese nationalist government in Nanjing. This last accomplishment was a step toward resolution of what Tojo and his cadres had in the late 1920s identified as the Manchurian-Mongolian problem. That, for Tojo, dovetailed neatly with a perceived need to burnish his curriculum vitae with battlefield success; it came at the cost of a widening war in China from which no exit strategy presented itself. In both the border dispute and the Inner Mongolian operation, Tojo embraced the traditions of the Kwantung Army and took an extremely aggressive approach while ignoring both government policy and the orders of the central military authorities in Tokyo. He was, as he himself acknowledged, engaging freely in *gekokujo*. In another military establishment Tojo might well have expected some form of reprimand. He himself half wondered whether he would be forced into premature retirement. Instead his well-earned reputation as a hardliner vis-à-vis China earned him his next appointment, as vice army minister.

5
RETURN TO TOKYO
1938–1939

TOJO HIDEKI'S PROFILE WAS rising. He had, by virtue of his lightning campaign in Inner Mongolia and his hard-line stance against diplomatic negotiations with Chiang Kai-shek, become the darling of the Imperial Japanese Army's most hawkish elements. He was, moreover, widely regarded as a man with a "gift" for "meticulous planning." He was universally recognized to have been so close to Nagata Tetsuzan as to have been akin to his "little brother." Nagata would have become, at least, a vice army minister, and Tojo was now expected to serve as Nagata's "successor" or replacement in that role and others.[1] Certainly in Xinjing in late 1937, rumor had it that Tojo was in line to succeed Umezu Yoshijiro as the next vice army minister.[2] These rumors circulated all the more freely after Tojo flew back to Tokyo in early April 1938 so he could join the current army minister, Lieutenant General Sugiyama Hajime, and others at luncheon with the emperor.[3]

Meanwhile, the undeclared war in China was taking a course contrary to Tojo's expectations. In Tokyo the Imperial Diet passed the State General Mobilization Law, which paved the way for unprecedented government intervention in all aspects of national economic life. Prime Minister Konoe Fumimaro only secured the law's passage through the Diet by disavowing any attempt at invoking the bill so long as the fighting continued on the continent; it nonetheless indicated the Japanese government's acceptance of the fact that it now found itself fighting a total war against China. The course of the war itself confirmed this reality. Japan's Central China Area Army and North China Area Army joined in mid-March and attacked the new center of Chinese resistance at Xuzhou, in the central Yangtze River region. The battle followed a familiar pattern: Xuzhou fell in mid-May, but Japanese troop numbers were not sufficient to encircle the enemy, and the Chinese forces escaped.[4] Konoe now despaired of his publicly declared refusal to deal with the Chinese nationalist government, the Kuomintang, for if the Japanese Army was unable to defeat Chinese forces in a decisive battle, Chiang was unlikely to surrender. An endless war in China was hardly palatable, and this raised the unavoidability of some form of truce negotiations, which would necessarily involve the legitimate Chinese government. It was time for a new policy direction, and Konoe decided to make sweeping changes to his cabinet.

Among the more notable changes was the removal of the ineffectual foreign minister, Hirota Koki. Replacing him was a wily retired general, Ugaki

Tojo proceeds to the Imperial Palace in his capacity as Kwantung Army chief of staff, early April 1938.

Kazushige, who was in hearty agreement concerning the need to overturn the *aite to sezu* (no deals with [the nationalist government]) pronouncement and to seek peace with China. Konoe also signaled what would become a lifelong fascination with reviving and resuscitating the Japanese Army's *kodoha* (Imperial way faction) by bringing into his cabinet General Araki Sadao. Perhaps most important, Konoe enlisted the emperor's assistance in convincing the army to replace Lieutenant General Sugiyama Hajime with Lieutenant General Itagaki Seishiro. The emperor had himself lost patience with what he regarded as Sugiyama's bumbling ineptitude and prevailed on Prince Kan'in Kotohito to take up the issue with his uniformed military colleagues. The army's "big three" granted this wish, although Sugiyama went only reluctantly. The entire process took about one week.[5]

On his way out of the cabinet, Sugiyama ordered Tojo back to Tokyo and appointed him army vice minister. This was a bald attempt at shoring up the hard-line position Sugiyama had consistently advocated. He based this presumption on Tojo's hawkish views toward China and his increasingly confident and forceful personality. He worked also from assumptions about Itagaki's reputation for agreeableness and affability and his distinct lack of any firm convictions; Tojo should, according to this reckoning, prove able to push Itagaki into a hard-line stance. Within the army there was also awareness of the contrast between Itagaki's and Tojo's careers: the incoming minister was first and foremost a field officer with vast experience in China but practically none in Tokyo, while his freshly minted deputy had forged his career in the army's political and operational nerve center in Tokyo. Tojo was no fool, and well understood that his administrative experience and capacity was the perfect foil for Itagaki. He recognized it would fall on him to ensure orderly processes in the Army Ministry, and he expected that, by so doing, he would consolidate a hard-line approach to China.

Tojo was driven also by personal ambition. His predecessor, Umezu, had been an unusually strong presence, "in reality the key figure in the Army Ministry."[6] Tojo determined to replicate that dynamic (and, to that end, gleefully took on a simultaneous role as chief of the Army Aeronautical Department). He had every reason to expect the enthusiastic support of his allies and supporters who were in key positions throughout the ministry. Among them were Nakamura Aketo, chief of the important Military Affairs Bureau; Tanaka Shin'ichi, chief of the Army Affairs Section; Iwakuro Hideo, Nagai Yatsuji, and Nishiura Susumu, also of the Army Affairs Section; Kagesa Sadaaki of the Military Affairs Section; Sanada Shoichiro of the Economic Mobilization Bureau; and Anami Korechika, chief of the Personnel Bureau. These men and others reveled in the sharpness of Tojo's mind and character, and took to referring to him as the Razor.[7] He felt, not without reason, that his time was nigh.

TOJO ARRIVED IN TOKYO approximately one week before Itagaki and set immediately to work. His most pressing task was to lead the Army Ministry in reconsidering its China policy, for he was convinced that he must greet Itagaki on his arrival with a coherent and cogent policy program. The result was a memorandum, "Shina Jihen shido ni kansuru setsumei" (Explanation of guidance on the China Incident), that called for a reaffirmation of the policies underpinning the *aite to sezu* declaration and for a clear-cut policy of Japanese leadership in East Asia. It envisioned a new China that dispensed with its "anti-Japanese" policies and programs and instead cooperated with Japan's anticommunism goals. The memorandum insisted on a continued "aggressive strategy" in China that included not only military operations but also "political maneuvering" (*boryaku*) in an effort to undermine the Kuomintang. It allowed for the pursuance of peace negotiations, if Chiang initiated the negotiations and accepted that his government would be nothing more than one of the regional regimes.[8]

Tojo and his subordinates sought also to envision the China Incident within a wider policy framework. They regarded the "overthrow of Anglo-American influence in China" among the army's war aims and foresaw the possibility of war in China developing in such a way that not China but the Soviet Union and Britain became the principal targets of Japanese policy. They called for armament expansion programs to prepare for that possibility and for a foreign policy that dropped any pretense at cooperation with the Anglo-American powers and instead sought a strengthened relationship among the Anti-Comintern Pact partners, Germany and Japan, as well as the pact's newest signatory, Italy.[9]

Tojo greeted Itagaki with his "Explanation," and Itagaki fronted a conference of five ministers with its policy prescriptions on June 16, 1938; also present were Finance Minister Ikeda Seihin, Prime Minister Konoe, Foreign Minister Ugaki, and Navy Minister Yonai Mitsumasa. Ugaki spoke of a very different approach, in which Japan revised its existing China policies, pursued a conciliatory policy toward Britain, and sought British mediation in bringing an end to the China Incident. The gap between

Itagaki and Ugaki was unbridgeable, and the conference ended without agreement on any substantial issue.[10]

The five ministers reconvened their conference on June 24. Agreement was possible only on two very broad platitudes. First, the Konoe cabinet would seek to "achieve all war objectives" and "resolve" the China Incident before the year was out. Second, the cabinet would be amenable to "amicable mediation" by third nations.[11] The precise objectives for which Japan fought remained undefined and subject to further debate. So, too, did the "third nations" whose mediation might extricate Japan from the undeclared war in China.

Under Tojo's watchful eye, the Army Ministry set about defining the objectives for which Japan fought in China and the policies most likely to attain them. The result was a set of policy prescriptions that fleshed out an extremely hard-line approach. With regard to Japan's objectives in China, the ministry sought a "new China" that Japan would "assist" in determining "all financial and economic policies." Japan would reserve to itself the sole right to "assume actual control over the development of national defense resources" in North China and Inner Mongolia. In Central China, Japan would "usually" cooperate with other nations in "industrial development projects." Across Central and South China, Japan would accept the principle of "free competition" in trade.[12]

The Army Ministry's hopes for foreign policy centered on a strengthened German-Italian-Japanese relationship. This would enable Japan to dissuade the Soviet Union from participating in the China Incident, to pressure Britain to abandon its policy of material support for Chiang Kai-shek, and to convince the United States to remain neutral. In a burst of optimism, Tojo and his colleagues allowed themselves to hope even for a strengthened Japanese-US economic relationship.[13]

Tojo had, in the meantime, contacted officers on the ground in China, staking out an extremely hard-line position. "Peace negotiations" with the "Chiang regime," he wrote, were "unacceptable." Some in the Japanese Army had begun advocating negotiations with China's nationalist government if Chiang resigned. Underpinning this position was a perceived need to devise an exit strategy from China while maintaining true to the form of Konoe's *aite to sezu* pronouncement. Tojo, however, denounced such thinking. Chiang's "resignation," he insisted, would change nothing. For Tojo, "peace negotiations" with the nationalist government remained out of the question even if Chiang resigned.[14]

TOJO'S ATTENTION SHIFTED IN mid-July 1938 to an obscure hillock located at the juncture of northeast Korea, southeast Manchukuo, and the Soviet Maritime Province near Psyet Bay. Known to the Japanese as Changkufeng, the hillock was occupied by a few dozen Soviet soldiers on or around July 10. Tojo first learned of the Soviet occupation on July 13, when the Korea Army commander in chief, General Koiso Kuniaki, alerted him—as well as the vice chief of staff, Lieutenant General Tada Hayao, and the Kwantung Army chief of staff, Lieutenant General Isogai Kensuke—to what Koiso called an "unlawful" Soviet action. Koiso presented a picture of moderation, making clear his disinclination to take any military "countermeasures." He thought it ought to suffice simply to demand the Soviets' withdrawal. Only if the Soviets did not comply, Koiso wrote, should the army consider using "all its might to drive the Soviet soldiers out of the area."[15]

In Tokyo, Tojo and Tada each accepted the propriety of resolving the border incident diplomatically. The General Staff was planning massive operations to capture Canton and Wuhan in the hope of securing a decisive victory against Chiang Kai-shek and extracting Japan from what was otherwise looking increasingly like a "quagmire" in China. The military simply did not have the troop strength to consider simultaneous operations against the Soviets.[16] Tojo cabled Koiso and expressed agreement with the idea that Japan ought to resort to force only if diplomacy failed to dislodge the Soviets from Changkufeng. "In the unlikely event the Soviets do not respond to our demands and do not withdraw," he wrote, "careful consideration must be given as to whether or not to resort immediately to force to destroy [Soviet forces at Changkufeng]." In a separate cable, Tada indicated his concurrence with Koiso's views. He also informed Koiso of his intention to enlist the Foreign Ministry's assistance in issuing a "stern protest."[17]

The Moscow embassy's chargé d'affaires, Nishi Haruhiko, met on July 15, 1938, with the Soviet deputy foreign minister, Boris Stomonyakov. He protested the Soviet troops' occupation of Changkufeng and requested their "immediate withdrawal." Stomonyakov refused on the grounds that Changkufeng was "Soviet territory."[18] That same day, Soviet forces shot and killed a Japanese officer reconnoitering the area, which led to a round of diplomatic protests and counterprotests.[19] The central military authorities in Tokyo responded to the Soviet diplomatic obstinacy by ordering the Korea Army's Nineteenth Division to concentrate in the vicinity of Changkufeng. The idea was to test Soviet resolve and to bolster Japan's diplomatic efforts. Ambassador Shigemitsu Mamoru met with Soviet Foreign Minister Maksim Litvinov on July 20. "It is exceedingly clear," Shigemitsu stated at this juncture, "that the area at issue is Manchukuoan territory." He reminded Litvinov that Japan had committed itself, in solemn treaty form, to the maintenance of Manchukuoan security and stated that, in case it proved necessary, Japanese forces would "not delay" in taking all "necessary actions" in defense of Manchukuoan territory. Litvinov showed "no sign of compromise," insisting that Japan's "threats" had "no effect in Moscow."[20]

The central military authorities in Tokyo concluded that diplomacy had failed and only force would shift Soviet forces from Changkufeng. None envisioned a large-scale war. To the contrary, all agreed on the need to limit the fighting so that it achieved nothing other than retaking Changkufeng. Tojo departed for Keijo (Seoul) to keep Korea Army headquarters on a tight leash (Tojo may also have been attracted to the prospect of being nearer the center of the action). Meanwhile, Prince Kan'in went to the Imperial Palace to seek the emperor's approval for the Korea Army's retaking of Changkufeng. The emperor had already learned from Ugaki of the Soviets' diplomatic obstinacy. Unbeknownst to Prince Kan'in, the foreign minister had also maintained that it was not yet time to resort to force. The emperor rebuked Prince Kan'in for having failed to coordinate with Ugaki. He also asked Prince Kan'in whether a border war at Changkufeng might develop into a "total war." Prince Kan'in bungled this question badly, admitting that he could not guarantee against such an eventuality, and the emperor refused to approve a resort to force.[21] A chastened Prince Kan'in cabled Korea Army headquarters and clarified the need for "prudence." The Korea Army, he wrote, must not "provoke" any military "conflict."[22]

Prince Kan'in's cable perplexed Tojo. He had assumed that the emperor's approval to retake Changkufeng was more or less a matter of course. He was also convinced that an assault was better sooner, rather than later, for Korea Army staff officers had apprised him of the Soviets' ongoing preparations for war in the area and of the increasing power imbalance this would impose. Concerned lest the opportunity was lost, Tojo cabled the Military Affairs Bureau director, Major General Nakamura Aketo, on July 21 and inquired as to any changes in army policy. Nakamura's response arrived that evening: There had been "no change" in army policy. Diplomacy remained the preferred means by which to resolve the incident; only if there were a drastic change in the situation would there be any reconsideration of policy.[23]

Tojo flew back to Tokyo in a bullish frame of mind. He convened an extraordinary meeting of the ministry's bureau directors and demanded to know, "What is wrong with you lot?" The Korea Army, he insisted, should be engaging the Soviets at Changkufeng, and he demanded to know why this was not the case. He learned not only of Prince Kan'in's audience with the emperor but also of a subsequent ill-tempered audience the emperor had granted Itagaki. In Tojo's absence, Itagaki had appeared before the emperor underprepared and with a series of slipshod or perfunctory points. The emperor, raging at Itagaki, accused the army of having made a habit of acting arbitrarily and without orders. He specifically mentioned the Manchurian Incident. The emperor also excoriated the army for the war in China, which had expanded against his wishes and continued without an end in sight. Having lambasted the army for its repeated and all-too-apparent willingness to disregard government policy, the emperor decreed that, in this latest incident, the army "must not move a single troop" unless and until he ordered otherwise. Itagaki was aghast and ready to resign. His subordinates approached the emperor's aides-de-camp and asked whether the emperor indeed sought Itagaki's ministerial resignation. The emperor, who was adamant that he was no autocrat but instead a constitutional monarch, disavowed any such intention. Even so, the emperor's reaction to the situation on Changkufeng caused Tojo to change his tune dramatically. Without even pausing to draw breath, Tojo ordered the bureau chiefs to "give up" all hope of a military solution and to prepare instead for a diplomatic solution; his reversal was so immediate and so complete that one subordinate later commented, "No ordinary man could have done this."[24]

The issue might have ended there but for a Japanese-Soviet clash on July 29, 1938. Sparking the incident was a small Soviet patrol on a hill some two kilometers north of Changkufeng. A few dozen Japanese troops attacked and annihilated the patrol. The situation escalated, and in the early hours of July 31 the Nineteenth Division stormed Changkufeng. The battle adhered closely to classic Japanese military doctrine insofar as it was decided by infantry in hand-to-hand combat, and the Japanese had driven all Soviet defenders off Changkufeng by sunrise.[25]

It was necessary to report these developments to the emperor, but Prince Kan'in refused to do so. It fell on his terrified deputy Tada, who informed the emperor that Japanese troops had not taken "one step" inside Soviet territory and had only resorted to arms to defend themselves against an "unlawful" Soviet attack. He also explained that the central military authorities remained committed to the twin policies of "nonexpansion" of the incident and resolution by "diplomatic negotiation." On these grounds, the emperor offered his ex post facto approval of the Nineteenth Division's actions.[26]

Tada emerged from the audience, cabled the Korea Army, and reinforced the need to end the border war expeditiously. He was adamant that the diplomats ultimately resolve the incident. Tojo echoed the message in a separate cable to the Korea Army. The army, he wrote, was "adhering to the policy of nonexpansion of the incident," regarding it as a "local issue" to be resolved by "diplomatic negotiation."[27]

The Soviets bucked expectations and on August 1 sent massive reinforcements, including a few hundred aircraft. The Japanese declined to respond in kind, hoping thereby to keep the incident localized. The fighting paused on August 5. Tojo now began calling for the unilateral withdrawal of the Nineteenth Division from Changkufeng. He was adamant that the army avoid "getting caught up" in the fighting and not concern itself with saving face.[28] The proposed withdrawal met with strong opposition from the General Staff, and it did not go ahead. Nor was the General Staff willing to consider reinforcements. This left the outgunned Nineteenth Division no choice but to dig in and defend its hopeless position until the diplomats hammered out truce terms, which required more time than the opponents of unilateral withdrawal had hoped.

Officers in both the Army Ministry and the General Staff breathed a sigh of relief when on August 10 Shigemitsu cabled truce terms he had negotiated with Litvinov. Key terms included both the Japanese and Soviet armies ceasing all "acts of hostilities" beginning at midnight on August 11, and Japanese forces withdrawing from their positions, while Soviet forces would not advance but would "maintain" their "current position."[29] Once the truce went into effect, Tojo got his way, and the Japanese effected a complete and unilateral withdrawal from the entire area surrounding Changkufeng. This opened the way for Soviet forces to occupy all of the high ground, including Changkufeng.

IT IS EASY TO imagine Tojo breathing a sigh of relief at the conclusion of the Changkufeng Incident. It had brought the Japanese Army to the brink of full-scale war with the Soviet Union. Such an outcome might have struck Tojo, in other circumstances, as a welcome opportunity. But the nine divisions maintained by the Kwantung and Korean Armies would clearly require reinforcements in the event a border war, like that at Changkufeng, expanded into something much larger. This was, in mid-1938, beyond the army's capacity. Twenty-four active service divisions were engaged in operations in Central China; only Imperial Guard units remained on the Japanese home islands. At least until the undeclared war in China was brought to a conclusion, the army had nothing left to give.[30]

Never one to sit on his laurels, Tojo now counseled a strengthening of the Anti-Comintern Pact. A strengthened alliance would, in his estimation, confront the Soviets with the possibility of a two-front war in the west (against Germany) and the east (against Japan). This should, Tojo reckoned, be cause for circumspection in Moscow and thereby reduce the likelihood of any future clashes along the Korean-Manchukuoan-Soviet border.

Even as the Changkufeng Incident unfolded, Tojo presided over the preparation of a policy document, which Itagaki submitted to the five ministers conference on July 19, 1938. It called for two alliance relationships, one each with Germany and Italy. The proposed alliance with Germany would target the Soviet Union, while the proposed alliance with Italy would target Britain. Each was an offensive-defensive alliance, which would provide for a mutually planned offensive or for assistance in the case of attack on a signatory. The idea of two alliance relationships—as opposed to a single, German-Italian-Japanese alliance—was in all likelihood an attempt at steering through the all-important German-Japanese alliance. The Imperial Japanese Navy and the Foreign Ministry were mounting opposition to an alliance that included Britain among its targets. Tojo and his professional military colleagues seemed to be indicating—however obliquely—a willingness at least to shelve an Italian-Japanese alliance if they got their way with the proposed German-Japanese pact.[31]

Agreement on a German-Japanese pact proved more difficult than Tojo and others anticipated. Ugaki refused to countenance it. As a sop to the army, he proposed to strengthen German-Japanese political ties. To Tojo and others in the Army Ministry, this seemed to miss the point entirely. Matters were brought to a head in early August, when a German proposal for a strengthened German-Italian-Japanese alliance arrived in Tokyo. The proposal included provision for discussion of "common action" in the event an alliance partner faced "diplomatic difficulties"; an obligation to "offer all political and diplomatic assistance" in the event of a "threat" to an alliance partner; and an obligation to "give military assistance" in the event an alliance partner came under attack. Tojo and his colleagues were in hearty agreement. Ugaki, however, insisted on changes to the second and third clauses. His revisions, which the five ministers conference accepted on August 26, called for an obligation to "offer all political and economic assistance" in the event of an "unprovoked attack" on one of the signatories and to "enter into discussions concerning military assistance" in the event an alliance partner came under "unprovoked attack."[32]

Tojo contacted the military attaché to the Berlin embassy, Lieutenant General Oshima Hiroshi, and explained that the Japanese government hoped "to conclude this treaty as soon as possible." In a separate cable to Oshima, Tojo explained that the government had forged consensus on an "extension of the existing Anti-Comintern Pact." Any new agreement, he wrote, would have to be "directed principally against the Soviet Union." He added that it was necessary to avoid including any "word or phrase" that might give "any impression" that Britain and the United States were "direct enemies." Here Tojo seemed quite deliberately to leave open the possibility of an alliance that indeed targeted the Anglo-American powers but did not do so explicitly. (That was almost certainly how Oshima understood Tojo's cable.) Tojo was more forthright in his treatment of the need for "discussion prior to the extension of military assistance" so that the "responsibility for granting military aid" was neither "instantaneous" nor "unconditional."[33]

Tojo misrepresented the situation within the Japanese government. The navy minister, Vice Admiral Yonai Mitsumasa, opposed the alliance outright. He told a five ministers conference on August 8 that a German-Japanese alliance targeting not just the Soviet Union but also Britain would cause the United States to "join hands" with the latter. The farsighted Yonai worried that the Anglo-American powers might subject Japan to "crushing economic pressures." He related his concern lest a Japan allied to Germany and Italy be ultimately unable to avoid war against the Anglo-American powers, and he stated his deep-seated conviction that "there would be absolutely no chance of Japan's winning a war of this nature."[34]

Yonai's representations revealed a worldview very different from that predominating in the army. Whereas uniformed army officers remained overtly focused on the continent, their naval counterparts set their collective gaze on the wide expanses of the Pacific Ocean. While Tojo and his professional colleagues assumed that Korea, Manchukuo, Mongolia, and North China made up the crux of Japanese overseas interests, navy officers focused instead on what they called the *nan'yo* (south seas), and they regarded Japan's colonial possession of Taiwan as the gateway. According to historian Mark Peattie, the army felt "the landward pull of the neighboring continent" while the navy felt instead "the maritime impulse to move out on the open seas."[35] These outlooks had remained fundamentally unchanged since the late Meiji period, when the army saw Russia as its primary hypothetical enemy and the navy saw the United States as the enemy.

For Tojo, a German-Japanese alliance made sense primarily because it promised to serve as a giant diplomatic and military pincer movement against the Soviet Union. The fact that the Germans wanted a pact that also targeted Britain was, for Tojo, a bonus insofar as Japan's undeclared war in China was being fought in the Yangtze River Valley stronghold of Britain's East Asia interests. Mention of an alliance that targeted Britain had, however, impinged directly on what the navy considered its prerogative. Thus, when Yonai stated that a German-Italian-Japanese alliance was dangerous because it courted the possibility of war against the Anglo-American powers, his voice was determining. And because the Japanese decision-making process required unanimity, there would be no strengthening of the Anti-Comintern Pact until Yonai or his ministerial successors changed their mind.

TOJO MIGHT IN OTHER circumstances have taken up the debate with Yonai's deputy and his opposite number, Vice Admiral Yamamoto Isoroku, the navy vice minister. Tojo found himself locked instead in argument with the vice chief of the General Staff, Tada Hayao. Tada, like Itagaki, boasted long experience in China. He had, in the early days and weeks after the Marco Polo Bridge Incident, joined with Ishiwara Kanji in arguing for nonescalation of the fighting and a localized resolution. He had opposed Konoe's *aite to sezu* proclamation and thereafter had fretted about the impossibility of extracting Japan from the China Incident in the absence of truce negotiations with Chiang's nationalist government. This concern had become, for Tada, all the more pressing following the Changkufeng Incident. Unlike Tojo, Tada was unenthusiastic about a strengthened Anti-Comintern Pact; he thought it important that Japan seek to end the China Incident by its own strength and on its own terms. He worried, moreover, about the danger of pursuing large-scale operations in Central China, leaving the Manchukuo-Soviet border exposed. He wanted a conclusion to the China Incident but was not convinced this was possible by force of arms alone. He wanted a softening of the *aite to sezu* policy, and he wanted truce negotiations.[36]

Against this backdrop, on August 22 the General Staff ordered an attack on the most populous and industrialized urban area on the central Yangtze River—namely, Wuhan's sister cities of Hankou, Hanyang, and Wuchang. This was an enormous operation that involved fourteen divisions from

Japan's Central China Area Army, five divisions from the Eleventh Army, four divisions from the Second Army, and an air corps. The attack aimed at Wuhan's capture, but—in a clear sign of the pessimism permeating the General Staff—there was no expectation of a decisive battle. The General Staff was, in other words, not convinced that this operation would compel Chiang to acknowledge the hopelessness of his situation. This reality left Tada and like-minded officers on the General Staff convinced of the need for peace negotiations, which would be most effective if they coincided with the capture of Wuhan.[37]

A gulf separated the Army Ministry and the General Staff. With Tojo leading the way, the Army Ministry was advocating an extremely hawkish position, while the General Staff, under the relatively dovish Tada, was a voice of relative moderation and caution. Itagaki became the unwitting prize. Tada called frequently on Itagaki in his office, habitually bypassing Tojo. An affronted Tojo was unsettled by the thought that the all-too-affable Itagaki might agree to a softening of China policy behind his back. He repeatedly insisted that the vice chief of staff must, as a matter of protocol, call on the vice minister and state his business before making his way to Itagaki's office. Tada showed no inclination to comply. He shared a breezy familiarity with Itagaki, which was partly attributable to the fact that both men traced their family origins to Iwate Prefecture (as did Tojo, but his personality did not lend itself to such easy relationships). Tada was, moreover, three years Tojo's senior, and one year Itagaki's senior, and was disinclined to follow the orders of a junior officer he regarded as disagreeable and unlikable. Tada also pointed out that, because Prince Kan'in remained atop the General Staff, many of the day-to-day tasks that ordinarily were the province of the chief of staff had devolved onto him and he was therefore higher in the pecking order than Tojo. None of these arguments made any impression on Tojo. He took the issue to Itagaki, who seemed conflicted and did nothing. This effectively left Tada, on his frequent visits to the Army Ministry building, free to continue to ignore an exasperated Tojo.[38]

Into this frayed atmosphere stepped Ishiwara Kanji. His relationship with Tojo's successor as Kwantung Army chief of staff, Lieutenant General Isogai Rensuke, had been little less fractious than his relationship with Tojo. His nervous disposition deteriorated precipitously, and he pleaded with Isogai to fire him. Isogai did not have such authority, but he did grant convalescent leave to Ishiwara, who then left for Tokyo.[39] He should have remained in Manchukuo, and Tojo insisted this was a breach of discipline that must not go unpunished. Tada defended Ishiwara, and Itagaki showed little inclination to discipline his onetime Manchurian conspirator in arms. In the ensuing weeks Tada and Tojo squabbled continuously over Ishiwara's fate.

Tojo's relationship with Itagaki also began to fray. Itagaki had agreed, in conversation with Privy Council President Hiranuma Kiichiro, to make available discretionary military funds to Iino Kichisaburo. Neither Hiranuma's nor Itagaki's intentions are clear, but Iino was a fortune teller and self-proclaimed holy man who some decades earlier had gained influence in aristocratic and military circles. Tojo looked down his nose at Iino, regarding him as a self-absorbed hack and peddler of magic tricks. Tojo was also affronted at what he regarded as a departure from proper procedure. He confronted Itagaki and insisted (correctly) that he, as vice minister, was responsible for all decisions concerning the military's discretionary budget. He undertook to make a one-off payment to Iino, but he was adamant in his refusal to agree to any future expense not first rigorously examined and investigated; he pointedly asked Itagaki to refrain from making any other promises that subverted due process. Itagaki did not enjoy the admonishment and began avoiding Tojo to the extent that he was able.[40]

THE ATTACK ON WUHAN was launched on October 26, 1938. The outcome was never really in question; when Wuhan fell on November 11, the Japanese controlled all of China's principal railways and waterways. Japan's Twenty-First Army had in the meantime landed at Bias Bay near Canton Province. It took Canton in little more than a week. The Japanese now controlled practically the entire Chinese coastline. There was nonetheless a problem: Chinese forces—as foreseen—had proved able to avoid a decisive battle against their better-armed, better-trained Japanese opponents. From his new stronghold in distant Chongqing in Sichuan Province, Chiang Kai-shek showed every intention of remaining in the fight.[41]

On November 3 Konoe proclaimed publicly Japan's efforts at establishing a new order in East Asia. According to Konoe, Japan sought the noble objectives of East Asian stability and a new era of cooperation among China, Japan, and Manchukuo. He spoke of other ideals informing Japanese conduct, including international justice, joint defense against communism, and the creation of a new culture. Most important, Konoe modified his *aite to sezu* declaration. He noted that Chiang's government had been reduced to a local regime and that Japan would, if necessary, crush it. China's nationalist government was welcome to participate in the new order only if it repudiated its anti-Japanese policies and improved the quality of its leadership.[42]

Konoe's new East Asian order proclamation prompted the military authorities in Tokyo to reconsider and reconceptualize Japanese Army policy. This necessitated bridging the gulf dividing the Army Ministry and the General Staff. To this end, Itagaki hosted a weeklong series of meetings in November that brought together the leadership of both offices. At this juncture, Itagaki sided with Tada's moderate standpoint, and the army now proved willing not only to consider dealing diplomatically with China's nationalist government but also to entertain the possibility of entering peace negotiations with Chiang Kai-shek himself.[43]

On conclusion of the week of meetings, army policy on ending the war centered on three key conditions: First, the Chinese nationalist government had to overturn its existing "anti-Japanese, procommunist policies" and commit to personnel changes to cement such a policy change. Second, the nationalist government had to cooperate with the various councils and governments the Japanese Army had fostered in occupied areas and must commit to the eventual establishment of a new central government. Third, the new central government, once established, had to normalize diplomatic relations with Japan. In an appended note, the army wrote of its willingness to negotiate with Chiang Kai-shek as long as he took "responsibility" for the war and resigned "immediately" thereafter.[44]

These terms and conditions ran directly counter to Tojo's counsel. He had argued since his arrival in Tokyo in June that Japan could not accept Chiang's continued leadership. Major Horiba Kazuo of the War Guidance Office confronted Tojo on precisely this point. If Japan refused to accept Chiang as leader, Horiba asked, with whom would Japan negotiate peace terms? And was not the question of national leadership properly a domestic issue for the Chinese themselves to decide? Such thinking infuriated Tojo, and he harangued not only Horiba but also Vice Chief of Staff Tada and Army Minister Itagaki. Ultimately, it fell on the Intelligence Bureau chief, Major General Higuchi Kiichiro, to "mediate." Higuchi suggested that an insistence on Chiang's resignation might best be added as a "supplementary" or "appended" term. Horiba added his own touch so that the "supplementary" term clarified Japan's insistence on Chiang's resignation while implying that Chiang might postpone the resignation indefinitely. Tojo exploded, insisting that the supplementary term instead clarify Japan's demand for Chiang's retirement "immediately" after truce negotiations. He got his way on this point, but the overall policy direction diverged sharply with Tojo's position.[45]

Tojo had lost the debate, but he showed an utter disinclination to fall into line. He shocked Itagaki and others with a public statement on November 28 in which he forecast a two-front war against China and the Soviet Union and warned also of continued deterioration in Japan's relationships with Britain and France. The Soviets were aiding the "Chiang regime" from the northwest, while the Franco-British powers were delivering aid via Southeast Asia (he noted that the United States was maintaining its "neutrality," and added his hope that it would continue to do so). Tojo said little more about the French, but he noted that Japan's continental policy was "rattling Britain's rights and interests in China" and posed a long-range threat to British colonies and possessions in Asia. He specifically mentioned Australia, India, and Singapore, and suggested none too obliquely that Japan was on a collision course with the British Empire.[46]

The British were, however, of considerably less interest to Tojo than were the Soviets. "The Soviet Union supports the Chiang regime, and is doing everything in its power to have him continue resisting Japan," Tojo stated. "It is thereby strengthening and expanding its own power in China. It is causing China to fall into extreme exhaustion and is, in this way, conniving to make [China into] a hotbed of Bolshevization." He added ominously that the Soviets were preparing for an "*inevitable* Japanese-Soviet clash in the near future": they were increasing their troop strength, industries, and railways in East Asia, and they were trying to ensure that Japan wasted its strength in a protracted war of attrition in China. Tojo even spoke of what he regarded as Moscow's intention to form a Sino-Soviet coalition before launching operations against Japan. As for Japanese policy, he echoed Konoe's words about a "construction of a new order in East Asia." Significantly, he added, "*Until we see the anti-Japanese Chiang regime annihilated,* we will without doubt be unable to quell the troops." He ended, "The army will conclude the current Incident, while preparing for a future *two-front war against China and the Soviet Union.*"[47]

Tojo's grandstanding infuriated Itagaki. Nothing in Tojo's public statement had directly contradicted the army's freshly minted policy position, but talk of the inevitability of a Japanese-Soviet war and the need to prepare for a two-front war on the continent seemed to suggest a major expansion of the current hostilities, even as the Japanese Army was searching for a way out of those hostilities. One biographer records Itagaki complaining bitterly about Tojo: "The fellow is like a bombshell. He sticks to his own ideas and forces them on others." Itagaki added for good measure that Tojo was an "obstinate chap" who preferred argument over "compromise."[48] Itagaki had, perhaps, missed Tojo's purpose, for Tojo was signaling his continued adherence to the hawkish opinions that had informed him throughout his time as vice minister. In so doing he was reminding the army's hard-liners that he remained their presumptive leader. This came at a price: Itagaki summoned Tojo to his office and demanded his vice ministerial resignation. Tojo declined to comply unless Tada were also forced to resign. This Itagaki refused to contemplate, and Tojo thus remained in his post.

THIS ALL COINCIDED WITH meetings in Shanghai between two Japanese Army officers and members of Chiang Kai-shek's Kuomintang. The negotiators reached agreement on Sino-Japanese peace terms, including joint defense against communism; China's recognition of Manchukuo; and prioritization of Japan's economic rights in China, with special consideration given in the development of North China's resources. The first term made provision for the stationing of Japanese troops in Inner Mongolia and in the Peking-Tianjin area in Hebei Province; all other troops would be withdrawn from China within two years of the restoration of peace. The negotiators also discussed the possibility of Chiang Kai-shek's deputy, Wang Jingwei, assuming nominal leadership of the nationalist government and entering peace negotiations with Japan.[49] This all seemed promising enough for the Army Ministry to appoint Lieutenant General Doihara Kenji—who had shared membership with Tojo in the Futaba Club and had long experience in behind-the-scenes Sino-Japanese political maneuvering—to assist in the "creation of a new central government" in China.[50]

These new policy directions were captured in a document, "Ni-Sshin shin kankei chosei hoshin" (Policy for the adjustment of new Sino-Japanese relations," that was discussed and ratified at the cabinet level and also at liaison conferences that brought together the cabinet and the Army and Navy General Staffs. An Imperial conference convened on November 30 at which the emperor offered his approval, albeit in a formulaic and predetermined manner, to this new effort at peace.[51]

Tojo fell in behind the new policy. Cabling the Central China Area Army and North China Area Army in early December, he wrote in reverential tones of the "Imperial sanction" the new policy had received and insisted that the "endgame of the holy war" was nigh. All that remained was for

Japan to maintain its "steadfast resolution." He sought to moderate any wilder ambitions that might exist, stating outright that the "permanent stationing of troops" in China was not necessary. As if to reinforce the point, he called for a "softened" attitude toward China. He now posited himself as a voice of moderation and Sino-Japanese amity, writing of the need to "avoid upsetting the [Chinese] people." He asked the field armies to ensure against a situation whereby the administrations and councils the Japanese Army had fostered in occupied areas led the way in opposing truce negotiations between the Japanese government and Wang.[52]

Tojo's about-face was stunning to behold. He now presented himself as positively dovish in his outlook on China, suddenly downplaying any role for the regional regimes across China he had hitherto championed. The fact that the emperor himself had sanctioned the peace maneuvers was, for Tojo, the game changer. Tojo had fallen in behind his emperor during the Changkufeng Incident; in late 1938 he again proved willing to forsake his own stance to follow his emperor's will as it related to China.

TOJO NONETHELESS PURSUED A vendetta against Itagaki and Tada. First, in early December he released another sensitive public statement on his own authority. This time he waded fearlessly into what was, for a soldier, the unfamiliar world of private capital and dividends. Sparking his involvement were newspaper reports quoting Finance Minister Ikeda Seihin as having disavowed any intention of restricting the profits a company might return to its shareholders. The army was not united on this issue, but Tojo and like-minded officers wanted to ensure that munitions industries retained sufficient capital to expand their production facilities if the need arose. This emphasis on each individual company's capital management meant that Tojo supported precisely what Ikeda had disavowed—namely, dividend limitations.[53]

The head of the Army Ministry's Media Division (and a key Tojo supporter), Lieutenant Colonel Sato Kenryo, took newspaper reports of Ikeda's statement to Tojo's office. He also took a statement he had drafted for media release that stated clearly and unequivocally, "The army wants dividend limitations." It linked dividend limitations with the "establishment of a wartime structure," an "urgent necessity" if Japan hoped ever to extricate itself from the China Incident. It ended with an appeal to higher motives and aspirations: "When front-line [troops] are marching forward while holding the remains [of their fallen brethren], moneymaking on the home front should not be tolerated."[54]

Tojo read both the newspaper reports and Sato's draft statement, and he questioned Sato: Would releasing the draft statement not open an irreversible divide between Ikeda and Itagaki? Would this cause the collapse of the Konoe cabinet? Had the newspapers represented Ikeda's words accurately? Would it not be simpler just to have Ikeda retract his statement? Sato remained adamant, and Tojo agreed on the spot to the draft statement's release. The statement cemented Tojo's status as the no-nonsense darling of the army's most hawkish elements. It also, unsurprisingly, infuriated Itagaki.[55]

Tojo's separation from the army leadership became complete when he used his vice ministerial authority over the *kenpei* (military police) and ordered the arrest of the Concordia Association's Asahara Kenzo. Tojo despised Asahara for his longtime role as a labor activist, but in December 1938 Tojo was less interested in Asahara's left-wing politics than he was in Asahara's close association with Ishiwara Kanji, as well as Itagaki and Tada. On Tojo's orders, on December 12 the *kenpei* ignored diplomatic convention, which stipulates that authorities of the host country may not enter the premises of a foreign diplomatic mission without express permission, and stormed the Manchukuo embassy to make the arrest.[56]

THE SO-CALLED ASAHARA INCIDENT WAS, for Itagaki, the last straw. He called Tojo into his office and once again demanded his resignation. Tojo again demanded Tada's figurative head on a platter and, this time, Itagaki was prepared to oblige him. He shifted Tada to command of the Third Army in Manchukuo and Tojo to the newly created position of inspector general of army aviation. Tada grumbled at what was essentially a demotion; Tojo came to relish his new role. For one thing, he had long been convinced of the airplane's essential role in modern warfare. In a Japanese Army pamphlet released in 1934, he had written, "The future of national defense is right in the sky."[57] He also came to recognize that his new role was, in fact, a step up from the vice ministerial role he had vacated. As inspector general he was responsible for all administrative, budgetary, operational, and educational issues pertaining to the army's air forces. He was, at least so far as the air forces were concerned, something akin to the minister, chief of staff, and inspector general of military training all rolled into one.

And, in a practice not dissimilar to that of the military's "big three," he reported directly to the emperor.

Tojo called almost immediately for a new set of operational guidelines. The existing guidelines read, "The main purpose of air operations is the quick destruction of the enemy's air power. However, depending on the circumstances, [air forces] may in a timely manner cooperate with ground forces or carry out political attacks." Like many of his military colleagues, Tojo was unhappy with these guidelines, which gave expression to a philosophy of an independent air force. He readily acknowledged that army aviation units ought necessarily to aim at "destruction of the enemy's air power," but he wanted a new set of guidelines that emphasized the links between air and ground operations. In particular, Tojo wanted clarification of the key point, whereby air units remained in conformity with the "requirements of the entire operation."[58] The new guidelines took a little more than twelve months to complete. They not only reflected Tojo's desire for the integration of an air fleet into existing military structures but also included his key point about conformity. He was indeed pleased, and presented the freshly minted guidelines to the emperor on February 24, 1940.[59]

TOJO WAS PARTICULARLY ENERGETIC in his efforts at expansion of the air fleet. As he put it to his subordinates, the expansion of Japan's air power was integral not only to attainment of Japan's objectives in its "holy war" in China but also to its ability to "sweep away all pending problems in East Asia." He acknowledged that "human and materials shortages" would be "serious," and called for redoubled efforts at overcoming all obstacles.[60]

This was no mean feat given that the undeclared war in China was soaking up the lion's share of the military budget. Tojo was too smart to waste his time and energy requesting more planes than the army could afford. Besides, he was a "total war" officer who had long since recognized that war preparation required vastly more than crash course mobilization programs. He therefore authored what might appropriately be called an expansion in depth program that focused less on planes than on enhancing the training of pilots and building the capacity of ground crews, enhancing an industrial base, and improving technologies, including aeronautical communications.[61]

Tojo was building an impressive record. This was due in no small part to his commitment to improving the army's air arm and thereby building the army's overall fighting capacity. He was also ambitious and regarded his role atop army aviation as a dress rehearsal for higher honors. He wanted to join the army's "big three." An opportunity would arise sooner, perhaps, than he expected.

The Konoe cabinet had resigned in mid-January 1939, after Konoe had lost hope in peace negotiations with China. Hiranuma Kiichiro led the next cabinet. Itagaki and Yonai continued to represent the armed services and continued to wrangle over the propriety of a German-Japanese military alliance. Itagaki became even more strident after the Kwantung Army provoked in May a bloody border war at Nomonhan with the Soviets, but Yonai held his ground and received able support from Foreign Minister Arita Hachiro. The Germans lost patience with what they regarded as Japanese foot-dragging, and on August 23—even as the border war at Nomonhan raged—they announced that they had concluded a nonaggression pact with the Soviet Union. The Germans and the Soviets proceeded to carve up Poland between them. The British and the French, fulfilling their solemn treaty promise to come to Poland's aid, declared war on Germany. The reverberations were also felt in Tokyo, where a stunned Hiranuma resigned as prime minister even as he professed an inability to comprehend European politics. Succeeding him was retired general Abe Nobuyuki.

The army recognized the need for a new cabinet-level representative. Itagaki had staked his reputation on a German-Japanese alliance that included the Soviet Union as a target. He could not possibly remain now that Germany had joined hands with the Soviets. On August 23, as soon as news of the German-Soviet pact had reached Tokyo, army officers one level beneath the "big three" met to discuss the issue of Itagaki's ministerial successor. Included in this meeting were Vice Chief of Staff Lieutenant General Nakajima Tetsuzo; the chief of the General Staff's General Affairs Bureau, Lieutenant General Kasahara Yukio; the vice minister, Lieutenant General Yamawaki Masataka; and the Personnel Bureau chief, Lieutenant General Iinuma Mamoru. The conclusion was unanimous: The army needed Tojo as its next minister.[62]

Discussion continued over the ensuing days. Tojo remained the clear choice of most officers in Tokyo; there was a sense that he was best able to lead the military in a rethinking of its policies. Itagaki, however, expressed concern lest Tojo as minister refuse to compromise with his contemporaries and get bogged down in endless arguments. Iinuma suggested Tada as a possible compromise candidate in the event that Tojo's appointment proved impossible. This appealed to Itagaki, who, on August 26, secured "big three" agreement to Tada as his ministerial successor.[63]

News of Tada's presumptive ministerial appointment shocked and dismayed Tojo's supporters. From Xinjing, the Kwantung Army demanded a rethinking of the situation. One officer in the Army Affairs Section was heard to shout, "We'll see blood over this!" The Tokyo provost marshal, Colonel Kato Hakujiro, foresaw a reemergence of the deadly factionalism that had been such a prominent feature of politics in the army in the early and mid-1930s.[64]

The emperor saved the Japanese Army from itself. He met on August 28 with Abe and ordered him to form a cabinet. He issued a raft of instructions, including that the cabinet must strictly uphold due constitutional process and must seek to regulate relations with the Anglo-American powers. He spoke of his long-standing "dissatisfaction" with the army and of the need to "enforce discipline." He insisted that, among the upper echelons, there were no "suitable" ministerial candidates other than General Hata Shunroku or Lieutenant General Umezu Yoshijiro. He dared the army's "big three" to disagree with him, stating that even if they named a different officer as candidate, he would ignore them and appoint either Hata or Umezu.[65] The army settled on Hata, who served in the short-lived Abe cabinet. Tojo remained as inspector general of army aviation, where he continued to raise the effectiveness and profile of the army's air arm, and where he stayed in full view of his supporters and allies among uniformed army officers.

TOJO HAD TAKEN ON the vice minister's role with a self-confidence bordering on bravado. He involved himself in all of the key debates, the vast majority of which revolved around Japan's aims and endgame in the China Incident. On all the key issues he relished the opportunity to stake out a hard-line position at sharp variance with that of other army leaders. In a continuation of policies he had championed while still with the Kwantung Army, he argued incessantly for independence for North China and Inner Mongolia. Tojo envisioned a future in which British influences, particularly, were expelled from the Yangtze River basin. He argued for a military alliance with Germany in the expectation that the alliance would coerce the Soviet Union and deter it from any move that might result in it fighting on two fronts against Germany and Japan. He consistently and angrily denounced so much as the notion of truce negotiations with Chiang Kai-shek. In so doing he burnished his reputation as the leading hawk in the army's upper echelons.

Only twice did Tojo change and soften his stance. In the first instance, he reined in his aggressive instincts and counseled a diplomatic solution to a small border war with the Soviet Union. He remained a picture of moderation even after the Soviets took the disputed territory at Changkufeng. In the second instance, he accepted the possibility of a post–China Incident future for Chiang Kai-shek. Specifically, he accepted an endgame of war strategy that centered on the merger of Chiang's Chongqing-based government with that of prominent defector and collaborationist Wang Jingwei. In each case, Tojo's softened stance owed to the express wishes of his emperor and Tojo's absolute fealty to him.

During his time as vice army minister, Tojo alienated himself from his contemporaries in the army's upper echelons. His immediate superior, Army Minister Itagaki Seishiro, sacked him amid complaints of his argumentative and obdurate ways. Shifted instead to the Inspectorate General of Army Aviation, Tojo cooled his heels for some eighteen months. He remained dutifully aloof from discussions of policy toward China and toward the outbreak of World War II in Europe, and focused his attentions almost solely on building the capacity of the army's air arm. In so doing he showcased his considerable administrative talent and established himself as a clear contender for the army minister's role. His entire career had prepared him for it, and he felt ready.

6 EMERGENCE AS ARMY MINISTER 1940

TOJO HIDEKI REMAINED AS inspector general of the Imperial Japanese Army's aviation unit in mid-January 1940, when the cabinet of Prime Minister Abe Nobuyuki collapsed amid disagreement and recriminations over the armed services' budget. The emperor took the unusual step of "recommending" that Admiral Yonai Mitsumasa be appointed prime minister.[1] Hata Shunroku, deferential to his emperor's wishes, stayed on as army minister. Tojo kept his counsel, although feelings ran particularly high among his supporters. Recalling Yonai's earlier standoffs with Itagaki Seishiro, they regarded Yonai as "antiarmy" and reciprocated with barely disguised "feelings of ill will" and even "repugnance" toward Yonai and his cabinet.[2] Tojo's supporters in the army charged Yonai with being an obstacle to the successful conclusion of the war in China, and they criticized his cabinet for what they regarded as its political weakness. The Yonai cabinet had, they charged, failed to unite the nation. They called for a "new political structure" that would repudiate Yonai's disinclination to act on the army's demands for national mobilization, and would instead support the military in its ongoing attempts at ending the war in China.[3]

Tojo remained silent on all of these matters, including Sino-Japanese peace. His sole focus, as was only right and proper for an officer in his position, was army aviation. He was nonetheless well aware of widespread confidence in the army concerning the prospects of peace with China. Some believed that when the army eventually brought down the Yonai cabinet, it did so at least partly to ensure that it did not get credit for reestablishing Sino-Japanese peace.[4] In March the army oversaw establishment of a new regime in Nanjing under Wang Jingwei's leadership, and army officers were hopeful it might merge with Chiang Kai-shek's nationalist government in Chongqing. What Tojo made of these maneuvers is undocumented.

Whatever Tojo's proclivities may have been, so-called Operation Kiri in March 1940 brought together Japanese officers as well as representatives from both Chongqing and Nanjing in covert, quasi-official negotiations in Hong Kong. This so heartened the army vice chief of staff, Lieutenant General Sawada Shigeru, that he reported on Operation Kiri to the emperor on March 15. Sawada explained that, in spite of contentious issues such as recognition of Manchukuo, all sides had agreed on an "outline of peace terms."[5] By late June the negotiators agreed that Itagaki (who had taken command of the China Expeditionary Army) would conduct ceasefire talks with both Chiang and Wang. The Japanese Army's leadership was so enthusiastic as to accept Chongqing's putative terms virtually in their entirety. Most important, peace would not be contingent on Chinese recognition of Manchukuo; this thorny issue would be set aside until after peace had been concluded. Nor would the Japanese Army insist on occupying tracts of China after the conclusion of peace; it would instead accept conclusion of a treaty of mutual assistance, signed between sovereign equals, which would allow for the stationing of Japanese troops in Inner Mongolia and North China. Vice Chief of Staff Sawada met with little opposition from within the army when, on June 24, he spoke of pursuing peace "as soon as possible" on such terms.[6]

Occurring alongside Operation Kiri was Adolf Hitler's blitzkrieg in Europe. In April–May 1940 the German Army overran Belgium, Denmark, Luxembourg, the Netherlands, and Norway with dizzying rapidity. France fell in early June, and most in Japan believed that Britain's time was nigh. The unflappable Yonai continued to insist on maintaining Japan's position of neutrality toward the European war.

Tojo's supporters and allies in the army were infuriated, ushering in the cry "Don't miss the bus!"[7] Their demands were twofold: Japan must ally itself militarily with Germany and Italy, and it must launch a forceful military advance into the suddenly defenseless colonial regions of Southeast Asia. The so-called southward advance appealed for two principal reasons. First, Southeast Asia abounded in oil, rubber, iron, tin, nickel, bauxite, and various other natural resources unavailable in the Japanese Empire but necessary if Japan were to construct a durable, self-sufficient system of national defense. Second, Anglo-American aid was reaching Chiang Kai-shek via Southeast Asia. A military advance into Southeast Asia—particularly French Indochina—would sever that supply route and would help convince Chiang that it was in his best interests to seek an end to the fighting. With a consensus fast emerging on these two points, the

Military Affairs Bureau's Military Affairs Section chief, Colonel Iwakuro Hideo, asked the Operations Bureau's Operations Section chief, Colonel Okada Juichi, whether the General Staff had prepared "operational plans for the capture of the Southern regions." The resulting plans, which were completed on June 25, forecast advances into French Indochina, Singapore, Thailand, and the oil-rich Dutch East Indies.[8]

By this time, army officers' dissatisfaction with Yonai had reached fever pitch. A cacophony of voices, with Tojo's supporters prominent among them, charged Yonai with a multitude of sins of both omission and commission. The Yonai cabinet was, Army Vice Minister Anami Korechika explained to the lord keeper of the Privy Seal, Kido Koichi, "extremely disadvantageous" so far as the "pursuit of talks with Germany and Italy" was concerned.[9] Yonai was also blocking the southward advance, and no new domestic political order seemed possible as long as he remained prime minister. In late June a revived and resuscitated Konoe Fumimaro asked the key question of the Military Affairs Bureau director, Lieutenant General Muto Akira, "Does the army intend to overthrow the [Yonai] cabinet?"[10]

Indeed it did. The army at this juncture dusted off a maneuver that General Uehara Yusaku had used during the Taisho political crisis. The army chief of staff, Prince Kan'in Kotohito, advised Hata on July 4 to resign from the "unenterprising and retrogressive" Yonai cabinet, which Hata did on July 16.[11] Yonai asked the army to name his ministerial successor, the army refused to comply, and because a cabinet could not function in the absence of a minister, it collapsed. Konoe presented as the only remotely suitable candidate to serve as Yonai's successor.[12]

All the while, the army's most hawkish officers agitated for Tojo's nomination as Hata's ministerial successor. They expected Tojo to help forge cabinet consensus on a German-Italian-Japanese military alliance, an advance into the suddenly defenseless and resource-rich colonial regions of Southeast Asia, and an improvement in Japan's strained relationship with the Soviet Union. There was also the expectation that Tojo would capitalize on the promise of Sino-Japanese peace. The most active pro-Tojo voices were Vice Minister Anami, Military Affairs Bureau Chief Muto, and Army Affairs Section Chief Iwakuro. The three men agreed on the need to ward off the possibility of the emperor again imposing on the military his choice as minister. This was something less than a vote of confidence in Hata as presiding minister and owed to a feeling that, at the highest counsels of state, the mild-mannered Hata was less forthright than he ought to be. Anami, Muto, and Iwakuro, wanted Tojo because he would, in their estimation, restore the army to what they regarded as its rightful, predominant position in the Japanese policymaking process. Tojo was, according to Anami, true to his nickname, the Razor: he cut through issues because he was able to "manage things without worrying about other people's feelings"; for that reason, he was "extremely good at getting things done."[13]

It was first necessary to convince Tojo himself to agree to take the post. In late June Anami asked Yamanaka Minetaro, a former army officer turned novelist and a close mutual friend, to approach Tojo about the position. But Tojo vehemently refused even to consider the post. He stated that, on the basis of what he had seen during his earlier stint as vice army minister, a ministerial post was fundamentally similar to the job of a "barmaid." He voiced a passionate disdain for the task of keeping all comers happy, avowed he had been "trained to command armies," and stated in no uncertain terms that a ministerial post meant nothing to him.[14]

This was Tojo at his typical, brusque best. It was also a performance. His protestations notwithstanding, Tojo was an intensely political officer. Yet the Meiji Emperor had, by means of the Imperial rescript to soldiers and sailors some six decades earlier, expressly forbidden uniformed officers from involving themselves in politics. This being the case, Tojo felt it unseemly to express interest in a ministerial post. In likening a ministerial job to that of a barmaid and insisting he was far more interested in commanding troops, Tojo was establishing his apolitical credentials. That being accomplished, he relented when Yamanaka approached him a second time about the position.[15]

Having secured Tojo's agreement to serve, Anami, Muto, and Iwakuro next sought the emperor's imprimatur. In late June Anami took news of the army's desire for Tojo to the lord keeper of the Privy Seal, Kido Koichi, who relayed to the emperor the army's intention to name Tojo its next minister. The emperor, however, reacted unfavorably. He told Kido that only those with significant command experience should be appointed army minister. He noted that Tojo had never even served as division commander, and he named General Nishio Toshizo, the commander in chief of the China Expeditionary Army, as his preferred ministerial candidate. Kido took the news to Anami on July 2.[16]

Anami, Muto, and Iwakuro had no intention of granting the emperor his wish. They wanted Tojo, and they impressed the imperative of his ministerial appointment on Hata. The outgoing minister agreed that Tojo was the logical choice.[17] On these grounds, Tojo made his debut as the "new minister"—in fact, if not yet in name—and on July 17 chaired a meeting of the Army Ministry's bureau directors. He opened the meeting by announcing that the army's 1941 budget would replicate that of the previous year, and he forbade profligate spending. He then made a seemingly simple statement: "The navy seems concerned about scrap iron and oil." He then added a question: "How about the army?"[18]

The chief of the Economic Mobilization Bureau, Major General Yamada Seiichi, answered. "Without US oil," he said, "our planes cannot fly." He then explained the military's intention to seek "resources" from Southeast Asia, one benefit of which would be an end to the nation's reliance on US oil. British colonies and possessions, including Burma, Hong Kong, Malaya, and Singapore, were the army's "first target," followed closely by the oil-rich Dutch East Indies. The Army General Staff and Army Ministry were, Yamada explained, agreed on the need for a forceful southward advance, even as the China Incident continued unabated. There was also agreement on the need to "adjust diplomatic relations" with the Soviet Union, the better to focus attention on Britain. Yamada raised the need for closer "cooperation with Germany and Italy" and spoke of broad agreement between the ministry and the general staff concerning efforts to "avoid friction" with the United States.[19]

Yamada spoke also of policy toward the Southeast Asian territories the Japanese Army intended to occupy. He stated that military rule should be imposed, and all occupied areas should be made "Japanese territory." The army would not support a laissez-faire approach to the occupied territories' development but would insist on its role as overseer of all development projects. As if to underscore such a role, Yamada clarified the army's intention to issue, throughout occupied territories, the same military scrip being used in southern China.[20]

Tojo said nothing. He was, of course, aware of the German Army's stunning successes in Europe, and during his time as inspector general of army aviation, he had not completely cordoned himself off from his service's fever-pitch excitement at the sudden defenselessness of European colonies in Southeast Asia. Tojo was hardly surprised at Yamada's enthusiasm for the southward advance, and he doubtless expected Yamada to identify the two most likely obstacles—the Soviet Union and the United States—standing between Japan and a forceful advance. Tojo could see as well as anyone that Japan could not undertake a southward advance while fighting China and at the same time entertain the possibility of war against the Soviet Union. Yamada had raised the most obvious solution, according to which Japan would follow in Germany's footsteps, shelve its ideological revulsion for the communist experiment, and seek to adjust relations with the Soviets. With regard to the United States, Yamada had asserted that Japan could advance forcefully into Southeast Asia without sparking a Japanese-US war. This was a succinct statement of the army's basic position.

Yet Tojo's statement regarding the Imperial Japanese Navy's concerns about oil and scrap iron indicates his awareness of the navy's different understanding of probable US responses to a Japanese southward advance. Whereas the army believed it should be possible to attack British positions in Southeast Asia without also inviting hostilities with the United States, the navy insisted instead on Anglo-American indivisibility. This interservice difference was substantial: So long as the United States remained aloof from any fighting, the distressed European powers were in no position to slow—much less stop—a forceful Japanese southward advance. Yet if the advance so provoked the United States that it embargoed commodities like oil and scrap iron or even entered the hostilities, then the prospects of a successful Japanese advance into Southeast Asia became far less certain. The possibility of war against the United States had fueled the Japanese Navy's expansion programs since the early aftermath of the Russo-Japanese War of 1904–1905, and some in the army seethed at what they believed was the navy's double game: citing the possibility of war against the United States to secure materiel and budget but also to warn against an overly ambitious agenda in the Pacific Ocean region. The issue was a vexing one, and Tojo during his debut ministerial performance chose against making any grand pronouncements about possible solutions.[21]

THE JAPANESE ARMY HAD still to overcome the emperor's leeriness of Tojo. Hata's last task as army minister was to ensure that the emperor, whether he liked it or not, at least acquiesced in the choice of Tojo. This Hata did in his final ministerial report to the emperor on July 18. Ostensibly, Hata wanted to explain the reasons for his resignation, which had brought down the Yonai cabinet. That alone was quite the task, for the emperor had not taken kindly to the treatment afforded his handpicked prime minister. Yet Hata was informed by a second objective: He took care to tell the emperor that Tojo would succeed him as army minister (and that Yamashita Tomoyuki would replace Tojo as inspector general of army aviation). In so doing Hata overstepped his ministerial prerogatives. Convention placed responsibility for reporting ministerial appointments to the emperor on the shoulders not of an outgoing minister but instead of the incoming prime minister. The emperor rebuked Hata for the indiscretion, promptly summoned Lord Keeper of the Privy Seal Kido Koichi, and relayed his displeasure with the army for having dispensed with convention. Hirohito then summoned his chief aide-de-camp, Hasunuma Shigeru, and told him that Hata's actions must not create a "precedent."[22]

Hirohito's reaction was at least partly attributable to his penchant for following established practice. Doubtless he was annoyed at Hata for having shown contempt for the prime minister's office and its prerogatives. It also seems possible that mention of Yamashita Tomoyuki as inspector general of army aviation provoked a stronger reaction than might otherwise have been the case, for Hirohito's distrust of Yamashita had been visceral ever since the latter's involvement in the failed coup d'état of February 26, 1936. Above all, however, the emperor's rigid adherence to convention should be understood as a frustrated reaction to the army's attempt at outmaneuvering him: Hata's report was official and formal, which so constrained the emperor that he felt unable to insist on his own preference for army minister. The Army General Staff now regarded Tojo's ministerial appointment as a "fait accompli."[23] The army had not only toppled the emperor's handpicked prime minister but had foisted on him a soldier he did not want as army minister.

Tojo had in the meantime departed Tokyo for a monthlong tour of the continent. He was inspecting Kwantung Army air installations, which he had championed as inspector general of army aviation. The tour had the added bonus of removing him from Tokyo, thereby freeing him from at least the appearance of complicity in the machinations surrounding his ministerial nomination. After Hata emerged from his fateful audience with the emperor, he ordered Tojo to cut short his inspection tour. Tojo departed immediately, but bad weather grounded him in Heijo (present-day Pyongyang) and he only reached Tokyo at 9:40 p.m. on July 18. He proceeded directly to the army minister's residence, where he learned officially that he was the army's choice to represent it in the next cabinet. His colleagues—in reference not only to the inclement weather he had encountered on his flight but also the lightning campaign he had led in Inner Mongolia following the outbreak of war against China, as well as the expectation that he would ensure an alliance with the proponents of lightning warfare in Germany—dubbed him the Lightning-Strike Minister.[24]

One of Tojo's first calls of business was a meeting Konoe had arranged in his capacity as incoming prime minister. This was the so-called four pillars conference that brought together the four most important members of the incoming cabinet, including the prime minister and the army, navy, and foreign ministers. Known also as the Ogikubo Conference, after Konoe's summer residence in Ogikubo, it was Konoe's attempt at forging a meeting of minds even before his cabinet had been inaugurated.[25]

Tojo traveled to Ogikubo in the knowledge that Konoe had already aligned himself with the army's agenda. The Military Affairs Bureau director, Muto Akira, a key Tojo supporter, had a day or two earlier shared with Konoe an army document bearing the presumptuous title "Sogo kokusaku kihon yoko" (Fundamental outline of overall national policy). It prioritized prompt resolution of the war in China, establishment of a Sino-Japanese-Manchukuoan economic bloc, construction of a "new order" across East and Southeast Asia, and a tripartite German-Italian-Japanese alliance. Domestically, the outline prioritized establishment of a "national security system" that would harness Japan's "entire national strength," as well as a "powerful political structure" to unite "officials and the people." In conversation with Muto, Konoe had indicated his agreement with the army's agenda, and Muto had offered Konoe the army's "complete cooperation."[26]

Tojo could also be reasonably confident about incoming foreign minister Matsuoka Yosuke. We have seen that Tojo and Matsuoka had worked together as members of the *ni-ki san-suke* (two -ki and three -suke) group in Manchukuo; Matsuoka's stint with the South Manchurian Railway had forged in him a continent-centric vision of the Japanese Empire that aligned reasonably neatly with that of most army officers. In July 1940 Matsuoka also maintained unshakable confidence in a total German victory in Europe, and he regarded the resource-rich colonial regions of Southeast Asia as ripe for Japan's picking. Possessed of an abrasive personality, Matsuoka owed his presumptive ministerial position to Konoe's belief that he could wrest control of foreign policy from the armed services. Matsuoka also shared a curious similarity with Tojo: The emperor did not want him in the cabinet. Hirohito had twice conveyed to Konoe his mistrust of Matsuoka, but Konoe, in a rare act of decisiveness, refused to give ground and clung to his choice of Matsuoka as foreign minister.[27]

Tojo knew relatively little about the fourth pillar at Ogikubo. Yoshida Zengo was a vice admiral who had served as navy minister in the Abe and Yonai cabinets. He had supported both cabinets' policies and seemed to possess an outlook fundamentally similar to that of Yonai. Yet the stunning success of the German blitzkrieg had captivated the Japanese Navy's lower and middle echelons, and they were little less enthusiastic about a southward advance and a German-Italian-Japanese military alliance than were Tojo's subordinates in the army. Whether Yoshida would seek to restrain his subordinates, or whether he would champion their hard-line stance, remained uncertain. Tojo probably did not overthink it, but he almost certainly looked forward with heightened curiosity to Yoshida's policy stance.

At the Ogikubo Conference, Konoe spoke to notes Matsuoka had prepared in advance. He opened with mention of the war in China and the need to put the Japanese economy on a war footing. Konoe also raised the "new world situation" brought about by the German blitzkrieg, as well as the perceived need for a timely response. He spoke of the opportunity that now presented itself: Japan could incorporate Southeast Asia into a "new East Asian order." Konoe made clear that any effort to this end required "strengthening of the Japanese-German-Italian axis," as well as a nonaggression pact with the Soviet Union.[28]

Konoe outlined a way out of the wearying war in China. A move into Southeast Asia would cut the routes by which the Anglo-American powers

The Ogikubo Conference, July 19, 1940. Seated, from left to right, are the so-called four pillars—namely Konoe Fumimaro, Matsuoka Yosuke, Yoshida Zengo, and Tojo.

were aiding Chiang Kai-shek. This, combined with continuing military operations in China and the government's aid to defector Wang Jingwei, should cause Chiang's government in Chongqing to lose morale and compel it to seek peace. Konoe pointed out that Chiang need only agree to Japan's terms of a "joint East Asian defense" and an "East Asian economic bloc," commit to no future wars against Japan, and coalesce in the merger of his government with that of Wang in Nanjing.[29]

Konoe spoke next about policy toward the United States. He predicated his remarks on the notion that Japan ought to avoid an "unnecessary clash" with the United States, but he also made clear that Japanese-US relations must proceed on Japanese terms. Most important, there should be no compromise regarding Japan's new East Asian order. Konoe acknowledged that such a policy courted the possibility of "forceful [US] intervention," but was steadfast in the conviction that Japan must "press ahead . . without consideration" for US policy.[30]

Konoe also spoke extemporaneously during the Ogikubo Conference. Tojo later recalled that Konoe placed particular emphasis on the need for "coordination between the government and the Supreme Command," for "army-navy harmony," and for military preparedness. These off-the-cuff remarks, no less than the prepared notes, fit neatly with army policy. Tojo said very little at the Ogikubo Conference; for the most part he sat, listened, and nodded.[31]

It later became apparent that the conferees took a very different set of understandings away from the conference. Tojo was convinced that agreement had been reached on a specific policy program, with a German-Italian-Japanese military alliance at its core. Yoshida begged to differ. He argued that he had agreed not to a military alliance but to strengthened relations with Germany and Italy. The difference, he insisted, was crucial. Besides, he argued that the conference was something of a "half measure": No notetakers had been present and no conferees signed off on any meeting record. He added, for good measure, that the Ogikubo Conference predated the cabinet's inauguration and conferees therefore spoke not with ministerial authority and responsibility but instead as individuals.[32]

THE TOJO-YOSHIDA SPLIT WAS yet to emerge when, at approximately 9:00 p.m. on July 22, 1940, Tojo took the short car ride from the Army Ministry in Tokyo's Ichigaya Ward to the Imperial Palace. This was his first audience as incoming army minister with the Showa Emperor. Immediately thereafter, he was scheduled to join his new cabinet colleagues, including Konoe, Matsuoka, and Yoshida, in an Imperial investiture ceremony in the palace's Phoenix Hall.[33]

Tojo eagerly anticipated the audience with the emperor. We have already encountered Tojo's fealty to his emperor; now, as minister, he spoke of the emperor as a "deity" and admonished his subordinates to contrast the emperor's "luster" with the dull ordinariness of his "vassals" (Tojo included).[34] We have also seen the various occasions—most recently as inspector general of army aviation—on which Tojo had already reported to the emperor. But now charged with reporting on matters of truly national import, he was genuinely excited at the prospect of fulfilling his constitutionally defined ministerial prerogative of giving "advice" to the emperor on all army-related matters.[35]

The meeting was no less notable for the Showa Emperor. He was, of course, well accustomed to meeting with new ministerial appointments, and he granted frequent audiences to uniformed army and navy officers. Indeed, he had granted Tojo an audience in the Imperial Library as recently as April 3, 1940.[36] The emperor's meeting with Tojo on July 22 was, however, far from formulaic. He had resolved to raise with Tojo his complete disenchantment with the army. When Tojo entered the Imperial Library, the emperor opened the conversation by speaking of his "distress" at the army's recent actions. The army was, he said, responsible for an ever-increasing number of "disgraceful incidents." It had "violated imperial instructions" and "sullied Our nation's history." He demanded that Tojo "look carefully into the causes" of the service's most recent indiscretions and "sweep away the root cause of the [Army] Ministry's evil."[37]

Tojo's reaction to these stinging words is not recorded anywhere. It certainly would have been out of character for him to remonstrate. It was doubtless not what Tojo had hoped for or envisioned, but it might reasonably be postulated that he sat in stunned silence for most of his first ministerial audience, giving careful thought to how he would act on his emperor's will and repair his service's relationship with its sovereign.

Before attending to the army-emperor relationship, Tojo had first to participate in policy discussions with his ministerial colleagues. Beginning on July 23, the cabinet met for three straight days to discuss basic policy. Satisfied that the Ogikubo Conference had already set the tone, Tojo contributed to the discussion in only general terms. For one thing, he spoke of the propriety of foreign policies that conformed with the "spirit" of *hakko ichiu* (eight corners of the world under one roof). In so doing he reprised a term from the eighth-century *Nihon shoki* (Chronicles of Japan), which, as Tojo himself understood it, stressed the emperor's integral role in "spreading virtue throughout the four seas and holding to virtue in relations with other countries." Tojo was, in effect, calling for the conceptualization and articulation of a distinctly Japanese and emperor-centric approach to world affairs. He also insisted on the imperative of Sino-Japanese-Manchukuoan unity, the "construction of Greater East Asia," and the establishment of a "national defense state."[38] These discussions and Tojo's contributions yielded a policy statement, "Kihon kokusaku yoko" (The main principles of basic national policy), which the cabinet approved on July 26. It was short on details, but it affirmed the cabinet's commitment to Tojo's contributions, including *hakko ichiu*. It also prioritized settlement of the war in China, reform of internal administrative structures, creation of a new political structure, and establishment of a planned economy.[39]

A liaison conference, which brought together the cabinet and the Army and Navy General Staffs, convened the following day, July 27; it approved another policy statement, titled "Sekai josei no suii ni tomonau jikyoku shori yoko" (Outline of the main principles for coping with the changing world situation). Tabled by the Supreme Command, this document had first been drafted in early July by middle-ranking Army General Staff officers, and had been revised following discussion and debate with the Navy General Staff. The document began from the basic premise that Britain would soon surrender to Germany, and it affirmed the government's pursuit of a strengthened relationship with Germany and Italy. It reiterated the government's determination to resolve the war in China and to take advantage of the war in Europe by launching the southward advance. In a departure from previous policy, it anticipated a southward advance—by force, if necessary—even if the war in China remained unresolved. Indeed, it made clear that the southward advance would facilitate an end to the war in China insofar as it would shut off the supply routes by which the Anglo-American powers were aiding Chinese nationalist leader Chiang Kai-shek. To facilitate the southward advance, it spelled out the need for a radically improved relationship with the Soviet Union. It also, at the Japanese Navy's insistence, acknowledged that the southward advance would in all likelihood have a deleterious impact on Japan's relationship with the United States and expressed preparedness for such an eventuality.[40]

Tojo emerged from this liaison conference and proceeded directly to Meiji Shrine and then Yasukuni Shrine. In what would become at least a weekly practice throughout his time as minister, he performed his ritual ablutions, prayed, and made offerings at each shrine. He then returned to the Army Ministry and briefed his subordinates. "We have decided on the 'main principles of basic national policy,'" he said, "and the Supreme Command's basic treatment of the [China] incident has also been decided." The cabinet and the Supreme Command were now, he declared, "united" behind fundamental policy. Only the "details" of the policy's "implementation" still needed to be determined.[41]

Satisfied with the Konoe cabinet's policy agenda, Tojo turned his attention to repairing the army's relationship with the emperor. In his estimation, this involved the reimposition of discipline and, to this end, he issued a jarring set of orders to his subordinates. No officer attached to the Army Ministry would henceforth be permitted "any speech or behavior" of a political nature in "private or public."[42] This, at a stroke, quashed the considerable freedom officers had enjoyed under Tojo's predecessors. Indeed, it guarded against precisely the kind of political maneuvering that had given rise to Tojo's own ministerial appointment. It also greatly empowered Tojo insofar as it ensured that he alone—rather than multiple subordinates each pulling in his own direction—would henceforth represent the army in the decision-making process.

A relaxed Tojo in the army minister's official residence soon after the army named him as its next cabinet-level representative, July 1940.

This is not to say that Tojo sought to stifle debate within the Army Ministry. Indeed, he readily conceded the importance of the free flow of information "up and down the chain of command." Yet, even here, he set limits: He forbade criticism of decisions already taken and identified "further debate of matters which have already been decided by superiors" as the "root of the evil of administrative retardation." Such practice, he avowed, must be "swept away." He also moved to prohibit *gekokujo* (insubordination). The importance of "obeying orders," he wrote, must not be undermined by unsanctioned actions undertaken in the guise of the "demands of the times." In return, and in a nod to his newly coined nickname, Lightning-Strike Minister, Tojo vowed fidelity to the concept of "lightning-strike management," which he defined as a policymaking process that did not "miss the opportunity" afforded by this "watershed moment" in world affairs.[43]

TOJO HAD IN THE meantime confronted the possibility of Operation Kiri shifting from quasi-official to official status. The operation's interlocutors agreed on July 22—the day of the second Konoe cabinet's inauguration—that Tojo's old boss, the China Expeditionary Army chief of staff, Lieutenant General Itagaki Seishiro, would meet in early August with T. L. Soong, a brother of the prominent Chinese nationalist politician (and Chiang Kai-shek's brother-in-law) T. V. Soong. The idea was that the two men would meet against the backdrop of a mutually agreed ceasefire to formally discuss the same peace terms that had been the subject of Operation Kiri's monthslong quasi-official and exploratory discussions.[44] The Army General Staff was eager to seize the opportunity and sought to appoint Itagaki to the conference as an Army General Staff representative. Tojo balked. He was concerned that the talks might go nowhere, and he wondered whether Chiang's government in Chongqing was engaging in this peace maneuver primarily to slow any moves Japan might make to recognize Wang's regime formally. He did not argue against the proposed meeting with T. L. Soong, but he did insist that Itagaki represent only the China Expeditionary Army.[45]

Tojo was no fan of Operation Kiri, and he made his displeasure with it readily apparent in the ensuing days. He argued that Itagaki, in his conversations with Soong, ought to present specific and unwavering peace terms. In so doing Tojo placed himself in direct opposition to the Army General Staff, which argued for terms that were broad, general, and elastic and which in staff officers' estimation should hopefully allow for sensible compromises. The issue of China's recognition of Manchukuo was a particular sticking point: The Army General Staff related its contentment with a statement from Chiang indicating a willingness to recognize Manchukuo at some indeterminate point in the future; Tojo insisted instead that Chiang must commit in clear and unambiguous language to recognizing Manchukuo after the conclusion of Sino-Japanese peace.[46] On July 30 Tojo delivered what was perhaps the clearest indicator of his leeriness toward Operation Kiri: He severely upbraided one of its principal Japanese participants, Colonel Imai Takeo, demanding to know "who in their right mind" had allowed such indeterminate talks.[47]

In early August Tojo executed a neat about-face. His reasons for doing so are not readily apparent. It is possible—but exceedingly unlikely—that he discovered within himself an otherwise uncharacteristic willingness to forsake his own stance in the interest of forging consensus within the Imperial Army. Infinitely more convincing is the likelihood that Tojo had become aware of his emperor's enthusiasm for Operation Kiri. The emperor had, on the eve of Tojo's ministerial appointment, spoken of the operation as "very promising," and he spoke in late July of his "high expectations" for it. When the emperor left Tokyo in early August for a tour of the Kure Naval District, he asked Chief Aide-de-Camp Hasunuma Shigeru to remain in Tokyo, precisely so he could remain in close contact with the army's political and operational nerve center regarding Operation Kiri.[48]

Tojo now softened his stance. On August 2 he allowed that some ambiguous phraseology regarding recognition of Manchukuo might serve the interests of peace. It helped that Military Affairs Bureau director Muto Akira offered reassurances about a way forward that relied on neither Chiang's goodwill nor his trustworthiness. According to Muto, Japan should assist with the establishment of such mechanisms as a Sino-Manchukuoan weather exchange bureau, which would normalize mundane (but necessary) contacts between China and Manchukuo and lead inexorably to China's eventual recognition of Manchukuo as an independent state.[49]

ALL THE WHILE, TOJO was encountering his share of difficulties over French Indochina. It certainly presented itself as an opportunity, for France had surrendered to Germany in mid-June, and its Southeast Asian colony now seemed (to borrow the phraseology of the time) like a low-hanging, overly ripe persimmon, waiting to be plucked from the tree. In accord with such thinking, the Army General Staff had been clamoring since late June to station troops in northern Indochina, whether the French authorities agreed or not.[50] Japan's South China Area Army, even more belligerent, was spoiling for a "military invasion."[51]

Tojo was satisfied that Japan ought to capitalize on France's distress and launch an Indochinese advance. His almost instinctive opportunism was, however, tempered by the will of his emperor. From the moment of France's fall, the emperor had insisted that the armed services not engage in "Machiavellian maneuvers like Frederick the Great, or Napoleon" toward French Indochina.[52] The ever-obedient Tojo was determined to give the emperor precisely what he wanted while at the same time delivering on an Indochinese advance. It would be a balancing act, but he would have to restrain the army's most bullish elements and ensure that the advance proceeded peacefully.

Tojo arranged for a July 29 meeting that brought together officers from the Army General Staff and the Army Ministry. He forbade his subordinates from agreeing to anything in French Indochina but diplomatic negotiations. Given the militancy of the General Staff, Tojo's instructions precluded any "coordination" of views, and attempts at uniting the Army Ministry and the General Staff over the ensuing days resulted only in "chaos." The General Staff's Operations Division, headed by the notoriously hawkish Major General Tominaga Kyoji, sought to break the deadlock and on August 8 spoke with Tojo as well as Muto and Iwakuro. To Tojo's likely chagrin, not only Indochina but also Hong Kong came under discussion. This doubtless reminded Tojo—if indeed he needed reminding—that the Army General Staff not only sought to cut off the Indochinese supply route by which the Anglo-American nations were aiding Chiang Kai-shek but also regarded Indochina as the first step in a much broader southward advance. Tojo did not disagree with this, but he was focused on northern Indochina and refused to accept the Operations Division's representations. General Staff officers again bemoaned the "chaos" Tojo's stance on the Indochinese issue was causing.[53]

Matsuoka had in the meantime opened negotiations with French Ambassador Charles Arsène-Henry. He reported on August 6 to his cabinet colleagues, including Tojo, concerning the threefold demand he had made of Arsène-Henry: the right of passage for Japanese forces through Indochina, the Japanese armed services' use of Indochina's airports,; and the right to provision Japanese forces on or near the Sino-Indochinese border. Notably, Matsuoka had refused to grant the sole concession the

French sought—namely, a guarantee of French Indochina's territorial integrity.[54] Tojo recognized that Matsuoka's negotiating position differed little, if at all, from the demands of even the aggressive South China Area Army. This held out the hope that diplomacy might deliver practically everything for which military officers might hope in Indochina. At issue, then, was not Japan's objectives in Indochina but instead the means by which those objectives might be attained. On August 6 Tojo reported to his subordinates in the Army Ministry and insisted on the pursuit of diplomatic negotiation.[55]

The divide between the Army General Staff and the Army Ministry nonetheless remained, and the issue of troop numbers only widened the gap. On August 10 the Army General Staff insisted that a twenty-thousand-man Imperial Guard division advance into Indochina. On Tojo's strict instructions, the Army Ministry stood adamantly opposed. It estimated the cost of maintaining such a division in Indochina to be 200 million yen annually, a prohibitively high cost. The General Staff suggested that Japan could capitalize on French distress and "borrow" the money from France. Tojo would have none of it. Insisting that "we must think not only of French Indochina," he admonished the General Staff to remain mindful of how the Indochinese advance would impact Japan's subsequent advance into other Southeast Asian colonies; he was particularly mindful of the oil-rich Dutch East Indies. In line with such thinking, Tojo demanded of the Army General Staff the minimum number of troops to be stationed in Indochina. He got his way. The Army General Staff conceded on August 12 that the twenty-thousand-man Imperial Guard Division could be stationed not in Indochina proper but on the Japanese-occupied island of Hainan. It moreover allowed that only three battalions, totaling thirty-three hundred men, need be stationed in Indochina proper.[56]

Matsuoka met again with Arsène-Henry on August 15. He continued to press Japan's demands and continued to ignore France's desire for a guarantee of Indochina's territorial integrity, but he made no headway.[57] He now urged the armed services to consider measures toward Indochina in the event that French authorities refused to accede to Japan's demands.[58] That complicated Tojo's efforts at ensuring the Japanese Army's acceptance of diplomacy vis-à-vis Indochina and also reopened the divide between the Army General Staff and the Army Ministry. General Staff officers now complained that diplomacy was causing a "delay" in Indochina that was "most unfavorably" impacting efforts at ending the war in China. That same day, the Chief of Staff, Prince Kan'in, approached Tojo and demanded an

August 20 deadline on diplomatic negotiations.[59] Tojo refused, insisting instead that Matsuoka soften his negotiating position and offer concrete details concerning troop numbers in Indochina. Tojo again got his way. His ministerial subordinates met the following day with their counterparts from the Army and Navy General Staffs and the Navy Ministry. They agreed that Matsuoka ought to affirm "France's suzerain rights in Indochina" and French Indochina's "territorial integrity." They limited the number of French Indochinese airports Japanese field officers would use, the number of Japanese troops required to guard those airports, and the Indochinese passageways Japanese forces would use.[60] This was all far more concrete than the information Matsuoka had hitherto received from the armed services and, notably, it served to delimit Japan's objectives in Indochina. On August 20 Arsène-Henry indicated French preparedness to consider Japan's demands.[61]

This might, in other circumstances, have been cause for celebration in the army. Yet the divide between the Army General Staff and the Army Ministry was deep. The General Staff noted that the French were yet to accede to any of Japan's demands and bemoaned the fact that it would "again" be necessary to outline those demands. At this juncture, two of Tojo's trusted subordinates—Lieutenant Colonels Nishiura Susumu and Nagai Yatsuji—spoke again of the cost of maintaining troops in Indochina. This enraged General Staff officers, who shuddered at this mention of money and denounced Nishiura and Nagai as "whores."[62]

THE DIVISION BETWEEN THE Army General Staff and the Army Ministry was only one issue confronting Tojo. He had also to contend with the Japanese Army's fraught relationship with its sister service, the Japanese Navy. Predictably enough, the issue of a German-Italian-Japanese military alliance was at issue. All had seemed well in early August, when Tojo's subordinates in the Army Ministry contributed to a joint army-navy draft alliance that took Britain as its target.[63]

Navy Minister Yoshida seems not, however, to have been consulted by his subordinates who participated in this process. He continued to oppose the alliance. The tipping point came on August 24 in the form of a cable from Japan's ambassador in Berlin, Kurusu Saburo. It announced that German Ambassador Heinrich Stahmer had left for Tokyo with the intention of negotiating—and concluding—a German-Italian-Japanese military alliance.[64] Yoshida remained steadfast in his refusal to countenance the alliance on the grounds that it would practically ensure US enmity. His stance confused and irritated Tojo. On one occasion, Tojo confronted Yoshida, brandished a set of notes he had made in the immediate aftermath of the Ogikubo Conference, and asked what had happened to the agreements the four so-called pillars had reached. Nowhere is Yoshida's response recorded; it nonetheless seems likely that he explained, for Tojo's benefit, the difference between strengthened political ties to which he had agreed and an alliance to which, he maintained, he had not agreed.[65] The interservice unity that seemed so readily forthcoming at the outset of the Konoe cabinet was already straining. Army officers began grumbling at the perceived need to "revise" the Konoe cabinet's fundamental policies and took to referring to Yoshida as "the navy minister who will not progress negotiations with Germany and Italy."[66]

Most army officers regarded the German alliance and the southward advance as two sides of the same coin. For them, Yoshida's insistence on nothing more than strengthened political ties with Germany called into question the Japanese Navy's commitment to the southward advance. Tojo's position was more nuanced. He and Yoshida were at odds over the issue of a German alliance, yet they were in basic agreement on the need to advance only peacefully into French Indochina. Yoshida, for his part, felt that Tojo's position on the German alliance was driven by the militancy of the Army General Staff. To try and bridge the gap between him and Tojo and between the two ministries and the Army and Navy General Staffs, he booked a table on August 29 at the famed Meiji-era restaurant Hoshigaoka Saryo. Also invited were the army chief of staff, Prince Kan'in Kotohito, and the navy chief of staff, Prince Fushimi Hiroyasu.[67]

In preparation for the meeting, Army and Navy General Staff officers met on August 27. The army officers wanted to know whether the navy's position had changed in the weeks since inauguration of the Konoe cabinet, and they wanted the navy to explain its basic stance on "resolution of the southern problem." Navy officers, in response, insisted on the consistency of their position. The southward advance should proceed "so far as possible, by peaceful means," and that any "decision to use force" in Southeast Asia required "extreme prudence." They continued to argue that a forceful southward advance raised the distinct possibility of US entry into the war, and they offered a forthright appraisal of the "chances of success" should this eventuate. They related their "confidence" in victory in the event the US Navy sought a decisive naval battle sometime soon after the outbreak of hostilities. They nonetheless acknowledged that the

United States would, in all likelihood, seek instead to fight a protracted war of attrition. Should this eventuate, the navy officers had "little confidence" in victory.[68]

Tojo, Yoshida, and Princes Fushimi and Kan'in met, as planned, on August 29. Difficult discussions were altogether avoided, and the conversation went little further than an exchange of pleasantries.[69] Yoshida's failing health provides the most likely explanation for this curious outcome. The strain of standing almost alone in his opposition to a German alliance had quite literally broken him. At the cabinet level he faced immense pressure not only from Tojo but also from Konoe and the garrulous Matsuoka. He had also to contend with his hawkish subordinates in the Japanese Navy. On the Navy General Staff, the notoriously pro-German Prince Fushimi assisted him little, if at all.[70] Yoshida's subordinates in late August were commenting about the extent to which Yoshida seemed incapacitated by "ill humor."[71] The isolated and harassed navy minister made his final stand on September 2, refusing to consent to a Foreign Ministry document, "Gunji domei kosho ni kansuru yoko" (Draft policy concerning negotiations for a military alliance), that ratcheted up the pressure on Yoshida insofar as it proposed to make not Britain but the United States the alliance's chief target.[72] Yoshida was hospitalized the following day, having suffered a debilitating physical and nervous breakdown.[73]

Even as Tojo sought to wear down Yoshida's resistance to a German-Italian-Japanese military alliance, he continued in his newfound, emperor-inspired enthusiasm for Operation Kiri. He seemed undeterred by the fact that the proposed conference between Itagaki and T. L. Soong, which was originally scheduled for early August had been indefinitely postponed. On August 13 he permitted Muto Akira to report on Operation Kiri to Foreign Minister Matsuoka. This was a step that would have seemed superfluous and even ridiculous had Tojo been anything less than guardedly optimistic about the operation's prospects for success.[74]

Tojo next received reports about Operation Kiri on August 21. Chongqing had raised the stakes by insisting that the Itagaki-Soong conference and simultaneous ceasefire could go ahead only if Japan revoked Konoe's *aite to sezu* (no deals with [the nationalist government]) pronouncement, which clarified his refusal to deal with Chiang. Chonqing also insisted that Japan must abrogate its existing agreements with Wang Jingwei. Tojo joined with Vice Chief of Staff Sawada to craft the army's response. They noted, for one thing, that Konoe's new East Asian order pronouncement of November 1938 had overturned his earlier *aite to sezu* pronouncement insofar as it specified Tokyo's willingness to "deal with Chongqing." Tojo and Sawada specified that Japan had concluded not treaties but merely "agreements" with Wang. They insisted that these agreements need not impede forthcoming "formal negotiations" between the Japanese government, Chiang's government in Chongqing, and Wang's government in Nanjing. Sawada's and Tojo's subordinates then drafted a conciliatory message for Chiang, which Tojo himself took to Konoe for his signature. (A separate letter from Itagaki to Chiang was also prepared.) Tojo and his subordinates now hoped that an Itagaki-Soong conference would take place in late September. Those hopes seemed realistic when a key Operation Kiri figure, Lieutenant Colonel Suzuki Takuji, reported in late August from Hong Kong on Chiang Kai-shek's apparent preparedness to conduct formal negotiations in the search for peace.[75]

In a neat coincidence, Matsuoka secured a deal in the course of his negotiations with French Ambassador Charles Arsène-Henry. In the Matsuoka-Henry Pact, concluded on August 30, France recognized Japan's "supreme interests" in the "economic and political sphere" throughout the Far East. Japan, in turn, pledged its respect for Indochinese "territorial integrity" and French "sovereignty" over Indochina. The pact was short on details, and it anticipated negotiations in Hanoi for the purpose of reaching agreement on Japan's concrete military demands.[76]

The Army General Staff and Army Ministry were divided over the issue of Japan's chief negotiator. The General Staff wanted Major General Nemoto Hiroshi, while the Army Ministry argued for Major General Nishihara Issaku. The former was the South China Area Army chief of staff and a proponent of aggressive action in Indochina; the latter was an urbane, French-speaking graduate of the Imperial University of Tokyo who, since late June, had taken a decidedly moderate approach in negotiations with French authorities in Indochina. The Army Ministry, under Tojo's increasingly assertive leadership, got its way; on August 26 Nishihara was confirmed as Japan's chief negotiator.[77]

The issue of the negotiations in Hanoi did not end there. The head of the General Staff's Operations Division, Tominaga Kyoji, departed Tokyo on August 27 for a two-week tour of Indochina.[78] Among other things, he delivered instructions to Nishihara. But he also conducted, of his own accord and without authority from Tokyo, negotiations with the Indochinese governor-general, Jean Decoux. He took an exceedingly hard line, and on September 2 he and his retinue drew their swords in an unseemly attempt at intimidating Decoux.[79]

On September 3 Indochinese authorities offered a proposal that would form the basis of an interim Franco-Japanese agreement known as the Nishihara-Martin Pact. Concluded on September 4, it specified the number of Japanese troops that could enter Indochina as well as the geographic limits of the advance. It barred a Japanese advance into Indochina until various other issues—including the date the advance would begin—were settled by diplomatic negotiation.[80]

On September 4 a formation of nine Japanese Army planes crossed the Indochinese border on three separate occasions. Then, on September 6, a battalion under the command of Lieutenant Colonel Morimoto Takuji crossed the border from China deep into French Indochinese territory. When the French Army protested, Morimoto withdrew. Tojo was incensed, shouting over the phone at the General Staff's Operations Section chief, Okada Juichi. Morimoto had, by his actions, reduced the Nishihara-Martin Pact to a dead letter. Tojo regarded this as an act of insubordination. At his heated insistence, Morimoto was court-martialed by the South China Army.[81] Tojo also saw to it that four of Morimoto's immediate superiors, including two generals and the brigade and regimental chiefs, were later relieved of their posts.[82]

The Morimoto battalion's brazen border crossing caused Tojo and Prince Kan'in to begin anew a search for consensus on all details of policy toward Indochina. Most important, Tojo now conceded the need to impose a deadline of September 22, 1940, on negotiations. Before the deadline, Japanese forces would advance only if agreement were reached with the Indochinese authorities; the use of force would become permissible if no Indochinese-Japanese agreement was forthcoming by the deadline.

ON SEPTEMBER 6 KONOE CHAIRED a four-minister conference. This was a reprisal of the so-called four pillars conference held at Ogikubo just before the inauguration of the Konoe cabinet, and it brought together the prime minister with the foreign, war, and navy ministers. There was one key difference: Yoshida's hospitalization had compelled his ministerial resignation, and the Japanese Navy had decided that the Yokosuka Naval District commander, Vice Admiral Oikawa Koshiro, would serve as his ministerial successor.

The September 6 conference was an inglorious debut for Oikawa. Under discussion was a military alliance with Germany and Italy, the very issue that had destroyed the health of his predecessor. Matsuoka had, moreover, ratcheted up the pressure by proposing an alliance that took the United States as its chief target. Tojo's position was clear: The army "agree[d] with the Foreign Ministry proposal."[83] So, too, did Konoe. Now everything hinged on Oikawa: Would he uphold the stance established and upheld by his predecessors in Yonai and Yoshida? Would he, in other words, refuse to countenance an alliance with Germany and Italy on the grounds that it would lead to an unwinnable war against the United States? Oikawa had no stomach for the intense politicking that a continued opposition to a German alliance entailed. He did not even ask for time to consult his subordinates—most of whom were, after all, clambering for a German alliance—and without giving it a moment's thought, he overturned his service's principled position.[84]

So far as Tojo was concerned, the issue of the German-Italian-Japanese military alliance was now more or less closed. He was happy to let Matsuoka take the lead in subsequent negotiations with German Ambassador Heinrich Stahmer, and again at the Imperial Conference, which met on September 19 to discuss the alliance. One of Tojo's few statements before the conference concerned Japan's need for oil. "The Government has a policy," he stated. "It desires to obtain materials peacefully from the Netherlands East Indies but, depending on circumstances, it could use force." Tojo otherwise let Matsuoka dominate the proceedings. The foreign minister insisted that the proposed alliance would improve relationships with the only two nations able to interfere with Japan's southward advance—namely, the Soviet Union and the United States. Germany could be expected "to serve as a mediator in improving diplomatic relations between Japan and the Soviet Union." He added that Japan—and, indeed, Germany—could also expect improved relations with the United States if only they dispensed with the idea of making a "few conciliatory gestures" and instead presented the United States with a "firm stand." That firm stand involved threatening the United States with a simultaneous two-front war in both Europe and the Asia-Pacific region in the hope of averting US entry into either the war in Europe or Japan's war against China. He was proposing a policy of coercion and bluster. It rested on the assumptions that the United States could be cowed into its isolationist shell; would remain within the confines of the North American continent; and would acquiesce in any wars of conquest Germany, Italy, and Japan, might launch in their respective spheres. At the Imperial Conference on September 19, only the emperor's mouthpiece, Privy Council President Hara Yoshimichi, raised the disturbing possibility of the United States accepting the challenge of simultaneous war against

Japan in the Asia-Pacific and Germany and Italy in the Atlantic Ocean region and Europe. Matsuoka insisted that the choice rested solely with the United States: It could either "stiffen" its attitude and "bring about a critical situation," or it could "levelheadedly reconsider." He seemed not to consider the possibility that the Japanese government might also "levelheadedly reconsider" its position. The odds of the Americans sparking a crisis were, according to Matsuoka, "fifty-fifty."[85]

Those odds seemed exorbitantly high to Hara. Days later he chaired a meeting of the Privy Council, where the two service ministers, Oikawa and Tojo, faced questions about the likely outcome in the event of war against the United States. Tojo responded flatly: War against the United States would involve "no more than an exceedingly small portion of the army's forces." This response drew on decades of war planning—recall the Imperial National Defense Policy in its various post-Russo-Japanese War iterations—and was an acknowledgment that, because the United States was the Japanese Navy's hypothetical enemy, forecasts concerning that war were solely the navy's responsibility. Oikawa, for his part, spoke confidently of Japan's chances in the event of a short war ending in a decisive battle, and he added it would be necessary to continue expanding the fleet to prepare for the possibility of a war of long duration. Tojo also took the opportunity to remind privy councilors that the Soviet Union, not the United States, was his main focus as army minister; he really only thought about war with the United States in the context of a war that also included the Soviet Union. He freely admitted that Japan could not expect to defeat two such powerful enemies simultaneously; his primary concern was therefore an "adjustment" and improvement in Soviet-Japanese relations. He also noted the need to ensure "resolution of the [China] Incident" before any "worst-case scenario" eventuated and Japan found itself at war with the United States. In response to a different question, Tojo implied that a southward advance ought not to spark a Japanese-US war, and he spoke of the need to secure an adequate supply of oil. He otherwise said little.[86]

The German-Italian-Japanese Tripartite Pact was concluded on September 27, 1940. Article 3 read, "Germany, Italy, and Japan ... undertake to assist one another with all political, economic, and military means when one of the three Contracting Parties is attacked by a power at present not involved in the European war or in the Sino-Japanese conflict." To clarify that the United States was indeed the target, article 5 noted that the pact did "not in any way affect the political status which exists ... between each of the three Contracting Parties and Soviet Russia." German Ambassador

Eugen Ott added in a supplementary letter that Germany would "consider it a matter of course to give Japan full support and assist her with all military and economic means" in the event Japan came under attack in the Pacific. Ott also promised that Germany would do "everything within her power to promote a friendly understanding" between Japan and the Soviet Union and stood ready "to offer her good offices to this end."[87]

OPERATION KIRI HAD, IN the meantime, ended in abysmal failure. In mid-September, T. L. Soong returned to Hong Kong following a brief stint in Chiang Kai-shek's makeshift capital in Chongqing; he brought with him the news that Chiang was dissatisfied with the peace terms under discussion. The Nanjing-based China Expeditionary Army, which had championed Operation Kiri from the outset, conceded that there was no longer any point in pursuing the operation.[88]

Colonel Imai returned to Tokyo and on October 1 reported to Tojo and his subordinates. Imai counseled that Operation Kiri had at least apprised Chiang's government in Chongqing of Japan's peace terms. His advice was twofold: Any future peace maneuvers ought to come at Chiang's initiative, and Japan ought henceforth to aid and assist the Wang regime. Tojo spoke up: "I totally agree with your thoughts on the Wang regime." He likened Operation Kiri to "divination" or "fortune-telling"; there was, he supposed, some chance that peace might have eventuated, but he found it unsurprising that nothing had come of it. He raised the possibility of German mediation of Sino-Japanese peace, as well as the possibility of direct Sino-Japanese peace talks. Either way, he noted that Japan's peace terms would remain unchanged from the terms it had set during Operation Kiri. And he expressed what he regarded as the need for the central authorities to direct, control, and take responsibility for all future peace maneuvers. Within the week, the Army General Staff issued orders suspending Operation Kiri.[89]

All the while, Tojo continued to grapple with the Indochinese advance and the tensions it had caused between the Army General Staff and the Army Ministry. On September 9 Prince Kan'in presented an opinion paper allowing that Japan ought to "express regret" at Morimoto's border crossing. It also argued for the imposition of a September 15 deadline on negotiations. Tojo now reckoned that the French Indochinese authorities were seeking merely to stall and prolong the negotiations, and he agreed to a deadline. Oikawa balked; he insisted that French forces would, in all likelihood, resist the advance, which would not proceed peacefully. This, for Oikawa, raised the prospect of a precipitous deterioration in Japanese-US relations and, in particular, heightened US pressure on Japan. His opposition did not last. Tojo spoke with Oikawa the following day and convinced him to accept a deadline.[90]

Oikawa's and Tojo's subordinates worked over the ensuing days with their counterparts in the General Staffs to forge a consensus on the deadline. At Tojo's insistence, the deadline was pushed back to September 22. Tojo also insisted that the advance must be "peaceful." Even after the deadline had passed, force was permissible only in the event the French sought to "resist."[91] Konoe hosted a four-minister conference on September 13. Agreement was reached on the need to express "regret" for Morimoto's unauthorized border crossing, and also on the need to secure French authorities' consent to a return to the agreement that had been scuttled as a result of Morimoto's actions. Consensus was also forthcoming on a deadline of September 22, after which a "friendly" and "peaceful" advance would automatically begin, regardless of whether a Franco-Japanese agreement had been reached.[92]

Matsuoka reported this new policy to the emperor on September 14, 1940. So, too, did Lieutenant General Sawada Shigeru (representing his immediate superior, Prince Kan'in) and Prince Fushimi. The emperor declined to give his approval. He explained to Lord Keeper of the Privy Seal Kido Koichi that the government (represented in this case by Matsuoka) had stressed a peaceful advance, while the Supreme Command (represented by Prince Fushimi and Sawada) had emphasized instead the possible use of force. He spoke later that same night with Princes Fushimi and Kan'in, as well as Sawada. He demanded to know specific measures the Supreme Command would take to ensure a peaceful advance in the event the French authorities accepted Japan's demands mere moments before the deadline. He also insisted that Japan's advancing forces must not respond in kind, even if they met with isolated incidents of French resistance. Only after receiving assurances on these points did he approve the advance. Prince Kan'in's orders to the South China Area Army made clear that a resort to force was permissible only if he himself issued orders to that effect.[93]

Konoe again hosted a four-minister conference on September 17. At this juncture, Matsuoka advised that the Tripartite Pact was nearing conclusion. He reiterated his belief that the pact would convince the United States to stay away from Japan's southward advance, and on those grounds, raised the possibility of extending the deadline for the Indochinese advance by a few days. Tojo immediately accepted a two-day extension, and Oikawa agreed. But they ran headlong into an argument with the Supreme Command concerning their constitutional prerogatives. The Navy General Staff took the lead. "The Army and Navy Ministers accepted the Foreign Minister's opinion without having consulted the Supreme Command," it asserted. "You have no right to do that."[94] In concert with the Army General Staff, it ill-humoredly indicated its willingness to accept a one-day extension.[95]

Tominaga Kyoji had, in the meantime, imposed his hawkish views on the policymaking process. He had flown on September 16 to Hanoi to deliver instructions to Major General Nishihara concerning the reopening of negotiations. He took the liberty of completely rewriting the terms Japan sought from the French authorities in Indochina. Thus it was that, on September 17, Nishihara presented to French negotiators exceedingly stiff terms: The number of troops to be stationed in Indochina was raised fivefold, to twenty-five thousand; not three but five air bases were sought; and even Hanoi was included as an area for the stationing of Japanese troops. There was also the suggestion that Japanese residents would be repatriated beginning September 19 and that Nishihara and his coterie would be withdrawn from Hanoi the following day. These latter two provisions seemed to promise anything but a peaceful Japanese advance.[96]

Tominaga's actions infuriated Tojo. The two men had spoken immediately before Tominaga's departure, and Tojo had emphasized two specific points—namely, the imperative of securing French agreement to a resuscitation of the agreements reached in early September before Morimoto's border crossing, as well as the overriding imperative of a peaceful advance. Tominaga had instead ratcheted up Japan's terms, with a presumed view to staving off any hope of Franco-Japanese agreement and thereby increasing the likelihood of a clash of arms. Such an outcome would directly contradict the emperor's will, and Tojo would have none of it. He raged against Tominaga: "What does he think the Imperial order of September 14 is?"[97] He snatched up a pen. "Orders must be issued," he wrote, "that even if the troop stationing is delayed, it is to be carried out peacefully." In his anger, Tojo disregarded the fragile consensus of the cabinet and Supreme Command regarding a one-day extension of the negotiations deadline and scrawled that it did "not matter" if the stationing were "delayed for two or three days." The Nishihara unit, he added, must not withdraw but instead "remain on the spot and continue negotiations to the end."[98]

For at least some, Tojo's note reopened the question of the independence of the Supreme Command. Those who sympathized with Tominaga on the General Staff began complaining that Tojo was "meddling" with the "prerogative of the Supreme Command." And there was a growing sense that Vice Chief of Staff Sawada had become little more than a "second vice army minister" insofar as he seemed to be doing Tojo's bidding.[99]

There is no record of Tojo's immediate response to such charges. His own thoughts can nonetheless be reconstructed with a high degree of confidence. On the one hand, it seems more than likely that he would have expressed fealty to the independence of the Supreme Command. On the other hand, he may well have spoken of the need, in an era of total war, to suspend ordinary constitutional process so that the chief of staff's operational concerns were subordinate to the broader vision of the army minister. This latter concept indicated a radical departure from Japan's constitutional procedure, but recall that Tojo lectured on precisely this point in the early 1920s when he taught military history at the War College. He continued to grapple with this issue over the ensuing weeks, months, and years.

THE FRENCH AUTHORITIES, HOURS before the deadline, proposed to offer Japan the use of four airfields in Tonkin Province, the stationing of up to six thousand Japanese troops, and the passage of twenty-five thousand troops through Tonkin Province. Nishihara affixed his signature, and the negotiations thereby concluded. The Fifth Division nonetheless sparked a fierce border clash with French Indochinese troops; the fighting lasted several days.

For Tojo, the advance into northern Indochina revealed just how problematic the issue of discipline within the army was. From the outset, field officers and General Staff officers had repeatedly defied orders, acting in accord with their own aggressive outlooks. This was precisely the issue the emperor had raised when he granted Tojo his first ministerial audience. Tojo now turned his attention to the reimposition of "military discipline." He admitted to Colonel Sato Kenryo the need to "make a costly sacrifice" for the cause of "justice."[100] Those sacrifices came in the form of personnel changes, over which Tojo now exercised ministerial authority. The sweeping changes he made were, to borrow the words of historian Hata Ikuhiko, "comparable to those that were made following the February 26 Incident."[101] Among the changes were that the ever-aggressive Tominaga Kyoji was shifted out of Tokyo, as were several of his hawkish subordinates. The South China Area Army commander, Lieutenant General Ando

Rikichi, was also relieved of his post. Then, on October 3, Prince Kan'in retired. Some wondered whether he was "taking responsibility" for the messy northern Indochinese advance.[102] Tojo declined to speculate openly, but as a member of the army's "big three," he contributed to the decision to replace Prince Kan'in with General Sugiyama Hajime.

The personnel sweep sent shock waves through an army that was already reeling from the failure of Operation Kiri to end the war in China. Nonetheless, Tojo and the cabinet on which he served had yielded two policy results that could not but appeal to the Imperial Japanese Army. The Konoe cabinet had concluded the German-Italian-Japanese Tripartite Pact, and it had taken the first step on an advance into the suddenly defenseless, resource-rich colonial regions of Southeast Asia. This was more than enough to satisfy widespread expectations within the army. Tojo was steering the army's agenda through the cabinet—at least as well as might be hoped.

But that was not the sum of Tojo's achievements. He took most seriously his responsibility to his emperor, and was convinced that the policy-making process could function effectively only if the relationship between emperor and army were harmonious. This was far from the case when he assumed his ministerial post. Restoring the emperor-army relationship to full health was no mean feat, especially for a man the emperor did not want as army minister. It required the reimposition of a discipline that had eroded precipitously, ever since Komoto Daisaku had assassinated Manchurian warlord Zhang Zuolin in 1928. Yet Tojo was cut of different cloth from his professional military colleagues. Military discipline had been a concern of his since at least the early 1930s, and he had acted decisively to impose discipline in Manchukuo in the immediate aftermath of the February 26 Incident. Now, in the summer and fall of 1940, he had begun imposing discipline across the entire Japanese Army and repairing its relationship with its sovereign.

7
DRAWING THE BATTLE LINES
SEPTEMBER 1940–APRIL 1941

TOJO HIDEKI HAD GIVEN little thought across his military career to Japan's relationship with the United States. The Americans had reacted to the conquest of Manchuria with a policy of nonrecognition; Tojo seems barely to have blinked. Following the Marco Polo Bridge Incident, he assumed a hawkish stance toward China without giving thought to the possibility of either staunch Chinese resistance or the likely American reaction. During his short stint as vice minister, he had raised the prospect of Japan fighting not only China but also the Soviet Union and possibly Britain. He not only excluded the United States from his list of likely enemies; he indicated his hope that the Japanese-US commercial relationship would continue unblemished.

That such thinking was overly optimistic became apparent in July 1939, when the administration of President Franklin D. Roosevelt registered its opposition to Japanese policy by giving Japan the mandatory six-month notice of its intention to abrogate the Japanese-US commercial treaty. Once the treaty expired in January 1940, the United States could legally discriminate against Japanese commerce. This action had no immediate material impact, but it raised the possibility of economic sanctions and even a trade embargo. The ramifications for Japan were enormous, not least because it imported over 90 percent of its oil from the United States.[1]

Against this backdrop Tojo and his colleagues in the second cabinet of Prime Minister Konoe Fumimaro had decided on the German-Italian-Japanese military alliance that specifically targeted the United States. And, as we have seen, Japanese forces launched an almost simultaneous advance into northern French Indochina. Tojo expected the United States to react to both. He braced himself for the possibility of an embargo on US oil to Japan. "The US attitude toward Japan is stiffening," he told his subordinates on

September 7, 1940. Although this "was to be expected," it raised important questions because Japan's war machine would be crippled if it lost access to US oil. Tojo asked resignedly whether there had been "any change" in Japan's "oil imports." There had not.[2]

The White House announced on September 26 that for the purpose of strengthening US defenses, it was revoking all export licenses for scrap metal and high-octane aviation gasoline. Roosevelt, in his proclamations and press releases, deliberately refrained from provocations and did not so much as hint at the possibility that the measure was aimed at Japan. Even so, there was no mistaking which nation was the principal target.[3] The German-Italian-Japanese Tripartite Pact was concluded one day later, and within the Imperial Japanese Army, discussion centered on whether the United States might take any further countermeasures.

Tojo spoke with his subordinates the day after conclusion of the pact. "This pact will inevitably exercise a major impact on Britain and the United States," he said. "Whatever the means of [Anglo-American] counterattack, we must consider the worst-case scenario and take all necessary precautions." He then turned his attention to what he called the newly instituted US "embargo" on the export of scrap iron and aviation gasoline to Japan. He noted that Japan relied almost exclusively on the United States for both resources and then stated the obvious: This reliance now had to change. Tojo noted the need to stockpile iron and oil—second-grade scrap and gasoline just marginally beneath aviation quality were the obvious alternatives—and also demanded intensive study of the recycling of scrap iron as well as the development of airplane technologies, including aviation fuel.[4]

TOJO, THEN, EXPECTED FURTHER injury to transpacific commerce as a result of American antipathy toward Japan's undeclared war in China, alliance with Germany and Italy, and southward advance. He gave the United States little additional thought, largely because he still presumed it would shy away from precisely what the Tripartite Pact threatened—namely, a two-front war in the Asia-Pacific region and in Europe. Most army officers were in agreement with this last point. In this way the halls of the Army Ministry were something of an echo chamber in which existing views about the US unwillingness to fight were reinforced and alternative ideas received next to no consideration.

At the cabinet level, Vice Admiral Yoshida Zengo had warned of the dangers inherent in threatening the United States with war. He had also insisted that a forceful southward advance would result in such a war. Yet, as we have seen, Tojo did not engage Yoshida's arguments on their merits. He indulged himself instead in self-righteous indignation at what he regarded as Yoshida's about-face on the Tripartite Pact. Yoshida had come and gone, and in his absence the Imperial Japanese Navy had consented to the Tripartite Pact on condition that the army and government provided the funding to accelerate the navy's preparations for the possibility of war against the United States.[5]

An October 22, 1940, meeting with retired admiral Nomura Kichisaburo provided an early instance in which Tojo again confronted views diverging sharply from his own. Nomura was an outspoken critic of the Tripartite Pact and one of the navy's most prominent America experts. He sought a meeting with Tojo because Matsuoka Yosuke and Oikawa Koshiro had approached him about the vacant ambassadorial post in Washington, DC. Tojo probably expected the meeting to be short and formulaic. Nomura, however, saw this as an opportunity to educate Tojo in what he regarded as the realities of the Japanese-US relationship.

The retired admiral opened with a brief lesson in naval strategy, including a frank admission of the Japanese Navy's inability to defeat its US counterpart in war. Japan's only chance, Nomura explained, was a "decisive battle" fought soon after the outbreak of hostilities. He insisted, however, that the United States would actively avoid giving Japan that chance. The US Navy would instead fight to its own strengths: It would conduct a "protracted war" that would bring into play America's immense industrial, scientific, technological, commercial, diplomatic, and political power. Japan could not compete in any of these fields and would, in the farsighted Nomura's opinion, meet eventually with crushing defeat.[6]

Nomura placed the current perilous state of Japanese-US commerce in precisely this context. The Roosevelt administration was not acting in a vacuum with its application of commercial and economic pressures; indeed, the "severance" of Japanese-US economic ties was a diplomatic weapon in its arsenal. This would deepen the "disarray" into which the Japanese economy was falling as a result of the yearslong China Incident, and in so doing would weaken Japan critically, even before a shot had been fired in the Pacific. Nomura castigated the Tripartite Pact for having brought Japan and the United States to the brink of war. He insisted that Japan had to defuse the situation by forswearing a forceful southward advance and allowing for the traditional US Open Door Policy of respect for Chinese sovereignty and equality of economic and commercial opportunity in China.[7]

Tojo proved no less enthusiastic than had Matsuoka and Oikawa about Nomura's ambassadorial appointment and asked Nomura to accept the post. Tojo can hardly be said, however, to have experienced an epiphany. He remained committed to the Konoe cabinet's policy program, including the Tripartite Pact and the southward advance, and following the collapse of Operation Kiri he sought victory in China that involved Wang Jingwei's collaborationist regime as well as a privileged commercial, economic, and industrial position for Japan. Tojo also continued in his presumption about America's unwillingness, beyond the application of economic and commercial pressures, to oppose Japan's policy program.

Tojo put much of this on record within twenty-four hours of his meeting with Nomura. On October 23 he joined with the newly installed army chief of staff, Lieutenant General Sugiyama Hajime (who was no less hawkish regarding China than Tojo), and approved as military policy a document that continued a yearslong attempt at defining victory in China. The "Shina Jihen shori yoko" (Outline of a policy to deal with the China Incident) had been drafted on Tojo's orders by the Military Affairs Bureau's Ishii Akiho before undergoing revision at the hands of Tojo's handpicked Operations Bureau director, Major General Tanaka Shin'ichi.[8] The outline sought to draw together the various threads that made up Japanese military policy; underpinning it was a focus not on the Pacific Ocean and the United States but instead on the Eurasian continent and, in particular, the nexus of China, Germany, and the Soviet Union. The outline thus captured a worldview that had informed Japanese Army officers for decades. It also went one step further and sought to locate Southeast Asia within that worldview.

The outline enunciated the need to extend formal diplomatic recognition to Wang Jingwei's regime in Nanjing. As long as Operation Kiri held out the possibility of a merger between Chiang Kai-shek and Wang Jingwei, the army had hesitated to take this step. Now that Operation Kiri had ended without success, there seemed no other way forward, even if there was little confidence in the Wang regime's ability to extend its governance beyond areas already under Japanese military control. The outline committed the Japanese Army, with a sense of irrevocability, to what was in essence a puppet regime. This, in turn, meant the army had little choice but to buckle down for what the outline called a "protracted war of endurance" in which Japanese troops would focus on defending occupied areas against external attack or internal disruption. The emphasis was very much on a low-intensity conflict supposed to lessen what had hitherto approximated an insatiable army appetite for budget and materiel.[9]

Despite the emphasis on a war of endurance, the outline divined a way out of the war. Chiang Kai-shek remained the linchpin in the exit strategy; the Japanese Army had to *compel* him to merge with the Wang regime. This could best be achieved, according to the outline, by causing Chiang to lose the will to continue in his struggle against Japan. This involved a concerted effort at isolating Chiang from his powerful patrons in London, Moscow, and Washington. This required an "adjustment" in Japan's relationship with the Soviet Union, as well as further advances southward, in the interest of cutting Chiang off from all remaining sources of Anglo-American aid. Of particular interest in this regard was the Burma Road, which the British reopened on October 17, 1940, so it could replace Indochina as the route by which to aid Chiang.[10] As if to emphasize this last point, the Military Affairs Bureau director, Lieutenant General Muto Akira, spoke of the need to "bomb" the road out of existence.[11]

SUGIYAMA AND TOJO ENVISIONED the outline informing not just military policy but indeed state policy. As a first step to that end, they sent it to the Navy Ministry and the Navy General Staff. This revealed the centrality of the armed services in Tojo's (and Sugiyama's) conception of the decision-making process. It also revealed an awareness of what the outline proposed: taking a key plank of decades-old naval strategy and policy—namely, the southward advance—and repurposing it in such a way as to incorporate it into army strategy and policy.

The outline touched off a furor in the Imperial Navy. Uniformed naval officers expressed incredulousness at the audacity of army policy, and they failed to see how extending the theater of operations and adding to Japan's enemies could possibly help in ending the war of the army's own making in China. In late October, officers on the Navy General Staff, in conference with their army counterparts, refused to accept that a southward advance could contribute to ending the China Incident. At issue was the likely US response to a southward advance: army officers hoped the Americans would remain aloof, whereas navy officers argued the opposite. They spoke of the folly of risking war against the imposingly powerful United States in a shortsighted attempt at ending the China Incident.[12] Army officers bristled at what they regarded as the navy's overly cautious approach. According to the Army General Staff's Colonel Arisue Yatoru, the navy sought to erase the "main point" of the army's endgame-of-war strategy.[13]

The navy's arguments perplexed Tojo. He sent the outline back to the Army Ministry's Military Affairs Bureau with questions about the impact of the China Incident on Japan's relations with the Anglo-American powers. Muto reported back to Tojo concerning the "strengthening of Anglo-American aid policies" toward Chiang Kai-shek. This trend, according to Muto, had become particularly noticeable since the conclusion of the Tripartite Pact. Japan had severed the Indochinese route by which the Anglo-American powers had aided Chiang; the British had, within weeks, opened the Burma Road and thereby opened a new aide route. Anglo-American policies were, Muto stated, "disadvantageous" for Japan insofar as they rendered unlikely "Chiang's surrender" in the "near future." "The United States will," he predicted, "adopt increasingly hard-line policies beginning next year." Muto counseled the need for Japan to press ahead with defense preparations. And, in a return to policies Tojo had championed as vice minister, he argued that the army must "cease all peace maneuvers" aimed at Chiang Kai-shek. He insisted that Japan deal with the Wang regime as China's sole, legitimate government and accept the diplomatic difficulties that would follow recognition of the Wang regime.[14]

On this basis Tojo agreed to delete from the outline all mention of a forceful southward advance. He did not, however, drop it from his policy objectives. He consoled himself with the thought that the Anglo-Americans' ongoing support for Chiang should eventually convince the navy to come around. He was, in effect, playing a waiting game, which in no way contradicted the call for protracted warfare in China. Once the navy indicated its acceptance of the revised outline, Tojo introduced it to Konoe and Matsuoka. He also presented a number of other army-penned documents, including a draft treaty to establish a formal diplomatic relationship with the Wang regime and a draft Chinese-Japanese-Manchukuoan declaration pledging military and economic cooperation, as well as fidelity to the "new order" in East Asia. Neither Konoe nor Matsuoka voiced substantial disagreement. Tojo next surprised everyone by calling for an Imperial conference. This was largely a reaction to what he saw as the navy's about-face on the Tripartite Pact in the early days of the Konoe cabinet. He intended to use the emperor in such a way as to prevent a repeat performance: Decisions reached at Imperial conferences were, in Tojo's conception, sacrosanct and nonnegotiable. He was, quietly and unassumingly, driving Japanese policy.[15]

The Eighth Imperial Conference convened on November 13, 1940. A raft of policy papers was presented, including not only the outline but also the proposed treaty and a joint Chinese-Japanese-Manchukuoan declaration. A silent emperor affixed his seal to this new direction in Japan's China policy.[16] Matsuoka seemed vaguely unsettled by the course Tojo was setting, and dallied briefly with an attempt at using German mediation to pressure Chiang into giving up the fight, and then with an effort at direct negotiations with the Chinese nationalist government in Chungking. Tojo learned, via undisclosed channels, that Chiang sought merely to delay Japan's formal recognition of the Wang regime in Nanjing. He prevailed on Matsuoka to exercise prudence, and was unsurprised when Matsuoka's last-gasp diplomatic efforts yielded no results.[17]

On November 30, Japan's ambassador to Nanjing, retired general and former Prime Minister Abe Nobuyuki, joined with Wang and signed off on the treaty concerning their "basic relations." It made provision for the stationing of Japanese troops in Inner Mongolia and North China; the evacuation of Japanese forces from elsewhere in China following the establishment of "peace and order"; "close cooperation" in the development of defense-related "mineral resources" in Inner Mongolia and North China; close cooperation also in the establishment of "facilities" that would enable the development elsewhere in China of "specific resources" Japan needed for "national defense"; and the abolition of Japan's extraterritorial rights in China.[18]

ADOPTION OF THE REVISED outline as state policy and recognition of the Wang regime in Nanjing as the sole, legitimate Chinese government took place against the backdrop of fresh questions about an advance into the defenseless colonial regions of Southeast Asia. A French Indochinese-Thai border dispute provided the impetus. The Japanese advance into northern Indochina in September had sparked Thailand's determination to reclaim territory previously ceded to France. Thai diplomats sought Anglo-American support, but by October that had yielded no results and Thailand turned instead to Japan.

The army's ever-aggressive staff officers saw an opportunity to launch advances farther south. They argued that mediation of the Indochinese-Thai dispute ought to open the way to an advance into the southern half of French Indochina. Specifically, they argued for access to air bases in Saigon and elsewhere in southern Indochina. Troops would be necessary, they argued, to protect the air bases, and they would require passage through southern Indochina. These terms and conditions would, staff officers believed, pave the way for further forcible advances on British Malaya and Singapore.[19]

Tojo was steering the outline through the state's policymaking mechanisms and was considerably more circumspect than officers on the Army General Staff. He joined a four-minister conference on November 5, 1940, and readily reached agreement on mediating the Indochinese-Thai dispute with a view to restoring to Thailand the territories it claimed. He also agreed on policy objectives, including Thailand's cooperation with Japan in establishment of a "New Order in East Asia," its amenability to an eventual alliance with Japan, its recognition of Manchukuo, and the conclusion of an economic pact that would enable Japan to "secure needed commodities" from Thailand. Swift ratification of a Japanese-Thai friendship treaty was also a basic expectation. These relatively lenient expectations were uncontentious and a product of Thai independence; Tojo and his colleagues' desire for Thailand's active identification with Japan's "new order" was genuine.[20] They were less certain when, some two and a half weeks later, they sought to define policy objectives vis-à-vis French Indochina. Scarcely concealed divisions over a possible resort to force underpinned these discussions. Agreement was reached on two points: French authorities would have to accept Thai annexation of the disputed territories, and they would have also to accept "military cooperation with Japan in the southern portion of Indochina."[21] This latter condition remained conspicuously undefined.

Indochinese and Thai forces clashed in late November. At about the same time, Thailand indicated its receptivity to Japanese mediation. Matsuoka met in early December with French Ambassador Charles Arséne-Henry and informally offered Japanese mediation. In the meantime, Army Chief of Staff Sugiyama ordered his subordinates to conduct a detailed study of both Japanese mediation and an advance into southern Indochina. Staff officers met with Tojo's subordinates on December 4 and cited the southern Indochinese advance as providing the necessary platform for Japan's entire southward advance.[22]

Matsuoka seemed to agree with at least prompt action in Indochina: He told Konoe, Tojo, and others on December 12 that Japan ought to "clean up" Indochina, and spoke specifically of sending troops into southern Indochina.[23] Within the week, France indicated its refusal to cede any Indochinese territory and rejected Japan's informal offer of mediation of the Indochinese-Thai border dispute. The Army General Staff reacted swiftly, insisting on a prompt decision to dispatch troops to southern Indochina. Tojo demurred.[24]

Tojo had, in late November, recommended that the four-minister conference be expanded to include the chiefs of the Army and Navy General Staffs. He suggested that this new consultative body, which superseded and appropriated the name of the earlier consultative body known as the liaison conference, ought to consider all matters straddling politics, diplomacy, and operational imperatives. (Recall that Tojo, as a War College instructor in the early 1920s, had lectured on the impossibility of separating operations and politics in an era of total war.)[25] The proposal met with enthusiastic acceptance, and the liaison conference met on December 26 to consider the Indochinese-Thai border dispute and the Japanese response. Conferees at the outset agreed on a policy document that prescribed the establishment of "inseparable" relations with Thailand. It specifically mentioned a "military-political pact" as well as a bilateral agreement regarding "economic cooperation." The document also stated that Japan must "pressure" Indochina to accept Japan's "demands." The nature of those demands remained a matter of contention and were again left undefined.[26]

Discussion at the liaison conference sought clarity on policy toward Indochina. Matsuoka opened proceedings by denouncing the French Indochinese authorities for having played Japan for a "fool." He recommended a "hard-line attitude" toward and "forceful pressure" on Indochina. Oikawa urged caution. He asked whether a hard-line attitude might negatively impact Japan's ongoing efforts at "resource acquisition" from across Southeast Asia, and he also argued for a policy that would not incite the Anglo-American powers. Tojo said little, but he supported Oikawa's position. Sugiyama indicated a preference for a hard-line attitude, but argued for "prudence" on the grounds that no decision for an advance farther south had been reached. The navy vice chief of staff, Vice Admiral Kondo Nobutake, who attended in place of the navy chief of staff, Prince Fushimi Hiroyasu, indicated his agreement with Sugiyama.[27]

The following day, Tojo spoke with officers from the Army General Staff and the Army Ministry. Some staff officers grumbled at what they regarded as the "weakening trend" concerning a "forceful southward advance," and Sugiyama was finding it difficult to restrain them. Tojo decided to intervene. He had to tread carefully, for he wanted to avoid accusations of trampling on the hallowed principle of General Staff independence. He nonetheless wanted to unify the Army Ministry and General Staff behind Southeast Asian policy. Lunch seemed the right option: It removed some of the formality that would otherwise characterize a meeting called by the army minister, and it allowed Tojo a freedom of speech that might otherwise have been ill advised. Over lunch Tojo explained clearly and unambiguously that there were two prerequisites that must be realized before Japan could launch a "forceful southward advance." First, "security vis-à-vis the Soviet Union" was an "absolute necessity." Second, "shipping [had] to be secured for full mobilization."[28]

TOJO'S LUNCH HAD THE desired impact. The focus within both the Army Ministry and General Staff shifted perceptibly to Tojo's prerequisites. The Soviet Union was the higher priority. This tied in with the need for an adjustment in the Japanese-Soviet diplomatic relationship, which the army had identified prior to the Konoe cabinet's inauguration. The vice chief of staff, Lieutenant General Tsukada Osamu, ordered his subordinates in early January 1941 to prepare a study of "negotiations for the adjustment of Japanese-Soviet diplomatic relations." There was a sense that the Soviets had made clear their "real intentions." They had, courtesy of their nonaggression pact with Nazi Germany and conversations with former Ambassador Togo Shigenori, identified with the revisionist powers and split with the Anglo-American powers; "now that things had come to this pass," there was "no need to sound out" the Soviets any further. It was time to cut a diplomatic deal.[29]

Decades-old enmities nonetheless died hard. Army officers emphasized "persistent diplomatic negotiations" based not on false professions of amity but instead on cold, hard calculations of "power." They remained adamant that Japan should protect its rights and not forsake them in pursuit of agreement with the Soviets. They expected a Japanese-Soviet nonaggression treaty or perhaps a neutrality pact.[30]

Tojo expected all of this and more. He viewed an adjustment in the Japanese-Soviet diplomatic relationship from the perspective of not only international politics but also army-navy rivalry over budget and materiel. A Japanese-Soviet nonaggression or neutrality treaty would not only reduce the risk of war but would lessen the army's need to prepare for precisely that possibility. This, in combination with the army's switch to low-intensity warfare in China, would minimize Japanese Army budgetary requirements. In anticipation of this reality, in mid-December Tojo granted the Imperial Navy's request for more funds and materiel.[31] He now fully intended to use this as leverage to press the navy to accept the southward advance and risk of war with the United States. In essence, Tojo was at least temporarily sacrificing the army's posture of preparedness against the Soviets in the interest of bolstering the navy's preparedness for war against the United States so as to cajole the navy into acceptance of the southward advance.

Matsuoka was working to his own timetable. In mid-January, the army learned through the navy that Matsuoka was preparing for a European sojourn. Berlin and Moscow were apparently on his itinerary. Army officers balked at the prospect of a freewheeling Matsuoka reaching agreements in Europe on his own initiative. They insisted on the need, before Matsuoka left for Europe, to "establish national policy," which could only be done once there was "complete agreement" between the cabinet and the Supreme Command. This required at least a meeting of the liaison conference. Tojo was very much in agreement with these demands: He did not like surprises, and he remained convinced that the army's voice in policy vis-à-vis the Soviet Union ought to be predominant.[32]

Matsuoka proved more forthcoming over the ensuing days, explaining that he was animated by a threefold objective. He sought, first, Soviet acceptance of German foreign minister Joachim von Ribbentrop's express desire for a German-Italian-Japanese-Soviet quadripartite pact. He also indicated his agreement with Ribbentrop's idea of dividing the world into blocs: Japan's bloc would incorporate China and Southeast Asia; the Soviet bloc would extend into the Middle East; Germany and Italy would carve up Europe and Africa; and North and South America would make up the US bloc. There was no room in such a world for the British Empire, and Matsuoka's second, interlinked objective was to secure Soviet "agreement" with the German-Italian-Japanese policy of "Britain's defeat." On these twin bases he sought his third objective—namely, to "adjust Japanese-Soviet diplomatic relations." He believed that various diplomatic issues, including the need for more clearly demarcated Manchukuoan-Soviet borders, were surmountable. And he argued that Japanese recognition of the Soviet "position" in Outer Mongolia should convince the Soviets to reciprocate and recognize Japan's position in Inner Mongolia and North China.[33]

ON JANUARY 7, 1941, TOJO gained the emperor's approval for issuance of a pocket-size booklet titled *Senjinkun* (Field service code). Begun during Tojo's time atop army aviation, *Senjinkun* was a joint undertaking between the Army Ministry and the Inspectorate General of Military Training. It owed authorship to Imamura Hitoshi and other officers, as well as novelist Shimazaki Toson, and it was conceived as a means of reinstilling discipline into an army that had descended into frequent orgies of theft, rape, violence, and murder across China. It instructed soldiers to stay away from "wine and women" and to uphold such laudable "moral tenets" as piety, obedience, simplicity, fortitude, integrity, and austerity. Yet, overshadowing all else in *Senjinkun* was the following exhortation: "Do not suffer the disgrace of becoming a prisoner."[34] In later years, suicide tactics in forlorn battles in the Pacific were at least partly attributable to this injunction against surrender, and after the war had been fought and lost, Tojo himself cited *Senjinkun* as requiring his own death. Japan's surrender and Tojo's failed suicide attempt was, nonetheless, in the distant and unforeseeable future; in early 1941 Tojo regarded *Senjinkun* as a "resource" for the "moral enhancement" of troops on the battlefield.[35]

Senjinkun was not, however, Tojo's highest priority; animating him, the emperor, and the army in the early days of 1941 was the southward advance. General Sugiyama fronted the emperor on January 13, and sought approval to rotate forces deployed to northern Indochina in such a way that both the departing force and the newly deployed force remained temporarily in Indochina. The resulting increase in troop numbers was designed specifically to pressure French Indochinese authorities. The emperor gave his approval but also expressed his fear of an "armed clash" in Indochina. Henceforth, Sugiyama focused on the need to avoid "repeating mistakes" made during the northern Indochinese advance.[36]

On January 24, 1941, France officially accepted Japan's offer of mediation. That same day, the emperor sought explicit assurances from Sugiyama that there would be no resort to force in the event that French Indochina proved amenable to Japan's demands.[37] This was all the convincing Tojo needed. He joined with Sugiyama and convened a meeting on January 25 that brought together their bureau and section chiefs. Consensus proved difficult. Sugiyama, trying to remain faithful to his emperor's wishes, argued for a "bloodless" advance. He was, however, having trouble controlling his subordinates. Tojo was typically forthright in demanding fealty to the emperor's wishes and, as was frequently the case, he sparked within the General Staff concerns for its independence from the cabinet.[38]

Tojo nonetheless secured consensus by holding out at least the possibility of a forceful advance. He suggested a late March deadline, before which the "use of force" was out of the question but after which it was, at least, conceivable. He remained mindful of the emperor's position, insisting that any decision for the use of force could only be reached at an Imperial conference. This would necessarily require an intensive preparatory effort at convincing his ministerial colleagues and the Navy General Staff to accept that all peaceful avenues had been exhausted and the time had arrived for the use of force. Securing the navy's agreement required army acknowledgment of a likely collision with "Anglo-American strategy," although Tojo and his professional military colleagues continued to hope it should prove possible to avoid what they called "unnecessary friction" with Britain and the United States.[39]

Japanese diplomats negotiated an Indochinese-Thai armistice on January 31. The clash that had continued unabated since November 1940 was brought to a close, laying the groundwork for Japanese mediation of the territorial dispute. A liaison conference had met in the meantime and agreed that close military, political, and economic ties with both Indochina and Thailand were necessary for Japan's "self-preservation and self-defense" (a phrase that over subsequent months became the catchcry of Japan's war hawks). The conferees allowed that Japan, in pursuit of these aims, should take all necessary measures. The possibility of the use of force against Indochina received mention, but consensus remained elusive on the timing of any such decision.[40] Tojo said little at this conference; there was no need, for the agreements reached adhered closely to army policy. He only intervened to rein in the impetuous Matsuoka and impress on him the need to avoid any statements or actions that might "incite" the Anglo-American powers.[41]

An international conference, convened with a view to ending the Indochinese-Thai border dispute, convened in Tokyo on February 7, 1941. Thailand opened with its maximum demand and claimed practically all territories it had previously ceded to Indochina. This France could not countenance, and the negotiations were deadlocked from the outset. The armistice originally scheduled to end on February 11 was extended to February 25. On February 17 Japanese negotiators proposed a compromise, but it fell on deaf ears. One week later, the negotiators convinced their guests to extend the armistice until March 7. The Japanese proposed another compromise and requested responses from both the French and the Thais by February 28. Thai diplomats quickly approved the Japanese compromise plan. As the deadline loomed, the French maintained their silence, and Japanese Army General Staff officers began agitating for a decision to use force against Indochina. Tojo would have none of it. Joining with Oikawa, he agreed that a decision for the use of force must only be reached after all diplomatic deadlines had passed. Army General Staff officers, including Vice Chief of Staff Tsukada, grumbled once again at what they regarded as Tojo's tendency to "infringe" on the Supreme Command's hallowed independence.[42]

Grumble they might have, but staff officers complied. Within days, another liaison conference agreed that France would be issued a request to accept the Japanese compromise plan no later than March 5. If the French did not comply, the use of force could commence three days later.[43] The French held out for as long as they felt able; not until March 6 did they accept Japan's mediation plan "in principle."[44] The armistice was again extended, and France and Thailand both formally accepted Japan's mediation proposal on March 10. The mercurial Matsuoka had, in the meantime, opposed the use of force against Indochina, and he refused to press French negotiators for the use of southern Indochinese air bases or the passage of Japanese troops through southern Indochina. Nor did he seek a friendship treaty with Thailand.[45] Army General Staff officers professed bewilderment at what they regarded as unrequited labor. Tojo was at least mildly sympathetic to this view but contented himself with having reined in the army's aggressive impulses and having, once again, enacted his emperor's will.

ALL THE WHILE, KONOE was pressing ahead with efforts at upending the domestic political landscape. The Japanese Army had long been enthusiastic about domestic political reform, and Konoe had professed his willingness to act in accord with the army's vision. Yet Konoe's movement toward a new political order seemed of relatively marginal interest to Tojo. There is a simple explanation: Tojo was a soldier, and he was a patriot who identified quite far to the right of Japan's political spectrum, but he was no ideologue. He remained more or less silent throughout discussions about the new political order. Konoe, for his part, was probably too eclectic a thinker to establish a coherent totalitarian party. He had also to contend with competing political groupings, including the political parties in the Imperial Diet, bureaucrats in the various government ministries, the extreme right wing, and, of course, the armed services. Each of these entities hoped to use Konoe's new political order for its own particular purposes. The result was a bewildering array of ideas, assumptions, and aspirations that gave little consistency to the movement, even when Konoe announced the creation of the Imperial Rule Assistance Association on October 12, 1940.[46]

Disappointment at Konoe and the Imperial Rule Assistance Association bubbled away in various sectors. The emperor himself criticized the association for seeking to usurp his position, in a manner not dissimilar to what the shogunate had done during Japan's feudal era.[47] There is no way of discerning whether Tojo was aware of the emperor's criticism; he was, however, made aware of disaffection in other quarters. Reporting to Tojo in late October 1940, Military Affairs Bureau Director Muto noted the high levels of dissatisfaction among reserve-list army officers, many of whom owed their allegiance to the *kodoha* (Imperial way faction). He expressed concern lest these throwbacks to the murderous army factionalism of the early and mid-1930s engage in an attempt at toppling the Konoe cabinet. He noted that the cabinet's downfall could only have a deleterious effect on the German-Italian-Japanese Tripartite Pact and also on the development of the Imperial Rule Assistance Association. Tojo's response revealed his satisfaction with the Imperial Rule Assistance Association and suggests that his expectations for domestic political reform did not exceed the modest accomplishments of the association. "Those who are working blindly for the overthrow of the cabinet will be severely punished," he said. "Put the *kenpei* [military police] on notice."[48]

Among the groups presumed to be working for the cabinet's overthrow, the East Asian League Association came in for Tojo's special focus. He trusted *kenpei* intelligence reporting, which confirmed the association's status as the leading antigovernment voice in Japan. Criticisms of the association were essentially sixfold: it recalled and at least partly revived the name and concept of the Anglo-American-centric League of Nations; its much-touted ideal of pan-Asian equality could only undermine Japanese leadership in East Asia; it envisioned the creation of an East Asian "suprastate," which left little space for Japanese sovereignty and the all-important *kokutai;* its emphasis on an emperor-centric East Asian leadership model ran directly counter to the *kokutai* (national essence, spirit); its adherence to racial equality and harmony threatened Japan's colonial rule in Korea; and it espoused policy positions that ran directly counter to state policy. The Konoe cabinet, with Tojo's enthusiastic backing, outlawed the East Asian League Association on January 14. That same day the cabinet issued a public statement accusing the association of espousing ideologies and theories "contrary to the spirit of the Empire's founding."[49]

For Tojo the furor surrounding the East Asian League Association went beyond ideology. At one level, it involved burning personal hatreds. The association was, after all, the brainchild of Tojo's bitterest enemy, Ishiwara Kanji. Despite professing no formal membership, Ishiwara was the association's chief ideologue, strategist, and even religious thinker. Other high-ranking officers who aligned themselves with the association included the prominent Tojo antagonist, Lieutenant General Tada Hayao, and a former Tojo ally turned adversary, Lieutenant General Itagaki Seishiro. The association took on an anti-Tojo hue, and in early February 1941 the *kenpei* reported that the organization aimed at nothing short of Tojo's "overthrow."[50] There was even a suggestion that the association was agitating for Ishiwara's appointment to the army's "big three" in the belief that he would press for an Imperial rescript ordering the military's immediate withdrawal from China.[51]

This last point encapsulated the other key point of difference between Tojo and the East Asian League Association. The association provided something of a rallying point for those officers who had long condemned the escalatory policies in China championed by Tojo. Ishiwara publicly charged Tojo with pursuing his own ambitions in China and disturbing Sino-Japanese peace. He labeled Tojo an "enemy of Japan" and called for his arrest and execution.[52] Such posturing could have only one effect: Tojo raged at Ishiwara and at what he called "Ishiwara's political movement." Some, including Prince Higashikuni Naruhiko and the army vice minister, Lieutenant General Anami Korechika, fretted at the likely reemergence of the murderous factionalism that had divided the army in the early and mid-1930s.[53] Certainly Tojo behaved in a manner befitting a veteran of that factionalism. He doubled down on Ishiwara and, in the worst-kept secret in the army, he determined to use his ministerial prerogative to retire Ishiwara forcibly. He also decided to remove Itagaki from his command post atop the China Expeditionary Army. Meanwhile, the *kenpei* intimidated, imprisoned, and in some cases tortured East Asian League Association members.[54]

Years later, after Japan experienced bitter defeat and near ruination, the emperor criticized Tojo's use of the *kenpei*. "He overused the *kenpei*," Hirohito said, "and offended public sentiment."[55] This criticism—however genteelly understated—was leveled principally at Tojo's later actions as prime minister; it presumably applied also to those pre–prime ministerial instances when Tojo used the *kenpei* to quash dissent. Tojo himself seems to have given the matter little thought. He had never known the army to be anything but brutal in its factionalism; that factionalism had ruined his father's career in the late Meiji-era Japanese Army and had been a constant feature of Tojo's own career. It had cost his closest friend and patron, Nagata Tetsuzan, his life, and it had taught Tojo the value of the otherwise despised and underestimated *kenpei*. He had used the *kenpei* to uphold law and order in Manchukuo following the February 26 Incident, and he had, as vice minister, used the *kenpei* against Ishiwara and his associates. In early 1941, he conflated the two, so that he regarded the *kenpei* as the upholder of law, order, and his own self-defined orthodoxy in the face of what he regarded as Ishiwara's politically minded pan-Asian heresies.

TOJO MIGHT HAVE, IN March 1941, compared his own position to that of General Araki Sadao in the early and mid-1930s. As Araki had done, Tojo moved with a ruthless efficiency against officers he deemed a threat to his own position atop the army. Araki had, however, underperformed in his dealings with his ministerial colleagues. He blustered and sloganeered, but he failed to secure his ministerial colleagues' agreement to army policy. He had, as a result, failed to make any meaningful contributions to state policy. This had underwhelmed Araki's supporters within the army, and he eventually resigned his ministerial position. Tojo would avoid the same fate by steering army policy through the highest counsels of state. Most important, he would see to it that Japan undertook the southward advance and brought an end to the China Incident.

The stars certainly seemed to be aligning. Most significantly, the money and materiel that Tojo and his ministerial colleagues had diverted to the Japanese Navy seemed to have had the desired effect, so that the navy expected by April 1941 to attain a 75-percent fleet ratio vis-à-vis the United States.[56] Tojo did not pretend to know much about maritime warfare, but he knew full well that Japan's naval strategists had, for decades, confidently predicted victory in a decisive naval battle in the Pacific if only the Japanese fleet was 70 percent the size of its US counterpart. Sailors like Nomura Kichisaburo, Yonai Mitsumasa, and Yoshida Zengo remained outside their service's mainstream insofar as they argued that a decisive battle would not eventuate, that a 70 percent fleet ratio was meaningless in predicting the likelihood of victory, and that—whatever the fleet ratio—Japan could not possibly hope to defeat the United States in war.[57] Tojo had no intention of wading into this debate among the admirals; he chose—quite simply and perfectly correctly—to accept the formally expressed opinions of the navy leadership.

In a neat coincidence, in February 1941 the Germans began using all available channels to press the Japanese government for an immediate attack against Singapore. Tojo's old Military Preparatory School classmate and Japan's freshly appointed ambassador to Berlin, Oshima Hiroshi, was a peculiarly amenable messenger. He cabled Tokyo in late February, following his initial meeting with German Foreign Minister Joachim von Ribbentrop, and relayed Ribbentrop's enthusiastic request for an immediate Japanese decision to attack Singapore.[58] Days later, Oshima cabled Tokyo after having presented his diplomatic credentials to Adolf Hitler. He reported Hitler as having spoken at length about the completion of all preparations—including, particularly, submarines and planes—for an assault on Britain. And he cited Hitler's stated confidence in the launch of operations against Britain sometime beginning in late March. The precise timing relied, Hitler said, on the weather. Whatever the start date, Hitler presumed rapid success in the skies and under the waves, predicting that German troops would invade Britain sometime in May. His intention was, he told Oshima, unwavering, and Germany would continue the war until Britain's "downfall." He made clear his belief that Japan ought to put Britain to the sword by attacking Singapore. He acknowledged the possibility of US intervention but dismissed what he called US "money politics" and questioned its ability to contribute in any meaningful way to the war's outcome. Hitler spoke also of the hostility he reserved for the Soviet Union. He denounced the Soviets for trying to "Bolshevize" their Slavic neighbors in Eastern Europe. He added that he had "no faith" in the German-Soviet nonaggression pact, and instead placed his faith in the one hundred German divisions amassed in eastern Europe.[59]

Tojo trusted Hitler and believed that he had brought Oshima into his innermost confidences. He relayed to his subordinates the news that Germany had, "by and large," completed "all preparations against Britain." He echoed Hitler's focus on planes and submarines and was satisfied that Germany now had the capacity for an invasion. Britain was, he believed, on its knees, and it was difficult to look past the opportunity this seemed to offer. Southeast Asia was ripe for the picking and, for Tojo, this held out the prospect of a way out of the undeclared war in China. He began savoring victory and announced that the "sacrifice" of so many Japanese youth on China's battlefields would henceforth form the "foundation" of Japan's "perpetual prosperity."[60]

The Germans continued throughout March to push for a Japanese attack against Singapore. Germany's ambassador in Tokyo, Eugen Ott, spoke on March 4 with Army Chief of Staff Sugiyama and asked rhetorically, "Is it not necessary that Singapore be conquered?"[61] Back in Berlin, Admiral Erich Raeder told Oshima on March 18 of the intensive planning that had gone into the forthcoming invasion of Britain. He assured Oshima that the invasion would be "easy" if only the forthcoming assault from the air and from beneath the sea could enable the landing on British shores of but "one mechanized division." Raeder added his government's ardent wish that Japan launch an attack against Singapore.[62]

In a happy confluence of events, Matsuoka departed for Europe on March 12, 1941. He nonetheless cabled Tokyo sparingly, and he chose against informing his colleagues in Tokyo of his meetings with Hitler and Ribbentrop. (He also maintained silence regarding his meetings with Italian dictator Benito Mussolini and Foreign Minister Galeazzo Ciano and with Pope Pius XII.) Vice Foreign Minister Ohashi Chuichi later argued that Matsuoka worried that other nations had broken Japan's diplomatic codes and were reading Japan's diplomatic traffic.[63] Such apologetics did not impress Tojo. He wanted—not at all unreasonably—to know what was being said in Europe. He had, to be sure, dispatched Colonel Nagai Yatsuji as a member of the touring party, but Matsuoka seemed unwilling to bring Nagai into his confidences. Tojo and his colleagues in Tokyo read about Matsuoka's doings in Berlin and Rome in the newspapers. Tojo fumed at what he regarded as Matsuoka's cavalier unconcern for proper policymaking processes.[64]

Tojo would have been interested to learn that Ribbentrop told Matsuoka on March 27 of the completion of all German preparations for an attack against Britain. He doubtless would have liked to know of Ribbentrop's prediction of British surrender within a few months. He would have been familiar with Ribbentrop's assertion that Japan should, as soon as possible, attack Singapore. Tojo's curiosity would undoubtedly have been piqued had he learned of Ribbentrop's admission that the Soviets seemed unlikely to join a quadripartite pact. Perhaps most notably, Tojo almost certainly would have noted the confidence Ribbentrop professed in Germany's ability to "crush" the Soviets militarily.[65] Tojo would very much have liked to learn that Hitler himself told Matsuoka of the "need" for Britain's defeat but that the "next enemies to come will be the United States and the Soviet Union." Tojo might have expected Hitler's importuning regarding a Japanese attack on Singapore, but he would have been most interested to learn of Hitler's insistence that Germany would march to war against the Soviet Union if it attacked Japan's rear during an attack on Singapore.[66]

In the absence of such information from Matsuoka, Tojo relied on the reporting of his old friend Oshima. The soldier-diplomat reported on April 1 that Hitler was "fulminating" against what he regarded as Soviet intrigues in Yugoslavia, where a recent coup d'état had replaced the pro-German Yugoslav government with one friendly to the Soviet Union.

Oshima placed particular emphasis on Hitler's assertion that 150 German Army divisions were in position to attack the Soviets.[67] Tojo's reaction went unrecorded.

On April 5 the Yugoslavs concluded a nonaggression treaty with the Soviets. The next day Hitler ordered the German Army to attack and destroy the new, pro-Soviet Yugoslav government. Sugiyama duly reported to a liaison conference on this new development. Vice Foreign Minister Ohashi Chuichi stated that Matsuoka was in Moscow and confident of the prospects for a Japanese-Soviet neutrality treaty. But the conferees were unsettled; a monumental shift seemed to be taking place in the war in Europe and, although nobody was ready to make any grand predictions about Hitler's next move, there was palpable concern about the impact on Japanese policy. At Sugiyama and Tojo's joint insistence, conferees agreed that any Japanese-Soviet agreement must not "weaken" German-Japanese ties. They also remained adamant that a merely platitudinal Japanese-Soviet agreement—one that did not diminish the prospect of a Japanese-Soviet war and therefore did not pave the way for a southward advance and contribute to conclusion of the war in China—was "unnecessary."[68]

Negotiations in Moscow were far from smooth. Even the impossibly self-confident Matsuoka began to doubt the possibility of diplomatic success.[69] A groundswell of opposition to Matsuoka arose within the army. "What has the Foreign Minister's European tour ultimately yielded?" went one line of questioning. "We can hardly say this was expected" went one refrain. "The nation's objectives remain difficult and distant" was another criticism.[70]

Matsuoka and Joseph Stalin met on April 12, 1941, and agreed to the terms of a neutrality treaty; the treaty signing took place at the Kremlin the following afternoon.[71] At an April 14 meeting of the Army Ministry's bureau directors, Tojo asked Muto to explain the course of the negotiations. Muto concluded his account with a forecast: The treaty would, he suggested, be the subject of much "debate" in Japan. It would "make waves" and come in for "criticism" by virulent anticommunists. The Japanese Army would, he insisted, take a nuanced stance. On the one hand, criticism of the neutrality treaty by uniformed officers was off-limits. On the other hand, the army would continue and indeed strengthen its "clampdown" on domestic communists, and it would continue military preparations vis-à-vis the Soviets. Shifting the focus beyond the Japanese Army, Tojo spoke of defusing the arguments of the right-wing ideologues by disseminating information about the benefits of the treaty and gaining the understanding of "the people."[72]

THE TIME FOR TOJO to consider a Southeast Asian advance now seemed at hand. Everything seemed to be falling into place. The Japanese-Soviet relationship had undergone significant adjustment, and he could be reasonably assured that the Red Army would not attack from the north as Japanese forces advanced deep into Southeast Asia. Just as important, the Japanese Navy now boasted a fleet ratio vis-à-vis the US Navy somewhere in the vicinity of 75 percent and, despite dissenting voices among the admirals, this seemed to provide a degree of confidence in victory in the event of a decisive battle fought soon after the outbreak of Japanese-US hostilities. As if to emphasize the navy's newfound preparedness for the possibility of war, Prince Fushimi stepped down as navy chief of staff on April 9. The aging admiral's retirement was hardly unexpected and not directly attributable to the proximity of war, but it removed an Imperial family member—and, at least in the minds of those who worried about such matters, the Imperial family collectively—from the decision-making process even as the nation moved perceptibly closer to war in the Pacific. Replacing Prince Fushimi was former Combined Fleet commander in chief and onetime navy minister Nagano Osami. Whatever his strengths and weaknesses, Nagano regarded a Japanese-US war as a practical certainty, at least so long as Japan remained allied to Nazi Germany by means of the Tripartite Pact.[73]

The long-awaited German assault against Britain was, for Tojo, the final piece of the puzzle. Yet, before the ink had dried on the Japanese-Soviet neutrality treaty, Tojo received the most concrete indication yet that German priorities had shifted. Oshima sent two cables on April 16. The first reported on separate conversations with Ribbentrop and Stahmer. Their message was consistent: Germany was about to march to war against the Soviet Union. Both Ribbentrop and Stahmer maintained that Germany had the capacity to attack the Soviet Union and Britain simultaneously, but the focus had clearly switched to the Soviets.[74] In his second cable Oshima applied a strategist's eye to this stunning development. The Germans would, in his view, only attack Britain after they had defeated the Soviet Union. Oshima believed Germany's attack on the Soviets would begin sometime between May and October, and he gave the Germans every chance of success. This bought Japan a degree of freedom, for the Soviets would be preoccupied, and unable to contemplate simultaneous operations in the Soviet Far East. Oshima recommended that Japan take the opportunity to capture Singapore. This was, he wrote, in Japan's self-interest and also served German interests insofar as it would mean the Anglo-American powers would focus on Japan and leave Germany to defeat the Soviets.[75]

Tojo had little time to consider Oshima's two cables before he was confronted by another major twist. Late in the day on April 17 the Foreign Ministry began receiving from Ambassador Nomura Kichisaburo in Washington a proposal for transpacific peace known as the Draft Understanding Between Japan and the United States. Nomura asked for approval to proceed with negotiations on the basis of the Draft Understanding. It required of Japan an elastic interpretation of its Tripartite Pact commitment to enter the war on Germany's side in case the United States opened hostilities against Germany. Japan had also necessarily to forswear a forceful southward advance and commit to peace terms with Chiang Kai-shek that echoed the terms tabled during Operation Kiri. So far as the United States was concerned, the Draft Understanding required that it reopen normal commercial relations with Japan, scale back its defensive preparations in the Pacific, and cooperate with Japan in its efforts at procuring natural resources from Southeast Asia. It also required that President Roosevelt use his good offices to bring Chiang Kai-shek to the negotiating table.[76]

The Draft Understanding contrasted sharply with everything Tojo had planned and anticipated. He had been waiting for the opportunity to strike south; the understanding demanded that Japan not launch a southward advance. He had anticipated the possibility of war between Japan and the United States; the understanding promised to return relations to a harmonious footing. He had regarded the United States as an impediment to successful conclusion of the China Incident; the understanding sought active US assistance in concluding it.

It is difficult to imagine Tojo giving the Draft Understanding much more than a moment's thought but for the hopelessly faulty assumptions that had hitherto informed all of his strategy and planning. He had falsely believed that Germany would soon defeat Britain, and he had mistakenly regarded Germany, Italy, Japan, and the Soviet Union as being united behind a shared commitment to overthrow the existing Anglo-American-centric world order. Hitler had turned everything on its head by turning away from the long-promised attack on Britain and planned to attack instead one of the presumed revisionist powers in the Soviet Union. What this meant for Japanese policy was far from certain. Tojo had, of necessity, to rethink.

The Draft Understanding commanded Tojo's attention; he could not help but notice that it held out the tantalizing prospect of an end to the China Incident. It was not the victor's peace for which Tojo hoped, but it went no further than the peace terms that had earlier informed Operation Kiri. It delineated such terms as Chinese "independence"; the "withdrawal of Japanese troops from Chinese territory"; no "acquisition of territory"; no "indemnities"; the resumption of the traditional US Open Door Policy in China, including freedom of commercial opportunity; the coalescence of the Chiang and Wang regimes; and "recognition of Manchukuo." The Draft Understanding departed from Operation Kiri in two essential ways: It made no mention of Inner Mongolia's and North China's independence, and it seemed to presume application of Open Door principles not only to South China but also to the Yangtze River basin and, indeed, across China. Even so, the Draft Understanding trumped Operation Kiri insofar as it made an eye-catching provision for Roosevelt to request Chiang Kai-shek's agreement to "negotiate peace with Japan."[77]

But Tojo had little time to consider the Draft Understanding before he received a cable, via military channels, from Washington, over the signature of Colonel Iwakuro Hideo. Iwakuro was one of the army's ablest mid-ranking officers, who had been among the staunchest advocates of both the Tripartite Pact and a forceful southward advance. He had supported Tojo's ministerial appointment, but his brash and cocky ways had seen him drop out of Tojo's favor. His two-year term atop the Army Affairs Section came to an end in February 1941; in a neat coincidence, Ambassador Nomura had on the eve of his nearly simultaneous departure for Washington requested that the army dispatch an officer to aid and assist him in forthcoming negotiations with US officials. Tojo had settled on Iwakuro—partly to keep an eye on Nomura, and partly to get Iwakuro out of his own hair. He had also half wondered whether Iwakuro, with his proclivity for political machinations and manipulations, might cook something up in Washington. He had heard nothing from Iwakuro since—which annoyed him immensely—and he was given to wondering about the extent to which Iwakuro's hand was discernible in the Draft Understanding.[78]

Iwakuro's cable made no mention of his involvement in authoring the Draft Understanding. His focus lay elsewhere: He pleaded for its rapid acceptance and the pursuit of negotiations with the United States. He wrote of the virtual "inevitability" of US entry into the European war, and in so doing admitted that the Tripartite Pact had failed in its high-handed attempt at scaring the United States away from war. In a further admission of the vacuity of the Tripartite Pact, Iwakuro wrote also that a forceful Japanese advance into Southeast Asia would in all likelihood trigger Japanese-US hostilities. The United States had called the Tripartite Pact's bluff, and Iwakuro fretted that a US war against Germany and Japan would became "protracted" and prohibitively costly. He added that the outcome would be "uncertain." The Draft Understanding, he suggested, offered a viable alternative. It would not only avert a Japanese-US war but would also contribute to resolution of the China Incident. A resumption of normal Japanese-US trade was another benefit. He recommended that Tojo lead the government in considering the Draft Understanding "as quickly as possible." He suggested a deadline of April 23, 1941 for the government to accept negotiations with the United States on the basis of the Draft Understanding.[79]

Tojo heard almost simultaneously from the military attaché to the Japanese embassy in Washington, Major General Isoda Saburo. Like Iwakuro, Isoda wrote of US intervention in the European war as if it were inevitable. He, too, argued that a forceful Japanese advance into Southeast Asia would spark a Japanese-US war. Isoda was convinced the Americans would fight a protracted war of attrition, which could only be disadvantageous to Japan. He was not satisfied that the Germans would emerge victorious over Britain (he was unaware that Hitler had turned his attention toward the Soviets), and he worried lest the Germans eventually conclude a negotiated peace with the British. Japan would, in this case, be left alone to fight the Anglo-American powers. Even if the British did surrender, the Americans would remain undefeated and, at least so far as Japan was concerned, undefeatable.[80]

According to Isoda, US interest in the Draft Understanding and in transpacific peace derived principally from a desire to avoid a two-front war in the Atlantic and Pacific regions. He was considerably more forthcoming than Iwakuro about the Draft Understanding's genesis: He noted his own involvement, as well as that of Ambassador Nomura; the naval attaché, Captain Yokoyama Ichiro; banker Ikawa Tadao; and Iwakuro. Isoda also wrote of the involvement of two Roman Catholic priests—Bishop James Walsh and Father James Drought—who had visited Japan in late 1940 and spoken with Muto Akira and others about the search for Japanese-US peace. They were private citizens with a connection—in the person of Postmaster General Frank Walker—to the Roosevelt administration. This was far more forthright than Iwakuro had been; Isoda nonetheless descended into a flight of fancy with his twin assertions that the Draft

Understanding had gained Roosevelt's "consent" and the United States had "agreed" to its terms.[81]

UNBEKNOWNST TO TOJO AND others in Tokyo, the Imperial Navy's top brass had played a crucial role in instructing Nomura's actions as he brought the Draft Understanding to fruition. The navy also took the lead in laying the groundwork for it by reopening discussions on April 5 with the army about the southward advance. In a case of exquisite timing, on April 17 the armed services agreed that Japan's objectives vis-à-vis Southeast Asia must be restricted, to a greater or lesser extent, to the economic and commercial sphere. Crucially, they agreed to attain those objectives by only "diplomatic means." This gave the Draft Understanding some possibility of success. It came at a price: The armed services, expressing their underlying determination, agreed also that Japan would resort to "military means" toward the south if its "self-existence and self-defense" were threatened by either a US embargo or a British-Chinese-Dutch-US encirclement. These seemed the likely outcomes in the event the Draft Understanding fell flat.[82]

On April 18 Konoe convened a liaison conference for the express purpose of studying the Draft Understanding. Sugiyama and Tojo attended with the understanding that "no decisions" be reached, and that the conference instead dedicate itself instead to "free discussion" of the document. Konoe presented the Draft Understanding to the conference as an "American proposal."[83] To Tojo, who reckoned he saw Iwakuro's fingerprints all over it, the idea that it was an "American proposal" sounded very much like a "cock and bull story" (*mayutsubomono*).[84] Yet he chose against correcting Konoe's misrepresentation. Instead he kept his silence and let Sugiyama launch into a barrage of questions:. Did the United States not hope by means of the Draft Understanding to "step up" aid to Britain? Did the Draft Understanding not "conflict with the Tripartite Pact"? Would "peace overtures to China" contradict Japan's past position and, in particular, its support for Wang Jingwei in Nanjing? Would the Draft Understanding undermine establishment of the Greater East Asia Co-Prosperity Sphere? Revisions were necessary. Should Japan "get started on an amended draft" or simply reject the Draft Understanding?[85]

Tojo maintained what was fast becoming a characteristic silence (or at least near silence) during the liaison conference. He saw little point in saying anything much. He was more interested in shifting the conversation down a level, in an effort at forging unity between the Army and Navy Ministries as well as the General Staffs. The result was an April 21 conference between Military Affairs Bureau director Muto Akira, Army General Staff Operations Bureau director Tanaka Shin'ichi, and their naval counterparts, Rear Admirals Oka Takazumi and Fukudome Shigeru. Here unity was forged on what conferees called "Ambassador Nomura's proposal" (thus rejecting Konoe's characterization of the Draft Understanding as an "American proposal"). They agreed that the Draft Understanding would facilitate US policies of aiding Britain, weakening the Tripartite Pact, and containing Japan's forceful southward advance. They also agreed that it held out the otherwise nonexistent prospect of an end to the China Incident. They felt it also promised to buy Japan the breathing space required to revive and resuscitate its national strength. On these grounds, the conferees believed it possible to turn the Draft Understanding to Japan's advantage. Key issues were, they agreed, fivefold: It would be necessary to ensure that the Draft Understanding did not "contradict" the spirit of the Tripartite Pact; contributed to "disposal" of the China Incident; did no damage to Japan's "international honor"; aided the "expansion" of Japan's "overall national strength"; and contributed to the restoration of "world peace."[86]

Later that same day, Fukudome and Muto met with the Foreign Ministry's American Bureau director, Terasaki Taro, and set about making revisions to the Draft Understanding. There were two notable revisions. The first involved the treatment of the US "attitude" toward the European war. The draft received from Nomura included the following statement: "The Government of the United States maintains that its attitude toward the European War is, and will continue to be, directed by no such aggressive measures as to assist any one nation against another." In an attempt at closing off ongoing US support for Britain, Muto, Fukudome, and Terasaki deleted the word "aggressive." The second revision centered on the treatment of the China Incident. The original draft's delineation of peace terms remained untouched; the revision came in the form of an appended "note" making clear the desirability of a US commitment to cut aid to Chinese leader Chiang Kai-shek if he refused to sit at the negotiating table with Japan. To soften the impact of this "note," Muto, Fukudome, and Terasaki agreed that it need not "be included in the actual text" of the Draft Understanding but could instead take the form of an auxiliary note. Crucially, the Draft Understanding's requirement that Japan pledge a "peaceful" advance into Southeast Asia went untouched.[87]

Tojo spoke late that afternoon with the emperor's chief aide-de-camp, General Hasunuma Shigeru, of what he now regarded as unity among the army, navy, and foreign ministries and also the Army and Navy General Staffs on the issue of diplomatic rapprochement with the United States in accord with the provisions of the Draft Understanding.[88] Diplomat Terasaki Taro agreed. He prepared for Nomura a cable indicating Tokyo's "in-principle agreement" with the Draft Understanding.[89]

TERASAKI NEVER SENT THAT cable. Vice Foreign Minister Ohashi Chuichi refused to allow its transmission, insisting that Terasaki await Matsuoka's return from Europe.[90] The wait was not a long one, for Matsuoka arrived home the following day. Konoe met Matsuoka at the airport and tried to broach the Draft Understanding with him. Matsuoka, however, showed no interest in speaking with Konoe. He proceeded directly to the Imperial Palace to report to the emperor.[91]

Tojo heard that same afternoon from Colonel Nagai Yatsuji, who had accompanied Matsuoka on his European tour. Nagai opened his report by mentioning Hitler's unshakable confidence in total German victory in Europe. Germany was, he added, better prepared for protracted warfare than during the previous world war. He spoke of the forthcoming intensification of German submarine warfare in the Atlantic and German acceptance of the unavoidability of US entry into the war. He related Hitler's "extreme indignation" at the Soviet Union and belief in the "need to strike a blow" against the Soviets. The invasion of Britain would, Nagai stated, be the final "act" of the war in Europe.[92]

Nagai also addressed German positions on Japanese policy. He revealed himself to be in agreement with the German government's desire for an immediate Japanese decision to attack Singapore. A proponent of what might be termed the "war sooner better than war later" thesis, Nagai based his call for an attack on Singapore on the observation that the United States was not yet prepared for war. Singapore aside, Nagai related a near complete German disinterest in the restoration of Sino-Japanese peace. The Germans were, he related, similarly dismissive of Japanese policy toward the Soviet Union. Ribbentrop had completely forsaken all hope of drawing the Soviet Union into alliance with Germany, Italy, and Japan. And Hitler seemed to think that any "adjustment" in Japanese-Soviet relations would only ever be shallow and therefore "easily" accomplished.[93]

Nagai concluded with a message from Oshima in Berlin. Oshima observed that German-Soviet relations had deteriorated so precipitously that the situation was utterly unlike what it had been in the latter months of 1940. He was satisfied that the Germans were in an unassailable position, and he expected the Soviets to "flirt" with the Germans in the interest of avoiding an unfavorable war. He nonetheless believed that Hitler would not revoke his decision to go to war against the Soviets. Oshima insisted that the long-awaited attack against Britain remained "Hitler's real intention," and it would commence sometime in 1941. He added that British surrender should take place in no more than four months after the invasion had commenced. It was in this context, Oshima suggested, that the Germans were so "extremely desirous" of a Japanese attack on Singapore; they believed that would signal the end of the British Empire and thereby end any prospect of Britain rising, phoenix-like, from the ashes of war.[94]

Tojo joined his colleagues at a liaison conference that evening. Matsuoka was intent on bathing in the glory of his European sojourn and professed little interest in the Draft Understanding and diplomatic rapprochement with the United States. In a rare instance of understatement, Matsuoka noted that it "differed from what he had in mind." He wanted to "think about it at his leisure," and suggested he might need two months to "consider it carefully."[95] Over the ensuing days Matsuoka argued for an attack on Singapore. Tojo met on April 25, 1941, with Konoe and Oikawa and registered his opposition to Matsuoka. He argued, and Oikawa agreed, that Japan ought first to "use the United States" to resolve the China Incident.[96]

Tojo spoke with the Army General Staff later that afternoon. He reported that Konoe wanted to proceed with negotiations on the basis of the Draft Understanding and that Oikawa wanted to do so promptly. Tojo then expounded on his own position. Resolution of the China Incident was, he stated, the "fundamental issue," and the Draft Understanding promised to resolve precisely this issue. Japan must not, he said, "miss this opportunity." Tojo next addressed German enthusiasm for an attack on Singapore. The Germans seemed to "forget," he stated, just how distant they were from East Asia. An attack on Singapore was impossible unless Japanese forces had access to bases in southern Indochina and perhaps also Thailand. He added that an attack on Singapore necessarily required near simultaneous attacks on the Dutch East Indies and the Philippines. This was primarily the navy's responsibility; even so, ten army divisions were a minimum requirement. So, too, were the ships needed to transport those divisions to the vicinity of the fighting. Arguments for the "capture of Singapore in one fell swoop" were, Tojo insisted, "perplexing." He concluded with what he regarded as the proper course for Japanese policy. Unconcerned by the fundamental incompatibility of the Draft Understanding and the southward advance, he argued that Japan should proceed simultaneously with both diplomatic rapprochement with the United States and the acquisition of bases in southern Indochina and Thailand. It only remained, in Tojo's estimation, to get such an approach into "Matsuoka's head."[97]

8
REDRAWING THE BATTLE LINES
APRIL–AUGUST 1941

TOJO HIDEKI LOOKED ON in exasperation as the policymaking process ground to a halt in late April 1941. He told the Policy Planning Board president, Suzuki Teiichi, of his desire to move on the Draft Understanding Between Japan and the United States and of his annoyance at Matsuoka Yosuke's obtuseness.[1] Matsuoka, for his part, pleaded ill and confined himself to his home. He emerged but once, to deliver a public address in which he singled out Prime Minister Konoe Fumimaro and Home Minister Hiranuma Kiichiro for fierce criticism. It was a self-serving publicity stunt that hinted at Matsuoka's own ambitions to be prime minister, and it ended any sense of ministerial collegiality and solidarity that had undergirded the Konoe cabinet. Konoe sulked and, like Matsuoka, confined himself to his home.[2]

The Japanese embassy in Washington, DC, fretted that the moment for diplomatic rapprochement might pass. Ambassador Nomura Kichisaburo regarded a clash between German submarines and the US Navy as imminent, and he worried about the pressure Japan would face to make good on its promise to come to Germany's aid—if for no good reason other than the fact that the German-Italian-Japanese Tripartite Pact had failed to scare the United States away from the war in Europe. He repeatedly cabled Matsuoka, as well as the naval authorities, in a forlorn effort at securing approval to proceed with negotiations on the basis of the Draft Understanding.[3] Colonel Iwakuro Hideo cabled Major General Muto Akira in late April and issued a similar plea for a timely agreement to proceed with negotiations.[4]

Then, on May 2, Iwakuro cabled Tojo. The rambling telegram included wide-ranging speculations—presented as incontrovertible fact—on the recent disempowerment of "anti-Japanese" voices in Washington. Iwakuro also sought to impress on Tojo that the United States would continue to strengthen its ongoing support for Britain. Iwakuro regarded US entry into the European war as a virtual inevitability, and he fretted about Japan's commitment to come to the assistance—including militarily—of Germany and Italy in that event. He asked for an end to what he called Matsuoka's diplomacy of "gesture," and he pleaded with Tojo to prod the government into "making a big move" and proceeding with negotiations. Iwakuro suggested that even if civilian ministers were unsympathetic, the armed services could act on their own initiative and order Nomura to explore the possibility of diplomatic rapprochement in his negotiations with US officials.[5]

Tojo had worked hard to rehabilitate the Imperial Japanese Army's relationship with the emperor. Tojo had no intention of undoing that good work by acting as a maverick; he would stay within established policymaking structures. An opportunity arose on May 3, when Konoe and Matsuoka both emerged from their self-imposed isolation to attend the first liaison conference held in almost a fortnight. Matsuoka was back to his curmudgeonly and blustery best. He floated far-reaching revisions to the Draft Understanding, including a demand that the administration of US President Franklin D. Roosevelt, first, accept Japan's unswerving determination to come to the aid of Germany and Italy should the United States continue aiding the Britain; second, deliver Chiang Kai-shek to the negotiating table on blind faith, because Matsuoka deleted any mention of peace terms Japan might offer Chiang; and, third, accept that Japan would make no promises about its intentions—peaceful or otherwise—in Southeast Asia. Tojo expected debate on Matsuoka's redraft, because it was considerably more strident than even the army thought necessary. Matsuoka, however, shifted the debate with bewildering rapidity across a series of side issues and loosely related thoughts and proposals. He raised and refuted rumors concerning his status as a German lickspittle, urged an attack on Singapore, insisted on the need for consultation with Japan's German and Italian allies, and floated an idea for a Japanese-US neutrality treaty. Disagreement with the neutrality treaty proposal was universal, as most felt it could only diminish the prospects of the Draft Understanding (in whatever iteration). Uncertainty reigned; none felt satisfied they knew what they had agreed to. Nonetheless, as the meeting came to a close, it "appeared" that everything was left to Matsuoka to decide.[6]

For reasons of his own, and in direct contradiction of the wishes of his colleagues, Matsuoka instructed Ambassador Nomura to float a Japanese-US neutrality treaty. This cavalier unconcern for his colleagues' opposition to the proposal annoyed Tojo, and another liaison conference on May 8 did nothing to brighten his mood. Matsuoka again stole the show, raising a series of hypothetical situations that, he insisted, would pit Japan and the United States in war.[7] He also taunted the armed services for their "pusillanimous" attitude.[8]

Tojo's patience was wearing thin. It seemed almost incomprehensible that the armed services could forge agreement on the Draft Understanding only to see everything unravel due to a loose cannon like Matsuoka. On May 9 he received a cable from the military attaché to the Japanese embassy in Washington, Isoda Saburo, who reported on what he regarded as the proximity of German-US hostilities and the high likelihood that Japan would soon have to decide whether to fulfill its alliance obligations and open war against the United States. Isoda also lambasted Matsuoka's Japanese-US neutrality treaty proposal, insisting that it was "necessary to proceed without delay with the Draft Understanding." Tojo spoke that same day with Vice Admiral Oikawa Koshiro, and they agreed that the time to confront Matsuoka had arrived. They met with him and were singularly unimpressed by his arguments that he was awaiting German affirmation of his policies. Oikawa and Tojo told Matsuoka to cable the revised Draft Understanding posthaste to Nomura, replete with instructions to deliver it to US officials.[9]

If anybody was ever going to confront Matsuoka about his revisions to the Draft Understanding, this was the moment. Yet Oikawa and Tojo declined to take the opportunity. What happened? In its original iteration the Draft Understanding had commended itself to Tojo precisely because it held out the promise of an end to the China Incident; a loosening of Japan's alliance with Germany and Italy was a price he was willing to consider. Now that Matsuoka had changed the Draft Understanding so that Japan was angling for a continuation and indeed amplification of its Tripartite Pact commitments, as well as victory in China, Tojo did nothing to stop him. His reasoning was simple: the Draft Understanding's primary focus was not the China Incident but Japanese-US diplomatic rapprochement. And Tojo presumed that because the Imperial Japanese Navy would bear the brunt of the fighting in the event of a Japan-US war, the navy of necessity had the greatest stake in the Draft Understanding. If Oikawa took overt issue with Matsuoka's redraft and argued against revisions that located the Tripartite Pact at the core of Japanese policy, Tojo was doubtless prepared to support Oikawa and speak up in defense of the original delineation of peace terms to be offered Chiang Kai-shek. From the viewpoint of interservice relations,

Tojo's logic was impeccable. Oikawa was not, however, the right man for the task at hand. He wanted to avoid war against the United States, but he was weak, vacillating, and utterly nonconfrontational. He would, in all likelihood, have offered his support had Tojo tackled Matsuoka's revisions to the Draft Understanding, but Oikawa declined to take the lead, as Tojo believed he must, and the moment was lost.

Matsuoka might have considered this something of a victory. He had succeeded in weaning the armed service ministers away from their earlier position of support—albeit guarded support—for the original iteration of the Draft Understanding. He nonetheless remained cantankerous and continued to await German affirmation of his policies. He did not cable the revised Draft Understanding to Nomura until May 12. Lest there was any doubt as to the purport of his revisions to the document, Matsuoka also sent a provocative memorandum with instructions to submit it to US Secretary of State Cordell Hull. The memorandum emphasized that Japanese-US rapprochement was possible only if the United States remained aloof from the war in Europe and washed its hands of China.[10]

So far as Japanese-US relations were concerned, there was little to do but wait for the US response to Matsuoka's revisions. The Americans were predictably disappointed at the heavy-handed revisions and were in no rush to respond; debate within the Japanese Army switched back to French Indochina. Two midranking officers who owed their positions to Tojo—the General Staff's Operations Section chief, Colonel Doi Akio, and the Military Affairs Section chief, Colonel Sato Kenryo—began arguing in early May for not just air bases and troop passage through southern Indochina but also the permanent stationing of troops in or around Saigon. They also wanted conclusion of a military agreement with Thailand. They rested their case on what they called "ABCD encirclement": they argued that the Americans (A) and British (B) were aiding Chiang Kai-shek (C) and also encouraging colonial authorities in the Dutch East Indies (D) to resist Japan's diplomatic efforts at procuring resources vital to its defense industries. These efforts, in Doi and Sato's estimation, were an attempt at encircling and containing Japan. They argued that a southern Indochinese advance would signal Japan's refusal to acquiesce in these ABCD policies. Middle-echelon navy officers were simultaneously making similar arguments in the halls of the Navy General Staff and Navy Ministry. Even so, Doi and Sato's enthusiasm for a southern Indochinese advance did not gain immediate favor within the army. Most important, the vice chief of staff, Lieutenant General Tsukada Osamu, opposed the advance on the grounds that its objectives were unclear. Tojo seemed content to allow Tsukada to play spoiler.[11]

Without any definite word from Tojo, the issue bubbled away among the army's middle echelons. By mid-May 1941, Tojo's subordinates in the ministry forged a consensus with their counterparts on the Army General Staff on the need for a southern Indochinese advance. Tojo finally intervened. He took no issue with the direction of the soldiers' discussions, but he nonetheless noted that Matsuoka had declined, when negotiating an end to the Indochinese-Thai border dispute, to apply pressure in pursuit of military agreements with either the Indochinese or the Thais. He anticipated Matsuoka's continued opposition to any such pursuit, and he made apparent his disinclination to push too hard on this score. Informing this position was Tojo's concern that he might isolate himself at the cabinet level with talk of further advances. He had earned the emperor's trust by fashioning himself as a model minister, and he was not turning back now. He signaled a refusal to make any "formal statements" at liaison conferences regarding southern Indochina and Thailand.[12]

Tojo made good on this promise and maintained a virtual silence at subsequent liaison conferences. Matsuoka felt no such need. In one of his more memorable performances, Matsuoka reported on May 22 on the failure of a monthslong diplomatic effort led by the former foreign minister, Yoshizawa Kenkichi. The mission had aimed to secure from the Dutch East Indies materials vital to Japanese defense industries. Extrapolating from the situation, Matsuoka launched into what can only have been an unscripted rant. In one breath, he forecast Japanese attacks against Malaya and the Philippines; in the next, he forecast a war in which a British-German-Soviet-US coalition fought against Japan. Tojo held his tongue, but Sugiyama Hajime could not resist. "For the Malayan part of this decision alone," he cried, "it will be necessary to lay the groundwork in Thailand and French Indochina." He lambasted Matsuoka for having failed, when mediating the Thai-Indochinese border dispute, to secure military agreements with the Indochinese and the Thais. Oikawa could not look past Matsuoka's suggestion of a British-German-Soviet-US coalition, and he openly questioned the foreign minister's sanity.[13]

RECALL THAT TOJO'S OLD friend and Japan's ambassador to Berlin, Oshima Hiroshi, had in mid-April apprised Tojo and others in Tokyo of the imminence of a German-Soviet war. Over the ensuing weeks, many uniformed officers in Tokyo suspected that this owed more to bluff and misinformation than to actual German intentions. The uncertainty ended following receipt of a May 28 cable from the military attaché to the Japanese embassy in Berlin, Banzai Ichiro. He wrote that the German Army had "completed its strategic deployment vis-à-vis the Soviets" and was "confident" in its ability to "bring a close to operations within three or four months."[14] Banzai wrote again on June 5: "The opening of a German-Soviet war is certain."[15] Oshima chimed in, sending on June 5–6 a series of telegrams reporting on his recent conversations with Adolf Hitler and Joachim von Ribbentrop. The tenor of those conversations was unmistakable: A German-Soviet war was not only "unavoidable" but imminent.[16]

In a neat coincidence, on June 5 Tojo learned from Iwakuro that Matsuoka's revisions to the Draft Understanding had drastically dimmed the prospect of Japanese-US rapprochement. The issues were essentially twofold. The first was that Matsuoka's twin aims of strengthening the Tripartite Pact and keeping the United States out of the war in Europe were unattainable; a German-US armed clash was a practical inevitability. The Roosevelt administration hoped that Japan might, via the Draft Understanding, divest itself of its solemn treaty-defined commitment to aid Germany politically, economically, and militarily in this event. This was not, however, a prerequisite of US policy toward the war in Europe, and the United States was prepared, if necessary, to go to war against Germany and risk a Japanese attack. The second issue centered on China. Iwakuro reported that Matsuoka's redraft had caused the United States to back away from any role in helping resolve the China Incident. Specifically, the Roosevelt administration was leery of the Matsuoka redraft's deletion of peace terms to be offered China and was "reluctant" to bring Chiang Kai-shek to the negotiating table with Japan. US policymakers might, moreover, have been forgiven had they decided it was better to leave Japan in the mess of its own making in China if Japan continued, by means of the Tripartite Pact, to threaten the United States with war in the Pacific Ocean region. In Iwakuro's estimation the Draft Understanding must now be regarded purely as the means by which Japan might divest itself of its alliance obligations to Germany if and when the United States went to war in the Atlantic. Even if Japan and the United States reached agreement, Iwakuro was unconvinced that any transpacific understanding would last. Partly because he foresaw an eventual Japanese-US "breakup," he suggested that Japan "should prepare for a southward advance."[17]

Army officers in Tokyo professed little interest in diplomatic rapprochement with the United States, but with a German-Soviet war on the horizon they saw an opportunity for a southward advance. The southern half of French Indochina provided the initial point of focus. Navy officers were in broad agreement on an advance. The army and navy agreed that it should preferably proceed peacefully and as a result of diplomatic agreement, but there was equally a focus on building military and naval preparedness for an advance if the French refused to accede to Japanese demands. Finally, and most strikingly, there was also a declaration of the armed services' determination to undertake the advance, even if doing so entailed the "risk" of war against Britain and the United States.[18]

Navy Chief of Staff Nagano Osami took the case for a southern Indochinese advance to a liaison conference. "We must build bases in French Indochina and Thailand in order to launch military operations. We must resolutely attack anyone who tries to stop us," he declared. "We must resort to force if we have to."[19] Tojo was only too happy to allow the suddenly bullish Nagano to take the lead. Tojo had, only weeks earlier, sworn off any attempt at steering a southern Indochinese advance through the decision-making process. He had no intention of standing apart from his cabinet colleagues and haranguing them about an advance. Now, however, the Navy General Staff was forging ahead, and a southern Indochinese advance could no longer be considered an army initiative. The difference was critical, and Tojo saw every reason to support Nagano in his enthusiasm for the advance. Yet, at least so far as Tojo and the army were concerned, the southern Indochinese advance was only ever an interim measure. The real question was what Japan should do *after* such an advance.

THE JAPANESE ARMY'S OPERATIONAL and political nerve centers were hives of activity as uniformed officers debated what should follow the southern Indochinese advance. At one end of the debate were officers who regarded the advance as a springboard for further advances south. In their view, access to Southeast Asia's abundant raw materials was necessary before the army launched large-scale operations against the Soviets.[20] At the other end of the debate were those who prioritized a northward advance against Soviet forces stationed in the Far East. They argued against advancing further southward than Indochina on the grounds that it would land Japan in war against the Anglo-American powers and render war against the Soviets impracticable.[21] Army Chief of Staff Sugiyama Hajime was, for his part, satisfied that the use of force was "inevitable," but he professed uncertainty at the "question of north or south." Consensus was forged among staff officers in early June around the concept of the "use of force in the south *and* north at the first opportunity."[22]

Tojo and his subordinates in the Army Ministry were at significant variance with Sugiyama and the General Staff. Whereas General Staff officers were confident of a total and rapid German victory, Tojo and his subordinates considered the possibility whereby the Germans found themselves in a Soviet quagmire, in which defeat seemed unlikely but victory remained elusive. This cautious appraisal of Germany's prospects led to a relatively moderate approach. On June 9 Tojo approved a policy paper that held a threefold emphasis: First, it elucidated the need for preparedness to join the war against the Soviets in the event a German victory seemed imminent. Second, it called for preparedness to advance into Southeast Asia if a German victory over Britain became apparent. Third, it insisted that Japan must remain true to its Tripartite Pact obligations in the event the United States entered the war in Europe, but it also insisted that Japan must decide for itself the timing and manner of its response.[23]

Even as this debate played out in the army, Matsuoka opposed the advance into southern French Indochina, worried that it might "provoke Britain and the United States."[24] Tojo might have been forgiven had he asked what happened to the man who only weeks earlier had taunted the armed services for their reluctance to attack Singapore. Yet he kept his counsel and allowed Matsuoka to lurch wildly, in the space of a few days, from opposition to a southern Indochinese advance, to agreement with the advance, and back again to spirited opposition. Without any prodding from Tojo, Matsuoka was creating an image of himself as unruly, intractable, and undisciplined. Within the army, a new view of Matsuoka was taking hold. "When Matsuoka is good he is good," wrote one officer, "but when he is bad he really is bad."[25] Tojo had long since reached a similar conclusion; now, however, he wanted agreement on the southern Indochinese advance. "If we don't finish the job before the end of the year," he warned on June 16, "we will have to abandon our policy of establishing the Greater East Asia Co-Prosperity Sphere." Then, in a comment aimed perhaps as much at the curiously quiescent Konoe as at Matsuoka, Tojo stated simply, "After the preparations are completed, *what we need is a decision.*"[26] Matsuoka held out until June 21, but he finally indicated his agreement with a southern Indochinese advance.[27]

Sugiyama and Tojo had, in the meantime, brought together their subordinates in the interest of forging consensus on the use of force in the north or south after the southern Indochinese advance. At Tojo's insistence, all officers agreed that whatever the army did in response to the German-Soviet war, it had necessarily to contribute to resolution of the China Incident. The southern Indochinese advance fit precisely this bill, at least as an interim measure, insofar as it would allow Japanese forces to put pressure on the Burma Road, by which the Anglo-Americans were now funneling aid to Chiang Kai-shek. Officers acknowledged that this raised the prospect of war against the Anglo-American powers, and they insisted Japan would make any decisions about war in the Pacific "independently" of its alliance partners. Japan's uniformed military officers nonetheless continued to hope that it would be unnecessary, and they agreed to continue to pursue diplomatic rapprochement vis-à-vis the United States. They evinced a determination to use force to the north in the event German victory over the Soviet Union seemed imminent and agreed that Japan ought to intervene against the Soviets as soon as an "exceedingly favorable" opportunity arose. Japan must, for the meantime, prepare for such a likely eventuality. Finally, they agreed to guard against any move that might dissipate Japan's national strength, setting aside any thought of advancing north and south simultaneously. In this way they agreed that war against an Anglo-American-Soviet coalition was beyond Japan's capacities; Japan had to fight either the Anglo-American powers or the Soviets. Their opportunistic instincts were so finely tuned that none spoke of neutrality or of standing aloof from the war that was quickly engulfing the globe.[28]

On June 18 the Army General Staff's Operations Section drafted an operational plan to reflect this new military policy. The plan, titled "Junbijin taisei" (Preparatory-formation setup), allowed for possible action in both the north and the south. The envisioned troop basis, in the north, totaled sixteen divisions: twelve in the Kwantung Army, two in the Japanese Korean Army, and two more divisions transferred from Japan. Conversely, five divisions would be placed on standby to advance southward. This plan also allowed for the maintenance of twenty-two divisions in China. If the decision were subsequently reached to advance north, nine more divisions would be transferred (five from Japan and four from China), giving the Kwantung Army a total of twenty-four divisions to fight the Soviets. If, however, the decision were reached to advance south, five more divisions would be transferred from Japan for a total of ten divisions in Southeast Asia.[29]

This operational plan spooked the Imperial Navy, whose officers could not help but see in the setup a predetermined focus on the army's traditional enemy to the north. The navy fretted at the money and materiel the army would need in a war against the Soviets. This would come at the navy's expense and result in a critical slowdown in its fleet expansion programs even as the US Navy engaged in the greatest shipbuilding program in history. To this end, the navy sought specific assurances that the army would adopt a policy of "ripe persimmon-ism" toward the Soviet Union. This entailed waiting for evidence that German victory was nigh and the ripe Soviet Far Eastern "persimmon" would fall off the tree with only minimal prodding from the Japanese Army. The navy also took issue with the army's desire for an ex ante commitment to strike if and when an opportunity arose in either the north or south and insisted that any decision involving the use of force must necessarily take into consideration the circumstances at the time an opportunity arose.[30]

Tojo prioritized army-navy unity and proved willing to accept the navy's suggestions. Some in the army grumbled at what they regarded as an army-navy "proposal for preparedness sans a decision."[31] At issue, so far as uniformed army officers were concerned, was the navy's refusal to address unequivocally its willingness to go to war with the United States. Major General Tanaka Shin'ichi put this very question to uniformed navy officers. They responded that the navy had only two choices if Japanese-US relations became "critical": it could either fight or it could retreat and submit to US demands. In a show of bravado that revealed more about interservice rivalry than it did about the navy's prospects in a Pacific war, the admirals insisted that sailors did not—could not—retreat, and the navy would, if necessary, fight. This did little to reassure Tanaka, who believed that his naval counterparts spoke without conviction but with a view merely to maximizing the navy's budgetary claims. Tojo may well have entertained similar doubts but he remained, at least outwardly, steadfast in his emphasis on a united army-navy stance.[32]

EVEN AS TOJO WAS uniting the army behind the preparatory-formation setup, the US revisions to the Draft Understanding arrived in Tokyo. The revisions required that Japan explicitly divest itself of the Tripartite Pact, accept a significantly diminished US role in delivering Chiang Kai-shek to the negotiating table, forswear a forceful advance into Southeast Asia, and bow to the US disinclination to negotiate a new transpacific commercial treaty. Tojo gave this US version of the Draft Understanding little thought. He noted that it diluted, almost beyond recognition, any US role in bringing an end to the China Incident. The Draft Understanding had originally commended itself to Tojo precisely because it held out the tantalizing promise of an end to the war in China; he now concluded that this latest iteration held no appeal whatever. There was nothing in the US counterproposal that might have caused Tojo and the army to rethink the fundamental direction of Japanese policy.[33]

Within twenty-four hours of receipt of the US counterproposal, German forces launched their assault on the Soviet Union. Soviet fronts in the north, south, and center disintegrated as German panzer columns advanced with breathtaking rapidity. This sparked in the Japanese Navy a neurotic concern that its sister service might abandon the southward advance and instead march to war against the Soviets. The admirals drew everyone's attention back to the immediate issue at hand—namely, the southern Indochinese advance. They also championed a wait-and-see approach toward both the Soviets in the north and the colonial areas beyond Indochina in the south. Tojo was only too happy to step back and allow the navy to take the lead. Consensus was forged on the southern Indochinese advance on June 25, 1941.[34]

The wait-and-see approach toward the German-Soviet war was the subject of considerable debate, and Matsuoka provided the principal dissenting voice. At a series of liaison conferences across consecutive days in late June, he argued passionately for an immediate decision for war against the Soviets. Tojo spoke sparingly; his interventions were icy and telling. Matsuoka argued, for example, that the Germans were concerned by the "movement of Soviet Far Eastern troops to the West"; Tojo counseled that this was Germany's problem and Japan "should not feel strongly" about it.[35] Matsuoka argued for greater consultation with the Germans concerning Japan's next move; Tojo ended this line of argument with a simple and dismissive observation: "Germany has not consulted us."[36] Matsuoka argued at length for a policy of "first strike north, and then go south" even if it was necessary "to give up to a certain extent in China"; Tojo insisted that the "China Incident must be continued and settled."[37]

Tojo's message was clear. He would not be forced into making any rash decisions, and the army did not take its marching orders from Matsuoka. As Tojo's foreign affairs expert, the Military Affairs Bureau director, Major General Muto Akira, explained on June 27, the army took threefold issue with Matsuoka. First, the army made no promises to foreign powers about its future intentions. Muto thought it likely that the "loud-mouthed" or "loose-lipped" Matsuoka had promised an attack on Singapore during his European sojourn—and had returned to Tokyo in the blithe expectation that his arguments for an attack on Singapore would win the day—and Muto thought Matsuoka was now calling for a northward advance precisely because it was what the Germans wanted him to do. Second, the army remained committed to the southern Indochinese advance, because it should (among other things) convince the British to close the Burma Road and thereby close the last remaining route by which Anglo-American aid was reaching Chiang Kai-shek. Third, the army remained to be convinced of a total German victory over the Soviet Union. On this last point Muto acknowledged that German forces were "tearing the Soviet Union apart" and the Soviets' "complete collapse" within the space of a few months seemed entirely possible. Specifically, he thought it possible that the regime of Joseph Stalin might collapse as German forces closed inexorably on Moscow. Yet grim experience in China had taught Japanese soldiers that the capture of cities—even capital cities—did not necessarily end wars. In the absence of a decisive battle in which the bulk of enemy forces was annihilated, there remained the possibility that the Soviets might replicate Chiang Kai-shek's war of attrition.[38]

What did this mean for Japan? Muto regarded the Soviet Far East as a "ripe persimmon." The only uncertainty was whether it would fall on its own or whether it would prove necessary to pluck it from the tree. Muto leaned toward the latter scenario, noting the likelihood of Japan being "unable to take the persimmon unless it uses troops." Mixing metaphors, he acknowledged the desirability of "eradicating" the "root of all evil to our north," but he counseled a relatively cautious approach at least until it became clear whether the Soviets were able to grind the Germans down in a protracted war of attrition. He added that, even if Japan downsized its troop presence in China and used force immediately in the north, it would gain little while expending valuable resources. It would be, he said, "bad strategy."[39]

TOJO MAINTAINED A HIGH degree of control over his subordinates, and officers attached to the Army Ministry were in virtual lockstep with the wait-and-see approach he championed. Sugiyama was having a harder time of it at the Army General Staff. Staff officers took up the cudgel, arguing incessantly for war against the Soviets. Tojo worried that Matsuoka might stir up trouble by seeking to connect with anti-Soviet passions running rampant on the General Staff. Tojo also wondered about Konoe, who one moment expressed a desire to withdraw Japan from the Tripartite Pact and the next moment brought into his confidences Tojo's onetime friend and forcibly retired leader of the army's *kodoha* (Imperial way faction), Obata Toshiro, whose freely expressed personal enmity toward Tojo was matched only by his arguments for an immediate northward advance.[40] Tojo's reaction was almost reflexive: He ordered *kenpei* (military police) surveillance of public debate and of those who might lead it.[41]

Staff officers believed that Tojo was veering away from his cautious approach toward their more bullish approach. The catalyst for the change of heart, they believed, was a June 29 conversation between Tojo and one of the General Staff's most outspoken proponents of a northward advance, the Operations Bureau chief, Major General Tanaka Shin'ichi. The hawkish Tanaka had earned a reputation for raising his voice and behaving threateningly toward officers who did not share his views; he refrained from such bullying tactics when he met with the tough-as-teak veteran of army factionalism, Tojo. Tanaka did, however, succeed in impressing on Tojo the need to ramp up preparations for war and the imperative of fighting the Soviets before the frigid Siberian winter. Tojo emerged from their conversation accepting the need to proceed with war preparations, with September 1 as the presumed start date for the opening of war against the Soviets.[42]

The General Staff's war hawks took heart from Tojo's agreement with Tanaka, and some now assumed that war would begin almost automatically on September 1. They underestimated Tojo. He had *not* agreed that war against the Soviets must begin on September 1; he had instead agreed that, *if war did begin,* it must do so by September 1. The difference was critical and can best be understood in the context of Tojo's understanding of the complex relationship between the emperor, the government, and the Army and Navy General Staffs. Tojo accepted the Army General Staff's insistence on a timetable and a deadline, and because these were designed to maximize Japan's chances of victory in war against the Soviets, it followed that such operational imperatives must necessarily inform any decision for war. Yet Tojo refused to accept that the emperor might reach decisions for war or peace solely or even principally on the basis of technical military (or naval) advice. No less an authority than the lead author of the Meiji Constitution, Ito Hirobumi, had insisted that the emperor decide on war or peace on the "advice of his Ministers."[43] The cabinet's role in any decision for war was, then, critical. Tojo understood his own role, as army minister, to involve coordination of the views of the cabinet and the supreme command. This did not, in his estimation, entail an automatic falling into line behind operational imperatives; it instead required a concerted attempt at discerning and allowing what were properly the General Staff's prerogatives—things like timetables for war preparations and deadlines for war—without ceding the cabinet's role in informing any decision for war. It was the most delicate of balancing acts, but Tojo worked hard to get the balance right. His reading of the Meiji Constitution, and its delineation of duties between the cabinet and the Supreme Command, was impeccably accurate. In late June 1941, it meant his agreement on war preparations and a timetable did not and would not result automatically in war.

Tojo's stance became apparent at a June 30, 1941, meeting of the prestigious but largely powerless Supreme War Council. Prince Asaka Yasuhiko criticized the army's fence-sitting posture toward both north and south, arguing it would be "better to go north first." Tojo shot back, stating that "anybody" could reach such a decision "in the abstract." "If it weren't for the China Incident," Tojo added, "it would be easy."[44]

Tojo had agreed to a timetable for war against the Soviets but continued to withhold the actual decision for war, which created difficulties for the General Staff. Officers responsible for war preparations questioned whether they could discharge their duties. How, they asked, was it possible to prepare for war if Tojo and his ministerial colleagues refused to concede that war would in fact begin? Colonel Hattori Takushiro, another hawkish anti-Soviet officer whom Tojo had recently appointed to the General Staff's Operations Division, devised the solution. He suggested the army adopt the wording "decision to prepare for the opening of war." This would, he argued, enable war preparations just short of full mobilization. Tojo was well satisfied with the proffered solution. On this basis, he agreed on the need to call up reserves, deliver vast amounts of materials and equipment (including horses and aircraft) to the Kwantung Army, put units in Manchukuo on a war footing, and observe the movements of Soviet Far Eastern forces. All would be done in the strictest secrecy. This buildup began on July 1 and became known as *Kantokuen,* shorthand for *Kantogun tokushu enshū* (Kwantung Army special maneuvers).[45]

TOJO HAD, IN LATE June, telephoned Oikawa and spoken of the need for an Imperial conference to formalize the twin decisions for a southern

Indochinese advance and preparedness to advance either north or farther south. Oikawa readily agreed, if only because he hoped an Imperial decision might prevent the army from peremptorily marching to war against the Soviets. The preparations were made, and an Imperial conference met on July 2. The twin decisions were reached, but not before Matsuoka spoke out. The garrulous foreign minister spoke in favor of a northward advance against the Soviets (receiving support from the Privy Council president, Hara Yoshimichi), and he warned that war against the Anglo-American powers might arise as a result of the southern Indochinese advance. His representations led to one fascinating exchange with Tojo. Matsuoka stated that the possibility of war in Southeast Asia and the Pacific existed because Japanese Army officers "on the front line" were "aggressive" and "convinced" that Japan should "use force." An incensed Tojo took these comments personally. He was, he stated, "responsible for supervising soldiers and military personnel" and reminded his colleagues that he had taken "severe disciplinary measures" following indiscretions during the northern Indochinese advance of September 1940. He added that the army acted solely "on orders issued by the emperor."[46]

The twin decisions reached at the Imperial conference allowed the army to move ahead with the Kwantung Army's special maneuvers. Tojo spoke on July 4 with Tanaka and listened patiently as the general launched into a diatribe against a cautious wait-and-see approach. Tojo then approved "full-scale mobilization" of the Korean and Kwantung Armies; combined, they would comprise 850,000 men (as compared to their combined peacetime standing of 350,000 men).[47]

Even so, Tojo refused to concede that the Kwantung Army's special maneuvers would lead automatically to war against the Soviets. As he put it to his subordinates on July 5, the nation remained undecided whether it would advance to the north or the south. In this situation, the army's attention, he said, must naturally remain on "northward preparations." (He presumed the navy would likewise remain focused on southward preparations.) Tojo wanted the utmost secrecy, and although he acknowledged the difficulty in hiding war preparations, he hoped it might prove possible to cause other nations to think that the army's sudden activity was for the purpose of the China Incident. He insisted that the army adopt a "wartime budget," and he wanted a threefold focus on "mobilization, transport, and fortifications." Tojo suspended any army-sponsored research not directly and immediately relevant to war against the Soviets, and he ordered that the Kwantung Army's divisions be organized immediately for war. Insisting that the era of total war had finally arrived, he noted a blurring of the distinction between the battle lines and the home front. He spoke specifically of the need to mobilize female factory workers so that they were animated by the same spirit as the men on the front lines.[48]

THE EMPEROR KNEW FULL well that Tojo stood in the way of the Japanese Army's most hawkish elements and their burning desire for war against the Soviets. He was nonetheless concerned lest even Tojo lose control of the situation. The sheer magnitude of the Kwantung Army's special maneuvers was cause for concern. So, too, was the noise emanating from the army. The emperor also worried about the possible impact of the southern Indochinese advance on Japan's relationships with the Anglo-American powers. And he continued, as always, to wonder how the army proposed to end the war in China.

The emperor spoke with Sugiyama and Tojo on July 7, 1941—the fourth anniversary of the opening shots of the China Incident—and voiced his concerns in a series of difficult questions. Was it possible to maintain secrecy while mobilizing on the scale envisioned by the army? Did the army remain committed to ending the China Incident? Or was it merely responding to opportunities as they arose in the north and the south? What now made up the army's primary point of focus—China, Southeast Asia, or the Soviet Union? Might the Kwantung Army replicate past behavior, take the bit between the teeth, and of its own volition start something in the north? The emperor also wanted to know more about the southern Indochinese advance. Might not the British, buoyed by the prospect of at least a few months' respite in Europe thanks to Hitler's decision to attack the Soviets, respond with armed force? What were the prospects of a "bloodless" southern Indochinese advance?[49]

Sugiyama was first to respond. He allowed that it was impossible to maintain absolute secrecy during the Kwantung Army's special maneuvers but insisted that the British were highly unlikely to resort to force in response to the southern Indochinese advance. The prospects of a bloodless advance were, he said, high. Tojo sought to reassure the emperor that the army continued to prioritize resolution of the China Incident. Curiously, he said nothing about the impact of the forthcoming southern Indochinese advance on the prospects of ending the war in China. He spoke instead of ongoing military operations in China as well as a curious but doomed peace maneuver involving Shanxi warlord and one-time premier Yan Xishan.[50]

Tojo's hope in the doomed-from-the-outset Yan Xishan peace maneuver owed more to desperation than to a clearheaded assessment of its prospects. Still, the emperor's intervention confirmed that Tojo's delicate balancing act was fundamentally the right course. He would continue to sanction preparations for war against the Soviets, but he would not—yet—demand from his ministerial colleagues a decision for war. Thus it was that, on July 8, he secured from his cabinet colleagues a discretionary budget, which would fund not only the Kwantung Army's special maneuvers but various other necessities. High on Tojo's list was the need for home island defenses. He was particularly concerned that Soviet bombers might raze Tokyo, and on July 9 he ordered his subordinates to focus on aerial defenses. The navy, too, required funding for the possibility of a southward advance. The armed services' budgetary needs were now so great that Tojo acknowledged the need for a precipitous rise in taxes and a reduction, wherever otherwise possible, of government expenditure. This would impose privations on the people. Tojo saw a need to reduce to the "lowest limits" such matters as "food security" and maintenance of the "people's livelihoods." Foreseeing that oil stocks would barely meet the armed services' requirements, he also insisted that civilian automobiles no longer run.[51]

THE KONOE CABINET SOUGHT a Franco-Japanese diplomatic accord that would establish Japan's right to station troops in southern Indochina as well as air and naval bases at Camranh Bay and in Saigon. Some, including Konoe, deluded themselves into believing that this might convince the Roosevelt administration to regard the southern Indochinese advance as the product not of aggressive opportunism but instead of diplomatic agreement.[52] Others, Tojo prominent among them, were less optimistic.

Tojo's foremost foreign affairs adviser, Muto Akira, was convinced the United States would respond to the southern Indochinese advance by slapping a complete trade embargo on Japan. Muto figured this would trigger a Japanese advance into the Dutch East Indies.[53] Tojo accepted that a transpacific trade embargo would necessitate the search for an alternative source of oil, and an advance into the Dutch East Indies was Japan's only real option. He nonetheless wanted the freedom to choose where to advance, and he hoped it might prove possible to dissuade the United States from imposing trade sanctions, at least until the Soviet situation had become clearer.

Tojo's hope rested with Matsuoka. To be more precise, Tojo's hope rested with Matsuoka's forthcoming removal from ministerial office. This was at Konoe's initiative and had widespread support. Certainly Tojo had no qualms; he was satisfied that Matsuoka had long since outlived his usefulness. By neat coincidence, the Roosevelt administration had recently issued an oral statement in which it deplored the difficulty of reaching a Japanese-US diplomatic settlement so long as "some" in the Japanese decision-making process remained "definitely committed" to a course calling for "support of Nazi Germany and its policies of conquest."[54] The statement did not specify any individual, but there was no need. It was perfectly apparent to all concerned that Matsuoka was persona non grata in Washington. The Japanese government formally rejected the US statement, but Konoe and some others convinced themselves that Matsuoka's removal from office might somehow revive the Draft Understanding and rekindle the search for Japanese-US diplomatic rapprochement. Tojo's expectations were considerably more qualified: He hoped that the proverbial delivery of Matsuoka's head on a platter might be enough, at least for a short while, to dissuade the United States from responding to the southern Indochinese advance by imposing stringent sanctions on Japan.

The Konoe cabinet resigned en masse on July 16, 1941. Succeeding it was another cabinet headed by Konoe. Oikawa and Tojo continued to represent the armed services; Toyoda Teijiro replaced Matsuoka. A retired admiral, Toyoda was reputedly pro-Anglo-American but had in September 1940 played the key role in overturning the navy's long-standing opposition to a military alliance with Germany.[55] Tojo cared little either way. Japanese policy was set, and he refused to countenance that Toyoda might somehow steer the ship of state on a different course. At the new cabinet's inaugural July 17 meeting, Tojo reminded his ministerial colleagues of the sacrosanctity of the emperor's "sacred decision" reached at the July 2 Imperial conference. The armed services, he said, would continue to operate on the basis of that sacred decision, and he insisted that national policy must not "move an inch." He wanted, in short, agreement among "all government organs" so the new cabinet could "show its true colors" as a "so-called wartime cabinet."[56] Later that day, he put it to his subordinates that the cabinet change had "no impact whatsoever" on the General Staffs' insistence on a southern Indochinese advance.[57] Toyoda duly took up negotiations with the Vichy French authorities on July 18. Within the week, he had secured all of Japan's substantial demands, including eight air bases, two naval bases, and freedom of movement for Japanese forces in southern Indochina.[58]

Speculation within the army focused on the likely Anglo-American response to the advance. On July 23 Muto told officers attached to the Army Ministry that "a series of economic pressures, such as a US asset freeze and Britain's tightening of export controls, must be anticipated as a matter of course." He reckoned that US trade sanctions were also highly likely, and he stated that Japan would have little choice but to overcome an Anglo-American economic stranglehold by preparing for an "armed clash with the United States and Britain."[59] Tojo, for his part, continued to hope that the Anglo-American response would not force Japan's hand so that he could retain the freedom to choose whether to advance north or south.

Vichy French authorities made public on July 24 the agreements concluded with Japan. The next day, Roosevelt froze Japanese assets in the United States. The British Empire quickly followed suit, as did the Dutch East Indies colonial authorities, who for good measure tore up a raft of commercial agreements concluded only weeks earlier with Japan. Meanwhile, the United States was working hard to convince South American nations to do the same. Addressing his subordinates on July 30, Tojo admitted that Japanese trade with the outside world would henceforth be restricted to French Indochina and Thailand. There was, from Tojo's viewpoint, no longer any choice but to establish something akin to the Britain's Imperial preference policy; he spoke specifically of a trading bloc under the rubric of the Greater East Asia Co-Prosperity Sphere.[60]

The asset freezes raised, for Tojo, the immediate prospect of Japan losing all access to oil imports. Speaking with his subordinates on July 30, he noted that in 1939 Japan had imported 89 percent of its oil from the United States. Since then it had increased oil imports from the Dutch East Indies, but that was small consolation given recent developments. It would very soon prove necessary, Tojo stated, to begin drawing on Japan's oil stocks. Those stocks were distressingly low and would stretch no further than approximately eight and a half months. He acknowledged the need to "impose restrictions" on the civilian use of gasoline, and he foresaw the armed services facing "extremely vexing" oil shortages.[61]

Tojo began turning over in his mind the difficulties an inability to access oil posed for a northward advance against the Soviets. Oil was not the only issue. Most important, the Soviets seemed to be absorbing the German onslaught. Even the Army General Staff's incurably aggressive middle echelons had begun questioning whether Hitler had been mistaken in his calculations of a decisive victory soon after the invasion.[62] Tojo told his subordinates on July 30 that, despite the immense pressure on their western front, the Soviets had been able to maintain "twenty-some divisions" in their Far Eastern provinces. (An ill-tempered emperor was, almost simultaneously, asking Sugiyama whether the Kwantung Army's special maneuvers ought to be suspended; among other things, Emperor Hirohito insisted that the special maneuvers had been self-defeating and had alerted the Soviets to the need to maintain troop levels in the Far East.)[63] So far as Tojo was concerned, the Soviet Far Eastern persimmon had not ripened anywhere near as much as anybody had hoped. The Kwantung Army's special maneuvers, Tojo now averred, aimed not to overwhelm but merely to match the Soviet Far Eastern troop presence. Restraint was the order of the day, and Tojo insisted it was "impossible to think of opening war immediately against the Soviets."[64]

Tojo met the following day with that most outspoken advocate of war against the Soviets, Tanaka Shin'ichi. Predictably enough, Tanaka spoke about beating the frigid Siberian winter by marching to war against the Soviets no later than September 1. With barely a month left, he pleaded with Tojo to secure before August 10 the cabinet's agreement to a decision for war. Tojo's response brought together numerous issues into one coherent whole. He opened his remarks by returning for the first time in weeks to the emperor's insistence that the China Incident must necessarily be the army's "first priority." He referenced the brunt of the fighting the army had borne for four wearying years in China, and in an implicit acknowledgment of the imperative of a southward advance he noted that any attempt at "cutting through" the nation's current difficulties must necessarily rest not with the army but with the navy. There would, accordingly, be no decision for war against the Soviets by August 10. Tojo refused to entertain any further discussion on this score, ending his remarks by stating that this would be, if necessary, his final act of service to his emperor.[65]

Tojo was enacting, as best as he was able, the emperor's will. He had stared down operational imperatives and, by declining to seek his cabinet colleagues' acquiescence in a decision for war against the Soviets, exercised his ministerial prerogative. He also cited the need for a continued focus on resolving the China Incident. This was all in keeping with the emperor's wishes. But, in one key sense, Tojo hopelessly misread Hirohito. Tojo seemed somehow unable to conceive of a policy option that did not require the use of armed force, and as implied in his conversation with Tanaka, he now looked to the navy to launch a southward advance.

The navy chief of staff, Admiral Nagano Osami, reported to the emperor on July 30, making the case for a southward advance and war. Nagano told Hirohito that the Tripartite Pact rendered a Japanese-US war a practical inevitability and added that, in the event of war, Japan's oil stocks would be exhausted within a year or two. This meant there was no choice but to strike southward immediately and secure access to the Dutch East Indies' oil. He admitted that this almost necessarily meant war against the United States and, to the emperor's chagrin, Nagano allowed that he had no confidence in the prospect of victory over the United States. Over the ensuing days, the emperor repeatedly expressed his complete loss of faith in Nagano.[66]

On August 1 the Roosevelt administration slapped a total embargo on the export of oil to Japan. The British and the Dutch followed suit. This, in Tojo's view, forced Japan's hand: Japan needed oil, which required an advance against the Dutch East Indies. Hope remained in the Army General Staff for a northward advance against the Soviets; the argument now rested on the supposed likelihood of a preemptive Soviet air strike against Kwantung Army positions. Tojo allowed the navy to take the lead in quashing these forlorn hopes. The result was a policy document, authored by a naval staff officer, Captain Ono Takeji. It proscribed "provocative actions" vis-à-vis the Soviet Union and advocated a "totally defensive posture" even in the event of a Soviet "frontal attack." Tojo was content to let the Imperial Navy bear the Army General Staff's discontent, maintaining near total silence when the document was adopted at a liaison conference on August 6.[67] He looked on as the Army General Staff dropped any hope of launching a northward advance before year's end and switched instead to arguments for a forcible southward advance no later than the closing days of November.

IT HAD NOT COME easily, but Japan's course now seemed set. An advance on the Dutch East Indies now presented itself as the only possible way forward. That required an attack on British positions in Malaya and Singapore; Japan would soon enough find itself at war with Britain. The navy was convinced it also meant war with the United States; Tojo was at least willing to accept that war against both Britain and the United States was highly possible.

Tojo entertained some doubts, mostly centered on the navy. Nagano's performance before the emperor in late July engendered little confidence;

Tojo was nonetheless convinced that the problems owed less to Nagano than to Oikawa. It would be necessary, he reckoned, to draw Oikawa out and have him exercise his ministerial responsibilities and prerogatives more frontally. At the very least, it would be necessary to compel Oikawa to confront the consequences of the decisions to which he had contributed and the policy course he had helped set.

9
THE DEADLINE FOR WAR AND THE SUMMIT PROPOSAL
AUGUST–OCTOBER 1941

IN THE EARLY AFTERMATH of the asset freeze and the trade embargo, Tojo Hideki determined to steer national policy in the direction of a forceful southward advance. This entailed no radical departure from existing policy but was instead a logical progression from decisions already reached. His mind turned, almost reflexively, to an Imperial Army-Navy agreement of mid-April 1941; it specified that a British-Dutch-US trade embargo would trigger a forceful southward advance.[1] At issue was oil: Tojo believed that Japan had no choice but to take the oil-rich Dutch East Indies, and he accepted that a southward advance entailed the risk of war against the United States. This, too, he based squarely on existing policy, including the Imperial conference decision of July 2 to advance south even if it ultimately resulted in war with the United States.[2]

Tojo was hardly alone. He took his cue, logically enough, from the man the constitution designated responsible for operational planning in the event of war in the Pacific, Navy Chief of Staff Nagano Osami. As recently as July 21, Nagano had stated, "If we could settle things without war, there would be nothing better. But if we conclude that conflict cannot ultimately be avoided, then I would like you to understand that as time goes by we will be in a disadvantageous position."[3] Nagano's concern was twofold. First, the oil embargo meant that Japan's oil stocks must invariably dwindle and eventually dry up. The ramifications for the Japanese Navy were enormous; in the words of naval historian Ikeda Kiyoshi, "battleships without oil cannot move."[4] Nagano was no less concerned by US President Franklin D. Roosevelt's naval expansion programs. These were of such magnitude that, within a few short years, they would render hopelessly unattainable the holy grail of Japanese naval strategy, a 70 percent fleet ratio vis-à-vis the US Navy. On the back of these twin pressures, Nagano concluded that war sooner was better than war later. Only Vice Admiral Oikawa Koshiro was able to challenge or silence Nagano, and although he privately fretted about the prospects of victory in a Pacific war, he was singularly unsuited to his ministerial duties and was in late July and early August nearly catatonic. Tojo reasoned quite rightly that Nagano spoke—even if only by default—for the navy.

Debate and discussion between the Army and Navy General Staffs confirmed Tojo's basic position. Navy staff officers met with their Army counterparts on August 16, and proposed that diplomacy and war preparations continue side by side until the end of October. "In the event that Japan and the United States have not reached a settlement by mid-October," asserted the navy officers, "steps to exercise our power will be taken." Army officers liked the deadline but were "extremely dissatisfied" with what they regarded as weasel words concerning the exercise of power; they wanted a more concrete commitment to war. The subsequent debate included not just the General Staffs but also the Army and Navy Ministries; Tojo assigned Major General Muto Akira to participate. Interservice agreement was reached by the end of August, with officers agreeing to "complete preparations for war, with the last ten days of October as a tentative deadline, resolved to go to war with the US, UK, and the Netherlands if necessary."[5]

AT THIS CRITICAL JUNCTURE, Prime Minister Konoe Fumimaro stood as an obstacle in the way of a southward advance and Pacific war. He met with both Oikawa and Tojo on August 4 and proposed to revive Japanese-US diplomacy by joining Roosevelt in a summit meeting. Oikawa was receptive, but Tojo was unenthused.[6] Once out of Konoe's earshot, he muttered about "politicians" and their inclination to reach "careless" decisions on even "great matters," only to "throw out" those decisions "like an old pair of sandals" when things went against their wishes. The problem, according to Tojo, owed at least partly to Konoe's utter lack of "conviction" and "honor." Ultimately it was not politicians but soldiers and sailors who put their lives "at risk" for the nation, and Tojo was convinced the army and navy should therefore be the locus of any decisions hinging on war or peace. With specific regard to the summit proposal, Tojo stated, "If he leaves [for a summit meeting] thinking that the talks will go easily, he will have a terrible time of it."[7]

Tojo took Konoe's summit proposal back to his military colleagues. They were even less impressed, and wondered whether a summit meeting could possibly achieve Japanese-US diplomatic rapprochement. Was Konoe proposing to make concessions and reach agreements without regard for existing policies and decisions. Was there any prospect of diplomatic success? How, for that matter, did one define *diplomatic success?* What far-reaching concessions might it require? Was Konoe planning to torpedo the German-Italian-Japanese Tripartite Pact? Would he renounce the use of force in Southeast Asia? Could he make such concessions on the spot, without consulting affected parties—and, particularly the army?[8]

Tojo shared these doubts, but he did not want to be the cabinet's sole naysayer. He refused to jeopardize his ongoing efforts at rehabilitating the army in the emperor's esteem and so did not want the army bearing the blame for aborting Konoe's summit proposal. Besides, he was too savvy a political operator to sink his efforts and energies into blocking what he regarded as a half-baked scheme with (as he put it to Army Chief of Staff Sugiyama Hajime) "no chance of success."[9]

Tojo responded formally and in writing to Konoe's summit proposal. He openly expressed his skepticism and indeed his principled objection, labeling a summit meeting "inappropriate" because it would "weaken" the Tripartite Pact and leave the Japanese public confused about the direction of national policy. He nonetheless—in at least an outward show of "respect" for Konoe—allowed that the summit meeting might go ahead. He attached two conditions. First, Konoe must remain within the bounds of established Japanese policy. Concretely, he must seek Roosevelt's agreement to the revisions Matsuoka Yosuke had made to the Draft Understanding Between Japan and the United States back in early May: accept Japan's fidelity to the Tripartite Pact, deliver Chiang Kai-shek to the negotiating table even though Japan made no promises about the peace terms it might offer, accept Japan's refusal to renounce the use of force in Southeast Asia, and reopen normal trade relations with Japan. Tojo's second condition also aimed at roping Konoe back into the realm of existing policy decisions: He must, Tojo stipulated, accept responsibility in the event he proved unable to revive Japanese-US diplomacy and lead the nation to war in the Pacific.[10]

Tojo's conditions were unyielding, and he refused to accept the idea that there was anything wrong with that. As he saw it, he was guarding against any sudden, ill-conceived change in policy based on little other than prime ministerial whimsy. He had, at least, accepted that the summit meeting might go ahead. That was enough for Konoe and Foreign Minister Toyoda Teijiro, who instructed Ambassador Nomura Kichisaburo to float the summit proposal with the Roosevelt administration. Nomura did as instructed when he met with US Secretary of State Cordell Hull on August 8, and again when he met with Roosevelt on August 17.[11]

Konoe had a trick up his sleeve, about which he kept Tojo and most other decision-makers in Tokyo deliberately uninformed. Konoe intended, if the summit meeting went ahead, to bypass ordinary policymaking processes such as liaison conferences and Imperial conferences. Tojo did not know that Konoe hoped to improvise, devising an extraordinary policymaking procedure whereby he would cable the emperor directly from the summit meeting and seek Imperial approval of any agreements he might strike with Roosevelt. How Tojo would have reacted, had he learned of Konoe's plans, is necessarily a matter for conjecture.

TOJO SAW NO COMPELLING need to avoid war against the United States. For a man who had marked himself since the early 1920s as a total war officer, he was curiously dismissive of arguments concerning America's national strength. Certainly he was brusque in his reception of Colonel Iwakuro Hideo, who arrived back in Tokyo in mid-August following a monthslong stint at the Japanese embassy in Washington, DC. Iwakuro was unaware of the particulars of Konoe's summit proposal, but when he met with the army leadership on August 15, he counseled the need to make meaningful concessions in diplomacy with the United States. The Roosevelt administration remained willing to compromise, and Iwakuro stated his belief that any Japanese-US agreement need not preclude the continued stationing of Japanese troops in North China. The alternative was war in the Pacific. He echoed Nomura in stating that US national strength was so immense as to render war against that nation "reckless." Unimpressed, Tojo asked Iwakuro whether he (and Ambassador Nomura) had been "seduced" by the United States. He transferred Iwakuro to southern Indochina.[12]

Seemingly unaffected by concerns about US national strength, Tojo showed little interest in Konoe's summit proposal and played only the most peripheral of roles. His principal priority rested with ensuring that Japan remain in position to launch a southward advance if, as he thought highly likely, the summit proposal fell flat. This entailed guarding against any attempts at winding back existing policy. Tojo reacted strongly in mid-August to Toyoda's efforts at developing a policy that would guarantee Thai neutrality in return for British concessions. "The acquisition of military bases in Thailand has already been approved in Imperial conferences on several occasions," Tojo told Toyoda on August 14. "It is not possible to change that at this point."[13]

Throughout August Tojo continued to watch for any indications that Konoe and Toyoda might try to soften existing policy in the hope of placating the United States. On August 25, Tojo invited the army leadership to his ministerial residence to vet a message Konoe and the Foreign Ministry had drafted for delivery to Roosevelt, as well as an accompanying written statement purporting to explain Japan's reasons for advancing into southern Indochina. With Tojo leading the discussion between and among the soldiers, both documents received the army's grudging approval.[14] Both the Konoe message and the written statement were adopted, and Nomura delivered them to Hull and Roosevelt on August 28.[15]

Roosevelt perhaps felt it was the season for summit meetings—he met "somewhere in the Atlantic" in mid-August with British Prime Minister Winston Churchill—and he received the Konoe message warmly. Hull was decidedly less receptive and warned Nomura of the need for agreement on key issues before a summit meeting. Policymakers in Tokyo nonetheless continued with preparations for a Konoe-Roosevelt summit meeting. Tojo, for his part, appointed Colonel Arisue Seizo, General Doihara Kenji, Lieutenant Colonel Ishii Akiho, Major General Muto Akira, and Lieutenant General Tsukada Osamu to accompany Konoe in the event the summit meeting went ahead. A minor controversy arose when the General Staff pushed to include as a delegate General Terauchi Hisaichi, the son of the man who had forced Tojo's father into premature retirement. This opened old wounds; Tojo would not—could not—appoint Terauchi to accompany Konoe to the United States, and Terauchi was excluded from the military delegation. Tojo thus achieved three objectives: He exacted a small measure of revenge on Terauchi and on Choshu; he remained exemplary in his ministerial conduct and continued to cooperate with Konoe on the summit proposal; and he put in place a mechanism so that the army could keep an eye on Konoe's every move before, during, and after the summit.[16]

ON SEPTEMBER 1 TOJO MET with Sugiyama and discussed, in the frankest possible terms, the army's position on diplomacy vis-à-vis the United States. The two men agreed that the army and state must "hold fast" to the Tripartite Pact. They agreed to proceed with the southward advance and "complete" construction of the Greater East Asia Co-Prosperity Sphere. They added, almost vehemently, that the army would "not withdraw troops" from China at the United States' behest.[17] By staking out such a position, Tojo was courting a split with Konoe. Sugiyama pointed to the likely outcome: Tojo would at some point in the foreseeable future resign his ministerial post and bring down the Konoe cabinet. Sugiyama seemed to welcome this likelihood. He told Tojo of his hope that the army would "take responsibility" for the subsequent direction of state policy. He was suggesting, even if only obliquely, that Tojo lead the subsequent cabinet.[18]

Tojo had no intention of tearing down the Konoe cabinet by resigning his ministerial post. He had only to recall the circumstances leading to his own ministerial appointment and the damage done to the Japanese Army's relationship with its emperor. This fealty to the emperor's desires dovetailed with Tojo's growing self-confidence. He was thriving in the hurly-burly of the decision-making process. His role, as he understood it, was to represent the army on the cabinet and also to represent the cabinet's positions and decisions to the army. He was, in this way, the mediator between operational imperatives and state policy. Few of his ministerial predecessors in recent memory had played this role anywhere near as well as Tojo was doing. He was not merely warming the army minister's seat; he had carved out for himself a position that aligned neatly with his decades-old conception of the army as the ultimate arbiter of the emperor's will and state affairs. A lesser officer might have thrown up his hands at the absurdity of it all. How was it possible to mediate between the General Staff's arguments for a southward advance and war against the United States, and Konoe's efforts by means of the summit proposal to avoid war with the United States? Ironing out this significant difference would be no mean feat. It was a challenge Tojo confronted with relish.

Tojo joined with his liaison conference colleagues on September 3 and endorsed two documents. The first, titled "Nichi-Bei kosho hoshin-an" (Japanese-US negotiations: Draft policy) had been prepared by Toyoda and his subordinates in the Foreign Ministry. According to this document, Japan undertook to advance no further south than Indochina, interpret its obligations to Germany and Italy "independently" in the event the United States entered the war in Europe, and seek peace with and then withdraw troops from China. In return, it required that the United States undertake to restore normal Japanese-US commercial relations. Neither Tojo nor anybody else took exception to this draft policy.[19] The second document endorsed had been in development by the Army and Navy General Staffs since mid-August.

It prescribed the pursuit of Japanese-US negotiations and the preparations for war against the United States. Most tellingly, it sought to impose a deadline on negotiations so that, in the absence of diplomatic success, Japan would go to war in the Pacific by the last ten days of October.[20]

The import of this deadline seemed to escape Konoe. He consented to it because he continued to believe he would meet Roosevelt and resolve all Japanese-US issues at a stroke during a summit meeting. Konoe had brought Toyoda into his confidence, and Toyoda, too, hoped that a Konoe-Roosevelt summit meeting would end any need for the deadline. In the aftermath of the September 3 liaison conference, Toyoda busied his subordinates in the Foreign Ministry with yet further attempts at drafting the terms, demands, and concessions that would henceforth inform Japanese diplomacy with the United States. Of the demands, a lifting of the trade embargo and a prompt return to a normal Japanese-US commercial relationship was perhaps the most noticeable. Concessions were noticeably few. Certainly the cause of the trade embargo—the southern Indochinese advance—was addressed at best circuitously, so that a Japanese troop withdrawal from Indochina was promised only after the end of the China Incident.[21] Tojo remained aloof from these efforts. He intervened only to guard against any extravagant promises about troop withdrawals from China as well as any concessions that might weaken the Tripartite Pact.[22]

Toyoda had barely put the finishing touches on his diplomatic strategy when Roosevelt's formal response to Konoe's summit proposal arrived. Roosevelt would meet with Konoe only after preliminary negotiations had resolved to the US State Department's satisfaction those issues that had bedeviled the Japanese-US negotiations since Nomura's arrival in Washington in early 1941. This condition clarified that the summit meeting would not go ahead unless Japan first addressed US concerns with Japan's obligations to its alliance partners in Germany and Italy, with Japan's war in China, and with Japan's intentions in Southeast Asia.[23]

Konoe and Toyoda remained somehow hopeful about the prospects for diplomatic success, and they acquiesced in the scheduling of an Imperial conference. Its purpose was twofold: It would adopt and formalize Toyoda's latest diplomatic strategy, and it would impose a late October deadline for war. In the lead-up to the conference, the emperor railed against the deadline and what he regarded as the prioritization of war over diplomacy. He also expressed puzzlement and astonishment at the unquestioned presumption that Japan could defeat the United States in war. These were but exercises in Imperial futility.[24]

The Imperial conference convened on September 6, 1941. Tojo remained silent throughout, letting others, including Konoe, Nagano, and Sugiyama, speak. Thus it was that they bore the brunt of the emperor's embittered puzzlement. Tojo felt justified in maintaining his silence and told himself that he had played only a minor role in establishing a deadline. It was, after all, an operational imperative, the province of the Supreme Command. Whatever the case, the outcome of the conference was predetermined; the Imperial conference imposed the late October deadline for war.[25]

The emperor now turned to Tojo. He did so indirectly, using Prince Higashikuni Naruhiko as a go-between. Higashikuni spoke with Tojo on September 7, relaying the "great worry" the "Japanese-US problem" was causing the emperor. Hirohito was "pouring his heart and soul into an adjustment of Japanese-US diplomatic relations," and placing much "hope" in Konoe's summit proposal. Tojo reassured Prince Higashikuni that he "totally understood" his emperor's concerns. He expressed fealty to those concerns, but he wrapped that fealty in his own distinct set of assumptions and conceptions.[26]

Tojo expounded on what he considered the fundamental incompatibility of Japanese and US policy. For one thing, the United States was demanding that Japan "dissociate" itself from its alliance partners in Germany and Italy and instead identify with the Anglo-American powers. Should Japan do this, he stated, the Anglo-Americans would enlist Japan's cooperation in defeating Germany, only to turn their guns subsequently against Japan. He then listed, in rapid-fire fashion, various other US demands he "could not accept." First was the demand for the withdrawal of Japanese forces from Indochina. Next were the interrelated demands for the withdrawal of Japanese forces from China, peace with Chiang Kai-shek via Anglo-American good offices, a return to the situation as it existed before the China Incident, renewed acceptance of the Open Door Policy, and equality of commercial opportunity in China.[27]

Tojo did not pause to consider that some of what he labeled US demands were rooted firmly in Japanese policy. To cite perhaps the most obvious example, even Matsuoka had sought Roosevelt's good offices in bringing Chiang Kai-shek to the negotiating table. It is difficult to comprehend how Tojo could possibly have twisted this into an "unacceptable" US demand. Indeed, this only begins to make a vague sort of sense if viewed through the prism of Tojo's heightened exasperation at what was looking increasingly like the failure of yet another peace maneuver and the dreaded prospect of unending war in China.[28]

During his conversation with Prince Higashikuni, Tojo revealed himself as utterly mistrustful of American motives. His thinking aligned neatly with—and doubtless took its cue from—Tokyo's leading war hawk, Navy Chief of Staff Nagano Osami. Tojo allowed that Japan could seek to avoid war by accepting America's demands, but he saw the subsequent peace lasting "no more than two or three years." The Roosevelt administration was, in his view, biding its time until it had so expanded its fleet that it was assured of an absolute preponderance of maritime strength. Only after it could be assured of victory in the Pacific would it visit war on Japan. Until then it would seek "somehow to avoid war" and, all the while, seek to "weaken" Japan and minimize its capacity to fight.[29]

This, then, was the context in which Tojo regarded Konoe's summit proposal. He nonetheless professed his determination to enact the emperor's will, promising to make "every effort" to ensure the summit went ahead. "If there is even the slightest hope of success in a Japanese-US summit," he said, "I think we should do it." He was nonetheless convinced that the chances of success were "no better than three in ten." Even so, he regarded earnest pursuit of Konoe's summit proposal as "beneficial" because it would enable the government to stand before "the people" and "rally and unite" them behind the notion that Japanese-US relations had collapsed "despite all Japan's efforts." It would, in other words, justify a subsequent decision for war by demonstrating that war was indeed the last resort.[30]

Prince Higashikuni took fundamental issue with Tojo. He stated baldly that the United States would defeat Japan if it came to war and insisted that Japan should avoid courting such a calamitous possibility. He insisted that the emperor prioritized success in a Konoe-Roosevelt summit meeting, and he told Tojo he should "resign" his ministerial post if he would not "obey." Tojo brushed Higashikuni aside. He noted that the United States had taken the lead in establishing ABCD (American-British-Chinese-Dutch) encirclement of Japan, which was "squeezing" the life out of Japan. Unless Japan did something, it would invariably "perish." Far better than submitting meekly to such a fate was a decision for war, in which Tojo curiously rated Japan's chances of victory as "fifty-fifty."[31]

TOYODA HAD HOPED THAT assurances about Japan's obligations to its alliance partners—and particularly its determination to interpret those obligations "independently"—might be enough to convince the Roosevelt administration to proceed with Konoe's summit proposal. That view proved altogether too optimistic. On September 10 US Ambassador Joseph Grew handed Toyoda a note highlighting US concern with Japanese intentions regarding China.[32] Toyoda accepted that the war in China was very much the army's prerogative and invited Tojo to appoint an army officer to participate in the drafting of peace terms for China. Tojo ordered Muto Akira to participate in that process. The "basic terms" came to include provision for the merger of the regimes of Chiang Kai-shek and Wang Jingwei, the indefinite stationing of Japanese troops in Inner Mongolia and North China, Sino-Japanese economic cooperation for the exploitation of militarily important natural resources, and China's recognition of Manchukuo. Tojo joined his liaison conference colleagues on September 13 to approve these "basic terms."[33]

It was now apparent that Toyoda's diplomatic strategy vis-à-vis the United States involved several component parts, and it seemed expedient to bring everything together into one umbrella statement. Toyoda decided to exhume the Draft Understanding Between Japan and the United States (which had remained in a state of abeyance since Hull had delivered the US revisions on June 21). Muto once again represented the army in the revision process, and the revisions were completed on September 18. According to this latest iteration of the Draft Understanding, Japan would interpret and apply its obligations to its alliance partners in Germany and Italy "independently," commit to no advances farther south than Indochina, forswear a northward advance against the Soviets, and commit to peace with China in accord with the aforementioned "basic terms" of Sino-Japanese peace. Toyoda's revisions also required a commitment on the part of the United States to restore normal commercial relations with Japan. He called a liaison conference meeting on September 18 in the confident expectation that the revisions to the Draft Understanding would secure ready and universal approval.[34]

Toyoda was sorely mistaken. Even as the conference was scheduled to begin, Sugiyama sent word that his men had not had sufficient time to study Toyoda's revisions, and he declined to attend the conference. The obvious implication was that the revisions had sparked opposition within the Army General Staff. Sugiyama's no-show infuriated Tojo. He invited Sugiyama and his deputy, Lieutenant General Tsukada, to his ministerial residence and demanded to know whether the General Staff intended to cooperate with the government or "destroy" the government's efforts at avoiding war in the Pacific. Sugiyama insisted that the General Staff had no intention of interfering with government policy. When Tojo demanded to know why the General Staff had aborted the liaison conference, Tsukada reiterated the official excuse—namely, that the General Staff needed more time to study Toyoda's revisions to the Draft Understanding.[35]

Tojo had not accepted this excuse in the first instance, and he did not accept it now. The subsequent conversation is nowhere recorded, although the postwar musings of one of Tojo's trusted subordinates, who was present at the meeting, enable at least a tentative reconstruction. Colonel Ishii Akiho later wrote that the constitution afforded the General Staff and the Cabinet *mutual* independence: The Cabinet was to refrain from interfering in operational matters, and the Supreme Command was to refrain from interfering in matters of state policy. He wrote in scathing terms of the General Staff's intrusion, in this instance, into the finer points of diplomacy vis-à-vis the United States. By airing its displeasure at Toyoda's revisions to the Draft Understanding, the General Staff had stepped all over Tojo's own responsibilities as the army's representative on the cabinet. That made it personal: Tojo discharged his ministerial duties with precision and exactitude and was ever careful in his delineation of where his own responsibilities began and ended. If others—Sugiyama very much included—did not respect that delineation of duties, they were displaying either carelessness or dissatisfaction with Tojo's ministerial performance.[36]

Any opposition Sugiyama and Tsukada may have felt toward Toyoda's revisions to the Draft Understanding evaporated in the face of Tojo's airtight logic and imposing personality. There was but one exception: They insisted that any mention of a northward advance be excised from the document. Tojo agreed and allowed that Sugiyama might take the case to a liaison conference, which Sugiyama did on September 20. This latest iteration of the Draft Understanding Between Japan and the United States, minus any promises concerning a northward advance, was approved and adopted as state policy.[37]

THE JAPANESE DECISION-MAKING PROCESS in late September proceeded along the two tracks established by the September 6 Imperial conference. The first track involved the search for an adjustment of the Japanese-US diplomatic relationship, and the second involved ongoing preparations for war against the United States. The first track promised to be difficult for the simple reason that Toyoda's revisions to the Draft Understanding were far more attuned to the demands of the Japanese Army than they were to the Roosevelt administration's expectations. Ambassador Nomura delivered the latest iteration of the Draft Understanding to the US State Department on September 27, and there was little left to do but to await the US response.[38]

The Supreme Command had settled on October 15, 1941, as the deadline for negotiations with the United States, and a liaison conference was scheduled for September 25 for the express purpose of discussing that deadline. Nagano and Sugiyama jointly prepared a memorandum outlining the demand.[39] Oikawa intervened and persuaded Nagano against formal submission of the memorandum.[40] The Army General Staff was disgruntled but, in the interest of maintaining interservice unity, it agreed to shelve the document and content itself with oral representations concerning the need for an October 15 deadline. Throughout all of this Tojo said little; he saw no need. Sugiyama and Nagano spoke from the viewpoint of operational demands, which was their prerogative. Besides, there was nothing outrageous in their demand; they were merely holding the cabinet to account for a decision to which it had contributed.[41]

Konoe, unsettled, called a cabinet meeting. He asked his ministerial colleagues—in a forum that specifically excluded the chiefs of staff—whether they thought the Supreme Command's demand for an October 15 deadline was "tough." Tojo was measured in his response. He reminded Konoe that the demand for an October 15 deadline was based on the September 6 Imperial conference decision. The Army and Navy General Staffs' demand required "no changes" to the existing decision, and it contained no surprises. It was time, Tojo said, to pinpoint a final deadline for negotiations. The gulf separating Konoe and Tojo was now plain for all to see: Konoe was equivocating on the deadline, while Tojo sought to uphold it. Playing mediator, Oikawa suggested that the opening of hostilities should not be automatic. He proposed the convening of another Imperial conference, on or around October 15, to debate the issue of war or peace. For those, like Konoe, who were uneasy at the prospect of war against the Anglo-American powers, this suggestion held out at least the possibility of reversing the earlier decisions. Yet, if that were to happen, those who did not want war were going to have to do more than simply rely on the emperor to enforce an about-face. They were going to have to convince Tojo of the propriety of their position *before* any Imperial conference, and this would require a compelling explanation of what had changed since they had agreed, on September 6, to impose a deadline for war. The debate promised to be robust, and Tojo looked forward to it. He readily agreed to the need for another Imperial conference on or around October 15.[42]

THE SUPREME COMMAND'S CALL for an October 15 deadline raised the pressure, creating fissures throughout the policymaking process. Konoe descended into a funk of self-pity, holed himself up in his villa in Kamakura, and mused about resigning. The Army General Staff was in an uproar. Staff officers fulminated against the "evil" Oikawa for having prevented formal submission of the Supreme Command document calling for an October 15 deadline. They now "welcome[d]," they said, the possibility of the Konoe cabinet's downfall. The ever-hawkish Operations Bureau director, Tanaka Shin'ichi, lost all patience with the decision-making process and pleaded once and for all for a "decision for war."[43] At practically the same time, the commander in chief of the Combined Fleet, Admiral Yamamoto Isoroku, told Nagano flatly of the need, "so far as possible," to "avoid war." His reasoning was simple: Japan should not fight a "war with such little confidence in victory."[44] Meanwhile, the two services "clashed," with army officers declaring their "antagonistic attitude" was unavoidable so long as the navy sought to extend the October 15 deadline.[45]

Tojo sought clarity amid the chaos. He met with Oikawa on September 27 and demanded a clear and unambiguous statement concerning the September 6 Imperial conference decision. Did Oikawa continue to support that decision, or had he changed his mind? Tojo also wanted to know why Oikawa had intervened to prevent the chiefs of staff from formally presenting their written demand for an October 15 deadline. Was there a division emerging between the Navy General Staff and the Navy Ministry? Why was Nagano insisting on a deadline for negotiations, and why was Oikawa prevaricating? Tojo got answers to none of these questions. Oikawa was adamant that he did not want to "change the Imperial conference decision," yet he also expressed concern that Japan might rush into war, even as the "world situation changed from one moment to the next."[46] Tojo was dissatisfied with this response but took solace in the thought that he had pinpointed—for Oikawa's benefit—divisions within the navy as the basic cause of the cracks appearing in the policymaking process.

US diplomacy exacerbated the issues dividing the naval leadership. On October 2 the Roosevelt administration responded formally to the latest Japanese iteration of the Draft Understanding. The response requested Japan's consideration of four principles Secretary of State Hull had raised repeatedly throughout the negotiations in Washington: respect for each nation's territorial integrity and sovereignty, noninterference in another nation's internal affairs, equality of commercial opportunity, and alteration of the status quo only by peaceful means. It suggested that Japan give these principles concrete application by withdrawing troops from China and Indochina. It also sought clarification on the issue of Japan's obligations to its German and Italian allies.[47] Admiral Nagano needed no further convincing. He fronted a liaison conference on October 4, insisting there was "no longer time for discussion." "We want quick action," he said. There was considerable ambiguity in his remarks. Was he arguing for an end to discussion between the Japanese and US governments, and for quick action in opening hostilities in the Pacific? Or was he instead calling for an end to discussion among Japanese decision-makers and for quick action concerning the approaching deadline and the need for a definite decision for either war or peace? If the former, he was vastly overstepping his prerogatives as navy chief of staff, which did not extend to the issue of war or peace. If the latter, he was merely voicing the operational demand for certainty—one way or another—and remaining well within the limits of his policymaking role. Tojo expected Oikawa to fulfill his constitutional role by clarifying the situation, but Oikawa remained infuriatingly silent. Tojo himself was a model of moderation, calling merely for further "study" of the latest US memorandum.[48]

Tojo was more forthcoming in his appraisal of US diplomacy when he chaired a meeting of army officers the following day at his official residence. The Americans were, he noted, making a threefold demand of Japan: "unconditional approval" of Hull's four principles, the withdrawal of Japanese troops from China and Indochina, and Japan's departure from the Tripartite Pact. All present agreed that diplomacy had failed and discussion turned quickly to war in the Pacific. There prevailed a belief in the need to secure from Germany an agreement not to conclude a separate peace. Tojo interjected: "Placing our trust in a country like that is no good! Japan will go it alone!"[49]

Tojo met that evening with Konoe. He characterized the US position as demanding "unconditional application" of Hull's four principles, withdrawal of Japanese troops from China, and Japan's secession from the Tripartite Pact. On these points, he stated, "Japan should not yield." Konoe advised Tojo to forget about Hull's four principles and the issue of Japan's alliance with Nazi Germany. The US focus, he asserted, was on the issue of Japanese troops in China. He suggested that Japan accept the US insistence on the withdrawal of Japanese troops, but then leave at least a portion of its troops in China on a pretext, such as the "securing of resources." "But that," Tojo countered, "would be a ruse." Undeterred, Konoe argued that troop withdrawals required "circumspection" and that the United States would not regard such as "delaying tactics." Konoe raised with Tojo the alternative. In the event of war, he asked, were the United Kingdom and the United States separable? Konoe was suggesting that war in the Pacific would necessarily involve both Britain and the United States, implying that victory in such a war was beyond Japan's capacity. Tojo did not address this implication. He simply cited the navy's research on the matter and stated his belief in Anglo-American inseparability.[50]

Unlike Konoe, Tojo was disinclined to make any predictions about war in the Pacific. Anglo-American inseparability, and its implications for Japan's fortunes in war, was not his concern. That was the navy's responsibility, and he deferred to the navy on this matter. For this reason, Tojo had no interest in Konoe's thoughts concerning Japan's chances of victory in the Pacific, as Konoe possessed neither a navy officer's education nor experience. As a civilian, he had never participated in—much less understood—any of the navy's war-gaming or war plans. Konoe's voice, from Tojo's perspective, was considerably less than authoritative on this matter. It counted for naught.

BUREAU AND DIVISION CHIEFS from both the Army and Navy General Staffs and Ministries met on October 6. The soldiers entered the meeting insistent that there was no longer any prospect for diplomacy; the sailors argued that a willingness to make concessions on the issue of troops in China raised the prospect of diplomatic success. To strengthen the case for a continuation of diplomacy, the chief of the Navy General Staff's Operations Division, Rear Admiral Fukudome Shigeru, stated flatly that he had "no confidence" of victory in a war across the Pacific and Southeast Asia.[51] Agreement was not forthcoming on anything other than the need to shift the conversation to the armed services' leadership.[52]

Tojo prioritized a united front with Sugiyama. He was, in essence, guarding against the kind of split that now wracked the navy, which was visiting chaos on the entire decision-making process. Tojo and Sugiyama agreed readily that Japanese-US negotiations had failed. They clarified their refusal to accept any change in existing policy concerning the stationing of troops in China, and they agreed that Hull's four principles were unacceptable. They nonetheless felt there was nothing to gain by arguing with colleagues concerning the prospect of success in the Japanese-US negotiations. They agreed simply to hold colleagues to the existing decision to impose a deadline on negotiations. They agreed, in other words, to a continuation of the Japanese-US negotiations until October 15. Finally,

Sugiyama and Tojo wanted clarity from their naval counterparts on two key questions: Was the navy confident of victory in the Pacific and Southeast Asia? And was it seeking to change the September 6 Imperial conference decision to impose a deadline on negotiations and a deadline for war?[53]

Sugiyama approached Nagano with these questions on October 7. That Nagano might face such questions had been obvious enough, and his subordinates had prepared his talking points in advance. He was supposed to explain that the cabinet ought not to decide lightly on an extension of the deadline for negotiations. Pursuing "aimless" diplomacy, and then later asking the Supreme Command to devise a successful war plan, was unacceptable. A decision to extend the deadline required a decision to "moderate" Japan's diplomatic demands so as to facilitate "prompt resolution" of all issues separating Japan and the United States. Nagano, however, departed from this carefully prepared script. He agreed with Sugiyama that there was no prospect of success in the Japanese-US negotiations and agreed on the need for a prompt decision for war.[54]

Tojo's meeting with Oikawa also took place on October 7. It proceeded very differently from the Sugiyama-Nagano meeting. Tojo opened with the army's understanding of the situation. He accused the Americans of trying to "force Japan, in both name and reality, to surrender." He related his dissatisfaction with the Americans' threefold insistence on Japan's withdrawal from the Tripartite Pact, the realization of Hull's four principles, and the withdrawal of Japanese troops from China. He recounted his willingness to make concessions on most other points, but on these three points he insisted that Japan "must stand firm." He then asked Oikawa whether the Japanese-US negotiations could possibly succeed and reminded Oikawa of the need to "respect" the Supreme Command's insistence on an October 15 deadline. Oikawa insisted that diplomatic success remained possible, though he conceded that it was unlikely before the October 15 deadline. Yet he insisted also that the Supreme Command's October 15 target ought not be "restrictive" and he stated there must remain "scope" for its extension. Tojo was measured in his response. It was necessary, he said, to "respect the Supreme Command's desired deadline." He made clear that he took no issue with the pursuit of diplomacy up until the deadline, but he remained insistent on the parameters within which diplomacy must proceed. "On the matters of the four principles and also of troop withdrawals ... we cannot make any concessions," he reiterated.[55]

Tojo asked Oikawa whether any of the assumptions underlying the September 6 Imperial conference had changed. Oikawa said nothing had changed. Tojo then went straight to the point. "Are you confident of victory in war?" he asked. Oikawa admitted he had "no confidence." He explained that the Navy General Staff's predictions of victory did not extend beyond the second—or possibly third—year of war in the Pacific. The prospects of victory thereafter, he said euphemistically, remained under study. Oikawa's frankness was fleeting. He told Tojo that under no circumstances would he repeat before anyone else his pessimistic forecast of war in the Pacific; he would leave the question of war or peace to Konoe.[56]

An angered Tojo left the meeting with Oikawa. "The Navy Minister says that the [decision for] war ... is the government's responsibility and that [the prospects of victory in war] are currently under study," he told his subordinates. "If that is the case, this means there were no prospects of victory when the September 6 Imperial conference decision was made!" In other words, the Imperial conference decision was based on faulty assumptions that were a direct result of Oikawa's inexplicable refusal to represent his service clearly and unambiguously. The "issue," thundered Tojo, was one of "responsibility!"[57] He then marched into a cabinet meeting and railed against the Americans, the British, and even the Germans for having meddled in domestic Japanese matters. He called for a "fight to the bitter end," demanding that the nation "prepare to meet its fate."[58]

Tojo's initial anger gave way to uncertainty. Oikawa had voiced a complete lack of confidence in even the possibility of victory in war against the Anglo-American powers, and his voice could not be dismissed lightly. Tojo responded with alacrity. His political fixer, Muto Akira, told Chief Cabinet Secretary Tomita Kenji that same day of the need to continue diplomatic negotiations with the United States. Muto also said that the army was willing to make concessions on the vexing issue of Japanese troops in China.[59] Tojo himself spoke again that day with Oikawa, and freely admitted to being "unable to make up his mind." For the first time, he wavered on the issue of troop withdrawals from China. "Tens of thousands of lives have been lost on my watch in the China Incident, and deserting them is impossibly unbearable," he said. "Yet, if I think of the many more tens of thousands of lives which will be lost in a Japanese-US war, then I must consider troop withdrawals [from China]."[60]

TOJO WENT ALMOST DIRECTLY from his meeting with Oikawa to one with Konoe. The indecision he had confessed to during his meeting with Oikawa was undetectable. Tojo was now incisive and, indeed, feisty. He opened proceedings by affirming the need to set an October 15 deadline. Konoe asked whether, in the interest of diplomatic success, the army would agree to troop withdrawals from China. As he had done previously, Konoe indicated that the pace and timing of any troop withdrawals should accord with the army's operational requirements. Tojo was emphatic in his response. "Utterly impossible!" he snapped. The two men haggled over Hull's four principles before Konoe blurted out, "A reexamination [of the September 6 Imperial conference decision to impose a deadline] is necessary." Tojo questioned the purpose of any such reexamination. "It is of grave importance," he snapped, "if you intend to demolish an Imperial conference decision."[61]

Konoe tried to shift the conversation away from the mechanics of the domestic decision-making process, seeking instead to focus Tojo's attention on what he regarded as the real issue at hand. He told Tojo of his belief in the likelihood of Japan's ultimate defeat in the event of war in the Pacific. Tojo refused to countenance Konoe's concerns and turned the conversation back to the decision-making process. "The September 6 decision was the joint responsibility of the government and the Supreme Command," he said. He then reminded Konoe that strategy, operations, and calculations of battlefield success were the purview solely of the Supreme Command. In so doing Tojo was telling Konoe of the irrelevance of his prime ministerial thoughts on Japan's chances in war. Konoe tried to wrest back the initiative by defining ministerial responsibilities in any decision for war. "It is necessary to think further about a just cause for this war," he said. Tojo granted this point but tied it back to the crucial issue of time. It was not, he said, sufficient reason to extend or revise the Supreme Command's insistence on an October 15 deadline. It was, he suggested, possible to define a just cause for war without extending the deadline. Outdebated and outmaneuvered, Konoe lashed out weakly at Tojo. "Soldiers and sailors," he quipped, "are apt to think too readily about war." Tojo famously replied, "Sometimes a man has to jump, with his eyes closed, from the veranda of Kiyomizu Temple."[62]

Tojo's performance left Konoe in a most pessimistic frame of mind. Konoe spoke with the lord keeper of the Privy Seal, Kido Koichi, on October 9, relaying how the Japanese-US negotiations had not proceeded as he hoped. The deadline now loomed, and Konoe admitted he was "extremely worried." The consequences of his earlier actions were—belatedly—weighing on him, and he seemed utterly bereft of ideas.[63] Yet Konoe misread Tojo. He *was* willing to reconsider withdrawing troops from China. But there was a precondition: Oikawa, not Konoe, had to profess openly, clearly, and unambiguously the navy's inability to defeat the United States in war. Muto Akira put the case to his naval counterpart, Rear Admiral Oka Takazumi. "If the navy says it cannot fight the war," Muto suggested, "the army will reconsider. If the navy cannot fight, then please say so."[64]

Oikawa had already told Tojo that the Japanese Navy could not emerge victorious from war in the Pacific. Yet he had also made clear that he would not state this openly at cabinet level, at a liaison conference, or at an Imperial conference. He hoped that Tojo would see things from his perspective and that the Army and Navy Ministries would forge unity on this basis. Naval Affairs Bureau chief Oka adhered closely to this policy. "The navy," he told Muto, "refuses to say that it can or cannot fight." Muto took the news to Tojo, who exploded in anger. "Why won't the Navy Minister make himself clear?" he thundered. "If the Navy Minister speaks out clearly, then I too will have to think again. Yet the Navy Minister is leaving all responsibility to the Prime Minister. This is truly deplorable!"[65]

ON OCTOBER 12, 1941, Tojo accepted an invitation to Konoe's Ogikubo residence. So, too, did Oikawa, Toyoda, and the Policy Planning Board director, Suzuki Teiichi. In the lead-up to the Ogikubo conference, Chief Cabinet Secretary Tomita Kenji telephoned Tojo's political fixer, Muto Akira. He explained that Oikawa intended to leave the decision for war or peace to Konoe's "discretion." Muto took the news to Tojo, who refused to back away from his own position, which Muto relayed to Tomita and Naval Affairs Bureau director Oka Takazumi. "This just won't do," Muto told Oka and Tomita. "Leaving [the question of war or peace in the Pacific] to the discretion of the prime minister? He alone can do nothing about an issue like this. Shouldn't the navy itself . . . state clearly that it can't fight? If it does so, I myself will suppress jingoism within the ministry."[66] Tojo's position was clear: He would accept the navy's forecast of defeat in war in the Pacific and would adjust army policy accordingly. Conversely, he would refuse to countenance Konoe's assertions about the outcome of war in the Pacific. The question was whether Konoe, Oikawa, and Toyoda would heed this warning.

Toyoda opened proceedings at the Ogikubo conference. "There is," he said, "scope for agreement in the Japanese-US negotiations." According to Toyoda, transpacific agreement merely required reconsideration of the twin issues of troops in China and Indochina. Tojo disagreed. There was, he said, "no scope for agreement" because the United States had shown "no intention of compromising." Oikawa took these two contrasting statements and noted that Japan was at the "crossroads" of war or peace. He submitted that a decision either way should properly be that of the prime minister. Tojo snapped back at Oikawa, "The issue is not that simple!" He reminded his colleagues that the Supreme Command was independent of the cabinet, and as such was under no compulsion to accept a prime ministerial decision. He himself "could not blindly obey . . . the prime minister's decision." Any decision to pursue diplomacy and forsake the option of war, Tojo averred, required a firm basis, and he made it apparent that he was yet to learn of that basis. Taking a verbal swipe at the "irritating" Toyoda, whose opening remarks had effectively pinpointed the army as the chief hindrance to Japanese-US agreement, he noted that the army's movements accorded with Imperial conference decisions.[67]

If Tojo hoped his comments might compel Oikawa to speak up, those hopes went unfulfilled. Toyoda commented that the September 6 Imperial conference decision to impose a deadline on diplomacy had been "rash." Tojo shouted him down: "That is troubling!" Konoe then spoke. "There are prospects [of victory] in the first year or two of war," he said. "In the third and fourth years [of war] I have no confidence and am anxious." He made clear his refusal to participate in a decision for war in which he had "no confidence." Tojo dismissed Konoe's lack of confidence, stating that this should have arisen at the September 6 Imperial conference.[68]

His colleagues' haphazard approach to decision-making flabbergasted and angered Tojo. A lesser politician than Tojo at this juncture might well have resigned his ministerial post and brought down the Konoe cabinet. He could certainly have reasoned that the current situation, in which Konoe was arbitrarily trying to overturn an Imperial conference decision, justified what was otherwise regarded as a heavy-handed political maneuver. And he would have done so with his service's unflinching support, as army officers were by now virtually unanimous in their contempt for the "pitiful" Konoe cabinet.[69] Tojo nonetheless remained mindful of the emperor's likely reaction to his resignation. His political instincts were, moreover, finely attuned. His resignation would solidify the Konoe-Oikawa-Toyoda triumvirate and enable the men to portray him and his service as the lone troublemaker in a chaotic policymaking environment.

Rather than resign, Tojo suggested that the negotiations in Washington continue. He imposed two conditions: There must be no concessions concerning the stationing of Japanese troops in China nor any agreements that might "undermine" the prospect of "success" in China. For his part, he would seek to secure from the Army General Staff an agreement to "abort" ongoing preparations for war until the last ten days of October.[70] Tojo secured just such an agreement on October 13 from Sugiyama.[71]

Tojo fretted in the aftermath of the Ogikubo conference. He made no effort to contact his ministerial colleagues and refused even to speak with most army officers. His irascible subordinate, Colonel Sato Kenryo, was one of very few people brave enough to confront Tojo. Sato asked whether Tojo might consider speaking casually and over drinks with Oikawa. Tojo spat back at him, "Are you suggesting we decide the great affairs of state by means of behind-the-scenes political dealings?" Sato was not cowed. He reminded Tojo of the money the navy had spent over the decades precisely so that the Combined Fleet might keep pace with its US counterpart. He reckoned it must be almost impossible for the navy now to admit that it could not fight. Even so, Sato asked Tojo to keep in mind the possibility of Japan being "crushed" in war with the United States and again asked him to speak with the navy leadership. Tojo refused. Nagano and Oikawa "could not speak the truth" at an Imperial conference, he said, so it was folly to think they might do so informally.[72]

Tojo had reached the point of no return; he could no longer work with his ministerial colleagues. He made this apparent when he met with Konoe on October 14. Konoe argued for the possibility of success in the Japanese-US negotiations if only the army would soften its stance on the stationing of troops in China. Tojo would not budge. "The army," he said, "cannot make concessions on the issue of the stationing of troops." Konoe responded by once again noting his unease at the prospect of war against the Anglo-American powers. Tojo chastised Konoe for being overly concerned about Japan's weaknesses and demanded he educate himself about Anglo-American weaknesses.[73]

The two men then proceeded directly to a cabinet meeting, where Tojo held the floor. "The army's movements," he said, "are based on Imperial decision." He gave his ministerial colleagues a short but stinging lesson in responsibility, reminding them that they had each "studied," "deliberated on," and consented to the deadline before submitting it for Imperial decision at the September 6 Imperial conference. He quoted the decision at some length: "In the event that there is no prospect of our demands being met by *the first ten days of October* through ... diplomatic negotiations ... , we will immediately decide to commence hostilities." He then stated, simply, "It is now [October] 14."[74]

Konoe and Tojo pose for a photo amid their bruising battle over the deadline for war, October 1941.

Tojo turned on those of his colleagues now arguing for further concessions so as to facilitate the Japanese-US negotiations. "It is not the case that military affairs are hindering diplomacy," he said. "Diplomacy is obstructing military affairs." He asked why diplomacy was "not proceeding as promised," but he did not wait for an answer. Instead he noted that the situation they now found themselves in had arisen because diplomacy had "not kept to schedule."[75]

Tojo left the cabinet meeting and went directly to the Imperial Palace. He spoke with Kido, who accepted that the Konoe cabinet must now fall, and added that the next cabinet somehow would have to manage the divide between the Army and Navy Ministries. Kido reminded Tojo that the Navy Ministry remained "uneasy" about war; Tojo merely stated that Oikawa had repeatedly expressed his satisfaction with the September 6 Imperial conference decision. Kido granted the point, but asked Tojo to try and bridge the gap with Oikawa for the sake of the next cabinet. This required a shift in focus, and Tojo told Kido he would immediately "discontinue" arguments with Konoe about the "issue of responsibility" and would instead take up with the navy the question of whether or not to proceed with "national policy as it currently stands."[76]

The interservice conversation took place slightly lower than ministerial level and involved the Military Affairs Bureau director, Muto Akira, and the Naval Affairs Bureau director, Oka Takazumi. Muto issued a set of questions that demanded straight answers: Did the navy believe there was a need to reach a diplomatic settlement with the United States? Was there any "scope" for a diplomatic settlement of issues? If there were no hope of diplomatic success, should Japan "unavoidably" go to war in the Pacific?[77] Oka forwarded the questions directly to Oikawa, who almost immediately called a meeting that included Rear Admiral Fukudome Shigeru, Vice Chief of Staff Ito Seiichi, Rear Admiral Oka Takazumi, and Navy Vice Minister Sawamoto Yorio. Nagano was notably absent. The naval leaders were unable to reach any firm answers; even as the Konoe cabinet limped into its final days, they were only able to agree that they found themselves "between a rock and a hard place."[78]

Tojo, for his part, refused to blink. "If the navy would simply say that it cannot take on a war, then we might be compelled to reexamine the decision of the [September 6] Imperial conference," he said. "If at this point they say they have no confidence, there will be no choice but to call everything off and start all over again."[79] Tojo's logic was impeccable. He and other decision-makers had presumed, when they imposed a deadline on the negotiations, that war in the Pacific was a viable option. The naval leadership had not given them cause to believe otherwise. Tojo was now demanding that Oikawa and the navy come clean. He was setting the tone for the future of interservice cooperation and, by extension, state policy.

10
LEADING THE NATION TO WAR
OCTOBER–DECEMBER 1941

IN THE LAST DAYS of the third cabinet of Prime Minister Konoe Fumimaro, Tojo Hideki began moving his personal belongings from his official ministerial residence to his home in Tokyo's Setagaya Ward. He harbored no regrets; he was satisfied that he had discharged his ministerial responsibilities to the best of his ability. The Konoe cabinet would soon collapse, and whatever others said, Tojo was convinced this owed not to his actions but those of his ministerial colleagues. Tojo was quite certain of at least one thing: There was little basis to rumors swirling within the Imperial Japanese Army that he might emerge as the next prime minister. He assumed he would play no role in setting the future course of Japanese policy, and he prepared for duties that were not ministerial, including a likely stint as a prestigious but largely ceremonial military councilor.[1]

Like others in Tokyo, Tojo confronted the question as to whether the army's lower and middle echelons would acquiesce in any decision to avert war in the Pacific. The question arose at least partly because the pursuit of diplomacy with the United States raised the prospect of an end to the war in China not on the Japanese Army's terms but instead on US terms. And as recently as October 2, 1941, the United States had gone on record as demanding the withdrawal of all Japanese troops from China. Whether the army's younger officers would accept a Sino-Japanese peace imposed from across the Pacific was an open question. Fears of a disturbance along the lines of the February 26 Incident were everywhere discernible, and Tojo himself professed uncertainty as to whether the army could be "brought under control."[2]

Tojo believed that extraordinary times called for extraordinary measures. He wondered whether the emperor might appoint an Imperial prince to succeed Konoe as prime minister. This would mark a break with precedent—not since the Meiji Restoration of 1868 had an Imperial prince served as prime minister—but Tojo specifically named Prince Higashikuni Naruhiko as the most likely candidate. He believed that Prince Higashikuni could command the soldiers' loyalty by virtue of both his Imperial lineage and his military career. Tojo's suggestion made its way, by circuitous means, to the Imperial Palace on October 15. Neither the lord keeper of the Privy Seal, Kido Koichi, nor the emperor himself were particularly receptive. The emperor wondered whether Prince Higashikuni might make a good army chief of staff—he was a general on active military service—but he insisted that "serious thought" was necessary before breaking with precedent and thrusting an Imperial prince into the prime minister's position. The emperor's concern was that the prince would prove unable to avert war. He was looking ahead to the question, in the event Japan lost the war, about the future of the Imperial institution.[3]

The Konoe cabinet resigned en masse late on the afternoon of October 16. The following day Kido hosted a meeting of the *jushin* (former prime ministers) to settle on a likely successor. Numerous possibilities were discussed and discarded before Kido pushed Tojo as Konoe's successor. This was another break with precedent, for the lord keeper of the Privy Seal, by convention, remained little more than a passive witness to the debate among the *jushin*. Kido knew full well that Konoe and others were charging Tojo with having torn down the cabinet on which he served; Kido was nonetheless sympathetic to Tojo's version of recent events, and he regarded Konoe's charges as self-serving apologia. Indeed, Kido admired what can only be called Tojo's political acumen and was satisfied that he had represented the army with aplomb. Kido now hoped that a prime ministerial appointment would force Tojo to look beyond only an army perspective and to approach the issue of war or peace from a truly national perspective. Kido suggested yet another break with precedent: Whereas admirals Okada Keisuke and Yonai Mitsumasa had resigned from active service on the eve of their respective prime ministerial appointments, Kido suggested that Tojo ought, as prime minister, to remain on the Japanese Army's active service list (as had Yamagata Aritomo during the Meiji period). This would enable Tojo to serve concurrently as army minister. Kido believed this was important, because he was convinced that Tojo alone could suppress the army's unruly elements and prevent or at least quash a coup attempt, in the event the cabinet enacted the emperor's wishes and avoided war against the United States. Several of the *jushin* were unsettled by the thought of Tojo as prime minister, but none voiced outright opposition.[4]

Kido took the suggestion to the emperor, who reacted with dismay and reluctance. As he put it to Grand Chamberlain Hyakutake Saburo, he was deeply frustrated with the army for having "interfered" incessantly in politics since the February 26 Incident. He lambasted the army for having repeatedly obstructed orderly "cabinet formation" processes and for having caused the "downfall" of numerous cabinets. It grated on him that the army had arrogated to itself powers that were properly his constitutionally defined "prerogatives" (*daiken*), and it bothered him that he was now in a position in which he had little choice but to reward the army for its repeated infractions by offering the prime ministerial position to an army general.[5]

The idea of asking Tojo to remain on active service deepened the emperor's discomfiture. He told Hyakutake this was "inimical to the spirit of the Meiji Restoration," and he spoke of his "grief" at what struck him as a return to the "warrior governments" of "times past." The emperor fretted at the likelihood of Tojo becoming a modern-day "shogun" who, in a manner not unlike Japan's feudal-era warrior rulers, usurped the emperor's powers and prerogatives. The emperor found this all the more galling because, as he saw it, Tojo had contributed directly to the "dire" situation in which Japan now found itself.[6]

The absurdity of the situation irked the emperor: He was being asked to trust the Konoe cabinet's leading war hawk to steer the nation away from war. Yet he accepted Kido's logic and figured—if through gritted teeth—that Tojo might at least prove able to control the army in the event he somehow averted war. In a subsequent conversation with Kido, the emperor acknowledged the risks, likening Tojo's prime ministerial appointment to entering a "tiger's den" in order to "catch a tiger cub."[7] But there were no viable alternatives. Hyakutake telephoned Tojo and, at the emperor's behest, summoned him to the Imperial Palace.[8]

Tojo had been nervously awaiting a phone call from the Imperial Palace, and he now braced himself for a severe upbraiding. He had little idea what the emperor had heard or believed, and he merely hoped he might be given the opportunity to offer his own version of recent events. He expected that Army Chief of Staff Sugiyama Hajime would also be called, and he advised Sugiyama to prepare himself for an upbraiding. In the meantime, Tojo's subordinates worried that the emperor might demand the withdrawal of all troops from China. They prepared a lengthy report, which made the army's

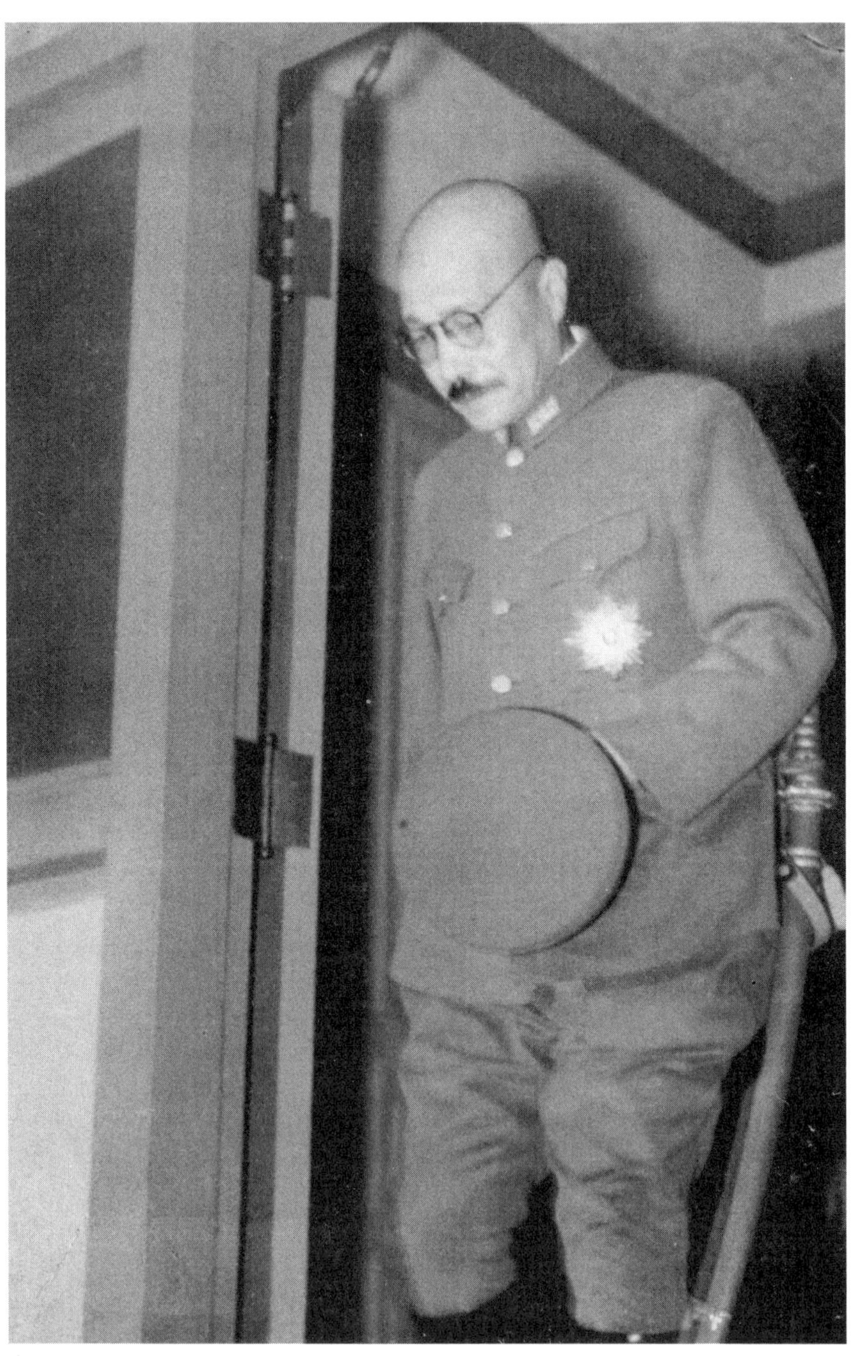

Tojo makes his way to the Imperial Palace following the collapse of the Konoe cabinet, 4:47 p.m., October 17, 1941. Tojo is half expecting a severe scolding by Hirohito.

Tojo leaves the Imperial Palace after the emperor asked him to serve as prime minister, 6:27 p.m., October 17, 1941.

case for the continued stationing of troops in China, and submitted it to Tojo in the expectation that he would deliver it to the throne. Tojo refused outright. He remained, in what he presumed was his final ministerial act, faithful to his emperor. "If His majesty says this is the way it will be, that is that as far as I am concerned: I will say 'yes sir' and withdraw," Tojo insisted. "I will not argue with His majesty." Tojo's nerves jangled when he arrived at the palace and learned that the emperor would dispense with the usual courtesies and not invite him to take a seat during his audience. Tojo turned to his secretary, Colonel Akamatsu Sadao, and whispered about what he supposed was the emperor's "anger" with him.[9]

Tojo entered the Imperial Library and waited. The emperor joined him and said, "I command you to organize a cabinet." He then made two demands. First, he ordered Tojo to "abide by the provisions of the constitution." Second, he implored Tojo to build "greater cooperation between the army and navy." Tojo remained in a stupefied silence when Vice Admiral Oikawa Koshiro entered the Imperial Library. The emperor explained, for Oikawa's benefit, that Tojo would serve as the next prime minister, and he repeated his demand for army-navy unity. The emperor then left the two men. After approximately thirty minutes, Kido joined Oikawa and Tojo and repeated the emperor's demand for army-navy unity, explaining the terms on which the armed services must unify. They were first to "reexamine ... the situation at home and abroad." On the basis of that reexamination, they were to discard the September 6 Imperial conference decision to impose a deadline on diplomacy and, after "careful consideration," to reset national policy. This was the emperor's much-heralded "wipe-the-slate-clean" message.[10]

Tojo left the Imperial Palace and ordered his driver to take him directly to Meiji Shrine. He prayed to the deified spirits of the Meiji Emperor and his wife, the Empress Shoken. Next Tojo moved on to the nearby Togo Shrine, where he prayed to the deified spirit of Fleet Admiral Togo Heihachiro. When he ordered his driver to take him next to Yasukuni Shrine, Colonel Akamatsu plucked up the courage to ask the hitherto silent Tojo what had happened in the palace. "I thought His majesty was angry, but he ordered me to form a cabinet," Tojo said. "I was awestruck and unable to respond. His majesty gave me a reprieve, called ... Oikawa, and ordered him to cooperate with me. I consulted at length with ... Kido, who told me to prepare to form a cabinet.... I figured there was no way to make those preparations other than by means of the gods' patronage. Thus, it all depends on these shrine visits." Tojo then climbed out of the car and prayed to the deified spirits of Imperial Japan's war dead in Yasukuni Shrine.[11]

WHEN HE RETURNED TO the official army minister's residence late that afternoon, Tojo was greeted by Vice Army Minister Kimura Heitaro and Military Affairs Bureau Chief Muto Akira. They had wondered about the possibility of Tojo's prime ministerial appointment and in anticipation had prepared a list of the army's preferred ministerial candidates. Tojo refused to look at the list. "Until now, I have been army minister," he said, "but now that I have received the Imperial command, I am no longer [solely] army minister." He then redefined his prime ministerial relationship with Kimura and Muto. "Army men must not involve themselves in cabinet formation," he said. "I don't need your list. It is not for you to submit it." Lest anybody misunderstand his intent, Tojo continued, "I will not listen to the army's ideas about forming this cabinet. I will [instead] ask those related to the cabinet for their help." He then moved with the Home Ministry's Inada Shuichi to another room, and forbade entry to Kimura and Muto—and, indeed, to all military men.[12]

Tojo worked to a very tight, self-imposed deadline: He presented the emperor with his finalized list of ministerial choices the following morning. Included among his personnel preferences were Hoshino Naoki as chief cabinet secretary and Kishi Nobusuke as commerce and industry minister. Tojo had worked with these two men in the so-called *ni-ki san-suke* (two -ki and three -suke) group in Manchukuo; one may infer from these personnel choices that Tojo had paid little attention, even as minister, to expanding his personal and political network beyond his professional military colleagues and a relatively small existing network of civilians. Tojo named as his preferred foreign minister the diplomat Togo Shigenori, who accepted the post only after Tojo agreed to reconsider the issue of Japanese troops in China.[13]

Tojo remained not only as army minister (per Kido's wishes) but served also as home minister. These positions gave him control over the *kenpei* (military police) and the police, which he believed would be necessary in the event war was averted. He later explained to Akamatsu, "His majesty said to restart the Japanese-US negotiations from a blank slate, and he also said he was giving careful consideration to avoiding war so far as that was possible. There may well have been an uprising greater than the February 26 Incident in the event we respectfully carried out

His majesty's wishes, did not go to war, and yielded to the US proposals. In that event, it would have been necessary to ditch our tears and to suppress the uprising. It was therefore necessary to take the concurrent posts of army minister and of home minister, which had control of the [*kenpei* and the] police."[14]

For the navy minister's post the Imperial Japanese Navy settled on the commander of Kure Naval District, Admiral Toyoda Soemu, who informally accepted the position on October 17, 1941. Tojo balked at the news. Toyoda had a well-earned reputation for being outspokenly antiarmy, and he was also adamantly opposed to war against the United States. Tojo was convinced that he and Toyoda would be unable to work together, and he was concerned lest divisions between the antiwar Toyoda and the prowar Nagano Osami plunge the navy into a prolonged period of infighting and indecision. If the navy insisted on Toyoda's ministerial appointment, he told Oikawa, he would decline the prime minister's post.[15]

Tojo's refusal to work with Toyoda split the navy leadership. Vice Minister Sawamoto Yorio was concerned about the "bad precedent" the navy would set if it dropped Toyoda at Tojo's insistence. Concerned that army-navy cooperation would be entirely on Tojo's terms, he recommended

Tojo in the home minister's office. The photo is undated, but taken between October 1941 and February 1942.

that the navy stand firm behind Toyoda. The navy vice chief of staff, Vice Admiral Ito Seiichi, agreed. Oikawa, however, insisted that the navy not be responsible for aborting the Tojo cabinet. He walked out of the meeting and went straight to Toyoda. He began to apologize but Toyoda cut him short, disavowing any ministerial ambition and then offering some sage advice for whoever assumed the navy minister's post: "Japan cannot fight this war!" The following morning Sawamoto asked Toyoda to indulge the polite fiction that he had declined the navy minister's post. Toyoda obliged in his characteristically forthright manner. "There is no way I could cooperate with [Tojo]," he said. "Because I'd be unable to realize my principled belief in [the imperative of] peace, I voluntarily decline [the ministerial post]."[16] The navy leadership had in the meantime settled on the Yokosuka Naval District commander, Admiral Shimada Shigetaro, as a compromise candidate. Whatever his positive attributes, Shimada was possessed of a weak personality and was singularly unsuited to staring down the advocates of war within his own service, let alone challenging Tojo and the army. Tojo accepted the nomination, and Shimada joined Tojo and the other incoming ministers at the cabinet's Imperial investiture ceremony on October 18.[17]

The importance of this brief episode can hardly be overstated. It contains the origins of a conception among navy officers of Shimada as a Tojo lackey who so prioritized agreement with Tojo that he seemed oblivious to the navy's own strategic outlook. Herein, moreover, are the seeds of Tojo's eventual fall from political power. But that was not evident in October 1941. Indeed, Tojo might have been forgiven had he congratulated himself for having stared down what he regarded as the navy's more obstreperous elements. He now had a yes-man as navy minister and, from Tojo's immediate perspective, this augured well not only for interservice cooperation but also for greater cohesion within the navy.

ON OCTOBER 18 THE EMPEROR inaugurated the Tojo cabinet. He also promoted Tojo to full general. The promotion was extraordinary (divisional command was but one basic expectation to which Tojo could not lay claim), but the army was satisfied that his prime ministerial appointment warranted the promotion. This did not mean, however, that Tojo had any greater degree of control over the Supreme Command than might otherwise have been the case. The Army and Navy General Staffs remained, as always, independent of the cabinet.

Tojo and Admiral Shimada Shigetaro, October 18, 1941. Shimada was the compromise candidate for navy minister after Tojo rejected its first choice, Toyoda Soemu.

Herein lay a major flaw with Kido's clean-slate message. He delivered the message to Tojo, but to neither General Sugiyama nor Admiral Nagano. This only deepened the mutual independence of the cabinet and the General Staffs at the very outset of Tojo's time as prime minister. Tojo himself was determined to act on what he himself understood to be the emperor's "command" to "wipe the slate clean."[18] His subordinates in the Army Ministry did not dare cross him, and they professed the need to "reexamine" existing policy, including the deadline for war. On the other side of the divide, staff officers were adamant that the "new cabinet must be an opening-of-war cabinet." Even after the Army Ministry on November 18 apprised staff officers of the clean-slate message, they remained convinced there was "no room for reconsideration" of existing policy, and they griped that the deadline for war had now passed. They also wondered about Tojo. He had, they complained, "toppled" the Konoe cabinet on the grounds there was "absolutely no prospect" of success in the Japanese-US negotiations. Now he seemed determined to pursue those same negotiations. Was this not "disadvantageous," even fraudulent?[19] To borrow the words of Sugiyama, "Things have already been delayed one month. . . . Hurry up and go ahead."[20]

Tojo would not, however, be hurried. He decided to reinvestigate the very basis of the mid-October deadline for war. He demanded clearheaded forecasts of both the European war and Anglo-American preparedness in the Pacific. He wanted to know Japan's prospects of acquiring Southeast Asia's resources, as well as its shipbuilding capacity and ability to replace ships invariably lost in a war of attrition. He wanted also to know the impact of a southward advance on Chiang Kai-shek, as well as the minimum diplomatic demands that might plausibly be made of the United States. Tojo issued these questions to all government ministries on October 18, almost as soon as he emerged from the Imperial investiture ceremony.[21]

Tojo's questions and the ministries' responses fueled a weeklong debate among his cabinet ministers and the Supreme Command. The debate was dominated by uniformed army and navy officers, most of whom had been involved in the earlier decision to impose a deadline for war; scarce was the officer who changed his outlook or position. Finance Minister Kaya Okinori was perhaps the most outspoken civilian minister, but estimates of Japan's preparedness for total war were almost solely the province of the Cabinet Planning Board. It was dominated by a younger generation of "total war" officers from both the army and navy, and it was headed by Tojo's longtime colleague Suzuki Teiichi. Day after day that late October, in debate after grueling debate, Suzuki revealed himself in favor of a decision for war. Informing his position were two expectations: Japan could, at the outset of war, occupy Southeast Asia and thereby gain access to the region's abundant raw materials; and Japanese shipbuilding industries could keep pace with projected losses of shipping in the Pacific. Suzuki buttressed his position with an impressive array of statistics and figures. The numbers had, however, been falsified so that estimates of shipping attrition rates were downsized and estimates of ship construction were increased. Tojo and others thus reached hopelessly faulty and wildly optimistic conclusions about Japan's capacity to wage total war.

The debate was moving inexorably toward its logical conclusion. Yet, so far as the Army General Staff was concerned, it was not moving nearly fast enough. Staff officers on October 25 complained that "discussion of the vital issue" of war or peace still seemed a lamentably "long way off."[22] They attributed the blame primarily to Tojo; some, like Operations Bureau chief Tanaka Shin'ichi, accused Tojo of having failed to impress strategic realities on the emperor. Tojo had been, according to this view, altogether too solicitous of the emperor's whims and fancies, based as they were on hazy notions of international goodwill and peace; Tanaka and others spoke derisively of Tojo's "palace cabinet." From that criticism stemmed a second, related criticism: Tojo was, as prime minister, neglecting his role and responsibilities as army minister. He ought, as army minister, to be convincing his cabinet colleagues of the strategic imperatives underpinning the Army General Staff's insistence on an immediate decision for war; instead he was insisting on a thoroughgoing reexamination of state policy. Some advocated the Tojo cabinet's "downfall"; others pushed instead for Tojo's forced resignation from the army minister's post.[23] These arguments gained such traction among staff officers that Sugiyama felt compelled to intervene with a statement of unstinting "support" for Tojo.[24]

Only on October 30—at the very end of this weeklong debate—did the conferees turn their attention to the possibility of an outcome other than war. Consensus was not forthcoming: Foreign Minister Togo "gave everyone a strange feeling" with his talk of accepting America's diplomatic demands, while most agreed there was "no hope" of at least short-term diplomatic success. There was a pervading sense that the pursuit of diplomacy would reduce Japan to the position of a "third-rate country." Over Sugiyama's objections, Tojo ordered the study of three options: "avoid war and undergo great hardships"; "decide on war immediately"; or "decide on war but carry on war preparations and diplomacy side by side." Tojo declined to indicate his preference but insisted that a decision be reached within two days.[25]

Tojo could be reasonably certain of the navy's support for his own unstated position. To be sure, Nagano's fire-eating subordinates in the Navy General Staff were vociferous in their criticism of Tojo and asked whether he had ever really wanted war or whether his performance in the Konoe cabinet had been a charade.[26] Even so, Nagano took a more nuanced position than he had previously, offering his qualified support for reexamining state policy. "We were to have reached a decision in October, and yet here we are," he said on October 24. "So I want to see our study and discussion kept concise. The navy is consuming 400 tons of oil an hour. The situation is urgent. We want it decided one way or the other quickly." In this way Nagano allowed Shimada some space to reach his own conclusions. Shimada went through the motions that might be expected of a new minister in a new cabinet: He consulted widely, pored over studies, and thought deeply about such matters as Japanese-US fleet ratios and Japan's oil supplies. By the end of October he opted to fall into line behind what he understood was Tojo's policy position, determining it would be best to pursue both diplomacy and war preparations simultaneously. He spoke with Tojo on October 31 and put a price on the navy's acquiescence in a decision for war: the service needed a massive allocation of materiel—including 1.1 million tons of steel in 1942—to support its fleet-building programs.[27]

This was a price Tojo was willing to pay. He turned his attention to securing Sugiyama's agreement to the continuation of war preparations and diplomacy. He went so far as to suggest an end-of-November deadline for diplomacy. Tojo's plan placed Sugiyama in a difficult position. Staff officers were bitterly critical of Tojo for prioritizing his prime ministerial duties over and above his responsibilities as army minister. He was, in their estimation, playing "politics," to the neglect of sound military strategy. They regarded Tojo's plan as an unedifying, indeed "corrupted" attempt at convincing others in his cabinet to agree to war. As distasteful as they found Tojo's newfound enthusiasm for another month of Japanese-US negotiations, staff officers saw little possibility of his stepping away from the position. They carved out a fallback position: "Resolve immediately on the abandonment of negotiations and the opening of war, conduct sham diplomacy in the forthcoming negotiations with the United States, and start war in the beginning of December."[28] Tojo quashed such thinking. He told Sugiyama of the need to give "due regard to the emperor," who would "not tolerate a diplomacy of deception."[29]

The two generals remained at loggerheads when a liaison conference met on November 1, 1941. It was a marathon, seventeen-hour affair. Tojo held firm, arguing for pursuit of "both diplomacy and military operations simultaneously." He got what he wanted, and the conferees agreed on a new deadline: If diplomatic success was not forthcoming by midnight of November 30, war would begin on December 1. That settled, the hitherto quiet foreign minister, Togo Shigenori, outlined his approach to the negotiations, putting forward what he called Proposals A and B. Proposal A sought resolution of the major issues dividing Japan and the United States. It delineated Japan's intention to occupy Inner Mongolia and North China for up to twenty-five years but otherwise to withdraw troops on the conclusion of peace, keep troops in French Indochina until the China Incident was settled, adhere to the principle of nondiscrimination in trade in China and the Pacific, and interpret independently its responsibilities as defined in the German-Italian-Japanese Tripartite Pact. Proposal B, narrower in scope, sought to return the Japanese-US relationship to the situation as it existed prior to the outbreak of the German-Soviet war. Not without reason it is referred to as a modus vivendi: It offered the withdrawal of Japanese troops from southern Indochina in return for a commitment by the United States to lift the trade embargo and unfreeze Japanese assets.[30] Tojo had seen Proposal A but not Proposal B beforehand, but he overcame his surprise and supported his foreign minister. Sugiyama was aghast. To borrow the words of historian Tsunoda Jun, he and Vice Chief of Staff Tsukada Osamu "went through the roof."[31] Tojo talked them down, securing a hard-earned consensus.

Nagano, Sugiyama, and Tojo appeared jointly before the emperor on November 2. Tojo reported, through tears of trepidation, on the previous day's decision to pursue diplomacy and to prepare for war simultaneously. He also explained the decision to impose a new deadline on diplomatic negotiations. The emperor admonished the tearful Tojo to do his "utmost" to realize a "breakthrough in the Japanese-US negotiations." He also importuned Tojo to "investigate" the possibility of "settling this difficult situation through the pope." (This curious suggestion went unheeded.) The emperor also asked whether, in the event of diplomatic failure, Tojo would seek his approval to go to war. Tojo was quick to grasp the emperor's purport: He would, for now, approve the simultaneous pursuit of diplomacy and war preparations, as well as the deadline, but he would continue to withhold a decision for war. (This neatly echoed the position Tojo had staked out in relation to the Kwantung Army's special maneuvers in June–July 1941.) Tojo reassured his sovereign of his intention to seek a formal decision for war in the event diplomatic success was not forthcoming by the deadline.[32]

This audience was an important milestone in Tojo's relationship with the emperor. He had wiped the slate clean and reinvestigated Japanese policy as the emperor's directive, but he had succeeded ultimately in little more than extending the existing deadline for war. He had not delivered what the emperor wanted, and he knew it. The emperor's likely reaction terrified Tojo. Perversely, his anguished tears, as well as his quick-witted grasp of the need to revisit the question of war or peace in early December, saw him rise exponentially in his emperor's estimation. Tojo himself sensed the shift. So, too, did his professional military colleagues. But while Tojo exulted in the emperor's newfound trust and indeed sought to burnish and enhance it, many staff officers remained intensely distrustful of him. Vice Chief of Staff Tsukada admitted to his subordinates that his "strenuous struggle" with Tojo had been "unbearable" and had moved him to "tears"; those same subordinates professed anger and bewilderment at Tojo's having forsaken his professional military colleagues and having instead made common cause with such "politically powerless" colleagues as Kaya and Togo.[33] An "influential general" told Tojo that the "extreme faith" with which he had greeted the new cabinet had evaporated, and he could no longer "suppress his disillusionment" at the cabinet's policymaking processes and decisions.[34] The disillusionment was widespread. According to one of Tojo's most trusted subordinates, Colonel Sato Kenryo, it owed primarily to the fact that Tojo was no longer making common cause with staff officers in arguing against any change to the original deadline but was instead insisting, over the objection of staff officers, on an extension of that deadline.[35]

Tojo had foreseen such tumult, and he was not turning back. He was enacting and implementing, as best as he was able, the emperor's will. This was not direct Imperial rule as envisioned by his mutinous factional enemies in the Japanese Army in the early and mid-1930s. Tojo was not upending and overturning the political system bequeathed him; he was working within constitutional limits. For this he was earning the emperor's approbation and this, in his estimation, more than compensated for the criticisms being leveled at him by his professional military colleagues. It also meant he was well positioned to contribute to the ongoing formation of the emperor's will.

First, it was necessary to formalize the simultaneous pursuit of diplomacy and war preparations, with a December 1 deadline. This required an Imperial conference, which convened on November 5. Tojo spoke at length about the Japanese-US negotiations, explaining that the Americans had hitherto demanded Japan's acceptance of US Secretary of State Cordell Hull's four principles. He acknowledged that the Konoe cabinet had notified the Americans of its acceptance. In so doing it had "conceded what it should not have conceded." His purport was clear: Japan would pursue diplomacy in all earnestness until December 1, but it would not accept such "strong [US] demands." He believed that the Americans would shrink from war against Japan, which created the conditions whereby Japan ought to be able to convince the administration of President Franklin D. Roosevelt to drop its insistence on Hull's four principles and to make concessions. Conversely, Tojo did not envision Japan making any concessions it had not already offered to make. This was a diplomacy of brinkmanship.[36] Muto explained the decision to the Army Ministry's bureau directors: "Japan is determined to go to war against the United States and Britain, in order to complete the Greater East Asia Co-Prosperity Sphere. The army and navy are to prepare [for that eventuality]. That said, it will be fine if Japan achieves its objectives via ongoing diplomatic negotiations. Yet, if [the negotiations] do not turn out as they should [by the beginning of December], we will commence operations."[37]

THE COURSE HAD BEEN set, and it was time to allow the diplomatic negotiations to run their course. In Washington, DC, Ambassador Nomura Kichisaburo presented Proposal A to Hull on November 7. Five days later, before Washington had formally responded, Togo admitted to Tojo and others that "negotiations with the United States have run into considerable difficulties." The problem, Togo explained, was one of time.[38] Tojo neither exulted nor despaired at the news. There was work to be done.

Among the most pressing issues was preparation of an exit strategy from the war that now loomed. The emperor himself had indicated this was a priority and had asked Tojo to treat it as such. It presented challenges. Japan was, after all, preparing for hostilities across an astonishingly wide area, including the Bismarck Archipelago, Burma, the Dutch East Indies, Guam, Hong Kong, Malaya, New Guinea, the Philippines, and Singapore. The traditional emphasis on ending war by concentrating forces and engaging the enemy in a decisive battle seemed unactionable. This extended to the maritime theater of war, in which regard it should be noted that Shimada's aforementioned demand for 1.1 million tons of steel in 1942 only made sense in the context of a long war of attrition. This was troubling, and Tojo freely admitted that, in the absence of a decisive maritime battle, Japan had "not the means to seal the fate of the enemy."[39] This brought him back to the sheer magnitude of the operations Japan was planning. Tojo was seen in his office, poring over a map, and in an unguarded moment he struck the pose of a man who, like his subordinates, was "racking his brains" in an attempt at envisioning a viable exit strategy from the war.[40]

The task of devising an exit strategy fell on Tojo's subordinates in the Army Ministry. The Military Affairs Section chief, Sato Kenryo, spoke openly of the "war's endgame" as the "most challenging" issue confronting decision-makers.[41] Another officer attached to the Military Affairs Section, Lieutenant Colonel Ishii Akiho, took responsibility for drafting an endgame-of-war strategy. After leading a desultory debate about Japan's war aims—uniformed military officers agreed that Japan would seek to assure its "self-existence and self-defense" and conflated this aim with establishment of a Greater East Asia Co-Prosperity Sphere—Ishii prepared a "draft proposal for hastening the end of the war."[42] According to this proposal, Japan would "quickly destroy American, British, and Dutch bases in the Far East . . . , endeavor at the same time to hasten the fall of the Chiang regime . . . work for the downfall of Great Britain . . . and . . . destroy the will of the United States to continue the war."[43] The proposal served Tojo's purposes insofar as it gave at least the appearance of an exit strategy. He submitted it to a liaison conference on November 15.

What did Tojo make of this exit strategy? For one thing, the rapid expulsion of Anglo-American and Dutch nations from Southeast Asia and the western Pacific was a feature of all operational planning and presented as eminently achievable. This would ensure access to vital materials and should also close off Chiang Kai-shek from all remaining avenues of Anglo-American support. Herein lay the hope of compelling Chiang's surrender, particularly among the large number of military officers—Tojo included—who had long since convinced themselves that Chiang would come on his knees to the negotiating table if only he could be isolated from his powerful Western patrons. British surrender was more problematic: Japan could hurt Britain by taking its Southeast Asian colonies and possessions, but British surrender was ultimately in the laps of Japan's German and Italian allies. Did this give Tojo pause? Was Germany not preoccupied with war against the Soviet Union? Could the Germans be relied on to defeat the Soviets quickly and then set their sights back on the British? Was Italy even a factor? These questions were imponderable, but if the British refused to surrender the Americans too would presumably stay in the fight. That spelled trouble for Japan's chances of emerging victorious from the war, so Tojo and his colleagues chose against giving it much—if any—thought. As we have seen, Tojo had advised Konoe of the occasional need to close one's eyes and jump from the veranda of Kiyomizu Temple; he was now preparing to take the plunge.

Tojo was also mindful of the need to define a moral justification for the looming war. Here, again, he was responding to the emperor's wishes; Tojo's orders filtered down to the Military Affairs Section's ever-dependable Ishii Akiho. Ishii rested Japan's case first on the assertion that Japan had negotiated with the United States in good faith. His next assertion followed logically: Japan had not reached a decision for war lightly, regarding war as the last resort. He insisted that Japan fought for ultimately peaceful purposes and for a "new order" in East Asia. Ishii contrasted Japan's desire for East Asian stability with the intentions of the Anglo-American powers. Their insidious intentions were, he claimed, on display in the China Incident: By aiding Chiang Kai-shek, the Anglo-American powers were "sacrificing" China even as they pursued their ultimate ambition of "domination of the Far East." Tojo presented this document at liaison conferences on November 15 and November 22; it later formed the basis of the Imperial rescript declaring war on Britain and the United States.[44]

The Roosevelt administration had, in the meantime, formally rejected Proposal A, which came as no real surprise to anyone in the Japanese government—Tojo included. Attention turned to Proposal B. Staff officers continued to clamor for war and "feared" a situation in which Washington saw merit in Japan's offer to withdraw from Indochina in return for renewed access to Japanese-US trade.[45] They blamed Tojo, asking whether he felt any "shame" at having forsaken the strategic imperatives driving army policy.[46] Criticisms of Tojo increased in volume and intensity: He was "weak-kneed"; he had used the army as a "springboard" for his "own advancement"; he ought to be "overthrown" or even "obliterated."[47] Assassination plots convinced Tojo to accept an around-the-clock *kenpei* escort.[48] He refused, however, to back away from Proposal B. In an ill-tempered outburst that can have done nothing to alleviate staff officers' concerns for what they saw as his disregard for the Supreme Command's independence of the cabinet, Tojo spoke on November 18 of "banishing" from active military service any general-rank officer who refused to follow his lead.[49]

Staff officers' fears lest the Roosevelt administration pursue diplomacy in accord with Proposal B were not entirely unfounded. Various policymakers in Washington, including Roosevelt himself, tried their hand at drafting their own modus vivendi proposal. This last-gasp search for Japanese-US peace foundered, however, on US concerns for the potentially explosive impact transpacific peace might have on Anglo-Sino-Soviet morale. Ultimately the Roosevelt administration chose against pursuing a modus vivendi. Instead Secretary of State Hull delivered on November 26 what Tojo himself referred to as the "Hull note." It made stiff demands of Japan. Before he had even seen the note, Tojo learned from the military attaché in Washington, Major General Isoda Saburo, that further negotiations were "hopeless." The note was, according to Isoda, "overbearing" in its insistence on a return to the situation as it had existed before the Manchurian Incident. Concretely, Isoda wrote that the note demanded "unconditional acceptance" of Hull's four principles, required the withdrawal of all Japanese troops from China and Indochina, demanded the explicit reduction of the Tripartite Pact to a "dead letter," and clarified the US refusal to recognize the regime of Wang Jingwei in Nanjing.[50]

Staff officers rejoiced; they regarded the Hull note as a "gift from Heaven."[51] Even Togo Shigenori, who had assumed the foreign minister's position on the condition that Tojo give diplomacy a chance, was now convinced that the United States had shut the door on negotiation and compromise.[52] Tojo himself was reflective. "The emperor said to return the Japanese-US negotiations to a clean slate and to reexamine [state policy]," he said. "I did just that, but we've reached the conclusion that, no matter what, we must now go to war." In an unguarded moment, he laughed at the officers who had criticized him since his prime ministerial appointment for his supposed "cowardice."[53]

TOJO BRACED HIMSELF FOR the penultimate—and what he regarded as perhaps the most important—step in the march toward war: He had now to convince his emperor to sanction the decision. Tojo had, all along, anticipated the need to convene an Imperial conference once the deadline had passed; in late November the emperor asked that the *jushin* be invited to participate. Tojo deflected this request by insisting that the *jushin* were uninformed and ultimately not responsible for contributing to a decision for war or peace. As a compromise, on November 29 Tojo met with and explained the fast-approaching deadline to the *jushin,* each of whom then spoke with the emperor. Retired admirals Okada Keisuke and Yonai Mitsumasa were particularly outspoken in their opposition to war. Okada suggested that the war would become protracted and questioned whether Japan could possibly meet its need for "material supplies." Yonai insisted that "getting smashed" (*dokamake*) in a fight in the Pacific was no solution to the diplomatic, economic, commercial, and financial pressures under which Japan now found itself. In a neat coincidence, the emperor met the following day with his younger brother, Prince Takamatsu Nobuhito, and learned that the Japanese Navy discerned no path to victory in the Pacific. According to Prince Takamatsu (an active-service officer who in late 1941 was serving on the Navy General Staff's Operations Section), the navy could hope at best for a stalemate and a truce and, on these grounds, wanted to avoid war altogether.[54]

It was at precisely this juncture that Tojo approached the emperor. He explained that the deadline had now passed; diplomacy had failed and an Imperial conference ought now to convene and sanction war. The emperor stopped Tojo in his tracks and asked whether the navy could possibly win a war in the Pacific. Tojo spoke of the Supreme Command's confidence in victory, insisting that its confidence was based almost solely on "naval strategy," and he invited the emperor to dispel any "misgivings" he might have by speaking with Nagano and Shimada. Hirohito then met with the two admirals, who confidently predicted victory. The emperor felt not so much reassured as he felt boxed in: The naval leadership seemed not to be heeding dissonant voices from within their service, but he could hardly discard the advice of the two men ultimately responsible for advising him on Japan's chances of victory in the Pacific.[55]

With this audience went the emperor's last hope of a peaceful resolution of the issues dividing Japan and the United States. Significantly, the emperor did not—could not—blame Tojo for the outcome because Tojo had avoided making any pronouncements about the prospects of victory. He had, as was only right and proper, pinned that responsibility on the naval leadership. At an Imperial conference convened on December 1, a silent Hirohito looked on as Tojo explained the Americans' refusal "to make even one concession." The conclusion, as Tojo put it, was inescapable: "Our Empire has no alternative but to begin war."[56] Imperial General Headquarters convened on December 2 and set December 8 (Japan standard time) as the commencement date for hostilities.

NOW THAT THE DECISION for war had been reached, Tojo learned of the war's opening gambit: The navy would attack the US fleet at Pearl Harbor at practically the same time as the army launched an invasion of Malaya. He received this privileged information not because he was prime minister but because his role as army minister meant he participated in meetings of the Imperial General Headquarters.[57] The distinction was critical. Tojo himself was highly conscious of the perceived need to distinguish between his duties as prime minister and as army minister, and he had gone so far as to divide his working hours between his two offices. When he learned of the war's two-pronged attack, he knew full well he was not at liberty to share the Supreme Command's highly classified operational secrets and so, however absurd it seems, Army Minister Tojo refused to divulge the twin Pearl Harbor and Malaya attack plan to Prime Minister Tojo.

As prime minister Tojo concerned himself with a declaration of war. Following the precedents set by the Russo-Japanese War and the declaration of war against Germany during World War I, this involved preparation of both a diplomatic notification of hostilities and a formal Imperial declaration of war. It also necessarily involved doing everything he could to maximize Japan's chances of victory. The latter imperative ensured that Tojo veered toward the Supreme Command's insistence that operational imperatives in wartime trump government policy. This seemed, to an officer like Tojo, almost axiomatic: The war could only be won if operations were successful, and staff officers had to plan and prepare for those operations while cabinet ministers had to do whatever they could to enable smooth implementation.[58]

The diplomatic notification of hostilities was something of a litmus test. Civilians on the cabinet—including, most prominently Foreign Minister Togo Shigenori—presumed that Japan would fulfill its diplomatic and legal obligations by notifying the Anglo-American powers on the eve of war of the forthcoming commencement of hostilities. The Supreme Command was unconvinced. It regarded the element of surprise as integral to the operational success of the twin attack plans and, even before receipt of the Hull note, had raised the "question of whether there should be a declaration of war." Tojo had joined his liaison conference colleagues in this debate but kept his counsel, while most—though not all—insisted on the need for just such a declaration.[59]

Receipt of the Hull note had reignited the debate. Some insisted the note was an ultimatum. They rested their case on international law, and specifically on the convention relative to the opening of hostilities, which Japan and other nations had concluded at the Hague in 1907. The Hague Convention clarified that hostilities "must not commence without previous and explicit warning, in the form either of a reasoned declaration of war or of *an ultimatum* with conditional declaration of war."[60] The argument was that the Hull note was an ultimatum and was therefore tantamount to a declaration of war. (Tojo himself would make precisely this case when on trial as a suspected war criminal in 1946–1948.) The naval leadership, by contrast, concerned itself little with what it regarded as international legal niceties. In late November Admirals Nagano and Shimada insisted that "diplomacy should be sacrificed in order to win the war," arguing that Japan ought "to carry on diplomacy in such a way that until the very last minute . . . our real plans will be kept secret."[61] Tojo maintained his silence, and consensus remained elusive.

The debate sharpened after the December 1 Imperial conference formalized the decision for war. The Foreign Ministry fired the opening salvo by drafting a final note for delivery to the United States. The draft clarified Japan's intention to "terminate negotiations" and placed responsibility on the United States "for any and all consequences that may arise in the future."[62] This latter assertion met the requirements of international law as they related to the commencement of hostilities. It was, in other words, a diplomatic way of saying that the United States had by its obtuseness invited the forthcoming state of hostilities. At a December 4 liaison conference, however, Foreign Minister Togo buckled before the Supreme Command's pressure and agreed to deletion of the phrase placing responsibility on the United States for any and all consequences. In this way Japan's last note failed to give notification of the commencement of hostilities and merely served notice of an intention to "sever" the Japanese-US negotiations.[63] In short, Japan was about to march to war without first declaring war.

At the December 4 liaison conference, Tojo himself dealt with the issue of the timing of the last note's delivery. If delivery were "too early," he said, it would "allow them time to get ready" for hostilities. Yet he was also concerned that, if it were delivered "too late," there would be "no point in delivering the note." He told Foreign Minister Togo that the "time of delivery must be coordinated with the requirements of the Supreme Command." Tojo must have known, based on his recent dealings with the Army General Staff, that Togo would struggle to win out in any disagreement concerning the timing of the delivery. But Tojo did not let this worry him. Indeed, he took no issue whatever with the Supreme Command's insistence on the importance of the element of surprise. He had spoken with colleagues of his belief that the armed services ought to "move" at midnight on December 8 and that a declaration of war could follow sometime thereafter. He sought—and received—assurances from the director general of the Cabinet Legislation Bureau, Moriyama Eiichi, that because combat was the prerogative of the Supreme Command and because declarations of war were the responsibility of the cabinet, there were "no constitutional issues" if operations preceded a declaration of war.[64] That was music to Tojo's ears for, as he told his liaison conference colleagues on December 4, the "most important thing" now was to "win the war."[65]

Tojo had in the meantime directed the Cabinet Affairs Section chief, Inada Shuichi, to take the lead in drafting an Imperial rescript on the declaration of war. Inada consulted with the armed services and the foreign ministry, and Tojo consulted with Lord Keeper of the Privy Seal Kido Koichi. Also involved were Yoshida Masuzo, an Imperial Household Ministry official and sinologist; Waseda University sinologist Kawada Mizuho; and the aging intellectual Tokutomi Soho. The emperor had long since made clear that he, too, wanted input, and Tojo took the draft to the Imperial Palace several times in early December. At the emperor's direct request, Tojo revised the Imperial rescript so that it included the following statement: "It has been ... *far from Our wishes* that Our Empire has now been brought to cross swords with America and Britain."[66]

The emperor also requested that the Imperial rescript specify Japan's commitment to its international legal obligations. He based this request on the precedent set by earlier Imperial rescripts on declarations of war, including those issued at the outset of the Sino-Japanese War of 1894–1895 and the Russo-Japanese War of 1904–1905. In what might have been a first for Tojo, he took direct issue with Hirohito's request. He explained that it might be necessary in the war's opening phase to land troops in Thailand. He added his hope that his cabinet's ongoing diplomatic efforts might convince the doggedly neutral Thais to accept these troop landings, but in the event the Thais rejected Japan's diplomatic overtures, it would be necessary to violate Thai neutrality and land troops in Singora in southern Thailand. Such action would be in direct contravention of Japan's international legal obligations.[67]

Troop landings that violated Thai neutrality were a comparatively minor infraction and, happily for Tojo, sufficed to secure the emperor's assent to no mention of international law in the Imperial rescript. There was much else that Tojo could have said, but which he deliberately and consciously left unstated. First, he maintained his silence on the war's opening shots and the armed services' prioritization of the element of surprise. He justified this silence by noting to himself that only Army Minister Tojo knew of the planned attacks against Pearl Harbor and Malaya; he was now reporting to the emperor in his prime ministerial capacity. Second, Tojo saw no need to explain to his emperor the precedent-shattering decision to dispense with a two-step declaration of war so that the Anglo-American powers would *not* receive diplomatic notification of hostilities but would only be presented with an Imperial rescript after the war had begun. The competent authorities, including the nation's top diplomat and the government's leading legal voice, had consented to this approach, and Tojo convinced himself there was no need to apprise his emperor of the details.

This is a good moment to pause and recall Tojo's public assertion, back in the early 1930s, that declarations of war were an anachronism. The almost prohibitively high risk inherent in the Pearl Harbor attack plan—one scholar suggests that the Combined Fleet commander in chief, Admiral Yamamoto Isoroku, proposed the plan in the counterintuitive hope that it would be rejected as too great a gamble—reinforced, for Tojo, the need to keep the enemy ignorant of Japan's intentions.[68] He clearly did not want to debate the issue with his emperor; he was doubtless convinced that Hirohito would hold to the gentlemanly standards of what Tojo believed was a bygone era and insist on observance of the letter of international law. At the same time, Tojo was overtly conscious of the constitution's provision for the emperor's inviolability, and he could not countenance so much as the possibility of the enemy using the Imperial rescript to impugn the emperor's character. For this reason, he used the issue of troop landings in neutral Thailand to convince his emperor of the propriety of erasing from the Imperial rescript any mention of Japan's international legal obligations.

THE IMPERIAL RESCRIPT WAS finalized on December 6, 1941. By this time, the tension was weighing on Tojo. His wife, Katsuko, found him late that night sitting up in bed, sobbing.[69] The following day he was unable to take what had become his daily early morning horse ride, and so he missed his principal form of not only exercise but also stress release.[70] Even so, tension and stress were not things to which Tojo was likely ever to admit. That night, amid confident predictions of victory, he told Vice Army Minister Kimura Heitaro and Vice Home Minister Yuzawa Michio that he "could not control his emotions." "I placed everything I know before His Majesty," Tojo explained, "and he consented." The decision for war was, in this way, not Tojo's decision but was instead "based completely on His majesty's decision." Here Tojo was not only congratulating himself for having convinced the emperor of the propriety of war but was also exulting in another, no less significant, victory: This was as near an instance of direct Imperial rule as could be imagined, and on these grounds Tojo expressed his "confidence in total victory."[71]

Tojo was thrown momentarily off-balance in the early hours of the morning on December 8. Foreign Minister Togo arrived at the prime minister's official residence with a conciliatory telegram Roosevelt had addressed to the emperor. Tojo later admitted that the telegram may have made a difference had it arrived a day or two earlier and explicitly nullified some of the Hull note's stiffer terms. But Roosevelt's telegram met neither of those conditions, so made no appreciable difference to the march toward war. Tojo went to bed sometime after 0300 hours on December 8. He was awakened some two hours later. By this time, Japanese forces had attacked Pearl Harbor before delivery in Washington of the note that served notice of an end to negotiations but did not declare war. Tojo professed less interest in international legal niceties than in early reports of success at Pearl Harbor. "Well done!" he muttered, before asking, "The Navy General Staff has reported to the emperor, right?"[72]

Later that morning, Tojo and his ministerial colleagues met with the Privy Council. Tojo then took the Imperial rescript to the emperor for final ratification before its public release. Hirohito, who had already received reports on the Pearl Harbor and Malayan attacks from Admiral Nagano and General Sugiyama, seems at this juncture to have asked Tojo whether Britain had received any diplomatic notification of the opening of hostilities. (It probably did not even occur to him that Japan's final note in the Japanese-US negotiations notified the United States of nothing more than a discontinuation of those diplomatic negotiations.) It might be surmised that Tojo stumbled and stalled in response. The emperor's shock was palpable. His immediate reaction was to harangue Tojo about his "heartbreak" at the turn of events. He recounted the warmth of Anglo-Japanese relations since his grandfather's reign, speaking with fondness of the kindnesses he had received in the United Kingdom when he toured as crown prince back in 1921.[73]

The emperor's disenchantment with what he regarded as Tojo's disregard for traditional Anglo-Japanese amity and also for international law only deepened with the passage of time. He later reflected on how Tojo had argued against inclusion of Japan's international legal obligations in the Imperial rescript, and he realized that Tojo had used Thai neutrality as a ruse. The emperor did not appreciate the half-truths in which Tojo engaged and in the early aftermath of surrender went so far as to vent his frustration with *New York Times* correspondent Frank L. Kluckhohn, saying he "had no intention to have the war rescript used as General Tojo [*sic*] used it."[74] In other words, Hirohito had believed the Imperial rescript would follow diplomatic notification of the commencement of hostilities. He had also taken on good faith Tojo's representations concerning Thai neutrality, troop landings in Thailand, and the need to refrain from mentioning international law in the Imperial rescript. This bothered him immensely, and in the early postsurrender period, he complained to the supreme commander for the Allied Powers, General Douglas MacArthur, about Tojo having "tricked" him into remaining silent on the matter of international law.[75]

This issue contrasted sharply with Tojo's efforts at implementing direct Imperial rule but, at least so far as Tojo was concerned, the success of the Pearl Harbor and Malayan operations justified his actions. He shared dinner that night with a number of soldiers and sailors, and they received updates on the Pearl Harbor attack as they ate. All told, eighteen US battleships, cruisers, and destroyers lay in ruins. Nearly two hundred planes had also been hit, and some twenty-four hundred US servicemen had died. "It was better than expected," said an ebullient Tojo. "Now Roosevelt must at last fall."[76] But Roosevelt bucked Tojo's expectations and turned a naval disaster into a powerful call to arms. The president stood before the US Congress and spoke of avenging "infamy," "treachery," and an "unprovoked and dastardly attack." A spontaneous battle cry rang out from the United States: "Remember Pearl Harbor!"[77] On the other side of the Atlantic Ocean, British Prime Minister Winston Churchill rejoiced in the fact that the United States was now in the war. "So," he wrote, "we had won after all!"[78] Tojo had led his nation *into* war against the imposingly powerful Anglo-American nations; only time would tell whether he would prove able to lead it *out*.

11
THE TRIUMPHANT TOTAL WARRIOR
DECEMBER 1941–DECEMBER 1942

THE OPENING SHOTS OF war released the pressure and tension under which Tojo Hideki had been operating since at least September 1941. The burning issue of war was now resolved, and in his quieter moments, Tojo congratulated himself for having crafted the composite of wills that underpinned the momentous Imperial decision for war. He did not, however, regard his job as complete. Nor did he sit idle. There was a war to be won, and he busied himself with the pursuit of victory.

The day the war began, Tojo indulged in some hearty self-congratulation. Successes on the battlefield, as well as unity on the home front, he attributed to a long-standing effort (in which he himself had played a central role) at "synthesizing materials, training, and spiritual strength."[1] Publicly he abstained from exultation in victory, and in a December 8 radio address he cut a stern figure as he explained why Japan fought. In clipped soldierly tones, Tojo blamed US obtuseness for the breakdown in transpacific diplomacy and stated that Japan fought for nothing less than its "self-existence and self-defense." He acknowledged the material might of the Anglo-American enemy and spoke of the likelihood of a long, drawn-out war. He cited Japan's proud history—never, he reminded his audience, in its 2,600-year history had Japan "known defeat in war"—and he called on all Japanese to devote their entire energies to the cause of victory. He asked them to remain animated by a phrase that had long enjoyed currency in the Imperial Japanese Army: "conviction in certain victory" (*hissho no shin'nen*). He added that Japan had to do more than defeat the powerful coalition of enemies arrayed against it; he also explained the need for Japan to fulfill its self-appointed role as the "architect of Greater East Asia."[2]

Tojo professed not to see any contradiction between a war fought for Japan's self-existence and self-defense and one fought also for Greater East

Asia. (This would remain the case after the war had been lost.) On trial for his life as a suspected war criminal, Tojo told international prosecutors, with his usual brusqueness, "Needless to say, the motive for the use of force was Japan's self-existence and self-defense." In his very next breath, he added, "After the war began, Japan began implementing its existing Greater East Asia policies, that is, it began building a new order of mutual prosperity in East Asia."[3] Tojo effectively collapsed the two aims into each other. It was a natural progression. Recall that army officers in the 1930s declared an ever-expanding area—which began with Manchukuo, then moved to

Tojo informs the Japanese people, via radio broadcast, of the opening of hostilities against the Anglo-American powers, December 8, 1941.

North China, and later included the Yangtze River basin—vital to efforts at building Japanese self-sufficiency. He seemed neither to notice nor care that the reexamination of state policy he had launched immediately after assuming the role of prime minister had barely touched on any Greater East Asian policies. Tojo was, in this way, taking such ambiguous phraseology as "Greater East Asia" and "mutual prosperity" and grafting it onto what he regarded as Japan's fight for existence against the ABCD (American-British-Chinese-Dutch) powers. In essence, he was arguing that Japanese autarchy (or self-existence and self-defense) only presented as possible in the context of a new, Greater East Asian, order.[4]

Animated by such thoughts, on December 10 Tojo took up with his liaison conference colleagues the question of the name to apply to the war Japan now fought. The naval leadership revealed itself less than beholden to Tojo's concept of a Japan-centric autarchic sphere and argued for the name Pacific War. This struck Tojo and indeed all army officers as altogether too partisan. He wanted a name that captured not only the Imperial Japanese Navy's war in the Pacific Ocean but also the ongoing China Incident, as well as wresting control of Southeast Asia from the Western powers. Above all, he wanted a name that made readily apparent the interconnections he himself made between Japanese autarchy and regional order. He forced the obsequious navy minister, Shimada Shigetaro, to forsake his service's position and forged consensus on the name Greater East Asian War.[5] Days later, the cabinet formally adopted the name, and Tojo dutifully reported the decision to the emperor.[6]

In the meantime, battlefield successes exceeded Tojo's expectations. The navy had destroyed the battle force of the US Pacific Fleet at Pearl Harbor, and the December 10 sinking of the British battleship *Prince of Wales* and battle cruiser *Repulse* ended Britain's hope of defending Malaya from the sea. Japanese troops thereafter advanced down the Malay Peninsula toward Singapore with breathtaking rapidity. Meanwhile, the December 8 attack on Clark Field had practically eliminated the US Far East Air Force and stripped the Philippines of its aerial defenses. As if to seal the Philippines' fate, Japanese forces took Guam on December 10 and set their sights on Wake Island (when it was captured on December 23, the nearest US base, at Midway, was some forty-five hundred miles from Manila). Shanghai's capture required no more than a few hours; Japanese troops began landing practically simultaneously on Hong Kong and within twenty-four hours were within sight of Kowloon. Tojo himself regarded these "unforeseen" victories as "gifts from heaven." The "gods" had, he reckoned, extended to Japan their "divine protection" precisely because his government had faithfully followed the emperor and "persevered" in pursuit of peace "to the last possible line of endurance."[7]

Tojo was not alone in waxing lyrical about these early battlefield successes. Nearly spontaneous outbursts of patriotism and confidence were everywhere discernible on the home front. "It is wonderful," wrote novelist Ito Seiichi with enchanting simplicity. Western-trained sculptor Takamura Kotaro wrote in a manner curiously reminiscent of American wartime propaganda: "Remember December 8!"[8] Tojo was satisfied that "these great victories in the first phase of the war have united and strengthened our people's will."[9] He nonetheless fretted about the durability of such sentiments. For a man who frequently lauded the Japanese people's spirit, comparing it favorably to what he supposed was the Anglo-American people's effeminate decadence, Tojo was unnerved by the possibility of defeat coming not on the battlefield but because of a crumbling home front attributable to Bolshevik revolutionaries, spineless politicians, and civilians without hope in ultimate victory. He was, in effect, recalling the debate he had witnessed in Germany at the end of the previous world war, wondering whether something similar might arise in Japan. Ever the authoritarian with a predilection for controlling dissident elements, he decided to legislate such possibilities out of existence. Within a week of the Pearl Harbor attack, Tojo introduced to the Imperial Diet a bill restricting freedom of speech, assembly, and association. Passage of the Press, Publication, Assembly, and Association Special Control Law was secured within twenty-four hours, but only after Tojo swallowed his pride and reassured Diet members that they were not among the law's targets and were not legislating themselves into repressed silence.[10] Diet members were spared but Western music was not. Zealous censors banned public performance of all Anglo-American music, and Tojo in early January 1942 was called before a disconcerted and discomfited emperor to explain himself.[11]

Days later, Tojo was back before Hirohito. This time he felt much more at ease, for he was reporting on what he and his aides regarded as an "epoch-making" speech he was scheduled to deliver to the Imperial Diet. Japanese forces had by now taken Hong Kong and Manila; Tojo hoped his speech would "shock the world" no less than had the Japanese forces' irrepressible advance.[12] His speech promised a Greater East Asian "order of coexistence and co-prosperity based on morality," and it went so far as to promise eventual independence for Burma and for the Philippines. (Tojo had planned also to promise eventual independence for the Dutch

East Indies but had run headlong into the Army General Staff's stiff opposition.) His speech acknowledged Japan's more utilitarian purposes and needs; there was, he said, an immediate and pressing need to "secure strategic bases in Greater East Asia and bring important resource areas under our control, thereby expanding our war potential." Here again Tojo was identifying Japan's autarchic goals with a restructured regional order. The emperor's reaction is impossible to ascertain, but it was presumably positive. Tojo delivered the speech as scheduled to the Imperial Diet on January 21.[13]

Tojo spoke against the backdrop of continuing battlefield success, for Japanese forces had, on January 23, captured Rabaul on the island of New Britain, northeast of New Guinea. He reached a most receptive domestic audience. The Imperial Rule Assistance Association (not unexpectedly) exulted in the laudable goal of "East Asian regeneration."[14] Keio University scholar Yamamoto Noboru agreed with Tojo about Japan's interconnected war aims; there was, he wrote, no contradiction in fighting for Japan's "existence" and also for "East Asian stability" and ultimately a region-wide "co-prosperity sphere."[15] Poet Kawada Jun composed a *choka* poem asserting that the war owed not only to the need to "defend our country" but equally to the "mission" to "save Asia's masses."[16] Even Tojo's old nemesis, Ishiwara Kanji, wrote publicly in support of the Greater East Asian War. He nonetheless departed from the government script and, in explaining Japan's war aims, used phraseology such as "East Asian league," which recalled past arguments with Tojo (and cannot but have antagonized Tojo).[17]

Tojo began speaking in early February 1942 of the imminent capture of Burma, the Philippines, and Singapore. Singapore was of particular significance—no less an authority than Winston Churchill labeled the "fall" of Singapore the "worst disaster and largest capitulation in British history"—and many in Japan were convinced that Britain was now practically "beaten."[18] Lord Keeper of the Privy Seal Kido Koichi told his personal secretary, Matsudaira Yasumasa, "The ABCD encirclement is broken, and it is now time to seize this excellent opportunity for peace."[19] Colonel Iwakuro Hideo, having returned to Tokyo from the front, sought to impress on Tojo and others that Singapore's capture provided the perfect opportunity to negotiate an end to the war.[20]

Tojo was unconvinced. "We should not," he said, "contemplate peace at this time."[21] He spoke with Foreign Minister Togo Shigenori of a grinding war of attrition lasting as long as ten or even twenty years.[22] In this context he regarded Japan's victories across Southeast Asia as but the first

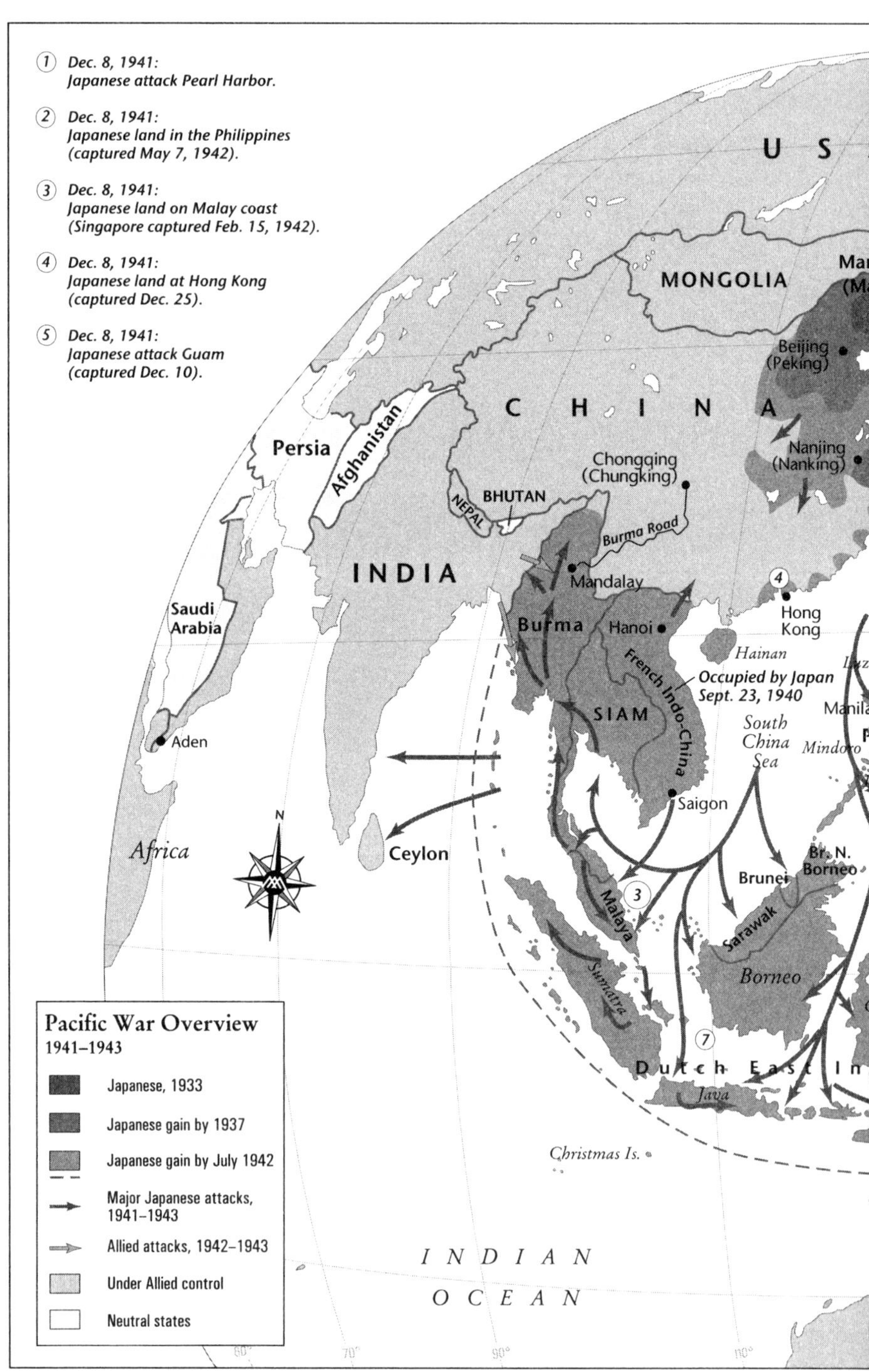

Map of Japan's war, December 1941–June 1942.

6 Jan. 4, 1942: Japanese aerial attack against Rabaul area (captured Jan. 23).
7 Feb. 27, 1942: Battle of Java Sea (Dutch East Indies captured Mar. 10).
8 May 3 – 8, 1942: Battle of Coral Sea.
9 Jun. 4 – Jun. 7, 1942: Battle of Midway.
10 Aug. 1942 – Feb. 1943: Battle of Guadalcanal.
Sea of Okhotsk
Bering Sea
60°
40°
20°
0°
JAPAN
Tokyo
Midway
9
Iwo Jima
Marcus Is.
1
Pearl Harbor
Wake Is.
Marianas
Saipan
5
Guam
Eniwetok
Truk
Kwajalein
Palau
Marshall Is.
Tarawa
Gilbert Is.
6
Ellice Is.
New Guinea
N. E. New Guinea
Solomon Is.
Terr. of Papua
10
Arafura Sea
Guadalcanal
Coral Sea
Western Samoa
New Hebrides
8
Efate
Fiji Islands
New Caledonia
150°
170°
150°

phase of the war, to which Singapore's imminent capture provided a rather neat end point. His refusal to consider otherwise lost Tojo support in the army. To cite the most prominent example, the Military Affairs Bureau director, Muto Akira, despaired at what he regarded as Tojo's obtuseness. He spoke widely—and incautiously—of the need to topple Tojo as prime minister if Japan were to explore early possibilities of peace. Some weeks later, in a sign of his growing intolerance of dissent, Tojo transferred Muto from Tokyo to the new Sumatran battlefront.[23] Rather than engage in a mistaken pursuit of peace, Tojo believed it was time to "establish a new policy" that accounted for Japan's battlefield successes in Southeast Asia and recalibrated the parameters of grand Japanese strategy.[24] He put Imperial General Headquarters on notice: This process was not the sole preserve of the general staffs; cabinet ministers would necessarily be involved. Few doubted that Tojo himself would be a prominent contributor to the process.[25]

The emperor provided a brief and curious diversion. At a February 14 audience in which Tojo reported on Singapore's imminent capture, the emperor wondered whether this might pave the way to a negotiated peace. He spoke with Tojo about Pope Pius XII drawing on his "spiritual authority" and serving as intermediary between Japan and its Anglo-American enemies. He asked Tojo to facilitate the dispatch of a diplomatic mission to the Vatican. This the ever-deferential Tojo did, and in April the Foreign Ministry appointed diplomat Harada Ken as special delegate to the Vatican.[26]

Tojo held out no hope for what he regarded as the emperor's papal flight of fancy. Even so, he was not averse to a Victory Day parade. Held on February 18—three days after the unconditional surrender of British forces in Singapore—in Tokyo's Hibiya Park, the parade provided the public with an opportunity at least to celebrate Japanese forces' successes in the opening months of war. Tojo nonetheless hushed the crowd when it began offering him three cheers. Then, when the emperor appeared on Nijubashi Bridge in formal military dress on horseback, Tojo himself led the crowd in a stirring three-peat rendition of "Long live his majesty the emperor!"[27]

That same day Tojo called a general election. He wanted to tap into heightened public morale, and he aimed, once and for all, to rid the Imperial Diet of what he regarded as its infernal factionalism and pluralism. This he saw as unfinished business, for the creation of the Imperial Rule Assistance Association and the simultaneous dissolution of the political parties in late 1940 had changed neither the composition of the Diet nor its propensity to divide along old party lines and loyalties. Tojo was determined to complete

Above: Tojo basks in the public's adulation following battlefield victories across Greater East Asia, March 1942. *Below:* Tojo burnishes the national spirit during a visit to Fukuoka, March 1942.

what former Prime Minister Konoe Fumimaro had started and to deliver what had long been a pet army project. He wanted to "consolidate" and unify the various institutions of Imperial prerogative and to ensure the Diet's support for his cabinet. He regarded this as pressing because, in the likely event the war became prolonged, unity among the cabinet, the armed services, the Diet, and the emperor would go a long way toward ensuring the home front did not collapse in a "commotion."[28]

The key issue was whether and how Tojo could intervene in the election. The sticking point was the Meiji Constitution, which forbade the government from nominating election candidates. To the chagrin of generations of army officers, including Tojo, political parties had long fulfilled this function. Seeking to short-circuit that practice, Tojo invited thirty-three prominent individuals to his prime ministerial residence on February 23 and asked for their assistance in forming a new political association to screen and nominate election candidates. Out of this conversation emerged the Imperial Rule Assistance Political Organization Council. Tojo hoped his old boss, the incisive yet divisive retired general and former prime minister, Hayashi Senjuro, might lead the council; when that proved impossible, Tojo maneuvered into the director's position another retired general and former prime minister, the mild-mannered Abe Nobuyuki.[29]

Tojo might have expected the navy to look askance at his political project. The admirals were convinced he was trying to tie together not just the Diet and the army but also the Imperial Palace. The key figure, in their estimation, was the emperor's political antenna, Kido Koichi. They worried about what they regarded as Kido's "deep interest in the formation of a people's organization" and also about his familial ties to Abe, whose son was married to Kido's daughter. These concerns did not translate into any concerted action, partly because Kido reassured them that he "neither encouraged nor recommended" Tojo's "screening" of election candidates but partly also because the ever-pliable navy minister, Admiral Shimada, did not take up the issue in any sustained manner with Tojo.[30]

Having set in motion this new approach to domestic politics, Tojo turned his attention in late February and early March back to the issue of grand strategy. He chaired a series of almost daily liaison conferences that sought to align opportunities and objectives. Conferees began on February 25 with what was perhaps an obligatory review of the successes with which Japanese forces had met: They had "dealt a great blow" to the Anglo-American enemy and had "annihilated Anglo-American bases in East Asia." Conferees also identified what was perhaps the single greatest issue

Tojo visits the Western District Army, headquartered in Fukuoka, March 1942.

now confronting Japan. "Under current circumstances, in light of Japan's national strength and the situation on the continent," they agreed, "we can expect neither immediate British capitulation nor US abandonment of its will to fight." Tojo and his colleagues now confronted a situation in which the Anglo-American powers had no intention of "compromise" or a negotiated peace, and instead intended to use their "superior war-making capabilities" to bring Japan "to its knees."[31]

On February 26 the Imperial Navy revealed itself to be particularly strained by the prospect of the United States harnessing its immense national strength to the war effort. The admirals foresaw a situation in which American armaments began to "rise exponentially" and expressed concern at the prospect of the United States launching a counterattack in the Pacific.[32] Tojo challenged this line of thinking. "US national power is supposed to increase rapidly," he said. "But will it actually do so?" He added, for good measure, that the United States would probably not gather the strength for a counterattack before late 1944. Navy Vice Chief of Staff Ito Seiichi took direct issue with Tojo. He spoke of America's massive shipbuilding capacity and insisted it would go on the counterattack as soon as late 1942. Tojo shifted his line of reasoning. "They can build warships," he said, "but won't they be short on personnel?" Ito again tackled Tojo and spoke of the large number of US Naval Academy graduates who had returned to civilian life but who could relatively seamlessly go back on active service. Tojo seemed unconvinced and turned the debate to other matters, including Soviet intentions.[33]

The debate between Tojo and Ito neatly encapsulated a gulf that now separated Japan's armed services. Tojo, for his part, accepted the virtual impossibility of enforcing US surrender. He was mindful of the likely need to turn Japan's guns at some point against the army's old enemy in the Soviet Union, and he revealed himself unimpressed by arguments about US strength. For these reasons he favored a strategy in which Japanese forces hunkered down for a protracted war of attrition in the Pacific, even as Southeast Asia's plentiful resources fed the material needs of Japan's armed services. Here again Tojo was blurring any distinction between Japanese autarchy and Asian interdependence. He asked his liaison conference colleagues, "What difference does it make if we call it a national defense sphere or a co-prosperity sphere?" Following some debate, which threw up "resource sphere" as another possible title for what Japan was building in Greater East Asia, Tojo partly answered his own question by noting that construction of a "national defense sphere" was a necessary step toward eventual construction of a "co-prosperity sphere." This vision was not Tojo's alone—army staff officers were its progenitors—and it gained wide currency in the military.[34]

This strategic vision filled Japan's uniformed navy officers with horror. They were convinced of the need to eliminate or at least neutralize strategic points from which the Anglo-American powers could launch a counterattack. They were also adamant that it was necessary to destroy the US fleet before the Americans could mobilize their industrial might and logistical capabilities. To this end, they argued for an offensive strategy that would capitalize on the success of the Pearl Harbor attack. Most immediately, they argued for operations to take the war in two different directions: southward to Australia and westward to India. Army officers, Tojo included, worried about further expansion of an already enormous theater of operations, but navy officers argued that it was necessary to remove Australia as a potential launching pad for any future Anglo-American counterattack, and the loss of India would remove the finest jewel from the British Empire's crown. Successful operations against Australia and India should, they argued, deal a body blow to the British Empire; they also anticipated a decisive battle that should hopefully put paid to the US fleet.[35]

Tojo helped cobble together a compromise between the armed services. He remained wedded to the army's essentially defensive concept of an "Imperial national resource sphere" centered on Japan, Manchukuo, and China that also incorporated recent gains across Southeast Asia. At the same time, he accepted the navy's offensive strategy. In this way some referred to Australia and India as components of a wider "strategic sphere"; Tojo preferred to think of them as part of a wider "supply sphere."[36] The army-navy compromise was encapsulated in a policy document Tojo delivered to the emperor on March 12, 1942. It started from the premise that Japan would continue in its efforts to compel British surrender and cause the United States to lose the will to continue the war. In a nod to the navy's offensive strategy, Japan would seek to "expand its wartime gains" and push toward both Australia and India. In the best-case scenario, this would lead to British surrender and at least puncture the US willingness to fight. Should these results not eventuate, Japan would resort to the army's defensive strategy and establish a posture of "long-term invincibility" by "promoting the development and use of [Southeast Asian] resources important to national defense" and "increasing national strength." Japanese forces would, in this reckoning, grind down American willingness to continue the fight.[37]

ON APRIL 4 TOJO ANNOUNCED publicly the recent capture of both the Burmese capital in Rangoon and the Andaman Islands in the Bay of Bengal. These were "crushing blows" against British land and sea positions in Burma and India, and he spoke of Japan's unwavering determination to "annihilate" the British. He insisted, by way of contrast, that Japan had no intention of "making enemies of India's 400 million people," and he spoke at length of Japan's identification with those advocating "India for the Indians."[38] Almost on cue, Japanese carrier-based bombers launched air strikes against Colombo. The sortie was destructive, but it was hardly sufficient to dislodge the British from India.

Days later, Japan itself came under aerial attack. A squadron of B-25s led by Colonel James H. Doolittle flew 668 miles from the carrier *Hornet* to bomb Tokyo. Damages were slight, but the implications were enormous for Japan, with its homes constructed of wooden frames with interior paper walls. The emperor was so unnerved that Tojo feared what he might say or demand. In a first for Tojo, he declined to report to the Imperial Palace.[39] He himself was "incensed" and took out his frustrations on the Eastern District

Army (headquartered in Tokyo) for misreporting the success of its aerial defenses during the so-called Doolittle Raid.[40] His professional military colleagues fretted at the inadequacy of army air defenses, including the patently insufficient number of high-speed fighter planes stationed around Tokyo. (Military officers were, conversely, impressed at the durability of civilian defenses.) They also worried about intelligence indicating that at least one B-25 bomber had landed in Soviet territory, and they were particularly exercised by the thought that the Soviets might end their neutrality and cooperate with the United States in its war against Japan.[41]

The Doolittle Raid had the unintended effect of injecting some energy and excitement into an otherwise stultified election campaign. Among the few other bright spots was an open letter penned by longtime party politician Ozaki Yukio, who denounced Tojo's effort at creating a "handpicked" Diet by means of the Imperial Rule Assistance Political Organization Council. Lest anybody failed to grasp his meaning, Ozaki charged Tojo with "election interference" and an "unconstitutional act."[42] Tojo was undeterred. He insisted, however disingenuously, that the council was a "people's movement" that could unite the "whole nation" in "support" of the war effort.[43]

People's movement or otherwise, in early April the council endorsed a roster of 466 candidates. To Tojo's chagrin, over half the candidates were incumbents—hardly the harbingers of the change for which he had hoped. The candidates had at least revealed themselves to be pliable, and Tojo resorted to the unedifying but effective tactic of buying their loyalty, with each Council candidate receiving 5,000 yen in campaign funding from the army's discretionary budget.[44] The election campaign was conducted under the censors' surveillance and included such colorless slogans as "One hundred million en masse conduct a proper election," "The election builds East Asia and a new Diet," and what historian Edward Drea has labeled a "joyless admonition ... to endure protracted warfare."[45] Dull it may have been, but the election campaign satisfied Tojo, who spoke on the eve of the election of the "robust national unity" on display.[46] The election was held on April 30, 1942, and 381 Imperial Rule Assistance Political Structure Association candidates were elected to office.

The Doolittle Raid also reignited debate between Japan's armed services over how best to fight the war. The army reverted to the notion of hunkering down for a grinding war of attrition in the Pacific, while the navy remained focused on the need to annihilate the US fleet and continued to insist on offensive operations. Tojo kept a low profile because he could not, as army minister, prosecute his service's case and at the same time play the prime minister's role of honest broker and consensus builder. Disgruntlement in the army with Tojo's performance ran high—the Operations Bureau chief, Tanaka Shin'ichi, for one, demanded Tojo vacate the army minister's post—and Tojo found himself defending his twin ministerial appointments and roles. Either way, his silence during the army-navy debate was critical and practically ensured that the navy got its way.[47]

The navy, then, took the offensive to the Anglo-American enemy. Curiously, it dispensed with what historians David Evans and Mark Peattie have called "one of the enduring principles of war" and chose not to concentrate its forces. A carrier division was detailed to the Coral Sea in the Southwest Pacific, while the Combined Fleet thrust across the Central Pacific toward Midway. The Battle of the Coral Sea, fought in early May, was tactically a draw, but it was enough to stop a seaborne invasion of Port Morseby. This stalled the attempt at cutting Australia off from the United States and marked a significant reversal for the Japanese Navy. Tojo seemed not to notice. His focus was instead on the army's near simultaneous Battle of Corregidor. This marked the final stage of the Philippines campaign, which had continued since the start of the war and which ended in final, ineluctable victory for the Japanese Army on May 7. "Recent events, all of which could have been fatal to the cabinet, have gone well thanks to this battlefield victory," he said, with an almost audible sigh of relief.[48] Particularly noticeable is the fact that Tojo seemed at least as interested in what the capture of the Philippines meant for his own domestic political fortunes as in what it meant for the Greater East Asian War.

In the Battle of Midway, June 4–7, 1942, Japan's Combined Fleet hoped for the decisive victory that might knock the Americans out of the war. The battle instead ended in resounding defeat for the Japanese Navy, ceding control of the Central Pacific to the US fleet. Tojo was horseback riding along Tamagawa River with other military officers, as well as the German and Italian military attachés, when rumors of the "fiasco" at Midway first began circulating. Army Vice Chief of Staff Tanabe Moritake was the principal source of information; he arrived late to Tamagawa River and relayed news that the Combined Fleet had lost four aircraft carriers (it also lost a heavy cruiser, hundreds of planes, and its most experienced pilots). Many fell into deep "dismay" and griped at the navy. "They did this over the army's objections," the officers grumbled, "and now look where we are."[49] Tojo might have been forgiven had he wondered whether he, too, might come in for criticism given that he had not represented the army's objections as forcefully as his professional military colleagues had wished. Whatever the case, the navy refused to acknowledge the extent of its losses at Midway: To a liaison conference that met on June 10, it reported the loss of not four aircraft carriers but just one.[50] Tojo sensed the navy was smarting and ordered his subordinates to ensure that it did not "lose heart."[51]

The loss at Midway convinced Tojo that he had been right all along about a protracted war of attrition. There was, he said, "no telling how many years" the war would continue.[52] This brought out some of his worst political instincts. He decided to withhold details of the Midway loss from the Japanese public on the grounds that he did not want to "discourage" them. In justifying this decision, he dismissed the "Japanese people" as "stupid" and unable to cope with the truth.[53] He came simultaneously to regard himself as utterly indispensable to the war effort and began speaking of the need to ensure that "the prime minister"—note the illeism—did "not fall" before bringing the war to its conclusion.[54] In a not unrelated development, he became highly sensitive to criticism; in one bad-tempered moment he launched into a tirade against any officials who had the temerity to be critical of cabinet policy.[55] Tojo toured Hokkaido in early July and started what can only be called the strange practice of random inspections of unsuspecting householders' rubbish bins; he returned to Tokyo and, on the basis of scraps he had found in people's bins, reported his satisfaction with the adequacy of food supplies in Japan's northernmost main island.[56]

IN LATE AUGUST TOJO encountered the first serious challenge to his cabinet. Foreign Minister Togo Shigenori revealed himself implacably opposed to Tojo's intention to establish a Greater East Asia ministry. Tojo championed this new ministry as the proper vehicle to administer Japan's relationships with its Greater East Asian neighbors. As he put it to Togo, diplomacy as practiced by the Foreign Ministry regulated Japan's relationships with independent foreign nations pursuing their own self-interests, whereas relationships within Greater East Asia ought to be defined instead by mutuality, consensus, and co-prosperity. He told Togo that the "independence" he had publicly promised for Burma and the Philippines "differed substantially" from the independence of nations outside Japan's sphere. This brought Tojo back to the idea that a new Greater East Asia ministry would be better placed than the Foreign Ministry to manage these relationships. Togo's opposition was trenchant. The proposal struck him as a power grab that promised to come at the Foreign Ministry's direct expense. It also struck him as expressive of an exploitative and colonial mindset that regarded Greater East Asia as little more than a storehouse of much-needed resources. He argued that Japan's relationships with its Greater East Asian neighbors must ultimately be placed in the realm of interstate diplomacy, which must necessarily remain the Foreign Ministry's responsibility. On these grounds Togo refused to agree to the creation of the new ministry.[57]

Tojo was unbending. This owed less to widespread support for a Greater East Asia ministry—even the Army General Staff was only lukewarm in its appraisal—than to the force of Tojo's will.[58] He took the proposal for a new ministry to the cabinet in late August. Togo, for his part, drew on outrage within the Foreign Ministry and stood firm in his opposition. He also refused to resign his foreign ministerial post, and because ministerial unanimity was a requirement of the cabinet decision-making process, Togo was threatening to compel the entire cabinet's resignation.[59] The key figure, so far as both men were concerned, was Lord Keeper of the Privy Seal Kido Koichi. His sympathies lay with Togo, but he was unconvinced that political upheaval was in the best interest of Japan's war effort.[60] This support from the palace was highly qualified, but it was enough for Tojo to chase Togo out of his cabinet. He expressed bewilderment at Togo's refusal to make "sacrifices" and insisted that Togo was "not qualified" to serve as a "minister of state" unless he displayed the same "level of commitment" as the "officers and men on the front line" who "were laying down their lives for the emperor."[61] Togo resigned on September 1, and Tojo temporarily assumed the foreign minister's duties. The same day, his cabinet agreed to establish the Greater East Asia Ministry and make it responsible for "affairs of state" within the region.[62]

The Japanese Army had, in the meantime, taken the fight to New Guinea in a renewed attempt at cutting transpacific lines and isolating Australia from the United States. Japanese forces landed at Buna in mid-August and struck out for Port Moresby. Within the week, US forces mounted a limited offensive against Guadalcanal and Tulagi, in the nearby Solomon Islands. Military officers in Tokyo—Tojo included—foresaw few difficulties, primarily because they clung to the belief that the United States would not be able to launch a major counteroffensive before late 1943 at the earliest. They were, moreover, mindful of other theaters and other possibilities. Chiang Kai-shek's makeshift capital in Chongqing was in the army's sights—an offensive aimed ultimately at Chongqing was scheduled to begin in December 1942—and the hope of finally compelling Chiang's surrender burned brightly in Tojo's breast. The possibility of pushing Britain closer to defeat also presented itself. Imperial General Headquarters was preparing for an invasion of Ceylon; there was also the promise of Germany focusing its attention back on Britain. This latter possibility arose out of renewed hope for German-Soviet peace, which owed principally to what Japanese Army officers regarded as the imminent fall of Stalingrad. So much hinged on this that decision-makers in Tokyo began envisioning Tojo traveling to Europe to meet with Adolf Hitler and Joseph Stalin and mediate German-Soviet peace.[63]

Tojo was at least mildly interested in a European sojourn. He had, since at least the Pearl Harbor attack, hoped the Germans might halt their war against the Soviets and turn their attention back to Britain. He based this hope not on German policy but instead on Japanese grand strategy, which required a coordinated attempt by Japan and its European allies against Britain. The Germans had their own ideas about what should comprise the principal point of focus and, as recently as July, had requested Japanese participation in the war against the Soviet Union. This might have given Tojo pause, yet he only realized the depth of German disinterest in a negotiated peace with the Soviets when he spoke in mid-November with German Ambassador Eugen Ott. At this point Tojo abandoned the notion of traveling to Europe and decided to send instead a relatively low-level delegation of bureau chiefs or perhaps vice ministers and vice chiefs of staff.[64]

This diplomatic setback coincided with a turn for the worse in the Southwest Pacific. US forces had in late August taken Guadalcanal in what Tojo and others in Tokyo believed was a raid. They were satisfied that Guadalcanal could be retaken with relative ease. Then, in late August, a six-hundred man detachment was annihilated at the hands of the US Marines it was trying to clear from Guadalcanal. In mid-September, the six-thousand-man Kawaguchi force (named after its commander, Kawaguchi Kiyotake) met with a bloody end in another failed attempt at dislodging the US Marines from Guadalcanal. The Army General Staff rushed in reinforcements from other theaters; the drive on Port Moresby from Buna was halted, and preparations for the offensive against Chiang's makeshift capital in Chongqing were delayed. At the same time, Admiral Yamamoto committed Combined Fleet units to a series of battles in the waters around Guadalcanal. Not without reason did Tojo acknowledge in early November that Guadalcanal had become the "focal point" of Japan's war.[65]

Tojo was, nonetheless, beginning to entertain misgivings about Guadalcanal. The cost of retaking the island was proving exorbitant: The army had suffered heavy losses in men, troopships, and cargo ships. The navy, too, was losing ships, airplanes, and pilots. Tojo's subordinates charged the Army General Staff with pursuing a mistaken strategy. Colonel Nishiura Susumu argued that the army ought to "take one step back" from Guadalcanal and build defenses at points already in Japan's possession.[66] The Military Affairs Bureau director, Major General Sato Kenryo, asked what the point was of staking the "fate of the nation" on a "virtually uninhabited" island "nobody in Japan even knows."[67] Reports of emaciated and malnourished troops reached Tojo. He was utterly incensed at the thought that the army had sent troops to a distant island at the far end of its supply lines and was now allowing those troops to starve. Recall that in the late 1920s and early 1930s Tojo's troops referred to him as the "kindly commander"; once again, his solicitude for the troops came to the fore. He registered his "extreme concern" with the Army General Staff and demanded the troops be adequately supplied and fed.[68]

Tojo now revealed a preparedness to withdraw from Guadalcanal. One biographer records him telling Nishiura and Sato, "We need not concern ourselves with recapturing Guadalcanal."[69] That was, however, an operational decision beyond his ministerial purview. Staff officers, for their part, remained fiercely protective of their constitutional right to plan operations without any government interference. They also remained fixated on victory in Guadalcanal.

Tojo was able to inject himself into a debate over Guadalcanal on November 4, when Tanaka spoke with him about the shipping required to send reinforcements and supplies to Guadalcanal. Shipping was, by convention, not regarded as a purely operational matter but a cabinet prerogative. Tojo seized the opportunity, telling Tanaka there were limits to the men, materials, and shipping Japan could afford in Guadalcanal.[70] The Army Ministry and General Staff jostled for almost a fortnight. Then, on November 16, Tanaka and the Operations Section chief, Colonel Hattori Takushiro, marched into Tojo's office and demanded an eye-watering 370,000 tons in shipping for forthcoming operations in Guadalcanal. Tojo balked. Diverting the lion's share of the nation's shipping to the army in Guadalcanal would mean the navy's needs went largely unmet (the navy was simultaneously demanding 250,000 tons); it would also mean shortages in merchant marine tonnage. This would impact not only maritime operations but also people's livelihoods, and it would deny Japanese industry the steady stream of Southeast Asian resources needed for wartime production. Tojo refused outright the General Staff's demands. Tanaka gave as good as he got and insisted the men already on Guadalcanal would starve unless they began receiving much-needed supplies. Tojo's blood boiled. "If the 30,000 men [on Guadalcanal] starve to death," he screeched, "that is the General Staff's responsibility! If it comes to that, I won't look at you for as long as I live! I'll see you in hell!"[71]

Tanaka fought passionately for another three weeks. He insisted that the loss of Guadalcanal would irreparably puncture the line that must be established—and held—in the Southwest Pacific if Japan were to fight a protracted war of attrition against the Americans. On December 5, debate between Tanaka and the Military Affairs Bureau director, Sato Kenryo, descended into fisticuffs.[72] Tojo found himself wondering about General Sugiyama Hajime. Was it not his responsibility to ensure that his subordinates' operational planning remained tethered to reality? Was Sugiyama not shirking that responsibility, leaving the unpopular decisions to Tojo and thus contributing to a divide between the Army Ministry and the General Staff? Staff officers, for their part, returned to a pet theme, accusing Tojo of minimalizing his responsibilities as army minister because of his responsibilities as prime minister. Tojo refused to budge.[73]

The matter came to a head when Tanaka stormed into the prime ministerial office in the late hours of December 6. He and Tojo engaged in a screaming match. Tojo insisted that Tanaka's shipping demands would mean a drastic reduction in merchant marine tonnage and the "ripping up" of Japan's wartime economy. He challenged Tanaka's understanding of the Supreme Command's independence by arguing that operational planning had necessarily to remain "within the scope of cabinet decisions." Tanaka shot back at Tojo, insisting that anything less than the tonnage he demanded meant abandoning Guadalcanal. Doing so, he said, would render impossible any attempt at establishing the defensive posture in the Southwest Pacific that informed the army's overall strategy. He accused Tojo of neglecting his duties as army minister and of overplaying his hand as prime minister. Tojo put Tanaka in his place and told him he had no choice but to "obey." An infuriated Tanaka responded with a string of angry personal insults, and a seething Tojo reassigned Tanaka from Tokyo to Singapore.[74]

Days later, a liaison conference met in the presence of the emperor. Tojo used the occasion to end the debate that had raged within the army. He announced the army would be allocated not 370,000 tons but 170,000 tons in shipping. "The government has made every effort—and will continue to make every possible effort—to meet the demands of the Supreme Command. It has reduced the people's livelihoods to the barest minimum, and has kept general production extremely low," he said. "I respectfully request that the Supreme Command pursue its operational objectives with complete understanding of this situation."[75] Neither Sugiyama nor anybody else voiced any opposition. Tojo had gotten his way.

WITH MIDWAY, AND NOW with Guadalcanal, Japan lost what had been its viselike grip on the strategic initiative. Tojo scrambled to wrest it back, not in the Pacific but in the China theater. His options were nonetheless limited, for Guadalcanal had so drained men and resources that the planned assault on Chongqing was now paused indefinitely. Tojo decided to try instead to hurt Chiang politically. He called a liaison conference on October 29 and forged consensus on the need to strengthen the regime of Wang Jingwei in Nanjing. Two specific measures were agreed on: First, the Wang regime should be granted its oft-expressed wish to declare war on the Anglo-American powers; second, Japan should divest itself of what historian John Hunter Boyle has aptly called "some of the most conspicuous infringements on Chinese sovereignty" by agreeing to retrocede Japanese concessions in Hankou, Tianjin, and elsewhere, while also allowing the Wang regime to assume administrative control over the Shanghai International Settlement.[76]

Tojo met on October 30, 1942, with the emperor and explained this departure in China policy. The emperor admonished Tojo to distance himself from the "mistaken" mindset that conceived of Japanese policy toward China and Greater East Asia as being driven solely or even primarily by "force." Tojo promised his cabinet's "very best efforts" in devising a new China policy.[77] He departed the Imperial Palace and began speaking in tones that, had he not been acting on his emperor's express wish, would have seemed utterly out of character. "In order to win the Greater East Asian War, we simply must win the hearts and minds of other peoples," he told his secretary in early December. "It is, I think, essential that the armed services prepare for any eventuality, while leaving the rear to China. That, I think, is the way to strengthen [Wang's] Nationalist Government, and that is how I intend to turn around the way we guide China."[78] Here again Tojo was enacting direct Imperial rule, at least as he understood it.

Tojo convened an Imperial conference on December 21. He spoke about the need to "break the deadlock" in the Sino-Japanese relationship by "strengthening" the Wang regime. He sought to "annihilate" Chongqing's "anti-Japanese" raison d'être and hoped to prosecute the war together with a "rejuvenated China." The Imperial conference formalized the twofold decision to allow the Wang regime to declare war on the Anglo-American enemy and to retrocede Japanese concessions in China; conferees also agreed, in the presence of the emperor, on a completely new China policy. First and foremost, Japan would cease intruding on the Wang regime's decision-making processes and would henceforth treat it as more than a mere puppet. Japan would encourage the empowerment of the Wang regime so that it came to exercise authority over the regional regimes the Japanese Army had fostered throughout China. To this end, conferees committed to a thoroughgoing revision of the Sino-Japanese Basic Treaty of November 1940, agreeing to erase many of the most onerous provisions that had forestalled the Wang regime's independence. Finally, conferees foreswore the pursuit of peace negotiations with Chiang Kai-shek.[79]

Tojo met twice with Wang in late December. Wang lamented his regime's abject dependence on the Japanese military and its inability to strike deeper roots among the people under its notional rule. Tojo reassured Wang that his government was "not weak" but was instead in a developmental stage. In Confucian but also vaguely patronizing tones, Tojo likened the relationship between the Japanese government and the Wang regime to that between a parent and child. He spoke of his own government's willingness to foster the Wang regime's development, and granted Wang's desire to declare war on the Anglo-American powers. He did so not because of some unrealistic belief in the efficacy of the armed forces at Wang's disposal but because he recognized this as a necessary step if the Wang regime were to begin earning legitimacy. This would not only enable Tojo to retain Hirohito's trust but it would also pave the way for the armies bogged down in the China theater to be redeployed to the Pacific theater.[80]

TOJO ENDED 1942 IN a rare, reflective mood. "I wonder how many years it took to end the atmosphere of *gekokujo* [insubordination in the army]," he said to his personal secretary on December 26. He congratulated himself for having "reversed" the situation so that junior officers now obeyed their superiors, even when the junior officer was of general rank, as had been the case with Tanaka in the prolonged dispute over Guadalcanal. Tojo next admitted, "When I was army minister, I tried hard to stand with Prime Minister Konoe but, in hindsight, I did not do enough." He allowed he had then been the army's "captive," but he insisted that his approach as prime minister was totally different. He disparaged those who allowed themselves to be carried along by "inertia"—they would never, in his estimation, "succeed"—and he spoke of his refusal to be a "passive" leader who simply did the army's bidding.[81] Tojo was, in other words, intent on being his own man. Whether that would be enough to stem the tide of the US counterattack remained to be seen.

12
TOJO CHALLENGED
JANUARY–DECEMBER 1943

IMPERIAL GENERAL HEADQUARTERS (IGHQ) met on December 31, 1942 and resolved to reset Japanese strategy in the South Pacific region. Tojo Hideki attended as army minister, but in keeping with the hallowed notion of the independence of the Supreme Command, said nothing of substance; he was an observer rather than an active participant. In recognition of the momentousness of the decisions being reached, the emperor also attended. Here Tojo and his emperor witnessed the twofold decision to "discontinue" operations aimed at Guadalcanal's "recapture" and to establish a defensive line from Isabel and New Georgia in the Solomon Islands and across to Lae, Madang, and Salamaua along New Guinea's northeastern coastline. Both services agreed on the need for an "offensive defense" whereby the Imperial Japanese Navy envisioned its air arm launching attacks against Guadalcanal from the central Solomon Islands while the Imperial Japanese Army prepared for a fresh overland assault against Port Moresby in New Guinea.[1]

Tojo awoke the following morning and visited Hie, Meiji, and Yasukuni Shrines. As was customary on New Year's Day, he worshipped and prayed for the year ahead. He did so in a private capacity rather than as a cabinet minister or army general on active service; even so, it is not difficult to picture him petitioning the deified spirits of the Meiji Emperor at Meiji Shrine and the war dead at Yasukuni Shrine for success in the next twelve months of warfare. Of particular interest is his visit to Hie Shrine. Here, it can be safely assumed, he prayed to enshrined deity and supernatural guardian of the Imperial Palace, O-yama-kui-no-kami; it seems axiomatic that Tojo prayed for the palace's ongoing protection. Not since the Doolittle Raid, when he had refused to report to his emperor, had Tojo revealed even the slightest unease at the war situation. Now, in prayer, he let down his guard and revealed—to a god, if nobody else—his concern lest the Imperial Palace itself come under attack.[2]

January 4, 1943.

Even as Tojo performed his New Year's Day oblations, his leadership came in for public criticism in the form of an op-ed, "Senji saishoron" (On wartime prime ministership), in Japan's largest daily newspaper, *Asahi Shimbun*. Authored by prominent right-wing Imperial Diet member Nakano Seigo, the piece drew lessons from precedents set by such luminaries as Chancellor Otto von Bismarck during the Franco-Prussian War and Prime Minister Katsura Taro during the Russo-Japanese War, arguing that Japan needed "strong" wartime leadership powered by "dedication" to the emperor, "self-discretion," and "incorruptibility."[3] The piece passed government censors; Tojo, however, understood Nakano to mean that he lacked the leadership qualities of the men discussed in the op-ed. He angrily ordered confiscation of the *Asahi Shinbun* issue, but most copies had already been delivered, so the order had little practical effect. Tojo bottled up his rage and awaited an opportunity for revenge against Nakano.[4]

Others were also beginning to question Tojo's war leadership. Two of his more prominent critics were his old sparring partner and predecessor as prime minister, Konoe Fumimaro, as well as the emperor's younger brother, Prince Takamatsu Nobuhito. This was for Tojo a potentially destabilizing coalition, involving as it did one of the more active members of the extraconstitutional group of former prime ministers known as the *jushin,* and a member of the Imperial family who also happened to be a middle-echelon naval officer. Both Konoe and Prince Takamatsu were "pessimistic" about Japan's prospects of victory. Konoe was particularly troubled by what he regarded as Tojo's misplaced "optimism." Tojo met with the two men on January 7, seeking to dispel their concerns by expounding on his grand strategy.[5]

Tojo opened by acknowledging that the possibility of defeat had exercised him since the war's opening. Should defeat come, he suggested, it would be attributable to three factors in isolation or in combination. He declined to list burgeoning US strength among the possible causes of defeat and instead nominated army-navy disunity, domestic disunity and dissent, and the Soviet Union's entry into the war against Japan. He launched directly into a discussion of what he designated "the most important" issue—namely, "assembling and amassing public support" for the war. He bemoaned what he estimated was the "10 percent" of the population who were "falling out of step" with each other and with their government. He stated his own preference for "martial law," but acknowledged it was anathema to the emperor. He added that his government's post–Pearl Harbor legislative program—including various bills he intended to introduce to the Imperial Diet's forthcoming eighty-first regular session—was regimenting the people's everyday lives in ways not dissimilar to martial law. It remained, he said, "necessary to regulate the people to an even greater extent."[6]

What Konoe and Prince Takamatsu made of Tojo's domestic program is a matter for conjecture; they said little and instead turned Tojo's attention to the possibility of mediating German-Soviet peace. Konoe took the opportunity to remind Tojo of an earlier, unfulfilled hope to bring the Soviets into the German-Italian-Japanese Tripartite Pact so that it became a quadripartite pact, and he stated that a prompt end to the German-Soviet war would be very much to Japan's advantage. Konoe and Prince Takamatsu postulated that successful Japanese mediation of the German-Soviet war might give rise to one of two possible outcomes. First, peace with the Soviets would allow Germany to reorder its priorities so it once again shared with Japan and Italy a focus on compelling British surrender. Second, they wondered whether German-Soviet peace might shake the world no less than had the opening of the German-Soviet war, and Konoe suggested it might present a "possibility for peace in the Greater East Asian War."[7]

Tojo acknowledged his ongoing interest in mediating an end to the German-Soviet war. He nonetheless noted that the Germans had asked Japan to do the precise opposite—join the war against the Soviets—and he insisted he would only take up mediation if the Germans specifically requested it. He counseled against any panic-stricken, doomsaying reappraisal of Germany's war prospects and spoke of the Germans emerging from the war with an autarchic sphere encompassing at least North Africa. He added that, whatever the Germans' proclivities, the Soviets were no longer likely to embrace Japanese mediation. He estimated the Soviets had mobilized perhaps 60 percent of their national strength; they were only just beginning to hit their stride, and it seemed most unlikely they would want a prompt end to the war. He told Konoe and Prince Takamatsu that not even a Japanese ultimatum—either enter truce negotiations with Germany or prepare for war in the Far East—would compel the Soviets to accept Japanese mediation. This owed to Japan's inability, at least for the duration of its war against the Anglo-American enemy in the Pacific Ocean region, to do anything more than occupy the Soviet Union's Maritime Provinces. And that, Tojo admitted, could "not hurt" the Soviets. With all these factors in mind, he insisted he would—unless and until Adolf Hitler changed course—only speak with the Germans about "fighting to the bitter end."[8]

Tojo sought also to temper any expectations of a prompt end to the Greater East Asian War. He spoke of his willingness to attend a "peace conference" but sought to dispel any misplaced optimism about a conference being called anytime soon. The war, he explained, was yet to "stabilize." The United States was on the cusp of taking Guadalcanal, and it seemed unlikely—to say the least—to opt out of the war after having finally wrested some initiative in the Pacific. The Americans would look to launch a counteroffensive from Guadalcanal, and Tojo was placing his hope in the Japanese armed services' ability to hold the Solomon Islands–New Guinea line to which IGHQ had committed approximately one week earlier. Here, in a most immediate sense, cooperation between the armed services was integral, because the defense Tojo envisioned was by no means static. It involved the free lateral movement of troops protected by overhead cover and the rapid deployment of naval units to any point along the defensive line that came under US counterattack. Wherever the Americans landed, the defenders would seek to delay them and inflict maximum casualties by fighting, if necessary, to the very last man. In the meantime, highly mobile forces would be brought up to encircle and annihilate the enemy. Defenses went considerably behind the IGHQ-designated line so that the bastion on Rabaul made for a robust system of defense with very considerable depth. Until this defense would grind down US forces in a war of attrition, Tojo thought it folly to assume the Americans would succumb to "war weariness."[9]

Tojo spoke also of the China front, not of winning but of "calming" the situation in China by "strengthening" the regime of Wang Jingwei. He noted his "resolve" to replace the China Expeditionary Army's commanding officer and chief of staff if they proved anything but supportive of his new China policy. He regretted that Chiang Kai-shek seemed unlikely, for the foreseeable future, to consider "cooperation" with Japan, which he attributed not to grievances arising from the Japanese Army's decade or more of aggression in China but to the political empowerment of the anti-Japanese Madame Chiang Kai-shek and her equally anti-Japanese brother, Foreign Minister T. V. Soong. Tojo reckoned their views had gained currency at least partly because of widespread confidence in Chongqing in eventual US victory. Such estimates would evaporate, he assumed, once Japanese forces held their defensive line and engaged their US counterparts in a grinding war of attrition in the South Pacific.[10]

In these ways Tojo's grand strategy rested on the presumption of protracted warfare in the Pacific. He was satisfied that Japan's successes in the early weeks and months of the war, as well as its long-range preparations for war, left it well placed. The conquest of Southeast Asia meant that Japan had "plenty of resources"; it had denied the Anglo-American enemy access to those resources. He added that "production of Manchukuo's resources" was booming. He cited the specific—and all-important—example of steel: Tonnage produced in 1943 would, he emphasized, would be as much as double what had been produced in 1942. He expressed complete confidence in Japan's capacity to produce whatever it needed—and in the quantities it needed. There would be no labor shortages, nor would there be any need to take women out of the home and inject them into the workforce; Tojo spoke instead of using "Korean and Chinese labor."[11]

Tojo ended his conversation with Konoe and Prince Takamatsu with a show of confidence. He acknowledged that he and Konoe had been divided, before Pearl Harbor, on the "optimism" or "pessimism" with which they had forecast Japan's war prospects against the Anglo-American powers. He argued that those pre–Pearl Harbor forecasts were now largely irrelevant. His grand strategy brought together the home front and the armed services, as well as allies, neutrals, and adversaries in a comprehensive fashion that mitigated against "pessimism."[12]

The politeness with which Tojo treated Konoe and Prince Takamatsu was affected and highly exaggerated. Before long, as we shall see, he would be complaining bitterly about high-society types and their dreams of Japanese-Soviet cooperation and peace in the Pacific. He nonetheless felt constrained by Konoe's and Prince Takamatsu's proximity to the throne. His baser instincts, as well as the limits to his capacity to act on those instincts, were more properly on display in the army. The focus of his wrath in January 1943 was Lieutenant General Hirabayashi Morito, who in the early aftermath of the Pearl Harbor attack spoke with his subordinates on the battlefields of China about the folly of war against the Anglo-American powers. "With Japan's current war potential, there is absolutely no chance of victory," Hirabayashi had insisted. He maintained this was the case "even if Japan were to engage in a war of attrition." He figured Japan would "in less than a year" be "outnumbered" and "eventually defeated." He lamented the fact that Tojo had not been forced into retirement before he could lead the nation into an impossible war and dismissed Tojo as lacking the "capacity" to "deal with" the situation for which he bore primary responsibility. Word filtered back to Tojo, who used his ministerial power over personnel decisions to banish Hirabayashi in January 1943 to the army reserve list.[13]

Tojo's sensitivity to criticism was on full display during a January conversation with friend, journalist, and wartime propagandist Takamiya Taihei. The two men met against the backdrop of wartime privations, for coal shortages meant Tojo filled the hibachi brazier not with coal but with pine needles. He spoke about reducing waste—pine needles left in the garden would, he explained, only "rot" away—but Takamiya was unimpressed. He allowed that the pine needles were doing an admirable job of heating the room, but he pleaded with Tojo to forget such trivial matters and turn his mind instead to "recovering the war situation." Tojo was incensed and screamed at Takamiya, "Get out! And don't come back!"[14]

Tojo quickly regathered his composure and called Takamiya back. He explained in an uncharacteristically meek tone, "I don't need you to tell me that. I am thinking about it." He went on to liken warfare to rolling a boulder down a hill: It required enormous initial effort to get things started, but it quickly gathered momentum and became an ineluctable force. This sounded to Takamiya as though Tojo were confessing to a lack of control over the situation. Unsettled, Takamiya asked whether there was at least a possibility of Japan rolling inexorably toward "utter defeat" (*tokoton haisen*). Tojo responded, "I don't want to let that happen, but it may well come to that." The possibility was weighing on Tojo, who admitted to having considered resigning and "releasing" himself from the burden of leading Japan's war effort. That, however, would be akin to deserting his emperor, and he refused to consider it further. Besides, Tojo could not believe that anybody else could do nearly as good a job as he was doing. So he would continue to lead Japan, but he worried about various impediments to victory. Once again, he seemed to look straight past the preponderance of power the United States was just beginning to bring to bear in the Pacific; he listed instead the perennial problem of the fraught army-navy relationship as well as the "prestige" he himself had "lost" during his bruising battles with IGHQ.[15]

TOJO'S TRIALS CONTINUED THROUGHOUT January. He woke on January 15 with a fever and, as a precautionary measure, excused himself from a prescheduled meeting with Hirohito. He came down with a nasty bout of influenza and was bedridden for much of the remainder of January. Some—Konoe prominent among them—thought Tojo might not recover and began considering a prime ministerial successor. Such thinking was fanciful. Tojo's strength began returning in late January; he had received from the emperor and empress a gift of soup, ice cream, and sherbet to aid in his recovery. At least so far as Tojo was concerned, this was more than mere courtesy, it was a show of ongoing support. The gesture fortified him.[16]

Tojo roused himself from his sickbed on January 28 for the opening of the Imperial Diet's eighty-first regular session. (In a historical first, the emperor had delayed the opening of the session to give Tojo every chance to attend.)[17] He delivered a stirring address that reprised and developed the pan-Asian themes he had introduced some twelve months earlier. Independence for Burma and the Philippines again received mention. The contributions of Manchukuoan industry to the war effort were a highlight; so, too, were the increasing levels of reciprocity between the Japanese government and the Wang regime in Nanjing. All told, two ideas were paramount: First, Tojo presented Japan's war as a joint, mutual undertaking among all Greater East Asian nations and societies. Second, he presumed that Japan was the natural leader of Greater East Asia. Japan was not only making the main contribution to the war effort but was also (in Tojo's estimation) best able to determine and direct specific measures each Greater East Asian nation must take on its path to independence.[18]

The address exhausted Tojo, and he returned to his sickbed for a few days. Before the month was out, and before he had fully recovered his strength, he found himself drawn once again into heated dispute with the Army General Staff. At issue was the army's steel allocation for 1943; staff officers confronting Tojo expressed their "extreme dissatisfaction" with what they regarded as a plainly inadequate allocation. Despite telling Konoe and Prince Takamatsu just a few weeks earlier of the massive quantities of steel being produced, Tojo now confronted the reality that production was not nearly enough to meet Japan's burgeoning needs. He was not happy with the Army General Staff's latest intervention: His cabinet and IGHQ had in December agreed—in the emperor's presence, no less—on materiel allocations for 1943, and Tojo was in no mood to revisit those decisions. Indeed, he received the staff officers' representations in a foul temper. They were nonetheless insistent that, without more steel, the army would be unable to prepare for the possibility of war against the Soviets. Tojo argued that greater steel allocations for the army could only come at the expense of the merchant marine. Such a decision would necessarily have a deleterious effect on Japan's overall national strength, for the nation needed shipping to move materiel from Southeast Asia. He ended the conversation by refusing outright the General Staff's demands.[19]

All the while, Tojo and his professional military colleagues looked on anxiously at the withdrawal from Guadalcanal, which was completed by February 7, 1943. He attributed the loss, at least partly, to US productive capacity and technological prowess. Other factors had contributed; chief among them, in Tojo's estimation, had been Japan's impossibly overstretched supply lines. Extrapolating from such assessments, he consoled himself with the thought that the Americans were yet to understand "the strength of the Japanese armed services," which he located in the "triumph of the Japanese spirit."[20] This was perhaps the only way Tojo could explain away the fact that Japanese troops had engaged the Americans in adverse conditions on Guadalcanal and lost. In so doing he—wittingly or otherwise—began reprising and repackaging the language of his old factional enemies, the *kodoha* (Imperial way) officers, who in the early and mid-1930s had espoused a military doctrine that prioritized men and morale over mechanization and weaponry. Perhaps it was the force of circumstance, but Tojo was presenting once again as both a forward-thinker and a traditionalist. To be more specific, he was a "total war" officer who refused to grant the army what he regarded as its shortsighted materiel demands precisely because he prioritized maintenance of Japan's total national strength. Yet he also sounded every bit the traditionalist with his overt show of faith in the superior morale of Japan's troops.

THE GUADALCANAL WITHDRAWAL COINCIDED neatly with a meeting in Casablanca between US President Franklin D. Roosevelt and British Prime Minister Winston Churchill, along with their staff officers. The principal business was campaign planning for the year to come. Debate over European operations was robust, but the war in the Pacific was, for all intents and purposes, an almost solely American affair. The British were hardly in a position to take issue with US insistence on ongoing operations to pressure Japanese forces, throw them off balance, and deny them freedom of action. Concretely, the Anglo-American powers agreed on the need in the south to continue the limited offensives in New Guinea and the Solomon Islands with a view to the eventual capture of Rabaul, in the north to seize the westernmost Aleutian Islands, and in the Central Pacific to prepare for the fleet's advance through the Caroline, Gilbert, and Marshall Islands. During the conference, Roosevelt spoke with newspaper reporters of the Anglo-Americans' determination to fight until they had crushed the German,

Italian, and Japanese governments and ideologies. They would fight, he said, until they had secured "unconditional surrender."[21]

Tojo greeted this definition of Anglo-American war aims with silence. Nearly twelve months later, he publicly branded unconditional surrender a "laughingstock," castigating Churchill and Roosevelt for treating Japan like a "third-rate nation."[22] If nothing else, it made plainly apparent what Tojo already believed—namely, that there was no prospect of truce negotiations anytime soon. This reinforced Tojo's belief in the need to build Japan's national strength so it could meet the demands of the total war he had long since envisioned.

If the announcement of unconditional surrender served to confirm for Tojo the fundamental soundness of his thinking about the war in the Pacific, a near simultaneous victory for the Soviets over the German Army in the six-month Battle of Stalingrad presented Tojo with pause for thought about the war in Europe. Tojo reported to the emperor on February 12 on the "unfavorable war situation" in which Germany now found itself. He nonetheless insisted that, seen from the "big picture," the German defeat at Stalingrad was "not a big problem." He thought the Germans should prove able to stop the Red Army's advance, and he reassured Hirohito that Germany still had the "human resources," the "industrial strength," and the "oil" to pursue the war, unhindered, for at least the remainder of 1943.[23]

Tojo's failure to grasp the significance of the Soviet victory at Stalingrad owed in large part to his stubborn overestimation of German national strength, as well as a perceived need to allay any concerns the emperor might be feeling. Nonetheless, the enormity of the Battle of Stalingrad—some 150,000 German troops died and another ninety thousand surrendered—confronted Tojo and his colleagues with the need to reassess Germany's war in Europe and reconsider what it meant for Japan's war in Asia and the Pacific. The conclusion was clear: The chances of a German invasion of Britain were now almost nonexistent. As Tojo put it to a liaison conference on February 27, it no longer seemed feasible to "work for the surrender of Great Britain in cooperation with Germany and Italy," which was supposed to contribute to "destroy[ing] the will of the United States to continue the war." For this reason, Tojo spoke of the need for a "reinvestigation" of the grand strategy that had informed Japanese policy since the eve of Pearl Harbor. This was a stunning admission: Tojo had led Japan into war on the basis of what had proved a patently faulty exit strategy. But he seemed barely to blink, simply flipping the existing endgame-of-war scenario on its head so that Japan would seek to destroy the Americans' will to fight and force them to the negotiating table, compelling the British to acknowledge the hopelessness of their cause. He told his liaison conference colleagues of the pressing need to exploit US "weaknesses," paramount among them "shipping issues" and especially "morale issues." Japan's exit strategy now depended in large part on what Tojo called "divisions" among the American people, as well as their "war weariness."[24] Here Tojo was falling back on preconceived notions of American weaknesses rather than clearheaded appraisals of the actual state of affairs in the United States.

Tojo's new strategy at least ended what had been Japan's overt reliance on its German ally. Japan would henceforth decide its own war fortunes. Much hinged on the defense in depth that the was armed services were establishing in the South Pacific. They were, however, unable to agree on priorities: the army, prioritizing New Guinea, expected the navy's support in the form of both aerial warfare and protection of convoy and supply shipping; the navy continued to prioritize the Solomon Islands, where it hoped to establish a defense that would enable it to prepare for a decisive maritime battle against the US fleet in the Central Pacific. All the while, the United States was shifting ever higher numbers of planes into the South Pacific.[25] Then, on March 3 and 4, a force of land-based American and Australian warplanes overtook a sixteen-ship Japanese convoy enroute from the bastion in Rabaul to Lae in New Guinea. With the loss of only a few of its planes, the enemy sank eight troop transports and four destroyers. Some three thousand Japanese troops perished in the Battle of the Bismarck Sea, and IGHQ decided against any further significant attempts at reinforcing or resupplying forces in New Guinea and the Solomons.[26] By late March, the armed services reached the obvious conclusion: Air superiority was proving decisive on the battlefield and "measures such as the comprehensive display of air power, supply, and aerial defense" were the "most important" strategic issues confronting Japan in the South Pacific.[27]

THE BATTLE OF THE Bismarck Sea notwithstanding, there was a lull in the South Pacific in the spring of 1943 as both Japan and the United States gathered themselves for the next round of fighting. Tojo found himself locked in a wearying army-navy brawl over steel allocations. The demands of shipbuilding meant the navy had an almost insatiable appetite for steel, and navy officers were wont to make the case that a navy without ships could not fight. Tojo's right-hand man, the Military Affairs Bureau director, Sato Kenryo, was angered by such arguments. In one heated exchange, he asked whether the navy would have the army fight with "bamboo spears." Tojo took up the cudgels and in mid-May told Navy Minister Shimada Shigetaro that the army could no longer "cut itself to the bone" in the interest of interservice unity. He would henceforth accept nothing less than a fifty-fifty army-navy split in steel allocations. The navy, however, would not budge, and Tojo decided against pressing the army's case. He forced his service to accept a compromise plan that allocated steel tonnage in the ratio of thirteen to twelve for the navy and the army, respectively.[28]

Steel allocations aside, Tojo directed his attention to the eighty-first regular Diet session, at which his cabinet introduced an astonishing eighty-nine bills. Of particular interest to members was a "special wartime administrative law" (*senji gyosei shokken toku-reiho*) that proposed to bolster wartime industrial production and, to that end, sought to increase Tojo's prime ministerial power over the economic ministries. To bolster his case, Tojo spoke of the need to boost production so that "two plus two" became not "four" but "five" and eventually "eighty." This foray into what the press called "Tojo arithmetic" was doubtless designed to spur the people onto ever-greater efforts in pursuit of victory; the unmistakably Orwellian undertones should not be ignored.[29] Also of interest were proposed revisions to the Meiji-era local autonomy act (*shisei choson sei kaisei-an*). Tojo regarded these revisions as being aimed at the "renovation of domestic leadership." Most important, he wanted "government leadership to penetrate officialdom at all levels."[30] The revisions proposed, for example, that hitherto democratically elected officials at the prefectural or municipal level instead be appointed by the Home Ministry. In this way Tojo hoped to magnify central government control over all levels of government across the nation. Then there were revisions to the "special wartime criminal law" (*senji keiji tokubetsu ho*) that Tojo had introduced to the Diet only twelve months earlier, which aimed at increasing the government's powers of surveillance over the Japanese public. Driving the supposed need for these revisions was what Tojo called "cheap" talk among the "upper classes." Of particular concern were those—presumably including Konoe—discussing matters like peace vis-à-vis the Anglo-American powers and a Japanese-Soviet alliance. Tojo told his military colleagues of his desire to "enforce strict controls" over anyone engaged in this "most dangerous" chatter.[31]

The government agenda touched a raw nerve in the Imperial Diet, and Tojo faced searching questions concerning the restrictions he was placing on the Japanese people's freedoms, as well as his own dictatorial ambitions. An atmosphere of "Tojo bashing" took hold in the Imperial Diet.[32] Tojo did not enjoy the treatment, and he complained bitterly about politicians and their "godlike" affectations.[33] Yet, not wanting to make too many "enemies" in the Diet, he sought to reassure members that he harbored no dictatorial ambitions.[34] The bills passed into law, which he reported to the emperor on March 26, 1943. To Tojo's chagrin, Hirohito identified with the Diet members who had accused the prime minister of trampling on individual liberties. Specifically, the emperor warned Tojo against "placing too great a burden on the people."[35]

Policies toward Greater East Asia provided Tojo with some comparative joy. He flew to Nanjing and met with Wang Jingwei; he then turned his attention to Burma. His cabinet had joined with IGHQ in January and agreed to encourage Burma's conspicuously pro-Japanese leader, Ba Maw, to prepare for national independence by August.[36] A liaison conference convened in early March and decided to invite Ba Maw to Tokyo.[37] Tojo met with him on March 22, going out of his way to treat his guest not as a colonial subject but a brother-in-arms. He spoke matter-of-factly about the decision to grant independence to Burma by August 1, which Tojo placed in the broader context of Japanese policy since the early 1930s. He first explained how Japan had not conquered Manchuria but had instead fostered the newly independent state of Manchukuo (he did not pause to consider the many strings the Kwantung Army had attached to Manchukuoan independence). He offered a creative reimagining of Japan's motivations when it marched to war against China: Japan had all along, he asserted, fought selflessly to liberate China from malicious Anglo-American influences. Truthful or otherwise, this struck a chord with Ba Maw, who above all else wished to extricate Burma from British colonial rule. Tojo next added that Burma and Japan were like "brother nations in East Asia" and spoke of his desire for a "long and prosperous" Burmese-Japanese relationship. Ba Maw later recalled leaving the meeting impressed, convinced that the Burmese and Japanese were as "two Asian peoples who were waging an Asian war together."[38]

Some two weeks later, Tojo pored over a cable authored by Japan's ambassador to the Wang regime, Shigemitsu Mamoru. Dated April 5, the cable assured him that the "new China policies" Japan had been pursuing since late 1942 had made a "deep impression" on the Chinese people. Shigemitsu called for a continuation and enhancement of these new China policies. It was necessary, he wrote, to "respect China's independence"

Tojo and Wang Jingwei, Nanjing, March 13, 1943.

and strengthen the Wang regime politically so it could unite the entire nation. He wrote also of the need to strengthen the Wang regime economically, through policies designed to "unify currencies" in areas under the Wang regime's control and with infrastructure projects designed to "unify freight." Shigemitsu also identified a need for a new Sino-Japanese treaty to replace the existing one, which had been concluded in November 1940 and contained many unequal provisions.[39]

Tojo recalled Shigemitsu to Tokyo. The ambassador expounded on the need to ensure that the "new China policy" would inform policies toward Greater East Asia as a whole. There was a need to actualize "East Asian liberation," a "general policy of neighborly friendliness," economic "liberation" based on principles of "equality and mutual benefit," and "freedom of trade." Tojo found himself nodding furiously in agreement, for Shigemitsu was precisely what he now needed. In contrast to Foreign Minister Tani

Masayuki and Greater East Asia Minister Aoki Kazuo, both of whom owed their positions to their willingness to do Tojo's bidding, Shigemitsu had not only an independent vision but also the purposefulness and self-confidence to hold his own during debate with cabinet ministers and IGHQ. Tojo was growing as a leader. He requested—and received—Shigemitsu's service as foreign minister amid pledges of "strongest support" for his policies.[40]

Shigemitsu's conception of a new China policy framed within a wider Greater East Asia context empowered Tojo to take initiatives, such as when he flew to Manila in early May for a lightning tour. He was greeted by hundreds of thousands of Filipinos shouting "Banzai!" and waving Japanese flags. The locals were acting on orders, but the show of Greater East Asian solidarity left Tojo (to borrow historian Jeremy Yellen's felicitous expression) "trembling with excitement."[41] He returned to Tokyo satisfied that he had won over the Filipinos with his "sincerity."[42]

Tojo was now convinced of the need for a summit meeting drawing together leaders from around Greater East Asia. He called an Imperial conference, so the emperor himself could approve and lend legitimacy to Tojo's Greater East Asian policies. But he was subjected to two shocks before the conference convened. First was a disastrous turn in the war

Tojo attends a mass rally in the Philippines, May 6, 1943.

fortunes of Japan's European allies: 275,000 German and Italian troops in Tunisia surrendered on May 13 to Anglo-American forces, summarily ending the Axis presence in North Africa. Tojo's immediate reaction was to consider the consequences for Japan of the reopening of the Suez Canal; British ships bound for the Indian Ocean would no longer have to round the Cape of Good Hope. This confronted Tojo with the likelihood of British maritime and aerial superiority in the Indian Ocean, raising the need for Japan to bolster defenses in Burma, Java, Sumatra, and Thailand. There were not, however, enough troops to go around. "I wonder," Tojo asked, "if one of our divisions can take on ten enemy divisions?"[43]

Then came a shock in the Aleutian Islands. The Japanese had sought to reinforce their Aleutian Island possessions, but the efforts were patently inadequate. Amphibious US forces landed on Attu in mid-May and caught Tojo—and the rest of the military and government—completely off guard. There was nothing anyone could do to help the doomed Japanese garrison; Tojo could only encourage it to "fight heroically."[44] The Japanese defenders, almost to the last man, chose death over surrender and shattered like broken jewels (*gyokusai*) in a suicidal charge on May 29. At least one trustworthy biographer places hot tears of burning anguish on Tojo's cheeks at the news of this grim outcome; the emperor sought explicit assurances that this would be the first and last instance of *gyokusai,* or suicidal tactics.[45] IGHQ decided to evacuate all troops from neighboring Kiska before the Americans landed there, resetting Japan's northern defensive line much farther south, in the Kurile Island chain.

These twin shocks took the gloss off the Imperial conference Tojo had called in the immediate aftermath of his Manila tour. The conference, which met on May 31, agreed to hold an October summit meeting to bring together leaders from around Greater East Asia. Imperial conferees also agreed on a series of "political strategies" designed to set the stage for the October summit meeting, including encouraging the Wang regime to begin "political maneuvers" vis-à-vis Chiang's government in Chongqing; enhancing "mutual cooperation" with Thailand; remaining on course and granting independence to Burma; granting independence "as soon as possible" to the Philippines; and developing capacities in Borneo, Celebes, Java, Malaya, and Sumatra to supply natural resources while also seeking to win the "hearts" of the people in those territories.[46]

Explaining to his Imperial conference colleagues the imperative of these Greater East Asian policies, Tojo made two startling admissions. First, there was considerable uncertainty about the "world situation," which he attributed to the "state of the German-Soviet war." Tojo might not have said it in so many words, but he was acknowledging that it was no longer possible to predicate Japanese grand strategy on German victory in Europe. This was an admission of the vacuousness of Japanese strategy since at least the conclusion of the Tripartite Pact in September 1940. Then there was the "intensifying" American counteroffensive in the Pacific. Tojo said little more about it at least partly because he had been knocked off balance by the loss of the Aleutians. He nonetheless forecast—in however guarded a fashion—the difficulties that operations in the South Pacific would henceforth pose. The twin shocks of German-Italian surrender in North Africa and the loss of the Aleutians had forced Tojo to confront the difficulties inherent in concluding the war successfully. In view of this unpromising situation, he acknowledged that only one area for "initiative" remained: "political strategies" designed to "unite Greater East Asia."[47]

Days after the Imperial conference, Tojo learned from General Sugiyama Hajime that efforts at reinforcing and supplying the New Guinea–Solomon Islands defensive line had not progressed as planned. The enemy's aerial superiority in the South Pacific was impeding Japan's ability to move ships; New Guinea and the central Solomons now seemed to promise a repeat of the situation on Guadalcanal. Withdrawal was, however, impossible. Hundreds of thousands of Japanese troops in the South Pacific were dangerously exposed, and naval staff planners were worried that the Marshall Islands in the Central Pacific were now vulnerable to enemy attack. This, Sugiyama explained, the navy could not countenance. Continuing to hope for a decisive fleet encounter in the Central Pacific, the Combined Fleet insisted the Marshall Islands be held at all costs (*haisui no jin*). The army, for its part, worried that the Marshalls were beyond Japan's logistics capability and wanted to draw a defensive line considerably farther west. The message for Tojo was unmistakable: The army was dangerously overstretched and lacking confidence but, for now, had no choice other than to do its best in joining the navy in defense of the northern New Guinea–central Solomon Islands line it had declared defensible some six months earlier.[48]

Sugiyama's operational pessimism struck at the very heart of Tojo's grand strategy. The in-depth defense Tojo had envisioned in the South Pacific now presented itself as utterly unfeasible, and he dispensed with the war of attrition he had presumed would pave the way to a negotiated peace with a disheartened United States. Tojo lurched instead to an endgame-of-war scenario that more nearly approximated naval operational planning and strategy. As he put it to the emperor on June 7, he now embraced a "decisive battle" as the most likely way of defeating the United States and ending the war.[49]

Other factors seemed to Tojo to support this newfound enthusiasm for a decisive battle. On the home front, the Japanese public confronted what liberal journalist Kiyosawa Kiyoshi called "food problems." This was directly attributable, according to Kiyosawa's diary, to Japan's "low-grade, stupid" leadership.[50] Tojo's knee-jerk reaction was to reprise his strangely folksy way of determining the people's dietary intake: He again began conducting early morning inspections of food scraps in household rubbish bins. He convinced himself he did this because he cared about the people, but others saw things differently. Military councilor General Nishio Toshizo, for one, was prepared to go on public record with derisive comments about Tojo as "the guy who gets up early every morning and scrounges through the city's rubbish bins."[51] An infuriated Tojo banished Nishio from the army's active service. That action might have been personally satisfying, but it did nothing for the situation at hand. Tojo told his cabinet on June 11 that the people would henceforth have to eat "whatever is edible." To reinforce the point, he presented his ministerial colleagues with a stomach-turning lunch of pigweed, burdock roots, asters, and mulberry leaves. To a crowd of schoolgirls in mid-June he explained, "You can eat anything as long as it's not poisonous." He sought to lead the way and ripped up the lawn at the official prime ministerial residence, replacing it with sweet potato vines. He reminisced about having collected leaves and other edibles as a youth and spoke of the attractiveness of "getting back to a simpler lifestyle."[52] Whether he genuinely believed this is open to question; what mattered most was the fact that the home front seemed increasingly poorly prepared for a grinding war of attrition. A decisive battle held out hope that food shortages would not become as big a factor in Japan's war as they had been in Germany's defeat in the World War I.

All the while, the issue of shipping allocations created not only an army-navy split but also divisions between the Army and Navy General Staffs and the cabinet. IGHQ repeatedly bewailed the inadequacy of shipping allocations, eyeing shipping allocated to the merchant marine. Tojo was aghast. He stood firm behind the merchant marine's needs, arguing that any "interference" with the "movement of goods" would mean a reduced industrial output that in turn would impact future operations, including the all-important decisive battle. He got his way, and on June 29 an agreement was finally reached on shipping allocations. The General Staffs ill-humoredly acquiesced, griping at what they regarded as plainly inadequate allocations. This prompted Tojo to admit to IGHQ that the "current front" was "stretched way beyond the nation's capacities." He pleaded with the armed services to allow a reset in Japanese grand strategy by undertaking for the meantime to "do the impossible" in New Guinea and the Solomon Islands.[53]

THE US COUNTERATTACK IN the South Pacific began some two months earlier than expected. On June 30, 1943, American and Australian forces landed unopposed some fifteen miles south of Salamaua at New Guinea's Nassau Bay. That same day, US forces began moving up the Solomon Island chain, making bloodless landings on New Georgia Island and neighboring Rendova Island. For the army, the principal concern was whether and how quickly enemy forces at Nassau Bay could connect with Australian forces at Wau, some twenty-five miles south of Salamaua; the navy fretted about the loss of its airfield at Munda, on New Georgia's southwestern tip. Military officers' pessimism ran deep, and they even began questioning whether the bastion on Rabaul was any longer defensible. The navy, for its part, insisted that the loss of Rabaul would render Truk Island (the navy's main forward base in the Caroline Island chain) indefensible, which would mean the loss of the Marshall Islands. In that case, naval staff planners argued, the Japanese home islands would be "denuded" and all sea lanes linking Japan to Southeast Asia would be cut. A decisive maritime battle would also be out of the question. Mutual interservice recrimination was the almost inevitable outcome.[54]

Tojo did not intervene in this fresh round of army-navy controversy, immersing himself instead in what he had designated as the sole area that still allowed for some initiative: He turned his attention back to Greater East Asia. A liaison conference met in late June and agreed to return to Thailand territories the British had long since incorporated in Malaya, to take concrete steps on the path to independence for the Philippines, and to begin involving the Javanese in self-governance.[55] With these policies in his hip pocket, in early July Tojo embarked on another tour of Southeast Asia. Stops included Jakarta, Singapore, and Thailand. In the words of historian Theodore Friend, the tour was "filled with marshalled crowds, militant rhetoric, fatiguing ceremony, and forced conviviality."[56] Tojo secured from Greater East Asian leaders, including the Indian National Army commander, Subhas Chandra Bose, agreement to attend a conference later that year in Tokyo.[57]

Tojo returns to Tokyo following a visit to the southern front, July 1943.

Tojo's respite lasted little longer than his Southeast Asian sojourn. By the time he returned to Tokyo, Anglo-American forces had landed on Sicily, and rumors of Italian surrender swirled around Tokyo. Domestic opposition to Tojo mounted. Four former prime ministers—Hiranuma Kiichiro, Konoe Fumimaro, Okada Keisuke, and Wakatsuki Rejiro—met on July 17 and agreed that Japan had to extricate itself from the war. They believed that Tojo was unlikely to make this happen and ought to be replaced as prime minister.[58]

Tojo joined the *jushin* for lunch on July 23. He regarded at least Konoe and Okada as oppositional, and he had long since resented what he regarded as the *jushin*'s propensity to criticize from the sidelines. He was on his guard but by no means on the defensive. Indeed, he outlined his grand strategy with clarity and simplicity. Japan had, he explained, to "secure" the victories it had scored across Greater East Asia in the early weeks of the war. It had to "strengthen" its relationship with Germany and Italy. It had to "persevere" in the Pacific by making full use of its "superior strategic position" and adopting a posture of "offensive defense." It had to keep the Japanese public united and unified. And it had to "mobilize Greater East Asia" to "ensure victory, regardless of what comes of the war in Europe."[59]

The *jushin* quartet was unconvinced that this amounted to an exit strategy. Okada contacted the emperor's political antenna, Lord Keeper of the Privy Seal Kido Koichi, and raised the possibility of removing Tojo from all positions of ministerial authority. To avoid trouble from Tojo and any of his diehard supporters, Okada thought the army might be prevailed upon to appoint him chief of staff in Sugiyama's stead. The timing for such a maneuver must have seemed propitious given that Italian leader Benito Mussolini was toppled from power on July 25. (Tojo reported on Mussolini's downfall to the emperor on July 26, admitting that Italian surrender now seemed only a matter of time; when Italy surrendered on September 8, Tojo denounced the "treacherous act" by what he and his government now regarded as an "enemy nation."[60]) Kido was not, however, convinced Tojo should be discarded just yet. In fact, he told Tojo on July 26 that Mussolini's downfall increased the imperative of a renewed attempt at "improving" Japanese-Soviet relations and exploring the possibility of using Soviet mediation to bring an end to Japan's war against the Anglo-American powers.[61]

Only a few weeks earlier, Tojo had bitterly criticized what he regarded as the effete upper-class types advocating a diplomatic pivot toward the Soviet Union. Now that one of the emperor's closest aides had raised just such a move with him, he was more circumspect. "Making an enemy of a certain country or making an ally of a certain country is a big issue," he muttered.[62] Before the month was out, he spoke with Cabinet Intelligence Bureau director Amo Eiji, Chief Cabinet Secretary Hoshino Naoki, and Foreign Minister Shigemitsu Mamoru about the prospects of a German-Soviet truce.[63]

Force of circumstance shifted Tojo's attention away from any diplomatic pivot and back to Greater East Asia. His government had committed to granting Burmese independence as soon as August 1, and he fronted the Privy Council on July 29 to explain this policy. He acknowledged that Burma was but a "small country" without the capacity to throw off the yoke of British colonialism. It owed its independence instead to the Japanese Army's strength and largesse, and although he disavowed any agreement that formally subjugated Burma, he was satisfied that it would be "up to Japan to take action" if "issues" ever arose there. Burmese independence, as understood by Tojo, was highly qualified.[64]

Increasing aircraft production was Tojo's other key point of focus in late July and early August. He spoke on July 23 of the need to prioritize "aerial superiority" and significantly increase airplane manufacture.[65] Then, at a liaison conference in early August, he forged agreement on the need "to strengthen the nation's all-out war potential, centering on a dramatic increase in direct air power to overwhelm Anglo-American forces." Conferees agreed it would henceforth be necessary to divert resources from the civilian sector, which they acknowledged would result in reductions in the public's living standards. At the same time, it would also be necessary to mobilize the labor force so that airplane production targets might be met. Tojo quietly shelved his earlier statements about leaving Japanese women in their homes and relying instead on Korean and Taiwanese labor; he now accepted that even high school students were required in the factories. He consoled himself with the thought that herein lay a far surer path to victory than that presented by a diplomatic pivot toward the Soviet Union.[66]

OPERATIONS IN THE SOUTH Pacific were faring poorly. In a repeat of the situation that had unfolded in Guadalcanal, the armed services were unable to resupply and reinforce either New Guinea or the Solomons, with predictable effects. In the Solomon Islands, the defense of New Georgia—replete with the critical Munda airfield—collapsed in early August. Japanese forces in the central Solomons scrambled to withdraw to the heavily garrisoned Kolombangarra Island, but US forces bypassed it, and on August 6, the Japanese Navy lost three destroyers farther north, in the Battle of Vella Gulf. In New Guinea, overstretched supply lines left the troops suffering from malnutrition and disease; the Eighteenth Army was scrambling simply to maintain day-to-day operations, let alone prevent American and Australian landings behind its lines. The strongholds at Lae and Salamaua were isolated, and it was only a matter of time before they were abandoned.[67]

Against this backdrop, on August 11 Tojo made what was supposed to be a routine report to the Imperial Palace. Operations in the South Pacific were properly the subject of the Supreme Command's reports to the throne and were not on Tojo's agenda. Even so, the emperor revealed himself "deeply troubled" by the situation in the South Pacific and confided in Tojo, "Not once have [the armed services] defeated an enemy landing. At times, I ask Nagano [Osami] and Sugiyama [Hajime] where it will be possible to crush an enemy landing, but they seem to have no idea. What in the world will become of this war?"[68] Tojo staggered out of the meeting. Any complacency he might have felt at Japan's deteriorating war situation—any inclination to allow IGHQ the time it needed to iron out the real differences in operational outlook between the army and navy—disappeared that instant. He was going to ensure that, henceforth, operations and policy reflected the emperor's voice.

Returning to the Army Ministry, Tojo summoned his trusted subordinate, the Military Affairs Bureau director, Sato Kenryo. In a state of obvious agitation, he ordered Sato to "go ask the Supreme Command where in hell it plans to bury the enemy." Sato tried to explain the difficulties in planning the timing and locale of a decisive battle now that the United States had wrested all initiative in the Pacific. Tojo shouted back, "Where are we going to check the enemy's advance? That's all I want to know!" He then ordered Sato to open discussions with IGHQ and the Navy Ministry with a view to devising a defensive line that made grand strategic sense, incorporated the best of both political and operational planning, and provided a launching pad for a decisive counterattack that would "pulverize" enemy forces. He would take up the conversation with Sugiyama, to ensure unity among the Army Ministry and the General Staff. In this way, and at the emperor's behest, Tojo took the initiative in what otherwise would have been regarded as the Supreme Command's prerogative.[69]

Thus began planning for what an Imperial conference on September 30 called the "absolute defense perimeter." Forces fighting in the Solomon Islands and western New Guinea fell outside this perimeter; they had simply to engage the enemy for as long as possible in a holding operation to buy time for the establishment of a new, retracted line of defense. That line encompassed; the Kurileand Ogasawara Islands; the Mariana and Caroline Islands in the Central Pacific; western New Guinea; the Dutch East Indies, Malaya, Burma, and at least parts of India. So long as Japanese forces held this perimeter, the defense of the home islands against aerial attack, the defense of resource-rich Southeast Asia against enemy attack, and the defense of sea lanes connecting the two would be practically assured. The necessary first steps toward establishing the perimeter involved strengthening defenses—and particularly aerial defenses—in western New Guinea and also in the Caroline and Mariana Islands in the Central Pacific; some saw renewed scope for operations against Chiang Kai-shek in Chongqing.[70]

Tojo's contribution to the absolute defense perimeter took three forms. First, he insisted that the war had to be won (he refused to concede that it might be lost) in 1944. The timing he based on his reading of Japan's waning national strength. Problems were discernible everywhere. He told his cabinet in late August that labor shortages were critical. He had also to admit there was "no hope" of importing any more than 50 percent of

Japan's needs in steel and aluminum. Oil shortages remained a problem. Pre–Pearl Harbor expectations of oil flowing freely from the Dutch East Indies now seemed wildly optimistic, and all Tojo could suggest was a heightened focus on developing synthetic oil. He might not have said it in so many words, but Japan was being stretched beyond the limits of its war-making capacity. A decisive battle fought no later than the second half of 1944 was Japan's last, best hope. "We must," he told his cabinet on August 24, "win the war next year at any cost."[71]

Tojo's second contribution was to increase and tighten government control over what remained of Japan's national strength, with a view to maximizing the nation's war-making capacity. As he put it to his cabinet colleagues on September 21, it was necessary to ensure that the nation was "correctly poised for the decisive battle." Such a posture of preparedness, he explained, entailed converting "all Greater East Asian resources into combat materials," as well as a preparedness to put "all Japanese citizens into combat positions."[72] Here Tojo was bringing together the next-generation total war officer's concern with harnessing all available national strength and the hitherto elusive decisive battle so that he was envisioning a truly cataclysmic end to Japan's war in the Pacific.

So far as Tojo was concerned, preparing for a decisive battle involved more than the marshaling of human and material resources; it also involved increasing his own powers of stewardship over Japan's decision-making, governing, and administrative processes. He sought to "tighten" the relationship between the cabinet and IGHQ, with a view to increasing his own capacity to coordinate administrative and operational matters. He also sought the power to take "thorough measures" against anyone who threatened to "divide national opinion," as part of a larger attempt at establishing a unified "ideological" outlook among the Japanese public. And he sought maximum control over Japan's war-related industries—increasing airplane production remained his main priority—to which end he presented his cabinet in late September with a plan to amalgamate the Ministry of Commerce and Industry and the Cabinet Planning Board and to create instead a munitions ministry. Unsurprisingly, he intended to assume this new ministerial role.[73]

Tojo's third principal contribution to the absolute defense perimeter concept involved a concerted attempt at folding his Greater East Asian policies directly and explicitly into this latest iteration of his grand strategy. He fronted a plenary session of the House of Peers in mid-June and spoke of the ever-increasing levels of "trust" Greater East Asian "nations and peoples" placed in Japan, as well as the "sincerity" of their "voluntary co-operation" with Japan's "unyielding policy" of "freeing Greater East Asia forever from the Anglo-American yoke." In this context, he declared the proximity of Burmese independence; his government's intention to bestow the "honor of national independence" on the Philippines before the year was out (which he compared favorably to the "empty independence" the United States had earlier promised the Philippines); forthcoming measures to establish popular political participation in Borneo, Celebes, Java, Malaya, and Sumatra; and his own "heartfelt sympathy" for Indian independence.[74] In making these pronouncements Tojo was addressing both domestic and Greater East Asian audiences. Foremost in his mind was, however, his supposed Anglo-American audience. It was, he told his aides, a "big thing" to be able to use the Imperial Diet to broadcast his Greater East Asian policies; he supposed the impact of his speech equated to the "strength of about five divisions."[75] Seeking yet greater injections from what he consciously labeled "political strategy" (*seiryaku*)—as distinct from "military strategy" (*senryaku*)—he secured the cabinet's and IGHQ's agreement to a conference in Tokyo in early November that drew together leaders from Burma, China, India, Japan, Manchukuo, the Philippines, and Thailand.[76]

Tojo used the time available to him to lay the groundwork for the Greater East Asia conference. He met with Wang Jingwei in late September and produced a new Sino-Japanese treaty draft that promised to erase all the unequal provisions of the existing treaty. Notably, it provided for the withdrawal of Japanese troops following the establishment of peace and for the end of all Japan's "special interests" in Inner Mongolia and North China. This was largely the handiwork of Foreign Minister Shigemitsu Mamoru, and in keeping with the "new China policy" Tojo had pursued since late 1942, it was designed to bolster the Wang regime. Tojo's personal contribution took the form of an insistence that the Wang regime undertake peace maneuvers toward the Chiang government in Chongqing. Indeed, he saw the new treaty and peace overtures between Chongqing and Nanjing as two sides of the same coin. "Treaty revision ... will be concluded with the Nanjing government," Tojo told Wang on September 22, "and it is believed that this will cause Chongqing to lose the pretext of its war of resistance."[77] Tojo left subsequent negotiations concerning the draft treaty to the diplomats, and a Sino-Japanese treaty of alliance was concluded on October 30.

Tojo had met in the meantime with the Philippines leadership, including Benigno Aquino, José P. Laurel, and Jorge B. Vargas. This was the final preparatory step before the formal granting of Filipino independence, and Tojo sought to impress on his guests Japan's ardent desire for the "construction of a new Philippines." He took particular care to explain his vision of a Philippines that actively opted for the closest "political, military, diplomatic, and economic" embrace with Japan. Most immediately and concretely, he wanted to extract from them a declaration of war against the Anglo-American powers in return for independence. The Philippines leaders refused, offering only to afford Japan the use of military and naval facilities in prosecution of the war.[78] Tojo was nonplussed but pressed ahead, and the Philippine Republic was inaugurated on October 14, 1943.[79]

The groundwork for a Greater East Asian conference was thereby laid. Tojo was genuinely excited at the thought of playing host to a wide array of "guests" from across the region.[80] But, before he did so, an opportunity to settle an old score presented itself. Nakano Seigo was arrested on October 21 by the Special Higher Police. Recall that Nakano had published an opinion piece in January 1943 that was critical of Tojo's wartime leadership; Nakano had, in the meantime, made tentative contact with Konoe and various other anti-Tojo figures and involved himself in a nebulous plan to remove Tojo from power.[81] On the heels of Nakano's arrest, Tojo summoned Home Minister Ando Kisaburo, and Justice Minister Iwamura Michio, among others. Branding Nakano's actions "inexcusable," he said he wanted to "treat definitively" what he regarded as a "very serious problem."[82] Whatever Tojo's proclivities, the Special Higher Police were concerned at the lack of evidence against Nakano. They handed him over to the *kenpei* (military police), who extracted a confession. Nakano was released and on October 26 returned home, where he committed *seppuku* (ritual suicide) while under twenty-four-hour *kenpei* surveillance. People "everywhere" were talking about his death; most seemed to think the *kenpei* had demanded his suicide in return for guarantees of his family's safety.[83] Tojo was one of the very few people who did not want to talk about it; he received reports of Nakano's suicide on October 26 and then warned old friend Takamiya Taihei that conversation about Nakano would imperil their relationship.[84]

One other piece of business demanded Tojo's attention before he could devote his energies to the Greater East Asian conference. On October 31 he secured the Privy Council's approval to establish the Munitions Ministry. This was the final, formalized step in the process Tojo had begun several weeks earlier when he fronted his cabinet with a plan to increase munitions production—including especially aircraft—by amalgamating the Cabinet

Planning Board and the Ministry of Commerce and Industry. He explained directly to the emperor that he would henceforth serve not only as prime minister and army minister but also as munitions minister. The emperor shifted the conversation in a direction that, incidentally, signaled just how significantly Japan's war fortunes had deteriorated: Hirohito asked Tojo to pay "particular attention" to "aerial defenses."[85]

The Greater East Asia Conference met in the Imperial Diet Building on November 5–6, 1943. Invitees included Burmese Prime Minister Ba Maw; the Indian National Army commander, Subhas Chandra Bose; Philippines President José P. Laurel; Thailand's deputy prime minister, Prince Wan Waithayakon; the Nanjing regime's Wang Jingwei; and Manchukuoan Prime Minister Zhang Jinghui. This was, by Tojo's own design, a "historic moment," and he delighted in "his place in it."[86] He took "great pleasure" in delivering a formal address of welcome to his guests. He denounced the "scourge" of Anglo-American hegemony, which he contrasted with Japan's "righteous cause." That cause was animated by a "spirit of justice," relations of "brotherly amity," "respect" for Greater East Asia's "glorious traditions," and "close economic cooperation," as well as political, economic, and cultural contributions to worldwide "advancement."[87] These principles received further treatment in the Joint Declaration of the Greater East Asia Conference that Tojo's government and IGHQ had approved in advance and to which all conferees affixed their signatures on November 6.[88]

In mid-November Tojo made an overnight trip to Ise Grand Shrine. He petitioned the sun goddess Amaterasu (the mythical progenitor of the Imperial line and spiritual resident of this holiest Shinto site) for victory in the war, praying that his Greater East Asian policies would deflate enemy morale and that Japanese defenders in the South Pacific would prove able to hold their positions long enough to allow successful establishment of the absolute defense perimeter. He prayerfully acknowledged that this latter plank of his grand strategy had gotten off to a bad start, for Anglo-American forces had landed on Bougainville, making such inroads that he could only conclude the central Solomons were lost. He nonetheless pinned his hopes on the Rabaul garrison—replete with its 100,000 Japanese defenders and plentiful provisions, munitions, weapons, and supplies—which he presumed was the principal Anglo-American target in the South Pacific. There a bloodletting operation that bought valuable time presented itself as not only possible but likely.[89]

In late November the US Navy captured the Makin and Tarawa Atolls in the eastern Gilbert Islands. This was the first step in an altogether new American offensive through the Central Pacific, aimed at not only the Gilberts but also the Caroline, Mariana, and Marshall Islands. This new offensive quite neatly resembled decades-old war planning in both the US and Japanese navies—both of which had long since planned for a decisive fleet encounter in the Western Pacific after the US fleet steamed across the Central Pacific—but, most immediately, it served to isolate and neutralize Rabaul.

Tojo now confronted twin enemy offensives: one in the South Pacific, the other in the Central Pacific. Once again he was knocked completely off balance, and he began questioning his grand strategy. He still, to be sure, had good reason to hope for a decisive battle fought along the absolute defense perimeter. Aside from any other consideration, it should hopefully mean that the home islands remained outside the range of Pacific-based US bombers. It should also guard against the dreaded possibility that the war in the Pacific would drag on long after the European war had ended, freeing the Soviets to strike out against an emaciated and emasculated Kwantung Army. Even so, he professed to his army chief of staff, General Sugiyama Hajime, uncertainty as to whether a battle that "determined victory" was possible any longer. He insisted on devising a fallback option. "No matter how we do it," he told Sugiyama, "we must plan to perpetuate this war."[90] Tojo's grand strategy, which had undergone several drastic changes during the course of this fateful year, was on a knife's edge.

13
TOJO OVERWHELMED
JANUARY–JULY 1944

TOJO HIDEKI GREETED THE New Year of 1944 with his customary ablutions and prayers at Meiji and Yasukuni Shrines. On January 6 he returned to Ise Grand Shrine, where he repeated his earlier prayers to the sun goddess Amaterasu for success in the Greater East Asian War. He returned to Meiji and Yasukuni Shrines on January 8 and again on January 21. There was an immediacy, even urgency, to his prayers; ultimate success in the war required that Japan's garrisons outside the absolute defense perimeter hold out long enough to allow both a peak in Tojo's crash-course aircraft production program and the completion of preparations inside the perimeter for a massive and decisive counterattack.[1]

Tojo was also preparing for at least the possibility that the enemy would pierce the absolute defense perimeter and attack the home islands. On January 7 he secured the emperor's approval of an enforcement order that sought to bolster Japan's aerial defenses, delineating these defenses the responsibility of military commanders and naval district commanders. The order also established a system whereby these commanders would present prefectural governors with air defense plans. Beyond fighter jets, the plans ran the gamut of surveillance, communication, alarms, light control, dispersion and evacuation, conversion, disguise, firefighting, fire prevention, evacuation, rescue, quarantine, distribution of emergency supplies, and emergency restoration. Tojo was paving the way for the armed services' ever deeper intrusion into not just prefectural politics but everyday life.[2]

Public sentiment was not, however, in lockstep with Tojo. Liberal critic Kiyosawa Kiyoshi confided in his diary that "everything" seemed "extremely grim." The Tojo cabinet had appropriated "legal dictatorial power" and instigated the "regulation of everything." The result was a "stillness like death." "Anxiety about the future of the war" was discernible everywhere, yet because the newspapers were practicing self-censorship, actual knowledge of the war situation was scarce. The "problem of food supplies" was inescapable, and black marketeers were profiting handsomely. No one could discern a "way to improve conditions." Tojo himself seemed unable to explain the war and its privations in such a way that made it all seem worthwhile, and Kiyosawa wrote caustically of Tojo's unwillingness or inability to speak about "postwar arrangements and a new order."[3]

Against such a backdrop, in late January Tojo fronted the Imperial Diet. He met with an unaccustomed silence as he approached the podium; despair hung in the air, and Diet members did not applaud him.[4] He nonetheless cut a confident figure as he spoke about his grand strategy. He acknowledged the increased pace and intensity of the Anglo-American counterattack in the Pacific Ocean region. He also allowed that Japan's sea-lanes of communication were under sustained assault. He nonetheless insisted that US productive capacity had long since reached "saturation point" and was now beset by "material and labor issues"; he added that Britain was "exhausted." By contrast, Japan's airplane production was "rising rapidly," and he now awaited a "good opportunity" to "deal the enemy a blow" by means of a "strategy of furious attack." He called on the "resolve" of Japan's "one hundred million" to continue to cooperate with the "augmentation" of the nation's "air power" in particular. The government would take all necessary steps in preparation for a "decisive battle," which he predicted would be fought that coming autumn. He explained that the enemy, who sought to avoid a war of attrition and was overly anxious to continue its counteroffensive, would trip itself up and thereby create chances for Japan's armed services to exploit. Japan had to use whatever time was available to continue to augment its "material and spiritual" strength (and, especially, air power) and had to launch a massive autumn offensive that would "bring the enemy to his knees."[5]

All the while, Tojo was engaged in a bruising battle with Imperial General Headquarters (IGHQ) concerning shipping needs. He had in late 1943 forecast monthly losses of 70,500 tons of shipping to enemy airplane and submarine attack and saw no need to augment the armed services' existing allocations. Actual losses far outstripped those estimates—290,140 tons in December 1943, and 420,950 tons in January 1944—and Tojo was in the unenviable position of having to block IGHQ's incessant demands for more ship bottoms. His position had changed little since the Guadalcanal campaign; the armed services' operational and logistical needs had necessarily to be balanced against the needs of the merchant marine and the national wartime economy.[6]

The enemy stepped up the pace in the Pacific. Anglo-American forces landed on January 31 on Bougainville, the largest of the Solomon Islands. This was hardly cause for optimism, but Tojo and others breathed a sigh of relief, for this at least seemed to signify an indefinite pause to the US fleet's drive through the Central Pacific.[7] How wrong they were. In late January the US Navy began moving against the Marshall Islands. The undefended Majuro Atoll fell on January 31; Tojo consoled himself with the thought that it was better to "anticipate" and dispatch forces ahead of time to the "point of encounter" so that those forces could prepare themselves to "attack the enemy."[8] He looked ahead to the fighting on the well-defended Kwajalein Atoll, but it fell barely one week later, ending in another rash of *gyokusai* (suicidal tactics) in which Kwajalein's eight thousand defenders died, almost to the very last man.

The lack of air cover available to Kwajalein's defenders had sealed their fate. This brought back into sharp focus the widely acknowledged need for more aircraft and set the Imperial Japanese Army and Imperial Japanese Navy against each other. Arguments arose because of wildly optimistic forecasting: In September 1943 the government had forecast production of 50,500 aircraft but later reduced the number to forty thousand. On the basis of the initial forecast, the armed services had agreed on what they considered equitable allocations of aluminum and other materials needed to produce their own aircraft, but they very nearly came to blows over the question of how best to divide the materials after the quantities had been reduced.[9] The split was so rancorous that Tojo wondered whether it would result ultimately in either the resignations of the chiefs of staff or the downfall of his cabinet. He prevailed on Navy Minister Shimada Shigetaro to join him on February 8 in a prayerful visit to Meiji and Yasukuni Shrines; two days later he met in the Imperial Palace with Admiral Nagano Osami, Shimada, and General Sugiyama Hajime.[10] The two admirals argued for the prioritization of the navy's air arm, insisting that the army alone absorb the reduction in materiel. Staring them down, Tojo secured their agreement to a more equitable distribution of airplane materiel, then boasted later to his secretaries that it had been "very easy."[11]

Forging that consensus might have been easy, but concerns with Tojo's leadership were discernible everywhere. Some in the army had taken to referring to him as Private Tojo (consciously or otherwise echoing an insult Ishiwara Kanji had coined when serving beneath Tojo in Manchukuo).[12] Even the almost embarrassingly servile Imperial Rule Assistance Political

Organization Council was calling—if only behind closed doors—for the Tojo cabinet's resignation.[13] Navy officers looked at the cabinet through the prism of the traditional army-navy rivalry, overtly conscious of the fact that their service's proudest political moments usually hinged on opposition to the army (as when, for instance, the navy in the late 1930s had opposed the army's enthusiasm for a military alliance with Nazi Germany). Many, including the Combined Fleet commander in chief, Admiral Koga Mineichi, were convinced that Shimada was too deferential to Tojo and "unfit" to continue representing the navy in the cabinet. Some went so far as to hope the service would find a new minister who would "oppose" Tojo and "destroy" his cabinet.[14]

On February 17 and 18, the enemy launched a devastatingly destructive two-day aerial assault against the prized naval base in Truk Atoll in the Caroline Islands. Forty-nine ships were either sunk or damaged, 270 airplanes were destroyed, and two thousand tons of installations (including oil tanks) sustained irreparable damage.[15] The Combined Fleet abandoned Truk for the relative safety of the Palau Islands, which severed Rabaul from all support and rendered hopeless its remaining defenses. At the same time, IGHQ ordered divisions be pulled from the Kwantung Army in Manchukuo and transferred to the Pacific. Tojo retreated ever deeper into the spiritual aspect of Japan's war. "No matter what difficulties we encounter," he said to his secretaries and aides, "our innermost hearts must not falter." He ordered them to be "more and more determined" in whatever they did. He even conceived of the war ending in national suicide. "We must," he said on February 18, "be prepared to cut short the enemy's life by cutting off our own legs, or by cutting our own stomach."[16]

THE MILITARY AFFAIRS BUREAU director, Lieutenant General Sato Kenryo, approached Tojo late on the night of February 18. "We just can't keep this up," he said. He suggested "abandoning" the absolute defense sphere and concentrating strength in the Philippines with the intention of fighting a "last-ditch, do-or-die decisive battle." Tojo was intrigued by a decisive battle fought in the Philippines, and he spoke of the need to begin focusing immediately on fortifying the "rear," including the home islands, Okinawa, and Taiwan. The politician in him nonetheless foresaw problems with forsaking the absolute defense sphere less than six months after its inception. The Supreme Command seemed unlikely to acquiesce in any such about-face, and Tojo looked ahead with a mixture of weariness and trepidation at the likelihood of long arguments between IGHQ and the government, and also between the armed services. Sato pressed his case, insisting that a "peace offensive" would be possible if only Japanese forces could "crush" the Americans in the Philippines. Tojo made no attempt to hide his attraction to the idea of a decisive battle in the Philippines, but he ordered Sato to drop any mention of a "peace offensive."[17]

Sato's suggestions gave Tojo a renewed sense of purpose. He saw in a decisive battle in the Philippines at least the kernel of a strategy that allowed for something other than one battlefield defeat after another. That approach had, however, to move beyond the purely strategic considerations animating IGHQ and necessarily had to incorporate calculations of overall national power. Herein, for Tojo, lay the root cause of his incessant, debilitating fights with the Supreme Command since at least the Guadalcanal campaign. He now decided to short-circuit those arguments by combining in his own person the hitherto distinct and separate positions of army minister and army chief of staff. He intended to remain as prime minister, army minister, and munitions minister; he also hoped to lessen army-navy squabbling by convincing Shimada to serve concurrently as navy minister and navy chief of staff. The idea shattered precedent and was arguably unconstitutional, but, at least so far as Tojo was concerned, hardly new. Recall Tojo, as a War College instructor in the early 1920s, lecturing that the Supreme Command and the cabinet could not remain independent of each other in the crucible of total war. Expecting opposition, he figured he needed the emperor's imprimatur. Late on the night of February 18, he floated the idea with Lord Keeper of the Privy Seal Kido Koichi.[18] The following day he presented it directly to a discomfited emperor, who asked Tojo repeatedly whether he intended for operational considerations to remain "distinct" from state policy. Hirohito was asking, in effect, whether and how Tojo intended to remain within constitutional confines. Anticipating this line of questioning, Tojo had devised a way to reassure the emperor of his intention to guard against IGHQ's operational concerns overwhelming the government's decision-making processes. He emphasized his intention to strengthen the cabinet, partly by means of a reshuffle but, more important, by holding all cabinet meetings in the Imperial Palace. He explained the move in terms of the ideal of "direct Imperial rule," which, he said, would ensure that "politics kept pace with operations in the current war situation."[19]

In his explanations to the emperor, Tojo chose not to acknowledge two causes of complaint among his contemporaries. The first was expressed succinctly by liberal journalist Kiyosawa Kiyoshi. "Conducting cabinet meetings at the palace," Kiyosawa wrote, was Tojo's way of remaining "hidden behind his majesty the emperor." Tojo had long since stifled public debate; Kiyosawa now saw Tojo seeking to snuff it out entirely, as he could claim his policies owed to the "benevolence of the emperor."[20] The second concern related to the wide-ranging powers Tojo was accumulating, something that disconcerted even his professional military colleagues. When the army's "big three" met on February 19, General Sugiyama refused to resign and received willing support from the inspector general of military training, Yamada Otozo. Both expressed dismay at Tojo's willingness to dispense with "tradition." Sugiyama went to the emperor with his concern lest Tojo establish a modern-day shogunate and concentrate power in his own hands at the direct expense of the emperor's prerogatives.[21] A similar situation played out in the navy, although opposition among the admirals centered on a knee-jerk insistence that the service must not follow blindly in the army's footsteps. This dovetailed neatly with widespread disgust at Shimada for being little more than Tojo's pawn.[22] Tojo's plan nonetheless prevailed; he and Shimada were formally appointed to their respective chief of staff roles on February 21.[23]

Coinciding with Tojo's latest appointment was the enemy's capture of Eniwetok Island. The Marshall Islands were now for all intents and purposes in enemy hands, even though the Americans had bypassed four atolls—Jaluit, Maloelap, Mili, and Wotje—on which the Japanese armed services had built airfields. These isolated atolls were as good as lost, but Tojo put on a brave face. "There will come a time," he insisted, "when we strike back and catch the enemy off guard." When that time arrived, he said, having bases "behind" enemy lines would prove advantageous and enable a "pincer attack."[24]

Less than forty-eight hours later, some two hundred US bombers raided the Mariana Islands, including Guam, Saipan, and Tinian. Japanese defenses were woefully inadequate, and the recently deployed First Carrier Division lost ninety of its ninety-three airplanes.[25] The admirals began worrying about an attack within as little as a week on the Ogasawara Islands in what would amount to a fast-track approach to the home islands.[26] Not entirely coincidentally, one of the nation's largest daily newspapers—*Tokyo Nichinichi Shimbun*—carried a frontpage headline, "We Can't Make Do with Bamboo Spears." Authored by naval journalist Shinmyo Takeo, the article warned that the nation faced "ruination" unless there were an immediate effort at bolstering the navy's air arm. It excoriated Tojo's ever-increasing emphasis on the Japanese people's martial spirit and reopened the divisive debate between the armed services over aircraft allocations. Tojo was incensed.[27] He nonetheless avoided a repeat of Nakano Seigo's martyrdom. There were no arrests, and the *kenpei* (military police) remained at arm's length. Instead the nearsighted thirty-seven-year-old Shinmyo was conscripted into the Japanese Army.[28]

Tojo wanted Shinmyo sent to a suitably dangerous battlefront, but the admirals pushed back hard against his conscription. Tojo chose not to dwell on the situation.[29] Weightier issues, including the all-important question of "how future policies and strategies ought to be implemented," demanded his attention. Most pressing was the need, as Tojo saw it, to upend the Army General Staff's planning practices. He was critical of his predecessor for having allowed himself to be "dragged along" by his lower- and middle-echelon subordinates, and he tried instead to usher in a "top-down" approach. He made clear to his subordinates that he would welcome their input, but he insisted that he himself would ultimately "clarify" decisions and positions. Once he had done so, he would tolerate no further debate.[30] Tojo's approach divided staff officers: some grumbled at his "bureaucratization" of staff planning, while others celebrated the efficiency he brought to the General Staff.[31]

Tojo's first major operational decision concerned the launch of the so-called Imphal operation. Long championed by the Fifteenth Army in Burma, the operation included among its objectives the seizure of India's Imphal area and installation there of the Free India Provisional Government. Tojo was intrigued by the possibility that Subhas Chandra Bose might capture Indian hearts and minds and undermine British colonial rule across the subcontinent—in January Tojo had given the operation his endorsement from, of all places, his household bathtub—but he continued to nurse concerns at what he rightly regarded as the slim chance of military success in Imphal. This ambivalence suggested treading carefully, which Tojo might have done but for two key factors. For one thing, Tojo was desperate for battlefield success somewhere. For another, in January Sugiyama had already received the emperor's sanction for the Imphal operation. Tojo had long since been unalterably opposed to changing anything on which the emperor had decided—he had brought down the cabinet of Prime Minister Konoe Fumimaro in October 1941 because it sought to overturn a deadline for war that an Imperial Conference had sanctified—and he was not about to start impugning his emperor's decisions now. He decided instead to scale back the operation.[32]

Tojo made another pilgrimage on March 11 to Ise Grand Shrine, again petitioning the sun goddess for success in the Greater East Asia War. He almost certainly included prayers for the success of the Imphal operation.[33] Well he might have. At least one of his subordinates on the General Staff had established contact with his old political nemesis, Konoe. Scathing in his assessment of Tojo's war leadership, Lieutenant General Sakai Koji condemned Tojo for having no strategy other than a fight "to the last soldier," which would leave Japan in a state of virtual "extinction" (*mestubo*).[34]

After Tojo's return from his pilgrimage, his subordinates on the General Staff presented him with a study that made the case for a decisive battle, fought within a few weeks, in and around the Philippines. The study implicitly acknowledged the need to dispense with the absolute national defense sphere, not yet twelve months old, that now lay in tatters. The Marshall and eastern Caroline Islands were now utterly "defenseless"—indeed, lost. So, too, was Rabaul. This owed primarily to "miscalculations" about the speed and strength of the enemy drive through the Pacific.[35]

There was now an immediate and pressing need to prepare for a "decisive battle" against the United States. This could not be a static war of defense but must instead comprise highly mobile operations fought in the Central and Southwest Pacific and in the Philippines, and it had necessarily to be fought the coming summer. Two factors informed this stringent timeline. First, Japan's "national strength" was in a state of decline; although Tojo had artificially ramped up aircraft production by diverting materials from other sectors, that program would end in August, and Japan's productive capacity thereafter would fall into precipitous decline. Second, German defeat now seemed a near certainty. Not only had the Soviet Red Army long since turned the tide, but a second Anglo-American front in western Europe was imminent. Even as the European war neared its endgame, the expiration in April 1945 of the Japanese-Soviet Neutrality Pact loomed, and Soviet entry into the war against an enfeebled Kwantung Army appeared certain in the not-too-distant future.[36]

The staff officers' study was sobering, but Tojo took heart from it, as it echoed Sato's call for a decisive battle in the Philippines and also included maritime operations, adding a depth and mobility that appealed to Tojo. Besides, the presumption of interservice unity in defense of a zone covering the western Carolines, Dutch New Guinea, the Marianas, and the Philippines would hopefully go a long way toward addressing what had become one of the emperor's key concerns: the ineffectiveness of existing army-navy efforts at cooperation. Tojo believed he now had a viable exit strategy. The study enabled him to see the long string of battlefield losses since Midway and Guadalcanal as part of a wider grand strategy in which the men on the front lines had given their lives to grind down the enemy even as it drew closer to the bulk of Japanese forces and the chief point of Japanese resistance in the western Caroline Islands, Dutch New Guinea, the Marianas, and the Philippines. Japanese defenses in the Pacific had not, in this view, irreparably cracked but instead had stretched like a rubber band. Buoyed by such thoughts, Tojo went public with a fresh round of exultations in the "Japanese spirit," which he equated with "taking the enemy's life" after having had one's own torso cut.[37]

Tojo remained confident that such pronouncements continued to inspire the Japanese people. "The people will follow along," he boasted, "even if I insist that a red thing is white."[38] The word on the proverbial street might have warned against such hubris. The pressure of the food shortage was now acute, and nobody had a "full stomach." Tojo himself seemed not yet to recognize it, but ever-lessening food rations was leading to one of his great fears, a diminution of morale on the home front. "If it comes to this," some hungry folks were reported to have said in response to the tightening of rice requisition quotas, "please stop the war!" The government sloganeered—"Control hoarding!" and "Obliterate the black market!"—but it seemed utterly bereft of ideas that might alleviate the people's hunger. Instead it sought to control public discourse. Thought police "swarmed" about, and people feared being "cruelly abused" by the *kenpei*. Again, Tojo might not have recognized it, but this had precisely the opposite effect for which he had hoped, and "animosity" toward him "spread in every quarter."[39]

Anti-Tojo sentiment had begun to reach into the innermost reaches of the Imperial Palace. The emperor and empress were joined on March 14, 1944, by Prince Takamatsu Nobuhito and his wife, Princess Kikuko. They watched a prerelease screening of a Morinaga Kenjiro documentary, *Tenkan kojo* (Converted factory), before the prince spoke with his elder brother about the absence of "hope" in Tojo's war leadership. He suggested that retired Lieutenant General Yanagawa Heisuke might succeed Tojo as prime minister, and Lieutenant General Anami Korechika might replace him as army minister. The emperor took up the conversation with his political fixer, Kido Koichi. He focused little on the question of "hope" in Tojo, nor did he dwell on how Tojo might be removed from power. Instead he launched into a blistering assessment of Yanagawa's character, recalling how he was forcibly retired from the army's active service owing to his support for the mutineers in the February 26 Incident of 1936. To make himself perfectly clear, Hirohito told Kido of his aversion to any plan "predicated" on a resuscitation of the abhorrent "factionalism" that had riven the army in the early and mid-1930s.[40]

Kido admonished Konoe, whom he suspected of hatching the plot to replace Tojo with Yanagawa. Konoe, as we have seen, had long since joined with Prince Takamatsu in despairing of Tojo's leadership; he had, in the meantime, continued in his fascination with reviving and resuscitating Tojo's old factional enemies, including not just Yanagawa but also General Masaki Jinzaburo and Lieutenant General Obata Toshiro. The *kodoha* (Imperial way) generals had all, like Yanagawa, been pushed into retirement following the February 26 Incident; they were now animated by a bizarre conspiracy theory according to which Tojo was enacting a long dormant plan—originally drafted by Tojo's assassinated friend and mentor, Nagata Tetsuzan—for a ruinous "fifty-year war." Whatever Konoe made of Nagata's posthumous influence over Tojo, he was haunted by the specter of a fifth column in the army that aimed to prolong the war and deepen the associated destruction and dislocation so as to lay the groundwork for both a communist revolution and an end to Japan's Imperial line. He thought the Imperial way generals might prove useful in checking Tojo and containing any fifth column in the army. Kido thought otherwise. He told Konoe of the emperor's refusal to countenance a revival of the Imperial way generals, speculating that the entire episode would have the "opposite effect" of what Konoe had intended. In other words, the emperor's fear of the mutinous Imperial way generals would lead him back to Tojo, who, whatever his faults, had at least proved capable of imposing order on the army.[41]

Kido seems to have at least partly misread Hirohito. He was correct in his understanding of the emperor's aversion to the Imperial way generals but, contrary to Kido's expectations, their mention did not cause the emperor to retreat behind Tojo. Indeed, the emperor spoke in late March with his chief aide-de-camp, General Hasunuma Shigeru, of his concern at the "worsening" war situation and regular pronouncements that Japan simply had to "do its best" and somehow "make it through." He openly wondered how Japan could possibly begin to rebuild after the war if it fought "to the last ditch," and he questioned whether the government was giving "adequate thought" to how to end the war.[42] Hirohito understood this required a decisive battle fought somewhere in the Pacific, which he hoped would lead to a negotiated peace. Yet, ever since Midway, the armed services had actively avoided any such decisive battle, repeatedly withdrawing behind retracting lines of defense. The emperor was now beginning to wonder whether Tojo was leading the nation into a ruinous fight to the finish against an imposingly powerful enemy.[43]

TOJO BUSIED HIMSELF OVER the subsequent weeks as he sought to wrest back the initiative in the Pacific. He designated the Philippines the "core" of what he now called the "absolute southern sphere." He ordered the Southern Expeditionary Army commander, Terauchi Hisaichi, to relocate his headquarters to Manila (recall that Terauchi's father had been part of the Choshu cabal that had chased Tojo's father out of the army, so it is not surprising that Tojo took great personal pleasure in overriding Terauchi's shrill objections), and he placed all military forces in the south under Terauchi's command. Tojo reckoned fighting in the Philippines would begin by late July, and he scheduled delivery of four air divisions to Manila before then. The anticipated decisive battle would in this way capitalize on another of Tojo's initiatives—namely, aircraft production. The decisive battle zone would also cover the western Caroline and the Mariana Islands, primarily the navy's responsibility, and Tojo agreed to move shipping from the waters around New Guinea to the Central Pacific. He ordered divisions and detachments to Guam, Saipan, and Truk. He also placed the recently activated Thirty-First Army, which included garrison forces on Guam and Saipan, under the Japanese Navy's command. He began bolstering defenses to the rear of the Carolines-Marianas-Philippines axis, with a particular focus on the Ryukyu Islands and Taiwan. Finally, in acknowledgment of the grim possibility whereby the enemy cut the sea-lanes connecting the Philippines to the Japanese home islands, Tojo ordered Terauchi to prepare to continue independently of IGHQ with a protracted war of attrition.[44]

The enemy scuttled Tojo's plans even as he was laying them. Amphibious enemy landings on the weakly defended Admiralty Islands, off New Guinea's north coast, utterly neutralized eastern New Guinea. Then, in late March, the enemy launched air raids against Hollandia in Dutch New Guinea. When it fell a few weeks later, Tojo admitted that Japanese defenders could not possibly hold Biak and Sarmi (farther west of Hollandia), but he insisted the westernmost end of Dutch New Guinea was defensible. Left unstated, but no doubt understood, was the absolute need to hold that westernmost end so as to deny the enemy that stepping stone to the Philippines.[45]

Also in late March, enemy forces resumed the drive through the Central Pacific with a series of highly destructive aerial assaults against the Combined Fleet's main bastion in the Palau Islands, in the western Carolines. The Combined Fleet commander in chief, Admiral Koga Mineichi, quickly abandoned the Palaus—having only weeks earlier abandoned Truk—as his easternmost base in the Central Pacific. This action protected the Combined Fleet but came at a cost. Koga died when his plane crashed enroute to Davao in the Philippines. The navy lost approximately 150 airplanes and seven oil tankers, and in mid-April confronted Tojo with a demand for more tankers if it were to engage the enemy fleet in the Mariana Islands. Tojo, however, was still hopeful that the Combined Fleet might engage the enemy farther east. He still anticipated a US invasion of Truk and believed the navy would fight to hold it.[46]

Tojo worked also to bolster Filipinos' fidelity to the cause. He spoke with a visiting Philippine delegation in late April, seeking to "encourage and inspire" them with talk of "Oriental pride" and "Oriental spirit." He sought to impress on the delegation his unshakable faith in victory and, looking to the postwar future, spoke of Manchukuo as providing a model for Philippine development. Whether the Manchukuo model inspired his guests is uncertain; they nonetheless must have wondered at Tojo's silence on the Joint Declaration of the Greater East Asia Conference, which was not yet twelve months old.[47]

The Philippines was not Tojo's only concern. He also worried that the enemy might take the Marianas and use them as a stepping stone toward the Bonin and Ogasawara Islands and Japan. He was also aware that airfields on Saipan would put the Japanese home islands within range of America's new, long-range B-29 bombers. He worried about the political impact should Tokyo come under sustained aerial attack. He assigned Tokyo's aerial defenses to the Tenth Aerial Division, instructing Division Commander Yoshida Kihachiro to prepare to defend the skies above Tokyo even at the cost of his own life.[48]

Tojo had also to reckon with the possibility of Tokyo coming under aerial attack by US bombers flying from airfields in China. This concern became apparent as early as January 1944, when staff officers raised with Tojo (then in his ministerial capacity) plans for a massive campaign codenamed Operation Ichigo, which promised to pry open an overland route from North China all the way to Indochina. "What is the actual, ultimate goal?" Tojo had demanded. He had only offered his ministerial assent on the understanding that knocking American airfields out of China was Op-

Tojo studies Tokyo's aerial defenses, November 27, 1943.

eration Ichigo's sole "operational objective." The emperor had also given his approval to the operation. In a virtual repeat of the Imphal campaign, Tojo as army chief of staff would not rescind something that had received Imperial sanction. He did, however, insist that Operation Ichigo aim only at the destruction of American airfields to the east of the Canton-Hankow Railway. This would protect the home islands and also supposedly the sea-lanes of communication connecting Japan to Southeast Asia.[49]

SHIMADA, TOJO, AND THEIR immediate subordinates in IGHQ met in the emperor's presence on May 2. They aimed to decide on a fresh grand strategy based on an unheralded degree of army-navy cooperation that would "crush the brunt of the enemy's attack" and "turn around" an increasingly bleak war situation. Tojo learned, to his chagrin, that the navy regarded Truk as "unavoidably" lost. Various other points of contention arose; agreement was nonetheless readily forthcoming on three essential points. First, enemy advances in both the Central and Southwest Pacific were converging on the Philippines. Second, the enemy would launch aerial attacks against the home islands and Southeast Asia as soon as it was able. Third, Japanese forces had to secure what Tojo and the generals now called the Imperial national defense sphere while at the same time preparing for a "decisive battle" encompassing the Caroline and Mariana Islands, Dutch New Guinea, and the Philippines. That battle would involve fleet operations to the east of the Philippines, in the Mariana and western Caroline Islands. Army air forces would cooperate with and contribute to naval operations, while troops would defend their island bases and airfields against attack. Meanwhile, the army would hold the western end of Dutch New Guinea by defending a line that extended from Geelvink Bay to Manokwari to Solong to Halmahera. It would also take all US airfields in eastern China, thereby guarding against aerial attacks on the home islands, Southeast Asia, and the sea-lanes connecting the two.[50]

Whatever sense of purpose Tojo took from this new grand strategy was quickly punctured by bad tidings from the Imphal operation. In early May Tojo had dispatched his vice chief of staff, Lieutenant General Hata Hikosaburo, to the continent to observe the Imphal campaign. Hata returned to Tokyo in mid-May and informed Tojo and others in IGHQ that the operational outlook was "extremely challenging." The Fifteenth Army was within sight of Imphal but was running critically short on ammunition, supplies, and food. Recalling his ambivalence about the Imphal operation, Tojo's emotions churned. He screamed at Hata and humiliated him by criticizing his weakness. He demanded a fight "to the end." On Tojo's insistence, and against the better judgment of practically everyone in Tokyo, IGHQ continued throughout May to urge the Fifteenth Army to fight against the odds, relying on its determination and fighting spirit.[51]

At about the same time as he was shouting down Hata, Tojo confronted criticisms from the emperor's younger brother, Prince Chichibu Yasuhito. The prince, who had risen to the army's general rank, raised with Tojo his concern that the nation was hurtling, "planned or unplanned," toward ruinous defeat. He expressed dismay at Tojo's having dispensed with the independence of the Supreme Command and questioned whether "political change" might be necessary to bring about a change in Japan's war fortunes. Tojo assured Prince Chichibu that he, in both his ministerial and command capacities, remained mindful of and faithful to the emperor's prerogatives. Then, to end the debate, he added he was answerable to nobody but his emperor, and if Hirohito believed that his loyalty was in some way "lacking," Tojo would atone for such a sin of omission by "disemboweling" himself before the emperor.[52]

Tojo's profession of loyalty to the emperor was nearly visceral. This must have been expected. He was now, however, *using* his fidelity to the emperor and the emperor's trust in him. His relationship with his emperor had become something akin to a talisman to protect himself from criticism, questioning, and political attacks. This dynamic was discernible even to outside observers. Liberal journalist Kiyosawa Kiyoshi was not privy to the exchange between Prince Chichibu and Tojo, but he had some weeks earlier noted, at least to himself, that Tojo was "trying to hide behind the august name of the emperor."[53]

Tojo's reliance on the emperor for his political survival presupposed the Imperial Palace's ongoing and unreserved support. That was no longer assured. Lord Keeper of the Privy Seal Kido Koichi, who had recommended Tojo's prime ministerial appointment in October 1941, had begun considering at least the possibility of a cabinet headed by someone other than Tojo. He consulted in mid-March with Admiral Yonai Mitsumasa about Generals Koiso Kuniaki, Terauchi Hisaichi, and Umezu Yoshijiro as possible prime ministerial successors.[54] Little over one month later, Kido "lambasted" Tojo for having repeatedly taken action too hastily and on the basis of "inadequate deliberation."[55] Tojo responded as only he could: He placed Kido's personal secretary, Matsudaira Yasumasa, under *kenpei* surveillance. (Some speculate that the *kenpei* even tapped Kido's phone.)[56]

Then, on May 18, IGHQ began receiving reports of enemy submarine activity in the waters around Saipan. Tojo barely blinked. "Technology alone does not win wars," he uttered with a certitude that must have struck those around him as at least slightly misplaced. His audience's reaction mattered little to Tojo, who again took cover behind the emperor. Victory, he insisted, was practically assured by the nation's "unique spirit of command," with the emperor at the apex as "supreme commander."[57] Tojo conveyed to the Navy General Staff his unshakable confidence in Saipan's defenses.[58] As if to knock Japanese forces completely off balance, US forces next landed, on May 27, on the island of Biak to the north of Dutch New Guinea. Biak's airfield would provide the Americans with control of the skies over much of New Guinea, and IGHQ decided on "emergency measures" to retake the island.[59] Shimada and Tojo duly reported these measures to the emperor.[60] A perturbed emperor spoke with Kido, who in turn suggested to Tojo that he consider resigning. Tojo, raising the stakes, announced his refusal to resign so long as he retained his emperor's "confidence."[61] Kido backed down. The emperor was wavering, but Kido could not—yet—be certain the emperor had forsaken Tojo.

Into this situation stepped former prime minister and retired admiral Okada Keisuke. He had connected with—indeed, had come to lead—anti-

Shimada and anti-Tojo sentiment within the navy. As Okada saw it, Shimada had adopted a posture of "blind obedience" to Tojo and the army. This meant the navy was "not fulfilling" its "responsibilities" in the decision-making process. It was neither "saying what it should say" nor "demanding what it should demand." Okada insisted that the decision-making process was dysfunctional and would remain so unless and until the navy "stood its ground" and "spoke from the gut" in dealing with Tojo and the army. This Shimada could not do, and Okada sought the admiral's resignation as both navy minister and navy chief of staff. Implicit in Okada's plan was the expectation that Shimada's ministerial successor would eventually cause such a deep rift as to compel Tojo's resignation. The main complication was the absence of admirals on active service who could conceivably stand up to Tojo, and Okada sought the restoration to active service of retired admirals Suetsugu Nobumasa and Yonai Mitsumasa so that they could serve respectively as navy chief of staff and navy minister. Yonai was the linchpin: In the late 1930s he had blocked the army in its enthusiasm for an alliance with Nazi Germany, and Okada now expected him to remain impervious to anything Tojo and the army threw at him. That Yonai enjoyed the emperor's implicit trust was certainly not lost on Okada.[62]

Okada's plan was masterful. It steered the narrative away from Tojo and the question of the emperor's trust in him. Shimada was the immediate issue. It was time, Okada explained on June 4 to naval elder Prince Fushimi Hiroyasu, to "despoil" (*kizumono ni suru*) Shimada of his twin positions atop the navy. Okada spoke on June 6 with Kido, and Prince Takamatsu, too, was brought into the anti-Shimada camp's confidences.[63] Kido took the case for Shimada's removal to Tojo's secretary, Colonel Akamatsu Sadao, on June 8. In a classic case of shooting the messenger, a visibly angered Tojo rebuked Akamatsu when the latter relayed Kido's message.[64]

Japan's fast-disappearing prospects of anything but crushing wartime defeat added urgency to Okada's efforts. An unsettled emperor learned on June 6 from Vice Admiral Nakamura Toshihisa that Anglo-American forces had opened a long-awaited second front in Europe.[65] Germany's fate seemed sealed, raising at least the likelihood that Japan would sooner or later be left fighting singlehandedly against not only the Anglo-American powers but also the Soviets. Such thoughts were enormously unsettling, but of far more immediate concern were reports in early June of a US Naval Task Force comprising over five hundred combat ships and transports carrying many more than 100,000 men setting course for the Marianas. Landings on Saipan began on June 15. Tojo had repeatedly declared Saipan defensible, and when he first received reports of US landings there, he insisted there was no need for "any fear at all."[66]

The emperor did not share Tojo's sentiment. As soon as he learned of the Saipan landings, he summoned Kido and conveyed how "acutely aware" he was of the "gravity of the situation." He sought updates later the same day from his staff officers, including Shimada and Army Vice Chief of Staff Ushiroku Jun. That afternoon, as if to offer a glimpse of what to expect if Saipan's defenses did not hold, enemy aircraft were sighted in the skies above the Ogasawara Islands. An attack on Tokyo did not eventuate, but the government's air raid warning system raised the alarm, and the emperor endured a sleepless night as he fretted over Saipan's fate, the likelihood of an unending string of air raids, and the future of Japan's war.[67]

Tojo remained confident that Saipan would hold. On June 16 he ordered the Thirty-First Army commander, Obata Hideyoshi, to "leave no stone unturned" in defending Saipan against the invading US troops.[68] That same day he reported to the emperor regarding his intention to send more troops, weapons, and ammunition to Saipan. In the report he noted a need also to bolster aerial defenses in and around the Marianas.[69] Emerging from the Imperial Palace, Tojo was confronted almost immediately by news of a US air raid against the Yahata Steel Works in Kyushu. Launched from airfields in China, the raid indicated that Tojo's hopes for Operation Ichigo remained unfulfilled and that US airfields in China were indeed a threat. Tojo acknowledged the impossibility of ignoring an aerial attack on the home islands, but he refused to accept that this was a fateful moment. "There is nothing surprising about this," he said, almost as if to reassure himself. "This is war." He declared the need "to expect this much" and, as if for good measure, added that the damages were no worse than a "mosquito bite."[70]

The emperor's reaction was at wide variance with Tojo's. Once he learned of the air raid on the Yahata Steel Works, he requested reports from Home Minister Ando Kisaburo and Chief Aide-de-Camp Hasunuma Shigeru. Precisely because the raid emanated from China, he worried about a war in which Japan had to fend off attacks from both the Pacific and the continent. He asked Foreign Minister Shigemitsu Mamoru what steps Japan might take to maintain Soviet goodwill and neutrality. Specifically, he floated with Shigemitsu the idea of Japan accepting Soviet annexation of the Baltic States, even if Germany requested Japanese recognition of their independence. Later that day, the emperor met with Aide-de-Camp Sato Jisaburo and learned about the state of Saipan's defenses; he spoke the following evening with Army Vice Chief of Staff Ushiroku Jun about the "need to secure Saipan."[71]

The twin shocks of the invasion of Saipan and the Kyushu air raid provided a stimulus for the navy's anti-Shimada and anti-Tojo forces. On June 17 Okada asked Shimada to resign from at least his ministerial post for two reasons. First was the issue of aerial bombardment. He insisted that the attack on the Yahata Steel Works was but a sign of things to come and stated that the Americans would fly ever greater numbers of planes against a growing list of targets that included not only cities across the home islands but also the sea-lanes of communication connecting Japan and Southeast Asia. Second was the "food problem," which, Okada said, was acute and in need of immediate resolution. Shimada addressed neither issue and refused to resign.[72]

After the conversation with Okada, Shimada did what might have been expected of him: he spoke with and took cover behind a typically unyielding Tojo. "If the emperor's confidence in us diminishes," Tojo told Shimada, "we should not be in a position, even for a moment, where we are responsible for giving him assistance as a vassal." There was, by contrast, not the "slightest need" to buckle before the demands of "outsiders" like Okada. Tojo advised Shimada not to worry about Okada, encouraging him to continue doing as much as he was able.[73] Later that same day the emperor made clear the price of his ongoing confidence. "We must, by all means, secure Saipan," the emperor told Tojo. He expressed his satisfaction at the fight being put up by Saipan's defenders, but he worried whether Japanese forces in and around the Marianas were "inadequate." This was all the more troubling because, as the emperor told Tojo, "If we lose Saipan, there will be frequent air strikes against Tokyo."[74]

Reporting to the emperor on June 19, Tojo allowed that there was no room for "complacency" but added that Saipan's defenders were "putting up a good fight." The fleet would engage in a "decisive battle" in the Philippine Sea, and the army, too, was preparing for a "decisive battle" in defense of Saipan. Tojo spoke of the need to send two more divisions to Saipan by early July and assured the emperor that the army and navy were doing "everything possible" to "annihilate" the enemy forces there. To emphasize this last point, Tojo explained that Saipan was now a higher priority than defensive preparations in New Guinea and the Philippines.[75]

Even as Tojo addressed the emperor, a Japanese carrier force engaged the enemy in the Battle of the Philippine Sea. This was, in historian Samuel Eliot Morison's telling, the "greatest carrier battle of the war."[76] It ended in devastating defeat for the Japanese Navy: Its three largest carriers were sunk, some 480 planes were destroyed, and a similar number of pilots were lost (by contrast, the Americans lost no ships, 130 planes, and seventy-six airmen). The United States, in the space of two days, wrested from Japan control of the seas and skies around Saipan.[77]

Tojo became aware on June 20 of the gravity of the situation. His subordinates on the General Staff quickly concluded that any effort at sending more troops to Saipan could only be an exercise in folly, not to mention callousness, for US aircraft would almost invariably send the reinforcements to their collective fate before they had even reached Saipan. This meant that a decisive battle aimed at the annihilation of the invading forces in Saipan was no longer feasible. At best, the Japanese Army could hope to settle into a grinding war of defense and hold its position on Saipan. Even that would be difficult given that the defenders could expect no air cover. Loss of control of the skies over the Marianas had wider ramifications. Until now Tojo had regarded the Bonin Islands, the Palau Islands, the Philippines, the Ryukyu Islands, and Taiwan as forming strong defensive points behind the front line in the Marianas. He now had to reckon with the likely possibility of one or several of these points becoming the front line.[78]

Even as he confronted the grim situation on Saipan, Tojo remained mindful of the emperor's reaction to the air raid on the Yahata Steel Works. He acknowledged that Japan could henceforth anticipate aerial assaults from both the China and Pacific theaters but dismissed their military and strategic utility. With specific regard to the attack on the steel works, he learned on June 19 that although sixty bombs had been dropped, infrastructure damage was negligible. He also learned that the raid killed 389 and seriously injured another 183. This was a price Tojo was willing to pay. He assured himself that public sentiment was "calm" and, indeed, "emboldened."[79]

Tojo could downplay the significance of the air raid, but he was fretful about the situation in the Pacific. The Combined Fleet's defeat in the Philippine Sea, he told his subordinates on the General Staff, was the "worst possible outcome." The number of planes and pilots the navy lost in the Philippine Sea devastated him. "Even if we strike the enemy's carriers," he told staff officers, "we are in trouble if our air forces cannot hold up." He began questioning the point of even trying to hold Saipan, acknowledging that the "prospects" for success were "grim." Besides, it now struck Tojo that even if Saipan proved defensible, there was no slowing the enemy advance. "Won't our air forces be crushed at Iwo Jima?" he asked.[80]

THE IMPOSSIBILITY OF DEFENDING Saipan now bested Tojo. He sent an intermediary to Prince Higashikuni Naruhito on June 20. "Recently, Tojo has lost his confidence," the intermediary stated. "He'd like to quit, if there is someone suitable [to succeed him]." Tojo equated his removal from power with an end to the war, and he was convinced that only an Imperial family member could steer events in that direction. Prince Higashikuni was his choice, but the prince would have none of it. He remonstrated with the intermediary, sending a message imploring Tojo to see out the war "to the bitter end." Uppermost in the prince's mind was the need, at some point in the postwar future, to insulate the emperor and indeed the Imperial institution against questions of war responsibility. Prince Higashikuni was convinced that Tojo must take responsibility for the war; removing him from power now could only complicate efforts at demonstrating that this had, from start to finish, been Tojo's war.[81]

A deflated Tojo fronted a *jushin* conference the following day. The *jushin* had been muttering among themselves about Tojo's propensity to speak with them in only the broadest platitudes; he offered on June 21 a most desultory report on the war. News of the navy's loss in the Battle of the Philippine Sea had, however, filtered out beyond the armed services, and the *jushin* wanted to know more. Tojo found himself on the defensive as he faced questions about the extent of the damage. He exaggerated US losses and estimated Japanese and US shipping losses in and around the Marianas at a ratio of sixty-forty, or even fifty-fifty. Okada lost patience. "What if you lighten your load a little?" he asked. When a dispirited Tojo asked what he meant, Okada insisted that combining the roles of prime minister, army minister, munitions minister, and army chief of staff in a single person must be overwhelming. He asked Tojo whether he was able to sleep at night, and repeated his suggestion that Tojo lighten his load.[82]

Tojo was ready to relinquish all his posts, but he refused to give Okada the satisfaction. He was determined that his removal from power come only at the emperor's direct behest. He sent his secretary, Akamatsu Sadao, to speak on June 23 with Kido's secretary, Matsudaira Yasumasa, about his desire to quit. He himself spoke with Kido, admitting he had been wrong when he recently advised the emperor about Saipan's defensibility. He acknowledged the emperor's concern about the aerial bombardment campaign the Americans would launch against the home islands, and he raised his desire to be relieved of all his posts. Tojo spoke also with the man he hoped would succeed him as prime minister. Calling on Prince Higashikuni, he admitted—just a little euphemistically—that the war had taken an "unfavorable" turn and announced his intention to resign from all posts. Prince Higashikuni would not hear of it. Resignation was, he said, "extremely irresponsible." Asked about future policies and plans, Tojo admitted he had no "clear" thoughts about how to extricate Japan from the war.[83]

Tojo awoke on June 24, 1944, in a state of trepidation. He and Shimada were scheduled to report to the emperor on the looming loss of Saipan, and although his conversation with Prince Higashikuni had not gone according to plan, he expected the emperor to relieve him of all decision-making posts. Tojo fortified himself for this moment of truth by praying that morning at Meiji and Yasukuni Shrines. At the Imperial Palac, he joined Shimada in explaining that the Americans had taken command of the skies over Saipan and it was not possible to wrest back control. This rendered impossible any effort at reinforcing Saipan's defenses. Saipan—and, indeed, the entire Mariana Island chain—were as good as lost.[84]

Tojo braced himself for the response, but he was not prepared for what he got. The emperor refused, for one thing, to accept Shimada and Tojo's advice about the Marianas and Saipan. He called a meeting of the hitherto almost purely ceremonial supreme military councilors in the hope that his field marshals and fleet admirals might lend their prestige to an outcome other than the forsaking of Saipan. This seemed to suggest that the emperor had lost confidence in Shimada and Tojo but, completely contrary to Tojo's expectations, Hirohito did not demand his or Shimada's resignation.[85]

Tojo emerged from the audience with a fresh sense of purpose. He had offered his proverbial head on a platter, yet the emperor had declined to take him up on it. Tojo took this to mean that the emperor had not lost faith in him. He received a further confidence boost the following day when, at a meeting of the emperor with the supreme military councilors (the fleet admirals, Prince Fushimi Hiroyasu and Nagano Osami, and the field marshals, Prince Nashimoto Morimasa and Sugiyama Hajime)—they voiced their "regret" at the impending loss of Saipan but allowed that loss of "command of the air and the sea" rendered the island indefensible.[86]

Tojo misread the emperor. Hirohito *had* lost faith in him, but he refused to involve himself directly in Tojo's removal from power. He had demanded General Tanaka Giichi's resignation as prime minister back in 1929, which he had come to regard as a youthful indiscretion, and he had no intention of making a similar demand of Tojo.[87] At issue was the emperor's self-conception: In contrast to Tojo's long-standing concern for direct Imperial rule, the emperor saw himself as a constitutional monarch and but "one component of the state."[88] He would remain strictly within the confines of constitutional due process. So it was that even though the emperor was satisfied that Tojo could not possibly bring the war to anything even approximating a successful conclusion, he was adamant that Tojo's removal from power must not come by Imperial diktat.

The emperor at this juncture connected with anti-Shimada forces in the navy. The occasion was a June 26 visit from Prince Fushimi for the ostensible purpose of receiving a formal communication recording the supreme military councilors' conclusions about Saipan. Once the formalities were complete, Prince Fushimi spoke with the emperor of the navy's desire to replace Shimada. The emperor well understood that by squaring off against Shimada, the navy was angling for Tojo's removal. The prince revealed himself, during his conversation with his aging uncle, as receptive to the navy's moves. The following day Prince Fushimi demanded Shimada's resignation. Shimada refused, on the grounds that his resignation might cause the downfall of Tojo's cabinet. One day later, Shimada, citing the need to guard against Prince Fushimi becoming "embroiled" in a "movement to overthrow the cabinet," ordered him out of Tokyo.[89]

Meanwhile, a reenergized Tojo decided to put a halt to what he regarded as Okada's "conspiracy" to overthrow his cabinet. Summoning the admiral to the prime minister's official residence on June 27, Tojo muttered a few words of greeting, then fell into an icy silence. Okada waited him out. Tojo eventually spoke up, labeling Okada's efforts at removing Shimada from atop the navy as "deeply regrettable." Okada stated that he acted only because the navy had rejected Shimada's leadership; he could not deliver the army-navy unity the emperor desired and the war demanded. Tojo denounced as "deplorable" the refusal of the navy's lower and middle echelons to accept Shimada's leadership. Okada, however, refused to allow that the opposition to Shimada owed its impetus to relatively junior officers. The service's lower and middle echelons were, he declared, "blameless." He himself, as a concerned elder officer, was the one leading the anti-Shimada charge. The conversation ended in disagreement: Tojo announced his refusal to consider a cabinet reshuffle, while Okada remained steadfast in his insistence on replacing Shimada.[90]

Okada kept up the pressure on Shimada. He and five other retired admirals, including Suetsugu Nobumasa, Suzuki Kantaro, Takahashi Sankichi, Yamamoto Eisuke, and Yonai Mitsumasa,, met on June 30 with Shimada. The atmosphere was tense; Suetsugu, in particular, peppered Shimada with questions about the war, and the retired admirals emerged from the meeting satisfied that Shimada had to go.[91]

Then came the final parting of ways between Tojo and the emperor. Tojo reported to Hirohito on July 1 concerning the failure of the Imphal operation: There was no longer any prospect of taking a corner of India, the hope of establishing a government led by Subhas Chandra Bose had proved ephemeral, and there would be no independence movements that could plausibly pressure the British colonial authorities. In view of this abject failure, Tojo significantly downscaled Japan's objectives, speaking merely of preventing the enemy from opening a communication route from India via Burma to China. Had the emperor needed any further convincing of Tojo's inability to forge an exit from the war, this was it. The equation, from the emperor's perspective, was simple: the looming loss of Saipan signaled the failure of Pacific strategy, the air raid on the Yahata Steel Works signaled the failure of the Operation Ichigo in China, and the scaling down of aims in Burma signaled the failure of the Imphal campaign. Tojo was presiding over a war that had everywhere failed, and the time for his removal had arrived.[92]

JAPAN'S POSITION ON SAIPAN crumbled. The emperor fretted about enemy attacks against the home islands and on July 5 demanded of Tojo a report on the Ogasawara Islands' defensibility.[93] On July 7 Tojo received Vice Admiral Nagumo Chuichi's final communication, announcing his decision to follow in the footsteps of Saipan's thirty thousand defenders who had committed *gyokusai*. (Nagumo shot himself in the head soon after sending the cable.)[94] That day, some two hundred members of the Imperial Diet met and, although they were not yet privy to the latest developments on Saipan, reveled in a torrent of anti-Tojo sentiment. They resolved that Tojo relinquish at least some of the posts he held. Some went so far as to speak of toppling Tojo's cabinet, even at the cost of their own lives.[95]

The question nonetheless remained: How could Tojo be removed from office? Tojo would not resign of his own free will, and Kido was adamant that the Imperial Palace not be the instigator of political "change." He bolstered the emperor's own inclinations, advising against demanding Tojo's resignation because he worried that Tojo's diehard supporters might level accusations of a "palace coup" and revolt against any post-Tojo political order. This dovetailed neatly with the emperor's and Kido's fear of an army freed from Tojo's strict and highly effective discipline and descending once more into the murderous chaos and rebellious disorder of the 1930s.[96]

Some despaired at what they regarded as the inability of due political process to keep pace with a fast-paced and long since failed war. A group of navy officers who had been forcibly retired following their involvement in the failed coup attempt of May 15, 1931, coalesced in the summer of 1944 around the navy's political antenna, Rear Admiral Takagi Sokichi. They plotted to assassinate Tojo by opening fire on his car as it passed the Navy Ministry Building. A separate assassination plot was brewing in the army, where a small group of midranking officers and civilians worked under the spiritual guidance of Tojo's old enemy, Ishiwara Kanji. Also involved was the emperor's youngest brother and junior army officer, Prince Mikasa Takahito, who agreed that Tojo must go but opposed the use of violence to remove him. The plot involved placing atop a pine tree bordering the Imperial Palace a lone bomber who would throw a highly destructive cyanide bomb at Tojo's car as it drove past. The assassination attempt was scheduled for July 18.[97]

Such extreme measures proved unnecessary. Tojo met with Kido in the early afternoon of July 13, speaking of his steely determination to stare down antiwar sentiment and "war weariness." He presented a five-point plan that would consolidate his own position and pave the way to ultimate victory. It comprised "true army-navy cooperation and unity"; a "strengthened" Imperial headquarters; a cabinet "reshuffle"; a change to the cabinet's approach to debate and decision-making; and a greater role for the *jushin,* including ministerial positions for General Abe Nobuyuki and Admiral Yonai Mitsumasa. Kido ignored the plan. He spoke of his concern that the emperor might bear the blame for Tojo's failings, and he insisted there could be no more missteps. The palace's ongoing support was contingent on Tojo's acceptance of three conditions. First, he had to accept and reinstate the independence of the Supreme Command. Second, he had to accept the navy's rejection of Shimada and secure his resignation. Third, he had to offer ministerial positions to several of the *jushin.* Tojo readily accepted the first and third conditions, but he balked at Kido's insistence on removing Shimada from atop the navy. He had long since recognized that the navy's anti-Shimada movement was angling ultimately for his own demise. He was too experienced a political operator to state this openly to Kido; he argued that Shimada's resignation would not appease but instead embolden the navy's middle echelons and might invite a rebelliousness akin to what had prevailed in the army in the mid-1930s. He left the palace without agreeing to this demand.[98]

Kido's three conditions—and, in particular, his insistence on Shimada's dismissal—confronted Tojo with a choice. He could presume that not just Kido but indeed the emperor had lost faith in him and resign. Or he could dispense with Shimada and try to enact his own five-point plan, with a view to strengthening his own political position and winning the war.[99] Shaken, Tojo leaned toward resignation, but his characteristic bullishness returned following a conversation with his subordinates.[100] That same afternoon he went to the Imperial Palace to speak with the emperor of his own five-point plan. He asked whether Kido's three conditions accorded with the emperor's "divine will," which Hirohito confirmed. Tojo now hoped to insulate himself from political turmoil by meeting the three conditions.[101] He spoke that evening with Shimada, tears streaming down his face as he asked for his resignation. Compliant to the last, Shimada agreed to fall on his sword in the hope that Tojo's own downfall might be averted.[102]

Tojo awoke on July 14, 1944, in a defiant mood. He determined to prosecute the war to a successful conclusion, excoriating those who were advocating compromise with and surrender to the Anglo-American powers. Following such a course of action would burden the people with a "humiliating sacrifice" and would create a rift between the Imperial family and the people. Tojo was casting himself as the crucial pipeline between the emperor and the people. He was also veering toward an evil-advisers-around-the-throne narrative, which had animated the two most prominent armed uprisings against the state in modern Japanese history—Saigo Takamori's Satsuma Rebellion of 1877 and the February 26 Incident of 1936. Tojo, however, remained in control and therefore had no need of violence. He would instead implement "tight security" measures against anyone who spoke of peace maneuvers and, in his estimation, threatened the Japanese Empire with "extinction."[103] Buoyed by such thoughts, Tojo proceeded to the Imperial Palace and announced his acceptance of Kido's three conditions.[104]

TOJO ENCOUNTERED ISSUES AT every turn. His first headache arose on July 15, when he reported in his capacity as chief of staff to the emperor. He opened with an admission that the war was drawing ever nearer to the home islands, and he spoke of the defensibility of the Ryukyu Islands, including Okinawa. He also nominated his deputy, General Ushiroku Jun, to succeed him as chief of staff, taking the first step toward meeting Kido's three conditions.[105] Military officers reacted with anger and animosity when they learned he had peremptorily named Ushiroku the next chief of staff. In a sign of just how weakened he suddenly was, Tojo swallowed his pride and retracted Ushiroku's nomination. After subsequent consultations with his subordinates, Tojo recalled from Manchukuo his old factional ally, General Umezu Yoshijiro, whom he nominated as the next chief of staff.[106]

All the while, Tojo fretted over the navy's efforts at locating Shimada's ministerial successor. He was not privy to negotiations among Prince Fushimi Hiroyasu, Kato Takayoshi, Nagano Osami, and Oikawa Koshiro, but "complications" in the navy's internal processes were apparent.[107] Tojo recalled the circumstances immediately preceding his own ministerial appointment in July 1940, wondering whether the navy would take a leaf from the army's playbook, refuse to nominate Shimada's successor, and bring down his cabinet. He misread the admirals, who were debating the propriety of recalling Yonai out of retirement and back to active service so he could serve as minister, per Okada's plan.[108] Either way, his inability to intervene put Tojo's nerves on edge. On July 15 he excused himself from the family dinner table and ate alone in a separate room. Not until the following afternoon, after the admirals had settled on Nomura Naokuni as the next minister, did Tojo begin breathing easier.[109]

Tojo spoke on July 16 with his new navy minister. It was necessary now to act on Kido's third condition. Tojo specified his intention to offer ministerial positions to General Abe Nobuyuki and Admiral Yonai Mitsumasa. The symmetry in bringing a soldier and a sailor onto his cabinet appealed to Tojo; Nomura agreed wholeheartedly and implied that his willingness to remain in the cabinet hinged on Yonai's acceptance of a ministerial role.[110]

Bringing Abe and Yonai into his cabinet was a two-step process. In the first instance, it involved making room for the two additions, as the number of cabinet ministers was limited by law. To this end, Tojo asked the minister without portfolio, Kishi Nobusuke, and the welfare minister, Koizumi Chikahiko, to resign their posts. Koizumi complied but Kishi did not. In characteristic fashion, Tojo sent the Tokyo Kenpei provost marshal, Shikata Ryoji, to "threaten" Kishi. But the tactic failed, and Kishi remained firm in his refusal to resign.[111] His stubbornness imperiled the second step in this process, the invitation to Abe and Yonai to join the cabinet. Tojo went ahead anyway. Abe was agreeable, but Yonai insisted he would serve only as navy minister.[112]

Tojo had proved unable to meet Kido's third condition, and his enemies among the *jushin* pounced. They met on the evening of July 17, and over

General Abe's objections, informed Kido of their belief that the Tojo cabinet was incapable of leading the nation out of the "crisis" in which it found itself. Kido concurred. He met the following morning with the emperor and relayed the *jushin*'s expression of no confidence in Tojo. The emperor met moments later with Tojo, who knew his fate was sealed, and he informed the emperor of his intention to resign.[113] Tojo convened a cabinet meeting for the morning of July 18, 1944, at which he introduced Nomura Naokuni as the new navy minister and spoke of his long-standing effort at uniting the government and Supreme Command behind a coherent grand strategy. He allowed for the need to revitalize the people's spirits and explained he had, in the last week or so, undertaken changes to his cabinet with precisely that end in mind. He lamented the insurmountable "obstacles" he had encountered in that effort and announced that the cabinet must now resign en masse.[114]

14
TOJO THE TROUBLEMAKER
JULY 1944–AUGUST 1945

FEW LAMENTED TOJO HIDEKI'S removal as prime minister from atop the nation's decision-making processes. The public held him responsible for having plunged Japan into the "misery" of an unwinnable war. Now "even a secret policeman" believed it was untenable for Tojo to live on "in shame," and the propriety of ritual suicide was a topic of at least private conversation. "I wonder," people asked, "if it is enough for him only to resign?"[1]

Tojo was not yet ready to accept obscurity, much less death. Almost immediately after his cabinet's resignation, Tojo joined a meeting of the army's "big three." He attended as army minister—a post he necessarily retained until the army's big three decided on his successor—while Generals Sugiyama Hajime and Umezu Yoshijiro attended as the incoming army chief of staff and incoming inspector general of military training. At Tojo's insistence, the big three agreed on the imperative of prosecuting the war to a successful conclusion, with a threefold approach. First, there must be a concerted attempt at uniting and unifying the Imperial Japanese Army and Imperial Japanese Navy. Second, Tojo's political downfall "must not influence operations." Third, measures were necessary to guard against any lowering of the Japanese people's morale that might arise as a result of enemy "propaganda, plots, and aerial bombardment." Tojo felt well satisfied with this threefold approach and readily indicated his agreement with Umezu's insistence that the army would henceforth forbid "any and all behaviors" that might impact the "successor cabinet."[2]

Later the same day, Kido Koichi asked for Tojo's thoughts concerning his prime ministerial successor. This was a bald attempt at guarding against the possibility of Tojo causing trouble from the sidelines. Tojo professed complete disinterest. He told Kido that the *jushin* (former prime ministers) bore "heavy responsibility" for the downfall of his cabinet, so he could only assume that they had some sort of plan regarding the next cabinet. He refused outright to offer his own thoughts on his successor, other than to note his opposition to the pursuit of peace and therefore to the appointment of an Imperial prince as prime minister.[3]

The *jushin* met with Kido in the Imperial Palace later that afternoon. On the agenda was the question of Tojo's prime ministerial successor. Agreement on a single candidate was not forthcoming, and when Kido emerged

Tojo, photographed almost immediately after the collapse of his cabinet, July 22, 1944.

from the meeting, he brought the emperor three possible candidates. All three were army generals: in the *jushin*'s order of preference, Terauchi Hisaichi, Koiso Kuniaki, and Hata Shunroku. The emperor, who knew his generals well and was thus perfectly aware of Tojo's personal enmity for Terauchi, noted it would be best to consult with him.[4]

By happenstance, the emperor was scheduled that very evening to preside over the formal appointments of Sugiyama as inspector general of military training and Umezu as new army chief of staff and. Tojo was scheduled to attend in his capacity as outgoing army chief of staff. In preparation for the occasion, the emperor had written an Imperial rescript thanking Tojo for his "meritorious exploits and efforts" and for having faithfully "discharged his duties ... as army chief of staff in this most difficult war situation." It furthermore ordered Tojo to continue to repay the emperor's "faith" in him by applying himself diligently to "military affairs."[5] The emperor also decided that Tojo should, in his final act as chief of staff, be given the opportunity to cite the operational imperatives that practically ensured against Terauchi's prime ministerial appointment. The motive was simple: The emperor hoped to give Tojo a voice and hence a stake in the selection of his successor.

When Tojo arrived at the palace that evening, the emperor's chief aide-de-camp, General Hasunuma Shigeru, pulled him aside and asked whether Terauchi's recall to Tokyo would be operationally injurious. In answering, Tojo avoided any mention of personal enmity. He was at his usual incisive best. Terauchi's prime ministerial appointment, Tojo stated, should be avoided "at all costs." He cited the intensification of the enemy's counterattack, and argued it was "impossible" to leave vacant the Southern Expeditionary Army's command post for so much as one day. The vicissitudes of the "domestic political situation," including the need to appoint his prime ministerial successor, must not be allowed to impact on the "morale" of frontline troops. Tojo furthermore predicted that Terauchi's recall would have a negative impact on nations in the Greater East Asia Co-Prosperity Sphere and also on neutral nations. His opposition to Terauchi's recall could not have been clearer.[6]

Having ensured against Terauchi's prime ministerial appointment, Tojo next spoke with Hasunuma about his own intentions. He was, he averred, far from "old and decrepit," and he made clear his intention to remain on the army's active service list. He stated his willingness to be removed from positions of "political responsibility," but drawing on the language of the Imperial rescript he had just received, he emphasized his intention to "busy himself with military affairs on the front line." He then, as scheduled, participated in Umezu's formal appointment as army chief of staff.[7]

The emperor reacted with equanimity when Tojo's advice concerning Terauchi reached him. He simply directed Kido to recall Koiso, as the next-choice prime ministerial candidate, from his post as Korean governor-general. Of far greater concern was Tojo's declared intention to remain on active service. The emperor, now second-guessing the wording of the rescript he had issued to Tojo, asked Kido whether Tojo intended to remain in the new cabinet as army minister.[8] The emperor was not alone in his concerns. Incoming prime minister Koiso Kuniaki met with Tojo on July 20, explaining that the emperor had ordered him to form a cabinet. He added that the navy was recalling Yonai Mitsumasa to active duty so he could serve as navy minister. Tojo announced that he could "not agree" with Yonai's recall to active duty. He also pushed very strongly for Shigemitsu Mamoru's continuation as foreign minister. Koiso broached the army minister's post, asking Tojo outright whether he intended to remain in the position. Tojo admitted he was undecided. Koiso wanted to replicate Tojo's assumption of both the prime and army minister's posts and advised Tojo to "give up" the latter. Tojo, however, refused to do so. Instead he insisted this was a "matter for a meeting of the big three to decide."[9]

There were limits to Koiso's ability to influence Tojo. He went directly from his meeting with Tojo to IGHQ and sought Umezu's assistance in removing Tojo from his last remaining ministerial post. Koiso also asked that he himself be allowed to return to the army's active service, so he could assume not only the prime minister's post but also that of army minister. Finally, he also asked Umezu whether he as prime minister could attend IGHQ meetings, and thereby exercise effective war leadership. Umezu promised answers to these questions following a meeting of the army's big three.[10]

The big three—Inspector General Sugiyama, outgoing Army Minister Tojo, and Chief of Staff Umezu—met on July 21. Umezu opened the proceedings by suggesting that either General Anami Korechika or General Yamashita Tomoyuki succeed Tojo as army minister. Tojo responded by making clear his intention to remain in the post. Umezu stated it was "inappropriate" for him to remain on the cabinet and added that he should not remain on active service. Tojo backed down meekly. He used what remained of his power to argue against incoming Prime Minister Koiso's desire to return to active service. He reprised the arguments he himself had faced—and overcome—when he first became prime minister, insisting that the prime minister should be a civilian. He also argued against Koiso's inclusion on IGHQ meetings. This was Tojo at his troublemaking best: he could not get the ministerial position he wanted, but he could at least obstruct and complicate matters for his successor. He got his way, and Sugiyama emerged as the compromise candidate for army minister.[11]

Tojo relished the opportunity of informing Koiso of these decisions. He emerged from his final big three meeting and handed the incoming prime minister a brief document. First and foremost, the big three had pledged the army's support for the Koiso cabinet, so long as the cabinet remained committed to the war's prosecution. They had also made clear that the army would not countenance Koiso's return to active service, rejecting outright Koiso's desire to serve concurrently as army minister. Next, the big three stated they could "not agree with the prime minister and other ministers attending Imperial Headquarters." Finally, they named Sugiyama as the army's choice for army minister.[12]

The Koiso cabinet was inaugurated the following day. Tojo had contributed substantially to the cabinet's makeup. He had ensured that Koiso, not Terauchi, would serve as prime minister. He had prevented Koiso from serving concurrently as army minister—Sugiyama assumed the post—and he had convinced Koiso that Shigemitsu should remain as foreign minister. Various others, including Ishiwata Sotaro, who had served in Tojo's cabinet as finance minister, remained in their posts.

TOJO NURSED SOME VERY specific, bitter grievances over his political downfall. Over dinner on July 22, he told his closest confidantes (all military men) that he had resigned his prime ministerial post only "reluctantly." He was adamant that the loss of Saipan did not "daunt" him, and although he acknowledged that the war would henceforth "intensify," he insisted this was a "matter of course." These insistences placed Tojo at odds with the emperor, who regarded the loss of Saipan as monumental and was now concerned about an aerial bombardment campaign against the home islands. Yet Tojo declined to see the gulf that now separated him from Hirohito. He blamed his political downfall on the *jushin,* complaining bitterly at their having rejected his efforts at reorganizing his cabinet. He nonetheless announced his intention to cooperate with the new cabinet and assist in its efforts at directing all of Japan's national strength to the war effort. He admonished his former confidantes to do the same.[13]

Some doubted the sincerity of Tojo's professions of loyalty to the Koiso cabinet. Lieutenant General Suzuki Teiichi, who knew Tojo as well as anyone, told Konoe that Tojo, "dreaming" of his own political revival, was "busying himself with schemes and plots" to that end. He was "spreading rumors" concerning the *jushin* role in his downfall, and practically all in the army agreed with him on this key point. This included even officers who personally opposed Tojo.[14]

There was some truth to what Suzuki said. Vice Army Minister Tominaga Kyoji attributed Tojo's downfall to a conspiracy or an "ingenuous plot" cooked up by the *jushin* who now sought a way out of the war. Similarly, Military Affairs Bureau director Sato Kenryo told a gathering of the Imperial Rule Assistance Association in late July that the Tojo cabinet had been toppled by a *jushin*-engineered "conspiracy." He criticized the alleged conspirators for having no plans, prospects, or strategies for "restoring" Japan's war fortunes, and he castigated the *jushin* for having used the people's "weeping and wailing" over the war situation as cover for taking Tojo down "without good reason."[15]

Such thinking was particularly prevalent among officers in the Army Ministry, the vast majority of whom—like Sato and Tominaga—owed their appointments to Tojo. Many spoke darkly about the unjust manner in which the *jushin* had "toppled" what they referred to as "Tojo's army cabinet." They were, moreover, convinced that the *jushin* based their actions on the belief that it was time to end the war. Unlike Tojo, they professed no loyalty to the Koiso cabinet, and outside the army, some were concerned that the mood among young army officers mirrored the situation in the leadup to the February 26 Incident.[16]

Tojo's own intentions remained a matter of uncertainty in the latter half of 1944. He was assiduously sending gifts to the Imperial Household Ministry's so-called Tojo fans (*Tojo raisansha*), and he was rumored to have secretly chauffeured Princes Chichibu Yasuhito and Takamatsu Nobuhito around Tokyo. He also sent gifts of food and garments to privy councilors, as well as to Count Makino Nobuaki and the surviving family of Count Kaneko Kentaro. These did not seem the actions of a man who had drifted quietly into retirement, and onetime cabinet minister and long-serving Imperial Diet member, Hatoyama Ichiro, expressed concern lest there occur a "Tojo revival."[17]

Those fears were overblown. Indignation within the Japanese Army at Tojo's downfall did not last, and Tojo found himself a forgotten figure. He attended monthly meetings of the *jushin,* as well as monthly meetings of the army's generals. No records of these meetings are known to exist, although one Tojo biographer has noted that even the generals did not go out of their way to solicit his opinions.[18] Tojo's time as a decision-maker had passed.

THE WAR CONTINUED TO develop unfavorably for Japan. This became startlingly apparent in late October 1944 in the Battle of Leyte Gulf. The Japanese Navy threw almost everything at the enemy in the hope of somehow averting ultimate defeat. Its losses were immense: three battleships, four carriers, six heavy cruisers, three light cruisers, eight destroyers, and six submarines. Much of what remained of Japan's once proud navy now lay at the bottom of the Pacific off the coast of the Philippines. Almost immediately, US forces began gathering themselves for an assault on Luzon. As if to emphasize the dire situation in which Japan now found itself, in October–November 1944, US B-29 bombers attacked Japanese cities from Saipan.

The Japanese Army, however, remained to be convinced that the war was irretrievably lost, and believed that something other than unconditional surrender was salvageable. It shifted primary responsibility for repeated battlefield defeats in the Pacific to its sister service, the navy, and from January 1945 began preparing for a "decisive home island battle." In one sense, this was a frank admission of the inability of Japanese forces to prevent the inexorable drive of US forces toward an invasion of Japan's home islands. Yet a home island battle, in the army's view, offered the best hope of contriving an outcome other than unconditional surrender. The army's confidence derived from a number of factors. A battle on the home islands afforded a logistical advantage it had hitherto not enjoyed. Such a battle, moreover, held out the beguiling prospect of the army and people uniting behind the imperative of repelling a supposedly nefarious and depraved invading force. And a decisive home island battle would be an all-army affair, and the Japanese Navy's inability to inflict any further meaningful losses on the US fleet would be immaterial to the final result. "We anticipate a turn in the war situation," said the director of the Army General Staff's Operations Bureau, Miyazaki Shuichi, in early February 1945, "due to the decisive home island battle."[19]

Tojo was quick to identify with the proponents of a home island battle. In conversation with staff officer Tanemura Sako in mid-February, Tojo identified the main impediments to such a battle. The "food situation" was "pressing," the "general public's morale" was "dropping," and the "intelligentsia's feelings of the inevitability of defeat" were of "truly great concern." Tojo also expressed concern that the Soviet Union would enter the war against Japan. It would be necessary to pay careful attention to its movements. He also issued an ominous warning. "Soviet entry into the war *will become inevitable,*" he said, "particularly if the enemy lands on the home islands." Tojo also spoke of mistakes he had made as prime minister—he seemed particularly animated by what he regarded as a missed opportunity to negotiate Soviet-German peace—before insisting, yet again, on army-navy unification.[20]

Tojo met on February 26, 1945, with the emperor, his first audience in some six months. He relished the opportunity. For the emperor this was the last in a series of audiences in which he met individually with the *jushin*. Hirohito's precise aim in holding these audiences is a matter for speculation; historian Noriko Kawamura argues persuasively that "the emperor was genuinely troubled by the [deteriorating war] situation and was seeking advice from the senior statesmen."[21] Retired admiral Okada Keisuke characterized the situation in typically straightforward fashion: Although peace sooner was better than peace later, Japanese forces were no longer able to secure a battlefield victory anywhere in the Pacific, which meant Japan had no way of compelling the United States to meet at the negotiating table. Thrice prime minister Konoe Fumimaro remained animated by the specter of a fifth column in the Japanese Army seeking to prolong the war, destroy the Japanese state, and facilitate a revolution. He urged immediate surrender.[22] Tojo's counsel was considerably less apocalyptic than that of Konoe. He argued that the war was far from lost, and although he acknowledged that Japan confronted a crisis, he was equally insistent that its enemies faced problems of their own. It was, he told the emperor, time for neither optimism nor pessimism.[23]

Tojo opened with observations concerning the Yalta Conference between British Prime Minister Winston Churchill, US President Franklin D. Roosevelt, and Soviet leader Joseph Stalin in February 1945. He acknowledged that Churchill and Roosevelt must be consulting with Stalin about the war against Japan, and he also acknowledged the Anglo-American desire for Soviet participation in the war against Japan. Yet Tojo reckoned that the Japanese Army had proved able to "obstruct the enemy's plans on the continent"—he cited the enemy's inability to launch aerial assaults against Japan from China as "evidence"—and he boasted that this had contributed to the Anglo-American "failure to involve the Soviet Union" in the war against Japan. Tojo also cited what he regarded as the failure of Anglo-American plans to "dispose of Germany" by the end of 1944. That Germany remained in the war was to Japan's advantage, because it meant that the Anglo-Americans could "not use adequate strength in the Pacific."[24]

Tojo conceded that Germany would eventually surrender. He believed that the Americans, British, and Soviets planned to "dispose" of Germany by April 25, and they would probably achieve that aim. He also believed that, by the same date, the enemy would try to render Japan helpless, "at the end of its tether." He cited the likelihood that the Soviet Union on or around April 25 would announce its intention to abrogate the nonaggression treaty it had concluded with Japan some four years earlier. Tojo also, in response to the emperor's questioning, rated the chances of Soviet entry into the war against Japan as fifty-fifty. (Here, presumably so as not to exercise a negative impact on the emperor's presumed resolve to press ahead with the decisive home island battle, Tojo softened his own earlier estimate of the inevitability of Soviet entry into the war.) Whatever the case, Tojo argued that US forces would prove utterly unable to annihilate Japanese forces in southern China and the Philippines. He was also dismissive of the utility of US aerial bombardment of Japan's urban centers, including Tokyo. The United States had resorted to aerial bombardment because it otherwise "lacked strength." He argued that aerial bombardment of the Japanese home islands had no real military application, insisting that the United States was merely "hoping for political results."[25]

Tojo also offered his thoughts on the future of Japan's war effort. He acknowledged that Japanese industry could not keep pace with its US counterpart. He recognized this meant an ever-increasing disparity in things like numbers of aircraft carriers. In the face of this unpromising situation, he counseled an increase in the use of kamikaze attacks: one or two planes or torpedo boats could sink a warship and nullify the US advantage. He also foresaw a distinct advantage for Japan in forthcoming battles: Whereas Japanese troops had hitherto been defending occupied islands in far-flung locales around the Pacific, the fight would soon switch to "Imperial soil."[26]

Tojo was looking forward to the near future, when Japan enjoyed the home advantage. He nonetheless warned the emperor about domestic impediments to successful prosecution of a home island battle. Most important, a "defeatist ideology" had emerged in some circles as a result of a combination of the "disadvantageous" war situation, aerial bombardment, and enemy propaganda. He acknowledged that daily life was "not easy," but he argued that the people were not starving and that they even had some disposable income. It was incumbent on the government, he said, to "deepen the people's awareness of war" while doing "everything" to ensure the people remained fed.[27]

Tojo also made recommendations concerning the decision-making process. He argued for "direct Imperial rule." He pleaded for a "sacred decision" to unite the army and navy. He criticized the continued existence of the separate Army and Navy General Staffs, and advocated instead for the creation of a single, unified General Staff under the emperor's direct command. He argued for a united strategy to defend the home islands, as well as northern China, Korea, and Manchukuo. Implicit in such arguments was the assumption that unification of the armed services would take place on the army's terms. A "final, decisive battle" was, Tojo argued, within Japan's capacity. "If we fight for justice and stand behind the spirit of Imperial immortality," he concluded, "pessimism will not rear its head."[28]

Grand Chamberlain Fujita Hisanori, a retired admiral, recorded in his memoirs the displeasure with which the emperor received Tojo's report.[29] Tojo returned to obscurity, and there he remained until Koiso resigned his prime ministerial post on April 5. At issue was Koiso's inability to turn around Japan's war fortunes. The fall of Saipan predated his appointment, but it practically ensured that he had presided over the loss of the entire Mariana chain, including Guam. Then had come the decisive battle in the Philippines in which Koiso—like Tojo before him—placed much faith; shuddering defeat on the sea and on the land had ensued, and the strategy to defend the Philippines was hopelessly compromised. Koiso's attention drifted—naturally enough for a Japanese general—to the continent, where he went against the advice of almost everyone in Tokyo to pursue a curious peace maneuver regarding Chiang Kai-shek, which, to nobody's surprise, went nowhere. All the while, the Americans took full advantage of their unchallenged superiority in the air and sea. In February US forces took Iwo Jima, and in April US forces landed on Okinawa. A US invasion of the Japanese home islands was now a practical inevitability. Koiso sought, all the while, to return to the army's active service so he could join meetings of IGHQ. He met with stinging rebuff from his professional colleagues, who called an end to his utterly ineffectual prime ministership.

The *jushin* convened on April 5 to recommend a successor. Tojo took center stage, insisting that the next cabinet must necessarily be the "final" wartime cabinet. It faced a choice between either ending the war and "submitting tamely to unconditional surrender" or fighting the war "to the last." The other *jushin* refused to engage Tojo's arguments, and instead took procedural issue with him. They argued it was not the role of the *jushin* to impose policies on an incoming cabinet and refused to accept any role other than that of recommending the next prime minister. The nearly unanimous choice was the aging admiral Suzuki Kantaro; a bristling Tojo offered the only dissenting voice. With the army about to defend the home islands and leading the entire nation into a battle for its very survival, Tojo insisted that the mantle of war leadership must go to an army general on active service. He named Field Marshal Hata Shunroku as the best possible candidate.[30]

The *jushin* stood firm behind Suzuki, whom the emperor ordered to form the next cabinet. Tojo refused to go down quietly, and he threatened political upheaval. He explained that, unless Suzuki took the "greatest care," the army would give him "the cold shoulder." He then issued a reminder of what this meant in practice. "If the army gives you the cold shoulder," he said, "the cabinet will fall." Retired admiral and fellow *jushin* Okada Keisuke challenged Tojo. "What do you mean?" he said. "[The army] will give the cold shoulder to one who has been named by the emperor at this moment of immense national crisis? Whose responsibility is national defense? Is it not the [responsibility of the] army *and* the navy?" Tojo refused to back down. "I am saying I want you to take care because I am concerned," he said.[31] Well he might have been, for even as he and the *jushin* spoke, the Soviets gave notice of their refusal to renew the neutrality treaty with Japan. Tojo—and everyone else in Tokyo—had now to reckon with the probability of the Soviet Union's eventual entry into the war.

TOJO AGAIN RETURNED TO obscurity. He might, in other circumstances, have hoped for easy access to—and even some degree of influence over—the new army minister, Anami Korechika. (Recall that Anami had played a key role in Tojo's initial ministerial appointment back in July 1940 and had served subsequently as Tojo's deputy.) The two men's relationship had, however, soured—Anami had been thoroughly disquieted by Tojo's relentless pursuit of Ishiwara Kanji—and neither man felt any remorse when Tojo had in April 1941 transferred Anami to the battlefields in China. The two men remained unreconciled, and Anami in 1945 kept Tojo at arm's length. He allowed Tojo a courtesy visit on April 12; not until July 28 did Tojo get another opportunity to speak with him.[32]

Tojo took to both meetings with Anami a fierce insistence on a decisive home island battle against an inevitable US invasion. Burning deep within him were romantic visions of an entire nation at arms, fighting gallantly to repel what he presumed to be a depraved and bloodthirsty invading force. At their meeting in late July, Tojo spoke about the decisive home island battle against the backdrop of the Potsdam Declaration. Released two days earlier by Chinese President Chiang Kai-shek, British Prime Minister Winston Churchill, and the new US president, Harry Truman (Roosevelt had died in April), the Declaration called on Japan to surrender or face "prompt and utter destruction." The destruction of as many as sixty Japanese cities by American B-29 bombers in the period since Tojo's downfall testified to this ominous warning. The Potsdam Declaration also outlined the treatment Japan might expect following surrender: The Allies would seek to eliminate the "authority and influence" of those responsible for Japan's war while meting out "stern justice" to all war criminals and reviving "democratic tendencies" in Japan. These objectives would be realized by means of military occupation.[33] Tojo was singularly unimpressed and, in his July 28 conversation with Anami, demanded fealty to the decisive home island battle.

Anami was no less invested in a decisive home island battle, and he did not invite Tojo back for any further pep talks. Then, on August 6, 1945, a US bomber dropped an atomic bomb on Hiroshima. Three days later, on August 9, the Soviets marched to war against Japan's Kwantung Army in Manchukuo. Later that same day, the United States launched another atomic attack, this time against Nagasaki. The twin shocks of the atomic bombs and Soviet entry into the war divided Japanese decision-makers. On one side of the divide, Anami—joined by the Navy chief of staff, Admiral Toyoda Soemu, and the army chief of staff, General Umezu Yoshijiro—argued for a decisive home island battle against a US invasion unless the enemy accepted four uncompromising conditions: preservation of the emperor's position, voluntary disarmament and demobilization of Japan's armed services, no foreign military occupation of the Japanese home islands, and prosecution of war criminals by the Japanese government. On the other side of the divide, Foreign Minister Togo Shigenori argued that the four conditions amounted to effective rejection of the Potsdam Declaration. With support from Kido and Yonai, Togo insisted instead on acceptance of the Potsdam Declaration, on the sole condition that the enemy guarantee the emperor's postwar position. Neither party backed down from its position until the emperor intervened with a "sacred decision" in the early hours of August 10. He sided with Togo and the proponents of single-condition surrender.[34] Later that morning, the Foreign Ministry cabled its representatives in neutral Sweden and Switzerland indicating the Japanese government's preparedness to "accept the terms enumerated" in the Potsdam Declaration, while at the same time seeking assurances that the enemy would do nothing that might prejudice the "prerogatives of His Majesty as a sovereign ruler."[35]

Tojo learned of the emperor's decision when he joined an extraordinary meeting of the *jushin* at the prime minister's official residence in the early afternoon of August 10. At this juncture Togo explained the government's offer to accept the terms and conditions of the Potsdam Declaration, so long as it did not affect "maintenance of the national polity." In explaining this decision, Togo stated that "war damages" were so great as to render "continuation of the war impossible." He added that Soviet entry into the war had "increased the difficulties" in continuing and that the emperor wanted peace "as soon as possible." Most of the *jushin* accepted Togo's version of events with equanimity. Koiso and Tojo did not. Setting aside their personal differences, they worked in tandem to question the validity of Togo's version of events. Koiso opened by asking whether the armed services agreed with the decision to accept the Potsdam Declaration. He also stated that "protection of the national polity" necessarily required troops and asked whether this would prove possible given the declaration's insistence on the disarmament and demobilization of Japan's armed forces. Recalling the army's founding principle and most basic function (protection of the emperor), Tojo stated that the enemy's declared intention to disarm and demobilize Japan's armed services meant that any agreement concerning postwar maintenance of the Imperial institution could only be a "form of empty rhetoric." He reminded Togo of the men and materiel Japan had already lost. Given the magnitude of these sacrifices, Tojo demanded that "cabinet ministers who had not died on the battlefield" make no mistakes at this crucial moment. His uncompromising position was singularly unaffected by either the atomic bomb attacks or Soviet entry into the war. He called for a decisive home island battle against the anticipated US invasion.[36]

Tojo and the other *jushin* proceeded directly from the prime minister's residence to the Imperial Palace. Relishing what was now for him a rare opportunity to counsel his emperor, Tojo held center stage. He was careful not to criticize Hirohito's decision, but he castigated members of the Suzuki cabinet for their actions. Indeed, he held the cabinet directly accountable for what he regarded as a terrible mistake that threatened to "ruin" the nation. He denounced the cabinet for using such fine-sounding phrases as "secure the throne and maintain the national polity" while doing nothing "concrete" to ensure that they were possible. Tojo nonetheless spoke to the emperor of a way forward: He foresaw the enemy rejecting the condition on which Japan sought to end the war, and he argued that in this event Japan should fight "to the last man."[37]

To bolster his case, Tojo also appealed to the emperor's concern for the ideals for which Japan fought. He reminded Hirohito that Japan's declaration of war in December 1941 had cited the noble objectives of East Asian "stability" and "world peace." He argued—rightly or wrongly—that Japan's conduct throughout the war had adhered closely to these objectives, and he insisted that Japan's cause was "moral," indeed "virtuous." He expressed concern at ending the war before the ideals of the Greater East Asian Co-Prosperity Sphere had been realized and worried that the region would hold Japan in "contempt." Tojo also revealed his concern with Japan's future generations and their view of its conduct in the war. Surrender would, he warned, pave the way for the enemy's "deconstruction" of Japan's "moral" wartime cause.[38]

Koiso and Tojo proceeded directly from the Imperial Palace to Anami's ministerial residence, where the three generals discussed the emperor's sacred decision. At least so far as Tojo was concerned, the discussion centered on a sad irony: The emperor's unprecedented intervention in the decision-making process closely approximated the model of direct Imperial rule Tojo had long advocated, yet the emperor had acted on the counsel of those who stood directly opposed to the army and its insistence on a continuation of the war and a decisive home island battle. All was not lost, however. Anami professed fealty to the approach Koiso and Tojo had adopted, and he promised to do everything possible to ensure "actual attainment" of the Imperial institution's postwar preservation. True to his word, Anami spoke the following morning with Hirohito of his "immense unease" with the prospects for preserving the Imperial institution. The emperor would have none of it, and he admonished Anami in the strongest possible terms.[39]

THE US RESPONSE TO Japan's surrender offer—called the Byrnes note after its principal author, Secretary of State James F. Byrnes—reached Japan by shortwave radio on the morning of August 12. The army's translation of the

Byrnes note quickly became available to Tojo. It did not reject Japan's surrender offer but it failed, as Tojo had plainly anticipated, to address concerns about the Imperial institution's postwar preservation. It made two key demands: the emperor would be "subject to" the authority of the forthcoming military occupation; and the Imperial institution must ultimately owe its existence to the "freely expressed will of the Japanese people."[40]

Tojo denounced the Byrnes note. He insisted on outright rejection and demanded the cabinet commit to continuing the war. His counsel was not, however, sought. He looked on from the sidelines as Generals Anami and Umezu, as well as Navy Chief of Staff Toyoda Soemu, led the charge against the Byrnes note. Tojo could only hope that others—including a suddenly proactive emperor—would also take issue with the Americans' ambiguous phrasing and resolve to continue the war. (This hope was not entirely unfounded, for the Byrnes note caused at least Prime Minister Suzuki Kantaro to reconsider his earlier willingness to concede defeat). It was not to be. The emperor himself spoke on at least three separate occasions on August 13 of his desire to accept the Byrnes note and for a prompt end to the war.[41]

In light of the emperor's resolve, Tojo executed a complete about-face and acknowledged that the war was over. He accepted that the government had agreed to the enemy's insistence on "unconditional surrender," and had attached only the one condition concerning "maintenance of the emperor's prerogatives." He did not, however, go down quietly. He decried what he regarded as Japan's having "succumbed" to the enemy's "propaganda." He lamented Japan's having forsaken the attempt at gathering all its remaining strength in one last heroic attempt at staving off invasion. He was so distraught he could "not even cry at the thought" of the "stain" the decision to surrender would leave on Japan's hitherto "splendid, three-thousand-year history." He denounced the government's "empty rhetoric" and wondered how the Imperial institution could possibly be maintained if there were no armed forces to protect it. Tojo seethed with impotent anger at the thought of the emperor and nation being "subordinated to the enemy."[42]

Now that the war would end in ignominious defeat, Tojo found himself reflecting on his cabinet's initial decision for war. He justified the decision, at least in his own mind, as a response to the enemy's "military, political, and economic pressure," which had been "suffocating." His cabinet had earnestly sought a diplomatic resolution, but he insisted that the Americans had caused the diplomatic rupture, and he pointed specifically to the so-called Hull note of November 26. Japan had responded by fighting for its "self-existence and self-defense," which he once again conflated with "East Asian stability." The armed services went to war in the confident expectation of eventual victory, but now the nation was bowing before the enemy's "threats." He recorded an apology (of sorts) to the emperor and to the people for his inability, in the leadup to Pearl Harbor, to foresee the "apathy," "lethargy," and "listlessness" that now gripped both the national leadership and the people. Looking ahead to the postsurrender period, he warned of "ever greater hardship" as the nation sought to rebuild.[43]

At an Imperial conference on August 14 the emperor made his second sacred decision to surrender. Tojo was not witness to the event but knew full well that the war was over. He penned a letter that same day to his longtime confidante, Akamatsu Sadao. He wrote of the "great responsibility" he felt toward the servicemen who had "sacrificed" their lives to a lost cause. It was now apparent that they had died a "dog's death," and Tojo wrote of his "moral" obligation to commit suicide. He wrote also of the forthcoming arrests of those the enemy deemed "criminally responsible" for the war. He knew he would be foremost on any list of criminal suspects, and he declared his intention to respond in "the Japanese way" and take his own life. This act of defiance would guard against so much as a hint that the emperor was "selling out" his senior statesmen and delivering them to the enemy. It also meant Tojo would not have to stand before the "enemy's court of law," whose jurisdiction he utterly rejected. He signed off with an expression of confidence in Japanese youth and an admonition against any military-inspired disturbances.[44]

That afternoon Tojo called on Anami. No record of this conversation is known to exist, but it can be assumed that the two men discussed the two diametrically different courses open to the Imperial Japanese Army. On the one hand, it could remain loyal to the emperor's sacred decision, lay down its arms, and accept humiliating defeat, disarmament, and demobilization. On the other hand, it could blame the evil advisers around the throne, rebel, take the emperor into custody, establish a military dictatorship, and lead the nation into glorious battle against the forthcoming invasion. Anami himself had encouraged the army's middle echelons in planning for just such an eventuality. Everything now hinged on him; his stance would determine the army's fate. It can be safely assumed that Tojo advised, in his characteristically blunt and forceful manner, against anything but the strictest loyalty to the emperor. Certainly he returned home and spoke with his son-in-law, Koga Hidesama, whom he suspected of involvement in the coup plans. "We must act in accord with Imperial orders," he demanded. "This is the life of a soldier."[45]

The war ended amid drama and tension on August 15, 1945. The emperor recorded for national broadcast an Imperial rescript imploring his people to endure the "unendurable" and suffer the "insufferable." Midranking army officers launched a last-gasp rebellion, but Anami and Umezu stood firm and upheld the emperor's sacred decision. The coup attempt was denied its central platform—the support of the military authorities—and ended desultorily. Anami had, in the meantime, turned his short sword on himself in an act of seppuku (ritual disembowelment); Tojo's son-in-law disengaged from the coup and shot and killed himself as national radio broadcast the Imperial rescript announcing surrender.

IN THE DAYS AFTER the surrender, Tojo reflected on his position. He accepted "complete responsibility" for Japan's failed war, and he planned to "clarify" his own responsibility by taking his own life.[46] He sent his children and their young families away from the family home in Tokyo. He incinerated most of his personal papers, which included decades' worth of memorandums and notes he had prepared on at least a daily basis. (In so doing he was following the lead of the military authorities, who ordered the destruction of any confidential records that might be used by the wartime enemy to assign war guilt or prosecute individuals as war criminals.) He also dismantled the underground air-raid shelter he had constructed during the war, for he expected the enemy to come and arrest him; he refused to give the enemy the satisfaction of imagining him hunkered down, underground, in fear of the terrible toll being exacted by the B-29 bombers.[47]

Several *kenpei* (military police) officers patrolled Tojo's neighborhood. They protected his person, but they could not—or, at least, did not—prevent a flood of hate mail from reaching him. Many letters denounced him as an "ogre" (*gokuakunin*) and a "brute" (*kichiku*). Just as many blamed him for the battlefield deaths of family members. Others questioned how and why his own sons had not been sent to die meaningless deaths on far-flung battlefields. Still others proposed to return his own adult children to him in coffins. More than a few demanded Tojo "get on with it and commit suicide!"[48]

Tojo bore this bitterness with a quiet equanimity. There was little else he could do. Besides, he recalled the death-before-dishonor *senjinkun* military code, which had gone out over his name in January 1941, and he regarded his own suicide in the face of his forthcoming arrest as a matter of course. He procured the pistol his son-in-law had turned on himself and, consulting a military physician, he marked on his chest the deadliest spot at which to point a pistol. Tojo drew on the bushido codes that had informed Japan's feudal-era samurai warriors, which the military had appropriated. So far as Tojo was concerned this meant, on the one hand, a refusal to contemplate an "ugly" and dishonorable death, in which regard the specter of Italian dictator Benito Mussolini haunted him.[49] On the other hand, it meant a conception of his final days and death as his final act of service to emperor and nation.[50] Concretely, it meant Tojo offering himself as a scapegoat, so that he—not the emperor—remained the "object of the people's resentment."[51] Approaching matters in this way, he felt a renewed sense of purpose, reinvigorated, and "refreshed."[52]

All the while, the first foreign military occupation in Japan's long history began. General Douglas MacArthur, whom US President Truman placed in charge of the occupation under the title Supreme Commander for the Allied Powers, arrived at Atsugi Airfield on August 30. He presided over the formal surrender ceremony on September 2, and then turned his attention to the twin tasks of the "destruction of Japan's ability to wage another war and the punishment of war criminals."[53] Tojo's moment of truth was drawing near, and he remained singularly unrepentant. He freely acknowledged his own "war responsibility" but insisted that Roosevelt bore the greater responsibility for the war's outbreak. He also "refused to accept" the enemy's conflation of responsibility for war and criminality. From Tojo's viewpoint, the mere suggestion of his criminality was but enemy propaganda and owed to a malicious American attempt at discrediting Japan's war.[54]

That last consideration gave Tojo pause. He thought, on occasion, about representing himself and his nation in the enemy's law court. He pictured himself propounding on his "convictions" and making a case for the righteousness of Japan's wartime cause and actions. Such thoughts owed primarily to his ongoing concern for the emperor, for whom Tojo wanted to "cause no trouble." He nonetheless insisted on being treated with dignity, and he was "prepared to take action" and take his own life in protest if the enemy treated him "unjustly" or "unreasonably" by, for example, trying to arrest him as a war criminal.[55]

With each passing day, Tojo's moment of truth drew nearer. Japan's last army minister, General Shimomura Sadamu, invited him to his ministerial residence on September 10 with the intention of convincing him to stand trial and protect the emperor. Tojo opened the conversation in a

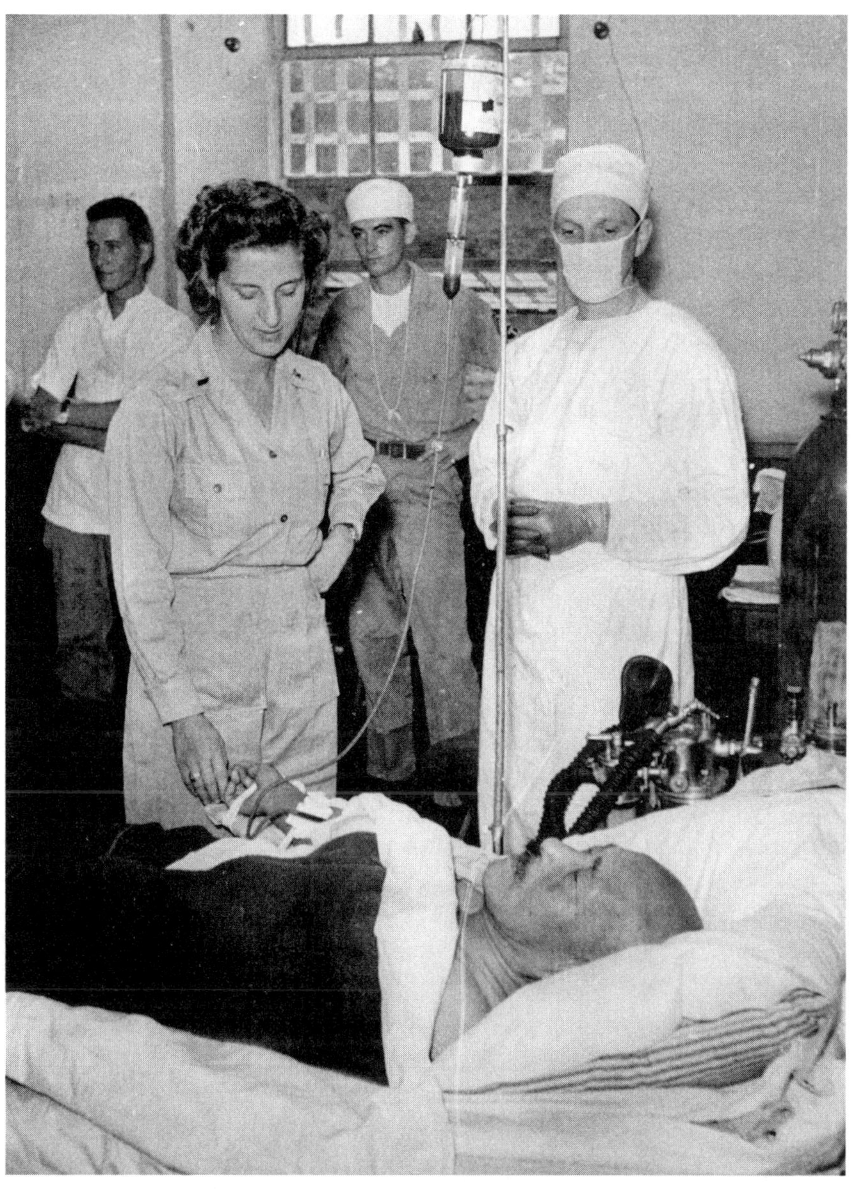

Tojo receives a blood transfusion following his failed suicide attempt, September 11, 1945.

characteristically feisty mood; he spoke of his "gravest responsibility" to both emperor and people and of his intention to "apologize" for Japan's lost war by taking his own life. Shimomura pushed back. He noted that the enemy would soon begin branding those responsible for the war as war criminals. He insisted that the emperor remain unsullied by any such appellation, and he stated that Tojo was best placed to ensure just such an outcome. Tojo conceded this point but argued he could "not infringe" the death-before-dishonor orders contained in the *senjinkun* military code he himself had published. Shimomura again pushed back. Because the nation had already surrendered, Tojo was unlike a soldier on the battlefield who had to make a choice between death and the ignominy of being taken prisoner. The Americans were unlikely to "humiliate" anyone they held responsible for the war (Shimomura did not say so, but he was hoping the occupation authorities would approach this issue with tact and order Japanese authorities to take suspected war criminals into custody). Tojo promised at least to "reconsider" his position.[56]

He did not have long to reconsider. The following day, General Headquarters Supreme Commander for the Allied Powers informed American press correspondents that Tojo would "be at once taken into American military custody."[57] Counter Intelligence Corps agents, thronged by the press, arrived in Tojo's front yard that same afternoon. Tojo leaned out of his office window and ascertained that he was indeed being placed under arrest. He closed the window, took out his son-in-law's pistol, and shot himself in the chest. The agents burst into his house and ignored Tojo's repeated requests that he be allowed to die. Over the next twelve hours, he lost half his normal blood supply and received a total of "six or seven" transfusions.[58]

15
TOJO'S LAST STAND
1945–1948

TOJO HIDEKI'S FINAL YEARS were characterized, above all, by a search for purpose. Such a search was no mean feat for a man who had dedicated his entire life to national defense and who now gazed out from a prison cell at his nation in ruins, under the first foreign military occupation in its long history. He was tried by the wartime enemy for an admixture of conventional war crimes and crimes against the peace. Tojo denounced the trial as victors' justice, convinced from the outset that his own guilty verdict and death sentence were predetermined. This he believed not because he accepted any charges or accusations leveled by the Allies but instead because he keenly felt his responsibility to the emperor and the people for Japan's lost war. He also embraced the opportunity to protect the emperor from any questions concerning the emperor's culpability. Tojo regarded the trial no less seriously than he had regarded the war, and he fought valiantly—if vainly—to the very end.

SEVERAL HOURS AFTER HIS suicide attempt, Tojo was taken to No. 98 Evacuation Hospital in Yokohama. His failed suicide was front-page news in Japan and abroad. Journalist Hasegawa Yukio reported that, even as Tojo lay in a pool of his own blood, he spoke of his desire to be remembered as a "demon of national defense." He also wanted others to remember the Greater East Asia War as a "just war" and to recognize the "national disgrace" the "victor's arbitrary trial" would necessarily entail. The latter two themes infused three separate suicide notes Tojo left on his desk—to the Anglo-American publics, to the Japanese public, and to Japanese youth. A Counter Intelligence Corps officer appropriated them. The occupation authorities rejected Tojo's twin insistences on the righteousness of Japan's wartime cause and the illegitimacy of any war crimes trials and, in keeping with a wide-ranging censorship regime, they decided against the notes' publication.[1]

Tojo's failed suicide attempt touched a raw nerve among the Japanese public. "You're an army minister," some complained, "and you can't even commit suicide." Others sneered at what they called Tojo's "sham suicide" (*kyogen jisatsu*).[2] "A true samurai," went a common line of reasoning, "never bungles the job." Many compared Tojo unfavorably with his compatriots—including not only Field Marshal Sugiyama Hajime but also his wife, Keiko—who took their own lives. According to the proverbial word on the street, it was "pretty bad when the wife of Marshal Sugiyama joins her husband in suicide and Tojo cannot do so well."[3]

Japan's military leadership also reacted to Tojo's failed suicide attempt. Army Minister Shimomura Sadamu complained about the occupation authorities' heavy-handedness, arguing that any attempt at taking criminal suspects into custody should be entrusted to Japanese authorities. He could point to a powerful precedent whereby Japan's armed services were proceeding in an orderly and efficient manner with their own demobilization after having been entrusted with this task by the Supreme Commander for the Allied Powers (SCAP), General Douglas MacArthur. Tojo's suicide attempt might have been averted, Shimomura argued, if only GHQ SCAP had apprised not American journalists but instead the Japanese government of the arrest.[4]

Foreign Minister Shigemitsu Mamoru was of like mind and directed the Central Liaison Office Yokohama branch director, Suzuki Tadakatsu, to take up the case with the occupation authorities (who remained in their temporary headquarters in Yokohama). On September 12 Suzuki requested of MacArthur's military secretary, Brigadier General Bonner Fellers, that GHQ SCAP at least inform the Japanese government of any future arrests. Suzuki went a step further when he spoke later that same day with the Allied Translator and Interpreter Section chief, Colonel Sidney Mashbir, and suggested that GHQ SCAP entrust Japanese authorities with any future arrests. Mashbir responded with the tantalizing suggestion that the Japanese government might consider investigating and punishing war criminals.[5]

Shigemitsu met the following day with MacArthur's chief of staff, Richard K. Sutherland. He emphasized the emperor's innocence of any crimes, then spoke of the government's determination to arrest and (in a nod to the Potsdam Declaration) "mete out stern and fair justice" to war criminals. Sutherland suggested that Japanese authorities might try anyone suspected of wartime maltreatment of prisoners of war. He insisted, however, that it was "nearly impossible" to conceive of the Japanese government trying and convicting Tojo (and others) suspected of the "political crime" of pursuing "aggressive" policies.[6]

Tojo was not privy to his government's diplomatic efforts, but he regarded his fate as sealed. He told Suzuki, who had secured the minor diplomatic victory of gaining the right to visit Tojo in the hospital, that the Americans had "not allowed" him to die because they wanted to prosecute him. He regarded this as part of a broader US attempt at discrediting, disgracing, and dishonoring Japan's war. Tojo took it on himself to define what the government needed of him; he assured Suzuki he would protect the emperor and confront the victors with the righteousness of Japan's wartime cause.[7]

As Tojo convalesced, the emperor publicly blamed him for the surprise attack on Pearl Harbor. On September 25, 1945, Hirohito provided *New York Times* reporter Frank L. Kluckhohn with written responses to a series of questions submitted in advance. Drafted by retired diplomat and soon-to-be prime minister Shidehara Kijuro, the responses included the avowal that the emperor had "no intention of having the war rescript used as General Tojo [*sic*] had used it." This was front-page news in Japan. It made for grim reading for Tojo, not because the emperor had disavowed complicity in the surprise attack but instead because Hirohito had been reduced to naming and shaming his wartime senior statesmen. Tojo discussed the Kluckhohn interview with Suzuki and reaffirmed his steely determination to play his role as the emperor's shield.[8]

TOJO REGAINED HIS HEALTH, and the occupation authorities transferred him on October 7 to the Omori Prisoner of War Camp, which had, since the beginning of the occupation, become XI Corps Stockade (No. 2). Tojo joined others under detention, including former cabinet colleagues Hashida Kunihiko, Ino Hiroya, Iwamura Michiyo, Kishi Nobusuke, Koizumi Chikahiko, Shimada Shigetaro, Suzuki Sadaichi, and Terashima Ken. Feelings of collegiality toward Tojo were, however, in short supply. His former colleagues referred disparagingly to him as "the supreme authority" and made no sustained attempt at speaking with him. Tojo, for his part, kept to himself. He became an avid reader; early twentieth-century novelist Natsume Soseki was his newfound favorite.[9]

Tojo at Omori Prison, late 1945.

Over time Tojo softened toward at least the other soldiers in captivity. Colonels Hashimoto Kingoro and Sakakibara Kazue became quite close to him; the latter was entrusted with the task of transcribing a monologue Tojo delivered in a couple of separate sessions in October–November 1945. In this monologue, Tojo expressed a newfound and unexpected admiration for the United States. He admitted to having once joined many of his professional military colleagues in presuming that US democracy meant debilitating domestic division and that American wealth meant an unpreparedness to endure wartime privations. He now realized that US democracy had harnessed and derived "strength" from domestic debate, which ultimately united the American people, and that US wealth meant that the people's living standards remained "stable" even as the government harnessed national strength for the war effort. On neither account was Japan able to compete with the United States. Tojo added that his failed suicide attempt had opened his eyes to yet another area in which the Americans excelled: medicine. He was convinced that Japanese doctors would have "despaired" of saving his life but that American doctors had been able to keep him alive precisely because US medicine was some "ten years" more advanced than Japanese medicine.[10]

Tojo also identified defects and flaws in the Japanese decision-making process that had contributed to Japan's cataclysmic defeat. He attributed the defects to the Imperial Japanese Army and spoke of the need for soldiers' "reflection" thereon. As if to begin that process, Tojo's monologue included his own reflections on what he pointed to as the twin evils of the independence of the Supreme Command and *gekokujo* (insubordination). Tojo took direct exception with the underlying principle of the independence of the Supreme Command, insisting that the attempt at creating a "pure strategy" by cordoning off the Imperial Army and Navy General Staffs from politics had given rise to a situation in which government policy exerted no appreciable influence over operational planning and strategy. Compounding this situation was the "philosophy of *gekokujo*," which had animated lower- and middle-echelon army officers ever since the Manchurian Incident. Their propensity to act in defiance of their superiors or in complete disregard of government policy had given rise to what Tojo called "government by staff officers." The net effect of these twin evils was a decision-making process dominated by the military officer's narrow strategic concepts.[11]

Tojo prescribed what he believed were radical measures to remedy these problems. There was an urgency to his prescriptions, for he reckoned that the Soviet Union and the United States were preparing for at least the possibility of the next war—as evidence, he pointed to the airfields the Americans were building across occupied Japan—and he presumed Japan would be not only on the front line but indeed an active participant in any Soviet-US war. It would, he reckoned, be necessary to end the independence of Japan's Supreme Command and ensure that operations and strategic planning remain under ministerial purview. In this way Tojo believed Japan might use the crisis in which it found itself to effect constitutional change and to subordinate the soldier to the civilian. (It did not occur to him that the occupation authorities would soon scrap Japan's Meiji Constitution and author a new constitution that renounced war and forbade maintaining an armed force.) Tojo sought also a cure for *gekokujo,* recommending that the War College abolish its "spiritual education." The army's upper echelons simply had to control their subordinates and instill in the rank and file complete subordination to the emperor's will.[12]

The remainder of Tojo's monologue presented a stark contrast. Completely missing was his capacity for reflection and introspection; on display instead was the feisty and unapologetic facade he intended to present at his forthcoming war crimes trial. He portrayed Japan as a nation consistently wronged by all its neighbors. Japan had earnestly sought to end the undeclared war in China but "China did not understand the Imperial nation's true intentions." Japan had sought throughout to keep the peace with the United States, but the administration of US President Franklin D. Roosevelt had "from the outset" showed "no intention" of responding in kind. The British and Dutch colonial authorities in Southeast Asia also viewed Japan as an "enemy," and by 1941, Japan found itself encircled by the ABCD (American-British-Chinese-Dutch) powers. Japan earnestly pursued negotiations in 1941 with the United States, but the Roosevelt administration only ever agreed to anything "in principle" and never took concrete steps to alleviate transpacific tensions. Only after the United States presented an ultimatum—in the form of the note from US Secretary of State Cordell delivered on November 26, 1941—did Japan finally resort to force.[13]

In this way Tojo's monologue rejected the charge of aggressor nation that the United States and its allies were leveling at Japan. Indeed, he charged the West with having long since pursued "Oriental conquest." He singled out the United States as having been particularly pernicious: it coined fine-sounding phrases like "the Open Door Policy" and trumpeted the principle of equal trade and investment, yet it had all along consciously and directly threatened Japan's lifeline in China. "Humanity has the freedom and right to exist," he mused. "When this is threatened, it becomes a cause of the outbreak of war." This last line was self-serving, seemingly indifferent to the possibility that, for example, Chiang Kai-shek might have leveled precisely the same charge at Japan. Nonetheless, Tojo was satisfied that he had located a key plank of his defense.[14]

ARRESTS OF WAR CRIMINAL suspects continued throughout October–December 1945. Joining Tojo in custody were generals Araki Sadao, Hata Hikosaburo, Hata Shunroku, Honjo Shigeru, Koiso Kuniaki, Matsui Iwane, Masaki Jinzaburo, and Minami Jiro. Civilians such as Hiranuma Kiichiro, Hirota Koki, and Matsuoka Yosuke were also arrested. Konoe Fumimaro took his own life in early December, evading arrest; the arrests (also in early December) of the lord keeper of the Privy Seal, Kido Koichi, and the emperor's uncle, Prince Nashimoto Morimasa, seemed to suggest that Japan's wartime enemies might be circling the emperor himself.[15]

This galvanized Tojo, who in early December refined the basic principles underlying his defense. The need to protect the emperor from any questions about war responsibility remained a bedrock principle. As a secondary aim, Tojo would seek to "reduce" or "alleviate" any responsibility attributed to former cabinet colleagues. This necessarily meant that Tojo himself must bear "full responsibility" for the war. To that end, he braced himself to "transcend" or "stand aloof" from concerns for his own life, and he refused to entertain the notion of "resiling even a little" before the "Anglo-Americans." He wrote also of his intention to use the forthcoming war crimes trial to reject any suggestion that Japan had somehow acted unlawfully in the 1930s and 1940s. He would "make clear to the world" Anglo-American hypocrisy and contrast Anglo-American "despotism" or "tyranny" with Japan's "righteousness" in its dealings with "East Asian peoples."[16]

The number of detainees was increasing dramatically (occupation authorities expected to arrest as many as fifteen hundred individuals), and this necessitated moving Tojo and his fellow inmates on December 8 from Omori to the considerably larger Sugamo Prison. The change in scenery did nothing for his relationship with his fellow detainees. They whiled away the time in the prison yard or gambling cigarettes in games of mah-jongg; he remained aloof and alone. Some expressed sympathy for Tojo and regretted his "solitary confinement."[17] Tojo himself seemed hardly to notice.

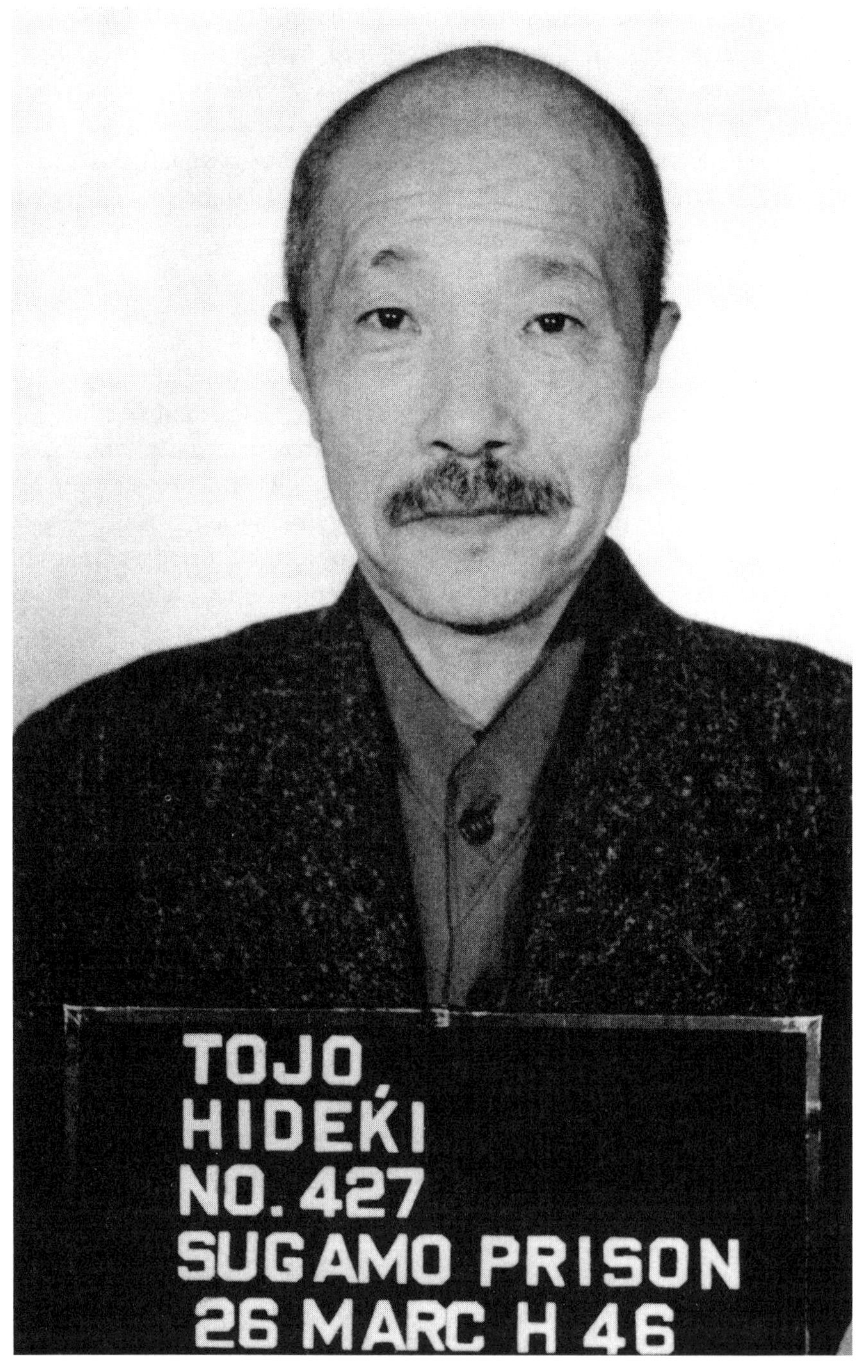

Tojo, awaiting trial as a war criminal suspect, March 26, 1946.

The war crimes trials loomed. The prosecution unit, known as the International Prosecution Section, arrived in Tokyo in early December. Many in Sugamo spoke with family members, friends, wartime colleagues, and former subordinates about their defense and began appointing lawyers. Tojo was defenseless; no one from either the Osaka or Tokyo Bar Associations deigned to defend him.[18] With seemingly nowhere else to turn, he "entrusted" selection of his defense counsel to the Japanese government.[19] At least some of his professional military colleagues in the occupation-era successor to the Army Ministry—the so-called First Demobilization Ministry—insisted that the government defend its wartime actions, as well as men like Tojo who faced prosecution for their wartime service. For example, Lieutenant General Oyama Masao insisted that the defense of men like Tojo was not an "individual issue" but a "national problem." Oyama went so far as to state it was an "issue of Japan versus America."[20] This the government could not countenance. It was obliged by the terms of surrender to cooperate with the war crimes trials. It could hardly appoint a legal team that would join a defiant, recalcitrant Tojo in denouncing the Allies' characterization of wartime Japanese policy. Besides, Foreign Minister Yoshida Shigeru seems to have regarded the war crimes trials as a useful expedient for eliminating anti-Anglo-American militarists like Tojo and establishing a cooperative policy toward the United States.[21]

On January 19, 1946, GHQ SCAP publicly proclaimed the establishment of the International Military Tribunal for the Far East (IMTFE, popularly known as the Tokyo trial). The proclamation charged Japan with having fought "illegal wars of aggression," and it clarified for Tojo offenses with which he might reasonably expect to be charged, including "crimes against the peace."[22] Over the next three and a half months, he and the other detainees underwent protracted interrogations by the International Prosecution Section. So far as Tojo was concerned, this equated to 124 hours of interrogation without counsel. The focus was, for the most part, on the period from the eve of Manchurian warlord Chang Tso-lin's assassination in June 1928 until the Pearl Harbor attack of December 1941.[23]

Tojo treated these interrogations with the utmost seriousness. He saw himself as the emperor's last line of defense and went to great lengths to portray Hirohito as a constitutional monarch who, at least from what Tojo saw during his four years of ministerial service, never sought to impose his personal preferences on the decision-making process. Tojo insisted that not the emperor but he as prime minister had exercised "supreme authority."[24] Other suspected war criminals agreed on the need to keep the emperor away from trial and distance him from any definitive interventions in Japan's wartime decision-making.[25]

Did Tojo reflect on the absurdity of it all? He had, throughout his time at the apex of Japan's decision-making process, tried to convince the emperor to become more of an autocratic figure whose voice would determine policy and operational decisions. Now Tojo was arguing the precise opposite, that the emperor had never done anything more than approve decisions recommended by cabinet and Imperial General Headquarters. So far as he was concerned, this was not a time to engage in protracted musings about the emperor's role in the Japanese decision-making process. The future of the Imperial institution seemed in peril, and Tojo was engaged in the most important of rearguard actions.

Unbeknownst to Tojo, the occupation authorities were pursuing a remarkably similar approach. General MacArthur informed the US Joint Chiefs of Staff in Washington, DC, in late January 1946 that "no specific and tangible evidence" connected the emperor to any acts of Japanese aggression. MacArthur was convinced that the Japanese people's submissiveness—and indeed the success of the occupation—owed in large part to the emperor's obedience to SCAP authority. He advised in the strongest possible terms against indicting the emperor. "Destroy him," MacArthur wrote, "and the nation will disintegrate."[26] Some US allies—most notably Australia and China—placed themselves at odds with SCAP, wanting the emperor tried as a war criminal. This galvanized the occupation authorities. MacArthur's secretary, Bonner Fellers, spoke with Admiral Yonai Mitsumasa in early March 1946, and the two men agreed that the "best way" of "exonerating" the emperor was to ensure that Tojo (along with Shimada) took "full responsibility" for the war.[27] Several months later, a "delighted" and doubtless relieved Tojo brandished newspaper reports quoting chief prosecutor Joseph B. Keenan's characterization of the emperor as "righteous" and beyond the reach of the Tokyo trial.[28]

THE INTERNATIONAL MILITARY TRIBUNAL for the Far East Charter was released on April 26, 1946. It set the framework for the trial and distinguished among three categories of offense, including crimes against the peace, conventional war crimes, and crimes against humanity, which came to be known as Class A, B, and C crimes, respectively.[29] The IMTFE indictment was issued three days later, on the emperor's birthday. It named twenty-eight defendants classified as being representative of a "criminal militaristic clique" that had planned, prepared, initiated, and waged "aggressive war." Besides Tojo, it named fourteen military officers, three naval officers, nine bureaucrats, and one nongovernmental ideologue.[30] All were summoned that night into a single room at Sugamo Prison, and each was presented with both English- and Japanese-language copies of the indictment, which included thirty-six counts of crimes against the peace. The first count summarized the so-called Class A war crimes. It charged the defendants with having led, organized, instigated or otherwise participated in a "conspiracy" to wage "declared or undeclared . . . wars of aggression" with the object of securing Japanese "domination" of Asia and the Pacific Ocean region. It also held the defendants responsible for "all acts performed . . . in execution of such plan."[31] This latter statement meant, in effect, that Tojo and his codefendants could be held accountable for any war crimes that occurred during the allegedly conspiratorial wars they had organized and led. They were, in other words, being charged with not only crimes against the peace (Class A) but also conventional war crimes (Class B).[32]

Tojo's legal counsel remained undecided. The First Demobilization Ministry had appointed eminent jurist Kiyose Ichiro to represent all military officers suspected of Class A war crimes; most had in the meantime appointed their own lawyers. Tojo was the sole exception. "I trust you," he told Kiyose, "and urge you to take on my defense."[33] Kiyose complied with this request, serving simultaneously as deputy head of the Japanese defense counsels. The occupation authorities insisted on a need for American defense counsel, reasoning that Kiyose and the other Japanese lawyers were not bilingual, nor were they familiar with procedures in an Anglo-American law court such as the IMTFE; the US lawyers were supposed to advise their Japanese counterparts. Tojo, vaguely suspicious, insisted that an American lawyer had to accept three conditions before joining his defense team: steadfast maintenance of the defensive nature of Japan's war, a refusal to countenance the emperor's responsibility for any wartime decision or action, and the argument that Japan had fought to liberate Asia from Western colonialism. George F. Blewett accepted the conditions and subsequently assisted Kiyose as Tojo's defense counsel.[34]

Formal proceedings began on May 3 in a repurposed War College auditorium. This was Tojo's first public appearance since his failed suicide attempt; one observer noted that Tojo and his coaccused, in their "ill-fitting prison garments," looked like "very ordinary, shrunken old men."[35] Be that as it may, there was no mistaking Tojo as the archvillain, and the press photographers trained their cameras squarely on him.[36] On the first day of proceedings, coaccused right-wing ideologue and Okawa Shumei provided a brief diversion by striking Tojo on the head. Amid the ensuing commotion, he denounced the trial in elliptical—almost delusional—terms. "This is," he shouted, "act one of the comedy!" Okawa sobbed into his handkerchief for much of the remainder of the day. He was removed from the courtroom and, in the anteroom, spoke of a compulsion to kill Tojo for the good of Japan. He was subsequently found mentally unfit for trial.[37]

On May 6, tribunal president and eminent Australian jurist Sir William Flood Webb asked each of the accused how he pleaded. All pleaded not guilty; the ever-exacting Tojo pleaded not guilty "on all counts."[38] In the trial's opening days, defense counsel Kiyose Ichiro submitted two separate motions: The first requested that Webb and several other judges recuse themselves, and the second challenged the IMTFE's jurisdiction. Both motions were rejected.[39] Tojo enjoyed Kiyose's needling, but he did not expect any finespun legal victories. The Tokyo trial was not, in his estimation, a noble international legal experiment. He saw it instead as a base political exercise in which the Anglo-American victors justified their own actions by shifting all blame onto the defeated. His own guilty verdict he regarded as predetermined. "Don't dream that this trial has anything to do with the gravity of my crime," he told his wife, Katsuko. "My heart is set only on serving [his Majesty] this one last time. I am not in the least bit concerned for myself."[40]

The prosecution began its case on June 4, 1946. In his opening statement, chief prosecutor Joseph B. Keenan likened Tojo and his coaccused to "murderers, brigands, pirates, and plunderers," charging them with having "declared war on civilization."[41] Tojo sat stone-faced. Keenan, in the space of a few short words, earned Tojo's enmity, and the general's disdain for the trial now took on a distinctly personal edge. Tojo had always been at his most formidable when a dispute became personal—consider his lifelong enmity for Choshu officers or his bitter feud with Ishiwara Kanji—and he now desperately wanted to best Keenan in a battle of wits.

Tojo was made to wait, for the prosecution required more than six months to present its case. He did not remain idle. In the dock each day, he reverted to type, taking copious notes. In his cell in the evenings, he prepared an affidavit. This was, at least partially, a response to the tribunal's decision in June 1946 to allow the use of affidavit evidence rather than direct oral examination for non-English-language speakers. Working on the affidavit sharpened Tojo's memory, helping him prepare for eventual battle with the prosecution. It was an exercise in exactitude. Several times each week, Tojo submitted draft sections of his affidavit to Kiyose, who then delivered them to Tojo's former secretary, Akamatsu Sadao. The redoubtable, almost sycophantic, Akamatsu consulted wartime diaries as well as former colleagues so he could add dates and other details. A team including Akamatsu, Kiyose, and others ensured continuity and consistency between sections so that the affidavit, once completed, read as a comprehensive, neat whole. Foreign Ministry translators created an English-language version, which Tojo's US lawyer combed through. This process had the bonus effect of giving Tojo an immense confidence boost: He suddenly felt less like an ailing, aging prisoner stripped of all honor, prestige, and power and more like an army general guiding his subordinates as he prepared to wage his last battle.[42]

THE PROSECUTION RESTED ON January 24, 1947. The defense promptly submitted motions questioning the court's jurisdiction and requesting declaration of a mistrial. These motions were rejected, and Chief Justice Webb recommended that the defense instead introduce individual motions for dismissal based on the grounds of insufficient evidence. A raft of motions ensued. Tojo's counsel insisted that the case against him be dismissed because the prosecution had provided "no positive legal evidence" of his role as a "leader, instigator, organizer, or accomplice" in any conspiracy to wage aggressive war. Nor was there any evidence of Tojo having "issued a single positive order" to commit any kind of atrocity. British associate prosecutor Arthur Comyns-Carr rebutted each motion. On February 3 the bench denied all of the defense motions, and the tribunal recessed for three weeks.[43]

When the tribunal reconvened, Tojo's counsel, Kiyose Ichiro, made an opening statement. He argued that it was a "mistake to think that there was one common and premeditated plan" throughout the Manchurian Incident, the war in China, and then the war in the Pacific. He took issue with the label "aggression," arguing that it was "impossible to define." He insisted that Japan's wars could not plausibly be labeled illegal, for international law distinguished between "war as an act of sovereign states and acts of brigands or pirates." He closed with an admonition against trying to prove "one party . . . entirely right and the other absolutely wrong," and he invited all who were present to consider "the deeper causes that prompt modern global wars." Such an approach, he averred, would mean the "guilt or innocence" of the accused would be "fairly determined" and at the same time pave the way toward "lasting world peace."[44]

Tojo was well satisfied with Kiyose's opening statement. Several of his coaccused were not. Many were concerned that Kiyose had prioritized defense of presurrender Japan, to the detriment of their own individual defenses. Some lawyers spoke up and indicated their clients' opposition to Kiyose's opening statement. The prosecution, naturally enough, demanded to know whom Kiyose's opening statement represented; Kiyose became "completely incoherent" as he bumbled his way through his response. The fact that he and his defense counsel were unable to forge consensus among the defendants was a sobering reminder for Tojo, who as prime minister had grown accustomed to getting his own way, of just how far he had fallen.[45]

Some four months of defense witness testimony followed. Throughout Tojo bristled at what he regarded as Anglo-American hypocrisy. The tribunal was charging Japan with a war of criminal aggression, and it purported to be saving the world from future wars. At the same time, the Soviet-US relationship, as Tojo put it to Sugamo inmate Kodama Yoshio, had reached an "all-time low," and the two superpowers had begun "combat training" for a "third world war." It was, Tojo said, "confounding" to listen to US military and naval aircraft in the skies above Sugamo Prison even as the United States used the tribunal to project itself as the defender of a world peace founded on "justice and humanity." He denounced the Tokyo trial as nothing more than an egregious case of "victor's justice."[46]

The tribunal recessed for six weeks beginning in late June 1947. Both the Japanese government and the prosecution sent intermediaries to speak with Tojo in Sugamo Prison; all sought assurances that Tojo intended to defend the emperor. Tojo laughed at the "fools" who thought he might betray Hirohito.[47] The tribunal reconvened in early August and, within weeks, individual defendants began taking the stand. Conflicts among the accused quickly surfaced, mainly—though not entirely—due to an ongoing difference between defendants (primarily uniformed army and navy officers) who prioritized the defense of presurrender Japan and defendants (primarily civilians) who prioritized their own individual defenses. Unedifying mudslinging ensued.

Tojo was dismayed by the discord. This was not the face he believed Japan ought to present to the wartime enemy. Determined not to stoop to such degrading levels, he finalized his preparations for his own looming cross-examination. Defense of the emperor remained his highest priority. To this end, he prepared, for his own reference, a paper concerning the "decision to open war and the emperor's responsibility." He started from the bedrock principle that state policy and military and naval operations were "not the emperor's responsibility." He drew from the language and spirit of the Meiji Constitution to demonstrate that the emperor was a constitutional monarch who acted in accord with the policy advice of cabinet ministers or the operational recommendations of the Supreme Command. He insisted that the emperor never rejected such counsel and never imposed decisions based on "his own personal volition." Tojo allowed that the emperor voiced his "opinion" and that the lord keeper of the Privy Seal's basic task was to convey the emperor's opinion to decision-makers in the cabinet and on the Supreme Command. Tojo nonetheless argued that the emperor did not "order" the prime minister or the chiefs of staff to enact his "independent will."[48]

Tojo argued that this dynamic was discernible in the final days before the Pearl Harbor attack in December 1941. He cited receipt of the so-called Hull note of November 26 as a galvanizing moment, the point at which the government and the Supreme Command determined to go to war. The emperor, for his part, clung to the "strong hope" that war might be avoided, yet he was "not in a position" to "reject" his advisers' counsel. Thus did the decision for war receive "Imperial sanction"; Tojo recalled the emperor's personal stance resulting in revisions to the Imperial rescript so it expressed the emperor's regret at the outbreak of war.[49]

Tojo did not content himself with mere recitation of the limits to the emperor's decision-making capacity. He noted that he had enjoyed unparalleled access to the emperor throughout his long period of service at the apex of the government and, on that basis, tried to pinpoint the emperor's contribution to the decision-making process. Tojo wrote first about the emperor's character, which he likened to a "finely polished mirror." The mirror analogy had various applications. For one thing, any "distortion" or "falsification" a cabinet minister or chief of staff reported to the emperor seemed somehow to reflect on the untruthful vassal. For another, cabinet ministers and the chiefs of staff alike sought to base their decisions on the emperor's innermost "intentions," and in this way the emperor's "will" reflected throughout the decision-making process. Tojo spoke also of the concern the emperor shared with his Imperial ancestors for the Japanese people's well-being. He recounted how this concern permeated the emperor's reaction to any policy or operational decision, and he contrasted the emperor's perspective with that of ministers and staff officers. (The former, in Tojo's rigid view, were supposed to represent only the perspective of the bureaucracy or service they represented on cabinet; the latter concerned themselves only with matters of operations and strategy.) Tojo also raised the emperor's abiding interest in international affairs as well as his solicitude for Japan's relationship with the Anglo-American powers. He recalled the emperor having raised, soon after the Pearl Harbor attack, the idea of writing to the British and US embassies and inquiring after the health of the interned diplomatic staff.[50]

Tojo concluded this exercise by reiterating Hirohito's distance from the decision-making process. He added, almost as an afterthought, his outright opposition to the suggestion that he had deceived the emperor and the Japanese people when he led the nation into war. This last assertion was somewhat perfunctory and perhaps, in Tojo's mind, was only necessary because he had been charged with leading a criminal conspiracy against the peace. Yet, by not developing this thought more fully, he left unreconciled three key propositions. He had contended, first, that the emperor's will permeated the thinking of his cabinet ministers and staff officers so that the decisions they reached reflected their emperor's thinking. Second, he had insisted that the decision for war in the Pacific had contradicted the emperor's will. Third, he held that he himself had not tricked or misled the emperor. Bringing consistency to these three propositions was no easy task, and we must take care not to hold Tojo to impossibly high standards. It was nonetheless the case that Tojo had left himself open to entanglement and possible befuddlement when he took the stand.[51]

TOJO TOOK THE STAND on December 26, 1947. This marked a high publicity point for a trial that had dragged on interminably and lost the interest of the wider Japanese public. (Outside Japan it had never attracted the same level of interest as had the Nuremberg trials of Nazi war criminals.) Tokyo residents who had long since forgotten about the trial suddenly thronged outside the courtroom in the hope of catching the words of the man they blamed for having led the nation to crushing defeat. The press gallery, too, was reenergized.

Tojo's defense began with an opening statement by Kiyose. His American lawyer, George Blewett, then needed a few days to read aloud to the tribunal the English-language translation of Tojo's affidavit, which presented a narrative at wide variance with that of the prosecution. For one thing, it only began with Tojo's appointment as army minister in July 1940. It insisted he had not earlier been in a position of decision-making responsibility, and it mostly disengaged from charges relating to Manchuria, the outbreak of war against China, or the border wars against the Soviet Union. In this way the affidavit rebutted the prosecution's insistence on one long war of criminal aggression dating back to the assassination of warlord Chang Tso-lin. It argued that what the indictment called a "criminal militaristic clique" had never, in fact, existed, and it portrayed Tojo as a reformer who had sought to regulate the relationship between the mutually independent cabinet and Imperial General Headquarters. It maintained that Japan had neither planned nor prepared for war against the Anglo-American powers; the war was primarily attributable not to Japanese aggression but to Anglo-American-Dutch provocation. Elsewhere it held that Japan had fought for its self-existence and self-defense, as well as for Greater East Asian liberation. It stated that Tojo had never ordered, permitted, or condoned any traditional war crimes or inhumane acts. The affidavit's treatment of the Pearl Harbor attack was the nearest it came to an acceptance of wrongdoing: it could not refute the fact that delivery of the last note had postdated the opening of the attack, but it argued that the Japanese government had taken every conceivable measure to deliver a lawful declaration of war before the opening of hostilities.[52]

Tojo's cross-examination was next on the agenda. General MacArthur was concerned that the witness stand might become Tojo's grandstand. He made clear to Keenan that there should be no cross-examination. Tojo should instead be made to "stand down" immediately on completion of his affidavit reading.[53] Keenan ignored MacArthur. Tojo's cross-examination promised to be good theater, and Keenan saw it injecting some life back into the trial. Tojo cannot have known of these machinations, but the opportunity to grapple with the prosecution—hopefully Keenan—and to defend presurrender Japan's actions had sustained him throughout what was otherwise a dreary existence in Sugamo Prison. He would have been crushed had that opportunity been taken away at the last moment. Keenan might not have known it, but he was playing right into Tojo's hands.

First, however, Tojo faced defense cross-examination. He fielded questions with ease, with one exception. He badly fumbled a question from Kido Koichi's American counsel, who asked whether Tojo could recall "any instance" in which Kido "acted or gave advice contrary to the emperor's wishes for peace." Tojo stoutly defended Kido, indicating there was "no such instance whatever." He should have stopped there. Instead he entangled himself in trying to explain the complexity of the Japanese decision-making process. "There is no Japanese subject who would go against the will of His Majesty," he said. As if to emphasize the point, he added that this was particularly the case among "high officials." Chief Justice Webb, acutely aware of his own government's desire to see the emperor join Tojo in the dock, interjected from the bench, "Well, you know the implications from that reply."[54] Tojo had let down his guard for the briefest of moments and had inadvertently raised questions about the emperor's role in the decision for war. He strengthened his guard.

Tojo was next the recipient of some good luck. The chief prosecutor, Keenan, on whom Tojo had focused his disdain and hatred, approached the bench and advised that he had "some questions" for Tojo. He added his hope that Tojo's pretrial interrogator, John W. Fihelly, might assist in the cross-examination. The trial had hitherto followed a one-prosecutor-per-defendant rule, but Tojo so desperately wanted to grapple with Keenan that

Tojo on the witness stand.

he made "no objection." Webb, however, stated that the bench was "against" Keenan's proposal. If Keenan wanted to question Tojo, he would have to do so without Fihelly, who had prepared for some two years for this moment. The hard-drinking, hopelessly unprepared Keenan decided in a burst of vainglorious enthusiasm that he deserved the accolades he presumed would ensue from cross-examining the archvillain Tojo, and he was determined to conduct the cross-examination in Fihelly's stead.[55]

Tojo had been hoping for years for precisely this moment. He needed no reminders of his personal enmity for Keenan, but the chief prosecutor delivered one anyway. He began his cross-examination by leveling a gratuitous insult at Tojo. "I shall not address you as a general," he said, "because, of course, you know there is no longer any Japanese Army." Keenan continued with this facile attempt at belittling Tojo. He called Tojo's affidavit an "insult to the intelligence of this Tribunal" and insisted that Tojo must be "ashamed" of Japan's wartime relationship with Germany. He harangued Tojo about precise numbers of casualties on Chinese battlefields and demanded that Tojo agree to the criminality of warfare. Webb warned Keenan that the bench was "getting no help from this type of cross-examination."[56]

Keenan's emphasis on scoring petty personal points was at least partly a defensive mechanism designed to hide his unpreparedness. His grasp of basic detail was wanting, and early in the cross-examination he pursued a befuddled line of questioning about US entry into World War I. Tojo asked repeatedly for clarification before offering to respond "in very great detail." Yet, by this time, Keenan realized that the entire topic served no particular purpose and told Tojo his response was "unnecessary." He shifted to a muddled question about the German-Italian-Japanese Tripartite Pact and US entry into the war in Europe. Realizing what little sense he had made, Keenan asked, "Do you understand my question?" Tojo pounced. "I can't ... comprehend where the point in the question is," he spat. Keenan explained himself clumsily, and Tojo barked at him in a manner he had once reserved for cadets or very young officers: "Was there a question?"[57]

Tojo exuded authority. Asked to explain the term "national difficulties," he insisted he could not "comprehend" what Keenan was getting at. He then took it on himself to define the question: "Now, is the point in the question this: national difficulties arising from internal difficulties?" A thoroughly discomfited Keenan replied, "I don't know." The topic switched to Tojo's ministerial appointment in July 1940, and Keenan tried to wrest back control. Tojo offered repeatedly to explain himself, but Keenan kept cutting him off and tried to get Tojo to speak about the period immediately preceding that appointment. Tojo shrugged. "Well [about] that I do not know anything, but if you do not desire an explanation there is no need on my part to make an explanation." Tojo eventually explained the general process by which the Japanese Army nominated its cabinet-level representative. Keenan pushed for specific details about the eve of Tojo's ministerial appointment, and Tojo alternated between elaborating on the general process of ministerial appointments and disavowing any knowledge of machinations prior to his own ministerial appointment. Eventually Chief Justice Webb interjected, "We are having difficulty here." Tojo took his cue from Webb, telling Keenan that he had already responded in "unnecessary detail" and suggesting that they move on to another topic.[58]

During the cross-examination, Tojo was wont to admonish Keenan, as when he stated, "Well, that is quite different to what I have been talking about. Your question is quite inconsistent." At times he advised Keenan on how best to proceed with his cross-examination. "May I ask," Tojo said at one point, "that you pursue your questions ... based on the original, separate document which is an exhibit in this case?" At other times Tojo highlighted the ambiguity and imprecision in Keenan's questions. The following exchange arose when Keenan pressed Tojo about the firm diplomatic stand the second Konoe cabinet adopted toward the United States:

> Q.: How far did you intend to go in your diplomatic measures by maintaining a firm attitude? Did you mean short of war or to include war if necessary?
> A.: What time are you referring to?
> Q.: Any time.
> A. The situation was different depending on the time.
> Q.: Will you please answer the question?
> A.: Unless you tell me the appropriate time I wouldn't be able to answer the question. That is why I am asking you for the time.

Tojo was toying with Keenan, like a cat with a mouse.[59]

Keenan's questions rarely seemed to contribute much to the prosecution's case. Or, at least, he did a terrible job of tying his questions back to the issue of Tojo's alleged participation in a criminal conspiracy that planned and prepared for wars of aggression across Asia and the Pacific. Tojo, by contrast, was more than capable of taking a seemingly random question and answering it in a way that contributed to his defense. At one point, in the midst of a series of confused questions about his cabinet's policy on the eve of Pearl Harbor, Tojo offered the following: "The question of entering war, or the question of trying to avoid war, trying to settle the question without entering war, the question of deciding on the rise or fall of a country, of a national defense state, is *not so simple a matter as you are trying to suggest.*"[60]

Tojo, growing in confidence, enjoyed small victories over the unsuspecting Keenan in even the unlikeliest moments. At one point Keenan began peppering Tojo with questions about the Japanese Army's advance in September 1940 into northern Indochina. Tojo responded by explaining how the military advance was the product of diplomatic agreement between the Vichy French and Japanese governments. Keenan tried to undermine Tojo's point by noting that the "Vichy Government was under the control of the Hitler Government." Then, as if to insult Tojo, he asked, "You know that, don't you?" Tojo responded as might have been expected: "I was well aware of the fact that the Vichy Government was operating under German occupation, but I considered the Vichy Government the legitimate government of France." But Tojo did not stop there. "It is just as the present Japanese Government, operating under the American Government, is the legitimate government of Japan," he added. An embarrassed Keenan quickly changed topic, asking Tojo about his cabinet's intention to march to war against the Dutch East Indies. Tojo shot straight back at Keenan: "The Netherlands itself declared war on Japan."[61]

Only for the briefest moment did Tojo oblige Keenan. This sudden burst of compliance was in response to Keenan's question about Tojo's own position "relative" to the emperor on the eve of the bombing of Pearl Harbor. This was Tojo's chance to repair any damage he had done with his earlier comments about Japanese officials' absolute loyalty to the will of their emperor. In direct reference to that statement, he explained that he had been speaking of his "feeling" as a "subject," adding that such feelings were "quite a different matter" from the issue of the emperor's responsibility for any decisions reached. With specific regard to the decision for war in the Pacific, he stated, "It is a fact that because of my advice and because of the advice given by the High Command the Emperor consented, though reluctantly, to the war."[62]

Tojo had done his duty. Keenan underscored this line of questioning by stating that Japan's emperor system was manifestly inferior to US presidential democracy. "The people of the United States choose their President every four years by direct voice," he stated. "That is not true in Japan." He then invited Tojo to comment. Webb, doubtless mindful of the fact that his own nation's head of state was not an elected president but a constitutional monarch, cut in to ask the "relevance" of this line of questioning. Tojo enjoyed the ensuing exchange between Keenan and Webb, which ended with a curt order from the chief justice: "We don't want to hear any more questions of that type."[63]

Keenan shifted to questions concerning the so-called Hull note of November 26, 1941, and the Nine-Power Treaty of February 1922. But Keenan had not the skill to obtain from Tojo any admissions or concessions. The prosecutor then shifted focus to the Pearl Harbor attack, asking Tojo whether he felt he had committed any "legal wrong" or "moral wrong." Tojo's response could not have been any clearer: "I committed no wrong. I feel that I did what was right and true."[64]

Keenan ended his cross-examination there. Tojo had been on the stand for the better part of a week, and he emerged the victor. He took grim satisfaction from what he believed was his last great battle. He now awaited a guilty verdict and death sentence, both of which he regarded as predetermined. He returned to the dock and whispered to Sato Kenryo of his willingness to submit to the jurisprudence not of the Tokyo trial but instead of King Enma, the great judge of Buddhist hell. Some days later, speaking again with Sato, Tojo remained vehement in his denunciation of the trial by "enemy nations" but spoke of the need to accept the verdict and sentence as if it were handed down by a Japanese tribunal. He allowed that he ought to be "torn to shreds" for what he called the "crime of defeat." He demanded that no excuses, explanations, or apologies be made on his behalf.[65]

Tojo took little interest in what others said of his cross-examination, but he earned plaudits. British prosecutor Arthur Comyns-Carr noted while Tojo was in the stand that he was "hanging Keenan"; after the cross-examination had ended, he applauded Tojo's "very fine performance."[66] New Zealand associate prosecutor Ronald Henry Quilliam noted how Tojo had controlled the debate, and he recorded people referring tongue-in-cheek to Tojo's "cross-examination of Keenan."[67] One of Japan's major daily newspapers, *Asahi Shimbun* editorialized about Tokyo's trains being atwitter with people speaking of how Tojo had "regained his popularity."[68] Keenan himself paid what was perhaps the greatest compliment: Immediately after Tojo returned to the dock, Keenan retreated to the resort town of Atami. In the words of Associated Press correspondent Frank White, Keenan sought to "recuperate" from his "bout" with Tojo.[69]

THE DEFENSE RESTED ON January 12, 1948, and the trial moved into the summations phase. After the tribunal adjourned on April 6, the judges spent the next seven months drafting the judgment. Throughout, Tojo and his coaccused remained in Sugamo Prison. Some seemed confident that they would walk free. Others thought they might get relatively light prison sentences. Tojo continued to regard himself as fated to the death sentence, but he no longer had anything with which to busy himself and therefore focused almost solely on his approaching mortality. This stirred his innermost being in ways to which he was utterly unaccustomed.

Shinto, or at least Shinto as Tojo knew it, was no help. He had always understood it as transactional in practice and national in outlook, so that the observance of prescribed rituals would convince the gods—including past emperors as well as the war dead in Yasukuni Shrine—to bestow favors on the nation. What good was that to him now? He had nothing to offer the gods to whom he had once prayed, and he was not at all sure they had anything much to offer him. The latter thought was particularly unsettling, and his religious outlook moved in what can only be described as the most astonishing ways. Shinto, he now professed, he did "not consider ... a religion." It existed solely to "inculcate reverence for the origin of the nation and for the ancestors." Tojo went so far as to renounce almost everything for which he had once worked. "The formation of nations comes from greed," he confessed, "and beautiful words talking about 'national existence' and 'self defense' ... are simply expressions of the national greed which culminates in what is known as war."[70]

Into Tojo's religious crisis walked Buddhist chaplain Hanayama Shinsho, who by happy coincidence belonged to the same True Pure Land Buddhism as Tojo's mother and wife. Tojo had first encountered Hanayama in March 1946, but he had remained utterly preoccupied with preparing for his moment on the stand. Now, however, Tojo was drawn to True Pure Land Buddhism's teachings on a paradisial afterlife, and he took hope from its promise of salvation for those who called on Amida Buddha. Tojo gladly received from Hanayama various texts, including Shinran's *Shoshinge* (Hymn of true faith) as well as a book exploring the Buddhist faith of several Japanese emperors. These he studied intensively, and from early

August on he began attending Hanayama's sermons and services. He took solace in Hanayama's avowal that the "new Japan must be built by those who have dwelt in Sugamo," and he was affected by the chaplain's gentle insistence on meeting death "in peace and calmness."[71]

The tribunal reconvened on November 4, and Chief Justice Webb needed a week to read the judgment. The tribunal threw out forty-five of the fifty-five charges; the ten counts retained included crimes against the peace (Class A) and conventional war crimes (Class B). The tribunal found that all these crimes had been proved.[72] So far as Tojo and his coaccused were concerned, it only remained to learn of their individual sentences. Surer than ever of his impending mortality, drawn ever deeper into Buddhist teachings, Tojo in the early hours of November 12 penned a poem: "Looking up, I hear reverently the voice of the Buddha calling me from the limitless clean sky."[73] In the courtroom later that day, Webb sentenced Tojo and six of his coaccused to death by hanging. In his final act of defiance, Tojo did not bother wearing his earphones to hear the translation.[74]

Tojo subsequently prepared a public statement, which he handed to Hanayama, in which he accepted that his death sentence was "deserved." He nonetheless allowed that the death sentence did "not absolve" him from the responsibility he bore to the large percentage of his fellow Japanese who had "suffered from the war." He regretted as "truly deplorable" the "atrocities and inhumanities" committed against Allied prisoners of war. He insisted that "a small part" of the Japanese Army was at fault for those atrocities, but he also accepted his own command responsibility. He pleaded with the Japanese people for "sympathy" for those who had fought and died on the battlefields of World War II. "If any crime has been committed in this war, it is men like me—the leaders—who are guilty," he declared.[75]

Tojo's final days were otherwise an exercise in almost uninterrupted meditative Buddhist prayer. The chant *Namu Amida Butsu* (I take refuge in Amida Buddha) was a prominent feature of his waking hours. At one point, he confessed to Hanayama that he was trying, even if unsuccessfully, "to imagine a Great Buddha enthroned above a Greater Solar System." He took to expressing himself in *tanka* poetry; for example,

Nothing now
Beclouds my soul
As with a full heart
I start my journey West.

Tojo and the other war criminals who had been sentenced to death were notified on December 21 that they would hang in the early hours of December 23. In his final afternoon, Tojo told Hanayama, "The most important thing is that through faith I can die and go to the Paradise of Amida-Butsu." He went to the gallows chanting *Namu Amida Butsu* and was declared dead by a US military physician at ten minutes after midnight.[76]

CONCLUSION

TOJO HIDEKI'S SELF-SACRIFICING PERFORMANCE at the Tokyo trial caught the Japanese public's attention. It even earned him some degree of sympathy and grudging respect.[1] This so spooked the occupation authorities that the Civil Intelligence Section of General Headquarters Supreme Commander for the Allied Powers (GHQ SCAP) blocked publication of Tojo's affidavit.[2] And to ward off the possibility of Tojo's final resting place becoming "canonized" and an incubator for indignance at the occupation-imposed postwar democratic order, GHQ SCAP decided to scatter his ashes "secretly" at sea.[3]

Tojo's resurgence in the Japanese people's estimation was, however, only ever ephemeral. He had been the object of "public indignation" long before the Tokyo trial began. Most particularly, his failed suicide attempt had made him a laughingstock.[4] Neither his performance at the trial nor his death washed that away. Only months after he was hanged for his crimes, Tojo was once again the target of bitterest criticism from practically all quarters. Left-wing literary figure Miyamoto Yuriko lambasted Tojo for his "despicable" performance at the Tokyo trial. She decried what she believed was his "conviction" in "fascism," and she wrote disparagingly of the bitter fruits of his "heroic leadership."[5] Economist Katsuta Teiji blamed Tojo for Japan's "economy of defeat" and invited his readers to hate Tojo with all their hearts.[6] Evangelical Christian pacifist Kagawa Toyohiko blasted Tojo and the other war criminals who "pretended to be heroes" with their "dreams of Asian invasion."[7] Former Imperial Japanese Navy officers, including the prolific Takagi Sokichi, continued to locate Tojo in their "virtuous navy, villainous army" narratives. In one essay, Takagi wrote approvingly of former Admiral Toyoda Teijiro's refusal even to talk to "army riffraff" like Tojo. He also criticized Tojo for having gone to war on the basis of the wildly inaccurate economic forecasting of Suzuki Teiichi, a retired army officer and Cabinet Planning Board minister.[8]

Against this backdrop, external pressure to prevent any Tojo resurgence in Japanese public opinion was probably unnecessary. It came anyway, in the form of the San Francisco Peace Treaty of September 1951, which made explicit provision for the Japanese government's acceptance of the

Tokyo trial's judgment.[9] In this way Japan returned to the community of sovereign nations on the understanding that the excision of Tojo and the others convicted by the Tokyo trial had been an integral part of a wider process of national rehabilitation imposed by the six-year-long foreign military occupation.

Literary magazine *Chuo koron* (Central review) greeted Japan's return to independence by publishing the three suicide notes that Tojo had prepared in the lead-up to his failed suicide attempt. These notes insisted that the United States had provoked the war, and they admonished the Japanese people to remain steadfast and to cultivate such virtues as loyalty and patriotism.[10] Lest anybody mistake this for an attempt at reviving and resuscitating Tojo's image, *Chuo koron* also carried a sharply critical response penned by Waseda University legal scholar Kai'no Michitaka. Kai'no had represented navy officers and others at the Tokyo trial; he now pilloried Tojo for presuming he could lay claim to "righteousness," and for his seeming obliviousness to his own heavy responsibility for the death, destruction, and devastation visited on the Japanese people.[11]

Business and political magazine *Daiyamondo* (Diamond) also carried a short piece attributable to Tojo. This he had dictated in the lead-up to his hanging. Here Tojo apologized to readers and acknowledged that his death would not "atone" for his responsibility to "those who died in the war and their bereaved families." He nonetheless refused to accept that he—or Japan—was guilty of an "international crime," and he denounced the Tokyo trial as a "political tribunal." He accused the Americans of their own war crimes, including "indiscriminate bombing" and especially the atomic attacks against Hiroshima and Nagasaki. He berated the Americans for having so disempowered Japan that it was powerless to prevent the communization of the region. He regarded a third world war as a virtual inevitability, and he wrote in hopeful tones of Japan's rearmament.[12]

Tojo was right about one thing: The Japanese people continued to hold him accountable for the death, destruction, and devastation of the war and refused to accept his death as atonement. In the words of his long-serving aide and secretary Akamatsu Sadao, the wider public continued to "heap abuse on Tojo" well after his death.[13] A government proposal in 1954 to increase assistance payments to the families of executed war criminals provides a case in point: The public and the opposition parties joined and expressed shock and dismay at the prospect of the government doubling the benefits provided to Tojo's widow. The daily newspapers joined the chorus. The *Yomiuri shimbun* labeled the proposal "extremely unfair," while the *Sankei shimbun* expressed incredulousness that the government would seek to "glorify the war criminal as a man of merit."[14]

All the while, the institution most concerned with honoring the war dead and promoting the welfare of bereaved families—the Japan War-Bereaved Families Association—refused to extend membership to war criminals' widows and children. Feelings ran high toward those convicted by the Tokyo trial, for association members regarded their own plight as directly attributable to Japan's wartime leadership. Tojo provided a particular point of focus and was denounced as the "enemy of the people" and the "source of all evil."[15]

JAPANESE WAR MEMORY MOVES little beyond a caricature of Tojo. This biography has offered a fresh look at the man. He was a complex figure in a tumultuous historical period, and inconsistencies in his approach to issues are readily discernible. He was intensely loyal to the Imperial Japanese Army, in which both he and his father served, but he despised with an unbridled passion the Choshu tribalism that ended his father's career and that remained a defining feature of army life until the early Showa period. He held firm to a lifelong insistence on the need for iron discipline in the army and refused in the early 1930s to accept any domestic military action that departed from due constitutional process. But Tojo was himself a leading figure in the anti-Choshu clandestine officer associations that mushroomed in the 1920s and early 1930s, and he supported those officers who in September 1931 launched the conquest of Manchuria without first seeking or receiving any kind of imprimatur from Tokyo. He played a key role in breaking Choshu dominance of the army's personnel affairs, but he and like-minded colleagues only managed in the early 1930s to replace it with another form of factionalism. This owed partly to petty jealousies and personal hatreds but also to genuine differences concerning the nature of twentieth-century warfare. Some officers who insisted on a traditional approach to military affairs prioritized strategic planning, placed their faith in morale, and lionized the infantryman. Other officers saw a tectonic shift away from warfare limited to the battlefield, insisting that victory had necessarily to be sought in such nontraditional indices of military strength as industry, commerce, technology, and finances. Tojo identified with the latter group; he was very much a "total war" officer, yet he never entirely dispensed with the traditionalists' belief in the primacy of men and morale. Tracing Tojo's participation in events, debates, and issues provides a useful lens through which to view the Japanese Army of the late Meiji, Taisho, and early Showa periods; it also suggests that consistency is perhaps an unreasonable expectation of any biographical subject.

Tojo found himself caught up in the maelstrom of army factionalism and, by the mid-1930s, the end of his military career seemed at hand. The consequences were far more serious for his friend and mentor, Nagata Tetsuzan, cut down in August 1935 by a sword-wielding junior officer. This was a defining moment for Tojo, who swore a blood oath of revenge. He was transferred to the fearsome garrison force known as the Kwantung Army, and from his post in Xinjing, Tojo looked on in February 1936 as junior officers in Tokyo launched a large-scale coup d'état. It did not escape his attention that the coup leaders were animated by the same revolutionary fervor as Nagata's assassin had been. Nor could Tojo ignore the support the coup leaders received from his factional enemies. Sympathizers in Manchukuo seemed poised to launch their own coup attempt; Tojo used the wide-ranging extrajudicial powers of the *kenpei* (military police) to crack down on anyone even remotely connected to the February 26 coup leaders. This action distinguished him from the military leadership in Tokyo, which seemed poised to throw its support behind the coup. Only after the emperor denounced the coup leaders as traitors did the army quash the coup attempt and purge Tojo's factional enemies from its ranks. It would be easy to conclude that the way was thereby paved for Tojo and his factional allies to dominate the army's highest echelons. That would, however, ignore Tojo's concern with the possibility of a Choshu revival. It would also overlook the fact that Tojo remained with the Kwantung Army and was, for at least a few years, removed from the army's administrative and operational nerve centers in Tokyo.

Tojo was still in Manchukuo in early 1937 when he took Japan to the brink of war with the Soviet Union. He was reacting to Soviet provocation; he was nonetheless dispensing with his own earlier insistence on the need to develop the sinews of Japan's national strength before hostilities against the Soviets could even be considered. Just as important, he was ignoring the orders of his superiors in Tokyo. Tojo himself acknowledged that he had engaged in a clear case of *gekokujo* (insubordination) and prepared for the likely consequences. Then came the Marco Polo Bridge Incident. Any disciplinary action Tojo might have expected was swept aside by the overriding need to devise a response to this outbreak of fighting in China. Tojo thought he knew how best to respond and again disregarded orders from Tokyo as he expanded the scene of hostilities far beyond the immediate vicinity of the fighting. In so doing he was acting on a twofold judgment: The Soviets had only just backed away from a fight and were highly unlikely to impose on the Japanese Army the nightmarish scenario of a two-front war on the Eurasian continent, and Japan's military might was far too great for Chiang Kai-shek to withstand in any sustained manner. In this way Tojo sought to capitalize on the situation so that Japan would come to control and industrialize the provinces of north China and Inner Mongolia; this would, he believed, strengthen Japan to such an extent that it could wage war against the Soviet Union in the confident expectation of victory. Yet when Chiang bucked expectations and refused to concede defeat, Tojo shrugged his shoulders, seeming only too willing to accept a widening sphere of hostilities across China in the ever-diminishing hope of delivering Chiang a decisive blow. We can and should see in Tojo's thoughts and actions the same hawkish opportunism that animated many uniformed military officers. That opportunism landed his army and nation in a quagmire in China.

The army's war hawks came to regard Tojo as their leading light. They spoke of the need for a military solution to the undeclared war in China and in 1938 celebrated Tojo's appointment as vice army minister. Tojo burnished his image by squaring off against the professional military colleagues who sought an exit from China by means of a negotiated settlement. Difficult and argumentative, he lasted only a few months in the role. He was transferred to army aviation, where he avoided controversy and put his extraordinary efficiency and administrative skills to the task of building the army's air arm. All the while, the army's war hawks agitated for his appointment as army minister. Some were afraid that the hawks might lose patience and resort to violence.

What should be made of Tojo's eventual ministerial appointment and subsequent role atop the army's policymaking process? It makes sense to begin with what he was *not*. Tojo was anything but the emperor's choice as army minister. Hirohito was disillusioned with the Japanese Army, he entertained misgivings about Tojo, and he went so far as to name another soldier as his preferred army minister. The army was, however, unyielding, and Tojo took the helm. He quickly proved himself, unlike most of his professional military colleagues, because he backed his frequent professions of loyalty to his emperor with concrete actions designed specifically to repair the fractured relationship between emperor and army. Principal among those actions was Tojo's insistence on—and maintenance of—discipline. This not only served to raise Tojo in the emperor's estimation but also had the bonus effect of *empowering* Tojo. Ill discipline among officers in the Army Ministry had hitherto meant the ministry spoke with a plethora of voices; during Tojo's time at the helm, his *was* the ministry's voice.

Tojo's opportunism was on full display as he tried to capitalize on the stunning success of Adolf Hitler's blitzkrieg in Europe. When Tojo first joined the cabinet of Prime Minister Konoe Fumimaro in July 1940, he was convinced of the near certainty of a total German victory over western Europe, including Britain. The resource-rich colonial regions of Southeast Asia seemed ripe for Japan's picking, and Tojo joined with his cabinet colleagues in developing a grand strategy designed to facilitate the so-called southward advance. That grand strategy sought, above all, to remove the obstacles posed by the two nations most able to intervene—namely, the Soviet Union and the United States. Tojo and his ministerial colleagues hoped to scare the United States away from a proactive stance by means of an offensive-defensive German-Italian-Japanese alliance that threatened simultaneous war in the Atlantic Ocean and Pacific Ocean regions. Regarding the Soviets, Tojo looked to shelve the army's traditional enmity for the Red Army and sought to replicate the Germans' turnaround in relations with the Soviets, the better to ensure calm to Japan's north. His grand strategy also sought an end to the war in China by means of Operation Kiri, which admittedly offered Chiang more moderate peace terms than Tojo thought desirable, but he saw it gaining momentum from the envisaged severance of Chiang Kai-shek from all sources of aid, including the Soviets in the north and the Western powers in the south. Finally, he saw a future in which Japan erected an impregnable Greater East Asian sphere, exploited Southeast Asia's natural resources, and built its national strength in preparation for future wars.

Problems with this grand strategy became apparent over the subsequent weeks and months. Conclusion of the German-Italian-Japanese Tripartite Pact coincided with Japanese forces' advance into the northern half of French Indochina; in Washington, DC, the administration of President Franklin D. Roosevelt signaled its refusal to be intimidated by the threat of simultaneous war in the Atlantic and the Pacific and slapped on Japan an embargo on scrap metal and aviation-grade gasoline. At practically the same time, Operation Kiri ended with barely a whimper; an unperturbed Tojo dispensed with Chiang and placed his faith instead in the collaborationist Wang Jingwei. Next came intelligence indicating that Hitler had delayed or abandoned the much-anticipated invasion of the United Kingdom and would instead turn his guns on the Soviet Union; Tojo's mind turned almost instinctively to the possibility of the Japanese Army marching to war against the Soviets. That would be a massive undertaking; Tojo wanted calm in the Pacific—he conceded that war against both the Soviets and the Americans was beyond Japan's capacity—and he now allowed for at least the possibility of diplomatic rapprochement with the United States. That latter possibility proved ephemeral, and Tojo joined a raging debate in Tokyo concerning Japan's next step: Should it advance north against the Soviets or south into Southeast Asia? He acquiesced in an interim response, according to which Japanese forces would advance into the southern half of French Indochina. The Roosevelt administration responded far more stringently than Tojo had anticipated, imposing a complete trade embargo and freezing Japanese assets in the United States. Tojo now shelved any thought of war against the Soviets and instead supported the insistence of Imperial General Headquarters (IGHQ) on a deadline for war in the Pacific. Throughout, the distinguishing feature of his actions was his willingness to upend what had been key planks of his grand strategy and change course completely. To be fair, it would be folly to suggest that Tojo should, for example, have stuck with the idea of a turnaround in Japanese-Soviet relations after Germany marched to war against the Soviets. Even so, it is very difficult to discern in Tojo *any* animating principle, other than a frank and unfettered opportunism. He was reacting to events, and his responses bore little consistency other than an insistence on military action.

Tojo eventually parted company with his cabinet colleagues on the issue of the deadline for war. Konoe Fumimaro, Oikawa Koshiro, and Toyoda Teijiro all found themselves second-guessing the wisdom of war in the Pacific and wanted to overturn the deadline. Tojo refused to yield. Konoe hid behind a conception of himself as a sage statesman and tried to portray Tojo as a furiously barking dog of war. This was, at best, only a caricature of the actual situation. Tojo insisted—correctly—that the decision to impose a deadline had never been merely a cabinet decision but had instead been reached by the mutually independent cabinet and IGHQ in the presence of the emperor. He maintained that such a decision could not be overturned on mere ministerial whim, and he insisted that Konoe and others should have voiced their concerns before the decision to impose a deadline had been reached. This was Tojo at his incisive best, and it owed at least in part to the fact that he had been grappling for decades with the question of the independence of the Supreme Command and its impact on the decision-making process. It owed also to the strength Tojo derived from the fact that the army spoke with one voice, which in turn owed to the common cause he made with Army Chief of Staff Sugiyama Hajime.

It is necessary to note one other feature of Tojo's refusal to consider erasing the deadline for war. Tojo worked from the basic premise that, because the navy would bear the brunt of the fighting in the event of war against the United States, it bore primary responsibility for any policy decisions that raised that prospect. Here again is evidence of Tojo's efforts at ensuring consensus between the cabinet and the Supreme Command or between policy and operational planning. Tojo's approach put much responsibility on the shoulders of Navy Minister Oikawa Koshiro, who frustrated Tojo by his failure to coordinate with the Navy General Staff and who infuriated Tojo by his spineless effort at leaving everything to Konoe. This Tojo refused to countenance. He was singularly dismissive of Konoe's forecasts of defeat in the Pacific, precisely because Konoe had neither access to nor understanding of maritime operations and strategy. So far as Tojo was concerned, Konoe's misgivings about war in the Pacific were vague, uninformed, and deficient in both virtue and value. Tojo placed his trust instead in the forecasts of Navy Chief of Staff Nagano Osami. This made a certain sense, but here again was evidence of Tojo's decidedly traditional approach to warfare, for he was privileging narrow strategic and operational concerns at the direct expense of broader views of national strength. Even so, he stood on firm ground because he was really only insisting that Konoe and others follow through on the decision they had long since reached to impose a deadline for war.

Konoe resigned in mid-October 1941 and at least forestalled the deadline to which he and his cabinet had agreed. To whoever would listen, he bitterly denounced Tojo. Others, including those closest to the throne, saw things differently. Tojo stood alone, in their view, as the only figure who in recent memory had proved capable of imposing order on the army. They regarded him highly because, unlike his contemporaries, Tojo had proved able to harness the army's immense institutional strength. Perhaps most impressive of all, he had changed the army's role in the domestic decision-making process, so that it was no longer a destabilizing force but had instead during the dying days of the Konoe cabinet stood for—and indeed *demanded*—an orderly approach to policymaking and statecraft.

The emperor nonetheless continued to harbor misgivings about the army, and he remained ambivalent about Tojo. It could hardly be otherwise, given that Tojo and the army were beating the drums of a war to which the emperor himself was unalterably opposed. Yet, it was undeniable: Tojo was the single most effective figure in the treacherous terrain of Japanese politics. The emperor, against his better judgment, ordered Tojo to form his own cabinet. Tojo did so with his usual efficiency. He then, on the emperor's request, launched a wide-ranging reexamination of state policy. This reexamination left many in the army wondering about Tojo's fidelity to the war he had hitherto advocated, but it resulted ultimately in little other than an extension to the deadline. The deadline passed, and amid hearty self-congratulations for having united Tokyo's fractious decision-making process, Tojo secured the emperor's acquiescence in war. The general then joined with IGHQ and prioritized operational success in the war's opening blows, including nearly simultaneous attacks against Malaya and Pearl Harbor. Meeting Japan's international legal obligations was relatively low on Tojo's list of priorities—he artfully dodged the emperor's questions about precisely this issue—and he presided over a decision-making process that dispensed with declarations of war against either Britain or the United States. Once again Tojo revealed himself opportunistic and beholden to no particular principle. He simply settled on his highest priority—in this case, success in Malaya and at Pearl Harbor—then did whatever he deemed necessary in an effort at ensuring the best possible outcome.

Criticisms can and should be made of Tojo's war leadership. Foremost among them must necessarily be the breathtaking frequency with which Tojo made fundamental changes to his grand strategy. He went to war in the hope that Japan and its allies might somehow force British and Chinese surrender and that the United States would thereby lose its will to stay in the fight. Weeks later he accepted the navy's arguments for a continued offensive that reached as far as Australia and India, but he also held fast a fallback position more neatly aligned with his own vision of a war of attrition in the Pacific. The maritime disaster at Midway convinced Tojo of the fundamental soundness of his own position. The subsequent loss of Guadalcanal was foreboding, but Tojo continued to hope that Japanese defenses in the Southwest Pacific might hold. Then came German defeat at Stalingrad, and Tojo had to accept that the Germans were no longer able to compel British surrender. He now turned his grand strategy on its head, envisioning that the Americans would lose their will to fight amid a grinding war of attrition in the Southwest Pacific and the British would acknowledge the hopelessness of their situation and come to terms with Germany and Japan. At the same time, he hoped that Wang would gain enough domestic political capital to convince Chiang Kai-shek that his own anti-Japanese cause was hopeless.

Problems manifested themselves everywhere. Japanese positions in the Southwest Pacific crumbled, and US forces also took back the Aleutian Islands at the northernmost extremity of Japan's hard-earned gains. Tojo seemed not to know which way to look. Then Japan's German and Italian allies surrendered their position in North Africa, and soon thereafter Italy dropped out of the war altogether. Tojo once again recalibrated his grand strategy. He accepted the need for a retracted defensive sphere in the Pacific, and at the same time he pinned his hopes on a decisive counterattack. The counterattack appealed to Tojo because it offered the opportunity of wresting back the initiative in the Pacific and of destroying US forces. Yet a prerequisite of any successful counterattack was the establishment of an impenetrable defensive position. This proved beyond Japanese capacity, and islands in the Central and Southwest Pacific fell to American forces with dizzying rapidity. Before he knew it, the Japanese home islands came within reach of the American B-29 bombers, courtesy of the fall of Guam. That was evidence of the vacuousness of Tojo's Pacific strategy; It coincided with the collapse of his continental strategy and the advent of an aerial bombardment campaign against the home islands by China-based B-29s. Tojo's ever-shifting grand strategy was lost, and he had nothing left to give other than disconcerting references to the propriety of national self-immolation.

Failings in Tojo's grand strategy were at least partly attributable to the gulf separating Japan's armed services. Military officers regarded the Chinese-Korean-Manchurian-Soviet nexus as the focal point for their collective attention, while their naval counterparts were primarily interested in the possibility of war against the Anglo-American powers on the expanses of the Pacific. This made perfect operational sense, but it made for a hopelessly bifurcated strategic outlook. Tojo did his best to bridge the divide: He overrode his professional military colleagues' objections in mid-1942 and accepted the navy's insistence on a decisive maritime battle at Midway; he repeatedly afforded the navy greater steel allocations than anybody in the army thought necessary; and, toward the end of his time atop the decision-making process, he placed the Thirty-First Army under naval command. Yet, as evidenced by his opening play as prime minister, when he rejected the navy's presumptive ministerial candidate in the argumentative Toyoda Soemu and got instead the compliant Shimada Shigetaro, Tojo presumed that the navy's outlook should be subordinated to that of the army. This presumption practically ensured that the admirals never bought into his subsequent arguments for greater union between the armed services. It also meant he closed himself off from the warnings of those admirals, like Toyoda, who were convinced that Japan could not hope to defeat the United States in war. Counterfactual thinking is risky, but we are left to ponder what might have been had Toyoda served on Tojo's cabinet. What would have happened had Toyoda held firm and refused to sanction war in the Pacific? One thing alone seems certain: It would have been unthinkable, even for as formidable a character as Tojo, to try and forsake the time-honored decision-making tradition that required a perfect unanimity of views between and among cabinet ministers and the chiefs of staff. Tojo would not, in other words, have been able to ignore or override Toyoda's obstructionism. Quite how Tojo would have navigated the competing pressures is anybody's guess, but the reexamination of the deadline for war that he launched in late October 1941 would have been far more pressurized and indeed interesting had Tojo had to contend with Toyoda.

The mutual independence of the cabinet and IGHQ was another complicating factor in Tojo's efforts at arriving at a coherent grand strategy. As army minister in the Konoe cabinet, he had been assiduous in making common cause with Army Chief of Staff Sugiyama Hajime. Maintaining that unity following his prime ministerial appointment proved difficult. It was commonsensical for Tojo, who remained as army minister, to continue to seek unity of purpose with the Army General Staff; as prime minister, he had necessarily to give due consideration to the views of all his cabinet ministers. This left him open to criticisms of what his professional military colleagues regarded as his neglect of the army's point of view, or his prioritization of his responsibilities as prime minister to the neglect of his duties as army minister. This dynamic was on full display during Tojo's heated wartime disputes with IGHQ over material allocations; unlike the chiefs of staff, he as prime minister had to remain mindful of the needs of the merchant marine. Tojo won the lion's share of these arguments. The disunity of purpose was nonetheless debilitating, and Tojo determined in early 1944 to take on the role of army chief of staff (his acquiescent navy minister likewise took on the role of navy chief of staff). This fusion of policy and operations was a classic case of too little, too late. The United States had by this time established a total preponderance of power in the Pacific. Nothing Tojo did could slow their momentum.

The doomed war effort was ultimately only the indirect cause of Tojo's downfall. He refused to fall on his figurative sword unless and until the emperor demanded he do so. This position was consistent with the principle of direct Imperial rule, which Tojo had worked hard to implement throughout his time as prime minister. In this sense, this would have been a fitting way for Tojo to go. The emperor was, however, loath to oblige. He fretted lest the army explode in indignation at his having acted against one of its own. Just as important, he was repudiating Tojo's vision of direct Imperial rule and was instead reasserting a conception of his self as but "one component of the state," according to which he ruled in concert with the various institutions of Imperial prerogative.[16] The story of how the emperor reconciled his self-conception with his subsequent so-called sacred decision to end the war is best left for another time; for now, it might merely be noted that in the absence of an Imperial diktat deposing Tojo, the Japanese Navy finally rediscovered its backbone and for a few months in 1944 worked actively to destabilize Tojo's power base. [17] Others, including Tojo's long-term civilian ally, Kishi Nobusuke, followed suit. This left the emperor to deliver the coup de grâce. On second thought, this was perhaps the most fitting way for Tojo to go.

What else might be said of Tojo's war leadership? His lack of concern for the people he led was a defining feature. He professed to care, and his random household rubbish bin inspections were supposed to be evidence of his solicitude for their well-being. Yet the loss of civilian life to aerial bombardment concerned him little; he continued to argue for a continuation of the war even *after* the atomic attacks against Hiroshima and Nagasaki. He wept following the first *gyokusai* (suicidal missions) in the Pacific, but not long thereafter he was speaking of the entire nation engaging in something akin to *gyokusai* in a cataclysmic decisive home island battle. He regarded the Japanese House of Representatives—the state organ purporting to represent the people—as a cesspit of corruption and disunity and was perfectly willing to brook charges of election interference in his efforts at ensuring its submissiveness. He almost instinctively withheld information from the people, and he was positively Orwellian in his "two plus two equals eighty" arithmetic, his thoughts about making the people see white in red, and his effort, at least his own mind, at making the deceased Nakano Seigo an unperson.

Criticisms might also be leveled at Tojo's vision of empire. He was unabashedly utilitarian in his approach and—to use terms he consciously adopted during the Japanese-US negotiations of 1941—he regarded the empire as necessary for Japan's self-existence and self-defense. To apply those terms to the specific example of Manchukuo, it served the needs of

Japan's self-existence insofar as it provided raw materials that would otherwise have to be sourced from outside the empire and, at the same time, it contributed to Japan's self-defense insofar as it provided a vital strategic locale in the event of war against the Soviets. Some in the Japanese Army, including the irascible Ishiwara Kanji, clung to a view of Manchukuo as an oasis of interracial Asian harmony; Tojo cared not at all for such idealism, showing interest only in policies and mechanisms designed to ensure Manchukuoan docility and servility. That same basic dynamic was discernible during the war in the Pacific, when Tojo was acutely aware of the Greater East Asia Co-Prosperity Sphere's utility to Japan and, for that reason, was unwilling to accept that nations in the sphere might want true independence.

Ultimately, Tojo's pre–Pearl Harbor failure to account for the enormity of US strength must necessarily be regarded as his greatest shortcoming. It is exceedingly difficult to reconcile Tojo's reputation as a total war officer with his myopic inability to recognize the preponderance of power the United States could bring to bear in war in the Pacific. How did he remain blind to the incredible economic, financial, technological, industrial, commercial, political, and diplomatic strength of the United States? Three interconnected answers present themselves. First, he was so bedazzled by the opportunity to strip the Western powers of their Southeast Asian colonies following the German blitzkrieg of 1940 that he failed to account for the pervasiveness of US power. Second, as was only right and proper in the Japanese decision-making process, he left practically all estimates and forecasts of US strength to the Japanese Navy. Third, he remained at some level beholden to traditional indices of military and maritime strength, and on those grounds, he reckoned that Japan's chances of victory over the United States were as good as they would ever be. On these grounds, it is perhaps unfair to conclude, as did International House of Japan mainstay Ian Mutsu, that Tojo was "shortsighted and stupid," but he was wrongheaded and blithely unconcerned by even the possible consequences of his embrace of war.[18]

Tojo embraced his responsibility for starting a war that ended in calamity for Japan, but his failed suicide attempt left very few satisfied that he had paid his dues. Then came the Tokyo trial, where Tojo defended Japan's actions in a feisty, defiant, and even authoritative performance. He embraced the role of scapegoat and took responsibility for all decisions reached during his time as prime minister. This was of course an exaggeration of wartime realities, but it folded neatly into other narratives that were contributing to the Japanese people's memory of the war, and especially the emperor's unprecedented intervention in the decision-making process to end the war. In this way Tojo created space for the emperor to burnish his own war-renouncing image and to work for the postwar survival of the Imperial institution. Protection of the emperor's dignity and safety had been a defining feature of Tojo's military career; this final effort was the only way Tojo could atone for his role in bringing things to such a pass.

NOTES

INTRODUCTION

1. "Akamatsu taisa e" [To Colonel Akamatsu], August 14, 1945, in "Tōjō moto Shushō shuki (Kiyose shiryō)" [Former Prime Minister Tojo's notes (Kiyose papers)], May 1966, 4A.22.2441, National Archives of Japan.
2. *Field Service Guide (Senzinkun)* (Tokyo: Tokyo Gazette Publishing House, 1941), 13.
3. Tōjō Yūko and Watanabe Shōichi, *Daitōa sensō no shinjitsu: Tōjō Hideki sensen kyōjutsusho* [The truth of the greater east Asian war: Tojo Hideki's sworn affidavit] (Tokyo: Wakku, 2005), 237.
4. These quotations are derived from a death row letter that Tojo penned to his family. The letter is quoted in full in Iwanami Yūko, *Issai kataru nakare* [Don't ever speak of me] (Tokyo: Yomiuri Shimbunsha, 1992), 131–137; the quotations herein are on 131, 132.
5. Yoshida Yutaka, "Senryōki ni okeru sensō sekinin-ron" [Debates about war responsibility during the occupation period], *Hitotsubashi rongi* [Hitotsubashi review] 105, no. 2 (1991): 134.
6. Jōhō Yoshio, ed., *Tōjō Hideki* (Tokyo: Fūyō Shobō, 1974), 5.
7. Satō Sanae, *Tōjō Hideki "waga munen"* [Tojo Hideki: "My chagrin"] (Tokyo: Kawade Shobō, 1997), 13.
8. Kiyosawa Kiyoshi, diary entry, July 20, 1944, in Kiyosawa Kiyoshi, *A Diary of Darkness: The Wartime Diary of Kiyosawa Kiyoshi,* ed. Eugene Soviak (Princeton, NJ: Princeton University Press, 1998), 228.
9. Iwanami, *Issai kataru nakare,* 80–81.
10. Konoe Fumimaro, *Heiwa e no doryoku: Konoe Fumimaro shuki* [My struggle for peace: Konoe Fumimaro's notes] (Tokyo: Nihon Denpō Tsūshinsha, 1946). See also Konoe Fumimaro, *Ushinawareshi seiji: Konoe Fumimaro-kō no shuki* [Failed politics: Prince Konoe Fumimaro's notes] (Tokyo: Asahi Shinbunsha, 1946).
11. For a former army officer's bitterly critical account of the "villainous army and virtuous navy" narrative, see Satō Akira, *Teikoku Kaigun "shippai" no kenkyū* [Research into the "failings" of the Imperial Navy] (Tokyo: Fuyō Shobō, 2000), 13.
12. Suzuki Kantarō, *Shūsen no hyōjō* [The face of the end of the war] (Tokyo: Rōdō Bunkasha, 1946), 8–10. See also Takagi Sōkichi, *Shūsen oboegaki* [Endgame-of-war memorandum] (Tokyo: Kōbundō Shobō, 1948); and Okada Keisuke, *Kaikoroku* [Reminiscences] (Tokyo: Mainichi Shimbunsha, 1951). General Koiso Kuniaki succeeded Tojo as prime minister; he resigned in April 1945 and was succeeded by Admiral Suzuki.
13. Tanaka Ryūkichi, *Haiin o tsuku: Gunbatsu sen'ō no jissō* [Probing the cause of defeat: The truth about the military clique's despotism] (Tokyo: Chūō Kōronsha, 1993), 61.
14. Miyatake Gaikotsu, *Amerikasama* [Dear America] (Tokyo: Zōroku Bunko, 1946), 6.
15. Maruyama Masao, *Thought and Behaviour in Modern Japanese Politics,* ed. Ivan Morris (London: Oxford University Press, 1969), 74, 87, 89, 120, 125, 128.
16. Tōjō Katsuko, "Omokage" [Shadows], in *Haisha: Tōjō Hideki fujin hoka senpan izoku no shuki* [The defeated: Notes by Tojo Hideki's widow and other war criminals' bereaved families], ed. Hayashi Ichirō (Tokyo: Futami Shobō, 1960), 63.
17. Itō Ken'ichirō, "Yuragu senbotsusha tsuitō, yuragu kokka: 1950-nendai kara 1970-nendai ni okeru Yasukuni Jinja o meguru gensetu no hensen o tōshite" [State, ambiguity, and war dead: Dispute on Yasukuni Shrine in postwar Japan from the 1950s to the 1970s],

Ritsumeikan kokusai kankei ronshū [Ritsumeikan journal of international studies] 9 (2009): 18.

18. Handō Kazutoshi, Hata Ikuhiko, and Hosaka Masayasu, "Shōwa Tennō 'Yasukuni memo' mikōkai bubun no kakushin" [The Showa Emperor's 'Yasukuni memo': The crux of the unreleased portion *Bungei shunjū* [Annals of art and culture], September 2009, 110–145.
19. Hata Ikuhiko, *Shōwashi no gunjintachi* [Soldiers and sailors of the Shōwa Period] (Tokyo: Bunshun Bunko, 1987), 64.
20. For reference to Tojo's "diabolical" image, see Tōjō Yūko, *Tōjōke no hahakogusa* [The Tojo family's cottonweed] (Tokyo: Kōbunsha 21, 2003), 11. For Tojo's granddaughter's criticism of the Japanese government, see Tōjō and Watanabe, *Daitōa sensō no shinjitsu,* 5–6.
21. Satō, *Tōjō Hideki,* 234.
22. Itō Shun'ya, dir., *Puraido: Unmei no toki* [Pride: The fateful moment], Tōei, 1998; released in the United States with English subtitles as *Pride,* DVD, Liberty International Entertainment/Cargo Films, 1998. See also Fukutomi Ken'ichi, *Tōjō Hideki: Tennō o moritōshita otoko* [Tojo Hideki: The man who protected the emperor] (Tokyo: Kōdansha, 2008); Matsuda Jukkoku, *Tōjō Hideki: Dai-Nippon Teikoku ni junjita otoko* [Tojo Hideki: The man who died for the Empire of Japan] (Tokyo: PHP Bunko, 2002); Shioda Michio, *Tennō to Tōjō Hideki no ku'nō: A-kyū senpan no isho to shūsen hiroku* [The emperor and Tojo Hideki's distress: The Class A war criminals' testaments and end-of-war records] (Tokyo: Mikasa Shobō, 1989); Ōkawa Ryūhō, *Tōjō Hideki: Daitōa sensō no shinjitsu o kataru* [Tojo Hideki: Speaking the truth of the Greater East Asian war] (Tokyo: Kōfuku no kagaku shuppan, 2013); and Takeda Kunihiko, *Naporeon to Tōjō Hideki: Rikei hakase ga seiri suru shin/kingendaishi* [Napoleon and Tojo Hideki: Truth in modern history as understood by a doctor of science] (Tokyo: Besuto Seraazu, 2016).
23. Furukawa Takahisa, *Tōjō Hideki: Taiheiyō Sensō o hajimeta gunjin saishō* [Tojo Hideki: The soldier-prime minister who started the Pacific war] (Tokyo: Yamakawa Shuppansha, 2009), 1.
24. Kōketsu Atsushi, "Tōjō Hideki: Dokusaisha ni narenakatta 'bakuryōchō'" [Tojo Hideki: The emperor's "chief of staff" who could not become a dictator], in Maeda Tetsuo and Kōketsu Atsushi, eds., *Tōgō Gensui wa nani o shita ka: Shōwa no sensō o enshutsu shita shōguntachi* [What did Fleet Admiral Togo do? The commanders who directed the Showa-era wars] (Tokyo: Kōbunken, 1989), 165, 168.
25. Robert J. C. Butow, *Tojo and the Coming of the War* (Princeton, NJ: Princeton University Press, 1961), 503. See also Alvin D. Coox, *Tojo* (New York: Ballantine Books, 1975); Peter Wetzler, *Hirohito and War: Imperial Tradition and Military Decision-Making in Prewar Japan* (Honolulu: University of Hawai'i Press, 1998), 61–81; Peter Wetzler, *Imperial Japan and Defeat in the Second World War: The Collapse of an Empire* (New York: Bloomsbury Academic, 2020), 89–145; Ben-Ami Shillony, *Politics and Culture in Wartime Japan* (Oxford: Clarendon Press, 1981); and see Edwin P. Hoyt, *Warlord: Tojo Against the World* (New York: Cooper Square, 2001).
26. For the documents that Tojo prepared in the final days of the war, see "Tōjō moto Shushō shuki." For the diarized accounts of Tojo's secretaries, see Itō Takashi, Hirohashi Tadamitsu, and Katashima Norio, eds., *Tōjō Naikaku Sōri Daijin kimitsu kiroku: Tōjō Hideki Taishō genkōroku* [Prime Minister Tojo confidential record: Record of General Tojo Hideki's words and deeds] (Tokyo: Tokyo Daigaku Shuppankai, 1990). Tojo prepared an account of the decision for war in the Pacific, in the margins of an anthology of Doi Bansui's poetry, during his postsurrender incarceration; see "Kaisen ni kansuru Tōjō Hideki Taishō no gokuchū shuki" [General Tojo Hideki's memorandum concerning the opening of war], Chūō sensō shidō jūyō kokusaku monjo 245, Center for Military History, National Institute for Defense Studies, Tokyo. This account is also available in Satō, *Tōjō Hideki.*

27. Kantōgun Shireibu, ed., "Tōri sakusen no sankō" [The Tōri campaign: References], Shōwa 12-nen 11-gatsu, Chūō Sensō Shidō Senkun 165, Center for Military History, National Institute for Defense Studies, Tokyo.
28. The official 102-volume *Senshi sōsho* series was published between 1965 and 1980 and has since been digitized in its entirety. See "Senshi shiryō / senshi zensho kensaku" [Library and historical records search system], Bōei Kenkyūjo [National Institute for Defense Studies], n.d., accessed April 5, 2022, http://www.nids.mod.go.jp/military_history_search/CrossSearch.
29. For the official history of Hirohito's reign, this book cites the unpublished volumes of *Shōwa Tennō jitsuroku,* which were made available to researchers in the Imperial Household Agency's Archives and Mausolea Department between September and November 2014. They have since been published; see Ku'naichō, ed., *Shōwa Tennō jitsuroku* [True documents of the Shōwa Emperor], 18 vols. (Tokyo: Tokyo Shoseki, 2015–2019). For the emperor's monologue, see Terasaki Hidenari, *Shōwa Tennō dokuhakuroku—Terasaki Hidenari Goyōgakari nikki* [The Showa Emperor's monologue: Imperial aide Terasaki Hidenari's diary], ed. Mariko Terasaki Miller (Tokyo: Bungei Shunjū, 1991); for an English-language translation, see Gordon M. Berger, Roger M. Brown, and Peter Mauch, eds., *The Emperor's Testimony: Hirohito's Monologue on Japan's War in Asia and the Pacific* (Cambridge: Cambridge University Press, forthcoming). Numerous courtiers' diaries and papers have become available in the years since the emperor's death; among the most recent are those of the Imperial Household Agency's first grand steward, Tajima Michiji. See Tajima Michiji, *Haietsuki* [Records of audiences], ed. Furukawa Takahisa, Chadani Seiichi, Tominaga Nozomu, Sebata Hajime, Kawanishi Hideya, Funabashi Seishin, eds., 5 vols. (Tokyo: Iwanami Shoten, 2021–2023).
30. Ichinose Toshiya, *Tōjō Hideki: "Dokusaisha" o enjita otoko* [Tojo Hideki: The man who acted as "dictator"] (Tokyo: Bunshun Shinsho, 2019). See also Furukawa, *Tōjō Hideki.* For a book that is not biographical but is pertinent, see Iwai Shūichirō, *1944-nen no Tōjō Hideki* [The Tojo Hideki of 1944] (Tokyo: Shōdensha Shinsho, 2020). For two excellent short biographies, see Tobe Ryōichi, "Tōjō Hideki," in *Shōwa no shidōsha* [Showa-era leaders] (Tokyo: Chūō Kōron Shinsha, 2019), 71–104; and Kiyotada Tsutsui, "Tōjō Hideki: Shōwa no higeki no taigensha" [Tojo Hideki: The embodiment of the Showa-era tragedy], in *Shōwashi kōgi: Gunjinhen* [Lectures on Showa era history: Soldiers and sailors], ed. Kiyotada Tsutsui (Tokyo: Chikuma Shinsho, 2018), 35–52. Hosaka Masayasu, *Tōjō Hideki to tennō no jidai (1) gunnai kōsō kara kaisen zen'ya made* [Tōjō Hideki and the era of the emperor (1) from intra-service conflict to the eve of the opening of the war] (Tokyo: Bungei Shunjū, 1988), and Hosaka Masayasu, *Tōjō Hideki to tennō no jidai (2) Nichi-Bei kaisen kara Tōkyō saiban made* [Tōjō Hideki and the era of the emperor (2) from the opening of the Japanese-U.S. war to the Tokyo trial] (Tokyo: Bungei Shunjū, 1988), are based on a wealth of source materials; Jōhō, *Tōjō Hideki,* is a compilation of sources as well as reminiscences by former army officers. For an older psychoanalytical study, see Hanzawa Hiroshi, "Tōjō Hideki," in *Gendai Nihon shisō taikei, 10: kenryoku no shisei* [Series on contemporary Japanese political thought, 10: The idea of power], ed. Kamishima Jirō (Tokyo: Chikuma Shobō, 1965), 327–350.
31. See, for example, Hans Speier, "Ludendorff: The German Concept of Total War," in *Makers of Modern Strategy: Military Thought from Machiavelli to Hitler,* ed. Edward Meade Earle (Princeton, NJ: Princeton University Press, 1948), 306–322; and Carl von Clausewitz, *On War,* trans. Michael Howard and Peter von Paret, (Princeton, NJ: Princeton University Press, 1976).
32. H. G. Wells, *The War That Will End War* (London: Frank and Cecil Palmer, 1914).
33. Michael A. Barnhart, *Japan Prepares for Total War: The Search for Economic Security, 1919–1941* (Ithaca, NY: Cornell University Press, 1987), 18.

34. Paul Kennedy, "Grand Strategy in War and Peace: Toward a Broader Definition," in *Grand Strategies in War and Peace*, ed. Paul Kennedy (New Haven, CT: Yale University Press, 1991), 2. See also Jeremy A. Yellen, "What Grand Strategy? Japan, 1931–1945," in *From Far East to Asia Pacific: Great Powers and Grand Strategy 1900–1954*, ed. Brian P. Farrell, S. R. Joey Long, and David J. Ulbrich (Berlin: De Gruyter, 2024), 221–249.
35. Harold D. Lasswell, "The Garrison State," *American Journal of Sociology* 46, no. 4 (1941): 455, 458–460.
36. Allan Mallinson, *Too Important for the Generals: Losing and Winning the First World War* (London: Penguin, 2017).
37. Kōketsu Atsushi, *Kenpei seiji: Kanshi to dōkatsu no jidai* [Kenpei politics: The era of surveillance and intimidation] (Tokyo: Shin Nippon Shuppansha, 2008), chapter 3, 87–136.
38. Kiyosawa Kiyoshi, diary entry, January 5, 1944, in Kiyosawa, *A Diary of Darkness*, 132.
39. See, for example, Robert King Hall, ed., *Kokutai no Hongi: Cardinal Principles of the National Entity of Japan*, trans., John Owen Gauntlett (Newtown, MA: Crofton, 1974); and Chigaku Tanaka, *What Is Nippon Kokutai? Introduction to Nipponese National Principles* (Tokyo: Shishio Bunko, 1935).
40. Hirobumi Ito, *Commentaries on the Constitution of the Empire of Japan*, trans. Miyoji Ito (Tokyo: Igirisu Hōritsu Gakko, 1889), 6–7, 24.
41. "The Imperial Rescript to Soldiers and Sailors," in *Sources of Japanese Tradition*, comp. Wm. Theodore de Bary, Ryusaku Tsunoda, and Donald Keene, vol. 2 (New York: Columbia University Press, 1964), 705–710.
42. Hall, ed., *Kokutai no Hongi*, 59, 67.
43. For a work that mischaracterizes army factionalism in the early 1930s but which nonetheless neatly summarizes military opposition to the organ theory, see Frank O. Miller, *Minobe Tatsukichi: Interpreter of Constitutionalism in Japan* (Berkeley: University of California Press, 1965), 210–215.
44. After the war had been fought and lost, the emperor recalled his embrace of the organ theory. See Berger et al., *The Emperor's Testimony*.
45. Japan uses a regnal calendar—that is, it marks time by Imperial reigns. Each reign is posthumously given a name, and when the emperor dies, he takes the name of the era with him. Mutsuhito ascended the throne in 1868 and began the Meiji era, and then when he died in 1912 he was named the Meiji Emperor; Yoshihito ascended the throne in 1912 and began the Taisho era, and then when he died in 1926 he was named the Taisho Emperor; Hirohito ascended the throne in 1926 and began the Showa era, and then when he died in 1989, he was named the Showa Emperor. Regarding "evil advisers," see Ben Ami-Shillony, *Revolt in Japan: The Young Officers and the February 26, 1936 Incident* (Princeton, NJ: Princeton University Press, 1973), 217.
46. See, for example, Ryoichi Tobe, "Tojo Hideki as a War Leader," in *British and Japanese Military Leadership in the Far Eastern War, 1941–1945*, ed. Brian Bond and Kyoichi Ichikawa (London: Frank Cass, 2004), 27.
47. The twin issues of the independence of the supreme command and the difficult relationships among Japan's armed services receive judicious treatment in Tobe, "Tojo Hideki as a War Leader."
48. See Berger et al., *The Emperor's Testimony*.
49. Ito, *Commentaries*, 85.
50. See, for example, Moriyama Atsushi, *Nihon wa naze kaisen ni fumikitta ka* [Why did Japan launch war?] (Tokyo: Shinchōsha, 2012).
51. Peter Mauch, "Prime Minister Tōjō Hideki on the Eve of Pearl Harbor: New Evidence from Japan," *Global War Studies* 15, no. 1 (2018): 36–37.
52. See, for example, Moriyama Atsushi, "Rekishi techō: Hyakutake Saburō nikki ni miru Shōwa Tennō no tai-Bei kaisen ketsui" [Historical note: The Showa Emperor's decision

for war against the United States as seen in the Hyakutake Saburo diary], *Nihon rekishi* [Japanese history] 903: 32–35.

53. See Berger et al., *The Emperor's Testimony.*
54. Berger et al., *The Emperor's Testimony.*
55. Audience record, July 14, 1950, in Michiji, *Haietsuki,* 182.

1 · TOJO'S YOUTH

1. "Charter Oath," in *Sources of Japanese Tradition,* vol. 2, comp. Wm. Theodore de Bary, Ryusaku Tsunoda, and Donald Keene (New York: Columbia University Press, 1964), 137.
2. Hosaka Masayasu, *Tōjō Hideki to tennō no jidai: gunnai kōsō kara kaisen zen'ya made* [Tōjō Hideki and the era of the emperor: From intra-service conflict to the eve of the opening of the war], vol. 1 (Tokyo: Bungei Shunjū, 1988), 21–23.
3. Hosaka, *Tōjō Hideki,* 1:21–23.
4. See Kawano Hitoshi, "Kindai nihon ni okeru gunji eriito no sentaku: Guntai shakai no 'gakureki shugi'" [Selection of the armed services' elite in modern Japan: The doctrine of "educational background" in the armed services' society], *Kyōiku shakaigaku kenkyū* [Educational sociology studies] 45 (1989): 163.
5. Edward J. Drea, *Japan's Imperial Army: Its Rise and Fall, 1853–1945* (Lawrence: University Press of Kansas, 2009), 59.
6. Jakob Meckel, "Yasenhō haisu beki no setsu" [The theory that field artillery should be abolished], in *Nippon no shin'ro* [Japan's course], ed. Itō Mio, vol. 1 (Tokyo: Ōishidō, 1888), 65–66.
7. Prince Arisugawa Taruhito to Oyama Iwao, February 24, 1888, "Tōjō Taii Doitsukoku ryūgaku no ken" [The matter of Captain Tojo's study in Germany], Meiji 21-nen Futatsudai Nikki 2-gatsu, futatsudai nikki, rikugunshō dainikki, Japanese Defense Ministry Archives (hereafter cited as JDMA), Japan Center for Asian Historical Records (hereafter cited as JACAR) reference code C06080647900.
8. "Rikugun hohei taii Tōjō Hidenori Doitsukoku ryūgakuhi mei no ken" [The matter of infantry captain Tojo Hidenori's orders to study abroad in Germany], March 10, 1888, Kanri shintai meiji 21-nen kanri shintai 4: Rikugunshō, dai-5-rui shokan shintai / kanri shintai, daijōkan / naikaku kankei, naikaku / sōrifu, gyōsei bunsho, National Archives of Japan (hereafter cited as NAJ), 2A-018-00, JACAR reference code: A00170100.
9. Tōjō Hidenori, "Reigen" [Preface], Nisshin sen'eki, Sen'eki, Rikugun ippan shiryō, JDMA, JACAR reference code C13110353100.
10. See, for example, Tsuge Hisayoshi, *Nichi-Ro Sensō meishōden: Jinbutsu de yomu gekitō no kiseki* [Biographies of famous commanders of the Russo-Japanese War: The locus of fierce fighting as read by human figures] (Tokyo: PHP Bunko, 2004), 58–59.
11. Ōsawa Hiroaki, "'Seishin yōhei kakuheki chōdan' to Ni-Sshin Sensō kenkyū" ["Operations against China: Inquiries into the matrix" and studies of the Sino-Japanese War], *Kumamoto hōgaku* 122 (2011): 102. See also Tsukamoto Takahiko, "Kyūrikugun ni okeru senshi hensan—gunji soshiki no yoru senshi e no torikumi no kadai to genkai" [Publications of military history by the Imperial Japanese Army—problems and limitations of military history undertaken by military organizations]: 70.
12. Tōjō Yūko and Fukudome Ken'ichi, *Tōjō Hideki no naka no Bukkyō to Shintō: Hito wa ikanishite shi o ukeirerunoka* [Buddhism and Shinto within Tojo Hideki: How do people accept death?] (Tokyo: Kōdansha Shinsho, 2010), 121.
13. Hosaka, *Tōjō Hideki,* 1:26–27.
14. Hosaka, *Tōjō Hideki,* 1:27.
15. For a partial translation of a popular play based on the folktale concerning Oiwa, see "Yotsuya Ghost Stories, Act Three," trans. Mark Oshima, in *Traditional Japanese Theater:*

An Anthology of Plays, ed. Karen Brazell (New York: Columbia University Press, 1998), 456–483.

16. Itō Shun'ichirō, *Shisei/tetsu no hito: Tōjō Hideki den* [Man of sincerity and iron: Tojo Hideki biography] (Tokyo: Ten'yū Shobō, 1942), 19. See also Hosaka, *Tōjō Hideki*, 1:31.
17. Ichinose Toshiya, *Tōjō Hideki: "Dokusaisha" o enjita otoko* [Tojo Hideki: The man who acted as "dictator"] (Tokyo: Bunshun Shinsho, 2019), 11–12.
18. Tanizaki Jun'ichirō, *Childhood Years: A Memoir*, trans. Paul McCarthy (Ann Arbor: University of Michigan Press, 2017), 82.
19. Regarding the minimum standard of education for aspiring cadets, see "Rikugun chihō yōnen gakkō jōrei" [Army local cadet schools ordinance], in *Rikugun shusshin shigansha hikei* [Handbook for those aspiring to the army] (Tokyo: Kōseidō, 1897), 431–434.
20. "Imperial Rescript to Soldiers and Sailors," in De Bary et al., *Sources of Japanese Tradition*, 2:705–710.
21. Nomura Rieko, *Rikugun Yōnen Gakkō taisei no kenkyū: Eriito yōsei to gunji/kyōiku/seiji* [A study of the Military Preparatory School system: Elite training and military/education/politics] (Tokyo: Yoshikawa Kōbunkan, 2007), 30–44.
22. Diary entry, July 5, 1939, in Itō Takashi and Terunuma Yasutaka, eds., *Zokugendaishi shiryō (4): Rikugun; Hata Shunroku nisshi* [Documents on contemporary history, continued (4): The army; Hata Shunroku's diary] (Tokyo: Misuzu Shobō, 1983), 218–219.
23. "Rikugun Yōnen Gakkō kyōiku kōryō" [Military Preparatory School educational plan], in *Kyōiku shiki* [Education commands], ed. Itō Yoshimatsu (Tokyo: Heiji Zasshisha, 1899), 87–88.
24. "Rikugun Yōnen Gakkō jōrei o sadamu" [Decision on the Military Preparatory School regulations], June 16, 1887, Kōbun ruijū dai-11-hen meiji 20-nen dai-15-kan heiseimongo heigaku ichi, NAJ, JACAR reference code A15111333000.
25. Imamura Bun'ei, *Rikugun Yōnen Gakkō no seikatsu* [Life at the Military Preparatory School], (Tokyo: Shōnen Tosho Shuppansha, 1944), 147–154. Regarding Tojo's entry to the Central Military Preparatory School, see *Kanpō* [Japanese government gazette] no. 5752, September 4, 1902, 65. Regarding his graduation from the Central Military Preparatory School, see *Kanpō* [Japanese government gazette] no. 6276, June 3, 1904, 54. *Kanpō* from 1882 to 1952 have been digitized and are viewable via Japan's National Diet Library Digital Collections (https://dl.ndl.go.jp/).
26. "Rikugun Chūō Yōnen Gakkō e Gyōgō no ken" [Concerning the Imperial visit to the Central Military Preparatory School], May 1903, Daiichi nikki, rikugunshō dainikki, JDMA, JACAR reference code C04013895100. See also "Rikugun Chūō Yōnen Gakkō e Gyōgō no ken" [Concerning the Imperial visit to the Central Military Preparatory School], May 1904, Daiichi nikki, rikugunshō dainikki, JDMA, JACAR reference code C04013980900.
27. This borrows from the language of the aforementioned Imperial Rescript to Soldiers and Sailors. See "Imperial Rescript."
28. Hosaka, *Tōjō Hideki*, 1:34.
29. Rikugun Shikan Gakkō, ed., *Rikugun Shikan Gakkō ichiran* [Military Academy conspectus] (Tokyo: Seishindō, 1908), 46, 59–60.
30. Bōeichō Bōei Kenshujo Senshishitsu (hereafter cited as BBKS), ed., *Senshi sōsho (8) Daihon'ei Rikugunbu (1) Shōwa 15nen 5gatsu made* [War history series (8), Imperial Headquarters, Army (1) until May 1940] (Tokyo: Asagumo Shimbunsha, 1967), 126.
31. Rikugun Shikan Gakkō, *Rikugun Shikan Gakkō ichiran*, 46.
32. Rikugun Shikan Gakkō, *Rikugun Shikan Gakkō ichiran*, 47. Regarding the fears of increased Russo-German cooperation and the importance attached to Prince Karl's visit, see John Albert White, *The Diplomacy of the Russo-Japanese War* (Princeton, NJ: Princeton University Press, 1964), 164.
33. Military preparatory school graduates gained direct entry into the Military Academy; those from civilian schools who sought entry first had to sit a highly competitive en-

trance examination. See Rikugun Shikan Gakkō, ed., *Rikugun Shikan Gakkō no shinsō* [The truth of the Military Academy] (Tokyo: Gaikō Jihōsha, 1914), 1.

34. Yamanaka Minetarō, *Rikugun hangakuji* [Army rebels] (Tokyo: Ohara Shoten, 1954), 184–187. "D" was shorthand for *daba,* which translates directly as a "pack horse" or a "horse of inferior breeding." "Donkey" is an idiomatic translation, which has the added value of starting with the letter *d.*
35. "Shikan Gakkō e gyōkō no ken" [Imperial visit to the Military Academy], March 22, 1905, Rikugunshō, Futatsu Dainikki, M38-3-51, JDMA, JACAR reference code C04014044000.
36. Andrew Gordon, "Social Protest in Imperial Japan: The Hibiya Riot of 1905," *Asia-Pacific Journal: Japan Focus* 12, no. 29 (2014): 3.
37. BBKS, *Senshi sōsho (8),* 126.
38. Hayashi Senjūrō, Tōjō Hideki, Itagaki Seishirō, and Ogawa Heikichi, *Roshiya kuru zo!* [Russia's coming!] (Tokyo: Teikoku Gunji Kyōkai, 1939).
39. Kimura Yoshiharu, ed., *Gendai ijin no genkō* [Words and deeds of great men of our time] (Tokyo: Fukōsha, 1909), 112.
40. Satō Sanae, *Tōjō Katsuko no shōgai: "A-kyū" senpan no tsuma to shite* [Tojo Katsuko's life as the wife of a "Class A" war criminal] (Tokyo: Jiji Tsūshinsha, 1987), 74–77.
41. Satō, *Tōjō Katsuko no shōgai,* 79. Tojo's eldest sister, Hatsue, was married to a soldier who was serving in Korea. She had therefore returned to her parents' home with her two children.
42. Tōjō Yūko, *Tōjōke no hahakogusa* [The Tojo family's cottonweed] (Tokyo: Kōbunsha, 2003), 14–17, 20.
43. Abiru Shōten Shuppanbu, ed., *Kakushu gakkō nyūgaku annai* [All schools' entry guide] (Tokyo: Abiru Shōten Shuppanbu, 1914), 81.
44. For the books that Tojo in all likelihood used in preparation for the entrance exam, see Tokyo Heirinkan, ed., *Kiō jūnenkan Rikugun Daigakkō hatsuban saiban shiken mondai tōanshū: Chikujō oyobi kōtsū, chikei no bu* [Collection of questions and answers from first and second Army War College entrance examinations for the past ten years: Fortifications, movements, and topography] (Tokyo: Heirinkan, 1910); Tokyo Heirinkan, ed., *Kiō jūnenkan Rikugun Daigakkō hatsuban saiban shiken mondai tōanshū: Heiki no bu* [Collection of questions and answers from first and second Army War College entrance examinations for the past ten years: Armaments] (Tokyo: Heirinkan, 1910); Tokyo Heirinkan, ed., *Kiō jūnenkan Rikugun Daigakkō hatsuban saiban shiken mondai tōanshū: Senjutsu no bu* [Collection of questions and answers from first and second Army War College entrance examinations for the past ten years: Tactics and operations] (Tokyo: Heirinkan, 1910). See also Kensū Gakkai, ed., *Kako ni okeru Rikugun Daigakkō hatsuban shiken sūgaku mondai oyobi sono tōkai ni tsuite* [Mathematical questions and answers from past Army War College initial entrance exams] (Tokyo: Kensū Gakkai, 1916).
45. Tōjō Hidenori, *Hohei kyōren no kan* [Infantry drill manual], vol. 1 (Tokyo: Heiji Zasshisha, 1906), 1, 7, 8.
46. Hosaka, *Tōjō Hideki,* 1:46–47.
47. Tojo Hideki to Tojo Hidenori, October 14, 1910, in Tōjō Yūko, *Kazokuai: Tōjō Hideki to Katsuko no ikuji nikki to tegami yori* [Familial love: From the parenting journal and letters of Tojo Hideki and Katsuko] (Tokyo: Kasuga Shuppan, 2008), 230.
48. Suyama Yukio, *Sakusen no oni Obata Toshirō* [Strategy demon Obata Toshiro] (Tokyo: Fuyō Shobō, 1983), 63.
49. For the written exam that Tojo passed in 1912, see Gunji Gakushishin, ed., *Rikugun Daigakkō hatsuban shiken mondai narabi kaitō* [Army War College written entrance exam questions and answers] (Tokyo: Gunji Gakushishinsha, 1912).
50. Tojo Katsuko, journal entry, December 12, 1912, in Tōjō, *Kazokuai,* 94.
51. BBKS, *Senshi sōsho (8),* 131.

52. The text appears in Shimanuki Takeji, "Nichi-Ro Sensō ikō ni okeru kokubō hōshin, shōyō heiryoku, yōhei kōryō no hensen" [The development of the national defense policy, the naval strength requirement, and the general plan for strategy since the Russo-Japanese War], *Gunji shigaku* [The Journal of Military History] 8, no. 4 (1973): 2–16.
53. For an army officer's book-length discussion of these issues, see Mitake Kakutarō, *Iryoku aru kokubō to seiei naru kokugun: Ichimei kyōdō hōkokuron* [Powerful national defense and the nation's best armed forces: One person's theory of cooperative patriotism] (Tokyo: Heirinkan, 1914).
54. Doris G. Bargen, *Suicidal Honor: General Nogi and the Writings of Mori Ōgai and Natsume Sōseki* (Honolulu: University of Hawai'i Press, 2006), 13.

2 · THE MAKING OF A POLITICAL OFFICER

1. Richard J. Smethurst, *A Social Basis for Prewar Japanese Militarism: The Army and the Rural Community* (Berkeley: University of California Press, 1974), 19.
2. These quotations draw from the War College's regulations, which were revised during Tojo's first year there, in 1913. See Jōhō Yoshio, ed., *Rikugun Daigakkō* [The War College] (Tokyo: Fūyō Shobō, 1973), 159, 240–242.
3. For a table of all instructors during Tojo's first year at the War College, see Jōhō, *Rikugun Daigakkō*, appendix 8.
4. Jōhō, *Rikugun Daigakkō,* appendix 8.
5. Sanbō Honbu, ed., *Meiji 37–38 nen Nichiro Senshi* [History of the Russo-Japanese War of 1904–1905], 9 vols. (Tokyo: Kaikōsha, 1912–1915). Reference to the War College's adoption of this official history as a textbook can be found in Jōhō, *Rikugun Daigakkō*, 267.
6. Tsukamoto Takayoshi, "Kyūrikugun ni okeru senshi hensan: Gunji soshiki ni yoru senshi e no torikumi no kadai to genkai" [Editing war history in the former army: Challenges and limitations of military organizations' approach to military history], *Senshi kenkyū nenpō* [Military history studies annual] 10 (2007): 70–71.
7. Tamon Jirō, *Yo ga sanka shitaru Nichi-Ro seneki* [The Russo-Japanese War in which I participated] (Tokyo: Zamajuku Shuppanbu, 1942).
8. Jōhō, *Rikugun Daigakkō* , 267.
9. Obata Toshiro, quoted in Takayama Shinobu, *Rikugun Daigakkō no senryaku/senjutsu kyōiku* [Education in strategy at the War College] (Tokyo: Fūyō Shobō, 2003), 100.
10. Jōhō, *Rikugun Daigakkō,* 267.
11. "Yasen setusbi jinchi no kōgeki," in *Senjutsu kenkyū no sankō, zokuhen* [Military science references, continued], ed. Rikugun Daigakkō (Tokyo: Kanjōdō, 1914), 1–67.
12. Muro Kenji, *Shokyū senjutsu kōju shubo* [Elementary war science: Lecture notes] (Tokyo: Tatekidō, 1914), 62.
13. Shiba Kōtarō, *Barukan senjutsusho* [Writings on Balkan strategy] (Tokyo: Tatekidō, 1914), 23.
14. Bōeichō Bōei Kenshujo Senshishitsu (hereafter cited as BBKS), ed., *Senshi sōsho (27) Kantōgun (1) tai-So senbi/Nomonhan Jihen* [War history series (27), the Kwantung Army (1), preparations vis-à-vis the Soviets/the Nomonhan Incident] (Tokyo: Asagumo Shuppansha, 1969), 28–29.
15. Gunjigaku Shishin, ed., *Jūkenjutsu kyōiku shishin* [Bayonet instruction guide] (Tokyo: Gunjigaku Shishinsha, 1909), 1–7.
16. *Yagai yōmurei* [War field duty manual] (Tokyo: Buyōdō, 1907), 6. Writing of the army's appropriation of *bushido,* Karl F. Friday, "Bushidō or Bull? A Medieval Historian's Perspective on the Imperial Army and the Japanese Warrior Tradition," *The History Teacher* 27, no. 3 (1994): 340, notes, "Hanging the label of '*bushidō*' on either the ideology of the Imperial Army or the warrior ethic of medieval Japan involves some fairly overt historian's sleight-of-hand."

17. Gunroshōkai Hensan, ed., *Gunjin seishin* [The spirit of soldiers and sailors] (Tokyo: Gunroshōkai, 1912), 1.
18. Heiji Zasshisha Kenkyūkai, ed., *Yūseigun ni taisuru shōjakugun no senjutsu* [Military operations for a numerically inferior force fighting a numerically superior force] (Tokyo: Heiji Zasshisha, 1913), 7.
19. "Yūsei naru teki ni taisuru kōgeki ni tsuite" [Concerning an attack against a numerically superior enemy], in Heiji Zasshisha Kenkyūkai, *Yūseigun ni taisuru shōjakugun no senjutsu,* 181–195.
20. Heiji Zasshisha Kenkyūkai, *Yūseigun ni taisuru shōjakugun no senjutsu,* 220, 335–336.
21. Tōjō Hidenori, *Senjutsu fumoto no chiri* [Strategic dust that has accumulated at the foot of a mountain], 2 vols. (Tokyo: Heiji Zasshisha, 1910). The title presumably references an Edo-era collection of printed ephemera titled "Fumoto no chiri" [Dust that has accumulated at the foot of a mountain]. The following discussion draws on a recent rendering of this work. See Izumi Shōshirō, ed., *Tōjō Hidenori "Nihon no sensōron" o yomu* [Reading Tojo Hidenori's "Japan on war"] (Tokyo: Bungei Shunjū, 2010).
22. Sugimori Hisahide, *Densetsu to jitsuzō: Shōwa jinbutsuden* [Legends and real images: Biographies of Showa-era personages] (Tokyo: Shinchōsha, 1967), 82.
23. Izumi, *Tōjō Hidenori "Nihon no sensōron,"* 25–37.
24. Izumi, *Tōjō Hidenori "Nihon no sensōron,"* 39–42.
25. Izumi, *Tōjō Hidenori "Nihon no sensōron,"* 23.
26. During a student officer's second year the War College classroom devoted some twenty hours to maritime strategy. See Jōhō, *Rikugun Daigakkō,* 164–167. Regarding the Twenty-One Demands, see, for example, Sōchi Naraoka, "A New Look at Japan's Twenty-One Demands: Reconsidering Katō Takaaki's Motives in 1915," in *The Decade of the Great War: Japan and the Wider World in the 1910s,* ed. Tosh Minohara, Tze-ki Hon, and Evan Dawley (Leiden, Netherlands: Brill, 2014), 189–210.
27. Mitake Kakutarō, *Ōshū sensō nichiroku hyōron* [Critical journal of the European war] (Tokyo: Hōkō Gakusha, 1915), 19.
28. "Rikugun Daigakkō heigaku kyōkan oyobi dōgakusei o kōkūki ni tōjō seshimuru ken" [Placing War College instructors and students aboard aircraft], Rikugunshō dainikki kanshū T4-2-14, Japanese Defense Ministry Archives (hereafter cited as JDMA), Japan Center for Asian Historical Records (hereafter cited as JACAR) reference code C02030735600.
29. Tojo Hideki, quoted in Hosaka Masayasu, *Tōjō Hideki to tennō no jidai: Gunnai kōsō kara kaisen zen'ya made* [Tojo Hideki and the era of the emperor: From intraservice conflict to the eve of the opening of the war], vol. 1 (Tokyo: Bungei Shunjū, 1988), 58.
30. *Kanpō* [Government bulletin] no. 1012, December 15, 1916, 381.
31. Hosaka, *Tōjō Hideki,* 1:59.
32. Rikugun Daijin Kanbō, ed., *Rikugun seiki ruiju* [Army regulations] (Tokyo: Senryūdō Kobayashi Matashichi, 1916).
33. James E. Sheridan, "The Warlord Era: Politics and Militarism Under the Peking Government, 1916–1928," in *The Cambridge History of China,* vol. 12, *Republican China, 1912–1949, Part 1,* ed. John K. Fairbank (Cambridge: Cambridge University Press, 1983), 303.
34. The text of the revised Imperial National Defense Policy remains undiscovered, and is presumed to have been incinerated in the immediate aftermath of Japanese surrender in World War II. For analysis, based on other relevant documentation, see BBKS, ed., *Senshi sōsho (8) Daihon'ei Rikugunbu (1) Shōwa 15nen 5gatsu made* [War history series (8), Imperial Headquarters, Army (1) until May 1940] (Tokyo: Asagumo Shimbunsha, 1967), 217–223. See also Saitō Seiji, "Kokubō hōshin daiichiji kaitei no haikei: Dainiji Ōkuma naikakka ni okeru rikukairyōgun kankei" [The background of the first revision of the national defense plan: Army-navy relations during the Ōkuma cabinet], *Shigaku zasshi* [Journal of historical science] 95, no. 6 (1986): 1007–1042.

35. James William Morley, *The Japanese Thrust into Siberia, 1918* (New York: Columbia University Press, 1957), 308.
36. "Dai12 shidan shotai no ichibu shisatsu ni kansuru ken (Tōjō Taii)" [Concerning inspection of Twelfth Division troops (Captain Tōjō)], Seimitsu jūdai nikki, Rikugunshō dainikki, JDMA, JACAR reference code C07060610100.
37. "Tōjō, Takahashi hohei taii, Ishiguchi, Ishii, Ōta hōhei taii kaigai shucchō no ken" [Overseas trip for infantry captains Tōjō and Takahashi and artillery captains Ishiguchi, Ishii, and Ōta], August 6–8, 1919, 5-1-10-0-4_1_003, JFMA, JACAR reference code B07090462700.
38. "Kakushu chōsa iinkai monjo: Rinji Gunji Chōsa Iin geppō dai-56-gō" [Various investigative committee documents: Extraordinary Research Commission into Military Affairs monthly report number 56], December 20, 1919, Taseikan / naikaku kankei, i-00124100, National Archives of Japan, JACAR reference code A05021015700. The reports that Tojo filed from Switzerland and later from Germany have been lost to history. The quotations in this paragraph are taken from an Extraordinary Research Commission into Military Affairs report. It should, in this regard, be noted that the commission based its research in large part on the reporting of Japanese military officers based in Europe. See "Rinji Gunji Chōsa Iin gyōmu jisshi no keikyō oyobi dō dai-1-nenpō chōsei hōkoku no ken" [Concerning implementation of Extraordinary Research Commission into Military Affairs business and compilation of the commission's first annual report], Rikugunshō ōuke dainikki T6-5-35, JDMA, JACAR reference code C03024767500.
39. See, for example, Abe Shōhei, "Daiichiji sekai taisen no Nihon rikugun ni oyoboshita eikyō: hohei senjutsu e no tekiō o chūshin to shite" [The first world war's influence on the Japanese army: Focusing on adaptations to infantry tactics], *Senshi kenkyū nenpō* [Military history studies annual] 18 (2015): 5–9.
40. Rinji Gunji Chōsa Iin, *Kokka sōdōin ni kansuru iken* [Views on national mobilization] (Tokyo: Rikugunshō, 1920), 2–3, 10.
41. See, for example, Mori Yasuo, *Nagata Tetsuzan: Heiwa iji wa gunjin no saidai sekimu nari* [Nagata Tetsuzan: The maintenance of peace is the greatest obligation of soldiers and sailors] (Kyoto: Minerva Shobō, 2011), 43–86. See also Kawada Minoru, *Shōwa rikugun no kiseki: Nagata Tetsuzan no kōsō to sono bunki* [Trajectory of the Showa-era army: Nagata Tetsuzan's vision and its ramifications] (Tokyo: Chūō Kōron Shinsha, 2011), 5–24.
42. Mori, *Nagata Tetsuzan,* 80–81.
43. Takahashi Masae, *Shōwa no gunbatsu* [Showa-era military cliques] (Tokyo: Kōdansha Gakujutsu Bunko, 2003), 81–83. See also Leonard A. Humphreys, *The Way of the Heavenly Sword: The Japanese Army in the 1920s* (Stanford, CA: Stanford University Press, 1995), 34–36.
44. Nakamura Kikuo, *Shōwa rikugun hisshi* [History of the Showa-era army] (Tokyo: Banchō Shobō, 1968), 137–138.
45. Kawada, *Shōwa rikugun no kiseki,* 8.
46. Takahashi, *Shōwa no gunbatsu,* 101.
47. Hosaka, *Tōjō Hideki,* 1:72–73.
48. Satō Kenryō, *Satō Kenryō no shōgen* [Satō Kenryō's testimony] (Tokyo: Fuyō Shobō, 1976), 38. For another student officer's account of Tojo's teaching of the Battle of the Marne, see Inada Masazumi, "Tōjō san no hen'ei" [A glimpse of Tojo], in *Tōjō Hideki,* ed. Jōhō Yoshio (Tokyo: Fūyō Shobō, 1974), 634–635.
49. Gerhard Ritter, "Foreword," in *The Schlieffen Plan: Critique of a Myth* (London: Oswald Wolff, 1958), 8, 12.
50. Ichinose Toshiya, *Tōjō Hideki: "Dokusaisha" o enjita otoko* [Tojo Hideki: The man who acted as "dictator"] (Tokyo: Bunshun Shinsho, 2019), 46–47.
51. Kitaoka Shin'ichi, *Kan'ryōsei to shite no Nihon Rikugun* [The Japanese Army as a bureaucratic system] (Tokyo: Chikuma Shobō, 2012), 88.

52. J. P. Clark, *Preparing for War: The Emergence of the Modern U.S. Army, 1815–1917* (Cambridge, MA: Harvard University Press, 2017), x.
53. See BBKS, *Senshi sōsho (8)*, 244–264. See also Yokoyama Hisayuki, "Nihon Rikugun no gunji gijutsu sen'ryaku to gunbi kōsō ni tsuite (2 kan): Daiichiji Sekai Taisengo o chūshin to shite" [Concerning the Japanese Army's technological strategies and arms programs (2): Focusing on the period after the First World War], *Bōei Kenkyūjo kiyō* [National Institute for Defense Studies security studies] 3, no. 3 (2001): 79–100.
54. See, for example, "Santō shuppei kankei" [Related to the Shantung expedition], May 24, 1927–May 25, 1927, A.6.1.5, Diplomatic Archives of the Ministry of Foreign Affairs of Japan, JACAR reference code B02031866100.
55. See Gunjika, "Taisōgi rikugun Gyōmu Iin ninmei no ken" [Commission of the army's Imperial Funeral Management Committee], December 27, 1926, Rikugunshō dainikki, Shōwa 1–2, JDMA, JACAR reference code C10050066600.
56. "Rikukaigun shohei shikikan: Taisōgi no sai ni okeru gishiki jisshi nikansuru ken" [Army and navy commanders: Matters concerning the execution of rituals during the Imperial funeral], February 10, 1927, Rikugunshō dainikki, Shōwa 1–2, JDMA, JACAR reference code C10050088800.
57. BBKS, ed., *Senshi sōsho (9) rikugun gunju dōin (1) keikakuhen* [War history (9), army munitions mobilization (1), planning volume] (Tokyo: Asagumo Shimbunsha, 1967), 241, 243.
58. Tōjō Hideki, "Dainishidan sen'yōhin seibi kensa hōkoku" [Survey report of the Second Division's mobilization of war materials], November 30, 1928, in "Dōin keikaku ni motodzuku sen'yōhin seibi kensa ni kansuru ken" [Concerning the inspection of military supplies based on mobilization planning], Mitsu Dainikki, Rikugunshō Dainikki, JDMA, JACAR reference code C01003802000.
59. Tōjō, "Dainishidan sen'yōhin seibi kensa hōkoku." Regarding the "bifurcation" of the officer class, see James B. Crowley, "Japanese Army Factionalism in the Early 1930s," *Journal of Asian Studies* 21, no. 3 (1962): 311–312.
60. Okamura Yasuji, diary entry, January 16, 1927, in *Shina hankengun sōshireikan Okamura Yasuji taishō* [China Expeditionary Army commander-in-chief, General Okamura Yasuji], ed. Funaki Shigeru (Tokyo: Kawade Shobō Shinsha, 2012), 165. See also Takahashi, *Shōwa no gunbatsu,* 82.
61. From the fifteenth class, Komoto Daisaku and Yamaoka Shigeaki were chosen; from the sixteenth class, Doihara Kenji, Kuroki Chikanori, Nagata, Obata, Okamura, Itagaki, Isogai Rensuke, Ono Hiroki, and Ogasawara Kazuo; from the seventeenth class, Kudo Yoshio, Matsumura Masakazu, Tojo, and Watari Hisao; and from the eighteenth class, Nakano Naozo, Okabe Naosaburo, and Yamashita Tomoyuki. See Ōe Shinobu, *Chōsakurin bakusatsu: Shōwa Tennō no tōsui* [The bombing death of Zhang Zuolin: The Showa Emperor's command] (Tokyo: Chūkō Shinsho, 1989), 33–34.
62. Takahashi, *Shōwa no gunbatsu,* 82–84.
63. See, for example, Alvin D. Coox, *Nomonhan: Japan Against Russia, 1939* (Stanford, CA: Stanford University Press, 1985), 1–16.
64. Louise Young, *Japan's Total Empire: Manchuria and the Culture of Wartime Imperialism* (Berkeley: University of California Press, 1998), 31.
65. For a study that contrasts Shidehara's China policy with that of Tanaka, see Nobuya Bamba, *Japanese Diplomacy in a Dilemma: New Light on Japan's China Policy, 1924–1929* (Kyoto: Minerva, 1972).
66. Kawada, *Shōwa rikugun no kiseki,* 11–12.
67. Kawada, *Shōwa rikugun no kiseki,* 12–13.
68. Regarding Tanaka's policies, see Bamba, *Japanese Diplomacy,* 303–339.
69. Ōe, *Chōsakurin bakusatsu,* 3–30.
70. Terasaki Hidenari, *Shōwa Tennō dokuhakuraku: Terasaki Hidenari Goyōgakkari nikki* [The Showa Emperor's monologue: Imperial aide Terasaki Hidenari's diary], ed. Mariko

Terasaki Miller (Tokyo: Bungei Shunjū, 1991), 22–23. See also Gordon M. Berger, Roger M. Brown, and Peter Mauch, eds., *The Emperor's Testimony: Hirohito's Monologue on Japan's War in Asia and the Pacific* (Cambridge: Cambridge University Press, forthcoming).

71. Okamura Yasuji, diary entries, January 12 and 17, 1929, in Funaki, *Shina hankengun sōshireikan*, 200–201.
72. Okamura Yasuji, diary entries, January 12, 1929, January 17, 1929, February 13, 1929, and February 23, 1929, in Funaki, *Shina hankengun sōshireikan*, 201–202.
73. Daily entries, March 27, 1929, June 27, 1929, and July 5, 1929, in Ku'naichō, ed., *Shōwa Tennō jitsuroku* [True documents of the Shōwa Emperor], vol. 16, Imperial Household Agency, Archives and Mausolea Department, 17–18, 99, 104. The directness of the emperor's demand for Tanaka's resignation only became apparent with the publication of the emperor's so-called monologue. See Terasaki, *Shōwa Tennō dokuhakuroku*, 22–23.
74. Audience record, May 30, 1952, in Tajima Michiji, *Shōwa Tennō haietsuki: Hatsudai ku'naichō chōkan Tajima Michiji kiroku, haietsuki 3 Shōwa 26nen 11gatsu–Shōwa 27nen 6gatsu* [Records of audiences with the Showa Emperor: The records of the Imperial Household Agency's first grand chamberlain, Tajima Michiji, audience records 3, November 1951–June 1952] (Tokyo: Iwanami Shoten, 2021), 227.
75. Michael A. Barnhart, *Japan Prepares for Total War: The Search for Economic Security, 1919–1941* (Ithaca, NY: Cornell University Press, 1987), 18.

3 · SHIFTING FORTUNES

1. Hohei Daiichi Rentai, ed., *Hohei Daiichi Rentai rekishi* [History of the First Infantry Regiment] (Tokyo: Hohei Daiichi Rentai, 1935), 22.
2. Takamiya Taihei, "Takamiya Taihei no kiroku" [Takami Taihei's record], in *Tōjō Hideki*, ed. Jōhō Yoshio (Tokyo: Fuyō Shobō, 1974), 660.
3. *Guntai naimusho* [Handbook for squad administration] (Tokyo: Buyōdō Shoten, 1922), 17.
4. Regarding equipment, see, for example, "Sen'yōhin kensa seiseki no ken" [Concerning the results of a survey of war equipment], Rikugunshō gunji kimitsu dainikki S4-4-4, Japanese Defense Ministry Archives (hereafter cited as JDMA), Japan Center for Asian Historical Records (hereafter cited as JACAR) reference code C01007453300. Regarding mobilization, see "Dōin keikaku ni kakaru shohōkoku teishutsu no ken" [Concerning the presentation of reports on mobilization planning], Rikugunshō gunji kimitsu dainikki S5-1-1, JDMA, JACAR reference code C01002592500. Regarding medical supplies, see "Sen'yō eisei zairyō kanri kensa seiseki no ken" [Concerning the results of survey of management of wartime medical supplies], Rikugunshō mitsu dainikki, S5-3-5, JDMA, JACAR reference code C01003929600.
5. Leonard A. Humphreys, *The Way of the Heavenly Sword: The Japanese Army in the 1920s* (Stanford, CA: Stanford University Press, 1995), 121.
6. Sugimori Hisahide, *Densetsu to jitsuzō: Shōwa jinbutsuden* [Legends and real images: Biographies of Shōwa-era personages] (Tokyo: Shinchōsha, 1967), 65.
7. Sugimori, *Densetsu to jitsuzō*, 65.
8. Itō Shun'ichirō, *Shisei/tetsu no hito: Tōjō Hideki den* [Man of sincerity and iron: Tojo Hideki biography] (Tokyo: Ten'yū Shobō, 1942), 57.
9. Matsuzaki Akira, "Tōjō rentaichō" [Regimental commander Tojo], in Jōhō, *Tōjō Hideki*, 673–674.
10. Hosaka Masayasu, *Tōjō Hideki to tennō no jidai: Gunnai kōsō kara kaisen zen'ya made* [Tōjō Hideki and the era of the emperor: From intraservice conflict to the eve of the opening of the war], vol. 1 (Tokyo: Bungei Shunjū, 1988), 90, 97.
11. Itō, *Shisei/tetsu no hito*, 59–60.
12. Takahashi Masae, *Shōwa no gunbatsu* [Showa-era military cliques] (Tokyo: Kōdansha Gakujutsu Bunko, 2003), 100.

13. See, for example, Kawada Minoru, *Shōwa rikugun no kiseki: Nagata Tetsuzan no kōsō to sono bunki* [Trajectory of the Showa-era army: Nagata Tetsuzan's vision and its ramifications] (Tokyo: Chūō Kōron Shinsha, 2011), 19–20.
14. Okamura Yasuji, diary entries, August 24, 1929, and February 11, 1930, in *Shina hankengun sōshireikan Okamura Yasuji taishō* [China Expeditionary Army commander-in-chief, General Okamura Yasuji], ed. Funaki Shigeru (Tokyo: Kawade Shobō Shinsha, 2012), 207, 211.
15. Daily entries, February 13 and 14, 1930, in Ku'naichō, ed., *Shōwa Tennō jitsuroku* [True documents of the Shōwa Emperor], vol. 17, Imperial Household Agency, Archives and Mausolea Department, 19–20.
16. Okamura Yasuji, diary entries, February 15 and 23, 1930, in Funaki, *Shina hankengun sōshireikan,* 213, 214. Regarding Kanaya's appointment, see daily entry, February 19, 1930, in *Shōwa Tennō jitsuroku,* 17:22.
17. For a brief account of the so-called March Incident, see Edward J. Drea, *Japan's Imperial Army: Its Rise and Fall, 1853–1945* (Lawrence: University Press of Kansas, 2009), 167–168.
18. Hosaka, *Tōjō Hideki,* 1:98–105, quotations on 101, 105.
19. Okaumura Yasuji, diary entry, March 15, 1931, in Funaki, *Shina hankengun sōshireikan,* 227.
20. Hosaka, *Tōjō Hideki,* 1:101.
21. See, for example, Seki Hiroharu, "The Manchurian Incident, 1931," in *Japan Erupts: The London Naval Conference and the Manchurian Incident, 1928–1932; Selected Translations from "Taiheiyō sensō e no michi: Kaisen gaikō shi,"* ed. James William Morley (New York: Columbia University Press, 1984), 163–164.
22. The general outline is quoted in its entirety in Seki, "The Manchurian Incident," 176.
23. Concerning the lead-up to the Manchurian Incident, see Seki, "The Manchurian Incident," 139–230. For an excellent military history, see Shimada Toshihiko, "The Extension of Hostilities, 1931–1932," in Morley, *Japan Erupts,* 241–335.
24. Okamura Yasuji, diary entry, September 21, 1931, in Funaki, *Shina hankengun sōshireikan,* 234–235.
25. See Shimada, "Extension of Hostilities," 242–247.
26. Okamura Yasuji, diary entry, September 24, 1931, in Funaki, *Shina hankengun sōshireikan,* 235–236.
27. Imamura Hitoshi, *Imamura Hitoshi kaikoroku* [Imamura Hitoshi's reminiscences] (Tokyo: Fuyō Shobō, 1993), 193.
28. Okamura Yasuji, diary entry, September 25, 1931, in Funaki, *Shina hankengun sōshireikan,* 236.
29. Rana Mitter, *The Manchurian Myth: Nationalism, Resistance, and Collaboration in Modern China* (Berkeley: University of California Press, 2000), 85.
30. Imamura, *Imamura Hitoshi kaikoroku,* 198–199.
31. Okamura Yasuji, diary entry, October 26, 1931, in Funaki, *Shina hankengun sōshireikan,* 240.
32. Imamura, *Imamura Hitoshi kaikoroku,* 205–208.
33. Kawada, *Shōwa rikugun no kiseki,* 56–57.
34. Araki Sadao, *Shōwa Nippon no shimei* [Showa Japan's mission] (Tokyo: Shakai Kyōiku Kyōkai, 1932), 18–20.
35. See Tsutsui Kiyotada, *Rikugun Shikan Gakkō jiken: Ni-ni-roku jiken no genten* [The Military Academy incident: The origins of the February 26 incident] (Tokyo: Chūkō Sensho, 2016), 21.
36. "Jikyoku shori yōkō" [Outline for dealing with the situation], December 22, 1931, Manshū jihen sakusen shidō kankeisetsu bessatsu sono 2, Chūō sensō shidō jūyō kokusaku monjo 546, JDMA, JACAR reference code C12120036400.

37. Yano Shintarō, “Araki Sadao no kōjutsu kiroku: Manshū jihen nit suite” [Araki Sadao’s oral record: Concerning the Manchurian incident], *Kindai Chūgoku kenkyū ihō* [Report on modern Chinese studies] 43 (2021): 66.
38. Mori Yasuo, *Nagata Tetsuzan: Heiwa iji wa gunjin no saidai sekimu nari* [Nagata Tetsuzan: The maintenance of peace is the greatest obligation of soldiers and sailors] (Kyoto: Minerva Shobō, 2011), 181–182.
39. Daily entry, January 8, 1932, in Ku’naichō, ed., *Shōwa Tennō jitsuroku* [True documents of the Shōwa Emperor], vol. 19, Imperial Household Agency, Archives and Mausolea Department, 7–8.
40. Katakura Tadashi, diary entry, January 8, 1932, in Katakura Tadashi, “Manshū Jihen kimitsu seiryaku nisshi sono yon” [Confidential political diary, part four, of the Manchurian Incident], in *Gendaishi shiryō 7: Manshū Jihen* [Documents on contemporary history 7: The Manchurian Incident], ed. Kobayashi Tatsuo and Shimada Toshihiko (Tokyo: Misuzu Shobō, 1964), 337–338.
41. Katakura Tadashi, diary entry, January 8, 1932.
42. Matsuda Jukkoku, *Tōjō Hideki: Dainippon teikoku ni junjita otoko* [Tojo Hideki: The man who died for Imperial Japan] (Tokyo: PHP Bunko, 2002), 111–112. It is at least possible that the author here used literary license. As this book is not scholarly and includes no citations, it is, at least, difficult to verify this quotation.
43. Regarding the Shanghai Incident, see Peter Mauch, *Sailor Diplomat: Nomura Kichisaburō and the Japanese-American War* (Cambridge, MA: Harvard University Asia Center, 2011), 80–87.
44. Okamura Yasuji, diary entries, February 7, February 14, and February 20, 1932, in Funaki, *Shina hankengun sōshireikan,* 249–250.
45. Ichinose Toshiya, *Tōjō Hideki: “Dokusaisha” o enjita otoko* [Tojo Hideki: The man who acted as “dictator”] (Tokyo: Bunshun Shinsho, 2019), 78.
46. Araki Sadao, quoted in Maruyama Masao, *Thought and Behavior in Modern Japanese Politics* (London: Oxford University Press, 1979), 67.
47. Suyama, *Sakusen no oni,* 267.
48. See, for example, Ian Nish, *Japan’s Struggle with Internationalism: Japan, China, and the League of Nations, 1931–1933* (London: Routledge, 1993), 25–26, 80–82, 158–163.
49. Bōeichō Bōei Kenshujo Senshishitsu (hereafter cited as BBKS), ed., *Senshi sōsho (8) Daihon’ei Rikugunbu (1) Shōwa 15nen 5gatsu made* [War history series (8), Imperial Headquarters, Army (1) until May 1940] (Tokyo: Asagumo Shimbunsha, 1967), 338–341. See also Kitaoka Shin’ichi, *Kanryōsei to shite no Nihon Rikugun* [The Japanese Army as bureaucracy (Tokyo: Chikuma Shobō, 2012), 240.
50. BBKS, *Senshi sōsho (8),* 338–341.
51. Suyama Yukio, *Sakusen no oni Obata Toshirō* [Strategy demon Obata Toshiro] (Tokyo: Fuyō Shobō, 1983), 66.
52. BBKS, *Senshi sōsho (8),* 339–340.
53. Ichinose, *Tōjō Hideki,* 82.
54. Tsutsui, *Rikugun Shikan Gakkō jiken,* 26.
55. Other younger officers joining Tojo alongside Nagata were Hattori Takushiro, Horiba Kazuo, Ikeda Sumihisa, Kagesa Sadaaki, Katakura Tadashi, Nagai Yatsuji, Nishiura Susumu, Sanada Shoichiro, Shikata Ryoji, and Tsuji Masanobu. See Yamaguchi Kazuki, “1930 nendai zenhanki ni okeru Rikugun habatsu tairitsu—kōdōha/tōseiha no taisei kōsō” [The factional conflict within the army in the first half of the 1930s], *Ritsumeikan daigaku jinbun kagaku kenkyūjo kiyō* [Ritsumeikan University Institute of Humanities, Human and Social Sciences bulletin] 117, no. 4 (2019): 272.
56. Yamaguchi, “1930 nendai zenhanki,” 272. See also Nishiura Susumu, *Shōwa sensōshi no shōgen: Nihon Rikugun shūen no shinjitsu* [Testimony concerning Showa-era war history: The truth of the end of the Japanese Army] (Tokyo: Nikkei Bijinesujin Bunko, 2013), 32–36.

57. Tsutsui, *Rikugun Shikan Gakkō jiken,* 21.
58. Shimada Toshihiko, "Designs on North China, 1933–1937," in *The China Quagmire: Japan's Expansion on the Asian Continent, 1933–1941; Selected Translations from "Taiheiyō sensō e no michi: Kaisen gaikō shi,"* ed. James William Morley (New York: Columbia University Press, 1983), 59.
59. Chūō Kōronsha, ed., *Hijōji kokumin zenshū* [Nation in crisis: Collected works], 8 vols. (Tokyo: Chūō Kōronsha, 1933–1935). Other than the army volume, there were individual volumes dedicated to naval affairs, foreign affairs, economic affairs, industrial affairs, the people's livelihoods, and aviation.
60. Tōjō Hideki, "Shōhai no bunkiten wa shisōsen" [At the juncture of victory or defeat is the battle of ideas], in *Rikugunhen: Hijōji kokumin zenshū* [Nation in crisis: Army volume] (Tokyo: Chūō Kōronsha, 1935), 54.
61. Tōjō, "Shōhai no bunkiten wa shisōsen" 55, 60. Regarding the naval disarmament treaties concluded in Washington, DC, and London, Tojo completely ignored the opinion of the Japanese Navy's so-called treaty faction, which regarded the treaties as being in Japan's best interests. He peremptorily sided with the navy's so-called "fleet faction," which emphasized Japan's sovereign right to arm itself as it saw fit. For treatment of this debate as it played out in the Japanese media, see Peter Mauch, "Return to Great Power Competition: Imperial Japan's Rejection of the Washington System," in *The Road to Pearl Harbor: Great Power War in Asia and the Pacific,* ed. John H. Maurer and Erik Goldstein (Annapolis, MD: Naval Institute Press, 2022), 38–62.
62. Mauch, "Return to Great Power Competition," 62–64.
63. Mauch, "Return to Great Power Competition," 63–64.
64. See Sasaki Takashi, "Araki rikushō to goshō kaigi" [Army minister Araki and the five ministers' conference], *Shigaku zasshi* [Journal of historical science] 88, no. 3 (1979): 37–51.
65. Masaki Jinzaburō, diary entries, January 31 and February 3, 1934, in Masaki Jinzaburō, *Nisshi* [Diary], vol. 1, ed. Itō Takashi, Sasaki Takashi, Suetaka Yoshiya, and Teranuma Yasutaka (Tokyo: Yamakawa Shuppansha, 1981), 134, 135–136.
66. Suzuki Teiichi, diary entry, February 15, 1933, in Itō Takashi and Sasaki Takashi, "Suzuki Teiichi nikki—Shōwa kyū nen" [Suzuki Teiichi diary—1934], *Shigaku zasshi* [Journal of historical science] 87, no. 4 (1978): 63.
67. Nishiura, *Shōwa sensōshi no shōgen,* 82.
68. Masaki Jinzaburō, diary entries, May 7, 1934, July 10, 1934, July 14, 1934, and July 25, 1934, in Masaki, *Nisshi,* 1:194, 246, 250, 256.
69. Masaki Jinzaburō, diary entries, July 31, 1934, August 2, 1934, and August 6, 1934, in Masaki, *Nisshi,* 1:260–261, 262, 264.
70. Akamatsu Sadao, *Tōjō hishokan kimitsu nisshi* [Secret diary of Tojo's secretary] (Tokyo: Bungei Shunju, 1985), 259. See also Hosaka, *Tōjō Hideki,* 1:135.
71. Nagata Tetsuzan, "Kokka sōdōin to seinen kunren (kōhō)" [National mobilization and youth training (posthumous manuscript)], in *Seinen jikyoku tokuhon* [Youth affairs reader] (Tokyo: Aoyama Shoin, 1941), 283–284.

4 · RESURRECTION IN MANCHUKUO

1. Kishi Nobusuke, quoted in Shin'ichi Yamamuro, *Manchuria Under Japanese Dominion,* trans. Joshua Fogel (Philadelphia: University of Pennsylvania Press, 2006), 4–5.
2. Ogino Fujio, ed., *Chian ijihō kankei shiryō* [Historical documents relating to the Peace Preservation Law], vol. 4 (Tokyo: Shin-Nippon Shuppansha, 1996), 753.
3. Hoshino Naoki, "Kenpei Shireikan Tōjō Hideki" [Provost Marshal Tōjō Hideki], *Bungei shunjū* [Annals of art and culture] 33, no. 12 (1956): 143.
4. Shimizu Hideko, "Tai-Man kikō no hensen" [Changes in Manchurian organizations], *Kokusai seiji* [International politics] 37 (1957): 147–148.

5. Hoshino, "Kenpei Shireikan Tōjō Hideki," 144.
6. Ben-Ami Shillony, *Revolt in Japan: The Young Officers and the February 26, 1936 Incident* (Princeton, NJ: Princeton University Press, 1973), 143.
7. Shillony, *Revolt in Japan,* 146, 149–150.
8. Takebe Rokuzō, diary entry, March 3, 1936, in Takebe Rokuzō, *Nikki* [Diary], ed. Taura Masanori, Furukawa Takahisa, and Takebe Ken'ichi (Tokyo: Fuyō Shobō, 1999), 106.
9. James B. Crowley, *Japan's Quest for Autonomy: National Security and Foreign Policy, 1930–1938* (Princeton, NJ: Princeton University Press, 1966), 274.
10. Kōketsu Atsushi, *Kenpei seiji: Kanshi to dōkatsu no jidai* [Kenpei politics: The era of surveillance and intimidation] (Tokyo: Shin Nippon Shuppansha, 2008).
11. Takebe Rokuzō, diary entry, March 4, 1936, in Takebe, *Nikki,* 107.
12. See, for example, Nakagane Katsuji, "Manchukuo and Economic Development," in *The Japanese Informal Empire in China, 1895–1937,* ed. Peter Duus, Ramon H. Myers, and Mark R. Peattie (Princeton, NJ: Princeton University Press, 1989), 133–157. The group's title referenced the last syllables of its members' given names: Hoshino Naoki and Tojo Hideki were the "two -ki" while Ayukawa Yoshisuke, Kishi Nobusuke, and Matsuoka Yosuke were the "three -suke."
13. Hironori Sasada, *The Evolution of the Japanese Developmental State: Institutions Locked in by Ideas* (London: Routledge, 2013), 73–74.
14. Masaru Udagawa, "The Move into Manchuria of the Nissan Combine," *Japanese Yearbook on Business History* 7 (1990): 5–11.
15. Takebe Rokuzō, diary entries, April 30 and May 4, 1936, in Takebe, *Nikki,* 117–118.
16. Sugimori Hisahide, *Densetsu to jitsuzō: Shōwa jinbutsuden* [Legends and real images: Biographies of Shōwa-era personages] (Tokyo: Shinchōsha, 1967), 82.
17. Takebe Rokuzō, diary entries, February 25 and March 1, 1937, in Takebe, *Nikki,* 180.
18. Toko Hideki, quoted in Usui Katsumi, "1937-nen Ni-Chū kankei bekken" [A study of Sino-Japanese relations in 1937], *Tsukuba hōsei* [Tsukuba review of law and political science] 11 (1988): 8–9.
19. Regarding the border crises in the early and mid-1930s, see Alvin D. Coox, *Nomonhan: Japan Against Russia, 1939* (Stanford, CA: Stanford University Press, 1985), 92–101, quotation on 104. See also Stuart D. Goldman, *Nomonhan, 1939: The Red Army's Victory That Shaped World War II* (Annapolis, MD: Naval Institute Press, 2013), 17–20.
20. Bōeichō Bōei Kenshujo Senshishitsu (hereafter cited as BBKS), ed., *Senshi sōsho (27) Kantōgun (1) tai-So senbi / Nomonhan Jihen* [War history series (27), the Kwantung Army (1), war against the Soviet Union / the Nomonhan Incident] (Tokyo: Asagumo Shuppan, 1969), 328–329.
21. BBKS, *Senshi sōsho (27),* 333.
22. "Shina Jihen boppatsu zengo (1937-nen natsu goro)" [Before and after outbreak of the China Incident (summer 1937)], Manshū jihen oyobi Shina jihen: jūyō jiki ni okeru tai-So (tai-Shi) josei handan 2 / 2, Chūō: sensō shidō, sono ta 11, Rikugun ippan shiryō, Japanese Defense Ministry Archives (hereafter cited as JDMA), Japan Center for Asian Historical Records (hereafter cited as JACAR) reference code C14060829800.
23. Umezu Yoshijirō to Tojo Hideki, June 26, 1937, Riku-Man mitsudainikki S12-15-62, Rikugunshō dainikki, JDMA, JACAR reference code C01003269500.
24. Tojo Hideki to Umezu Yoshijiro and Imai Kiyoshi, June 28, 1937, Riku-Man mitsudainikki S12-15-62.
25. Shigemitsu Mamoru to Hirota Koki, three cables, June 29, 1937 (two), and June 30, 1937 (one), in *Nihon gaikō bunsho: Shōwaki III daiikkan* [Documents on Japanese foreign policy: Shōwa period III], vol. 1, ed. Gaimushō (Tokyo: Gaimushō, 2014), 341–349.
26. Umezu Yoshijiro to Tojo, June 29, 1937, Riku-Man mitsudainikki S12-15-62.
27. Ueda Kenkichi to Hirota Koki, June 30, 1937, in Gaimushō, *Nihon gaikō bunsho: Shōwaki III,* 1:350. See also BBKS, *Senshi sōsho (27),* 335.

28. Hirota Koki to Shigemitsu Mamoru, June 30, 1937, in Gaimushō, *Nihon gaikō bunsho: Shōwaki III,* 1:350; and Shigemitsu Mamoru to Hirota Koki, July 1, 1937, in Gaimushō, *Nihon gaikō bunsho: Shōwaki III,* 1:351–353.
29. Ueda Kenkichi to Hirota Koki, June 30, 1937, in Gaimushō, *Nihon gaikō bunsho: Shōwaki III,* 1:351.
30. Shigemitsu Mamoru to Hirota Koki, July 2, 1937, in Gaimushō, *Nihon gaikō bunsho: Shōwaki III,* 1:360–363.
31. Ueda Kenkichi to Hirota Koki, July 2, 1937, in Gaimushō, *Nihon gaikō bunsho: Shōwaki III,* 1:363–364.
32. Ueda Kenkichi to Hirota Koki, July 3, 1937, in Gaimushō, *Nihon gaikō bunsho: Shōwaki III,* 1:366–367.
33. Ueda Kenkichi to Hirota Koki, July 5, 1937, in Gaimushō, *Nihon gaikō bunsho: Shōwaki III,* 1:367–368.
34. "Shina Jihen boppatsu zengo (1937-nen natsu goro)" [Before and after outbreak of the China Incident (summer 1937)], Manshū jihen oyobi Shina jihen: jūyō jiki ni okeru tai-So (tai-Shi) josei handan 2/2, Chūō: sensō shidō, sono ta 11, Rikugun ippan shiryō, JDMA. Jacar Reference no.: C14060829800.
35. Sugimori, *Densetsu to jitsuzō,* 83–84.
36. Sugimori, *Densetsu to jitsuzō,* 83–84.
37. The best history of Kwantung Army ambitions in North China remains Shimada Toshihiko, "Designs on North China," in *The China Quagmire: Japan's Expansion on the Asian Continent, 1933–1941; Selected Translations from "Taiheiyō sensō e no michi: Kaisen gaikō shi,"* ed. James William Morley (New York: Columbia University Press, 1983), 3–230. See also James Boyd, "In Pursuit of an Obsession: Japan in Inner Mongolia in the 1930s," *Japanese Studies* 22, no. 3 (2002): 289–303.
38. BBKS, ed., *Senshi sōsho (86) Shina Jihen rikugun sakusen (1) Shōwa 13-nen 1-gatsu made* [War history series (86), China Incident army strategy (1), until January 1938] (Tokyo: Asagumo Shuppan, 1975), 153, 159, 167. See also Usui, 1937-nen Ni-Chū kankei bekken" 9.
39. Regarding the adoption of the term "China Incident," see "Kakugi kettei" [Cabinet decision], September 2, 1937, in *Nihon gaikō bunsho: Nitchū Sensō* [Documents on Japanese foreign policy: Sino-Japanese War], vol. 1, ed. Gaimushō (Tokyo: Gaimushō, 2011), 93.
40. Takebe Rokuzō, diary entry, July 18, 1937, in Takebe, *Nikki,* 210.
41. Ueda Kenkichi to Hirota Kōki, July 13, 1937, in *Nihon gaikō bunsho: Nitchū Sensō* [Documents on Japanese foreign policy: Sino-Japanese War], vol. 1, ed. Gaimushō (Tokyo: Gaimushō, 2011), 17–18.
42. "Gaimu/rikugun/kaigun sanshō no jikyoku shushu hoshin" [The ministries—foreign, army, and navy—policy of settling the incident], July 23, 1937, in Gaimushō, *Nihon gaikō bunsho: Nitchū Sensō,* 1:29.
43. "Kantōgun Shireibu jōsei handan" [Kwantung Army Headquarters' estimate of the situation], July 24, 1937, in Gaimushō, *Nihon gaikō bunsho: Nitchū Sensō,* 1:30–35.
44. "Kantōgun Shireibu jōsei handan."
45. "Kantōgun Shireibu jōsei handan."
46. "Chaharu Sakusen hakki ni itaru made no keii" [Circumstances until the initiation of Operation Chahar], Chaharu Sakusen kimitsu nisshi (Shina Jihen dai-3 kan), Chūō: sensō shidō jūyō kokusaku monjo 552, JDMA, JACAR reference code C12120048100. See also BBKS, *Senshi sōsho (86),* 220.
47. "Chaharu Sakusen hakki ni itaru made no keii." See also BBKS, *Senshi sōsho (86),* 227.
48. Takebe Rokuzō, diary entry, July 31, 1937, in Takebe, *Nikki,* 214.
49. "Chaharu sakusen hakki ni itaru made no keii." See also BBKS, *Senshi sōsho (86),* 227, 241.
50. "Chaharu Sakusen hakki ni itaru made no keii."

51. "Chaharu Sakusen ji 12-nen 8-gatsu 11-nichi itaru 12-nen 10-gatsu 17-nichi" [Operation Chahar, August 11, 1937–October 17, 1937], Shina, Shina Jihen zenpan 142, Rikugun ippan shiryō, JDMA, JACAR reference code C11110439300.
52. "Chaharu Sakusen hakki ni itaru made no keii."
53. "Chaharu Sakusen hakki ni itaru made no keii." See also "Chaharu sakusen ji 12-nen 8-gatsu 11-nichi itaru 12-nen 10-gatsu 17-nichi"; and BBKS, *Senshi sōsho (86),* 241–242.
54. "Chaharu Sakusen hakki ni itaru made no keii."
55. "Chaharushō hōmen seiji kōsaku kinkyū shori yōkō" [Outline of emergency measures involving the political stratagem in Chahar Province], August 13, 1937, in Kantōgun Shireibu, "Tōjō Kantōgun Sanbōchō no chūmō heidan Ishimoto sanbōchō ni taisuru kondan yōshi" [Outline of Kwantung Army Chief of Staff Tōjō's conversation with Ishimoto, chief of staff of the corps stationed in Inner Mongolia], December 1937, Katakura shiryō 73, Chūō: sensō shidō jūyō kokusaku monjo 555, Bōeishō bōei kenkyūjo senshi kenkyū sentaa.
56. Hata Ikuhiko, *Gendaishi no sōten* [The issues on Japan's modern history] (Tokyo: Bungei Shunjū, 1998), 201–204.
57. "Kantōgun Chaharu haken no kakuheidanchōno sakusenjō no keii" [The Kwantung Army dispatch to Chahar: Circumstances of each unit's war leadership], Chūō: sensō shidō jūyō kokusaku bunsho 552, Rikugun ippan shiryō, JDMA, Jacar Reference Code: C12120048500. For reference to Tojo's "lightning" campaign, see Izumi Kaiō, "Shōgen" [Testimony], in *Tōjō Hideki,* ed. Jōhō Yoshio (Tokyo: Fūyō Shobō, 1974), 631.
58. Ueda Kenkichi to Sugiyama Hajime, August 14, 1937, in "Shōwa 13-nen 'manju dainikki,' rikumanmitsu dainikki, rikugunshō dainikki," JDMA, JACAR reference code C01003364500.
59. Kantōgun Shireibu, "Taijikyoku shori yōkō" [Summary of disposal of the current situation], August 14, 1937, in "Shōwa 13-nen 'manju dainikki.'" See also BBKS, *Senshi sōsho (86),* 255–256.
60. Kantōgun Shireibu, "Taijikyoku shori yōkō."
61. Kantōgun Shireibu, "Taijikyoku shori yōkō."
62. Kantōgun Shireibu, "Taijikyoku shori yōkō."
63. Kantōgun Shireibu, "Taijikyoku shori yōkō."
64. "Kantōgun Chaharu haken . . . no keii."
65. Tojo Hideki to Umezu Yoshijiro, August 19, 1937, in "Shōwa 13-nen 'manju dainikki,'" rikumanmitsu dainikki, rikugunshō dainikki," JDMA, JACAR reference code C01003364500.
66. Umezu Yoshijiro to Tojo, August 20, 1937, in "Shōwa 13-nen 'manju dainikki.'"
67. "Chaharu Sakusen ji 12-nen 8-gatsu 11-nichi itaru 12-nen 10-gatsu 17-nichi."
68. Dokuritsu Konsei Dai-11 Ryodanchō—Dai-5 Shidanchō sakusen shidōjō no keii [Circumstances of war leadership of Independent Eleventh Mixed Brigade commander—Fifth Division commander], Chūō: sensō shidō jūyō kokusaku bunsho 552, Rikugun ippan shiryō, JDMA, JACAR reference code C12120048400.
69. "Chaharu Sakusen ji 12-nen 8-gatsu 11-nichi itaru 12-nen 10-gatsu 17-nichi."
70. Hosaka Masayasu, *Tōjō Hideki to tennō no jidai: Gunnai kōsō kara kaisen zen'ya made* [Tōjō Hideki and the era of the emperor: From intraservice conflict to the eve of the opening of the war], vol. 1 (Tokyo: Bungei Shunjū, 1988), 159–160.
71. Tojo Hideki to Umezu Yoshijiro and Imai Kiyoshi, August 28, 1937, in "Chaharushō seiji kōsaku ni kansuru ken" [Matters relating to political work in Chahar Province], Rikugunshō, Rikumanmitsu dainikki S12-19-66, JDMA, JACAR reference code C01003290700. See also "Chaharu Sakusen ji 12-nen 8-gatsu 11-nichi itaru 12-nen 10-gatsu 17-nichi."
72. Umezu Yoshijiro to Tojo, August 29, 1937, in "Chaharushō seiji kōsaku ni kansuru ken."
73. Tojo Hideki to Umezu Yoshijiro, August 30, 1937, in "Chaharushō seiji kōsaku ni kansuru ken."
74. Tojo Hideki to Umezu Yoshijiro and Imai Kiyoshi, September 3, 1937, in "Cha-Nan Jiji Seifu ni kansuru ken" [Concerning the South Chahar Autonomous Government], Rikugunshō, Rikumanmitsu dainikki S12-20-67, JDMA, JACAR reference code C01003293900.

75. Journal entry, September 4, 1937, in "9-gatsu: Kita Shina Jihen gyōmu nisshi" [September: North China Incident operational record], Chūō—sensō shidō jūyō kokusaku bunsho 1281, JDMA, JACAR reference code C12120364700.
76. "Cha-Mō shori yōkō sōfu no ken" [Concerning delivery of the outline of management of Chahar and Mongolia], September 4, 1937, Rikugunshō, rikushi kimitsu dainikki S12-2-89. JDMA, JACAR reference code C01005636100.
77. "Cha-Mō shori yōkō sōfu no ken."
78. Tojo Hideki to Umezu Yoshijiro and Imai, September 5, 1937, in Kanden 224 gō [Kwantung cable no. 224], Rikugunshō, Rikumanmitsu dainikki S12-21-68, JDMA, JACAR reference code C01003297500.
79. Tojo Hideki to Umezu Yoshijiro and Imai Kiyoshi, September 7, 1937, in "Cha-Nn seimu shidō ni kansuru ken" [Concerning political guidance in South Chahar], Rikugunshō, Rikumanmitsu dainikki S12-19-66, JDMA, JACAR reference code C01003291000.
80. Umezu Yoshijiro to Tojo Hideki, September 8, 1937, in "Cha-Nan seimu shidō ni kansuru ken."
81. "Daidō kōryaku no keii oyobi kaku heidanchō no senshidō" [The capture of Datong and the unit commanders' war leadership], Chaharu sakusen kimitsu nisshi, Chūō: sensō shidō jūyō kokusaku monjo 552, Rikugun ippan shiryō, JDMA, JACAR reference code C12120048600.
82. "Daidō kōryaku no keii oyobi kaku heidanchō no senshidō." See also "Kicha shōkyō toppago ni okeru dai-5 shidan shiyō hōmen kettei made no keii" [Circumstances leading to the deployment of the Fifth Division after breaking through the border], Chaharu sakusen kimitsu nisshi, Chūō: sensō shidō jūyō kokusaku monjo 552, Rikugun ippan shiryō, JDMA, JACAR reference code C12120048200. Regarding the massacre, see Hata, *Gendaishi no sōten,* 205–206.
83. "Daidō kōryaku no keii oyobi kaku heidanchō no senshidō." See also "Kicha shōkyō toppago ni okeru dai-5 shidan shiyō hōmen kettei made no keii."
84. Takebe Rokuzō, diary entry, October 16, 1937, in Takebe, *Nikki,* 234–235.
85. Kantōgun Shireibu, "Tōjō Kantōgun Sanbōchō."
86. Tojo Hideki to Umezu and Imai, November 29, and December 23, 1937, in Kantōgun Shireibu, "Tōjō Kantōgun Sanbōchō."
87. Mark R. Peattie, *Ishiwara Kanji and Japan's Confrontation with the West* (Princeton, NJ: Princeton University Press, 1975), 232.
88. Katakura Tadashi, "Shōgen" [Testimony], in Jōhō, *Tōjō Hideki,* 549.
89. Peattie, *Ishiwara Kanji,* 311.
90. Tobe Ryōichi, *Shōwa no shidōsha* [Shōwa-era leaders] (Tokyo: Chūō Kōron Shinsha, 2019), 81.
91. See Hoshino Naoki, *Mihatenu Yume: Manshūkoku gaishi* [The impossible dream: Manchukuo's unofficial history] (Tokyo: Daiyamondosha, 1963), 271–276; and Y. Tak Matsusaka, "Managing Occupied Manchuria, 1931–1934," in *The Japanese Wartime Empire, 1931–1945,* ed. Peter Duus, Ramon H. Myers, and Mark R. Peattie (Princeton, NJ: Princeton University Press, 1996), 105–107, 116–117.
92. Coox, *Nomonhan,* 103; Umemoto Sutezō, *Tōjō Hideki to sono jidai* [Tojo Hideki and those times] (Tokyo: Miyakawa Shobō, 1968), 135; Iwai Shūichirō, *Tada Hayao den: 'Nitchū wahei' o mosaku shitudzuketa rikugun taishō no mu'nen* [Tada Hayao biography: The regrets of the army general who continued to grope for "Sino-Japanese peace"] (Tokyo: Shōgakkan, 2017), 196; Handō Kazutoshi, Hosaka Masayasu, and Fukuda Kazuya, *Shōwa rikukaigun no shippai: Karera wa naze kokka o hametsu no fuchi ni oiyatta no ka* [Failures of the Shōwa-era army and navy: Why did they drive the nation into the abyss of ruination?] (Tokyo: Bungei Shunjū, 2007), 33.
93. Katakura, "Shōgen," 550. See also Peattie, *Ishiwara Kanji,* 314.
94. Tanaka Shin'ichi, "Ishiwara Kanji to Tōjō Hideki" [Ishiwara Kanji and Tojo Hideki], *Bungei shunjū* [Annals of art and culture] 44 (1966): 263.

95. BBKS, ed., *Senshi sōsho (8) Daihon'ei Rikugunbu (1) Shōwa 15nen 5gatsu made* [War history series (8), Imperial Headquarters, Army (1) until May 1940] (Tokyo: Asagumo Shimbunsha, 1967), 516–518.
96. Daily entry, January 15, 1933, in Harada Kumao, *Saionji kō to seikyoku* [Prince Saionji and the political situation], vol. 2 (Tokyo: Iwanami Shoten, 1950), 420; Usui Katsumi, "The Politics of War," in Morley, *The China Quagmire,* 310–311.
97. Tojo Hideki, quoted in Takahashi Hisashi, "Ni-Kka Jihen o meguru gunji/gaikō senryaku no bunretsu to sakugo—Shōwa 12–13 nen" [Fissures and errors in military/diplomatic strategy during the Sino-Japanese Incident, 1937–1938], in *Hendōki no Nihon gaikō to gunji: Shiryō to kentō* [Japanese diplomatic and military policy in a time of transition: Documents and analysis], ed. Kindai Gaikōshi Kenkyūkai (Tokyo: Hara Shobō, 1987), 125.
98. Takahashi Hisashi, "Ni-Kka Jihen o meguru gunji/gaikō senryaku no bunretsu to sakugo—Shōwa 12–13 nen," 125.

5 · RETURN TO TOKYO

1. Sugawara Setsuo, *Rikugun no chi'nō kyūnin otoko: Jidai rikugun o shou hitobito* [The army's nine wise men: The people who will carry the army into the next generation] (Tokyo: Kyō no Mondaisha, 1936), 29–31.
2. Takebe Rokuzō, diary entry, October 23, 1937, in Takebe Rokuzō, *Nikki* [Diary], ed. Taura Masanori, Furukawa Takahisa, and Takebe Ken'ichi (Tokyo: Fuyō Shobō, 1999), 238.
3. Daily entry, April 5, 1938, in Ku'naichō, ed., *Shōwa Tennō jitsuroku* [True documents of the Shōwa Emperor], vol. 25, Imperial Household Agency, Archives and Mausolea Department, 40–41.
4. Bōeichō Bōei Kenshujo Senshishitsu (hereafter cited as BBKS), ed., *Senshi sōsho (8) Daihon'ei Rikugunbu (1) Shōwa 15nen 5gatsu made* [War history series (8), Imperial Headquarters, Army (1) until May 1940] (Tokyo: Asagumo Shimbunsha, 1967), 539–542.
5. Yoshitake Oka, *Konoe Fumimaro: A Political Biography* (Tokyo: University of Tokyo Press, 1983), 73–74.
6. Inada Masazumi, "Senryakumen kara mita Shina Jihen no sensō shidō" [War leadership during the China Incident as seen from a strategic perspective], *Kokusai seiji* [International relations] 15 (1961): 154.
7. Tobe Ryōichi, *Shōwa no shidōsha* [Shōwa-era leaders] (Tokyo: Chūō Kōron Shinsha, 2019), 82.
8. BBKS, *Senshi sōsho (8),* 549.
9. BBKS, *Senshi sōsho (8),* 549. Regarding the Anti-Comintern Pact, see Ōhata Tokushirō, "The Anti-Comintern Pact, 1935–1939," in *Deterrent Diplomacy: Japan, Germany, and the USSR, 1935–1940: Selected Translations from "Taiheiyō sensō e no michi: Kaisen gaikō shi,"* ed. James William Morley (New York: Columbia University Press, 1976), 9–111.
10. BBKS, *Senshi sōsho (8),* 550.
11. "Kongo no Shina Jihen shidō hōshin" [China Incident guidelines], June 24, 1938, in *Nihon gaikō bunsho: Nitchū Sensō* [Documents on Japanese foreign policy: Sino-Japanese War], vol. 1, ed. Gaimushō (Tokyo: Gaimushō, 2011), 299.
12. "Jikyoku gaikō ni kansuru rikugun no kibō" [The Army's hopes regarding current foreign policies], July 3, 1938, in Gaimushō, *Nihon gaikō bunsho: Nitchū Sensō,* 1:326–329. For an English-language translation, see "Appendix Three: The Army's Hopes Regarding Current Foreign Policies," July 3, 1938, in Morley, *Deterrent Diplomacy,* 268–272.
13. "Jikyoku gaikō ni kansuru rikugun no kibō."
14. Hata Shunroku, diary entry, June 23, 1938, in Itō Takashi and Terunuma Yasutaka, eds., *Zokugendaishi shiryō: Rikugun (4); Hata Shunroku nisshi* [Documents on contemporary history, continued (4): The army; Hata Shunroku's diary] (Tokyo: Misuzu Shobō, 1983), 139.

15. BBKS, *Senshi sōsho (8),* 553.
16. BBKS, ed., *Senshi sōsho (27) Kantōgun (1) tai-So senbi/Nomonhan Jihen* [War history series (27), the Kwantung Army (1), preparations vis-à-vis the Soviets/the Nomonhan Incident] (Tokyo: Asagumo Shuppansha, 1969), 341–342.
17. BBKS, *Senshi sōsho (8),* 554.
18. Shigemitsu Mamoru to Ugaki Kazushige, July 20, 1938, in *Nihon gaikō bunsho: Shōwaki III daiikkan* [Documents on Japanese foreign policy: Shōwa period III], vol. 1, ed. Gaimushō (Tokyo: Gaimushō, 2014), 369–370.
19. Alvin D. Coox, *Nomonhan: Japan Against Russia, 1939* (Stanford, CA: Stanford University Press, 1985), 128. The Soviets' counterprotest rested on the claim that the officer had violated the Soviet boundary.
20. See the series of telegrams from Shigemitsu Mamoru to Ugaki Kazushige, July 20 and 21, 1938, in Gaimushō, *Nihon gaikō bunsho: Shōwaki III,* 1:369–371.
21. Daily entry, July 20, 1938, in Ku'naichō, *Shōwa Tennō jitsuroku,* 25:97.
22. BBKS, *Senshi sōsho (27),* 350–351.
23. BBKS, *Senshi sōsho (27),* 351–352.
24. Iwakuro Hideo, *Shōwa rikugun: Bōryaku hisshi* [The Showa-era army: A secret history of its machinations] (Tokyo: Nihon Keizai Shimbun Shuppansha, 2015), 103. Regarding Itagaki's audience with the emperor, see daily entry, July 20, 1938, in Ku'naichō, *Shōwa Tennō jitsuroku,* 25:97. See also Harada Kumao, *Saionji kō to seikyoku* [Prince Saionji and the political situation], vol. 7 (Tokyo: Iwanami Shoten, 1952), 46–54.
25. Stuart D. Goldman, *Nomonhan, 1939: The Red Army's Victory That Shaped World War II* (Annapolis, MD: Naval Institute Press, 2013), 120–121.
26. BBKS, *Senshi sōsho (27),* 367. Daily entry, July 31, 1938, in Ku'naichō, ed., *Shōwa Tennō jitsuroku* [True documents of the Shōwa Emperor], vol. 27, Imperial Household Agency, Archives and Mausolea Department, 101.
27. BBKS, *Senshi sōsho (27),* 367.
28. BBKS, *Senshi sōsho (27),* 401.
29. Shigemitsu Mamoru to Ugaki Kazushige, August 10, 1938, in Gaimushō, *Nihon gaikō bunsho: Shōwaki III,* 1:399.
30. BBKS, ed., *Senshi sōsho (79) Chūgoku hōmen kaigun sakusen (2) Shōwa 13-nen 4-gatsu ikō* [War history series (79), naval operations in the China theater, (2) after April 1938] (Tokyo: Asagumo Shuppansha, 1975), 77–78.
31. "Nichi-Doku oyobi Nichi-I sūjiku kyōka ni kansuru hōsakuan" [Draft policies concerning Japanese-German and Japanese-Italian strengthened axes], July 19, 1938, in *Nihon gaikō bunsho: Dainiji Ōshū taisen to Nihon* [Documents on Japanese foreign policy: The second great European war and Japan], vol. 1, ed. Gaimushō (Tokyo: Roku-ichi Shobō, 2012), 37–39.
32. An English-language translation of the German proposal is reproduced in Ōhata, "The Anti-Comintern Pact," 51. Ugaki's revised draft is reproduced in *Nihon gaikō bunsho: Dainiji Ōshū taisen to Nihon,* 1:39–40. An English-language translation of Ugaki's draft is reproduced in Ōhata, "Anti-Comintern Pact," 61.
33. Tojo to Oshima, August 29, 1938, in Gaimushō, *Nihon gaikō bunsho: Dainiji Ōshū taisen to Nihon,* 1:40–41.
34. Yonai Mitsumasa, quoted in Sadao Asada, *From Mahan to Pearl Harbor: The Imperial Japanese Navy and the United States* (Annapolis, MD: Naval Institute Press, 2006), 216.
35. Mark R. Peattie, *Nan'yō: The Rise and Fall of the Japanese in Micronesia, 1885–1945* (Honolulu: University of Hawai'i Press, 1988), 1. See also J. Charles Schencking, "The Imperial Japanese Navy and the Constructed Consciousness of a South Seas Destiny," *Modern Asian Studies* 33, no. 4 (1999): 769–796.
36. See Iwai Shūichirō, *Tada Hayao den: "Nitchū wahei" o mosaku shitudzuketa rikugun taishō no mu'nen* [The Tada Hayao biography: The regrets of the army general who continued

to grope for "Sino-Japanese peace"] (Tokyo: Shōgakkan, 2017), 192–198. See also Katō Yōko, *Mosaku suru 1930 nendai: Nichibei kankei to rikugun chūkensō* [Seeking the 1930s: Japanese-US relations and the army's middle echelons] (Tokyo: Yamakawa Shuppansha, 2012), 132.

37. BBKS, *Senshi sōsho (8),* 563.
38. Hosaka Masayasu, *Tōjō Hideki to tennō no jidai: Gunnai kōsō kara kaisen zen'ya made* [Tōjō Hideki and the era of the emperor: From intraservice conflict to the eve of the opening of the war], vol. 1 (Tokyo: Bungei Shunjū, 1988), 179–181.
39. See Kobayashi Kazuhiro, *Shina'tsū: Gunjin no hikari to kage; Isogai Rensuke den* [China hand: A soldier's light and shadow; Lt. Gen. Isogai Rensuke biography] (Tokyo: Kashiwa Shobō, 2000), 167.
40. Akamatsu Sadao, *Tōjō hishokan kimitsu nisshi* [Secret diary of Tojo's secretary] (Tokyo: Bungei Shunju, 1985), 271–272.
41. BBKS, *Senshi sōsho (8),* 564.
42. See, for example, Oka, *Konoe Fumimaro,* 79–80.
43. Horiba Kazuo, *Shina Jihen sensō shidō shi* [A history of war leadership during the China Incident] (Tokyo: Hara Shobō, 1973), 217. See also Katō, *Mosaku suru 1930 nendai,* 134.
44. Horiba, *Shina Jihen sensō shidō shi,* 217.
45. Horiba, *Shina Jihen sensō shidō shi,* 218.
46. Tojo Hideki, quoted in Itō Shun'ichirō, *Shisei/tetsu no hito: Tōjō Hideki den* [Man of sincerity and iron: Tojo Hideki biography] (Tokyo: Ten'yū Shobō, 1942), 91–95.
47. Tojo Hideki, quoted in Itō, *Shisei/tetsu no hito,* 91–95, emphasis added.
48. Hosaka, *Tōjō Hideki to tennō no jidai,* 1:183.
49. See the documents authored by Colonel Imai Takeo on November 20, 1938, in Gaimushō, *Nihon gaikō bunsho: Nitchū Sensō,* 1:417–423.
50. "Doihara chūjō ni ataeru shiji" [Lt. Gen. Doihara's instructions], in Gaimushō, *Nihon gaikō bunsho: Nitchū Sensō,* 1:423–428.
51. See "Ni-Sshin shin kankei chōsei hōshin" [Policy for the adjustment of new Sino-Japanese relations], November 30, 1938, in BBKS, *Senshi sōsho (8),* 576–577.
52. Tojo's telegram is quoted in full in BBKS, ed., *Senshi sōsho (89) Shina Jihen rikugun sakusen (2) Shōwa 14-nen 9-gatsu made* [War history series (89), China Incident, army strategy (1), until September 1939] (Tokyo: Asagumo Shuppan, 1976), 259–260.
53. Satō Kenryō, *Tōjō Hideki to Taiheiyō Sensō* [Tojo Hideki and the Pacific War] (Tokyo: Bungei Shunjū Shinsha, 1960), 105.
54. Satō, *Tōjō Hideki to Taiheiyō Sensō,* 107.
55. Satō, *Tōjō Hideki to Taiheiyō Sensō,* 105–107.
56. See Iwai, *Tada Hayao den,* 199–200; and Kōketsu Atsushi, *Kenpei seiji: Kanshi to dōkatsu no jidai* [Kenpei politics: The era of surveillance and intimidation] (Tokyo: Shin Nippon Shuppansha, 2008), 89–90.
57. Tojo Hideki, quoted in Ichinose Toshiya, *Tōjō Hideki: "Dokusaisha" o enjita otoko* [Tojo Hideki: The man who acted as "dictator"] (Tokyo: Bunshun Shinsho, 2019), 88.
58. Tojo Hideki, quoted in BBKS, ed., *Senshi sōsho (78) rikugun kōkū no gunbi to un'yō (2) Shōwa 17 nen zenki made* [War history series (78), army air armaments and operations (2), until early 1942] (Tokyo: Asagumo Shuppansha, 1974), 216.
59. Daily entry, February 24, 1940, in Ku'naichō, *Shōwa Tennō jitsuroku,* 27:27–28.
60. BBKS, *Senshi sōsho (78),* 214.
61. BBKS, *Senshi sōsho (78),* 203, 207–211.
62. Tsutsui Kiyotada, "Tennō shimei rikushō no tōjō—Shōwa 14-nen ni okeru tennō, rikugun, shimbun" [Entrance of the emperor-appointed war minister—the emperor, the army, and the newspapers in 1939], in *Shōwashi kōgi 2: Senmon kenkyūsha ga miru sensō e no michi* [Lectures on Shōwa period history: The road to war as seen by specialists], ed. Tsutsui Kiyotada (Tokyo: Chikuma Shinsho, 2016), 200. See also Iwai, *Tada Hayao den,* 212.

63. Tsutsui, "Tennō shimei rikushō no tōjō," 201–202. See also Iwai, *Tada Hayao den,* 212.
64. Tsutsui, "Tennō shimei rikushō no tōjō," 202–205.
65. Daily entry, August 28, 1939, in Ku'naichō, ed., *Shōwa Tennō jitsuroku* [True documents of the Shōwa Emperor], vol. 26, Imperial Household Agency, Archives and Mausolea Department, 105–106.

6 · EMERGENCE AS ARMY MINISTER

1. Terasaki Hidenari, *Shōwa Tennō dokuhakuroku: Terasaki Hidenari Goyōgakari nikki* [The Showa Emperor's monologue: Imperial aide Terasaki Hidenari's diary], ed. Mariko Terasaki Miller (Tokyo: Bungei Shunjū, 1991), 49. For an English-language translation, see Gordon M. Berger, Roger M. Brown, and Peter Mauch, eds., *The Emperor's Testimony: Hirohito's Monologue on Japan's War in Asia and the Pacific* (Cambridge: Cambridge University Press, forthcoming).
2. Bōeichō Bōei Kenshujo Senshishitsu (hereafter cited as BBKS), ed., *Senshi sōsho (65) Daihon'ei Rikugunbu Daitōa Sensō kaisen keii (1)* [War history series (65), Imperial Headquarters, Army, the circumstances leading to the opening of the greater East Asian War (1)] (Tokyo: Asagumo Shuppansha, 1973), 304–305.
3. Ogata Taketora, *Ichigunjin no shōgai: Teitoku Yonai Mitsumasa* [One sailor's lifetime: Admiral Yonai Mitsumasa] (Tokyo: Wakōdō, 1983), 65–84.
4. Takagi Sōkichi, "Konoe dainiji naikaku seiritsu keii" [Circumstances of the establishment of the second Konoe cabinet], July 31, 1940, in *Nikki to jōhō* [Diary and reports], vol. 1 (Tokyo: Misuzu Shobō, 2000), 436–438.
5. Daily entries, February 21 and March 15, 1940, in Ku'naichō, ed., *Shōwa Tennō jitsuroku* [True documents of the Shōwa Emperor], vol. 27, Imperial Household Agency, Archives and Mausolea Department, 26–27, 38–39.
6. Hata Shunroku, diary entry, June 25, 1940, in Itō Takashi and Terunuma Yasutaka, eds., *Zokugendaishi shiryō: Rikugun (4); Hata Shunroku nisshi* [Documents on contemporary history, continued (4): The army; Hata Shunroku's diary] (Tokyo: Misuzu Shobō, 1983), 259.
7. See, for example, Peter Mauch, *Sailor Diplomat: Nomura Kichisaburō and the Japanese-American War* (Cambridge, MA: Harvard University Asia Center, 2011), 116.
8. BBKS, ed., *Senshi sōsho (20) Daihon'ei Rikugunbu (2) Shōwa 16-nen 12-gatsu made* [War history series (20), Imperial Headquarters, Army (2), until December 1941] (Tokyo: Asagumo Shuppansha, 1968), 47.
9. Kido Koichi, diary entry, July 8, 1940, in Kido Kōichi, *Nikki* [Diary], ed. Kido Nikki Kenkyukai, vol. 2 (Tokyo: Tokyo Daigaku Shuppankai, 1966), 801.
10. Hata Shunroku, diary entry, June 27, 1940, in Itō and Terunuma, *Hata Shunroku nisshi,* 263.
11. "Daihon'ei rikugunbu sanbō sōchō yori rikugun daijin e no yōbō" [The army chief of staff's demands of the army minister], in diary entry, July 4, 1940, in Itō and Terunuma, *Hata Shunroku nisshi,* 267.
12. Peter Mauch, "The Shōwa Political Crisis, July 1940: The Imperial Japanese Army Courts a Breach with Its Sovereign," *War in History* 27, no. 4 (2020): 670–688.
13. Yamanaka Minetarō, *Rikugun hangakuji* [Army rebels] (Tokyo: Ohara Shobō, 1954), 190.
14. Yamanaka, *Rikugun hangakuji,* 198, 209.
15. Yamanaka, *Rikugun hangakuji,* 198, 209.
16. Kido Kōichi, diary entries, June 28 and July 2, 1940, in Kido Kōichi, *Nikki,* 2:797, 799.
17. BBKS, *Senshi sōsho (65),* 406.
18. Logbook entry, July 17, 1940, in Kinbara Setuzō, *Rikugunshō gyōmu nisshi tekiroku zenhen* [Army Ministry logbook summary part one], ed. Hatano Sumio and Chadani Seiichi (Tokyo: Gendaishiryō Shuppan, 2016), 183.

19. Logbook entry, July 17, 1940, in Kinbara, *Rikugunshō gyōmu nisshi tekiroku zenhen,* 183–184.
20. Logbook entry, July 17, 1940, in Kinbara, *Rikugunshō gyōmu nisshi tekiroku zenhen,* 184.
21. See Sadao Asada, *From Mahan to Pearl Harbor: The Imperial Japanese Navy and the United States* (Annapolis, MD: Naval Institute Press, 2006), 221–222.
22. Daily entry, July 18, 1940, in Ku'naichō, *Shōwa tennō jitsuroku,* 27:114.
23. BBKS, *Senshi sōsho (65),* 406.
24. See Tōkyō Saiban Kenkyūkai, ed., *Tōjō Hideki sensei kyōjutsusho* [Tojo Hideki's affidavit] (Tokyo: Yōyōsha, 1948), 4–5. See also Akamatsu Sadao, *Tōjō hishokan kimitsu nisshi* [Secret diary of Tojo's secretary] (Tokyo: Bungei Shunju, 1985), 14.
25. See Hosoya Chihiro, "The Tripartite Pact, 1939–1940," in *Deterrent Diplomacy: Japan, Germany, and the USSR, 1935–1940: Selected Translations from "Taiheiyō sensō e no michi: Kaisen gaikō shi,"* ed. James William Morley (New York: Columbia University Press, 1976), 216–221.
26. "Sōgō kokusaku kihon yōkō" [Fundamental outline of overall national policy], n.d., quoted in BBKS, *Senshi sōsho (65),* 409–410. For Muto's offer of the army's support, see BBKS, *Senshi sōsho (65),* 411.
27. See BBKS, *Senshi sōsho (65),* 408.
28. "Sokakuchū yonchū kaidan (ogikubo kaidan) kettei " [Decisions at the four pillars conference during the formation of the cabinet] in Inaba Masao, Kobayashi Tatsuo, Shimada Toshihiko, and Tsunoda Jun, eds., *Taiheiyō sensō e no michi: bekkan, shiryōhen* [Japan's road to the Pacific War: Supplementary volume: Documents] (Tokyo: Asahi Shinbunsha, 1963), 319–320.
29. "Sokakuchū yonchū kaidan (ogikubo kaidan) kettei."
30. "Sokakuchū yonchū kaidan (ogikubo kaidan) kettei."
31. Tōkyō Saiban Kenkyūkai, *Tōjō Hideki sensei kyōjutsusho,* 6.
32. Suikōkai, ed., *Teikoku Kaigun teitokutachi no ikō: Koyanagi shiryō* [The Imperial Navy's admirals' posthumous manuscripts: The Koyanagi papers], vol. 1 (Tokyo: Suikōkai, 2010), 17. See also BBKS, ed., *Senshi sōsho (101) Daihon'ei Kaigunbu, Daitōa Sensō kaisen keii (2)* [War history series (101), Imperial Headquarters, Navy, circumstances leading to the outbreak of the Greater East Asia War (2)] (Tokyo: Asagumo Shuppansha, 1979), 49–52. For the "half measure" quotation, see Yoshida Toshio, *Gonin no kaigun daijin* [Five navy ministers] (Tokyo: Bungei Shunjū, 1983), 169.
33. Daily entry, September 11, 1931, in Ku'naichō, ed., *Shōwa Tennō jitsuroku* [True documents of the Shōwa Emperor], vol. 18, Imperial Household Agency, Archives and Mausolea Department, 116.
34. Akamatsu, *Tōjō hishokan kimitsu nisshi,* 33.
35. For Tojo's own explanation of cabinet ministers' responsibility as the emperor's advisers, see Shiohara Tokisaburō, ed., *Tōjō memo: Kakute tennō wa sukuwareta* [Tojo memo: Thus was the emperor saved] (Tokyo: Handobukkusha, 1952), 28. Tojo was drawing explicitly on the language of article 55 of the Meiji Constitution, which stated, "Ministers of State shall give their advice to the Emperor, and be responsible for it."
36. Daily entry, April 3, 1940, in Ku'naichō, *Shōwa tennō jitsuroku,* 18:46.
37. Tojo later recalled (from Sugamo Prison) that the emperor had repeated what he told Terauchi following the February 26 Incident. See Satō Sanae, *Tōjō hideki "waga munen"* [Tojo Hideki: "My chagrin"] Tokyo: Kawade Shobō Shinsho, 1997), 41. For the emperor's words to Terauchi following the February 26 Incident, see daily entry, March 10, 1936, in Ku'naichō, ed., *Shōwa Tennō jitsuroku* [True documents of the Shōwa Emperor], vol. 23, Imperial Household Agency, Archives and Mausolea Department, 51.
38. Anami Korechika, diary entry, July 24, 1940, in 48 Nikki (jikan 2; rikugun jikan), Anami Korechika papers, Modern Japanese Political History Materials Room, National Diet

Library. Tojo's subsequent explanation of the "spiritual sense" of "eight corners of the world under one roof" can be found in "Kyokutō Kokusai Gunji Saiban kankei shiryō (Eibun) kyōjutsu chōsho: Tōjō Hideki" [International Military Tribunal for the Far East papers (English) investigator's record of oral statement: Tojo Hideki], January 14–18, 1946, Hōmu Daijin Kambō Shihō Hōsei Chōsabu, 4A.18.2420, National Archives of Japan.

39. "Kihon kokusaku yōkō" [The main principles of basic national policy], July 26, 1940, in *Nihon gaikō nenpyō narabini jūyō monjo, 1840–1945* [Chronology of Japan's foreign policy and major documents], ed. Gaimushō (Tokyo: Hara Shobō, 1965), 436–437. For Tojo's understanding of this policy document, see Tōkyō Saiban Kenkyūkai, *Tōjō Hideki sensei kyōjutsusho,* 8–9.
40. "Sekai josei no suii ni tomonau jikyoku shori yōkō" [Outline of the main principles for coping with the changing world situation], July 27, 1940, in Gaimushō, *Nihon gaikō nenpyō narabini jūyō monjo,* 437–438.
41. "Kachō kaigi" [Section chief conference], September 27, 1940, in Kinbara, *Rikugunshō gyōmu nisshi tekiroku zenhen,* 191. Regarding Tojo's visit to Meiji and Yasukuni Shrines, see Hosaka Masayasu, *Tōjō Hideki to tennō no jidai: Gunnai kōsō kara kaisen zen'ya made* [Tojo Hideki and the era of the emperor: From intraservice conflict to the eve of the opening of the war], vol. 1 (Tokyo: Bungei Shunjū, 1988), 199.
42. Akamatsu, *Tōjō hishokan kimitsu nisshi,* 15.
43. "Rikugun daijin kunji no ken" [Army minister's orders], July 25, 1940, Rikugunshō dainikki, Shōwa 14-nen mitsudainikki, Daisansatsu, Military Archival Library, National Institute of Defense Studies, Japanese Defense Ministry Archives (hereafter cited as JDMA), Japan Center for Asian Historical Records (hereafter cited as JACAR) reference code C01001781200.
44. The memorandum which the interlocutors exchanged on July 22 is reproduced in full in BBKS, ed., *Senshi sōsho (90) Shina Jihen rikugun sakusen (3) Shōwa 16-nen 12-gatsu made* [War history series (90), army strategy in the China Incident (3), until December 1941] (Tokyo: Asagumo Shuppansha, 1975), 250.
45. BBKS, ed., *Senshi sōsho (69): Daihon'ei Rikugunbu Daitōa Sensō kaisen keii (3)* [War history series (69): Imperial Headquarters, Army, circumstances leading to the outbreak of the greater East Asian War (3)] (Tokyo: Asagumo Shuppansha, 1973), 8.
46. BBKS, *Senshi sōsho (69),* 8.
47. BBKS, *Senshi sōsho (69),* 22. See also Imai Takeo, *Shina Jihen no kaisō* [A memoir of the China Incident] (Tokyo: Misuzu Shobō, 1964), 145.
48. Daily entries, July 18, July 23, and August 5, 1940, in Ku'naichō, *Shōwa tennō jitsuroku,* 27:114, 117, 125.
49. BBKS, *Senshi sōsho (69),* 9–10. See also Jōhō Yoshio, ed., *Gunmukyokuchō Mutō Akira kaisōroku* [Military Affairs Bureau director Mutō Akira's memoirs] (Tokyo: Fūyō Shobō, 1981), 162.
50. See BBKS, ed., *Senshi sōsho (68): daihon'ei rikugunbu daitōa sensō kaisen keii (2)* [War history series (vol. 68): General headquarters, army, circumstances leading to the outbreak of the Greater East Asian War (vol. 2)] (Tokyo: Asagumo Shuppansha, 1973), 4.
51. Hata Ikuhiko, "The Army's Move into Northern Indochina," in *The Fateful Choice: Japan's Advance into Southeast Asia; Selected Translations from "Taiheiyō sensō e no michi: Kaisen gaikō shi,"* ed. James William Morley (New York: Columbia University Press, 1980), 169.
52. Daily entry, June 20, 1940, in Ku'naichō, *Shōwa tennō jitsuroku,* 27:90.
53. Journal entries, July 29, August 1, August 8, and August 9, 1940, in *Daihon'ei Rikugunbu sensō shidō han: Kimitsu sensō nisshi,* vol. 1, ed. Gunjishi Gakkai (Tokyo: Ginseisha, 2008), 15–17.
54. See the telegram dated August 6, 1940, in *Nihon gaikō bunsho: Ni-Cchū Sensō* [Documents on Japanese foreign policy: Sino-Japanese War], vol. 4, ed. Gaimushō (Tokyo: Gaimushō, 2011), 2904–2906.

55. "Kyokuchō kaigi" [Bureau chief conference], August 7, 1940, in Kinbara, *Rikugunshō gyōmu nisshi tekiroku zenhen,* 194.
56. BBKS, *Senshi sōsho (68),* 28–29.
57. "Gaishō—Anrii taishi kaidan (15-8-15)" [Foreign Minister—Henry conversation (August 15, 1940)] in "Chūō ni okeru keii (1)" [Circumstances at the center (1)], Futsuin mondai keii 2, Jūyō kokusaku bunsho, Sensō shidō, Chūō, Rikugun ippan shiryō, JDMA, JACAR reference code C12120107300. See also the telegram dated August 17, 1940, in Gaimushō, *Nihon gaikō bunsho: Ni-Cchū Sensō,* 4:2915–2916.
58. BBKS, *Senshi sōsho (68),* 31.
59. Journal entry, August 15, 1940, in Gunjishi Gakkai, *Kimitsu sensō nisshi,* 1:19.
60. BBKS, *Senshi sōsho (68),* 32–33.
61. See the two telegrams dated August 21, 1940, in Gaimushō, *Nihon gaikō bunsho: Ni-Cchū Sensō,* 4:2917–2921.
62. Journal entry, August 20, 1940, in Gunjishi Gakkai, *Kimitsu sensō nisshi,* 1:20.
63. An English-language translation of the army-navy draft is reproduced in Morley, *Deterrent Diplomacy,* appendix 6, 289–297.
64. Kurusu Saburo to Matsuoka Yosuke, August 23, 1940, in *Nihon gaikō bunsho: Dainiji Ōshū taisen to Nihon, daiissatsu, Nichi-Doku-I Sangoku Dōmei/Ni-Sso chūritsu jōyaku* [Documents on Japanese foreign policy: The second European war and Japan, Japanese-German-Italian Tripartite Pact/Japanese-Soviet neutrality treaty], vol. 1, Gaimushō (Tokyo: Gaimushō, 2012), 203.
"Nichi-Doku-I dōmei jōyaku teiketsu yōroku" [Digest record of conclusion of the Japanese-German-Italian treaty of alliance], in *Nihon gaikō bunsho: Nichi-Doku-I Sangoku Dōmei kankei chōshoshū* [Documents on Japanese foreign policy: Records related to conclusion of the Tripartite Pact], ed. Gaimushō (Tokyo: Gaimushō, 2004), 17.
65. BBKS, *Senshi sōsho (101),* 51–52.
66. Journal entries, August 6 and August 12, 1940, in Gunjishi Gakkai, *Kimitsusensō nisshi,* 1:16–17, 18.
67. BBKS, *Senshi sōsho (101),* 66.
68. "Rikukaigun shunōbu kaidan no sai ni okeru 'Jikyoku shori yōkō' ni kanren suru shitsugi ōtō shiryō" [Questions and answers concerning the "Outline of main principles for coping with the changing world situation" for use at the conference of army-navy leaders], August 27, 1940, in Sugiyama Hajime, *Sugiyama memo* [Sugiyama's memorandums], vol. 1, ed. Sanbō Honbu (Tokyo: Hara Shobō, 2005), 16–22.
69. BBKS, *Senshi sōsho (101),* 66–67.
70. Regarding Prince Fushimi, see Nomura Minoru, *Tennō, Fushiminomiya to Nihon Kaigun* [The emperor, Prince Fushimi, and the Japanese Navy] (Tokyo: Bungei Shunjū, 1988).
71. Journal entry, August 27, 1940, in Gunjishi Gakkai, *Kimitsu sensō nisshi,* 1:21.
72. "Gunji dōmei kōshō ni kansuru yōkō" [Draft policy concerning negotiations for a military alliance], in "Nichi-Doku-I dōmei jōyaku teiketsu yōroku," 26–27.
73. BBKS, *Senshi sōsho (101),* 71.
74. BBKS, *Senshi sōsho (69),* 20.
75. BBKS, *Senshi sōsho (69),* 14–15, 21–22, 24.
76. For the Matsuoka-Henry Pact, see Morley, *The Fateful Choice,* appendix 2, 301–302.
77. Journal entry, August 26, 1940, in Tanemura Sakō, *Daihon'ei kimitsu nisshi* [Confidential supreme headquarters journal] (Tokyo: Daiyamondosha, 1952), 23.
78. Journal entry, August 27, 1940, in Gunjishi Gakkai, *Kimitsu sensō nisshi,* 1:21.
79. See Jōhō Yoshio, ed., *Satō kenryō no shōgen* [Sato Kenryo's testimony] (Tokyo: Fuyō Shobō, 1976), 177. See also Hata, "The Army's Move into Northern Indochina," 176–177.
80. Suzuki Takuji to Matsuoka Yosuke, September 4, 1940, in Gaimushō, *Nihon gaikō bunsho: Ni-Cchū Sensō,* 4:2940–2944.
81. BBKS, *Senshi sōsho (68),* 63.

82. Hata, "The Army's Move in Northern Indochina," 183.
83. Journal entry, September 5, 1940, in Gunjishi Gakkai, *Kimitsu sensō nisshi,* 1:24.
84. "Gunji dōmei kōshō ni kansuru hōshin'an" [Proposed policy regarding negotiations for a military alliance], September 6, 1940, in Sugiyama, *Sugiyama memo,* 1:27–33. See also "Nichi-Doku-I dōmei jōyaku teiketsu yōroku," 45.
85. "Imperial Conference, September 19, 1940," in *Japan's Decision for War: Records of the 1941 Policy Conferences,* trans. and ed. Nobutaka Ike (Stanford, CA: Stanford University Press, 1967), 3–13, quotation on 11. For a record of Matsuoka's negotiations with Stahmer, see "Matsuoka Gaishō / Stahmer Gōshi hikōshiki kaidan yōshi" [Outline of informal conversation between Foreign Minister Matsuoka and Ambassador Stahmer] September 9–10, 1940, in *Nihon gaikō bunsho: Dainiji Ōshū taisen to Nihon,* 1:215–27. For a detailed Foreign Ministry account of Matsuoka's negotiations with Stahmer, see *Nihon gaikō bunsho: Nichi-Doku-I Sangoku Dōmei,* 48–51.
86. "Nichi-Doku-I Sangoku Dōmei jōyaku teiketsu ni kansuru Sūmitsuin shinsa iinkai no giji gaiyō" [Summary of proceedings of Privy Council assessment committee concerning conclusion of the Japanese-German-Italian tripartite alliance], September 26, 1940, in *Nihon gaikō bunsho: Dainiji Ōshū taisen to Nihon,* 1:227–247, quotations on 229, 230.
87. An English-language translation of both the terms of the alliance and Ott's letter are reproduced in Morley, *Deterrent Diplomacy,* appendix 7, 298–301.
88. BBKS, *Senshi sōsho (69),* 28.
89. BBKS, *Senshi sōsho (69),* 32. Tojo's remarks remained within the confines of an agreement he reached with Matsuoka and Oikawa that same day. See "Tai-Jūkei wahei kōshō no ken" [Concerning peace negotiations vis-à-vis Chongqing] and the attachments in Gaimushō, *Nihon gaikō bunsho: Ni-Cchū Sensō,* 576–579.
90. BBKS, *Senshi sōsho (68),* 69.
91. BBKS, *Senshi sōsho (68),* 71–72.
92. Regarding the four-minister conference, see journal entries, September 12 and 13, 1940, in Gunjishi Gakkai, *Kimitsu sensō nisshi,* 1:26. See also "Futsuin mondai jigo no sochi ni kansuru ken" [Concerning future measures for the French Indochinese issue], September 13, 1940, in Gaimushō, *Nihon gaikō bunsho: Ni-Cchū Sensō,* 4:2949–2950.
93. Daily entry, September 14, 1940, in in Ku'naichō, *Shōwa tennō jitsuroku,* 27:145–146. Prince Kan'in's orders are reproduced in BBKS, *Senshi sōsho (20),* 91–92.
94. BBKS, *Senshi sōsho (68),* 87.
95. Journal entry, September 17, 1940, in Tanemura, *Daihon'ei kimitsu nisshi,* 27.
96. BBKS, *Senshi sōsho (68),* 88–90.
97. BBKS, *Senshi sōsho (68),* 79–80, 91.
98. Journal entry, September 18, 1940, in Tanemura, *Daihon'ei kimitsu nisshi,* 28.
99. Journal entry, September 18, 1940, in Gunjishi Gakkai, *Kimitsu sensō nisshi,* 1:27.
100. Satō Kenryō, *Tōjō Hideki to Taiheiyō Sensō* [Tojo Hideki and the Pacific War] (Tokyo: Bungei Shunjū Shinsha, 1960), 140.
101. Hata, "The Army's Move into Northern Indochina," 206.
102. Journal entry, October 3, 1940, in Tanemura, *Daihon'ei kimitsu nisshi,* 32.

7 · DRAWING THE BATTLE LINES

1. Edward S. Miller, *Bankrupting the Enemy: The US Financial Siege of Japan Before Pearl Harbor* (Annapolis, MD: Naval Institute Press, 2007), 78.
2. "Kyokuchō kaihō" [Bureau directors' meeting transactions], September 7, 1940, in Kinbara Setuzō, *Rikugunshō gyōmu nisshi tekiroku zenhen* [Army Ministry logbook summary part one], ed. Hatano Sumio and Chadani Seiichi (Tokyo: Gendaishiryō Shuppan, 2016), 215–217, quotation on 217.
3. Miller, *Bankrupting the Enemy,* 123–140.

4. "Kyokuchō kaihō" [Bureau directors' meeting transactions], September 28, 1940, in Kinbara, *Rikugunshō gyōmu nisshi tekiroku zenhen,* 224–227, quotation on 225–226.
5. See, for example, Prince Fushimi's statement, in "Imperial Conference, September 19, 1940," in *Japan's Decision for War: Records of the 1941 Policy Conferences,* trans. and ed. Nobutaka Ike (Stanford, CA: Stanford University Press, 1967), 13.
6. "Tōjō Rikushō to no kaidan yōshi" [Outline of conversation with Army Minister Tojo], October 22, 1940, Nomura Kichisaburō kankei monjo, Modern Japanese Political History Materials Room, National Diet Library. See also Peter Mauch, *Sailor Diplomat: Nomura Kichisaburō and the Japanese-American War* (Cambridge, MA: Harvard University Asia Center, 2011), 126–127.
7. See "Tōjō rikushō to no kaidan yōshi"; and Mauch, *Sailor Diplomat,* 126–127.>
8. Arisue Yatoru, "Gozen kaigi no keika" [Developments leading to the Imperial conference], in Sugiyama Hajime, *Sugiyama memo* [Sugiyama's memorandums], vol. 1, ed. Sanbō Honbu (Tokyo: Hara Shobō, 2005), 140–143.
9. "Shina Jihen shori yōkō" [Outline of policy to deal with the China Incident], October 21, 1940, in Bōeichō Bōei Kenshujo Senshishitsu (hereafter cited as BBKS), ed., *Senshi sōsho (69): Daihon'ei Rikugunbu Daitōa Sensō kaisen keii (3)* [War history series (69): Imperial Headquarters, Army, circumstances leading to the outbreak of the greater East Asian War (3)] (Tokyo: Asagumo Shuppansha, 1973), 72–74.
10. "Shina Jihen shori yōkō," 72–74. For Japan's terms in the event that Chiang sought a merger with the Wang regime (these terms did not differ substantially from the terms under discussion during Operation Kiri), see "Nippongawa yōkyū jōken shian" ["Draft of Japan's demands and terms"], in BBKS, *Senshi sōsho (69),* 74.
11. "Kyokuchō kaihō" [Bureau directors' meeting transactions], October 12, 1940, in Kinbara, *Rikugunshō gyōmu nisshi tekiroku zenhen,* 232–236, quotation on 232.
12. See Arisue, "Gozen kaigi no keika," 140–143. See also BBKS, ed., *Senshi sōsho (90) Shina Jihen rikugun sakusen (3) Shōwa 16-nen 12-gatsu made* [War history series (90), army strategy in the China Incident (3), until December 1941] (Tokyo: Asagumo Shuppansha, 1975), 298.
13. BBKS, *Senshi sōsho (90),* 77.
14. "Kyokuchō kaihō" [Bureau directors' meeting transactions], November 9, 1940, in Kinbara, *Rikugunshō gyōmu nisshi tekiroku zenhen,* 245–247, quotation on 245–246.
15. Arisue, "Gozen kaigi no keika," 140–143.
16. The documents tabled at the Imperial conference (including the "Outline" in its final version) are reproduced in Sugiyama, *Sugiyama memo,* 1:143–154.
17. Journal entry, November 22, 1940, in Tanemura Sakō, *Daihon'ei kimitsu nisshi* [Confidential supreme headquarters journal] (Tokyo: Daiyamondosha, 1952), 36.
18. "Treaty and Agreements Between Japan and the Wang Jingwei Regime in Japanese-Occupied China, Signed at Nanking, November 30, 1940," in US Department of State, *Foreign Relations of the United States: Japan, 1931–1941,* vol. 2 (Washington DC: Government Printing Office, 1943), 117–121.
19. BBKS, ed., *Senshi sōsho (20) Daihon'ei Rikugunbu (2) Shōwa 16-nen 12-gatsu made* [War history series (20), Imperial Headquarters, Army (2), until December 1941] (Tokyo: Asagumo Shuppansha, 1968), 118–119.
20. "Tai-Tai shisaku ni kansuru yonshō kaigi kettei no yōshi" [Summary of four-minister conference decision concerning policies toward Thailand], November 5, 1940, in *Nihon gaikō bunsho: Dainiji Ōshū taisen to Nihon* [Documents on Japanese foreign policy: The second great Europe war and Japan], vol. 2, no. 2, ed. Gaimushō (Tokyo: Gaimushō, 2013), 900.
21. "Taikoku no shitchi kaifuku assen ni kanren suru Tai-Tai narabi ni Tai-Futsuin shisaku no ken" [Concerning policies toward Thailand and French Indochina as they relate to

mediation and return of Thailand's lost territories], in Gaimushō, *Nihon gaikō bunsho: Dainiji Ōshū taisen to Nihon,* 2:2:902–903.

22. BBKS, *Senshi sōsho (20),* 174.
23. "12-gatsu 12-nichi dai-2-kai Renraku Kondankai" [2nd Liaison Conference, December 12, 1940], in Sugiyama, *Sugiyama memo,* 1:156.
24. BBKS, *Senshi sōsho (20),* 175.
25. "Renraku kondankai setchi no shui" [The aim in establishing the liaison conference], undated, in Sugiyama, *Sugiyama memo,* 1:155.
26. "Tai-Futsuin ni taishi toru beki Teikoku no sochi" [Measures that Japan should adopt toward Thailand and French Indochina], December 27, 1940, in Sugiyama, *Sugiyama memo,* 1:157.
27. "12-gatsu 27-nichi dai-3-kai Renraku Kondankai" [3rd Liaison Conference, December 27, 1940], in Sugiyama, *Sugiyama memo,* 1:156–157. This conference record does not include any statement by Tojo. Regarding Tojo's agreement with Oikawa, see BBKS, *Senshi sōsho (20),* 176.
28. Journal entry, December 27, 1940, in *Daihon'ei rikugunbu sensō shidō han: Kimitsu sensō nisshi* [Imperial headquarters, army, war guidance section: Confidential war journal], vol. 1, ed. Gunjishi Gakkai (Tokyo: Ginseisha, 2008), 53.
29. Journal entry, January 10, 1941, in Gunjishi Gakkai, *Kimitsu sensō nisshi,* 1:57. Regarding the conversations with former ambassador Togo, see, for example Hosoya Chihiro, "Japanese-Soviet Neutrality Pact," in *The Fateful Choice: Japan's Advance into Southeast Asia; Selected Translations from "Taiheiyō sensō e no michi: Kaisen gaikō shi,"* ed. James William Morley (New York: Columbia University Press, 1980), 41–46.
30. Journal entry, January 10, 1941, in Gunjishi Gakkai, *Kimitsu sensō nisshi,* 1:57.
31. Stephen E. Pelz, *Race to Pearl Harbor: The Failure of the Second London Naval Conference and the Onset of World War II* (Cambridge, MA: Harvard University Press, 1974), 218.
32. Journal entry, January 11, 1941, in Gunjishi Gakkai, *Kimitsu sensō nisshi,* 1:57.
33. Journal entry, January 14, 1941, in Gunjishi Gakkai, *Kimitsu sensō nisshi,* 1:58–59.
34. Imperial Japanese Army, *Field Service Code (Senzinkun)* (Tokyo: Tokyo Gazette Publishing, 1941), 1, 10–14.
35. "Rikukun daiichigō," January 8, 1941, in "Senjinkun ni kansuru ken: tsūchō" [Notes concerning the Field Service Code], Rikumitsu / Rikufu Shōwa 16-nen, Rikugunshō dainikki [Document files of the Army Ministry], JDM Archives, Japan Center for Asian Historical Records (hereafter cited as JACAR) reference code C01005234000.
36. Journal entry, January 14, 1941, in Gunjishi Gakkai, *Kimitsu sensō nisshi,* 1:60.
37. "1-gatsu 25-nichi nan-Futsuin ni taisuru sakusen junbi ni kanshi jōsō no sai okamon" [The emperor's questions in response to the report concerning preparation for operations against southern Indochina, January 25], in Sugiyama, *Sugiyama memo,* 1:163.
38. BBKS, *Senshi sōsho (20),* 183.
39. "Futsuin Tai shori yōkō" ["Outline of measures toward Indochina and Thailand"], January 25, 1941, in "Tai-Tai Furansu Indoshina kokusaku kettei monjo" ["National policy toward Thailand and French Indochina: Documents"], A-7-0-0-9_2_002, Japan Diplomatic Record Office, JACAR reference code B02032438600.
40. "Tai-Futsuin-Tai shisaku yōkō" ["Outline of policies toward Thailand and French Indochina"], January 30, 1941, in Sugiyama, *Sugiyama memo,* 1:167–168.
41. "1-gatsu 30-nichi dai-7-kai Renraku Kondankai" [7th Liaison Conference, January 30, 1941], in Sugiyama, *Sugiyama memo,* 1:165–167, quotation on 166.
42. Journal entries, February 27–28, 1941, in Gunjishi Gakkai *Kimitsu sensō nisshi,* 1:78–79.
43. "Futsugawa ga waga saigo chōteian o ōdaku sesaru baai no sotchi" [Measures in the event France does not accept our final mediation plan], March 2, 1941, in Sugiyama, *Sugiyama memo,* 1:187.

44. "3-gatsu itsuka dai-14-kai Renraku Kondankai" [14th Liaison Conference, March 5, 1941], in Sugiyama, *Sugiyama memo,* 1:188.
45. See, for example, Sadao Asada and Sumio Hatano, "The Japanese Decision to Move South," in *Paths to War: New Essays on the Origins of the Second World War,* ed. Robert Boyce and Esmonde M. Robertson (Basingstoke, UK: Macmillan, 1989), 394.
46. Gordon M. Berger, *Parties Out of Power in Japan, 1931–1941* (Princeton, NJ: Princeton University Press, 1977), 275–310.
47. Stephen S. Large, *Emperor Hirohito and Shōwa Japan: A Political Biography* (London: Routledge, 1992), 78.
48. "Kyokuchō kaihō" [Bureau directors' meeting transactions], October 30, 1940, in Kinbara, *Rikugunshō gyōmu nisshi tekiroku zenhen,* 239–241, quotation on 240.
49. Iokibe Makoto, "Tōa Renmei ron no kihonteki seikaku" [Ishiwara Kanji's East Asian League: Its fundamental features], *Ajia kenkyū* [Asian studies] 22, no. 1 (1975), 26; Higashikuni Naruhiko, diary entries, February 3 and 17, 1941, in *Kōzoku gunjin denki shūsei 11: Higashikuninomiya Naruhiko ō* [Collection of biographies of Imperial family soldiers and sailors 11: Prince Higashikuni Naruhiko], ed. Satō Motoei (Tokyo: Yumani Shobō, 2012), 25–27.
50. Higashikuni Naruhiko, diary entry, February 3, 1941, in *Kōzoku gunjin denki shūsei 11,* 25–27.
51. Takagi Sōkichi, diary entry, February 20, 1941, in Takagi Sōkichi, *Nikki to jōhō* [Diary and reports], vol. 2 (Tokyo: Misuzu Shobō, 2000), 514–516.
52. Mark R. Peattie, *Ishiwara Kanji and Japan's Confrontation with the West* (Princeton, NJ: Princeton University Press, 1975), 330.
53. Higashikuni Naruhiko, diary entry, February 3, 1941, in *Kōzoku gunjin denki shūsei 11,* 25–27.
54. Peattie, *Ishiwara Kanji,* 329.
55. Terasaki Hidenari, *Shōwa Tennō dokuhakuraku: Terasaki Hidenari Ggoyōgakkari nikki* [The Showa Emperor's monologue: Imperial aide Terasaki Hidenari's diary], ed. Mariko Terasaki Miller (Tokyo: Bungei Shunjū, 1991), 88. For an English-language translation, see Gordon M. Berger, Roger M. Brown, and Peter Mauch, eds., *The Emperor's Testimony: Hirohito's Monologue on Japan's War in Asia and the Pacific* (Cambridge: Cambridge University Press, forthcoming).
56. BBKS, *Senshi sōsho (20),* 136. See also BBKS, *Senshi sōsho (69),* 160.
57. See, for example, Sadao Asada, *From Mahan to Pearl Harbor: The Imperial Japanese Navy and the United States* (Annapolis, MD: Naval Institute Press, 2006), 239–246; and Mauch, *Sailor Diplomat,* 62–67, 70–74, 92–93, 124–125.
58. Oshima Hiroshi to Matsuoka Yosuke, February 26, 1941, in Gaimushō, *Nihon gaikō bunsho: Dainiji Ōshū taisen to Nihon* [Documents on Japanese foreign policy: The second great European war and Japan], vol. 1 (Tokyo: Roku-ichi Shobō, 2012), 330.
59. Oshima Hiroshi to Matsuoka Yosuke, March 2, 1941, in Gaimushō, *Nihon gaikō bunsho: Dainiji Ōshū taisen to Nihon,* 1:330–333.
60. "Kyokuchō kaihō" [Bureau directors' meeting transactions], April 5, 1941, in Kinbara, *Rikugunshō gyōmu nisshi tekiroku zenhen,* 284–288, quotations on 286, 287.
61. BBKS, *Senshi sōsho (69),* 372–374, quotations on 373.
62. Oshima Hiroshi to Konoe Fumimaro, March 18, 1941, in Gaimushō, *Nihon gaikō bunsho: Dainiji Ōshū taisen to Nihon,* 1:333–334.
63. Ōhashi Chūichi, *Taiheiyō Sensō yuraiki: Matsuoka gaikō no shinsō* [Pacific War memoir: The truth of Matsuoka's diplomacy] (Tokyo: Kaname Shobō, 1952), 56–57.
64. BBKS, *Senshi sōsho (69),* 385.
65. "Matsuoka-Ribbentrop kaidan yōshi" [Outline of Matsuoka-Ribbentrop conversation], March 27, 1941, in Gaimushō, *Nihon gaikō bunsho: Dainiji Ōshū taisen to Nihon,* 1:334–336.

66. "Matsuoka-Hitler kaidan yōshi" [Outline of Matsuoka-Hitler conversation], March 27, 1941, in Gaimushō, *Nihon gaikō bunsho: Dainiji Ōshū taisen to Nihon,* 1:336–337.
67. Oshima Hiroshi to Konoe Fumimaro, April 1, 1941, in Gaimushō, *Nihon gaikō bunsho: Dainiji Ōshū taisen to Nihon,* 1:337.
68. "4-gatsu 10-ka dai-17-kai Renraku Kondankai" [17th Liaison Conference, April 10, 1941], in Sugiyama, *Sugiyama memo,* 1:195–196. See also Tatekawa Yoshitsugu to Konoe Fumimaro, April 9, 1941, in Gaimushō, *Nihon gaikō bunsho: Dainiji Ōshū taisen to Nihon,* 1:339.
69. Tatekawa Yoshitsugu to Konoe Fumimaro, April 10, 1941, in Gaimushō, *Nihon gaikō bunsho: Dainiji Ōshū taisen to Nihon,* 1:339–340.
70. Journal entry, April 12, 1941, in Gunjishi Gakkai, *Kimitsu nisshi,* 1:89.
71. For an exhaustive account of Matsuoka's conversations with Vyacheslav Molotov and Joseph Stalin, see Boris Slavinsky, *The Japanese-Soviet Neutrality Pact: A Diplomatic History, 1941–1945* (London: Routledge, 2003), 32–56.
72. "Kyokuchō kaihō" [Bureau directors' meeting transactions], April 14, 1941, in Kinbara, *Rikugunshō gyōmu nisshi tekiroku zenhen,* 300–305, quotations on 301, 303.
73. See Peter Mauch, "Admiral Nagano Osami and Japan's Decision for War Against the United States," in *Planning for War at Sea: 400 Years of Great Power Competition,* ed. Paul Kennedy and Evan Wilson (Annapolis, MD: Naval Institute Press, 2025), 169–189.
74. Oshima Hiroshi to Konoe Fumimaro, April 1, 1941, in Gaimushō, *Nihon gaikō bunsho: Dainiji Ōshū taisen to Nihon,* 1:355–357.
75. Oshima Hiroshi to Konoe Fumimaro, April 1, 1941, in Gaimushō, *Nihon gaikō bunsho: Dainiji Ōshū taisen to Nihon,* 1:357–360.
76. Nomura Kichisaburo to Konoe Fumimaro, April 17, 1941, in *Nihon gaikō bunsho: Nichi-Bei kōshō 1941-nen* [Documents on Japanese foreign policy: Japan-US talks in 1941], vol. 1, ed. Gaimushō (Tokyo: Buntenkaku, 1990), 20–24. For an English-language rendition of the Draft Understanding, see "Proposal presented to the Department of State through the Medium of Private American and Japanese Individuals on April 9, 1941," US Department of State, *Foreign Relations of the United States: Japan 1931–1941,* 2:398–402. Regarding the Draft Understanding, see Mauch, *Sailor Diplomat,* 152–164. Regarding the timing of the Draft Understanding's arrival in Tokyo, see Konoe Fumimaro, *Konoe nikki* [Konoe diary] (Tokyo: Kyōdō Tsūshinsha, 1968), 187.
77. Nomura to Konoe, April 17, 1941, in *Nihon gaikō bunsho: Nichi-Bei kōshō 1941-nen,* vol. 1, 20–24.
78. BBKS, *Senshi sōsho (69),* 547.
79. Tsunoda Jun, "Confusion Arising from a Draft Understanding Between Japan and the United States," in *The Final Confrontation: Japan's Negotiations with the United States, 1941; Selected Translations from "Taiheiyō sensō e no michi: Kaisen gaikō shi,"* ed. James William Morley (New York: Columbia University Press, 1994), 44–46.
80. BBKS, *Senshi sōsho (20),* 253–256.
81. BBKS, *Senshi sōsho (20),* 253–256.
82. "Army-Navy Draft Policy of 17 April 1941," in Morley, *The Fateful Choice,* 303–304. Regarding the navy's role in bringing the Draft Understanding to fruition, as well as the interconnectedness of the Draft Understanding and the armed services' approach to the southward advance, see Peter Mauch, "A Bolt from the Blue? New Evidence on the Japanese Navy and the Draft Understanding Between Japan and the United States, April 1941," *Pacific Historical Review* 78, no. 1 (2009): 55–67. Regarding the army-navy agreement on the southward advance, see Asada and Hatano, "The Japanese Decision to Move South," 395–396.
83. Konoe Fumimaro, *Heiwa e no doryoku: Konoe Fumimaro shuki* [Endeavor for peace: Konoe Fumimaro's notes] (Tokyo: Nihon Denpō Tsūshinsha, 1946), 36.

84. BBKS, *Senshi sōsho (69),* 545.
85. "20th Liaison Conference, April 22, 1941," in Ike, *Japan's Decision for War,* 17–19.
86. "Nomura Taishi no teian ni taisuru iken" [Response to Admiral Nomura's proposal], April 21, 1941, in Inaba Masao, Kobayashi Tatsuo, Shimada Toshihiko, and Tsunoda Jun, eds., *Taiheiyō Sensō e no michi: Bekkan, shiryōhen* [The road to the Pacific War: Supplementary volume, documents] (Tokyo: Asahi Shinbunsha, 1963), 408–409.
87. "4-gatsu 21-nichi shūseian ryōgunbu oyobi Gaimu" (Armed services' and Foreign Ministry's revised draft, April 21), reel 4, Konoe Fumimaro Kankei Monjo, Modern Japanese Political History Materials Room, National Diet Library. See also Peter Mauch, "Documentary Discovery: Japan's Armed Services' Revisions to the Draft Understanding Between Japan and the United States, April 1941," *Journal of American-East Asian Relations* 20, no. 1 (2013): 79–89.
88. Kido Koichi, diary entry, April 21, 1941, in Kido Kōichi, *Nikki* [Diary], ed. Kido Nikki Kenkyukai, vol. 2 (Tokyo: Tokyo Daigaku Shuppankai, 1966), 870.
89. Konoe Fumimaro, "Dai-2-ji oyobi dai-3-ji Konoe naikaku ni okeru Nichi-Bei kōshō no keika (sōkō)" [Progress of the Japanese-US negotiations during the second and third Konoe cabinets (draft)], in Konoe Fumimaro, *Nikki* [Diary], Kyōdō Tsūshinsha Konoe Nikki Henshū Iinkai, ed., (Tokyo: Kyōdō Tsūshinsha, 1968), 197.
90. Konoe, "Dai-2-ji oyobi dai-3-ji Konoe naikaku ni okeru Nichi-Bei kōshō no keika (sōkō)," 197.
91. See "Matsuoka Gaimudaijin to-Ō fukumei naisō" [Foreign Minister Matsuoka's report to the emperor about his European trip], April 22, 1941, in *Nihon gaikō bunsho: Dainiji Ōshū taisen to Nihon,* 1:362–371.
92. BBKS, *Senshi sōsho (20),* 241–243.
93. BBKS, *Senshi sōsho (20),* 241–243.
94. BBKS, *Senshi sōsho (20),* 241–243.
95. "20th Liaison Conference, April 22, 1941," in Ike, *Japan's Decision for War,* 19–24, quotations on 20, 21.
96. Journal entry, April 25, 1941, in Gunjishi Gakkai, *Kimitsu sensō nisshi,* 1:97.
97. BBKS, *Senshi sōsho (20),* 264–265.

8 · REDRAWING THE BATTLE LINES

1. Konoe Fumimaro, *Konoe nikki* [Konoe diary] (Tokyo: Kyōdō Tsūshinsha, 1968), 199.
2. Peter Mauch, *Sailor Diplomat: Nomura Kichisaburō and the Japanese-American War* (Cambridge, MA: Harvard University Asia Center, 2011), 168.
3. Mauch, *Sailor Diplomat,* 168–169.
4. Bōeichō Bōei Kenshujo Senshishitsu (hereafter cited as BBKS), ed., *Senshi sōsho (69): Daihon'ei Rikugunbu Daitōa Sensō kaisen keii (3)* [War history series (69): Imperial Headquarters, Army, circumstances leading to the outbreak of the greater East Asian War (3)] (Tokyo: Asagumo Shuppansha, 1973), 564–565.
5. BBKS, *Senshi sōsho (69),* 565–567.
6. "21st Liaison Conference, May 3, 1941," in *Japan's Decision for War: Records of the 1941 Policy Conferences,* trans. and ed. Nobutaka Ike (Stanford, CA: Stanford University Press, 1967), 24–27.
7. "22nd Liaison Conference, May 8, 1941," in Ike, *Japan's Decision for War,* 27–31.
8. BBKS, ed., *Senshi sōsho (20) Daihon'ei Rikugunbu (2) Shōwa 16-nen 12-gatsu made* [War history series (20), Imperial Headquarters, Army (2), until December 1941] (Tokyo: Asagumo Shuppansha, 1968), 268.
9. Journal entries, July 29, August 1, August 8, and August 9, 1940, in *Daihon'ei rikugunbu sensō shidō han: Kimitsu sensō nisshi* [Imperial headquarters, army, war guidance section: Confidential war journal], vol. 1, ed. Gunjishi Gakkai (Tokyo: Ginseisha, 2008), 101.

10. Mauch, *Sailor Diplomat,* 175–176.
11. Ishii Akiho, "Nichi-Bei kōshō no shinsō" [The truth of the Japanese-US negotiations], in *Gunmukyokuchō Mutō Akira kaisōroku* [Military Affairs Bureau director Mutō Akira's memoirs], Jōhō Yoshio (Tokyo: Fūyō Shobō, 1981), 238. See also journal entries, May 10 and 13, 1941, in Gunjishi Gakkai, *Kimitsu sensō nisshi,* 1:102, 103. For these early arguments regarding ABCD encirclement, see "Dai-4-setsu Doku-So kaisen ni tomonau kokusaku no kakuritsu" [Section 4 establishment of national policy associated with the outbreak of the German-Soviet war], Jūyō kokusaku kettei no keii gaisetsu (dai-2-ji Konoe naikaku yori kaisen made), Chūō: sensō shidō jūyō kokusaku monjo, Rikugun ippan shiryō, Japanese Defense Ministry Archives (hereafter cited as JDMA), Japan Center for Asian Historical Records reference code C12120363600. With specific regard to the navy, see Sadao Asada, *From Mahan to Pearl Harbor: The Imperial Japanese Navy and the United States* (Annapolis, MD: Naval Institute Press, 2006), 248.
12. Journal entry, May 14, 1941, in Gunjishi Gakkai, *Kimitsu sensō nisshi,* 1:104. See also BBKS, ed., *Senshi sōsho (70) Daihon'ei Rikugunbu Daitōa Sensō kaisen keii (4)* [War history series (70), Imperial Headquarters, Army, the circumstances leading to the opening of the greater East Asian War (4)] (Tokyo: Asagumo Shuppan, 1974), 111–112.
13. "25th Liaison Conference, May 22, 1941," in Ike, *Japan's Decision for War,* 36–43, quotation on 39.
14. Banzai Ichiro, quoted in BBKS, ed., *Senshi sōsho (73) Kantōgun (2) Kantokuen/shūsenji no tai-Sosen* [War history series (73), Kwantung Army (2), Kwantung Army special maneuvers/war against the Soviet Union at the end of the war] (Tokyo: Asagumo Shuppansha, 1974), 5.
15. Banzai Ichiro, quoted in BBKS, *Senshi sōsho (70),* 142.
16. Oshima's cables, the more important of which were addressed not only to Matsuoka but also to Tojo and Sugiyama, are reproduced in *Nihon gaikō bunsho: Dainiji Ōshū taisen to Nihon* [Documents on Japanese foreign policy: The second great European war and Japan], vol. 1, ed. Gaimushō (Tokyo: Roku-ichi Shobō, 2012), 401–408.
17. Journal entry, June 5, 1941, in Gunjishi Gakkai, *Kimitsu sensō nisshi,* 1:110.
18. Journal entries, June 9, 10 and 11, 1941, in Gunjishi Gakkai, *Kimitsu sensō nisshi,* 1:113–116.
19. "29th and 30th Liaison Conferences, June 11 and 12, 1941," in Ike, *Japan's Decision for War,* 47–53, quotations on 50–51.
20. Journal entry, June 6, 1941, in Gunjishi Gakkai, *Kimitsu sensō nisshi,* 1:111–112. See also BBKS, *Senshi sōsho (20),* 300.
21. Journal entry, June 7, 1941, in Gunjishi Gakkai, *Kimitsu sensō nisshi,* 1:112–113. See also BBKS, *Senshi sōsho (20),* 301; and BBKS, *Senshi sōsho (70),* 147–148.
22. BBKS, *Senshi sōsho (20),* 302, emphasis added. See also BBKS, *Senshi sōsho (70),* 153–154.
23. Journal entry, June 9, 1941, in Gunjishi Gakkai, *Kimitsu sensō nisshi,* 1:113–114. See also BBKS, *Senshi sōsho (20),* 301.
24. "29th and 30th Liaison Conferences," 47–53, quotations on 50–51.
25. Journal entry, June 16, 1941, in Gunjishi Gakkai, *Kimitsu sensō nisshi,* 1:118–119, quotation on 119.
26. "31st Liaison Conference, June 16, 1941," in Ike, *Japan's Decision for War,* 53–56, quotations on 56, emphasis added.
27. BBKS, *Senshi sōsho (20),* 291.
28. For a useful summary, see BBKS, *Senshi sōsho (73),* 8. The final draft, dated June 14, 1941, has been lost to history. For a complete transcription of an earlier draft, dated June 13, 1941, see BBKS, *Senshi sōsho (20),* 303–304. See also BBKS, *Senshi sōsho (70),* 155–156.
29. BBKS, *Senshi sōsho (73),* 8.
30. Journal entry, June 21, 1941, in Gunjishi Gakkai, *Kimitsu sensō nisshi,* 1:120. See also BBKS, *Senshi sōsho (73),* 8.

31. BBKS, *Senshi sōsho (20),* 304.
32. BBKS, *Senshi sōsho (70),* 164.
33. Regarding the US counterproposal, see Mauch, *Sailor Diplomat,* 176, 181–182.
34. "32nd Liaison Conference, June 25, 1941," in Ike, *Japan's Decision for War,* 56–60.
35. "32nd Liaison Conference," 59.
36. "33rd Liaison Conference, June 26, 1941," in Ike, *Japan's Decision for War,* 60–64, quotation on 62.
37. "34th Liaison Conference, June 27, 1941," in Ike, *Japan's Decision for War,* 64–67, quotations on 65, 66.
38. "Kachō kaigi" [Section chief conference], June 27, 1941, in Kinbara Setuzō, *Rikugunshō gyōmu nisshi tekiroku zenhen* [Army Ministry logbook summary part one], ed. Hatano Sumio and Chadani Seiichi (Tokyo: Gendaishiryō Shuppan, 2016), 329–333.
39. "Kachō kaigi," June 27, 1941, 329–333.
40. Suyama Yukio, *Sakusen no oni Obata Toshirō* [Strategy demon Obata Toshiro] (Tokyo: Fuyō Shobō, 1983), 342.
41. "Kyokuchō kaihō" [Bureau directors' meeting transactions], June 28, 1941, in Kinbara, *Rikugunshō gyōmu nisshi tekiroku zenhen,* 333–335.
42. This reading of Tojo permeates the official military histories and has seeped into English-language scholarship. See BBKS, *Senshi sōsho (20),* 323–324; BBKS, *Senshi sōsho (70),* 278; and Alvin D. Coox, *Nomonhan: Japan Against Russia, 1939* (Stanford, CA: Stanford University Press, 1985), 1039.
43. Hirobumi Ito, *Commentaries on the Constitution of the Empire of Japan,* trans. Miyoji Ito (Kanda, Japan: Chū-ō Daigaku, 1906), 31.
44. For a translation of the "gist" of this Supreme War Council meeting, see Ike, *Japan's Decision for War,* 73–75.
45. Regarding Tanaka's enthusiasm for preparations for war, and for Hattori's wording, see BBKS, *Senshi sōsho (20),* 326, 328. For the July 1 start date of the Kwantung Army special maneuvers, see BBKS, *Senshi sōsho (70),* 276. For another instance in which Tojo spoke of making war preparations, see "37th Liaison Conference, July 1, 1941," in Ike, *Japan's Decision for War,* 75–77.
46. "Imperial Conference, July 2, 1941," in Ike, *Japan's Decision for War,* 77–90, quotations on 87, 89.
47. BBKS, *Senshi sōsho (70),* 279.
48. "Kyokuchō kaihō" [Bureau directors' meeting transactions], July 5, 1941, in Kinbara, *Rikugunshō gyōmu nisshi tekiroku zenhen,* 344–346.
49. Daily entry, July 7, 1941, in Ku'naichō, ed., *Shōwa Tennō jitsuroku* [True documents of the Shōwa Emperor], vol. 29, Imperial Household Agency, Archives and Mausolea Department, 6–7.
50. Daily entry, July 7, 1941, in Ku'naichō, ed., *Shōwa Tennō jitsuroku,* 29:6–7. For an account by the Japanese military officer at the heart of the maneuver, see Tanaka Ryūkichi, *Taiheiyō Sensō no haiin o tsuku: Gunbatsu sen'ō no jissō* [Pinpointing the cause of defeat in the Pacific War: The reality of the military clique's arbitrariness] (Tokyo: Nagasaki Shuppan, 1984), 14–17.
51. "Kyokuchō kaihō" [Bureau directors' meeting transactions], July 9, 1941, in Kinbara, *Rikugunshō gyōmu nisshi tekiroku zenhen,* 350–356, quotations on 350–353.
52. See, for example, Yoshitake Oka, *Konoe Fumimaro: A Political Biography* (Tokyo: University of Tokyo Press, 1983), 135–136.
53. "Kachō kaigi," June 27, 1941, 329–333, quotation on 330.
54. The Roosevelt administration delivered this "oral statement" to Ambassador Nomura at the same time as it delivered the US revisions to the Draft Understanding. See Mauch, *Sailor Diplomat,* 181–182.

55. See Peter Mauch, "Dissembling Diplomatist: Admiral Toyoda Teijirō and the Politics of National Security," in *Tumultuous Decade: Japan's Challenge to the International System, 1931–1941,* ed. Masato Kimura and Tosh Minohara (Toronto: Toronto University Press, 2013), 234–239.
56. The "Army and Navy Ministers' Joint Request" that Tojo delivered to the new cabinet is quoted in its entirety in BBKS, ed., *Senshi sōsho (101) Daihon'ei Kaigunbu, Daitōa Sensō kaisen keii (2)* [War history series (101), Imperial Headquarters, Navy, circumstances opening of the Greater East Asia War (2)] (Tokyo: Asagumo Shuppansha, 1979), 381.
57. "Kachō kaigi" [Section chief conference], July 17, 1941, in Kinbara, *Rikugunshō gyōmu nisshi tekiroku zenhen,* 375.
58. The diplomatic traffic is contained in *Nihon gaikō bunsho: Dainiji Ōshū taisen to Nihon* [Documents on Japanese foreign policy: The second great Europe war and Japan], vol. 2, no. 2, ed. Gaimushō (Tokyo: Gaimushō, 2013), 1024–1064.
59. "Kyokuchō kaihō" [Bureau directors' meeting transactions], July 23, 1941, in Kinbara, *Rikugunshō gyōmu nisshi tekiroku zenhen,* 382–385, quotation on 383.
60. "Kyokuchō kaihō" [Bureau directors' meeting transactions], July 30, 1941, in Kinbara, *Rikugunshō gyōmu nisshi tekiroku zenhen,* 408–412, quotations on 410.
61. "Kyokuchō kaihō" [Bureau directors' meeting transactions], July 30, 1941, in Kinbara, *Rikugunshō gyōmu nisshi tekiroku zenhen,* 408–412, quotations on 410.
62. Journal entry, July 29, 1941, in Gunjishi Gakkai, *Kimitsu sensō nisshi,* 1:139.
63. "Gokamon hōtō" [Answers to the emperor's questions], July 30, 1941, in Sugiyama Hajime, *Sugiyama memo* [Sugiyama's memorandums], vol. 1, ed. Sanbō Honbu (Tokyo: Hara Shobō, 2005), 284.
64. "Kyokuchō kaihō" [Bureau directors' meeting transactions], July 30, 1941, in Kinbara, *Rikugunshō gyōmu nisshi tekiroku zenhen,* 408–412, quotations on 412.
65. BBKS, *Senshi sōsho (70),* 304–306.
66. The best account of Nagano's July 30 audience with the emperor is contained in BBKS, *Senshi sōsho (101),* 404. Regarding the emperor's complete disenchantment with Nagano following the July 30 audience, see Asada, *From Mahan to Pearl Harbor,* 262.
67. "45th Liaison Conference, August 14, 1941," in Ike, *Japan's Decision for War,* 115–118. Regarding Tanaka's ongoing arguments for a northward advance, see BBKS, *Senshi sōsho (70),* 305–311. Regarding the need felt by the navy to suppress the Army General Staff's arguments for a northward advance, see BBKS, *Senshi sōsho (101),* 406.

9 · THE DEADLINE FOR WAR AND THE SUMMIT PROPOSAL

1. "Appendix 3: Outline of Policy Toward the South," in "Army-Navy Draft Policy of April 17, 1941," in *The Fateful Choice: Japan's Advance into Southeast Asia, Selected Translations from "Taiheiyō sensō e no michi: Kaisen gaikō shi,"* ed. James William Morley (New York: Columbia University Press, 1980), 303.
2. "Outline of National Policies in View of the Changing Situation," in "Imperial Conference, July 2, 1941," in *Japan's Decision for War: Records of the 1941 Policy Conferences,* trans. and ed. Nobutaka Ike (Stanford, CA: Stanford University Press, 1967), 78–79.
3. "40th Liaison Conference, July 21, 1941," in Ike, *Japan's Decision for War,* 103–107, quotation on 106.
4. Ikeda Kiyoshi, *Kaigun to Nihon* [The Navy and Japan] (Tokyo: Chūō Kōron, 1981), 121.
5. Bōeichō Bōei Kenshujo Senshishitsu (hereafter cited as BBKS), ed., *Senshi sōsho (101) Daihon'ei Kaigunbu, Daitōa Sensō kaisen keii (2)* [War history series (101), Imperial Headquarters, Navy, circumstances opening of the Greater East Asia War (2)] (Tokyo: Asagumo Shuppansha, 1979), 454–455. See also BBKS, ed., *Senshi sōsho (70) Daihon'ei Rikugunbu Daitōa Sensō kaisen keii (4)* [War history series (70), Imperial Headquarters,

Army, the circumstances leading to the opening of the greater East Asian War (4)] (Tokyo: Asagumo Shuppan, 1974), 491–495, 499–508. For the quotation concerning army staff officers' "extreme dissatisfaction" with the navy's wording, see BBKS, ed., *Senshi sōsho (90) Shina Jihen rikugun sakusen (3) Shōwa 16-nen 12-gatsu made* [War history series (90), army strategy in the China Incident (3), until December 1941] (Tokyo: Asagumo Shuppansha, 1975)434.

6. Konoe Fumimaro, *Nikki,* [Diary], ed. Kyōdō Tsūshinsha Konoe Nikki Henshū Iinkai (Tokyo: Kyōdō Tsūshinsha, 1968), 226–227.
7. BBKS, *Senshi sōsho (70),* 415.
8. BBKS, *Senshi sōsho (70),* 412–413.
9. BBKS, *Senshi sōsho (70),* 413.
10. Tojo's written response is reproduced in both BBKS, *Senshi sōsho (101),* 417, and BBKS, *Senshi sōsho (70),* 412.
11. Peter Mauch, *Sailor Diplomat: Nomura Kichisaburō and the Japanese-American War* (Cambridge, MA: Harvard University Asia Center, 2011), 196–197.
12. BBKS, *Senshi sōsho (70),* 495–499.
13. "46th Liaison Conference, August 14, 1941," in Ike, *Japan's Decision for War,* 118–120, quotation on 120.
14. Present at the meeting at Tojo's official ministerial residence were the army vice minister, Lieutenant General Kimura Heitaro; the Military Affairs Bureau director, Major General Muto Akira; and the Army Affairs Section director, Colonel Sato Kenryo. Representing the General Staff were the chief of staff, General Sugiyama Hajime; the vice chief of staff, Lieutenant General Tsukada; the Operations Bureau chief, Major General Tanaka Shin'ichi; and the Intelligence Bureau chief, Major General Okamoto Kiyotomi. See BBKS, *Senshi sōsho (70),* 446.
15. See Mauch, *Sailor Diplomat,* 199.
16. BBKS, *Senshi sōsho (70),* 455.
17. Journal entry, September 2, 1941, in *Daihon'ei rikugunbu sensō shidō han: Kimitsu sensō nisshi,* vol. 1, ed. Gunjishi Gakkai (Tokyo: Ginseisha, 2008) 152.
18. BBKS, *Senshi sōsho (70),* 511.
19. "'Nichi-Bei kōshō hōshin-an' (renraku kaigi kettei)" ["Japanese-US negotiations: Draft policy" (liaison conference decision)], September 3, 1941, in *Nihon gaikō bunsho: Nichi-Bei kōshō, 1941-nen* [Documents on Japanese foreign policy: The Japanese-US negotiations, 1941], vol. 1, Gaimushō (Tokyo: Gaimushō, 1991), 293.
20. "50th Liaison Conference, September 3, 1941," in Ike, *Japan's Decision for War,* 129–133.
21. For an English-language translation of the final draft of this document, see "The Minimum Demands of Our Empire to Be Attained Through Diplomatic Negotiations with the United States (and Great Britain), and the Maximum Concessions to Be Made by Our Empire," in Ike, *Japan's Decision for War,* 135–136.
22. BBKS, *Senshi sōsho (70),* 518–519, 527.
23. Mauch, *Sailor Diplomat,* 199.
24. The emperor engaged in a particularly feisty exchange with General Sugiyama in the lead-up to the September 6 Imperial conference. See, for example, the headnote to Imperial conference, September 6, 1941, in Ike, *Japan's Decision for War,* 133–134.
25. "Imperial Conference, September 6, 1941," in Ike, *Japan's Decision for War,* 133–163.
26. Higashikuni Naruhiko, diary entry, September 7, 1941, in *Kōzoku gunjin denki shūsei 11: Higashikuninomiya Naruhiko ō* [Collection of biographies of Imperial family soldiers and sailors 11: Prince Higashikuni Naruhiko], ed. Satō Motoei (Tokyo: Yumani Shobō, 2012), 82–84.
27. Higashikuni, diary entry, September 7, 1941.
28. Higashikuni, diary entry, September 7, 1941.
29. Higashikuni, diary entry, September 7, 1941.

30. Higashikuni, diary entry, September 7, 1941.
31. Higashikuni, diary entry, September 7, 1941.
32. "Statement Handed by the American Ambassador in Japan (Grew) to the Japanese Minister for Foreign Affairs (Toyoda) on September 10, 1941," in US Department of State, *Foreign Relations of the United States: Japan, 1931–1941,* vol. 2 (Washington DC: Government Printing Office, 1943), 610–613.
33. "52nd Liaison Conference, September 13, 1941," in Ike, *Japan's Decision for War,* 169–172. This meeting record includes the "Basic Terms of Peace between Japan and China."
34. For the text of Toyoda's revisions to the Draft Understanding, see Toyoda to Nomura, September 25, 1941, in *Nihon gaikō bunsho: Nichi-Bei kōshō, 1941-nen* [Documents on Japanese foreign policy: The Japanese-US negotiations, 1941] vol. 2 (Tokyo: Gaimushō, 1991), 367–377. See also "53rd Liaison Conference, September 18, 1941," in Ike, *Japan's Decision for War,* 172–173, headnotes.
35. BBKS, ed., *Senshi sōsho (76) Daihon'ei Rikugunbu, Daitōa Sensō kaisen keii (5)* [War history series (76), Imperial Headquarters, Army, the circumstances leading to the opening of the greater East Asian War (5)] (Tokyo: Asagumo Shuppan, 1974), 20–21.
36. BBKS, *Senshi sōsho (76),* 20–21.
37. "54th Liaison Conference, September 20, 1941," in Ike, *Japan's Decision for War,* 173–176.
38. Mauch, *Sailor Diplomat,* 201–202.
39. "Seisen no tenki ni kanren shi gaikō kōshō seihi no mitōshi kettei no jiki ni kansuru yōbō" [Demand concerning the timing of a decision concerning the forecast of success or failure in diplomatic negotiations and the related issue of the turning point between politics and war], September 25, 1941, in Sugiyama Hajime, *Sugiyama memo* [Sugiyama's memorandums], vol. 1, ed. Sanbō Honbu (Tokyo: Hara Shobō, 2005), 340.
40. Journal entry, September 27, 1941, in Gunjishi Gakkai, *Kimitsu sensō nisshi,* 1:159.
41. "55th Liaison Conference September 25, 1941," in Ike, *Japan's Decision for War,* 176–178.
42. Journal entry, September 27, 1941, in Gunjishi Gakkai, *Kimitsu sensō nisshi,* 1:159. See also Sawamoto Yorio, diary entry, September 26, 1941, in Sawamoto Yorio, "Sawamoto Yorio Kaigun Jikan nikki: Nichi-Bei kaisen zen'ya" [The diary of Vice Navy Minister Sawamoto Yorio: On the eve of the Japanese-US War], ed. Itō Takashi, Sawamoto Norio, and Nomura Minoru, *Chūō kōron* [Central review], January 1988, 454.
43. Journal entries, September 27 and 29, 1941, in Gunjishi Gakkai, *Kimitsu sensō nisshi,* 1:158–160.
44. BBKS, *Senshi sōsho (101),* 484.
45. Sawamoto Yorio, diary entry, September 30, 1941, in Sawamoto Yorio, "Sawamoto Yorio Kaigun Jikan nikki," 457.
46. Journal entry, September 27, 1941, in Gunjishi Gakkai, *Kimitsu sensō nisshi,* 1:158.
47. Nomura Kichisaburo to Toyoda Teijiro, October 2, 1941, in Gaimushō, *Nihon gaikō bunsho: Nichi-Bei kōshō,* 2:1–8.
48. "57th Liaison Conference, October 4, 1941," in Ike, *Japan's Decision for War,* 180.
49. BBKS, *Senshi sōsho (76),* 91.
50. BBKS, *Senshi sōsho (76),* 91.
51. Journal entry, October 6, 1941, in Gunjishi Gakkai, *Kimitsu sensō nisshi,* 1:163.
52. Sawamoto Yorio, diary entry, October 6, 1941, in Sawamoto Yorio, "Sawamoto Yorio Kaigun Jikan nikki," 460.
53. Journal entry, October 6, 1941, in Gunjishi Gakkai, *Kimitsu sensō nisshi,* 1:163–164.
54. Sawamoto Yorio, diary entry, October 7, 1941, in Sawamoto Yorio, "Sawamoto Yorio Kaigun Jikan nikki," 461. For a more complete version of the talking points that Nagano's subordinates had prepared in advance, see Shiryōchōsakai, ed., *Taiheiyō Sensō to Tomioka Sadatoshi* [The Pacific War and Tomioka Sadatoshi] (Tokyo: Gunji Kenkyūsha, 1971), 184–186.
55. BBKS, *Senshi sōsho (76),* 101–104.

56. BBKS, *Senshi sōsho (76),* 101–104
57. BBKS, *Senshi sōsho (76),* 104.
58. BBKS, *Senshi sōsho (76),* 105.
59. BBKS, *Senshi sōsho (101),* 493.
60. Sawamoto Yorio, diary entry, October 8, 1941, in Sawamoto Yorio, "Sawamoto Yorio Kaigun Jikan nikki," 462–463.
61. BBKS, *Senshi sōsho (76),* 105–107.
62. BBKS, *Senshi sōsho (76),* 105–107.
63. Kido Koichi, diary entry, October 9, 1941, in Kido Kōichi, *Nikki* [Diary], ed. Kido Nikki Kenkyukai, vol. 2 (Tokyo: Tokyo Daigaku Shuppankai, 1966), 912.
64. Fukudome Shigeru, *Kaigun no hansei* [The navy's reflections] (Tokyo: Nihon Shuppan Kyōdō, 1951), 75.
65. Fukudome, *Kaigun no hansei,* 75.
66. Satō Kenryō, *Satō Kenryō no shōgen* [Satō Kenryō's testimony] (Tokyo: Fuyō Shobō, 1976), 232.
67. "Jūgatsu jūninichi goshō kaigi" [October 12 five ministers' conference], in Sugiyama, *Sugiyama memo,* 1:345–347.
68. "Jūgatsu jūninichi goshō kaigi," 345–347.
69. Journal entry, October 13, 1941, in Gunjishi Gakkai, *Kimitsu sensō nisshi,* 1:168.
70. "Jūgatsu jūninichi goshō kaigi," 346–347.
71. Tōkyō Saiban Kenkyūkai, ed., *Tōjō Hideki sensei kyōjutsusho* [Tojo Hideki's affidavit] (Tokyo: Yōyōsha, 1948), 74.
72. Satō, *Satō Kenryō no shōgen,* 236–237.
73. "Jūgatsu jūyokka gozen jūichiji gojuppun yori yaku nijuppunkan kakugi ni okeru rikugundaijin setusmei no yōshi" [Outline of the Army Minister's explanation before the twenty-minute cabinet meeting at 11:00 a.m. on October 14], in Sugiyama, *Sugiyama memo,* 1:347–348.
74. "Rikugundaijin setusmei no yōshi," 347–348.
75. "rikugundaijin setusmei no yōshi," 347–348.
76. "Jūgatsu jūyokka kakugi ni oite rikugun daijin setsumeigo kyūchū ni okeru kido, tōjō kaidan yōshi" [Outline of conversation between Kido and Tojo following the war minister's explanation at the October 14 cabinet meeting], in Sugiyama, *Sugiyama memo,* 1:350–351. See Kido Koichi, diary entry, October 14, 1941, in Kido, *Nikki,* 2:915.
77. Takagi Sōkichi, diary entry, October 13, 1941, in Takagi Sōkichi, *Nikki to jōhō* [Diary and reports], vol. 2 (Tokyo: Misuzu Shobō, 2000), 569.
78. Sawamoto Yorio, diary entry, October 13, 1941, in Sawamoto Yorio, "Sawamoto Yorio Kaigun Jikan nikki," 465.
79. Tojo Hideki, quoted in Tsunoda Jun, "The Decision for War," in *The Final Confrontation: Japan's Negotiations with the United States, 1941; Selected Translations from "Taiheiyō sensō e no michi: Kaisen gaikō shi,"* ed. James William Morley (New York: Columbia University Press, 1994), 230.

10 · LEADING THE NATION TO WAR

1. Tsunoda Jun, "The Decision for War," in *The Final Confrontation: Japan's Negotiations with the United States; Selected Translations from "Taiheiyō sensō e no michi: Kaisen gaikō shi,"* ed. James William Morley (New York: Columbia University Press, 1994), 240.
2. Tsunoda, "The Decision for War," 232.
3. Daily entry, October 15, 1941, in Ku'naichō, ed., *Shōwa Tennō jitsuroku* [True documents of the Shōwa Emperor], vol. 29, Imperial Household Agency, Archives and Mausolea Department, 78. See also Kido Kōichi, diary entries, October 15 and 16, 1941, in Kido

Kōichi, *Nikki* [Diary], ed. Kido Nikki Kenkyukai, vol. 2 (Tokyo: Tokyo Daigaku Shuppankai, 1966), 915–916; and Satō Kenryō, *Satō Kenryō no shōgen* [Satō Kenryō's testimony] (Tokyo: Fuyō Shobō, 1976), 239.

4. Kido Kōichi, diary entry, October 17, 1941, in Kido, *Nikki,* 2:917.
5. Hyakutake Saburō, diary entry, October 18, 1941, *Hyakutake Saburō nikki: jijūchō ga mita Shōwa Tennō to sensō* [Hyakutake Saburō diary: The Shōwa Emperor and war as seen by the grand chamberlain], ed. Furukawa Takahisa and Chadani Seiichi (Tokyo: Iwanami Shoten, forthcoming).
6. Hyakutake Saburō, diary entry, October 18, 1941.
7. Daily entry, October 24, 1941, in Ku'naichō, *Shōwa Tennō jitsuroku,* 29:86.
8. Daily entry, October 16, 1941, in Ku'naichō, *Shōwa Tennō jitsuroku,* 29:80.
9. Daily entry, October 17, 1941, in Ku'naichō, *Shōwa Tennō jitsuroku,* 29:82; Akamatsu Sadao, "Hishokan memo," *Tōjō Hideki,* ed. Jōhō Yoshio (Tokyo: Fūyō Shobō, 1974), 81.
10. Daily entry, October 17, 1941, in Ku'naichō, *Shōwa Tennō jitsuroku,* 29:82–83. See also Kido Kōichi, diary entry, October 17, 1941, in Kido, *Nikki,* 2:917.
11. Akamatsu, "Hishokan memo," 81.
12. Hoshino Naoki, "Hoshino Naoki no kiroku" [Hoshino Naoki's record], in *Tōjō Hideki,* ed. Jōhō Yoshio (Tokyo: Fūyō Shobō, 1974), 83.
13. Hoshino, "Hoshino Naoki no kiroku," 83–84. See also Kishi Nobusuke, Yatsugi Kazuo, and Itō Takashi, *Kishi Nobusuke no kaiso* [Kishi Nobusuke's memoirs] (Tokyo: Bungei Shunjū, 1981), 49–50; and Tōgō Shigenori, *The Cause of Japan,* trans. and ed. Tōgō Fumihiko and Ben Bruce Blakeney (New York: Simon and Schuster, 1956), 54–55.
14. Akamatsu, "Hishokan memo," 81–82.
15. Diary entry, October 17, 1941, in Sawamoto Yorio, "Sawamoto Yorio Kaigun Jikan nikki: Nichi-Bei kaisen zen'ya" [The diary of Vice Navy Minister Sawamoto Yorio: On the eve of the Japanese-US War], ed. Itō Takashi, Sawamoto Norio, and Nomura Minoru, *Chūō kōron* [Central review], January 1988, 466–467. See also "Sanchōkan kaigi oyobi jūshin kaigi no moyō" [The meetings of the big three and the senior statesmen], in Sugiyama Hajime, *Sugiyama memo* [Sugiyama's memorandums], vol. 1, ed. Sanbō Honbu (Tokyo: Hara Shobō, 2005), 352.
16. Diary entries, October 17 and 18, 1941, in Sawamoto, "Sawamoto Yorio Kaigun Jikan nikki," 466–467. For Oikawa's conversation with Toyoda, see Toyoda Soemu, *Saigo no Teikoku Kaigun* [The last of the Imperial Navy] (Tokyo: Sekai no Nihonsha, 1950), 66.
17. Daily entry, October 18, 1941, in Ku'naichō, *Shōwa Tennō jitsuroku,* 29:83–85.
18. Nukata Hiroshi, "Shōgen" ["Testimony"], in Jōhō, *Tōjō Hideki,* 91.
19. Journal entries, October 17, 18, and 20, 1941, in *Daihon'ei rikugunbu sensō shidō han: Kimitsu sensō nisshi* [Imperial headquarters, army, war guidance section: Confidential war journal], vol. 1, Gunjishi Gakkai (Tokyo: Ginseisha, 2008), 171–173. For the Army Ministry's communication to the Army General Staff about the clean-slate message, see Bōeichō Bōei Kenshujo Senshishitsu (hereafter cited as BBKS), ed., *Senshi sōsho (20) Daihon'ei Rikugunbu (2) Shōwa 16-nen 12-gatsu made* [War history series (20), Imperial Headquarters, Army (2), until December 1941] (Tokyo: Asagumo Shuppansha, 1968), 524.
20. "59th Liaison Conference, October 23, 1941," in *Japan's Decision for War: Records of the 1941 Policy Conferences,* trans. and ed. Nobutaka Ike (Stanford, CA: Stanford University Press, 1967), 184–187, quotation on 186.
21. For Tojo's questions, see "Kugatsu Muika gozen kaigi kettei 'Teikoku kokusaku suikō yōrei' no gutaiteki kenkyū" [Concrete study of the "guidelines for the implementation of Imperial national policy" which was decided at the September 6 Imperial conference], October 23–October 30, in Sugiyama, *Sugiyama memo,* 1:363–370. For an English-language translation of Tojo's questions, see Tsunoda, "The Decision for War," 248–249.
22. Journal entry, October 25, 1941, in Gunjishi Gakkai, *Kimitsu sensō nisshi,* 1:175.

23. Satō, *Satō Kenryō no shōgen,* 117. See also Ishii Akiho, "Shuki: Nichibei kōshō no shinsō" [Memorandum: The reality of the Japanese-US negotiations], in *Gunmukyokuchō Mutō Akira kaisōroku,* ed. Jōhō Yoshio [Military Affairs Bureau director Mutō Akira's memoirs] (Tokyo: Fūyō Shobō, 1981), 271–272.
24. BBKS, ed., *Senshi sōsho (76) Daihon'ei Rikugunbu, Daitōa Sensō kaisen keii (5)* [War history series (76), Imperial Headquarters, Army, the circumstances leading to the opening of the greater East Asian War (5)] (Tokyo: Asagumo Shuppan, 1974), 209.
25. "65th Liaison Conference, October 30, 1941," in Ike, *Japan's Decision for War,* 196–199.
26. Ishii, "Shuki," 272.
27. See BBKS, ed., *Senshi sōsho (101) Daihon'ei Kaigunbu, Daitōa Sensō kaisen keii (2)* [War history series (101), Imperial Headquarters, Navy, circumstances opening of the Greater East Asia War (2)] (Tokyo: Asagumo Shuppansha, 1979),531–532. Shimada repeated his demand for 1.1 million tons of steel in 1942 at the November 1 liaison conference. See "66th Liaison Conference, November 1, 1941," in Ike, *Japan's Decision for War,* 199–207; the navy's demand is on 200–201.
28. Journal entry, October 31, 1941, in Gunjishi Gakkai, *Kimitsu sensō nisshi,* 1:177.
29. "Tōjō Rikushō to Sugiyama Sōchō to no kaidan yōshi" [Outline of discussion between Army Minister Tojo and Chief of Staff Sugiyama], November 1, 1941, in Sugiyama, *Sugiyama memo,* 1:370–372.
30. "66th Liaison Conference," 199–207. Proposals A and B are reproduced in the record of the November 5 Imperial conference. See "Proposal A" and "Proposal B" in Ike, *Japan's Decision for War,* 209–211.
31. Tsunoda, "The Decision for War," 261.
32. Daily entry, 2 November 1942, in Ku'naichō, *Shōwa Tennō jitsuroku,* 29:98. See also "11-gatsu futuska saikentō shūryogo Tōjō Sōri rikukai ryōsōchō retsuritsu jōsō no sai no gokamon hōtō" [The emperor's questions at the time of Prime Minister Tojo's and the army and navy chiefs of staffs' reports following the November 2 reexamination], in Sugiyama, *Sugiyama memo,* 1:386–388. Regarding Tojo's tears, see journal entry, November 2, 1941, in Gunjishi Gakkai, *Kimitsu sensō nisshi,* 1:181. See also Hosaka Masayasu, *Tōjō Hideki to tennō no jidai: Gunnai kōsō kara kaisen zen'ya made* [Tojo Hideki and the era of the emperor: From intraservice conflict to the eve of the opening of the war], vol. 1 (Tokyo: Bungei Shunjū, 1988), 299. The emperor's withholding of an automatic decision for war in the event the deadline passed without diplomatic success has been the subject of scholarly misunderstanding. Pulitzer Prize–winning historian Herbert Bix, for one, argues that the emperor made a decision for war at the November 5 Imperial conference; see Herbert P. Bix, *Hirohito and the Making of Modern Japan* (New York: HarperCollins, 2000), 424.
33. Journal entry, November 2, 1941, in Gunjishi Gakkai, *Kimitsu sensō nisshi,* 1:179–181, quotations on 180.
34. "Kyokuchō kaigi" [Bureau chief conference], November 5, 1941, in Kinbara Setuzō, *Rikugunshō gyōmu nisshi tekiroku zenhen* [Army Ministry logbook summary part one], ed. Hatano Sumio and Chadani Seiichi (Tokyo: Gendaishiryō Shuppan, 2016), 575–583, quotation on 575.
35. "Kachō kaigi" [Section chief conference], November 6, 1941, in Kinbara, *Rikugunshō gyōmu nisshi tekiroku zenhen,* 583–587, quotations on 585.
36. "Imperial Conference, November 5, 1941," in Ike, *Japan's Decision for War,* 208–239 (see especially "Essentials for Carrying out the Empire's Policies," 209; Tojo's remarks are quoted on 229).
37. "Kyokuchō kaigi," November 5, 1941, 575–583, quotation on 575.
38. "67th Liaison Conference, November 12, 1941," in Ike, *Japan's Decision for War,* 239–243, quotation on 240.

39. Tobe, "Tojo Hideki as War Leader," 30.
40. BBKS, *Senshi sōsho (76)*, 342.
41. "Kachō kaigi," November 6, 1941, 583–587, quotation on 585.
42. Regarding the debate about Japan's war aims, see BBKS, *Senshi sōsho (76)*, 341.
43. "Draft Proposal for Hastening the End of the War against the United States, Great Britain, the Netherlands, and Chiang, approved at the 69th Liaison Conference, November 15, 1941," in Ike, *Japan's Decision for War*, 247–249.
44. BBKS, *Senshi sōsho (76)*, 416–417.
45. Journal entry, November 13, 1941, in Gunjishi Gakkai, *Kimitsu nisshi*, 1:186.
46. Journal entry, November 18, 1941, in Gunjishi Gakkai, *Kimitsu nisshi*, 1:187.
47. Akamatsu, "Hishokan nisshi," 44.
48. "Kyokuchō kaigi" [Bureau chief conference], November 8, 1941, in Kinbara, *Rikugunshō gyōmu nisshi tekiroku zenhen*, 587–589, quotation on 587.
49. "Kyokuchō kaigi" [Bureau chief conference], November 15, 1941, in Kinbara, *Rikugunshō gyōmu nisshi tekiroku zenhen*, 596–599.
50. Journal entry, November 26, 1941, in Gunjishi Gakkai, *Kimitsu sensō nisshi*, 1:191.
51. Journal entry, November 27, 1941, in Gunjishi Gakkai, *Kimitsu sensō nisshi*, 1:191–192.
52. Historian Tosh Minohara argues that Togo's about-face owed to the shock and dismay he felt on receipt of the Hull note. That shock was, in Minohara's analysis, all the more palpable because Togo had sighted decrypted and decoded Chinese diplomatic traffic that indicated US preparedness to negotiate the terms of a modus vivendi. See Tosh Minohara, "'No Choice But to Rise': Tōgō Shigenori and Japan's Decision for War," in *Tumultuous Decade: Japan's Challenge to the International System, 1931–1941*, ed. Masato Kimura and Tosh Minohara (Toronto: Toronto University Press, 2013), 268–270.
53. Tojo Hideki, quoted in Hirohashi Tadamitsu, journal entry, December 1, 1941, in in "Tōjō Hideki Taishō genkōroku (Hirohashi memo)" [General Tōjō Hideki's words and deeds (Hirohashi memorandums)], in *Tōjō naikaku sōri daijin kimitsu kiroku: Tōjō Hideki Taishō genkōroku* [Prime Minister Tojo confidential record: Record of General Tojo Hideki's words and deeds], ed. Itō Takashi, Hirohashi Tadamitsu, and Katashima Norio (Tokyo: Tokyo Daigaku Shuppankai, 1990), 479.
54. Daily entry, November 30, 1941, in Ku'naichō, *Shōwa Tennō jitsuroku*, 29:124.
55. Daily entry, November 30, 1941, in Ku'naichō, *Shōwa Tennō jitsuroku*, 29:125.
56. "Imperial Conference, December 1, 1941," in Ike, *Japan's Decision for War*, 262–283, quotation on 263.
57. See Ryoichi Tobe, "Tojo Hideki as a War Leader," in *British and Japanese Military Leadership in the Far Eastern War, 1941–1945*, ed. Brian Bond and Kyoichi Ichikawa (London: Frank Cass, 2004), 26.
58. See, for example, "Kōshō shiryō dai36gō: Kaisen shōsho ni kansuru Tōjō no shōgen (yōshi)" [Document number 36: Tojo's testimony concerning the Imperial rescript declaring war (summary)], Daitōa Sensō zenpan 10, Japanese Defense Ministry Archives, Japan Center for Asian Historical Records (hereafter cited as JACAR) reference code C16120630000.
59. "71st Liaison Conference, November 22, 1941," in Ike, *Japan's Decision for War*, 253–254.
60. "Kaisen ni kansuru jōyaku ohijun no ken" [Ratification of treaty on opening hostility], Sūmitsu'in kankei monjo, goanka'an, Meiji 44nen, National Archives of Japan, JACAR reference code A03033082700, emphasis added.
61. "74th Liaison Conference, November 29, 1941," in Ike, *Japan's Decision for War*, 260–262.
62. Takeo Iguchi, *Demystifying Pearl Harbor: A New Perspective from Japan* (Tokyo: International House of Japan, 2010), 156.
63. "75th Liaison Conference, November 29, 1941," in Ike, *Japan's Decision for War*, 283–285.
64. See Satō Motoei, "Taibei sensen fukoku to Nittai gunji kyōtei mondai" [The military convention between Japan and Thailand just before the pacific war], *Chūō Daigaku*

Seisaku Bunka Sōgō Kenkyūjo nenpō [Chūō University Institute of Policy and Cultural Studies annual review] 17 (2013): 88.

65. "75th Liaison Conference," 283–285. The meeting record does not directly attribute these statements to Tojo; it merely notes that the comments were made. It nonetheless seems entirely within reason to surmise that Tojo made these comments.
66. Terasaki Hidenari, *Shōwa Tennō dokuhakuroku: Terasaki Hidenari Goyōgakari nikki* [The Showa Emperor's monologue: Imperial aide Terasaki Hidenari's diary], ed. Mariko Terasaki Miller (Tokyo: Bungei Shunjū, 1991), 81–82. Tojo included the italicized phrase at the emperor's request. For an English-language translation, see Gordon M. Berger, Roger M. Brown, and Peter Mauch, eds., *The Emperor's Testimony: Hirohito's Monologue on Japan's War in Asia and the Pacific* (Cambridge: Cambridge University Press, forthcoming).
67. Tokugawa Yoshihiro, *Jijūchō no igon: Shōwa tennō to no 50nen* [Grand Chamberlain's testament: 50 years with the Shōwa Emperor] (Tokyo: Asahi Shimbunsha, 1997), 47. See also daily entry, December 8, 1941, in Ku'naichō, eds., *Shōwa tennō jitsuroku,* 29:140.
68. Todaka Kazushige, "Shinjuwan wa sōteigai! Kaisen o tomerarenakatta 'sekinin' to 'gosan'" [Pearl Harbor was unexpected! "Responsibility" and "miscalculations" that were unable to prevent the opening of war], in Rekishi Kaidō Henshūbu, ed., *Nichi-Bei kaisen no shin'in to gossan* [The opening of the Japanese-US war: Real causes and misunderstandings] (Tokyo: PHP Shinsho, 2021), chapter 5.
69. Hosaka, *Tōjō to tennō no jidai,* 1:322.
70. Hirohashi Tadamitsu, journal entry, December 7–8, 1941, in "Hirohashi memo," 480.
71. See Peter Mauch, "Prime Minister Tōjō Hideki on the Eve of Pearl Harbor: New Evidence from Japan," *Global War Studies* 15, no. 1 (2018): 37.
72. Tojo Hideki, quoted in Hirohashi Tadamitsu, journal entry, December 1, 1941, in "Hirohashi memo," 479.
73. Terasaki, *Shōwa Tennō dokuhakuroku,* 81–82. See also Berger, et. al., eds., *The Emperor's Testimony.*
74. See Matsuo Takayoshi, "Shōwa Tennō wa Shinjūwan kōgeki no sekinin o Tōjō moto shushō ni tenka shita" [The Shōwa Emperor shifted responsibility for the Pearl Harbor attack onto former prime minister Tojo], *Ronza* [Forum], February 2007, 136.
75. Reporting on the emperor's first postsurrender meeting with MacArthur, political adviser George Atcheson reported the emperor as having said "he had been tricked by Tojo." See Peter Mauch, "Hirohito and General Douglas MacArthur: The First Meeting as Documented by *Shōwa tennō jitsuroku,*" *Diplomacy and Statecraft* 28, no. 4 (2017): 589–590.
76. Tojo Hideki, quoted in Hirohashi Tadamitsu, journal entry, December 7–8, 1941, in "Hirohashi memo," 480.
77. Emily S. Rosenberg, *A Date Which Will Live: Pearl Harbor in American Memory* (Durham, NC: Duke University Press, 2003), 12, 16.
78. Winston S. Churchill, *The Second World War,* vol. 3, *The Grand Alliance* (London: Cassell, 1950), 539.

11 · THE TRIUMPHANT TOTAL WARRIOR

1. Hirohashi Tadamitsu, journal entry, December 7–8, 1941, in "Tōjō Hideki Taishō genkōroku (Hirohashi memo)" [General Tōjō Hideki's words and deeds (Hirohashi memorandums)], in "Tōjō Naikaku Sōri Daijin kimitsu kiroku," [Prime Minister Tōjō confidential record], *Tōjō naikaku sōri daijin kimitsu kiroku: Tōjō Hideki Taishō genk Tōjō roku* [Prime Minister Tojo confidential record: Record of General Tojo Hideki's words and deeds], ed. Itō Takashi, Hirohashi Tadamitsu, and Katashima Norio (Tokyo: Tokyo Daigaku Shuppankai, 1990), 481.

2. "Taishō o haishimatsurite" ["On receipt of the Imperial rescript"], December 8, 1941, in Tōjō Hideki, *Daitōa Sensō ni chokumen shite: Tōjō Hideki enzetsushū* [Facing the Greater East Asia War: Tōjō Hideki's collected speeches] (Tokyo: Kaizōsha, 1942), 1–3.
3. Tōkyō Saiban Kenkyūkai, ed., *Tōjō Hideki sensei kyōjutsusho* [Tojo Hideki's affidavit] (Tokyo: Yōyōsha, 1948), 141.
4. On this point, see Hatano Sumio, *Taiheiyō Sensō to Ajia gaikō* [Japan's Asia policy during the Pacific War: Political struggles over Asian liberation] (Tokyo: Tokyo Daigaku Shuppankai, 1996), 8–10.
5. "12gatsu 10ka renraku kaigi kiroku ketsu" [December 10 liaison conference: Record lacking], in Sugiyama Hajime, *Sugiyama memo* [Sugiyama's memorandums], vol. 1, ed. Sanbō Honbu (Tokyo: Hara Shobō, 2005), 568. See also Bōeichō Bōei Kenshujo Senshishitsu (hereafter cited as BBKS), ed., *Senshi sōsho (35) Daihon'ei Rikugunbu (3) Shōwa 17nen 4gatsu made* [War history series (35), Imperial Headquarters, Army (3), until April 1942] (Tokyo: Asagumo Shuppansha, 1970), 192–194.
6. Daily entry, December 12, 1941, in Ku'naichō, ed., *Shōwa Tennō jitsuroku* [True documents of the Shōwa Emperor], vol. 29, Imperial Household Agency, Archives and Mausolea Department, 148.
7. Higashikuni Naruhiko, diary entry, December 11, 1941, in *Kōzoku gunjin denki shūsei 11: Higashikuninomiya Naruhiko ō* [Collection of biographies of Imperial family soldiers and sailors 11: Prince Higashikuni Naruhiko], ed. Satō Motoei (Tokyo: Yumani Shobō, 2012), 104–105.
8. See Donald Keene, *So Lovely a Country Will Never Perish: Wartime Diaries of Japanese Writers* (New York: Columbia University Press, 2010), 13, 15. Regarding US wartime propaganda, see Emily S. Rosenberg, *A Date Which Will Live: Pearl Harbor in American Memory* (Durham, NC: Duke University Press, 2003), 11–33.
9. Higashikuni, diary entry, December 11, 1941, 104–105.
10. See Edward J. Drea, *The 1942 Japanese General Election: Political Mobilization in Wartime Japan* (New York: Paragon Book Gallery, 1979), 20.
11. Daily entry, January 9, 1942, in Ku'naichō, ed., *Shōwa Tennō jitsuroku* [True documents of the Shōwa Emperor], vol. 30, Imperial Household Agency, Archives and Mausolea Department, 7.
12. Hirohashi Tadamitsu, journal entry, January 21, 1942, in "Hirohashi memo," 11.
13. "Daitōa kensetsu no kōsō" [The idea of Greater East Asia's construction], in Tōjō, *Daitōa Sensō ni chokumen shite,* 3–11, quotations on 3–6. For an analysis of the early drafts of this speech, which included a promise of independence for the Dutch East Indies, see Hatano, *Taiheiyō sensō to Ajia gaikō,* 23. See also daily entry, January 17, 1942, in Ku'naichō, *Shōwa Tennō jitsuroku,* 30:12.
14. Taisei Yokusankai Sendenbu, *Daitōa Sensō to sono zento* [The Greater East Asia War and the journey ahead] (Tokyo: Taisei yokusankai sendenbu, 1941), 1–2.
15. Yamamoto Noboru, *Shokumin seisaku* [Colonial policies] (Tokyo: Keiō Shuppansha, 1942), 144–145.
16. Kawada Jun, "Daitōa Sensō no igi" [The meaning of the Greater East Asia War], in *Shika taiheiyōsen* [Historical epic poems: War in the Pacific] (Tokyo: Yakumo Shorin, 1942), 17–20.
17. Ishiwara Kanji, *Kokubō seijiron* [Theories of national defense and politics] (Tokyo: Seiki Shobō, 1942), 34.
18. For Churchill's assessment of the "fall" of Singapore, see Winston S. Churchill, *The Second World War,* vol. 4, *The Hinge of Fate* (Boston: Houghton Mifflin, 1950), 81. For Japanese Army officers' reaction, see Masanobu Tsuji, *Singapore, 1941–1942: The Japanese Version of the Malayan Campaign of World War II* (Oxford: Oxford University Press, 1988), 280.

19. "Matsudaira Yasumasa Naifu Hishokanchō kōkyōshochū yori nukigaki" [Chief Secretary Matsudaira Yasumasa affidavit: Excerpt] in Gaimushō, ed., *Nihon no sentaku: dainiji sekai taisen shūsen shiroku* [Japan's choices: Historical records of the end of World War II], vol. 1 (Tokyo: Yamata Shobō, 1990), 59. See also "Yonai Mitsumasa kōkyōsho yori bassui" [Yonai Mitsumasa affidavit: extract], in Gaimushō, ed., *Shūsen shiroku,* vol. 1, 60.
20. Journal entry, April 6, 1942, in Gunjishi Gakkai, ed., *Daihon'ei rikugunbu sensō shidō han: kimitsu sensō nisshi* [Imperial headquarters, army, war guidance section: Confidential war journal], vol. 2 (Tokyo: Ginseisha, 2008).
21. Higashikuni Naruhiko, diary entry, December 29, 1941, in *Kōzoku gunjin denki shūsei 11,* 105–106.
22. "Tōgō Shigenori kyōjutsusho" [Togo Shigenori affidavit], in Gaimushō, ed., *Shūsen shiroku,* vol. 1, 32.
23. "Seiji jōhō" [Political information], February 24, 1942, in Takagi Sōkichi, *Nikki to jōhō* [Diary and reports], vol. 2 (Tokyo: Misuzu Shobō, 2000), 601–602. See also Tōgō Shigenori, *The Cause of Japan,* trans. and ed. Tōgō Fumihiko and Ben Bruce Blakeney (New York: Simon and Schuster, 1956), 228–229.
24. Journal entry, February 4, 1942, in "Tōjō Naikaku Sōri Daijin kimitsu kiroku," [Prime Minister Tōjō confidential record], *Tōjō naikaku sōri daijin kimitsu kiroku: Tōjō Hideki taishō genkōroku* [Prime Minister Tōjō confidential record: Record of Gen. Tōjō Hideki's words and deeds], ed. Itō Takashi, Hirohashi Tadamitsu, and Katashima Norio (Tokyo: Tokyo daigaku shuppankai, 1990), 13.
25. "Nigatsu futsuka dai-81-kai Renraku Kaigi" [81st Liaison Conference, February 2, 1942], in Sanbō Honbu, ed., *Sugiyama memo* [Sugiyama's memoranda], vol. 2 (Tokyo: Hara Shobō, 2005), 14–18, Tōjō's statement on 16.
26. Daily entry, February 14, 1942, in Ku'naichō, *Shōwa Tennō jitsuroku,* 30:30.
27. Hirohashi Tadamitsu, journal entry, February 18, 1942, in "Hirohashi memo," 486. See also Akamatsu Sadao, *Tōjō hishokan kimitsu nisshi* [Secret diary of Tojo's secretary] (Tokyo: Bungei Shunju, 1985), 66.
28. "Seiji jōhō," 601–602, quotation on 601.
29. Journal entry, February 23, 1942, in "Tōjō kimitsu kiroku," 18. See also Drea, *The 1942 Japanese General Election,* 22–27; and Ben-Ami Shillony, *Politics and Culture in Wartime Japan* (Oxford: Clarendon Press, 1981), 22.
30. "Seiji jōhō," 601–602.
31. "Sumiyaka ni Ei o kuppuku seshime Bei no sen'i o hōki seshimuru tame kitei keikaku no suikō nomi o motte jūbun to subeki ya" [Is enactment of existing plans sufficient to compel prompt British surrender and abandonment of the US will to fight?], February 25, 1942, in Gaimushō, *Shūsen shiroku,* 1:8–9.
32. "Sekai jōsei handan" [Assessment of the world situation], March 7, 1942, in Gaimushō, *Shūsen shiroku,* 1:11–18, quotations on 15. The record of the February 26 liaison conference makes apparent that an earlier draft of this document was under discussion then. See "Nigatsu nijūrokunichi dai-89-kai Renraku Kaigi" [89th Liaison Conference, February 26, 1942], in Sanbō Honbu, ed., *Sugiyama memo,* 2:38–41.
33. "Nigatsu nijūrokunichi dai-89-kai Renraku Kaigi" [89th Liaison Conference, February 28, 1942], in Sanbō Honbu, ed., *Sugiyama memo,* 2: 38–41.
34. "Nigatsu nijūhachinichi dai-90-kai Renraku Kaigi" [90th Liaison Conference, February 28, 1942], in Sanbō Honbu, ed., *Sugiyama memo,* 2:41–45, quotation on 42. For a brief illuminative account of the army's envisioned strategy, see BBKS, eds., *Senshi sōsho, (80) daihon'ei kaigunbu/rengō kantai (2) Shōwa 17nen 6gatsu made* [War history series, vol 80, Imperial headquarters, navy/combined fleet (vol. 2): until June 1942] (Tokyo: Asagumo Shuppansha, 1975), 116.
35. BBKS, *Senshi sōsho (80),* 116.

36. "Nigatsu nijūhachinichi dai-90-kai Renraku Kaigi," 2:41–45, quotation on 43.
37. "Kongo toru beki sensō shidō no taikō" [Outline of war leadership to be adopted], in Gaimushō, *Shūsen shiroku.* See also daily entry, March 11, 1942, in Ku'naichō, *Shōwa Tennō jitsuroku,* 30:49–50.
38. "Indo ni okeru wagagunji kōdō ni kansuru Tōjō Naikaku Sōri Daijin danwa" [Prime Minister Tōjō's talk about our military action in India], April 4, 1942, in Sanbō Honbu, ed., *Sugiyama memo,* 2:108–109.
39. "Shigatsu nijūshichinichi dai-100-kai Renraku Kaigi" [100th Liaison Conference, April 27, 1942], in, Sanbō Honbu, ed., *Sugiyama memo,* 2:116–117.
40. Satō Kenryō, *Satō Kenryō no shōgen* [Sato Kenryo's testimony] (Tokyo: Fuyō Shobō, 1976), 304.
41. Journal entry, April 18, 1942, in Gunjishi Gakkai, *Kimitsu sensō nisshi,* 2:239. See also journal entry, April 19, 1942, in "Tōjō kimitsu kiroku," 37–38.
42. Quoted in Drea, *1942 Election,* vii.
43. Tōjō Hideki, "Sōsenkyo ni nozomu seifu no taido" ["The government's attitude toward the general election"], *Shūhō* [Weekly bulletin], dai-282-gō, March 4, 1942, Naikaku jōhōkyoku kankei shuppanbutsu, Naikaku bunko, NAJ. Jacar reference code: A06031044400.
44. Shillony, *Politics and Culture,* 23.
45. Drea, *1942 Election,* 23, 26, 35.
46. Journal entry, April 29, 1942, in "Tōjō kimitsu kiroku," 42.
47. Journal entry, April 24, 1942, in Gunjishi Gakkai, *Kimitsu sensō nisshi,* 2:241.
48. Akamatsu, *Tōjō hishokan kimitsu nisshi,* 69.
49. Satō, *Satō Kenryō no shōgen,* 307.
50. "Rokugatsu tōka Renraku Kondankai" [Liaison conference, June 10, 1942], in Sanbō Honbu, ed., *Sugiyama memo,* 2:130–131.
51. Akamatsu, *Tōjō hishokan kimitsu nisshi,* 71.
52. Hirohashi Tadamitsu journal entry, August 22, 1942, in "Hirohashi memo," 490.
53. Tojo Hideki, quoted in Peter Wetzler, *Hirohito and War: Imperial Tradition and Military Decision-Making in Prewar Japan* (Honolulu: University of Hawai'i Press, 1998), 75.
54. Hirohashi Tadamitsu, journal entry, August 22, 1942, in "Hirohashi memo," 491.
55. Hirohashi Tadamitsu, journal entry, June 11, 1942, in "Hirohashi memo," 489.
56. Journal entry, July 13, 1942, in "Tōjō kimitsu kiroku," 63.
57. "Daitōashō secchi mondai ni kansuru Tōgō Gaishō to Tōjō Shushō to no kaidan" [Conversation between Foreign Minister Togo and Prime Minister Tojo concerning the issue of establishment of the Greater East Asia Ministry], July 12, 1942, in *Nihon gaikō bunsho: Taiheiyō Sensō* [Documents on Japanese foreign policy: Pacific War], vol. 2, ed. Gaimushō (Tokyo: Shiraminesha, 2010), 1437–1439.
58. For the Army General Staff's reaction to the Greater East Asia Ministry, see BBKS, eds., *Senshi sōsho (63) Daihon'ei Rikugunbu (5) Shōwa 17-nen 12-gatsu made* [War history series (63), Imperial General Headquarters, Army (5), until December 1942] (Tokyo: Asagumo Shuppansha, 1973), 115.
59. See "Tōgō Shigenori kōkyōsho" [Togo Shigenori affidavit], in Gaimushō, *Shūsen shiroku,* 1:33–34. See also Tōgō, *Cause of Japan,* 247–255.
60. "Kido Kōichi kōkyōsho" [Kido Kōichi affidavit], in Gaimushō, *Shūsen shiroku,* 1:56.
61. Hirohashi Tadamitsu, journal entry, September 2, 1942, "Hirohashi memo," 491–492.
62. "Kakugi kettei" [Cabinet decision], September 1, 1942, in *Nihon gaikō bunsho: Taiheiyō sensō,* 2:1439–1451, quotation on 1440. The Greater East Asia Ministry came into being in November 1942.
63. BBKS, *Senshi sōsho (63),* 92–101.
64. BBKS, *Senshi sōsho (63),* 101.

65. BBKS, *Senshi sōsho (63)*, 307.
66. Nishiura Susumu, *Shōwa sensōshi no shōgen: Nihon Rikugun shūen no shinjitsu* [Testimony concerning Showa-era war history: The truth of the end of the Japanese Army] (Tokyo: Nikkei Bijinesujin Bunko, 2013), 237–239.
67. Satō, *Satō Kenryō no shōgen*, 312.
68. BBKS, *Senshi sōsho (63)*, 304.
69. Hosaka Masayasu, *Tōjō Hideki to tennō no jidai(2) Nichi-Bei kaisen kara Tōkyō saiban made* [Tōjō Hideki and the era of the emperor (2) from the opening of the Japanese-U.S. war to the Tokyo trial] (Tokyo: Bungei Shunjū, 1988),68.
70. The record of this conversation is reproduced in BBKS, *Senshi sōsho (63)*, 306–308.
71. BBKS, *Senshi sōsho (63)*, 375.
72. BBKS, *Senshi sōsho (63)*, 452–453.
73. Journal entry, November 16, 1942, in Gunjishi Gakkai, *Kimitsu sensō nisshi*, 1:303. See also Nishiura, *Shōwa sensōshi no shōgen*, 237–239.
74. Journal entry, December 7, 1942, in Gunjishi Gakkai, *Kimitsu sensō nisshi*, 1:1, 310.
75. "Shōwa jūnananen jūnigatsu tōka dai-ikkai 'Gozen ni okeru Daihon'ei Seifu Renraku Kaigi' giji" [Agenda of first 'Imperial General Headquarters-Government Liaison Conference' before the Emperor, December 10, 1942], in Sanbō Honbu, ed., *Sugiyama memo*, 2:187–208, quotation on 187.
76. "Daihon'ei seifu renraku kaigi kettei" [Imperial General Headquarters—government liaison conference decision], October 29, 1942, in *Nihon gaikō bunsho: Taiheiyō Sensō* [Documents on Japanese foreign policy: Pacific War], vol. 1, ed. Gaimushō (Tokyo: Shiraminesha, 2010), 176–181. See also John Hunter Boyle, *China and Japan at War, 1937–1945: The Politics of Collaboration* (Stanford, CA: Stanford University Press, 1972), 308.
77. Journal entry, October 30, 1942, in "Tōjō kimitsu kiroku," 110.
78. Hirohashi Tadamitsu, journal entry, December 11, 1942, in "Hirohashi memo," 493.
79. "Dai-9-kai Gozen Kaigi" [9th Imperial Conference], December 21, 1943, in Sanbō Honbu, ed., *Sugiyama memo*, 2:310–342, quotations on 313. See also "Gozen Kaigi kettei" [Imperial conference decision], in Gaimushō, *Nihon gaikō bunsho: Taiheiyō sensō*, 1:182–192.
80. They met on December 21 and again on December 25. For records of these conversations, see Gaimushō, *Nihon gaikō bunsho: Taiheiyō sensō*, 1:192–206.
81. Hirohashi Tadamitsu, journal entry, December 26, 1942, in "Hirohashi memo," 494.

12 · TOJO CHALLENGED

1. For a record of the IGHQ meeting, see Bōeichō Bōei Kenshujo Senshishitsu (hereafter cited as BBKS), ed., *Senshi sōsho (28): Minami Taiheiyō rikugun sakusen (2) Gadarukanaru/Buna sakusen* [War history series (28), army operations in the South Pacific (2), the Guadalcanal and Buna operations] (Tokyo: Asagumo Shuppanhsa, 1969), 443. See also BBKS, ed., *Senshi sōsho (77) Daihon'ei Kaigunbu/rengō kantai (3) Shōwa 18nen 2gatsu made* [War history series (77), Imperial Headquarters, Navy / combined fleet (3): up to February 1943] (Tokyo: Asagumo Shuppansha, 1974), 498–500.
2. Journal entry, January 1, 1943, in "Tōjō Naikaku Sōri Daijin kimitsu kiroku" [Prime Minister Tōjō confidential record], *Tōjō naikaku sōri daijin kimitsu kiroku: Tōjō Hideki taishō genkōroku* [Prime Minister Tōjō confidential record: record of Gen. Tōjō Hideki's words and deeds], ed. Itō Takashi, Hirohashi Tadamitsu, and Katashima Norio (Tokyo: Tokyo daigaku shuppankai, 1990), 144.
3. Nakano Seigō, "Senji saishōron" [On wartime prime ministership], in *Tōjō Hideki*, ed. Jōhō Yoshio (Tokyo: Fūyō Shobō, 1974), 602–605.
4. Jōhō, *Tōjō Hideki*, 586. See also Ben-Ami Shillony, *Politics and Culture in Wartime Japan* (Oxford: Clarendon Press, 1981), 103.

5. Takamatsunomiya Nobuhito Shinnō, diary entries, December 30, 1942, and January 7, 1943, in Takamatsunomiya Nobuhito Shinnō, *Nikki* [Diary], vol. 5 (Tokyo: Chūō Kōronsha, 1996), 387, 421. See also journal entry, January 7, 1943, in "Tōjō kimitsu kiroku," 146–147.
6. Takamatsunomiya Nobuhito Shinnō, diary entry, January 7, 1943, in Takamatsunomiya, *Nikki,* 5, 426–428.
7. Takamatsunomiya Nobuhito Shinnō, diary entry, January 7, 1943, in Takamatsunomiya, *Nikki,* 5, 426–428.
8. Takamatsunomiya Nobuhito Shinnō, diary entry, January 7, 1943, in Takamatsunomiya, *Nikki,* 5, 426–428.
9. Takamatsunomiya Nobuhito Shinnō, diary entry, January 7, 1943, in Takamatsunomiya, *Nikki,* 5, 426–428.
10. Takamatsunomiya Nobuhito Shinnō, diary entry, January 7, 1943, in Takamatsunomiya, *Nikki,* 5, 426–428.
11. Takamatsunomiya Nobuhito Shinnō, diary entry, January 7, 1943, in Takamatsunomiya, *Nikki,* 5, 426–428.
12. Takamatsunomiya Nobuhito Shinnō, diary entry, January 7, 1943, in Takamatsunomiya, *Nikki,* 5, 426–428.
13. "Rikugun chūjō ga Taiheiyō Sensō o hihan: Hirabayashi Shidanchō, shōkō 40-nin no mae de enzetsu" [Lieutenant general criticizes Pacific War: Division Commander Hirabayashi's speech before 40 officers], *Chūnichi shimbun* [Central Japan news], December 7, 2009, http://www.chunichi.co.jp/article/national/news/CK2009120702000128.html.
14. Takamiya Taihei, *Shōwa no shōsui* [Shōwa-era commanders] (Tokyo: Tosho Shuppansha, 1973), 86. Takamiya's role as a wartime propagandist is attributable to his position with the Information Bureau; for a summary of the Intelligence Bureau's functions, see Janis Mimura, *Planning for Empire: Reform Bureaucrats and the Wartime Japanese State* (Ithaca, NY: Cornell University Press, 2011), 184–185.
15. Takamiya, *Shōwa no shōsui,* 86. Tojo's loss of confidence was shared by much of the army leadership, and many upper-echelon officers in January 1943 expressed their mortification at the loss of Guadalcanal. See BBKS, ed., *Senshi sōsho (66) Daihon'ei Rikugunbu (6) Shōwa 18nen 6gatsu made* [War history series (66), Imperial Headquarters, Army (6) until June 1943], (Tokyo: Asagumo Shuppansha, 1973), 66–68.
16. Daily entry, January 15, 1943, in Ku'naichō, ed., *Shōwa Tennō jitsuroku* [True documents of the Shōwa Emperor], vol. 31, Imperial Household Agency, Archives and Mausolea Department, 10–11. See also journal entries, January 15–January 27, 1943, in "Tōjō kimitsu kiroku," 149–152.
17. Takamatsunomiya Nobuhito Shinnō, diary entry, January 20, 1943, in Takamatsunomiya Nobuhito Shinnō, *Nikki* [Diary], vol. 6 (Tokyo: Chūō Kōronsha, 1997), 476.
18. Tōjō Hideki, *Hisshō no ōdōri: Tōjō Sōri Daijin gikai enzetsu tōbenshū* [The road to victory: Prime Minister Tōjō's Diet speech and collected answers] (Tokyo: Dōmei Tsūshinsha, 1943), 3–31. See also journal entry, January 28, 1943, in "Tōjō kimitsu kiroku," 152–153.
19. See journal entries, January 29–30, 1943, in "Tōjō kimitsu kiroku," 153; and BBKS, *Senshi sōsho (66),* 131. For the record of the December 10 liaison conference (including the various studies tabled at the conference) which decided materiel allocations for 1943, see "Shōwa jūnananen jūnigatsu tōka da-1-kai 'Gozen ni okeru Daihon'ei Seifu Renraku Kaigi' giji" [Minutes of the 'first IGHQ-Government Liaison Conference in the presence of the Emperor'] in Sanbō Honbu, ed., *Sugiyama memo* [Sugiyama's memorandums], vol. 2 (Tokyo: Hara Shobō, 2005), 187–302.
20. Hirohashi Tadamitsu, journal entry, February 9, 1943, in "Tōjō Hideki Taishō genkōroku (Hirohashi memo)" [General Tōjō Hideki's words and deeds (Hirohashi memorandums)] in *Tōjō naikaku sōri daijin kimitsu kiroku: Tōjō Hideki Taishō genkōroku* [Prime Minister Tojo confidential record: Record of General Tojo Hideki's words and deeds], ed. Itō Ta-

kashi, Hirohashi Tadamitsu, and Katashima Norio (Tokyo: Tokyo Daigaku Shuppankai, 1990), 499.

21. See, for example, Mark A. Stoler, *Allies in War: Britain and America Against the Axis Powers, 1940–1945* (London: Hodder Arnold, 2005), 89–91.
22. This is taken from a speech Tōjō delivered on December 8, 1943. It is reproduced in Gaimushō, ed., *Nihon no sentaku: dainiji sekai taisen shūsen shiroku* [Japan's choices: Historical records of the end of World War II], vol. 1 (Tokyo: Yamata Shobō, 1990), 106–109.
23. Kido Kōichi, diary entry, February 12, 1943, in Kido Kōichi, *Nikki* [Diary], ed. Kido Nikki Kenkyukai, vol. 2 (Tokyo: Tokyo Daigaku Shuppankai, 1966), 1011–1012.
24. See "Nigatsu nijūnananichi dai-137-kai Renraku Kaigi" [137th Liaison Conference, February 27, 1943], in Sanbō Honbu, ed., *Sugiyama memo,* 2:379–386. Direct quotations on pp. 379, 381. See also "Draft Proposal for Hastening the End of the War Against the United States, Great Britain, the Netherlands, and Chiang," November 15, 1941, in Nobutaka Ike, ed., *Japan's Decision for War: Records of the 1941 Policy Conferences* (Stanford, CA: Stanford University Press, 1967), 247–249, quotation on 247.
25. BBKS, ed., *Senshi sōsho (39): Daihon'ei Kaigunbu/Rengō Kantai (4) daisandan sakusen zenki* [War history series (39), Imperial Headquarters, Navy / Combined Fleet (4), stage three operations, early period] (Tokyo: Asagumo Shuppansha, 1970), 71, 90. See also BBKS, *Senshi sōsho (66),* 74.
26. BBKS, ed., *Senshi sōsho (40): Minami Taiheiyō rikugun sakusen (3) Munda/Saramoa* [War history series (40), army strategy in the South Pacific (3), Munda / Salamaua] (Tokyo: Asagumo Shuppansha, 1970), 55–62.
27. BBKS, *Senshi sōsho (39),* 113.
28. BBKS, *Senshi sōsho (66),* 494–495.
29. Oda Hisashi, *Kōkoku hyakunenshi: Taishō Shōwa* [A 100-year history of advertising: The Taishō and Shōwa periods] (Tokyo: Sekai Shisōsha, 1976), p. 250.
30. Journal entry, February 7, 1943, in "Tōjō kimitsu kiroku," 154.
31. Journal entry, February 13, 1943, in "Tōjō kimitsu kiroku," 157–158.
32. Takamatsunomiya Nobuhito Shinnō, diary entry, March 2, 1943, in Takamatsunomiya, *Nikki,* 6:72. See also Furukawa Takahisa, *Tōjō Hideki: Taiheiyō Sensō o hajimeta gunjin saishō* [Tojo Hideki: The soldier-prime minister who started the Pacific war] (Tokyo: Yamakawa Shuppansha, 2009), 63–68; and Shillony, *Politics and Culture,* 28.
33. Hirohashi Tadamitsu, journal entry, February 7, 1943, in "Hirohashi memo,"498–499.
34. Hirohashi Tadamitsu, journal entry, February 7, 1943, in "Hirohashi memo," 499.
35. Daily entry, March 26, 1943, in Ku'naichō, eds., *Shōwa Tennō jitsuroku,* 31:50.
36. "Daitōa Sensō kansui no tame Biruma no dokuritsu shisaku ni kansuru ken" [Measures for Burmese independence for the purpose of accomplishing the Greater East Asia War], January 14, 1943, in *Nihon gaikō bunsho: Taiheiyō Sensō* [Documents on Japanese foreign policy: Pacific War], vol. 2, ed. Gaimushō (Tokyo: Shiraminesha, 2010), 1344–1346.
37. "Biruma dokuritsu shidō yōkō" [Outline of guidance of Burmese leadership], March 10, 1943, in Gaimushō, *Nihon gaikō bunsho: Taiheiyō Sensō,* 2:1348–1355.
38. The record of Tojo's March 22 conversation with Ba Maw is reproduced in Gaimushō, *Nihon gaikō bunsho: Taiheiyō Sensō,* 2:1355–1361. The meeting record includes a document that Tojo handed Ba Maw and which formally records the Japanese decision to grant Burmese independence by August 1; brotherhood quotation on 1359. For Ba Maw's postwar recollection of this meeting, see Ba Maw, *Breakthrough in Burma: Memoirs of a Revolution* (New Haven, CT: Yale University Press, 1968), 310. For an interesting account of how Ba Maw accidentally left the aforementioned document in a hotel room in Manila en route to Burma, see Aung San, "Blueprint for Burma," in *The Political Legacy of Aung San,* ed. Josef Silverstein (Ithaca, NY: Cornell University Press, 1993), 87–88.

39. See the first attachment to "Tōjō sōri daijin Chin Kōhaku tokushi kaidan" [Record of meeting between Prime Minister Tojo and special emissary Chen Gongbo], April 9, 1943, in *Nihon gaikō bunsho: Taiheiyō Sensō* [Documents on Japanese foreign policy: Pacific War], vol. 1, ed. Gaimushō (Tokyo: Shiraminesha, 2010), 301–303.
40. "Oboe" [Memo], April 28, 1943, in Shigemitsu Mamoru, *Shuki* [Papers], ed. Itō Takashi and Watanabe Yukio (Tokyo: Chūō Kōronsha, 1986), 321–325, quotation on 322. See also "Shūsen ni kansuru hōshin taiyō" [Outline of policy concerning war's end], in Gaimushō, *Shūsen shiroku,* 1:65. Shigemitsu's ministerial appointment was but part of a wider cabinet reshuffle. Tojo brought into his cabinet several Diet members, including Oasa Tadao and Yamazaki Tatsunosuke; he also replaced Home Minister Yuzawa Michio with Andō Kisaburō, a retired general and the deputy director of the Imperial Rule Assistance Political Organization Council.
41. Jeremy A. Yellen, *The Greater East Asia Co-Prosperity Sphere: When Total Empire Met Total War* (Ithaca, NY: Cornell University Press, 2019), 147.
42. Hirohashi Tadamitsu, journal entries, May 12, 1943, in "Hirohashi memo," 502–503.
43. Hirohashi Tadamitsu, journal entry, May 19, 1943, in "Hirohashi memo," 504.
44. Hirohashi Tadamitsu, journal entry, May 28, 1943, in "Hirohashi memo," 506.
45. Hosaka Masayasu, *Tōjō Hideki to tennō no jidai: (2) Nichi-Bei kaisen kara Tōkyō saiban made* [Tōjō Hideki and the era of the emperor (2) from the opening of the Japanese-U.S. war to the Tokyo trial] (Tokyo: Bungei Shunjū, 1988), 92. For the emperor's reaction, see daily entry, August 2, 1943, in Ku'naichō, eds., *Shōwa Tennō jitsuroku,* 31:129. For an enlightening discussion of the army's reaction to this first instance of *gyokusai* in the Pacific, see Edward J. Drea, *Japan's Imperial Army: Its Rise and Fall, 1853–1945* (Lawrence: University Press of Kansas, 2009), 231.
46. "Daitōa seiryaku shidō taiyō" [Main points guiding political strategy toward Greater East Asia], May 31, 1943, in Sanbō Honbu, *Sugiyama memo,* 2:410–411.
47. "Gogatsu sanjūichinichi dai10kai gozen kaigi" [10th Imperial Conference May 31, 1943], in Sanbō Honbu, *Sugiyama memo,* 2:409–417, quotations on 412.
48. BBKS, *Senshi sōsho (39),* 338. See also BBKS, ed., *Senshi sōsho (67): daihon'ei rikugunbu (7) Shōwa 18nen 12gatsu made* [War history series (vol. 66): Imperial headquarters, army (vol. 7) until December 1943] (Tokyo: Asagumo Shuppansha, 1973), 139.
49. Kido Kōichi, diary entry, June 7, 1943, in Kido, *Nikki,* 2:1033.
50. Kiyosawa Kiyoshi, diary entries, May 20 and 27, 1943, in Kiyosawa Kiyoshi, *A Diary of Darkness: The Wartime Diary of Kiyosawa Kiyoshi,* ed. Eugene Soviak (Princeton, NJ: Princeton University Press, 1999), 28, 32.
51. Handō Kazutoshi, Yokoyama Yoshikazu, Hata Ikuhiko, and Hara Takeshi, *Rekidai rikugun taishō zenran: Shōwahen: Manshū jihen/Shina Jihenki* [Complete list of successive army generals: The Showa period; The Manchurian and China incidents] (Tokyo: Chūō Kōron Shinsha, 2013), chapter 4. See also Hirohashi Tadamitsu, journal entry, June 14, 1943, in "Hirohashi memo," 508.
52. Hirohashi Tadamitsu, journal entries, May 28, June 5 and 14, 1943, in "Hirohashi memo," 506–509.
53. "Rokugatsu nijūkunichi dai-149-kai Renraku Kaigi" [149th Liaison Conference, June 29, 1943], in Sanbō Honbu, *Sugiyama memo,* 2:437–440, quotation on 438. See also BBKS, *Senshi sōsho (66),* 499–503.
54. BBKS, *Senshi sōsho (67),* 139.
55. "Rokugatsu nijūrokunichi dai-148-kai Renraku Kaigi" [148th Liaison Conference, June 26, 1943], in Sanbō Honbu, *Sugiyama memo,* 2, 432–437.
56. Theodore Friend, *The Blue-Eyed Enemy: Japan Against the West in Java and Luzon, 1942–1945* (Princeton, NJ: Princeton University Press, 1988), 63.
57. See Joyce Chapman Lebra, *The Indian National Army and Japan* (Singapore: Institute of Southeast Asian Studies, 2008), 120.

58. "Okada Keisuke shōgen" [Okada Keisuke testimony], in Gaimushō, *Shūsen shiroku,* 1:115–116. See also Okada Keisuke, *Kaikoroku* [Reminiscences] (Tokyo: Mainichi Shinbunsha, 1950), 207–208. Tojo met with the *jushin* in late July but he was accompanied by various ministerial colleagues, including Shigemitsu and Shimada. See journal entry, July 23, 1943, in "Tōjō kimitsu kiroku," 206–208. The fact that he was not alone made it difficult for the *jushin* to grill him. See Wakatsuki Reijiro's reminiscence, quoted in Gaimushō, *Shūsen shiroku,*1:132–133.
59. Journal entry, July 23, 1943, in Shigemitsu, *Shuki,* 378–379. See also journal entry, July 23, 1941, in "Tōjō kimitsu kiroku," 206–208.
60. Hirohashi Tadamitsu, journal entry, September 9, 1943, in "Hirohashi memo," 515. See also "Daihon'ei Seifu Renraku Kaigi kettei: Ikoku ni taisuru shochi no ken" [IGHQ-Government Liaison Conference decision: Measures toward Italy], September 9, 1943, in Gaimushō, *Nihon gaikō bunsho: Taiheiyō Sensō,* 1:657–665.
61. Kido Kōichi, diary entry, July 26, 1943, in Kido, *Nikki,* 2:1043. See also Hirohashi Tadamitsu, journal entry, July 27, 1943, in "Hirohashi memo," 511.
62. Hirohashi Tadamitsu, journal entry, July 27, 1943, in "Hirohashi memo," 511.
63. Journal entry, July 29, 1943, in "Tōjō kimitsu kiroku," 210.
64. Hirohashi Tadamitsu, journal entry, July 29, 1943, in "Hirohashi memo," 511–513, quotation on 512.
65. Journal entry, July 23, 1943, in "Tōjō kimitsu kiroku," 206–208, quotation on 207.
66. "Shōwa 19nen kokka dōin keikaku sakutei ni kansuru ken" [Concerning formulation of a national mobilization plan for 1944], August 2, 1943, in Sugiyama, *Sugiyama memo,* 2:446–447.
67. For an army-centric view, see BBKS, *Senshi sōsho (67),* 27–78. For a navy-centric view, see BBKS, *Senshi sōsho (39),* 338–409.
68. Daily entry, August 7, 1943, in Ku'naichō, *Shōwa Tennō jitsuroku,* 31:148. See also Satō Kenryō, *Satō Kenryō no shōgen* [Satō Kenryō's testimony] (Tokyo: Fuyō Shobō, 1976), 324.
69. Satō, *Satō Kenryō no shōgen,* 323–325.
70. BBKS, ed., *Senshi sōsho (19) hondo bōkū sakusen* [War history series (19), aerial defense operations in the home islands] (Tokyo: Asagumo Shuppansha, 1968), 225–227. See also Hiroyuki Shindo, "The Japanese Army's Search for a New South Pacific Strategy, 1943," in *Australia 1943: The Liberation of New Guinea,* ed. Peter J. Dean (Cambridge: Cambridge University Press, 2013), 80–82. See also Hiroyuki Shindo, "From the Offensive to the Defensive: Japanese Strategy During the Pacific War, 1942–1944," in *Sharing Experiences in the 20th Century: Joint Research on Military History,* ed. Tomoyuki Ishizu and Frank Reichherzer (Tokyo: National Institute for Defense Studies Joint Research Series, 2022), 156.
71. Hirohashi Tadamitsu, journal entry, August 24, 1943, in "Hirohashi memo," 514.
72. "Naikaku sōri daijin kakugi setsumei yōshi" [Outline of the Prime Minister's explanation], September 21, 1943, in "Tōjō kimitsu kiroku," 232–235, quotation on 233.
73. "Genjōseika ni okeru kokusei un'ei yōkō-an" [Draft government operational outline in the current situation], September 21, 1943, in "Tōjō kimitsu kiroku," 230–232. See also "Sōri daijin no gunjushō (kashō) secchi ni kansuru hanketsu" [Decision concerning establishment of the prime minister's (tentatively named) munitions ministry], September 26, 1943, in journal entry, September 26, 1943, in "Tōjō kimitsu kiroku," 253.
74. "Dai-82-kai Teikoku Gikai Kizokuin honkaigi dai-1-gō" [82nd Imperial Diet House of Peers plenary session number one], June 16, 1943, in "Teikoku Gikai kaigiroku kensaku shisutemu" [Imperial Diet proceedings search system], https://teikokugikai-i.ndl.go.jp/#/detail?minId=008203242X00119430616¤t=1.
75. Hirohashi Tadamitsu, journal entry, June 18, 1943, in "Hirohashi memo," 509.

76. "Daitōa Kaigi ni kansuru ken" [Concerning the Greater East Asian Conference], October 2, 1943, in Gaimushō, *Nihon gaikō bunsho: Taiheiyō Sensō,* 2:1496–1498.
77. "Tōjō Naikaku Sōri daijin / Ō Shuseki Ken Gyōseiin Inchō kaidan yōshi" [Record of conversation between Prime Minister Tōjō and Executive Yuan President Wang], September 22, 1943, in "Tōjō kimitsu kiroku," 239–252, quotation on 251. For more detail on the new treaty, see "Daihon'ei seifu renraku kaigi kettei" [Imperial General Headquarters–government liaison conference decision], September 18, 1943, in Gaimushō, *Nihon gaikō bunsho: Taiheiyō Sensō,* 1:318–320. See also Hatano Sumio, *Taiheiyō Sensō to Ajia gaikō* [Japan's Asia policy during the Pacific War: Political struggles over Asian liberation] (Tokyo: Tokyo Daigaku Shuppankai, 1996), 141–154.
78. This is drawn from Tojo's address to a liaison conference on the eve of his meeting with Aquino, Laurel, and Vargas. See "Daihon'ei seifu renraku kaigi kettei" [Imperial General Headquarters–government liaison conference decision], September 29, 1943, in Gaimushō, *Nihon gaikō bunsho: Taiheiyō Sensō,* 2:1391–1393. For a record of the meeting, as well as the documents exchanged at the meeting, see journal entry, October 1, 1943, in "Tōjō kimitsu kiroku," 258–265.
79. See, for example, Friend, *The Blue-Eyed Enemy,* 123–127.
80. Hirohashi Tadamitsu, journal entry, October 20, 1943, in "Hirohashi memo," 523.
81. See Jōhō, *Tōjō Hideki,* 587–589.
82. "Nakano ippa ni taisuru shochi ni kansuru ken" [Concerning measures toward the Nakano clique], October 24, 1943, in "Tōjō kimitsu kiroku," 277–281.
83. Kiyosawa Kiyoshi, diary entry, November 1, 1943, in Kiyosawa, *Diary of Darkness,* 101.
84. Journal entry, October 26, 1943, in "Tōjō kimitsu kiroku," 282. See also Takamiya, *Shōwa no shōsui,* 93–94. For a recent account of Nakano's suicide, and Tojo's involvement therein, see Iwai Shūichirō, *1944-nen no Tōjō Hideki* [The Tojo Hideki of 1944] (Tokyo: Shōdensha Shinsho, 2020), 90–104.
85. Journal entry, October 31, 1943, in "Tōjō kimitsu kiroku," 284.
86. Ba, *Breakthrough in Burma,* 337.
87. "Address of Prime Minister General Hideki Tōjō Before the Assembly of Greater East Asiatic Nations," in *Japan's Greater East Asia Co-Prosperity Sphere in World War II: Selected Readings and Documents,* ed. Joyce C. Lebra (London: Oxford University Press, 1975), 88–93. Indonesia's independence leaders, including Mohammad Hatta and Sukarno, were not invited to participate; Tojo met with them a few days after the conference and tried to "assuage their disappointment." See Friend, *The Blue-Eyed Enemy,* 105–107. For the record of Tojo's conversation with Sukarno, see "Jawa Chūō Sangiinchō Sukaruno shi ikkō Tōjō Naikaku Sōri Daijin hōmon no sai ni okeru kondan yōshi" [Record of conversation when House of Councilors President Sukarno visited Prime Minister Tojo], November 15, 1943, in "Tōjō kimitsu kiroku," 366–367. Tojo met also with the North China Political Council chairman, Wang Kemin (who was at least nominally under the Wang regime's jurisdiction) and tried to reassure him that the Japanese government had not forsaken the council. See "Kahoku Seimu Iinkai Inchō Ō Kokubin shi no Tōjō sōri daijin raihō ni saishite no kaidan yōshi" [Record of conversation on North China Political Council Chairman Wang Kemin's visit with Prime Minister Tojo], November 15, 1943, in "Tōjō kimitsu kiroku," 361–365.
88. "Daihon'ei seifu renraku kaigi ryōkai: Daitōa kyōdō senden" [Imperial General Headquarters-government Liaison Conference understanding: Greater East Asia joint declaration], October 23, 1943, in Gaimushō, *Nihon gaikō bunsho: Taiheiyō Sensō,* 2:1504–1505. See also Yellen, *The Greater East Asia Co-Prosperity Sphere,* 157–158.
89. For details of Tojo's trip to Ise Grand Shrine, as well as a skeleton account of his prayers to the sun goddess Amaterasu, see journal entries, November 19 and 20, in "Tōjō kimitsu kiroku," 369–370.
90. BBKS, *Senshi sōsho (67),* 607.

13 · TOJO OVERWHELMED

1. Journal entries, January 1, 6, 8, and 21, 1944, in "Tōjō Naikaku Sōri Daijin kimitsu kiroku," [Prime Minister Tōjō confidential record], *Tōjō naikaku sōri daijin kimitsu kiroku: Tōjō Hideki taishō genkōroku* [Prime Minister Tōjō confidential record: Record of Gen. Tōjō Hideki's words and deeds], ed. Itō Takashi, Hirohashi Tadamitsu, and Katashima Norio (Tokyo: Tokyo daigaku shuppankai, 1990), 383, 384, 387, 389.
2. "Gyomei gyoji" [Imperial seal], *Kanpō* [Japanese government gazette], January 7, 1944, 75.
3. Kiyosawa Kiyoshi, diary entries, January 5, 6, 7, 8, 9, and 26, 1944, in Kiyosawa Kiyoshi, *A Diary of Darkness: The Wartime Diary of Kiyosawa Kiyoshi*, ed. Eugene Soviak (Princeton, NJ: Princeton University Press, 1999), 132–134, 140.
4. Okada Keisuke, *Kaikoroku* [Reminiscences] (Tokyo: Mainichi Shimbunsha, 1951), 213.
5. "Dai84kai Teikoku gikai ni okeru naikaku sōri daijin enzetsuan" [Draft of prime minister's address to the 84th Imperial Diet session], January 17, 1944, in Sanbō honbu, ed., *Sugiyama memo* [Sugiyama's memorandums], vol. 2 (Tokyo: Hara Shobō, 2005), 522–530.
6. See Bōeichō Bōei Kenshujo Senshishitsu (hereafter cited as BBKS), ed., *Senshi sōsho (71) Daihon'ei Kaigunbu/Rengō Kantai (5) daisandan sakusen chūki* [War history series (71), Imperial Headquarters, Navy/Combined Fleet (5) stage three operations, middle period] (Tokyo: Asagumo Shuppansha, 1974), 275; and BBKS, ed., *Senshi sōsho (75): Daihon'ei Rikugunbu (8) Shōwa 19nen 7gatsu made* [War history series (66), Imperial Headquarters, Army (8), until July 1944] (Tokyo: Asagumo Shuppansha, 1974), 4.
7. BBKS, *Senshi sōsho (75)*, 63.
8. Hirohashi Tadamitsu, journal entry, February 1, 1944, in "Tōjō Hideki Taishō genkōroku (Hirohashi memo)" [General Tōjō Hideki's words and deeds (Hirohashi memorandums)], in *Tōjō naikaku sōri daijin kimitsu kiroku: Tōjō Hideki Taishō genkōroku* [Prime Minister Tojo confidential record: Record of General Tojo Hideki's words and deeds], ed. Itō Takashi, Hirohashi Tadamitsu, and Katashima Norio (Tokyo: Tokyo Daigaku Shuppankai, 1990), 528.
9. BBKS, *Senshi sōsho (71)*, 214–215.
10. Journal entries, February 8 and 10, 1944, in "Tōjō kimitsu kiroku," 393, 394.
11. Hirohashi Tadamitsu, journal entry, February 10, 1944, in "Hirohashi memo," 528–529.
12. Hosokawa Morisada, diary entry, January 14, 1944, in Hosokawa Morisada, *Hosokawa nikki* [Hosokawa diary], vol. 1 (Tokyo: Chūō Kōronsha, 1979), 101.
13. Higashikuni Naruhiko, diary entry, February 19, 1944, in *Kōzoku gunjin denki shūsei 11: Higashikuninomiya Naruhiko ō* [Collection of biographies of Imperial family soldiers and sailors 11: Prince Higashikuni Naruhiko], ed. Satō Motoei (Tokyo: Yumani Shobō, 2012), 129–130.
14. Takagi Sōkichi, diary entries, February 18–19, 1944, in Takagi Sōkichi, *Nikki to jōhō* [Diary and reports], vol. 2 (Tokyo: Misuzu Shobō, 2000), 713–715.
15. BBKS, *Senshi sōsho (71)*, 246.
16. Hirohashi Tadamitsu, journal entry, February 18, 1944, in "Hirohashi memo," 531–532.
17. BBKS, *Senshi sōsho (75)*, 92–93.
18. Kido Koichi, diary entry, February 18, 1944, in Kido Kōichi, *Nikki* [Diary], ed. Kido Nikki Kenkyukai, vol. 2 (Tokyo: Tokyo Daigaku Shuppankai, 1966), 1089–1090.
19. Daily entry, February 19, 1944, in Ku'naichō, ed., *Shōwa Tennō jitsuroku* [True documents of the Shōwa Emperor], vol. 32, Imperial Household Agency, Archives and Mausolea Department, 26–27.
20. Kiyosawa Kiyoshi, diary entry, March 16, 1944, in Kiyosawa, *A Diary of Darkness*, 159.
21. BBKS, *Senshi sōsho (75)*, 97.
22. Okada, *Kaikoroku*, 214–215.

23. Daily entry, February 21, 1944, in Ku'naichō, *Shōwa Tennō jitsuroku,* 32:27–29.
24. Hirohashi Tadamitsu, journal entry, February 24, 1944, in "Hirohashi memo," 533.
25. BBKS, *Senshi sōsho (71),* 263–264.
26. BBKS, *Senshi sōsho (75),* 211.
27. Hosokawa Morisada, diary entry, February 26, 1944, in Hosokawa, *Hosokawa Nikki,* 1:138.
28. See Toshiya, *Tōjō Hideki: "Dokusaisha" o enjita otoko* [Tojo Hideki: The man who acted as "dictator"] (Tokyo: Bunshun Shinsho, 2019), 275–278. Conscription had become, for Tojo, a weapon of choice against domestic opponents. In 1943 Tojo raised the eligible conscription age from forty to forty-five, and the forty-two-year-old bureaucrat Matsumae Shigeyoshi was promptly conscripted. Matsumae had ordered a study into the difference in the productive capacities of Japanese and US industries; that report convinced him of the need to "overthrow the government as soon as possible" if Japan were to be saved. See Hosokawa Morisada, diary entry, November 16, 1943, in Hosokawa, *Hosokawa Nikki,* 1:21–22. See also Kōketsu Atsushi, *Kenpei seiji: Kanshi to dōkatsu no jidai* [Kenpei politics: The era of surveillance and intimidation] (Tokyo: Shin Nippon Shuppansha, 2008), 98.
29. The admirals regarded Shinmyo almost as one of their own, and after surrender, invited him to record a series of conversations in which they reflected on the navy's missteps before the war. See Shinmyō Takeo, ed., *Kaigun sensō kentō kaigi kiroku: Taiheiyō kaisen no keii* [A record of the conferences of former naval leaders: Examining the circumstances leading to the opening of the Pacific War] (Tokyo: Mainichi Shinbunsha, 1976).
30. Hirohashi Tadamitsu, journal entry, March 2, 1944, in "Hirohashi memo," 534.
31. Hayashi Saburō, *Taiheiyō Sensō rikusen gaishi* [The Pacific War: A brief history of the land war] (Tokyo: Iwanami Shoten, 1951), 128–129.
32. BBKS, *Senshi sōsho (75),* 245.
33. Journal entry, March 11, 1944, in "Tōjō kimitsu kiroku," 411–413.
34. Hosokawa Morisada, diary entry, March 10, 1944, in Hosokawa, *Hosokawa Nikki,* 1:147.
35. BBKS, *Senshi sōsho (75),* 271–272; Wada Tomoyuki, "Taiheiyō Sensō kōhanki ni okeru sensō shidō: rikugun no sensō shūketsu kōsō o chūshin to shite" ["War guidance in the second half of the Pacific War: Focusing on the army's conception of the endgame of war"], *Senshi kenkyū nenpō* [National Institute for Defense Studies military history studies annual] 13 (2010): 60–62.
36. BBKS, *Senshi sōsho (75),* 271–272; and Wada, "Taiheiyō sensō Sensō kōhanki ni okeru sensō shidō," 60–62.
37. Tojo's new strategy is drawn from his contemporaneous comments about *gyokusai* units and wartime tactics. See Hosokawa Morisada, diary entry, March 15, 1944, in Hosokawa, *Hosokawa Nikki,* 1:154–158. For Tojo's comments about winning after one's "torso" had been cut, see Hirohashi Tadamitsu, journal entry, March 15, 1944, in "Hirohashi memo," 563.
38. Hosokawa Morisada, diary entry, March 15, 1944, in Hosokawa, *Hosokawa Nikki,* 1:155.
39. Kiyosawa Kiyoshi, diary entries, February 10 and 13, 1944, and March 8, 13, 14, 16, and 23, 1944, in Kiyosawa, *A Diary of Darkness,* 144–145, 146–147, 154–156, 158–161, 164–165.
40. Daily entries, March 14–15, 1944, in Ku'naichō, *Shōwa Tennō jitsuroku,* 32:41–42. See also Hosokawa Morisada, diary entry, March 18, 1944, in Hosokawa, *Hosokawa Nikki,* 1:160; and Kido Koichi, diary entry, March 15, 1944, in Kido, *Nikki,* 2:1095.
41. Daily entries, March 14–15, 1944, in Ku'naichō, *Shōwa Tennō jitsuroku,* 32:41–42. Regarding Nagata's "fifty-year war" plan, see Suyama Yukio, *Sakusen no oni Obata Toshirō* [Strategy demon Obata Toshiro] (Tokyo: Fuyō Shobō, 1983), 347–349.
42. Hasunuma Shigeru, quoted in Suzuki Tamon, *Shūsen no seijishi, 1943–1945* [Japan's long road to surrender: A political history, 1943–1945] (Tokyo: Tokyo Daigaku Shuppankai, 2011), 61.

43. See Edward J. Drea, "Chasing a Decisive Victory: Emperor Hirohito and Japan's War with the West (1941–1945)," in *In the Service of the Emperor: Essays on the Imperial Japanese Army* (Lincoln: University of Nebraska Press, 1998), 169–215.
44. BBKS, *Senshi sōsho (75)*, 161–175, 252–264. See also BBKS, ed., *Senshi sōsho (6) chūbu Taiheiyō rikugun sakusen (1) Mariana gyokusai made* [War history series, vol. 6: Central Pacific army operations (vol. 1), until the Marianas gyokusai] (Tokyo: Asagumo Shuppan, 1967), 299–301.
45. BBKS, *Senshi sōsho (75)*, 211–212, 371.
46. BBKS, *Senshi sōsho (75)*, 239–244, 272–273, 371–374.
47. Hirohashi Tadamitsu, journal entry, April 29, 1944, in "Hirohashi memo," 540–541. See also journal entries, April 27–29, 1944, in "Tōjō kimitsu kiroku," 429–431.
48. BBKS, ed., *Senshi sōsho (19) hondo bōkū sakusen* [War history series (19), aerial defense operations in the home islands] (Tokyo: Asagumo Shuppansha, 1968), 249.
49. BBKS, ed., *Senshi sōsho (4) Ichigō Sakusen (1) Ka'nan no kaisen* [War history series (4), Operation Ichigo (1), the opening of the battle of Henan] (Tokyo: Asagumo Shuppansha, 1967), 29.
50. BBKS, *Senshi sōsho (75)*, 361–371. See also daily entry, May 2, 1944, in Ku'naichō, *Shōwa Tennō jitsuroku*, 32:68–69.
51. BBKS, *Senshi sōsho (75)*, 441–442.
52. Journal entries, May 16 and 17, 1944, in Gunjishi Gakkai, ed., *Daihon'ei rikugunbu sensō shidō han: kimitsu sensō nisshi* [Imperial headquarters, army, war guidance section: Confidential war journal], vol. 2 (Tokyo: Ginseisha, 2008), 527–530.
53. Kiyosawa Kiyoshi, diary entry, March 16, 1944, in Kiyosawa, *A Diary of Darkness*, 159.
54. Kido Koichi, diary entry, March 18, 1944, in Kido, *Nikki*, 2:1095.
55. Takagi Sōkichi, diary entry, April 25, 1944, in Takagi, *Nikki to jōhō*, 2:732.
56. Yatsugi Kazuo, *Tennō: Arashi no naka no gojūnen* [The emperor: Fifty years in the storm] (Tokyo: Hara Shobō, 1981), 24. Regarding the possibility that Kido himself came under kenpei surveillance, see for example Iwai Shūichirō, *1944-nen no Tōjō Hideki* [The Tojo Hideki of 1944] (Tokyo: Shōdensha Shinsho, 2020), 148.
57. For reports of submarine activity around Saipan, see journal entry, May 18, 1944, in Gunjishi Gakkai, *Kimitsu sensō nisshi*, 2:530–531. For Tojo's thoughts about Japan's command structure, see Hirohashi Tadamitsu, journal entry, May 19, 1944, in "Hirohashi memo," 542–544, quotation on 543.
58. BBKS, ed., *Senshi sōsho (45): daihon'ei kaigunbu / rengō kantai (6) daisandan sakusen kōki* [War history series, vol. 45: general headquarters, navy / combined fleet, vol. 6, third-stage operations, latter half] (Tokyo: Asagumo Shuppansha, 1971), 12.
59. Journal entry, May 29, 1944, in "Tōjō kimitsu kiroku," 444.
60. Daily entry, June 29, 1944, in Ku'naichō, *Shōwa Tennō jitsuroku*, 32:84.
61. Takagi Sōkichi, diary entry, May 29, 1944, in Takagi, *Nikki to jōhō*, 2:738.
62. See Takagi Sōkichi, diary entries, May 29 and June 8, 1944, in Takagi, *Nikki to jōhō*, 2:739–742. See also BBKS, *Senshi sōsho (45)*, 94–95.
63. See Takagi Sōkichi, diary entries, June 5, 8, and 10, 1944, in Takagi, *Nikki to jōhō*, 2:739–743.
64. BBKS, *Senshi sōsho (75)*, 501; BBKS, *Senshi sōsho (45)*, 95.
65. Daily entry, June 6, 1944, in Ku'naichō, *Shōwa Tennō jitsuroku*, 32:87.
66. Hirohashi Tadamitsu, journal entry, June 15, 1944, in "Hirohashi memo," 548.
67. Kido Koichi, diary entry, June 15, 1944, in Kido, *Nikki*, 2:1110. See also daily entry, June 15, 1944, in Ku'naichō, *Shōwa Tennō jitsuroku*, 32:90–91.
68. BBKS, *Senshi sōsho (75)*, 472. Obata was in Yap when the invading forces landed on Saipan. He hurried to the Palaus, but Tojo on June 16 ordered him back to Saipan immediately to lead the defense against US forces.
69. BBKS, *Senshi sōsho (45)*, 12–13.

70. Hirohashi Tadamitsu, journal entry, June 17, 1944, in "Hirohashi memo," 548.
71. Kido Koichi, diary entries, June 16–17, 1944, in Kido, *Nikki,* 2:1111. See also daily entries, June 16–17, 1944, in Ku'naichō, *Shōwa Tennō jitsuroku,* 32:91–93.
72. Takagi Sōkichi, diary entry, June 17, 1944, in Takagi, *Nikki to jōhō,* 2:743–744.
73. Akamatsu Sadao, *Tōjō hishokan kimitsu nisshi* [Secret diary of Tojo's secretary] (Tokyo: Bungei Shunju, 1985), 155.
74. BBKS, *Senshi sōsho (45),* 21.
75. BBKS, *Senshi sōsho (75),* 473–474. See also BBKS, *Senshi sōsho (45),* 14; and daily entry, June 19, 1944, in Ku'naichō, *Shōwa Tennō jitsuroku,* 32:93–94.
76. Samuel Eliot Morison, *The Two-Ocean War: A Short History of the United States Navy in the Second World War* (Boston: Little, Brown, 1963), 342.
77. BBKS, *Senshi sōsho (71),* 557–574.
78. BBKS, *Senshi sōsho (75),* 483.
79. Hirohashi Tadamitsu, journal entry, June 19, 1944, in "Hirohashi memo," 549–552.
80. BBKS, *Senshi sōsho (71),* 565. See also BBKS, *Senshi sōsho (45),* 28.
81. Higashikuni Naruhiko, diary entry, June 20, 1944, in Satō, *Kōzoku gunjin denki shūsei 11,* 132. See also diary entry, June 22, 1944, in Konoe, *Nikki,* 10–11.
82. Konoe Fumimaro, diary entry, June 21, 1944, in Konoe Fumimaro, *Konoe nikki* [Konoe diary] (Tokyo: Kyōdō Tsūshinsha, 1968), 6–7. See also journal entry, June 21, 1944, in "Tōjō kimitsu kiroku," 452–453; and Kido Koichi, diary entry, June 21, 1944, in Kido, *Nikki,* 2:1112.
83. Konoe Fumimaro, diary entry, June 24, 1944, in Konoe, *Konoe nikki,* 14–15; Kido Koichi, diary entry, June 23, 1944, in Kido, *Nikki,* 2:1112; Higashikuni Naruhiko, diary entry, June 23, 1944, in Satō, *Kōzoku gunjin denki shūsei 11,* 133.
84. Daily entry, June 24, 1944, in Ku'naichō, *Shōwa Tennō jitsuroku,* 32:97.
85. Daily entry, June 24, 1944, 97.
86. BBKS, *Senshi sōsho (75),* 484. See also BBKS, *Senshi sōsho (45),* 45, 33–36; and daily entry, June 25, 1944, in Ku'naichō, *Shōwa Tennō jitsuroku,* 32:97–98. Regarding Tojo's fresh sense of purpose (which Prince Higashikuni mistakenly attributed to his own admonition to Tojo), see diary entry, June 25, 1944, in Satō, *Kōzoku gunjin denki shūsei 11,* 133. See also Akamatsu, *Kimitsu nisshi,* 160.
87. Terasaki Hidenari, *Shōwa Tennō dokuhakuraku: Terasaki Hidenari Goyōgakkari nikki* [The Showa Emperor's monologue: Imperial aide Terasaki Hidenari's diary], ed. Mariko Terasaki Miller (Tokyo: Bungei Shunjū, 1991), 22. See also Gordon M. Berger, Roger M. Brown, and Peter Mauch, eds., *The Emperor's Testimony: Hirohito's Monologue on Japan's War in Asia and the Pacific* (Cambridge: Cambridge University Press, forthcoming).
88. Honjō Shigeru, diary entry, April 9, 1935, in *Emperor Hirohito and His Chief Aide-de-Camp: The Honjō Diary, 1933–36,* trans. Mikiso Hane (Tokyo: University of Tokyo Press, 1982), 133.
89. BBKS, *Senshi sōsho (45),* 36–37. See also daily entries, June 25–26, 1944, in Ku'naichō, *Shōwa Tennō jitsuroku,* 32:97–99; diary entry, June 27, 1944, in Takagi, *Nikki to jōhō,* 2:746–748; and Tatsumi Ineo, "Shūsen oboegaki sono ichi" [End of war memorandum part one] in Gaimushō, ed., *Nihon no sentaku: dainiji sekai taisen shūsen shiroku* [Japan's choices: Historical records of the end of World War II], vol. 1 (Tokyo: Yamata Shobō, 1990), 143. Tatsumi Ineo was a penname used by Takagi Sokichi.
90. Takagi Sōkichi, diary entry, June 27, 1944, in Takagi, *Nikki to jōhō,* 2:746–748, quotations on 747–748. For Tojo's denunciation of the "conspiracy" to overthrow him, see diary entry, July 2, 1944, in Konoe, *Konoe nikki,* 26–38, quotations on 28, 34.
91. Takagi Sōkichi, diary entry, June 30, 1944, in Takagi, *Nikki to jōhō,* 2:750.
92. Daily entry, July 1, 1944, in Ku'naichō, *Shōwa Tennō jitsuroku,* 32:101–102. Regarding the failure of the Imphal operation, see Asano Toyomi, "Japanese Operations in Yunnan and

North Burma," in *The Battle for China: Essays on the Military History of the Sino-Japanese War of 1937–1945,* ed. Mark Peattie, Edward Drea, and Hans van de Ven (Stanford, CA: Stanford University Press, 2010), 374.

93. Daily entry, July 5, 1944, in Ku'naichō, *Shōwa Tennō jitsuroku,* 32:103.
94. Journal entry, July 7, 1944, in "Tōjō kimitsu kiroku," 459–460.
95. See Hosaka Masayasu, *Tōjō Hideki to tennō no jidai(2) Nichi-Bei kaisen kara Tōkyō saiban made* [Tōjō Hideki and the era of the emperor (2) from the opening of the Japanese-U.S. war to the Tokyo trial] (Tokyo: Bungei Shunjū, 1988), 164–166.
96. Takagi Sōkichi, diary entry, July 8, 1944, in Takagi, *Nikki to jōhō,* 2:751–752.
97. See, for example, Iwai, *1944-nen no Tōjō Hideki,* 67–170.
98. Kido Koichi, diary entry, July 13, 1944, in Kido, *Nikki,* 2:1116–1118.
99. Journal entry, July 13, 1944, in "Tōjō kimitsu kiroku," 461–462.
100. BBKS, *Senshi sōsho (75),* 504.
101. Daily entry, July 13, 1944, in Ku'naichō, *Shōwa Tennō jitsuroku,* 32:108–109, quotation on 108.
102. Journal entries, July 13 and 14, 1944, in "Tōjō kimitsu kiroku," 461–464.
103. Journal entry, July 14, 1944, in "Tōjō kimitsu kiroku," 462–464, quotations on 463–464.
104. Kido Koichi, diary entry, July 14, 1944, in Kido, *Nikki,* 2:1118.
105. See daily entry, July 15, 1944, in Ku'naichō, *Shōwa Tennō jitsuroku,* 32:109–110; and journal entry, July 15, 1944, in Gunjishi Gakkai, *Kimitsu sensō nisshi,* 2:556–557.
106. Journal entry, July 17, 1944, in Gunjishi Gakkai, *Kimitsu sensō nisshi,* 2:557.
107. Journal entry, July 16, 1944, in Gunjishi Gakkai, *Kimitsu sensō nisshi,* 2:557.
108. BBKS, *Sensi sōsho (45),* 98.
109. Journal entries, July 15–16, 1944, in "Tōjō kimitsu kiroku," 464–466.
110. BBKS, *Senshi sōsho (45),* 98–99. See also "Nomura Naokuni shuki 'Tōjō naikaku hōkai no shinsō'" [Nomura Naokuni memo: "the truth of the collapse of the Tōjō cabinet"] and "Nomura Naokuni kōkyōsho" [Nomura Naokuni affidavit], in Gaimushō, *Shūsen shiroku,* 1:145–147.
111. Takagi Sōkichi, diary entry, July 16, 1944, in Takagi, *Nikki to jōhō,* 2:754–755. See also journal entry, July 17, 1944, in "Tōjō kimitsu kiroku," 466–467; and Hirohashi Tadamitsu, journal entry for the end of June through mid-July in "Hirohashi memo," 555–556.
112. Journal entry, July 16, 1944, in "Tōjō kimitsu kiroku," 465–466. See also BBKS, *Senshi sōsho (45),* 99.
113. Kido Koichi, diary entry, July 18, 1944, in Kido, *Nikki,* 2:1121. See also daily entry, July 18, 1944, in Ku'naichō, *Shōwa Tennō jitsuroku,* 32:12–114.
114. Terauchi Eiji kōkyō [Terauchi Eiji's affidavit], in Gaimushō, *Shūsen shiroku,* 169.

14 · TOJO THE TROUBLEMAKER

1. Kiyosawa Kiyoshi, diary entries, July 20 and 21, 1944, in Kiyosawa Kiyoshi, *A Diary of Darkness: The Wartime Diary of Kiyosawa Kiyoshi,* ed. Eugene Soviak (Princeton, NJ: Princeton University Press, 1998), 228–230.
2. Journal entry, July 18, 1944, in Gunjishi Gakkai, eds., *Daihon'ei rikugunbu sensō shidō han: kimitsu sensō nisshi* [Imperial headquarters, army, war guidance section: confidential war journal], vol. 2 (Tokyo: Ginseisha, 2008), 557–558. See also Hattori Takushirō, "Dai6hen dai7shō: Tōjō naikaku no sōjishoku (1)" [Draft 6 chapter 7: Resignation of the Tōjō cabinet (1)], in "Daitōa Sensō zenshi sōan" [Complete history of the greater East Asian war: Draft], 0975, Rikugun ippan shiryō, chūō zenpan, gaishi, JDMA (hereafter cited as JDMA), Japan Center for Asian Historical Records (hereafter cited as JACAR) reference code C13071337000.
3. Kido Koichi, diary entry, July 18, 1944, in Kido Kōichi, *Nikki* [Diary], ed. Kido Nikki Kenkyukai, vol. 2 (Tokyo: Tokyo Daigaku Shuppankai, 1966), 1121.

4. For a record of the *jushin* meeting and for the emperor's reaction to Terauchi, see Kido, diary entry, July 18, 1944, 1121–1127. See also Kido Kōichi, "Kyōsho (sōkiroku 269–271)" [Affidavit (stenographic notes 269–271)], in Gaimushō, ed., *Nihon no sentaku: dainiji sekai taisen shūsen shiroku* [Japan's choices: Historical records of the end of World War II], vol. 1 (Tokyo: Yamata Shobō, 1990), 175–184, quotation on 183.
5. Daily entry, July 20, 1944, in Ku'naichō, ed., *Shōwa Tennō jitsuroku* [True documents of the Shōwa Emperor], vol. 32, Imperial Household Agency, Archives and Mausolea Department, 115.
6. Daily entry, July 20, 1944 in *Shōwa Tennō jitsuroku,* 32, 115. See also Hirohashi Tadamitsu, journal entry, July 19, 1944, in in "Tōjō Hideki Taishō genkōroku (Hirohashi memo)" [General Tōjō Hideki's words and deeds (Hirohashi memorandums)], in *Tōjō naikaku sōri daijin kimitsu kiroku: Tōjō Hideki Taishō genkōroku* [Prime Minister Tojo confidential record: Record of General Tojo Hideki's words and deeds], ed. Itō Takashi, Hirohashi Tadamitsu, and Katashima Norio (Tokyo: Tokyo Daigaku Shuppankai, 1990), 556; daily entry, July 19, 1944, in "Tōjō Naikaku Sōri Daijin kimitsu kiroku," [Prime Minister Tōjō confidential record], in Itō et al., *Tōjō naikaku sōri daijin kimitsu kiroku,* 468; and Kido, diary entry, July 18, 1941, 1127.
7. Hirohashi, journal entry, July 19, 1944 556; daily entry, July 19, 1944, in "Tōjō kiroku," 468.
8. Kido, "Kyōsho," 175–184.
9. Daily entry, July 19, 1944, in "Tōjō kiroku," 468. See also "Ōi Atsushi oboegaki" [Ōi Atsushi memorandum], in Gaimushō, *Shūsen shiroku,* 1:192–193; daily entry, July 21, 1944, in Nakamura Seigo, *Nagatachō ichibanchi: Gaikō haisen hiroku* [Nagatachō number one: confidential records of the diplomacy of defeat] (Tokyo: Nyūsusha, 1946), 15–16; daily entry, July 20, 1944, in Shigemitsu Mamoru, *Shigemitsu Mamoru shuki: zoku* [Shigemitsu Mamoru Papers: continued], eds., Itō Takashi and Watanabe Yukio, (Tokyo: Chūō Kōronsha, 1986); and Konoe Fumimaro, diary entry, July 24, 1944, in Konoe Fumimaro, *Konoe nikki* [Konoe diary] (Tokyo: Kyōdō Tsūshinsha, 1968), 108.
10. Hattori, "Dai6hen dai7shō: Tōjō naikaku no sōjishoku (2)" [Draft 6 chapter 7: resignation of the Tojo cabinet (2)], in "Daitōa sensō zenshi sōan" [Complete history of the greater East Asian war: Draft], 1003, Rikugun ippan shiryō, chūō zenpan, gaishi, JDMA, JACAR reference code C13071337100.
11. Takagi Sōkichi, diary entry, July 28, 1944, in Takagi Sōkichi, *Nikki to jōhō* [Diary and reports], vol. 2, (Tokyo: Misuzu Shobō, 2000),758.See also Tanemura Sakō, diary entry, July 20, 1944, in Tanemura Sakō, *Daihon'ei kimitsu nisshi* [Confidential supreme headquarters journal] (Tokyo: Daiyamondosha, 1952); and Terasaki Hidenari, *Shōwa Tennō dokuhakuraku: Terasaki Hidenari Goyōgakkari nikki* [The Showa Emperor's monologue: Imperial aide Terasaki Hidenari's diary], ed. Mariko Terasaki Miller (Tokyo: Bungei Shunjū, 1991), 112.
12. Hattori, "Dai6hen dai7shō (2)."
13. Hirohashi Tadamitsu, memorandum, July 22, 1944, in "Hirohashi memo," 556–557.
14. Konoe Fumimaro, diary entry, July 20, 1044, in Konoe, *Konoe nikki,* 102–103.
15. For Tominaga's comments, see diary entry, July 19, 1944, in Gunjishi Gakkai, *Kimitsu sensō nisshi,* 2:558–559. For Sato's comments, see Satō Kenryō, *Satō Kenryō no shōgen* [Sato Kenryo's testimony] (Tokyo: Fuyō Shobō, 1976), 409.
16. Hosokawa Morisada, diary entry, September 11, 1944, in Hosokawa Morisada, *Hosokawa nikki* [Hosokawa diary], vol. 2 (Tokyo: Chūō Kōronsha, 1979), 302.
17. Hosokawa Morisada, diary entry, October 15, 1944, in Hosokawa, *Hosokawa nikki,* 2:316–317.
18. Hosaka Masayasu, *Tōjō Hideki to tennō no jidai(2) Nichi-Bei kaisen kara Tōkyō saiban made* [Tōjō Hideki and the era of the emperor (2) from the opening of the Japanese-U.S. war to the Tokyo trial] (Tokyo: Bungei Shunjū, 1988), 188.

19. Tanemura Sakō, diary entry, February 6, 1945, in Tanemura, *Daihon'ei kimitsu nisshi,* 209.
20. Tojo Hideki, quoted in Tanemura, *Daihon'ei kimitsu nisshi,* 212–213, emphasis added.
21. Kawamura, *Hirohito and the War,* 141. The emperor met not only with the *jushin* but also with former lord keeper of the Privy Seal, Makino Nobuaki.
22. John W. Dower, *Empire and Aftermath: Yoshida Shigeru and the Japanese Experience, 1878–1954* (Cambridge, MA: Harvard East Asian Monographs, 1979), 255–264.
23. Daily entry, February 26, 1945, in Ku'naichō, *Shōwa Tennō jitsuroku,* 33:52–60. See also "Fujita Hisanori kiroku" [Fujita Hisanori's record], in Gaimushō, ed., *Nihon no sentaku: dainiji sekai taisen shūsen shiroku* [Japan's choices: Historical records of the end of World War II], vol. 2, (Tokyo: Yamata Shobō, 1990), 275–282.
24. Daily entry, February 26, 1945, in Ku'naichō, *Shōwa Tennō jitsuroku,* 33:52–60.
25. Daily entry, February 26, 1945, in Ku'naichō, *Shōwa Tennō jitsuroku,* 33:52–60.
26. Daily entry, February 26, 1945, in Ku'naichō, *Shōwa Tennō jitsuroku,* 33:52–60.
27. Daily entry, February 26, 1945, in Ku'naichō, *Shōwa Tennō jitsuroku,* 33:52–60.
28. Daily entry, February 26, 1945, in Ku'naichō, *Shōwa Tennō jitsuroku,* 33:52–60.
29. Fujita Hisanori, *Jijūchō no kaiso* [Grand chamberlain's memoir] (Tokyo: Chūō Kōronsha, 1987), 80.
30. Tanaka [Kengorō?], "Suzuki naikaku no seiritsu" [Establishment of the Suzuki cabinet], undated, Daitōa Sensō zenshi sōan dai-10-hen, gaishi, zenpan, rikugun ippan shiryō: chūō, JDMA, JACAR reference code 13071342700.
31. Kido Koichi, diary entry, April 5, 1945, in Kido, *Kido nikki,* 2:1188–1194.
32. Anami Korechika, entries, April 12 and July 28, 1945, in "Memochō" [Notebook], File no. 59, Anami Papers, National Diet Library.
33. Potsdam Proclamation (Proclamation of the Three Powers—the United States, Great Britain, and China), July 26, 1945, in Gaimushō, ed., *Shūsen Shiroku,* 2:684–688.
34. See, for example, Sadao Asada, "The Shock of the Atomic Bomb and Japan's Decision to Surrender," *Pacific Historical Review,* vol. 67 no. 4 (1998): 477–512.
35. Tōgō to Kase (in Sweden) and Okamoto (in Spain), August 10, 1945, in Gaimushō, *Shūsen Shiroku,* 2:816–818.
36. Untitled memorandum (1), August 10, 1945, in "Tōjō moto shushō shuki (Kiyose shiryō)" [Former prime minister Tojo's notes (Kiyose papers)], May 1966, 4A.22.2441, National Archives of Japan.
37. Untitled memorandum (2), August 10, 1945, in "Tōjō moto shushō shuki (Kiyose shiryō)" [Former prime minister Tojo's notes (Kiyose papers)], May 1966, 4A.22.2441, National Archives of Japan.
38. Untitled memorandum (2).
39. Untitled memorandum (2). See also daily entry, August 11, 1945, in Ku'naichō, ed., *Shōwa Tennō jitsuroku* [True documents of the Shōwa Emperor], vol. 34, Imperial Household Agency, Archives and Mausolea Department, 37–38, quotation on 37.
40. Untitled, August 12, 1945, in "Tōjō moto shushō shuki (kiyose shiryō)" [Former prime minister Tojo's notes (Kiyose papers)], May 1966, 4A.22.2441, National Archives of Japan. For the English-language original, see US Secretary of State James F. Byrnesto the Swiss Representative, undated, in *Shūsen shiroku,* vol. 3, 860–862. The Byrnes note receives judicious treatment in Richard B. Frank, *Downfall: The End of the Imperial Japanese Empire* (New York: Random House, 1999), 300–303. See also Tsuyoshi Hasegawa, *Racing the Enemy: Stalin, Truman, and the Surrender of Japan* (Cambridge, MA: Belknap Press of Harvard University Press, 2005), 218–222.
41. Daily entry, August 13, 1945, in Ku'naichō, *Shōwa Tennō jitsuroku,* 34:38–41.
42. Untitled, August 13, 1945, in "Tōjō moto shushō shuki (kiyose shiryō)" [Former prime minister Tojo's notes (Kiyose papers)], May 1966, 4A.22.2441, National Archives of Japan.
43. Untitled, August 13, 1945.

44. "Akamatsu taisa e" [To Colonel Akamatsu], August 14, 1945, in "Tōjō moto Shushō shuki (Kiyose shiryō)" [Former Prime Minister Tojo's notes (Kiyose papers)], May 1966, 4A.22.2441, National Archives of Japan.
45. Regarding Tojo's meeting with Anami, see Hosaka, *Tōjō Hideki to tennō no jidai,* 2:208. Regarding the rebellious army officers, see Pacific War Research Society, ed., *Japan's Longest Day* (Tokyo: Kodansha International, 1968). Tojo's statement to Koga is taken from Koga's suicide note, recorded in Satō Sanae, *Tōjō Katsuko no shōgai: "A-kyū" senpan no tsuma to shite* [Tojo Katsuko's life as the wife of a "Class A" war criminal] (Tokyo: Jiji Tsūshinsha, 1987), 37.
46. Sakakibara Kazue, "Tōjō Hideki no kangai" [Tojo Hideki's deep emotions], in Jōhō Yoshio, *Tōjō Hideki,* ed. Jōhō Yoshio (Tokyo: Fūyō Shobō, 1974), 422.
47. Tojo had sent some of his children and their families away from the family home in mid-1944. He sent the remainder away following surrender. See Iwanami Yūko, *Issai kataru nakare: Tōjō Hideki ichizoku no sengo* [Don't speak about the past: Tojo Hideki's family after the war] (Tokyo: Yomiuri Shimbunsha, 1992), 54. Regarding the destruction of Tojo's personal papers, see Iwanami, *Issai kataru nakare.* The author of the book is Tojo's maternal granddaughter, Tojo Yūko; following its publication she changed her name from Iwanami to Tojo. Naval historian Sadao Asada has labeled the wholesale destruction of the military and naval record a "crime against history." See Sadao Asada, *From Mahan to Pearl Harbor: The Imperial Japanese Navy and the United States* (Annapolis, MD: Naval Institute Press, 2006), x. Regarding the extensiveness of the destruction, see Hara Takeshi, "Riku-kaigun monjo ni tsuite" [Concerning army and navy documents], *Senshi Kenkyū Nenpō* [War history studies annual] 3 (2000): 109. Regarding Tojo's dismantling of his air-raid shelter, see Hosaka, *Tōjō Hideki to tennō no jidai,* 2:214.
48. Tōjō Katsuko, "Omokage" [Shadow], in Hayashi Ishiro, ed., *Haisha: Tōjō Hideki fujin hoka senpan izoku no shuki* [The defeated: Notes of Tojo Hideki's wife and surviving families of other war criminals] (Tokyo: Futami Shobō, 1960), 58; Iwanami, *Issai kataru nakare,* 91.
49. Hosaka, *Tōjō Hideki to tennō no jidai,* 2:218.
50. HirohashiTadamitsu, journal entry, late August 1945, in "Hirohashi memo," 559.
51. Untitled memorandum, August 27, 1945, in "Tōjō moto shushō shuki (kiyose shiryō)" [Former prime minister Tojo's notes (Kiyose papers)], May 1966, 4A.22.2441, National Archives of Japan.
52. Hirohashi Tadamitsu, journal entry, late August 1945, in "Hirohashi memo," 559.
53. Douglas MacArthur, *Reminiscences* (New York: McGraw-Hill, 1964), 282.
54. Hirohashi Tadamitsu, journal entry, late August 1945, in "Hirohashi memo," 559–560.
55. Katakura Tadashi, "Shōgen" ["Testimony"], in Jōhō, *Tōjō Hideki,* 658.
56. Shimomura Sadamu, "Shūsen shori no kaiko" [Reminiscences about managing the war's endgame], in Jōhō, *Tōjō Hideki,* 422–424. See also Kiyose Ichirō, *Hitsuroku Tōkyō saiban* [Confidential records: The Tokyo trial] (Tokyo: Chūō bunko, 1986), 24.
57. Allied Powers General Headquarters statement, September 11, 1945, in *Nihon gaikō bunsho: Senryōki* [Documents on Japanese foreign policy: The occupation period], vol. 2, ed. Gaimushō (Tokyo: Gaimushō, 2020), 1523.
58. Robert J. C. Butow, *Tojo and the Coming of the War* (Princeton, NJ: Princeton University Press, 1961), 462.

15 · TOJO'S LAST STAND

1. The three notes are reproduced in Kiyose Ichirō, *Hitsuroku Tōkyō saiban* [Confidential records: The Tokyo trial] (Tokyo: Chūō bunko, 1986), 27–29. For a brief English-language account of these notes, see Robert J. C. Butow, *Tojo and the Coming of the War* (Princeton, NJ: Princeton University Press, 1961), 461–462.

2. Satō Sanae, *Tōjō Katsuko no shōgai: "A-kyū" senpan no tsuma to shite* [Tojo Katsuko's life as the wife of a "Class A" war criminal] (Tokyo: Jiji Tsūshinsha, 1987), 57.
3. Ted de Bary to Don Keene, September 24, 1945, in Otis Carey, ed., *War Wasted Asia: Letters, 1945–1946* (Tokyo: Kodansha International, 1975), 45–51, quotation on 50.
4. Kiyose, *Hitsuroku Tōkyō saiban,* 24.
5. Suzuki Tadakatsu, diary entry, undated (but following a September 12, 1945 entry), in Yajima Akira, "'Suzuki Tadakatsu nikki' hoi: 1945nen 8gatsu 29nichi—10gatsu 30nichi" ["Suzuki Tadakatsu diary" addendum: August 29, 1945–October 30"], *Meijō Daigaku hōgakkai* 71 nos. 3–4 (2022): 168–169. The Foreign Ministry established the Central Liaison Office as the official channel of communications between the Japanese government and GHQ SCAP. The Central Liaison Office Yokohama branch was a hive of activity in the initial days of the occupation because MacArthur established temporary headquarters there.
6. For Shigemitsu's memorandum of his conversation with Sutherland, see meeting record, September 13, 1945, in Gaimushō, ed., *Nihon gaikō bunsho: Senryōki* [Documents on Japanese foreign policy: The occupation period], vol. 2, ed. Gaimushō (Tokyo: Gaimushō, 2020), 1531–1532. GHQ SCAP implicitly accepted the Japanese government's request that it be entrusted with the future arrests of criminal suspects. See, for example, SCAPIN 296, "Apprehension of Japanese War Criminals," November 17, 1945, and SCAPIN 378, "Apprehension of Japanese Personnel," December 1, 1945, in Gaimushō, *Nihon gaikō bunsho: Senryōki,* 2:1534–1539.
7. On September 12, Japanese authorities recorded "uncertainty" at the possibility of meeting with Tojo. See "Shūsen renraku chūō jimukyoku: Tōjō Taishō ni kansuru jōhō" [War termination liaison committee: Information about General Tojo], September 12, 1945, in "Rengōkuni to sesshō kankei jikō sono 8 no 2" [Matters concerning negotiations with the Allied Powers, number 2 of 8], September 12–16, 1945, Bunko: yuzu 26, Japanese Defense Ministry Archives, Japan Center for Asian Historical Records reference code. For Tojo's conversation with Suzuki, see Suzuki Tadakatsu, diary entry, September 17, 1945, in Yajima, "Suzuki Tadakatsu nikki," 184–185.
8. Suzuki Tadakatsu, diary entry, October 2, 1945, in Yajima, "Suzuki nikki," 205. Regarding the emperor's interview with Kluckhohn, see Matsuo Takayoshi, "Sengokushi hiwa: Beikokujin kisha kaiken Shōwa Tennō wa Shinjūwan kōgeki no sekinin o Tōjō moto shushō ni tenka shita" [Secret story of the nation at war: US correspondents meeting, the Showa emperor transferred responsibility for the Pearl Harbor attack to former prime minister Tojo], *Ronza,* February 2007, 128–143.
9. Hosaka Masayasu, *Tōjō Hideki to tennō no jidai(2) Nichi-Bei kaisen kara Tōkyō saiban made* [Tōjō Hideki and the era of the emperor (2) from the opening of the Japanese-U.S. war to the Tokyo trial] (Tokyo: Bungei Shunjū, 1988), 230, 232, 235. Tojo recorded his delight in Natsume Soseki in a prison diary, which his granddaughter, Iwanami Yūko, quoted. See Iwanami Yūko, *Issai kataru nakare: Tōjō Hideki ichizoku no sengo* [Don't speak about the past: Tojo Hideki's family after the war] (Tokyo: Yomiuri Shimbunsha, 1992), 90.
10. Sakakibara Kazue, "Tōjō Hideki no kangai" [Tojo Hideki's deep emotions], in Jōhō Yoshio, *Tōjō Hideki,* ed. Jōhō Yoshio (Tokyo: Fūyō Shobō, 1974), 746–748. Tojo's thoughts on US medical prowess fit within a broader narrative shared by many soldiers concerning America's immense industrial capacity and its scientific and technological prowess. The long-range B-29 bomber and the atomic bomb were perhaps the two most prominent examples of advances in American science and technology; so far as Tojo was concerned, American field surgery was but another such example. On this point, see Sadao Asada, "The Shock of the Atomic Bomb and Japan's Decision to Surrender," *Pacific Historical Review,* vol. 67 no. 4 (1998): 505–508.

11. Sakakibara, "Tōjō Hideki no kangai," 747, 750.
12. Sakakibara, "Tōjō Hideki no kangai," 750–751.
13. Sakakibara, "Tōjō Hideki no kangai," 748–750.
14. Sakakibara, "Tōjō Hideki no kangai," 750.
15. See, for example, SCAPIN 296; and SCAPIN 378.
16. Tojo Hideki, quoted in Hosaka, *Tōjō to tennō no jidai,* 2:234.
17. Tōjō Yūko, *Tōjōke no hahakogusa* [The Tojo family's cottonweed] (Tokyo: Kakimonsha, 2003), 98.
18. "Hōmu daijin kanbō shihō hōsei chōsabu," undated, Kiyose Ichirō (Tōjō) / Kanzaki Masayoshi (Hata) chōshusho [Interview transcript], in "Hōmushō kyūzō Tokyo Saiban sensō saiban kankei shiryō dainibu," Japan Digital Archives Center (J-DAC) 06433100—001.
19. See "Hōmushingishitsu Daini Iinkai giji kiroku" [Minutes of Legal Affairs Counsel Office Second Committee], January 9, 1946, in *Nihon gaikō bunsho: Senryōki,* 2:1551–1555, quotation on 1551.
20. "Sensō Saiban Renraku Iinkai daisankai giji kiroku" [Minutes of third meeting of War Trial Liaison Committee], February 8, 1946, in *Nihon gaikō bunsho: Senryōki,* 2:1559–1564.
21. See Higurashi Yoshinobu, *The Tokyo Trial: War Criminals and Japan's Postwar International Relations* (Tokyo: Japan Institute of International Affairs, 2022), 175–176.
22. "Special Proclamation: Establishment of an International Military Tribunal for the Far East," January 19, 1946, in *Documents on the Tokyo International Military Tribunal: Charter, Indictment, and Judgments,* ed. Neil Boister and Robert Cryer (Oxford: Oxford University Press, 2008), 5–6.
23. Boister and Cryer, *Documents on the Tokyo International Military Tribunal,* 75. For the record of Tojo's interrogation, see Awaya Kentarō and Yoshida Yutaka, eds., *Kokusai kensatsukyoku (IPS) jinmon chōsho* [International Prosecution Section (IPS) interrogation records], vols. 5–6 (Tokyo: Nihon Tosho Sentā, 1993). His interrogator was former chief of the Criminal Division of the US Attorney General's Office, John W. Fihelly.
24. Shiohara Tokisaburō, *Tōjō memo: Kakute tennō wa sukuwareta* [Tojo memo: Thus was the emperor saved] (Tokyo: Handobukkusha, 1952).
25. Higurashi, *The Tokyo Trial,* 172.
26. Douglas MacArthur to Chief of Staff Eisenhower, January 25, 1946, in US Department of State, eds., *Foreign Relations of the United States, 1946: The Far East,* vol. 8 (Washington: US Government Printing Office, 1971), 396.
27. Tanaka Nobumasa, *Dokyumento Shōwa tennō* [The Shōwa Emperor: Documents] (Tokyo: Ryokufu Shuppan, 1993), vol. 8, 409.
28. Shigemitsu Mamoru, diary entry, June 16, 1946, in Shigemitsu Mamoru, *Sugamo nikki* [Sugamo diary] (Tokyo: Yoshikawa Kōbunkan, 2022), 22.
29. The category of crimes against humanity (Class C) was ultimately not used in the Asia-Pacific theater. See "Charter of the International Military Tribunal for the Far East," April 26, 1946, in Boister and Cryer, *Documents on the Tokyo International Military Tribunal,* 7–11.
30. Besides Tojo, the indicted were Generals Araki Sadao, Doihara Kenji, Hata Shunroku, Itagaki Seishiro, Koiso Kuniaki, Matsui Iwane, Minami Jiro, and Umezu Yoshijiro; Lieutenant Generals Kimura Heitaro, Muto Akira, Oshima Hiroshi, Sato Kenryo, and Suzuki Teiichi; Colonel Hashimoto Kingoro; Admirals Nagano Osami and Shimada Shigetaro; Vice Admiral Oka Takazumi; former Prime Ministers Hirota Koki and Hiranuma Kiichiro; former Foreign Ministers Matsuoka Yosuke, Shigemitsu Mamoru, and Togo Shigenori; career diplomat and former ambassador to Italy, Shiratori Toshio; Tojo's chief cabinet secretary, Hoshino Naoki; Tojo's finance minister, Kaya Okinori; long-serving Lord Keeper of the Privy Seal, Kido Koichi; and nongovernmental ideologue Okawa Shūmei. "Indictment," in Boister and Cryer, *Documents on the Tokyo International Military Tribunal,*

16–69 (defendants are named on 16). Selection of these individuals was supposed to be "representative" rather than "comprehensive." See Boister and Cryer, *Documents on the Tokyo International Military Tribunal,* 60.

31. "Indictment: Count I," in Boister and Cryer, *Documents on the Tokyo International Military Tribunal,* 18.
32. Only the IMTFE tried Class A suspects; nearly six thousand Japanese were tried by national trials for ordinary war crimes. See Sandra Wilson, Robert Cribb, Beatrice Trefalt, and Dean Askielowicz, *War Criminals: The Politics of Justice After the Second World War* (New York: Columbia University Press, 2017).
33. "Hōmu daijin kanbō shihō hōsei chōsabu."
34. Kiyose Ichirō, *Hiroku Tokyo saiban* [Secret record of the Tokyo trial] (Tokyo: Chūō Kōronsha, 1986), 33.
35. William J. Sebald, *With MacArthur in Japan: A Personal History of the Occupation* (New York: W. W. Norton, 1965), 153.
36. Shigemitsu Mamoru, diary entry, May 3, 1946, in Shigemitsu, *Sugamo nikki,* 9.
37. Eric Jaffe, *A Curious Madness: An American Combat Psychiatrist, a Japanese War Crimes Suspect, and an Unsolved Mystery from World War II* (New York: Scribner, 2014), 10–15. Two other accused—Matsuoka Yosuke and Admiral Nagano Osami—fell out of the tribunal's consideration, as they died of illness during the trial.
38. Arnold C. Brackman, *The Other Nuremberg: The Untold Story of the Tokyo War Crimes Trials* (New York: William Morrow, 1987), 94.
39. Kiyose argued that Webb's prior position as Australian government commissioner, investigating allegations of Japanese violations of the laws of war, rendered him biased. A number of scholars are in agreement with this point. See, for example, Boister and Cryer, *Documents on the Tokyo International Military Tribunal,* 83–84. Regarding the court's jurisdiction, Kiyose argued that Japan had surrendered in accord with the terms of the Potsdam Declaration (and had attached its own condition concerning the emperor's position). His key argument was that Japan's surrender had only ever been conditional, and the victorious allies therefore did not have unlimited authority. On this basis, Kiyose argued that the victorious allies had, in establishing the Tokyo trial, overstepped their rights and prerogatives. See Kiyose, *Hiroku Tōkyō saiban,* 35–48.
40. Iwanami, *Issai kataru nakare,* 84–85.
41. Brackman, *The Other Nuremberg,* 106–109.
42. Kiyose, *Hiroku Tōkyō saiban,* 148–155.
43. Brackman, *The Other Nuremberg,* 270–282, quotations on 272. Regarding Tojo's motion, see also Higurashi, *The Tokyo Trial,* 205–206.
44. Kobori Keiichiro, *The Tokyo Trials: The Unheard Defense* (Tokyo: Kodansha, 1995), 33–60, quotations on 41, 46, 59–60.
45. Higurashi, *The Tokyo Trial,* 191–192, 213–214. For more on the split between the "country before individual" defense strategy pursued by Tojo (and others) as opposed to the "individuals first" strategy pursued by (mostly) the civilians on trial, see Urs Matthias Zachmann, "Loser's Justice: The Tokyo Trial from the Perspective of the Japanese Defence Counsels and the Legal Community," in *Transcultural Justice at the Tokyo Tribunal: The Allied Struggle for Justice, 1946–1948,* ed. Kerstin von Lingen (Leiden: Brill, 2018), 290.
46. Kodama Yoshio, *Shibakusa wa fumaretemo: Sugamo senpan no kiroku* [Even if the grass is swept away: Records of a Sugamo war criminal] (Tokyo: Shin'yūkan Shinbun, 1956), 26.
47. Shiohara, *Tōjō memo,* 15.
48. "Kaisen kettei to Heika no gosekinin (Kiyose Ichirō bengonin ni yoru Tōjō hikoku no chōshusho)" [The war's opening and the Emperor's responsibility (Defendant Tojo's written report by defense counsel Kiyose Ichiro)] November 21, 1947, in "Hōmushō kyūzō Tokyo Saiban sensō saiban kankei shiryō dainibu," J-DAC 06739100.

49. "Kaisen kettei to Heika no gosekinin."
50. "Kaisen kettei to Heika no gosekinin."
51. "Kaisen kettei to Heika no gosekinin."
52. Tōjō Yūko, ed., *Daitōa Sensō no shinjitsu: Tōjō Hideki sensei kyōjutsusho* [The truth of the Greater East Asia War: Tojo Hideki's affidavit] (Tokyo: Wac, 2005).
53. Richard B. Finn, *Winners in Peace: MacArthur, Yoshida, and Postwar Japan* (Berkeley: University of California Press, 1992), 180–181.
54. John R. Pritchard, Sonia Zaide, and Donald C. Watt, eds., *The Tokyo War Crimes Trial: The Complete Transcripts,* vol. 15 (New York: Garland, 1981), 36520–36521. See also, for example, David Cohen and Yuma Totani, The *Tokyo War Crimes Tribunal: Law, History, and Jurisprudence,* (Cambridge: Cambridge University Press, 2018), 139–140. The Australian government had long insisted that the emperor's culpability remained at least open. See, for example, Yuma Totani, *The Tokyo War Crimes Trial: The Pursuit of Justice in the Wake of World War II* (Cambridge, MA: Harvard University Asia Center, 2008), 51.
55. Pritchard et al., *Tokyo War Crimes Trial,* 15:36533–36534. See also Totani, *The Tokyo War Crimes Trial,* 38; and Boister and Cryer, *Documents on the Tokyo International Military Tribunal,* 76.
56. Tojo's cross-examination is reproduced in its entirety in Pritchard et al., *Tokyo War Crimes Trial,* 15:36535–36840, quotations on 36535, 36546, 36570.
57. Pritchard et al., *Tokyo War Crimes Trial,* 15:36591–36592.
58. Pritchard et al., *Tokyo War Crimes Trial,* 15:36594, 36604, 36613.
59. Pritchard et al., *Tokyo War Crimes Trial,* 15:36654, 36667, 36692.
60. Pritchard et al., *Tokyo War Crimes Trial,* 15:36704.
61. Pritchard et al., *Tokyo War Crimes Trial,* 15:36721.
62. Pritchard et al., *Tokyo War Crimes Trial,* 15:36779–36780.
63. Pritchard et al., *Tokyo War Crimes Trial,* 15:36783–36784.
64. Pritchard et al., *Tokyo War Crimes Trial,* 15:36803.
65. Jōhō, ed., *Tōjō Hideki,* 484–485. Once Keenan ended his cross-examination, Tojo was questioned briefly by the bench. His answers were simple and direct, bereft of the defiance that had characterized his performance when Keenan was asking the questions. See Pritchard et al., *Tokyo War Crimes Trial,* 15:36804–36811.
66. Peter Lowe, "An Embarrassing Necessity: The Tokyo Trial of Japanese Leaders, 1946–48," in *Domestic and International Trials, 1700–2000,* vol. 2, *The Trial in History,* ed. R. A. Melikan (Manchester: Manchester University Press, 2003), 144.
67. Totani, *The Tokyo War Crimes Trial,* 40.
68. Jōhō, *Tōjō Hideki,* 480.
69. Brackman, *The Other Nuremberg,* 355.
70. Shinsho Hanayama, *The Way of Deliverance: Three Years with the Condemned Japanese War Criminals,* trans. Hideo Suzuki, Eiichi Noda, and James K. Sasaki (New York: Charles Scribner's Sons, 1950), 215.
71. Hanayama, *The Way of Deliverance,* 8–9, 34, 122, 126.
72. "Findings on Counts of the Indictment," in Boister and Cryer, *Documents on the Tokyo International Military Tribunal,* 594–597, quotation on 596.
73. Hanayama, *The Way of Deliverance,* 128.
74. Tojo's verdict is reproduced in Boister and Cryer, *Documents on the Tokyo International Military Tribunal,* 623–624. His refusal to wear earphones is mentioned in Sebald, *With MacArthur in Japan,* 166.
75. Hanayama, *The Way of Deliverance,* 200–201.
76. Hanayama, *The Way of Deliverance,* 224, 208–209, 216, 222, 254, 273. For the time of the declaration of his death, see Sebald, *With MacArthur in Japan,* 174.

CONCLUSION

1. Nakadate Yūki, "Tōkyō saiban kan: senryōka no Nihon kokumin wa Tōkyō saiban o dou mita ka" [Views of the Tokyo trial: How did the Japanese people view the Tokyo trial during the occupation?], *Hikaku shakai bunka kenkyū* [Social and Cultural Studies] (2013): 52–53. See also Yoshida Yutaka, "Senryōki ni okeru sensō sekinin-ron" [Debates about war responsibility during the occupation period], *Hitotsubashi rongi* [Hitotsubashi review] 105, no. 2 (1991): 131.
2. For the publication that ran afoul of the occupation-era censors, see Tōkyō Saiban Kenkyūkai, ed., *Tōjō Hideki sensei kyōjutsusho* [Tōjō Hideki: Affidavit] (Tokyo: Yōyōsha, 1948).
3. See Takazawa Hiroaki, "Amerika kokuritsu kōbunshokan ga shozai suru Tōkyō saiban hi shokeisha no itai shogū kankei shiryō" [Materials on disposal of the war criminals' bodies executed as a result of the International Military Tribunal for the Far East in possession of the US National Archives and Records Administration], *Nihon Daigaku Seisan Kōgakubu kenkyū hōkoku* [Journal of the College of Industrial Technology, Nihon University] 55 (2022): 1–43, quotations on 15, 16.
4. Prime Minister Shidehara Kijuro told the House of Peers in December 1945, "It is only natural that the people should feel public indignation toward those who insisted on and planned for war five years ago"; quoted in Inoue Toshikazu, *Sensō Chōsakai: Maboroshi no seifu monjo o yomitoku* [The War Investigating Committee: Reading rare government documents] (Tokyo: Kōdansha Gendai Shinsho, 2017), 20. The term "laughingstock" is taken from an article in a small newspaper published in Yamaguchi Prefecture. See Yamato Yumiko, "Sengo Nihon ni okeru senji shidōsha / sensō hanzai jinkan (ue): Yamaguchi-ken kankō no media ni miru Kishi Nobosuke-kan o tsūjite" [The view of wartime top leaders and war criminals through the local media (1): The case of Nobusuke Kishi], *Hikaku shakai bunka kenkyū* [Social and cultural studies] 27 (2010): 47.
5. Miyamoto Yuriko, *Heiwa no mamori* [Protecting peace] (Tokyo: Shin-Nihon Bungakkai, 1949), 39, 62.
6. Katsuta Teiji, *Shōwa 24-nen no Keizai dōkō dai-29* [1949 economic trends, vol. 29], (Tokyo: Dōtai Keizai Kenkyūjo Shuppanbu, 1949), 6.
7. Kagawa Toyohiko, *Shōnen heiwa dokuhon* [Peace reader for youth] (Tokyo: Yotokusha, 1951), 64.
8. Takagi Sōkichi, "Koboreta haiin" [Spilling the causes of defeat], *Chūō kōron* [Central review] 695, no. 1 (1951): 55.
9. See, for example, Yuma Totani, *The Tokyo War Crimes Trial: The Pursuit of Justice in the Wake of World War II* (Cambridge, MA: Harvard University Asia Center, 2008), 229.
10. The three notes are reproduced in Kiyose Ichirō, *Hitsuroku Tōkyō saiban* [Confidential records: The Tokyo trial] (Tokyo: Chūō bunko, 1986), 27–29. For a brief English-language account of these notes, see Robert J. C. Butow, *Tojo and the Coming of the War* (Princeton, NJ: Princeton University Press, 1961), 461–462.
11. Kai'nō Michitaka, "Tōjōteki musekininron" [A Tojo-like refusal to take responsibility], *Chūō kōron* [Central review], May 1952.
12. The article is reproduced in Kiyose, *Hitsuroku Tokyo saiban,* 195–200, and in Iwanami Yūko, *Issai kataru nakare: Tōjō Hideki ichizoku no sengo* [Don't speak about the past: Tojo Hideki's family after the war] (Tokyo: Yomiuri Shimbunsha, 1992), 131–137.
13. Akamatsu Sadao, *Tōjō hishokan kimitsu nisshi* [Secret diary of Tojo's secretary] (Tokyo: Bungei Shunju, 1985), 201.
14. Akazawa Shirō, "1950-nendai no gunjin onkyū mondai (1)" [The issue of pensions for soldiers and sailors in the 1950s (1)], *Ritsumeikan hōgaku* 333–334 (2010): 27–28.
15. Satō Sanae, *Tōjō Katsuko no shōgai: "A-kyū" senpan no tsuma to shite* [Tojo Katsuko's life as the wife of a "Class A" war criminal] (Tokyo: Jiji Tsūshinsha, 1987), 226–228.

16. *Honjō Shigeru,* diary entry, April 9, 1935, in *Emperor Hirohito and His Chief Aide-deCamp: The Honjō Diary, 1933–36,* trans. Mikiso Hane (Tokyo: University of Tokyo Press, 1982), 133.
17. Much has been written about the emperor's "sacred decision." An excellent starting point is Hatano Sumio, *Saishō Suzuki Kantarō no ketsudan: 'Seidan' to sengo Nihon* [Prime Minister Suzuki Kantaro's decision: The "sacred decision" and postwar Japan] (Tokyo: Iwanami Shoten, 2015).
18. Ian Mutsu, "Tojo: How He Was," in Edwin P. Hoyt, *Warlord: Tojo Against the World,* (Lanham, MD: Scarborough House, 1993), xi.

ACKNOWLEDGMENTS

I MUST BEGIN BY thanking Kathleen McDermott, who first encouraged me to consider writing a biography of Tojo Hideki. The mantle of editing the biography shifted to Emily Silk; I owe Emily an immense debt for everything she brought to this project, including her patience, her support, her ability to encourage, and her effectiveness in steering this book to publication.

My scholarly debts are many and are apparent in this book's notes. Among the weightier debts is that owed to David Walton, who read all fifteen draft chapters and remains a welcome source of friendship and support. Roger H. Brown has been unfailing in his academic generosity, and I look forward to working with him in the future. J. Charles Schencking proved a tower of support, and for this I am very grateful. Noriko Kawamura offered all manner of insights that proved extremely helpful and useful. This book otherwise owes much to the input of Hamai Kazufumi, Reto Hofmann, Andrew Levidis, Christopher Szpilman, and Sandra Wilson. Two Western Sydney University colleagues—Gregory Barton and Brett Bennett—have added color and vivacity to everyday academic life in Sydney. Political scientist Ito Go has kindly arranged several visiting professorships at Meiji University, which have allowed me sustained time in the archives in Tokyo. I offer my heartfelt thanks to Vanessa Bonesch, who took time out of her busy schedule to cast her lawyerly eye over my musings. I also owe a debt of gratitude to retired journalist Ueda Hiroaki, who graciously lent me photographs from his father's private collection. I must thank my old friend, Robert Eldridge, for introducing me to the general's great grandson, Tojo Hidetoshi. And I thank Tojo Hidetoshi, who accepted at face value my assurance that I sought neither to lionize nor demonize his great grandfather and granted me permission to use images stored in the Center for Military History, National Institute for Defense Studies in Tokyo.

ILLUSTRATION CREDITS

Frontispiece: Chūō zenpan shashin 14, Center for Military History, National Institute for Defense Studies, Tokyo.
Page 22: Chūō zenpan shashin sono ta 172 Tōjō Hideki shi no Shashin, Center for Military History, National Institute for Defense Studies, Tokyo.
Page 23: Chūō zenpan shashin sono ta 172 Tōjō Hideki shi no Shashin, Center for Military History, National Institute for Defense Studies, Tokyo.
Page 89: Courtesy of Ueda Hiroaki.
Page 95: Chūō zenpan shashin sono ta 172 Tōjō Hideki shi no Shashin, Center for Military History, National Institute for Defense Studies, Tokyo.
Page 97: Courtesy of Ueda Hiroaki.
Page 120: SuperStock / Alamy Stock Photo.
Page 150: Wikimedia Commons.
Page 154: SuperStock / Alamy Stock Photo.
Page 243: The Asahi Shimbun / Getty Images.
Page 248: Chūō zenpan shashin 12, Center for Military History, National Institute for Defense Studies, Tokyo.
Page 249: Chūō zenpan shashin 12, Center for Military History, National Institute for Defense Studies, Tokyo.
Page 252: Chūō zenpan shashin 12, Center for Military History, National Institute for Defense Studies, Tokyo.
Page 254: Chūō zenpan shashin 12, Center for Military History, National Institute for Defense Studies, Tokyo.
Page 272: Chūō zenpan shashin 12, Center for Military History, National Institute for Defense Studies, Tokyo.
Page 279: Chūō zenpan shashin 13, Center for Military History, National Institute for Defense Studies, Tokyo.
Page 279: Chūō zenpan shashin 13, Center for Military History, National Institute for Defense Studies, Tokyo.
Page 281: Chūō zenpan shashin 14, Center for Military History, National Institute for Defense Studies, Tokyo.
Page 295: Chūō zenpan shashin 14, Center for Military History, National Institute for Defense Studies, Tokyo.
Page 307: Box 1, Item 135, Wang Jingwei and Lin Baisheng Photo Collection 1940–1944, East Asia Library, Stanford University.
Page 308: Chūō zenpan shashin 14, Center for Military History, National Institute for Defense Studies, Tokyo.
Page 313: Japanese Military Photo Archives / Alamy Stock Photo.
Page 334: Chūō zenpan shashin 15, Center for Military History, National Institute for Defense Studies, Tokyo.
Page 350: ClassicStock / Alamy Stock Photo.
Page 367: Accession Number 019291, Australian War Memorial.
Page 372: Everett Collection Historical / Alamy Stock Photo.
Page 376: NAA: M1417, 23, National Archives of Australia.
Page 386: Carl Mydans / The LIFE Picture Collection / Shutterstock.

INDEX